States, Markets and Civil Society
in Asia Pacific

States, Markets and Civil Society in Asia Pacific

The Political Economy of the Asia-Pacific Region, Volume I

Joseph A. Camilleri

Professor of International Relations, School of Sociology, Politics and Anthropology, La Trobe University, Melbourne, Australia

Edward Elgar
Cheltenham, UK • Northampton, MA, USA

Published by
Edward Elgar Publishing Limited
Glensanda House
Montpellier Parade
Cheltenham
Glos GL50 1UA
UK

Edward Elgar Publishing, Inc.
136 West Street
Suite 202
Northampton
Massachusetts 01060
USA

A catalogue record for this book
is available from the British Library

Library of Congress Cataloguing in Publication Data

Camilleri, Joseph A., 1944–
    States, markets and civil society in Asia-Pacific / Joseph A. Camilleri.
    Includes bibliographical references and index.
    Contents: v. I. The political economy of the Asia-Pacific region —
    1. East Asia—Economic policy. 2. Pacific Area—Economic policy. 3.
East Asia—Politics and government. 4. Pacific Area—Politics and
government. 5. National security—East Asia. 6. National
security—Pacific Area. I. Title.

    HC460.5.C258 2000
    338.95—dc21   00–034816

ISBN 1 85898 838 1

Printed and bound in Great Britain by Bookcraft (Bath) Ltd.

Contents

Tables

Glossary of acronyms

ABC	Australian Broadcasting Commission
ABM	anti-ballistic missile
ABRI	Armed Forces of the Republic of Indonesia
ADF	Australian Defence Force
ANZUS	Australia, New Zealand, United States (treaty)
APEC	Asia Pacific Economic Cooperation
ARF	ASEAN Regional Forum
ASDF	Air Self-Defense Force (Japan)
ASEAN	Association of Southeast Asian Nations
ASEAN-4	Indonesia, Malaysia, Philippines, Thailand
ASEAN PMC	ASEAN Post-Ministerial Conference
ASEM	Asia–Europe Meeting
ASPAC	Asian and Pacific Council
ASW	anti-submarine warfare
AWAC	airborne warning and control (system)
BIS	Bank for International Settlements
BMD	ballistic missile defence
BN	Barisan Nasional (National Front, Malaysia)
BRA	Bouganville Revolutionary Army
CANDU	Canadian deuterium-uranium reactor
CCP	Chinese Communist Party
CFE	Conventional Armed Forces in Europe (treaty)
CIDA	Canadian International Development Agency
CIS	Commonwealth of Independent States
COMECON	Council for Mutual Economic Assistance
CPM	Communist Party of Malaya
CSCA	Conference on Security and Cooperation in Asia
CSBM	Confidence- and Security-Building Measures
DAP	Democratic Action Party (Malyasia)
DIFF	Development Import Finance Facility (Australia)
DOD	Department of Defense (United States)

DPR	Dewan Perwakilan Rakyat (House of Representatives, Indonesia)
DPRK	Democratic People's Republic of Korea
DRV	Democratic Republic of Vietnam
EAEC	East Asia Economic Caucus
EAEG	East Asia Economic Group
EEZ	exclusive economic zone
EPA	Economic Planning Agency (Japan)
EPB	Economic Planning Board (Korea)
EU	European Union
EXIM	Export–Import Bank
FDI	foreign direct investment
FEER	*Far Eastern Economic Review*
FLNKS	Kanak National Socialist Liberation Front (New Caledonia)
FLP	Fiji Labour Party
FPDA	Five Power Defence Arrangement
FY	fiscal year
G7	Group of Seven
GATT	General Agreement on Tariffs and Trade
GDP	gross domestic product
Golkar	Golongan Karya (the ruling political party during the New Order period in Indonesia)
GNP	gross national product
IAEA	International Atomic Energy Agency
ICBM	intercontinental ballistic missile
IMF	International Monetary Fund
INF	intermediate-range nuclear forces (treaty)
INFID	International Forum on International Development (Indonesia)
INTERFET	International Force on East Timor
IRBM	intermediate-range ballistic missile
ISEAS	Institute for Southeast Asian Studies (Singapore)
ISIS	Institute for Strategic and International Studies (Malaysia)
JCPDG	Joint Committee on the Promotion of Democratic Government (Hong Kong)
JCP	Japanese Communist Party
JDA	Japanese Defense Agency
JIM	Jakarta Informal Meeting
KMT	Kuomintang
LDP	Liberal Democratic Party (Japan)
MAF	Malaysian Action Front

MFN	most favoured nation
MITI	Ministry of International Trade and Industry (Japan)
MOF	Ministry of Finance (Japan)
MOU	Memorandum of Understanding
MPR	Majelis Permusyawaratan Rakyat (People's Consultative Council, Indonesia)
MSDF	Maritime Self-Defense Force (Japan)
MTCR	Missile Technology Control Regime
NAFTA	North American Free Trade Agreement
NAM	Non-Aligned Movement
NATO	North Atlantic Treaty Organization
NDPO	National Defense Program Outline (Japan)
NFP	National Federation Party (Fiji)
NGO	non-governmental organization
NGO-CORD	NGO Coordinating Committee for Rural Development (Thailand)
NIE	newly industrializing economy
NMD	National Missile Defense
NORAD	North American Aerospace Defence (agreement)
NPT	Non-Proliferation Treaty
NSC	National Security Council (United States)
OCC	open coastal city (China)
OCP	open coastal zone province (China)
ODA	overseas development assistance
OECD	Organization for Economic Co-operation and Development
OPM	Free Papua Movement
OSCE	Organization for Security and Co-operation in Europe
PAP	People's Action Party (Singapore)
PAS	Parti Islam Se-Malaysia (Malay Islamic Party)
PDI	Partai Demokrasi Indonesia (Indonesian Democratic Party)
PECC	Pacific Economic Cooperation Council
Phil DHRRA	Philippine Partnership for the Development of Human Resources
PHILSSA	Philippine Support Service Agencies
PKI	Communist Party of Indonesia
PLA	People's Liberation Army (China)
PNG	Papua New Guinea
PPBI	Centre for Working Class Struggles (Indonesia)
PPD	Party for Peace and Democracy (South Korea)
PRC	People's Republic of China
PRCR	Rally for New Caledonia in the Republic

RAAF	Royal Australian Air Force
RMAF	Royal Malaysian Air Force
ROK	Republic of Korea
SAVE	Society Against Family Violence (Singapore)
SBSI	Indonesia Prosperous Workers' Union
SDF	Self-Defense Forces (Japan)
SDI	Strategic Defense Initiative
SEANWFZ	Southeast Asia Nuclear Weapons Free Zone
SEATO	Southeast Asia Treaty Organization
SEZ	special economic zone
SLBM	submarine-launched ballistic missile
SPARTECA	South Pacific Regional Trade and Economic Co-operation Agreement
SPNFZ	South Pacific Nuclear Free Zone
SSBN	nuclear-powered ballistic missile submarine
START	Strategic Arms Reduction Talks/Treaty
TAC	Treaty of Amity and Co-operation
TMD	theatre missile defence
TNC	transnational corporation
TRA	Taiwan Relations Act
TVS	Thai Volunteer Service Foundation
UKUSA	United Kingdom–United States of America Agreement
UMNO	United Malays National Organization
UMP	Union of Moderate Parties (Vanuatu)
UNCED	United Nations Conference on Environment and Development
UNCTAD	United Nations Conference on Trade and Development
UNDP	United Nations Development Programme
UNESCO	United Nations Educational, Scientific and Cultural Organization
UNPROFOR	UN Protection Force
UNTAC	UN Transitional Authority in Cambodia
UNTAET	United Nations Transitional Authority in East Timor
USAKA/KMR	US Army Kwajalein Atoll/Kwajalein Missile Range
VOA	Voice of America
VP	Vanua'aku Pati
WALHI	Wahana Lingkungan Hidup (Environmental Forum, Indonesia)
WTO	World Trade Organization
ZOPFAN	Zone of Peace, Freedom and Neutrality

Preface

As originally conceived, the purpose of this book was to examine the development of multilateral approaches to economic and security co-operation in Asia Pacific. It soon became apparent, however, that regionalization as it evolved during the 1980s and 1990s could not be considered in a vacuum. The phenomenon – and its regional and sub-regional manifestations – could not be adequately characterized, let alone explained, without first placing it in its geopolitical, economic and cultural context. To compress this ambitious undertaking into one book proved an increasingly unmanageable task. Edward Elgar's suggestion of a two-volume study did not at first seem the appropriate course to take. It risked extending the duration of a project already several years in the making, and compounding the many difficulties associated with the conceptual and practical organization of the material. Yet, on reflection, there was much to be said for the idea. It promised a more comprehensive treatment of the issues involved, and at the same time offered a convenient line of demarcation between contextual background and the analysis of regionalization. And so the outline of this book, as the first of a two-volume study, gradually took shape. As the title indicates, it is an attempt to identify the multiple connections between states, markets and civil society which have over time given form and substance to the domestic and international environment of individual countries and the political economy of the region as a whole. The companion volume, *Regionalism in the New Asia-Pacific Order* builds on these conceptual and empirical foundations.

One of the recurring themes of the book is the speed and intensity of change. The rapid industralization of East Asia's economies, the end of ideological bipolarity, the sharpening conflict between authoritarian and democratic tendencies are suggestive of the profound transformation which the region has undergone in little more than two decades. These mutually reinforcing yet contradictory trends help explain why change has been neither uniform nor unilinear. As the events of the last few years have amply demonstrated, sustained economic growth can be followed by financial meltdown; seemingly immovable, highly centralized, coercive political regimes can be swept aside almost overnight by explosions of public dissent; significant expressions of democratic sentiment can be just as abruptly stifled; and relatively minor disputes can quickly escalate beyond the threshold of violence. Yet change coexists with continuity. It is therefore necessary in this study to distinguish between dominant trends and counter-trends, secular and cyclical factors, influences that are culturally or politically specific and those that have a wider regional or global reach. Integral to the analysis of change are several considerations: the structure–agency dichotomy, the relation of state to non-state actors, and the multiple levels of analysis from the local, to the micro-regional, national, macro-regional and global.

Rather than outline the theoretical framework in one or more introductory chapters and present the historical material quite separately in later chapters, the study seeks to connect conceptual and empirical analysis within each chapter. The book is divided into five main chapters, each covering either different periods, different actors or different themes. Each chapter, while it begins by clarifying the terms and concepts most relevant to the issues under consideration, has been constructed as part of a larger interconnected whole. By frequent cross-referencing and cumulative elaboration of ideas, the intention has been to develop an integrated perspective on the region's geopolitical, economic and socio-cultural landscape. Concluding reflections form the content of Chapter 6.

Given that its main purpose is to provide the necessary historical background for an examination of the last 20 or so years, Chapter 1 is primarily devoted to the Cold War period, and to the geopolitical currents which shaped the dynamics of ideological and strategic bipolarity. Drawing on a range of concepts partially or wholly derived from the study of geopolitics in both its classical and more recent formulations, the chapter examines the formation and functioning of Cold War alliances in the Asia-Pacific context, and their subsequent transformation or disintegration. Attention is drawn to the weaknesses as well as the strengths of the geopolitical imagination, and to the need for a more complex, less state-centric discourse that incorporates the insights of political economy and socio-cultural analysis.

In Chapter 2 the focus is on East Asia's economies and the exponential growth rates they achieved during the 1980s and 1990s. The aim here is not simply to describe the phenomenon of export-oriented industrialization but to assess its geopolitical as much as its economic significance, and to identify the factors contributing to the temporal and spatial qualities of the international division of labour. The financial crisis of the late 1990s is closely scrutinized to elucidate the salience and potency of the endogenous and exogenous pressures bearing upon those economies. As we shall see, the crisis offers rich insights into the hegemonic role of the United States and the increasingly complex relationships between the newly industrializing economies, transnational capital and international institutions, notably the International Monetary Fund.

The rapidly changing balance of economic capabilities reflected in the rise of Japan as an economic player of the first magnitude sets the stage in Chapter 3 for a more detailed examination of the fluctuating balance of interests between three main centres of power: the United States, Japan and China. At issue here is a complex set of questions: the changing form and function of hegemonic leadership, the interplay of competition and interdependence, and the economy–security nexus, all of which must be set in the context of three bilateral relationships, but also the triangular interaction of policies, perceptions and capabilities. We inject another element of complexity into the analysis by briefly examining Russia's engagement with Asia Pacific during the 1990s. The intention here is to identify the implications of Russia's relative decline, and more importantly the geopolitical elements of change and continuity between the Cold War era and its aftermath.

In Chapter 4 we introduce the concepts of periphery and semi-periphery to ascertain the degree of leverage or autonomy available to a range of smaller polities sometimes referred to as small and middle powers. The countries (South Korea, Indonesia, Malaysia, Australia, Canada and various Pacific island states) and variables (for example, stage of economic development, political system, diplomatic and strategic culture) to be considered have been carefully selected to illuminate the degree of externally or internally induced vulnerability experienced by these polities and the relative freedom of action which they enjoy.

In locating East Asian states within their economic and geopolitical environment we are able to identify the salient influences constraining their behaviour, remembering, of course, that these environmental conditions are seldom static. They are, however, potent precisely because they are internalized by the state. A great many agencies, notably corporations, financial markets, media networks and epistemic communities, may be said to constitute an intricate yet seamless transmission belt. Be that as it may, the state is more than just a blank page to be filled by exogenous actors. Indeed, both state and civil society are mutually constitutive of the political space within which a wide range of interests and values are articulated and maximized. In Chapter 5, state and civil society are examined with a view to clarifying the relation of state to market, the evolution of the developmental state, the role of the emerging middle classes, and the origins and scope of democratic discourse and practice. These questions are, as we shall see, central to an understanding of the political trajectory of East Asian societies, but also of the cultural, economic and geopolitical affinities and faultlines that are increasingly shaping both intra-regional and inter-regional relationships.

In setting the stage for a closer analysis of the new regionalism in Asia Pacific, this book's principal preoccupation is to. lay bare the complex mechanisms which on the one hand underpin Pacific Asia's heterogeneity and on the other connect it economically and geopolitically to the wider Asia-Pacific region and the rest of the world. In this study, Pacific Asia is understood to include the countries of Northeast and Southeast Asia, whereas Asia Pacific also encompasses Russia, Oceania and North America. The rationale for this definition of region and sub-regions and its implications for multilateral approaches to economic and security co-operation is developed in the companion volume.

Needless to say, this two-volume study would not have been conceived, much less completed, without the psychological support and intellectual insights offered by others too numerous to name. Mention must, however, be made of the rewarding exchanges I have had at a great many seminars and conferences in the region, and interviews with a wide range of scholars, officials, journalists and NGO representatives in Beijing, Shanghai, Manila, Bangkok and Kuala Lumpur. I am most appreciative of my association with the Council for Security and Co-operation in Asia Pacific, and in particular its Australian Committee. I owe a rather large debt to La Trobe University, in particular to the librarians for their unfailing assistance, to the Department of Politics for its general support, and to the secretarial staff for their wholehearted co-operation. I am especially indebted to Sue Chaplin, Nella Mete and Margherita Matera for their wonderful work on the computer.

Let me also acknowledge that this project would not have seen the light of day had it not been for the generous support of the Australian Research Council and for the enthusiastic and highly professional contribution of my research assistants, Andrew Cock, Amnon Varon and Michael O'Keefe. A special word of thanks goes to Michael for his unstinting and methodical assistance, on which I came to rely so heavily for the entire duration of the project. Finally may I express my sincerest gratitude to my wife, whose abundant patience and understanding were so crucial, especially during the more demanding stages of this project.

Joseph Camilleri

1. Geopolitical change: from the Nixon Doctrine to the end of the Cold War

Despite outward appearances of stability and quasi-permanence, the political and strategic order of the 1970s and 1980s, in Asia Pacific as in Europe, was characterized by unresolved tensions and ambiguities, which the Cold War system could only partially obscure. This was a period of considerable change marked by subtle but profound shifts in the global and regional organization of political space. The aim of this chapter is to analyse how power was exercised or, to be more exact, how it was spatially projected and distributed. It will examine the role of the United States and to a lesser degree the Soviet Union, and the function and centrality of their relationship, particularly with respect to regional security. Attention will also focus on the interaction between established and emerging centres of power, notably China and Japan, and its implications for the dynamics of regional conflict and co-operation. Central to the analytical framework will be the changing complexion of Cold War alliances which had for more than two decades defined and institutionalized the boundaries between rival military and ideological camps.

GEOPOLITICS REVISITED

Geopolitical discourse, with its emphasis on the relationship between politics and geography, or to be more precise between physical space, military power and the conduct of states, seeks to identify the environmental determinants of change in the pattern of international relations. Geopolitical interpretations may choose to highlight the function of any number of geographical variables, from climate to size of territory, topography, strategic position, availability of natural resources, or size of population. There is, however, more to geopolitics than meets the eye. Geopolitical change, the focal point of analysis in this chapter and a recurring theme in the study as a whole, is, as we shall discover, a multifaceted, at times troublesome, but nevertheless rewarding concept.

Friedrich Ratzel, one of the founding figures of modern geopolitics, was primarily concerned to establish the natural laws governing the territorial enlargement of states. For him the state was a living organism engaged in a competitive struggle for existence.[1] With the growth of culture and population came the need for *lebensraum* or 'living space', which normally proceeded by the annexation of smaller states. By making the struggle for living space between different cultures the engine of change and human progress, Ratzel had sought to apply biological notions of evolution to the conduct of statecraft. Like Ratzel, Rudolf Kjellén, a Swedish political scientist credited with being the first to coin the term 'geopolitics', viewed the state as 'a geographical organism or a phenomenon in space'.[2] He emphasized its natural and organic attributes, in other words its capacity for growth, and differentiated between first-rank 'world powers' and second-rank 'great powers'. These ideas were enthusiastically adopted by Karl Haushofer, for whom geopolitics was inseparable from practical politics. Attempting to build on the foundations of political geography, he defined the field as 'the science of the conditioning of political processes by the earth'.[3] In line with his pro-Nazi sympathies, Haushofer found in geopolitics a remedy for what he saw as Germany's 'continental narrowness' and the 'smallness in its world vision'.[4]

It should be readily apparent that questionable assumptions and polemical purposes can easily vitiate the usefulness of geopolitical theorizing. Reference has already been made to the crude application of evolutionary principles and the social Darwinist preoccupation with ideas of struggle and survival. Placed in this context, success became virtually synonymous with power, expansion and domination. An 'imperialist agenda' driven by different versions of cultural or national chauvinism – what Haushofer himself called the 'elemental craving for better scientific protection of the political unit' – seemed to colour many of these early excursions into geopolitical analysis. Is geopolitics, then, to be understood as objective scholarship or little more than an apologia for national self -aggrandisement? Excessive concentration on geographical constraints runs the obvious risk of geopolitical determinism, obscuring or neglecting the role of the subjective realm – and its various psychological, intellectual and cultural manifestations – which can radically modify the impact of geography on state behaviour. The geopolitical perspective on international relations, with its emphasis on the natural and the physical as the foundation of all knowledge, rests on the questionable division between the inner self and the world 'out there', and treats observed 'reality' as if it had a 'natural' existence entirely separate from and independent of the observer. By adopting what ÓTuathail has described as 'the Cartesian perspectivalist tradition', geopolitics may subordinate history to geography, and encourage 'the spatialisation of perceived phenomena rather than their historisation'.[5] The scenes and spectacles produced by the geopolitical imagination have no doubt a dramatic, almost riveting quality about them, but that is perhaps no more than a 'theatrical production of the illusion of order',[6] an attempt to impose on the world an imperial vision of space based on territorial divisions and power rivalries.

Another element in the critique of geopolitical discourse – perhaps one which synthesizes many of the others – is its alleged statism, its unquestioning assumption that the state effectively distinguishes between 'them' and 'us', irrevocably divides space between 'our' place and 'theirs'[7] and sets the stage across which military, economic and diplomatic battles are fought. The territorial state, struggling for power and wealth in what is an essentially hostile environment, thus becomes a unitary actor, an autonomous agent capable of defining values, setting goals, formulating strategies, and controlling and organizing resources. Quite apart from its various epistemological flaws, this representation of the state, and the spatialization on which it rests, has been described as a western conceptual system which deprives the world political map of its inherent heterogeneity in favour of a contrived homogeneity imposed by hegemonic centres of knowledge and learning.[8] Social power and agency, it is argued, may, in specific historical conditions, function through and be inseparable from the institutions of the state, but they can function equally well and for long periods of time through other modes of spatial organization. To put it simply, geopolitics asserts rather than demonstrates the centrality of the state.

Subjected to trenchant criticism, geopolitical models of international relations tended to lose favour in the aftermath of the Second World War, not least because of their perceived association with the policies of Nazi Germany. More generally, the conception of geopolitics as the state-centric manipulation of knowledge was considered politically dangerous and intellectually indefensible. Yet geopolitical discourse was far from monolithic. To begin with, it was closely connected to the academic discipline of political geography which, understood as the study of the political dimension of human activity viewed spatially, remained a highly respected field of inquiry. By the 1970s geopolitics itself was rediscovered as a useful meeting point for geography and political science.[9] A return to the geopolitical insights of the pre-Nazi period was now seen as making a valuable contribution to the study of international relations. There was certainly much to support the view that, suitably qualified and contextualized, a geographical perspective could illuminate, though not fully explain, the main axes of international conflict and their regional and global implications.

To elucidate the scope and limitations of geopolitical discourse, it may be useful to begin by referring, however briefly, to two somewhat dated but still relevant geopolitical interpretations – one advanced by Alfred Thayer Mahan and the other by Halford Mackinder – both of which rest on the proposition that the physical layout of lands and seas provides opportunities and sets limits which substantially shape the interests and strategies of states. While the positions they advanced were far from identical and in any case changed markedly over time, largely in response to changing circumstances, there were considerable commonalities of approach. Both Mahan and Mackinder were concerned as much to prescribe as to interpret; they wished to preserve the privileged position of the great power with which they passionately identified, the United States and Britain respectively; they sought to take account of change through time; they used history to buttress their geographical arguments; and they regarded conflict as the normal condition of international relations and military force as the principal ingredient of state power.[10] Similarities in the conclusions they reached are perhaps most readily observable between the early phase of Mahan's thinking and the later phase of Mackinder's theorizing.

According to Mahan, sea power had played a decisive role in modern history, as evidenced by the enormous strategic advantages which naval supremacy conferred on Britain during the eighteenth and the greater part of the nineteenth centuries. Mahan viewed sea power as both 'an abstraction and a concrete fact',[11] and the principles governing its exercise as belonging to 'the unchangeable, or unchanging, order of things'.[12] Naval power, he argued, had been critical to the development of production and commerce, the expansion of shipping and the acquisition and maintenance of colonies, and held therefore the key to much of the history of nations bordering the sea.[13] He viewed the acquisition of naval capability as critical to America's future rise to the front ranks of world power. For Mahan, the steady expansion of the Russian empire demonstrated the strength but also the weakness of land power.

Russia had accumulated enormous defensive power, but any attempt to expand towards the Indian and Pacific Oceans would be thwarted by virtue of its geographical limitations (poor access to the sea, long supply lines, inadequate internal communications) and the geographical assets of its principal rivals (Britain's insular position, the British Navy's possession of the best naval ports in every ocean, in particular around the rimlands of Asia, and control of such strategic connecting seas as the Suez Canal, the Gibraltar Strait, the English Channel and the North Sea). While they could not contemplate a frontal assault on the inner core of the Russian empire, the maritime powers could effectively contain Russia along its periphery. In time an equilibrium would be established between opposing forces of land and sea. Mahan's hypothesis, developed at the end of the nineteenth century, would soon be overtaken by events, not least Russia's defeat at the hands of Japan and Germany's rise as a major military and economic power. The prospect of future German dominance on both land and sea meant that, from the vantage point of the insular nations, the focus of containment would have to shift from Russia to Germany.[14] Notwithstanding its explanatory and predictive limitations, Mahan's theory foreshadowed Mackinder's notion of the Eurasian 'Heartland', and the strategic conception which would guide US attempts in the late 1940s and early 1950s to contain Soviet power and influence.

Mackinder shared Mahan's belief in the critical importance of sea power, which he attributed to the global continuity of the oceans,[15] but naval power, he argued, would ultimately depend on its land base, or to be more exact, on the economic and technological resources at its disposal.[16] As early as 1904, just after the completion of the trans-Siberian railway, he had predicted that the vast spaces occupied by the Russian empire and Mongolia, which he later referred to as the 'Heartland', would, once human and material resources had been fully harnessed, constitute the 'pivot area' of world politics.[17] This pivotal mass would not be susceptible to the pressures exerted by maritime powers, and, should it gain control over 'the marginal lands' of Eurasia, would in due course become a major sea power in its own right.[18] By virtue of its strategic location, the heartland could eventually dominate the World-Island, which in Mackinder's conception comprised Europe, Asia and Africa, not as three separate continents but as a single interconnected geographical entity. Control of the World-Island could in due course be translated into domination of the world.

Like Mahan, Mackinder subsequently turned his attention to Germany, which for a time he envisaged as the possible nucleus of a transcontinental Eurasian empire, capable of using 'the surplus of its vast resources to outbuild the British fleet'.[19] However, with the defeat of Germany in the First World War, which he attributed in part to the German strategic blunder of fighting simultaneously on two strategic fronts without a clear sense of priorities,[20] his concern gradually shifted back to the Soviet Union. During this second phase, extending from the early 1920s to the mid-1940s, his earlier hypothesis would undergo radical change. Whereas he had previously foreshadowed the growth of a single world empire, he now postulated the emergence of two centres of power. Reflecting on the experience of the First World War, he discerned a new dividing line between East and West, running not through the mid-Atlantic but along the Rhine. In Mackinder's view, North America and Western Europe were 'rapidly becoming the balanced halves of a single great community'.[21] Separate from this Atlantic community was the Soviet Union which, if it were to prove victorious in the war against Germany, would emerge as 'the greatest land power on the globe'. Yet, the heartland, though it constituted a potentially impregnable natural fortress, was unlikely to command the World-Island, let alone the world, because pitted against it was the combined industrial and military might of the United States and Europe, a coalition greatly enhanced by ideological affinities and rapidly expanding sea and air lines of communication.[22]

Notwithstanding a great many flaws in Mackinder's conceptual framework, several of the ideas he advanced would shed considerable light on subsequent strategic and diplomatic behaviour. Foremost among these was his argument that with the expansion of Europe into Africa, Asia, the Americas and Australasia, the world had become a closed political system in which:

> every explosion of social forces . . . [would] be sharply re-echoed from the farside of the globe, and weak elements in the political and economic organism of the world [would] be shattered in consequence.[23]

This 'closure' of the world was the culmination of a long historical process, which Mackinder described as 'the Columbian epoch'. With the period of discovery, expansion and conquest now at an end, the focus would shift from territorial expansion to the struggle for relative efficiency. In this single global space, events in one part of the world would have consequences in other parts. It would no longer be possible to treat one conflict in isolation from another. Mackinder had in effect foreshadowed the internationalization of conflict not merely in a geographical sense – a trend graphically illustrated by two world wars and the Cold War – but in the deeper political sense that even in local and regional conflicts strategic calculations, military deployments and capabilities, and diplomatic outcomes would increasingly acquire global dimensions.

Equally penetrating was the insight that both land power and sea power would have a critical role to play in the global configuration of forces, and the related and prescient conclusion that two major centres of power were emerging, one resting primarily on the 'heartland' quality of the Soviet land mass, and the other on the command of the seas held by a North Atlantic coalition whose leadership would by the end of the Second World War shift decisively to the United States.[24] Mackinder's scenario, though it was predicated on continuing co-operation between these two centres of power as a way of containing future German expansion, offered one of the earliest and sharpest articulations of the trend towards international bipolarity, and the contribution which land and sea would make to the structure and modality of bipolar conflict.

Mackinder's grand geopolitical generalizations did nevertheless suffer from a number of defects which severely limited their applicability to the post-1945 international order. To begin with, the co-operative Soviet–American relationship would not long survive the conclusion of the war. Second, the strategic significance of land and sea would be increasingly determined or at least mediated by technological innovation, and in particular by the advent of nuclear weapons and ballistic delivery systems capable of travelling continental distances. The net effect of modern military technology would be to blur the dividing line between the strategic value of land and sea, and shift the emphasis in military strategy from defence to deterrence in ways and to a degree that Mackinder could not have imagined.

One other shortcoming is worth noting here. Though for Mackinder the polarizing effects of land and sea on the constellation of forces were more muted than in Mahan's case, there is no mistaking the extent to which this polarization continued to dominate his geopolitical thinking. He was as a consequence unable to take sufficient account of a number of other factors, including technology, which were to have a significant bearing on the geopolitical equation. After all, the balance of power at any given moment is the outcome of a complex process of coalition building and alliance formation, which is itself a function of technological, economic, political, cultural and ideological variables, and not merely the expression of some natural geographical configuration. Alliances, as we shall see, would play a critical role in the internationalization of conflict, and in institutionalizing the bipolar structure of international relations. Bilateral and multilateral alliances would serve to connect regional and global axes of conflict and, as a corollary of this trend, help to establish a strategic bridge between one region and another.

Here, it is worth referring to Nicholas Spykman who, though influenced by Mackinder's heartland thesis, adopted an explicitly global perspective. Stressing the significance of the Eurasian 'rimlands', notably Western Europe, the Middle East, South Asia and East Asia, he argued that both maritime and continental powers had traditionally sought to secure control of the rimlands, with conflict the inevitable outcome. It was now possible, however, that a future great power would come to dominate the whole of this region, namely 'the girdle of marginal seas' stretching from the Baltic Sea to the Sea of Okhostsk.[25] In this sense, the alliances in both world wars could be said to have demonstrated the pivotal importance of the rimlands.

In the Second World War it was in the interests of the United States and Britain, the two dominant sea powers, to unite with the Soviet Union, the principal land power, to prevent 'the unification of the Old World centres of power', that is, Germany and Japan. For Spykman, the rimlands constituted a geographic centre of power comparable in scope to the World-Island and the heartland. More importantly, perhaps, the rimlands were likely to play a decisive role in the formation and subsequent development of military alliances. It was left to Mienig, writing in 1956, to refine Spykman's argument and adapt it to the strategic circumstances of the post-1945 period. He divided the rimlands into two parts, the 'extra-insular' and the 'intra-insular', the former looking outwards to the World-Island, and the latter looking inwards to the heartland.[26] Meinig's strategic representation of the world had two striking implications: both the continental and maritime powers would attempt to maximize their control over the rimlands, with alliances likely to prove the most feasible instrument of control. With each power pursuing the same strategy, the dividing line between their respective spheres of influence would fluctuate between uneasy stand-off and accidental or intentional collision.

Instructive though they are, the geopolitical interpretations proposed by Mahan, Mackinder, Spykman and others are in need of radical reformulation if they are to enrich our analysis of contemporary geopolitical change. To put it simply, the relation of forces, whatever its geographical and other determinants, must be placed in its historical context, examined in terms of the dynamics of change, and more closely connected to the economic but also cultural and psychological dimension of the security dilemma as it manifests itself in different regions and localities. States, it should be remembered, expand but also contract. Though the nation-state has since the nineteenth century achieved normative status as a principle of political organization, in only a few instances has a substantial and stable fit emerged between state and nation. In the majority of instances, either the nation came first, in which case the dominant nation used the levers of state power to secure or expand its dominant position *vis-à-vis* adjacent populations, or the state came first, in which case nationalism often became a lever for the consolidation and expansion of state power. As Parker aptly puts it, the policy of the state-nation was 'to centralise power in the core regions, and then, as part of the process of strengthening the state, to effect a cultural absorption of the conquered territories into the culture of the core regions'.[27] This process, in fact, characterizes the experience of much of eighteenth- and nineteenth-century Europe and of post-colonial Asia, except that in the latter case the post-colonial state has simply inherited the territories and boundaries bequeathed by the colonial power. Indeed, the disintegration of colonial empires left behind a large number of states whose viability was anything but assured and for which internal security posed an even greater threat than external security. The post-colonial project, though often promoted in the name of nation-building, was in practice an exercise in state-building. The fragility of the state and the political violence which often accompanied it would in turn become inextricably linked with international axes of conflict. To this extent at least the panoramic view of the state system, as captured by the 'geopolitical gaze',[28] with its emphasis on the geographical determinants of power, is tendentious if not misleading. It projects on to the political map of the world an air of stability and permanence at odds with the ceaseless and at times tempestuous fission and fusion of states. The global map of geopolitics had not yet adequately connected with, let alone incorporated, the maps of regions and localities.

Notwithstanding the caveats outlined above, there is much in geopolitical discourse to commend it. Placed within a more nuanced and encompassing interpretative framework, important strands in geopolitical thought can help us to decipher the architectural design of the Cold War and the structural weaknesses that eventually led to its demise. Five such strands are worth noting here. First is the paradoxical conclusion that geopolitics implies change. Behind the façade of geographical fixity is the reality of a continually evolving landscape, punctuated by moments of intense perturbation. Geopolitical analysis is helpful in discerning change but also in mapping its trajectory. Particularly relevant in this context is the notion of geopolitical order which John Agnew and Stuart Corbridge define as 'the routinized rules, institutions, activities and strategies through which the international political economy operates in different historical periods'.[29] Though any number of geographical variables (for example, the nature and scope of state territoriality, the spatial reach and connectedness of states and non-state actors, the elements and the gradations of power) will at any given time structure the international political economy, the particular combination of variables and the relationship between the geographical and psycho-social environment will vary from period to period.

The durability of any geopolitical order will depend on its congruence not only with geographical constraints and opportunities but also with societal norms and aspirations. However dominant a geopolitical model may be at a particular moment, other models reflecting other interests and other geographic constellations will vie for ascendancy. Nor is geopolitical analysis itself monolithic. By ascribing different weights to different variables, different periodizations are derived, none of which may be entirely satisfactory, but each of which may have a certain explanatory value. One approach to geopolitical order favoured by Robert Cox identifies three periods (1845–75, 1875–1945, 1945–65),[30] with the mode of social organization and the degree of fragmentation/integration of the world economy as key indicators. Other approaches include Immanuel Wallerstein's cycles of hegemony,[31] George Modelski's long cycles of world leadership,[32] Peter Taylor's periodization based on state-centric sequences and combinations of hegemony, rivalry and concert,[33] and Agnew's sequence of 'civilizational' (1815–75), 'naturalized' (1875–1945), and 'ideological' (1945–90) geopolitics.[34]

A second and closely related strand in geopolitical discourse revolves around notions of 'leadership', 'primacy' or 'hegemony'. Different models differ on the meaning of hegemony, the forms it assumes, the conditions under which it emerges and declines, and the function ascribed to the hegemonic state. The multiplicity of models need not, however, detract from, and may even enhance, the incisiveness with which key questions are formulated, especially with regard to the historical geography of primacy, the definition and maintenance of hegemonic boundaries, the institutional and ideological underpinnings of hegemony, and the relationship between economic and military power.[35] As we shall see, all these questions are critical to an understanding of the hegemonic spheres established during the Cold War years, and of the role of such geopolitical concepts as containment, domino effect, alliance management and burden-sharing in the maintenance or loss of hegemonic status. They are also suggestive of the spatial distribution of costs and benefits within the hegemonic sphere as well as of the duration of the phases that comprise the hegemonic age: from emergence to ascendancy, subsequent decline, and eventual dissolution.

Whereas hegemony and primacy are suggestive of a unipolar, not to say unitary, model, a third strand in geopolitical thought is its sensitivity to the numerous polarities that characterize the world system. Indeed, the geopolitical tradition is, as we have already seen, particularly attentive to the binary division of the world, to the actual or potential rivalry between land powers and sea powers, but also to the various other economic and ideological factors that consummated the East–West bifurcation of global space. The binary focus can, in any case, be usefully extended to encompass other dichotomies, some of which reinforced and others of which cut across the Cold War division of the world.[36] Relevant in this context is the North–South axis of conflict which in some respects provided the arena for the conduct of East–West rivalries, but which at the same time injected new elements of polarization, notably between rich and poor, colonizers and colonized, great and small powers, the included and the excluded,[37] with race, culture and religion emerging as potent symbols of global pluralism.

The fourth strand we wish to highlight is perhaps more clearly associated with 'critical' than with classical geopolitics. Instead of taking geopolitical reasoning for granted, it is possible to theorize in geopolitical terms by problematizing the very discourse of statecraft. The terms of geopolitical world order, including the geographical constructs articulated by ministers, diplomats, generals, administrators and others in positions of power and authority are amenable to critical scrutiny. In the process new light is shed on the exercise of hegemony both within and between states, and across the spaces occupied by other actors, be they epistemic communities, social movements, transnational corporations or international organizations. Particularly valuable in this regard has been the contribution of the French radical geographer Yves Lacoste, for whom geography is strategic knowledge structurally linked to political and military practices. Geography, he argues, is closely connected to, and often serves, the science and practice of warfare. More than that, geography is placed at the service of territorial administration and government itself.[38] *La géographie dominante* is therefore an appropriate field of study precisely because, once set in its political context, it can yield a more objective, or at least more detached, reading of the relationship between geography and the state. To put it differently, geopolitical visions, however state-centric, assume analytical significance not merely because they refer to actual spatial practices through which the international political economy is constituted, but because they illuminate the ways in which those practices are represented and contested.[39]

Paradoxically, then, what is most useful about 'new' geopolitics is that it reclaims the uniqueness of the geopolitical tradition, thereby distancing it from cruder versions of political geography and the interests of any particular state.[40] Geopolitics is thus able to recover the holistic perspective that is its distinguishing characteristic. By subjecting to scrutiny the totality of geographical space, that is global space, geopolitics makes it possible to place local and regional events and relationships within the larger systemic context of which they are an integral part. The synthesis – understood in both its Kantian and Hegelian senses – of the world political map, which lies at the heart of the geopolitical project, is, needless to say, especially relevant to the contemporary globalization of human affairs. Far from negating the importance of localities, cities or regions, the systemic perspective implicit in geopolitics can help to clarify the varying degrees and patterns of overlap, interpenetration and reciprocal influence between system and subsystem. It can more accurately represent the variety of spatial forms – not just local, national, regional and global, but also functional space[41] – and the cultural and ecological[42] norms which define and sustain them.

We are now in a position to place the security dilemma within its geopolitical context. Security complex theory, particularly as developed by Barry Buzan, represents one such attempt.[43] While recognizing the interaction between the decisions of individual states and the international system as a whole, Buzan posits the existence of regional subsystems as key units of analysis. Security interdependence is said to be markedly more intense between states inside the same complex than between states belonging to different complexes. Indeed, the security perspectives and interests of any state within a given complex are so interlinked that they cannot be analysed apart from one another. The patterns of amity and enmity among states within the complex and the distribution of power among the principal states are said to endow each security complex with its distinctive structure and dynamics. The degree to which outside powers penetrate a particular region thus becomes one of the crucial variables shaping both the internal structure of the complex and its relationship to other complexes.[44]

Towards the end of this chapter we shall return to Buzan's conceptualization of the security complex when we attempt to identify the dominant geopolitical trends of this 20-year period. It is worth noting, however, at the outset that the security dilemma is a more elusive phenomenon than either crude geopolitics or even security complex theory would suggest. There is more to security than the protection of state boundaries from military incursion by other states.[45] As the experience of several Asia-Pacific countries (for example, the Philippines, Indonesia, Papua New Guinea) – not to mention the disintegration of the Soviet Union – clearly indicates, it is not only external attack but domestic upheaval of various kinds which can endanger a state's territorial integrity. Nor is the use of force the only serious threat to existing boundaries. Any number of economic, political and ideological disturbances, be they internal or external, may produce the same effect. Though boundaries may remain more or less intact, ethnic, religious or class conflict may disrupt and even traumatize an entire society. Cambodia after 1975 is an extreme but by no means isolated example. The accommodation of ethnic and other minorities, whether in Malaysia, the Philippines or Indonesia, has been a highly sensitive and often intractable problem for the post-colonial state, with far-reaching implications as much for its internal security as for its external diplomacy.

A second consideration must inform the analysis of security, namely the complex interplay of geopolitics and geoeconomics.[46] The formation, management and eventual dissolution of alliances, and the wider network of security relations of which they are an integral part, cannot be divorced from the intensifying competition between national economies or from the related scramble for resources, markets and investment opportunities. Neither the Cold War system nor the other axes of conflict which have dominated the Asia-Pacific geopolitical landscape can be understood purely in terms of an anarchic system comprised of discrete, relatively self-contained states. By helping to shape the rationale and structure of military budgets, the pattern of arms transfers, and even the scale and intensity of regional conflicts and great power military interventions, the transnationalization of trade, production and finance has become a keystone of both global and regional security relations. Increasingly, the security decisions of states are not the key independent variables of the geopolitical equation but the product of an intricate web of local, national, supranational and transnational interests, in which the primary considerations are as much economic as strategic.[47]

A third qualification readily suggests itself. Though regional systems and subsystems have sufficient autonomy to constitute a useful framework for the analysis of security relations, such analysis must ultimately be placed in a global context. The wider geopolitical perspective is especially valuable in this respect. So far as Asia Pacific is concerned, the internationalization of the security dilemma was perhaps most pronounced in the case of Korea and Vietnam, but not altogether absent in a range of lesser conflicts (for example, Cambodia, Taiwan). The global implications of nuclear deterrence, the global strategies of superpowers and their capacity to project force on a global scale, and the development of global institutional responses, notably through the agency of the United Nations, have all contributed to the internationalization of conflict.[48] The net effect has been to deepen interconnections between different regions, on the one hand, and between regions and the global strategic system, on the other.

Consideration of the complex influences which shape a state's domestic environment prompts another qualification to the geopolitical equation, which Buzan readily acknowledges but does not adequately incorporate into his security complex theory. During the Cold War period it was widely assumed that the principal geostrategic division in Asia Pacific expressed the wider ideological confrontation between capitalism and communism. As we shall see, the US-led system of bilateral and multilateral alliances, with its much publicized commitment to the principles of liberal democracy and free enterprise, was designed to contain not only Soviet and Chinese power and influence but the growth of communist parties and revolutionary movements in the Asian rimlands and beyond. This overarching ideological polarization, though it was a distinguishing feature of the Cold War, in fact obscured several pre-existing fault lines, many of them deeply embedded in historical memory: the smouldering fears and animosities arising from the clash of Russian and Japanese imperialism; lingering East Asian resentment of Japan's aggressive policies during the Second World War and its attempts to impose an East Asian Co-prosperity Sphere; the continuing efforts of post-colonial societies to erase or overcome the painful legacy of colonial domination; and perhaps most importantly, the attempts of modern China to come to terms with the trauma of nineteenth-century western economic and military penetration. Subterranean cultural or civilizational currents may have been temporarily blunted or masked by the exigencies of the East–West confrontation, but it is doubtful whether a discerning narrative of the 1970s and 1980s, let alone of the ensuing decades, can overlook the political and strategic significance of culturally rooted experiences and traditions.

Though this chapter cannot do justice to all the strands, caveats and qualifications outlined above, an attempt will be made to convey, at least in preliminary fashion, something of the contemporary evolution of geopolitical discourse in Asia Pacific and the diverse geographical and political influences which helped to give it form and content. A more detailed and comprehensive exposition of these complex variables and their interaction will gradually unfold as subsequent chapters and the companion volume attempt to explain how state and non-state actors in Asia Pacific have negotiated the transition from rigid bipolarity to competitive interdependence.

THE COLD WAR IN ASIA PACIFIC

The tensions in Soviet–US relations which had been simmering during the latter part of the Second World War, particularly over the Second Front and post-war arrangements for Europe, soon gave rise to substantial conflicts on Iran, Poland and the future of Germany. In March 1946 Churchill spoke of a Europe divided by an 'Iron Curtain' extending from the Baltic to the Adriatic. The announcement of the Truman Doctrine in March 1947, which committed US support for anti-communist forces in Greece and Turkey, soon followed by the proclamation of the Marshall Plan, signalled the almost complete breakdown in East–West relations. The role of the Red Army in the forcible takeover of power by communist parties in much of Eastern Europe and the defeat of communist forces in Greece following the removal of communist parties from governments in Italy and France effectively cemented the ideological division of Europe. The Berlin blockade which began in June 1948 marked the first major crisis of the Cold War, and was soon followed by the formation of the North Atlantic Treaty Organization (NATO) in April 1949 and the division of Germany into two rival states.[49]

In Asia Pacific ideological and strategic bipolarity was not as sharply defined, at least at first. The United States, having emerged from the Second World War as the undisputed power in the Pacific, soon consolidated its force projection capabilities from Micronesia and Guam to the Philippines, Okinawa, and up to the Aleutians. It had no incentive, however, to enter into security commitments with countries with which it had little in common and whose contribution to collective security would be marginal at best. In the minds of US strategic planners the conditions prevailing in the Pacific did not warrant the establishment of alliance arrangements modelled on the North Atlantic Treaty.[50] There was, it is true, one important parallel: just as occupation policy in Germany was central to US plans for the restoration of European capitalism in Europe, so the occupation of Japan was designed, despite vigorous opposition from several US allies, to assist Japan's economic reconstruction and make it the anti-communist workshop of Asia. It was not, however, until the final victory of Mao's forces in China in October 1949 and the outbreak of hostilities in Korea in June 1950 that the United States proceeded to apply in earnest the policy of containment to Asia.

Unable to construct a single strategic alliance comparable to NATO, the United States was now prepared to entertain a number of separate security commitments. The aim was to create a loose network of defence arrangements with countries situated on the rim of the western Pacific. In due course military treaties or agreements would be concluded with the Philippines (the 1947 military bases agreement, which gave the United States full and rent-free control over 23 bases and installations for 99 years, was followed by a mutual defence pact in August 1951), and with Australia and New Zealand (the 1947 UKUSA agreement providing for intelligence co-operation with Australia, Canada and Britain, notably in the area of signals and communications, was followed by the ANZUS Treaty of September 1951). In the case of ANZUS, Australian diplomacy had produced a Pacific security agreement which, while accommodating the requirements of US policy, namely Washington's determination to conclude a peace treaty with Japan, could nevertheless be portrayed as neutralizing the possibility of a resurgent Japanese militarism.[51] These security links formed part of a larger strategic plan, which chief negotiator John Foster Dulles described as 'a chain of Pacific defence' stretching from the Aleutians through Japan, the Ryukyus, the Philippines, to Australia and New Zealand. US forces in Japan and the northern Pacific, the US presence in the Philippines, and some acceptable security arrangement with Australia and New Zealand were now referred to as 'the three spokes of a wheel', at the hub of which would be the United States.[52] The US grand design was a relatively simple one: to surround the Eurasian heartland with a ring of military power stretching from Europe to the rimlands of Asia. Dulles emphasized more than once that Japan had to be denied to the Soviet Union and 'attracted to the side of the Western democracies', as the ultimate Soviet aim was 'to get control over the great industrial capacity of Germany and Japan'.[53] To frustrate this aim was considered the overriding interest of the free world and the centrepiece of US containment policy in Asia.

The now famous survey of the US strategic position drafted in February–March 1950 (NSC-68) recommended a rapid US military build-up with a view to deterring Soviet expansion and enabling the United States to respond to 'any number of pressure points' without having to choose between capitulating and precipitating a global war.[54] The strategic assessment made by Truman at this time is vividly recreated in *Rise to Globalism*:

In June 1950 he [Truman] badly needed another crisis, one that would allow him to prove to the American people that he and the Democratic Party were not soft on Communism, to extend containment to Asia, to shore up Chiang's position on Formosa, to retain American bases in Japan, and most of all to rearm America and NATO. The whole package envisaged in NSC68, in short, could be wrapped up and tied with a ribbon by an Asian crisis.[55]

These diverse considerations converged on 25 June 1950, when North Korean forces crossed the thirty-eighth parallel. Within hours of the attack Truman ordered supplies to be sent to South Korea, despatched the US Seventh Fleet to the Formosa (Taiwan) Strait, and promised additional support for counter-revolutionary warfare in Indochina and the Philippines.

The Korean War had acted as the catalyst for a major shift in US strategic planning. The objective was no longer just to protect 'vital areas', but to oppose communism on every front. The first and most obvious consequence of the war was to bring Korea within the US security perimeter. In the aftermath of the war, the United States would maintain significant forces in South Korea, including two army divisions supported by nuclear weapons and six major airbases deploying some 100 combat aircraft.[56] The conflict had another important consequence: with Japanese industry supplying much of the US war effort, it contributed to Japan's economic recovery. At the same time, US bases in Japan, which played an active role in the war, were now seen as critical to the future defence of US strategic interests in the region. In due course the peace treaty with Japan (signed in September 1951), which excluded the Soviet Union and legitimized a continued US military presence, was complemented by security treaties with South Korea (in August 1953) and Taiwan (in December 1954).[57] By this time, the United States had also come to regard Southeast Asia as the target of a co-ordinated Soviet offensive and, therefore, a vital sector on the line of containment, hence its increasing support for France's colonial war against the Viet Minh. The signing of the Southeast Asia Treaty Organization (SEATO) in September 1954 effectively extended the US security system to Southeast Asia and the Indian Ocean. The essential function of the treaty was made explicit when the United States formally declared that its own obligations would be specifically limited to cases of communist aggression.

The complex alliance structure and extensive basing network which the United States had concentrated along the rimlands of Asia and across the Pacific served a number of distinct but closely related objectives. At its simplest, the strategic rationale was to project military power throughout the Pacific and into the Indian Ocean. More specifically, the aim was to enhance the ability of the United States to fight a global or regional war, and develop the necessary infrastructure, including planes, ships, missile testing sites and communications facilities, for a highly sophisticated nuclear deterrent system. Expressed in geopolitical terms, the world's pre-eminent naval power was intent on encircling the land mass occupied by the Soviet Union and China with a ring of military force, thereby denying them access to areas of strategic or economic interest to the United States. Important in this regard was the protection of ocean routes and sea lines of communication, widely regarded as the lifeline of western economies. 'Securing' the Pacific was, in this sense, part of a larger US design to create an international economic order guided by the principles of free trade and the free flow of capital.[58] Geopolitics had become inseparable from geoeconomics.

The Korean War has been rightly described as 'a watershed marking the beginning of a new period in which politics became truly global'.[59] Not only did the war crystallize the global character of America's strategic posture and capabilities, it highlighted the global dimensions of the East–West conflict, and in the process brought Asia to the centre stage of international politics. The fact that US military intervention was carried out under the auspices of the UN Security Council could not but endow the Korean conflict with added global significance. There was, however, one other critical factor in the globalization of geopolitics, namely the alliance concluded between China and the Soviet Union in February 1950.

Though Stalin had given the Chinese communists remarkably little support during the protracted civil war, he now saw the defeat of Chiang Kai-shek's forces as a unique opportunity to extend Soviet influence in Asia, and to apply greater pressure on the western alliance system. For Mao, the Soviet Union offered the only realistic source of economic aid and the only hope of countering US continuing support for the remnant Kuomintang, which had now established itself in Taiwan.[60] In return for a number of Chinese concessions, including continued Soviet operation of the Central Manchurian Railway until the end of 1952 and the granting of bases at Darien and Port Arthur, Stalin committed significant Soviet resources for China's industrialization, and made available Soviet and Eastern European ships for transporting badly needed merchandise to Chinese ports. Once the Korean War broke out, Stalin made it clear that there could be no Soviet participation; but as time went on the Chinese armed forces would be able to rely on the Soviet Union for a massive flow of arms, with a good number of Russian advisers and even pilots playing a part in China's military response to MacArthur's offensive in North Korea.[61] Indeed, it is arguably the Korean War which, more than any other factor, helped to cement the Sino-Soviet alliance. Though the Soviet Union did not become directly involved in the conflict, its role was nevertheless decisive in that it gave the Chinese the necessary confidence to intervene, and deterred the United States from expanding the war into China for fear of Russian intervention. MacArthur's preferred solution would have been to strike at China; but Truman, conscious of the risks involved, decided to limit US objectives to restoring the *status quo ante bellum.*

Just as opposing US and Soviet interests in the immediate aftermath of the Second World War had contributed to the partitioning of Korea (with ideologically hostile governments established in the North and the South), so the onset of the Cold War helped to consolidate the division. First the North Koreans (with Stalin's foreknowledge but not necessarily his enthusiastic support) and then the Americans had gambled on reunifying the country by 'liberating' the other half; but in the end the logic of nuclear and ideological bipolarity required both sides to accept division, both globally but also along the rimlands of Asia, as a quasi-permanent condition. However, by comparison with the division of Germany, there had developed in Northeast Asia a more complex geopolitical equation, attributable largely to China's role for which there was no exact parallel in Europe. The Sino-Soviet alliance represented a marriage of convenience between two radically different and independent communist movements, in which ideology was as likely to divide as to unite. The fluid, at times byzantine relationship between Pyongyang, Moscow and Beijing, as it gradually unfolded after the Korean War, demonstrated that the two blocs were not exact replicas of each other.

At least so far as Asia was concerned, China was as much a pole of attraction as the Soviet Union. Nowhere was this more strikingly evident than in the triangular relationship between Hanoi and the two communist giants. From 1945 to 1948 Stalin, preoccupied with consolidating communist gains in Europe, treated the Viet Minh with reserve and did little to champion their cause. Content to have the relationship channelled through the French communists, Moscow waited until 1950 to recognize the Democratic Republic of Vietnam (DRV), which Ho Chi Minh had proclaimed in 1945.[62] In the early stages of their struggle against France, the Viet Minh could count on little outside help. It was not until Mao's victory in China that substantial Chinese support became available, including the supply of munitions and artillery, extensive training on Chinese soil, and the despatch of Chinese cadres to Vietnam. China's pervasive political influence in Hanoi began to wane once the North Vietnamese leadership realised that the Chinese-inspired land reform programme had failed, and that the reunification of the whole of Vietnam would not proceed as envisaged by the 1954 Geneva Accords. Following extensive contacts between Hanoi and Moscow in 1957, the flow of Soviet and Eastern European aid to North Vietnam increased substantially. Within a year, China had been displaced as the DRV's principal source of economic aid, but the realignment of Hanoi's diplomacy was only partial and temporary, with the pendulum continuing to swing over the next decade from Moscow to Beijing and back again.[63]

The point of this necessarily brief overview has been to situate the Asia-Pacific region within the global context of the Cold War. Both the western and communist alliance systems in Asia Pacific entailed a considerable degree of ideological, political and economic as well as military institutionalization. Yet the integrative tendencies operating within each system were much less pronounced than in Europe, hence the absence on either side of anything remotely approaching the structural cohesion of NATO or the Warsaw Pact. Though the Korean War, the Vietnam War and the various Taiwan crises can be interpreted as the consequences, or at least the expression, of ideological and strategic polarization, the bipolar division of territory and spheres of influence was much less sharply defined than in Europe. The rimlands of Asia had themselves become an arena of contestation in a way that was not true of the rimlands of Europe. The uniqueness of China's position, the prevalence of bilateral as opposed to multilateral arrangements, the substantially different cultural traditions and stages of economic development encompassed by alliances in Asia, the unresolved legacies of colonial and pre-colonial conflict, no doubt all contributed to the looser structure of Cold War politics in this part of the world. The fact remains, however, that in Asia as in Europe collective defence arrangements spawned a complex web of bilateral and multilateral agreements governing the establishment and operation of forces, stationing of troops, co-operation in military training, and transfer of arms, technology and intelligence.[64] By and large these agreements provided both superpowers with opportunities to maintain or expand their respective strategic and economic spheres of influence. These opportunities were generally much greater for the United States by virtue of its much larger economic base, its vastly superior naval capabilities, and the absence of any ally with the will or capacity to question its strategic priorities.[65]

This is not to say that junior allies did not themselves derive a range of benefits from the policy of alignment. Most alliances could, after all, claim to have afforded their member states an effective guarantee for the defence of their territory and the preservation of the value system to which they subscribed. That was presumably the main intent of the Sino-Soviet alliance, which in effect withstood the severe challenge posed by the Korean War and deterred the United States from launching a major military offensive against China. Similarly, the US security guarantees extended to Taiwan deterred Beijing from using force in pursuit of its reunification objective. In addition, many allies, particularly those of the United States, not least the defeated power, Japan, were able to maintain defence capabilities financially far less demanding, even when measured as a proportion of GNP, than the burden borne by the superpower. For many governments, the policy of alignment also contributed to their own self-preservation and legitimacy (in the face of actual or potential domestic political opposition). This was true of a number of US allies (as in the case of South Korea and the Philippines), and to a lesser extent of Soviet allies (for example, North Korea). There were, moreover, economic benefits associated with the transfer of capital and technology and access to markets, which were to prove important factors in the subsequent development of the tiger economies (for example, South Korea, Taiwan). Japan, as we have already observed, was the principal economic beneficiary of the Korean and Vietnam Wars. Similarly, military and economic aid provided at different times by the Soviet Union to China, North Korea and North Vietnam performed a critical function in sustaining these ailing economies.

Given their meagre resource base, it should come as no surprise that for most junior allies 'benefit-sharing' was generally more important than 'burden-sharing'. Alliances were formed in peacetime with a view to organizing the peace as much as to deterring or conducting a future war. International bipolarity thus appeared to rest on unusually strong ideological, strategic and economic foundations. Unlike other parts of Asia, or most of Africa, Asia Pacific was much less attracted to the politics of non-alignment, thereby adding another layer of stability to these foundations. There were at best a few exceptions, and these were either temporary or partial.[66] Though Sukarno's Indonesia had played a leadership role in developing the principles and practices of non-alignment, the advent of the staunchly anti-communist Suharto regime signalled a far closer relationship with the United States. Malaysia's non-alignment, though rhetorically strong, was in practice diluted by its defence arrangements with Britain, Australia and New Zealand, all three of whom were allies of the United States. Cambodian and Laotian neutrality was effectively undermined by the Vietnam War. As for Burmese neutrality, it was more an expression of Burma's self-imposed diplomatic isolation than explicit identification with the strategies and aspirations of the non-aligned movement. No wonder, then, that theorists and practitioners alike came to believe that Cold War alliances, unlike the coalitions operating in the classical balance of power system of eighteenth- and nineteenth-century Europe, would somehow remain unchanging fixtures in the Asia-Pacific geopolitical landscape.[67] It was this fixation with the seeming rigidity, not to say immutability, of Cold War politics which led many scholars and policy-makers to ignore or seriously underestimate the winds of change blowing across the region. To cite but the most obvious example, the demise of the Sino-Soviet alliance, which had its origins in the late 1950s, substantially modified, at least regionally, the bipolar structure of international relations, yet even a decade later many had yet to recognise its far-reaching geopolitical implications.

US ALLIANCES AND THE REORIENTATION OF US STRATEGY

In the case of the United States it was not until the late 1960s, and then largely in response to the débâcle in Vietnam, that a re-evaluation of US national interests prompted a significant diplomatic and strategic readjustment to the realities of international life. The Guam doctrine, first enunciated in July 1969, recognized the domestic imperative for restraint in military intervention and the need for a new Asian balance. The new US strategic posture sought to stabilize relations with the Soviet Union, while at the same time bringing US commitments more closely into line with US interests and capabilities. To this end, American friends and allies would be expected to make a greater contribution to their own defence, thereby alleviating the enormous burden of the containment policy which the United States had shouldered for more than two decades.

The dilemma, as US strategic planners saw it, was how to extricate the United States from an unwinnable war in Vietnam while maintaining more or less intact the other elements of the complex network of alliances and security arrangements which had been painstakingly constructed during the 1950s. The Nixon Administration's response to that dilemma was the policy of Vietnamization.[68] By August 1969 the departure of the first 25 000 US troops had been completed, and by November 1971 only 196 000 troops remained, compared with a peak of 543 000 in February 1969. The Vietnamization strategy set out to strengthen and stabilize the South Vietnamese armed forces in the hope that they would continue the war effort but with less direct American participation on the ground. The combined American and South Vietnamese invasion of Cambodia in March 1970, the bombing strikes against North Vietnam in November 1970, the expansion of the war into Laos in February 1971, the decision to impose a blockade on North Vietnam and mine its ports in December 1972 were all designed to provide the Saigon regime with the breathing space it needed to establish a more effective political and military base. This was precisely the rationale offered by Nixon for the extension of the Vietnam War into Laos and Cambodia:

> The Cambodian sanctuary operations were not inconsistent with the plan for American disengagement. Rather they furthered the strategic purpose of insuring the Vietnamization and withdrawal programs.[69]

It was a case of the United States using its technological superiority to strengthen the fighting capacity of its ally (South Vietnam) while punishing its adversary (North Vietnam) and weakening its resolve, thereby facilitating and accelerating the process of military disengagement, or, in Nixon's words, 'achieving peace with honour'.

The Guam doctrine was, however, designed to have much wider application. As Nixon explained to Congress, 'the only responsible alternative to continuing to carry that full burden is to help our friends build the capacity to do the job with less assistance from us'.[70] By the same token, Nixon did not wish to give the impression of hurried disengagement, which might have damaging consequences for US economic and strategic interests in Asia Pacific. In his report to Congress in February 1970, he was anxious to spell out the scope and limitations of the new doctrine:

> The United States will keep all its treaty commitments. We shall provide a shield if a nuclear power threatens the freedom of a nation allied with us, or of a nation whose survival we consider vital to our security and the security of the region as a whole. In cases involving other types of aggression we shall furnish military and economic assistance when required and as appropriate. But we shall look directly to the nation threatened to assume the primary responsibility of providing the manpower for its defence.[71]

The strategy of promoting greater regional self-reliance in defence was ambiguous, to say the least, designed as it was to convey different messages to different audiences.[72] Not surprisingly, it encountered insurmountable difficulties in Indochina, hence the search for more fertile soil in other parts of the Asian rimlands. By the early 1970s the United States was developing closer economic and military links with a number of ASEAN governments as a way of buttressing US interests in the post-Vietnam era. In February 1971 a decision was made to reduce the number of US troops stationed in South Korea, but in the context of expanded US military assistance to South Korea's armed forces. The partial retraction of US military power in East Asia had come to depend, on the one hand, on the reaffirmation of US security commitments, especially in Northeast Asia, and on the other, on a policy of détente with the Soviet Union and rapprochement with China. The binary division of the world had lost at least some of its former sharpness.

The reformulation of US policy during the Nixon–Kissinger years was in part designed to coax the Soviet Union and China to exercise a moderating influence on communist and revolutionary movements and governments hostile to US political and military interests in the region. More generally, the intention was to entice Moscow and Beijing to abandon their revisionist goals in favour of greater participation in the management of the status quo. The inescapable dilemma facing the United States was whether it could achieve such a radical rearrangement of Cold

War relationships, while at the same time maintaining the confidence of its allies and the viability of its security arrangements. The military ineptitude of the Saigon regime, and its eventual collapse, coupled with the political fallout within the United States – not to mention the impact of the Watergate scandal – cast a shadow on the effectiveness of US diplomacy and the reliability of US commitments. The ten-year trauma of the Vietnam War culminating in humiliating defeat for the United States and the triumph of communist forces throughout Indochina, gave rise to the 'Vietnam syndrome'.[73] A wide cross-section of US public opinion, supported and nurtured by an influential policy-making elite, now questioned the wisdom of military intervention, and counselled against future participation in an Asian land war. Jimmy Carter's pledge during the 1976 election campaign to withdraw US troops from South Korea dramatized the emerging consciousness of the limitations of US military power. However, the Carter Administration, in response to powerful domestic pressures and changing perceptions of the international environment, would eventually reaffirm the continued presence of US troops in Korea. The United States now planned to strengthen its air and naval capability in the Pacific by introducing several advanced systems, including Trident nuclear missiles for its submarine fleet, cruise missiles for its B52s, airborne warning and control systems, and the latest advanced fighter aircraft, including F-14s for its carriers and F-15s for its airforce squadrons.[74] Yet the uncertainty and ambiguity which had characterized US policy in Asia since the early 1970s would not be easily dispelled.

Even before Reagan's election in 1980, the process of détente in Soviet–American relations had virtually collapsed. The United States sought to contain the expansion of Soviet power and influence in Asia Pacific by developing closer ties with Beijing. By 1979 a decision had clearly been made to play the 'China card'. The new American thinking was perhaps most concisely expressed by Carter's national security adviser, Zbigniew Brzezinski:

> Few actions will contribute more to the security and stability of our important position around the rim of Asia . . . than a constructive involvement with China. As we improve our relations with Peking, China will also wish to keep us involved in the region and not, as in the past, seek to drive us away . . . Normalisation consolidates a favourable balance in the Far East and enhances the security of our friends.[75]

The anti-Soviet thrust of Washington's new China policy would be maintained during Reagan's first presidential term. According to US official rhetoric, the Soviet grand design was to achieve 'maximum, geopolitical strength from which to project power and influence'.[76] More specifically, Moscow was intent on neutralizing Japan and weakening the US–Japan alliance, threatening the security of the sea lanes, increasing access to Vietnamese air and naval facilities, reducing ASEAN's links with the West, and discouraging closer West European and Japanese links with China. The Soviet threat thesis, which now became the guiding principle of US foreign policy, was meant to legitimize the rapid expansion of military expenditures, the strengthening of counter-force nuclear capabilities and a concentrated campaign against Soviet proxies,[77] not least in Asia.

The response of the Asia-Pacific region to the new US policy was less than enthusiastic. Though most governments welcomed a continuing US military presence, and many had their own reasons for maintaining a certain diplomatic distance from Moscow, few of them were entirely persuaded by official US assessments of the Soviet threat.[78] There was a general tendency to question the military significance of the Soviet presence at Cam Ranh Bay and the importance or durability of the Soviet–Vietnamese alliance. The structural weakness of the Soviet economy coupled with the enormous diplomatic and financial costs of the Soviet move into Afghanistan appeared to place severe limitations on the Soviet capacity for military intervention or infiltration in other parts of Asia.[79] To some the US preoccupation with the Soviet threat seemed a dangerous recipe for the expansion of Chinese military capabilities. To others it signalled added US pressure on allies to increase their defence spending. Needless to say, regional reactions to the new US strategic posture varied considerably from country to country, but even amongst US allies it provoked considerable discomfort and a sense that US priorities did not necessarily reflect regional needs or circumstances. In short, the Second Cold War was unlikely to reverse the slow but steady erosion of ideological and strategic bipolarity or insulate Cold War alliances from the corrosive impact of complex and interacting charges in the domestic, regional and global environment of member states. The rimlands would not be easily or fully integrated into the World-Island.

The Japan–US Alliance

The ensuing overview of the evolution of US alliances necessarily focuses on the US–Japan relationship, generally considered strategically the most important and one of the most solidly based alliances in Asia Pacific. For Japan the bilateral security treaty with the United States, signed only a few hours after the San Francisco Peace Treaty in September 1951, served two critical functions: it guaranteed Japan's territorial integrity, and it enabled it to concentrate its energies on economic development rather than military defence.[80] These two central tenets of the Yoshida Doctrine[81] implied two other advantages. First, the alliance with the United States, coupled with Japanese renunciation of the use or threat of force, promised to allay regional anxieties about Japan's future role, and to that extent contributed to Japan's rehabilitation as a legitimate and respected member of the international community. Second, a close relationship with the United States would enhance Japanese access to US markets and resources and more generally facilitate Japan's full participation in the new liberal economic and political order.

Substantial though they were, these benefits could not obscure the fact that the peace and security treaties were unequal agreements dictated largely by US strategic priorities. Not surprisingly, the Soviet Union, China and India did not sign the San Francisco Treaty, nor did Burma or North Korea. Australia, New Zealand and the Philippines were prevailed upon to sign, but only after expressing serious misgivings. The United States was from the outset intent on making Japan an integral part of its containment policy, hence its enthusiasm for Japanese economic reconstruction, and its willingness to curtail the reparations programme and remove production controls on war-related industries. As early as 1948 the National Security Council had secretly approved the creation of a 150 000-man armed Japanese constabulary force. By January 1951, Dulles was urging the Japanese to create a defence force of 300 000 to 350 000 – an idea which Prime Minister Yoshida himself resisted for fear of the damage that such rapid military expansion might do to Japan's financial and political stability.[82] Japanese leaders were especially anxious to avoid the development of military forces which might then have to be deployed in the Korean War.

The peace treaty was inseparable in content and meaning from the security treaty which gave the United States virtually free rein to maintain bases in Japan and to use them in support of operations in other parts of East Asia, without necessarily consulting the Japanese government. Similarly, the treaty permitted the United States to station in Japan any weapon, even if this did not accord with the wishes of its government. Moreover, it provided for the intervention of US forces in large-scale internal disturbances in Japan, a provision deemed by many incompatible with the country's sovereign status.[83] Significantly, the United States had not made an explicit commitment to protect Japan in case of attack, yet had acquired the right to veto any arrangement allowing a third power to introduce its forces into Japan. Finally, there was no provision for the termination of the treaty except by mutual consent.[84] All these provisions are perhaps best understood as the logical continuation of US occupation policy,[85] which helps to explain why they provoked widespread resentment within the Japanese body politic, most sharply expressed by, but by no means confined to, the Socialist and Communist parties.

Indicative of the asymmetrical structure of the alliance was the intense and ultimately successful pressure Washington exerted on Prime Minister Yoshida to withhold recognition from the People's Republic of China and establish instead diplomatic relations with Taiwan. Though the Treaty of Mutual Co-operation and Security of January 1960 removed several of the most offensive elements of the 1951 agreement, significant differences of outlook persisted. With the escalation of the Vietnam War in the mid-1960s, Japanese business profited handsomely as it supplied a substantial proportion of US arms procurements. By contrast, the pivotal role played by large US military bases in Okinawa in the prosecution of the war caused considerable disquiet, and greatly strengthened sentiment inside Japan for the return of Okinawa, a Japanese island held in trust by the United States since 1945. Following the Sato–Nixon communiqué of November 1969, Okinawa returned to Japanese sovereignty in 1972, but on the understanding that the United States would retain access to its military facilities. In addition, Prime Minister Sato indicated a substantial widening of Japan's security obligations, referring specifically to the possible use by US forces of Japanese areas and facilities in the event of conflict on the Korean peninsula and expressing firm support for US treaty commitments to Taiwan.[86] The Japanese government had reconciled itself to the fact that the deployment of substantial US land, naval and air forces throughout the Japanese archipelago and particularly on Okinawa was designed not merely to defend Japan against external attack, but to sustain a capacity for US power projection in both Southeast and Northeast Asia. Japan had been assigned a crucial role in 'securing' the rest of the Asian rimlands.

The reconciliation of US and Japanese interests had enabled Tokyo to enjoy the benefits of the US security umbrella yet avoid the high costs of large-scale remilitarization, but at a price. Following the establishment of the National Defense Agency, Japan proceeded with the formation of the Ground, Air and Maritime Self-Defense Forces, which over the next decade would oversee the steady expansion of the defence budget and the emergence of a sizeable military-industrial infrastructure.[87] US pressure was no doubt the decisive factor in the gradual reinterpretation of Japan's peace constitution, which is not to say that Japanese interest in maintaining access to military training and technology and domestic conservative political pressures did not also play a part. Japanese governments did, it is true, periodically reaffirm their commitment to Article IX of the Constitution. The Three Principles on Arms Exports and the Three Non-Nuclear Principles were in large measure enunciated in order to accommodate pacifist sentiment within Japan. Yet the definition of these principles would prove no less elusive than constitutional interpretation. In theory, Japan was precluded by virtue of the Three Non-Nuclear Principles from producing nuclear weapons, possessing them or allowing them to be introduced on its territory.[88] In practice, Japanese governments substantially diluted these principles, first by allowing US warships to make regular visits to Japanese ports without challenging the US Navy's 'neither confirm nor deny' policy, and subsequently by agreeing to participate in Strategic Defense Initiative (SDI) research.

It would be misleading to suggest that the ambiguities in Japanese security policy were attributable entirely to the tensions within the alliance. The Japanese policy-making process, as we shall see more clearly in a later chapter, was itself subject to multiple and often contradictory pressures. There is no denying, however, the impact of external factors. With the passage of time Japan's extraordinary economic success, coupled with the declining competitiveness of the US economy in the late 1960s and early 1970s and the reduction of US forces in the Asia-Pacific theatre consequent upon the Nixon Doctrine, prompted a concerted US campaign for a new approach to burden-sharing.[89] Japan was now expected to make a greater contribution to the common defence effort, which, in practical terms, meant increased Japanese military spending, greater financial support for the US military presence, defence technology-sharing and more US arms exports to Japan.[90] In responding to these pressures the Japanese government, mindful of the divergence of views within both its own ranks and the bureaucracy, not to mention public sensitivities, was inclined to accommodate US demands, but by pursuing a strategy based on gradualism and *ad hoc* improvization.[91]

Perhaps the first substantive response came in 1976 with the approval by Cabinet of the National Defense Program Outline (NDPO), which redefined the purpose of the Self-Defense Forces (SDF) as raising the cost of aggression against Japan by establishing the military capability to resist a limited invasion. Japanese pronouncements and actions fell, however, short of US demands and expectations. To appease domestic criticism of the NDPO, Prime Minister Miki Takeo set a 1 per cent of GNP ceiling on defence expenditure, thereby limiting the degree to which Japan would accommodate US pressures for burden-sharing. Soon after Reagan's election US pressure intensified. In March 1981, US Defense Secretary Weinberger called for a more rational division of labour among Japan, Europe and the United States. In May 1981, following discussions between President Reagan and Prime Minister Suzuki, in which defence featured as a major issue, a statement was issued that Japan could 'within the framework of the constitution' protect its sea lines of communication to 1000 nautical miles, and that this goal would be adopted as national policy. In June 1981, Washington called for a Japanese defence posture capable of dealing with the Soviet fleet and its associated Backfires.[92] In the summer of 1982 the Suzuki government announced an increase in its projected purchase of

F-15 Eagle fighters from 100 to 155 and of P-3C Orion anti-submarine planes from 45 to 74.[93]

It was not, however, until Nakasone came to office in November 1982 that Japan's defence policy became more closely aligned with US strategic planning. Before becoming prime minister, Nakasone had clearly articulated several related themes: that Japan needed to develop its military potential; that it should move towards closer military collaboration with the United States; and that it was necessary to change Japan's public opinion in favour of greater self-reliance in defence. During his first official visit to Washington, soon after becoming prime minister, Nakasone described Japan and the United States as 'two nations with a single destiny'.[94] At the G7 Summit in Williamsburg in May 1983, Japan for the first time endorsed a joint statement setting out the West's common strategic purpose:

> It is our first duty to defend freedom and justice on which our democracies are based. To this end, we shall maintain sufficient military strength to deter any attack, to counter any threat to ensure the peace.[95]

A change was clearly under way in the perceptions of the governing Liberal Democratic Party, to which the opposition parties, including the Socialist Party, and even public opinion were not entirely immune.

During 1983–5 Japan's defence spending increased at a faster rate than its economic growth. At a time of fiscal stringency, Japanese military expenditures in the first half of the 1980s registered annual increases of between 6.5 per cent and 7.8 per cent. In 1985 Nakasone persuaded the Cabinet and the National Defense Council to approve a $75 billion five-year defence plan, which provided for the acquisition of 246 T-74 tanks, five submarines, nine destroyer escorts, 50 P-3C maritime reconnaissance aircraft, 63 F-15 fighters and six squadrons of 'Patriot' surface-to-air missiles. Though these planned acquisitions were subsequently revised, there was no denying that Japan had embarked on the procurement of state-of-the art hardware. In January 1987 the Cabinet formally lifted the 1 per cent ceiling on defence expenditure, allowing the defence budget for FY1987 to rise to $24 billion (or 1.004 per cent of GNP). The government appropriated about $29.5 billion for FY1988 and submitted to the Diet a FY1989 budget of $31.4 billion (or 1.006 per cent of estimated GNP). The strengthened yen had considerably increased Japan's military spending in dollars terms, making it comparable to that of the larger European NATO countries.[96] By the late 1980s, Japan's ground forces could boast 1150 tanks, its air force 473 combat aircraft, and its navy over 50 destroyers and 15 submarines.[97] Japan's increased defence budget had also made possible a greater contribution to the cost of US forces stationed in Japan (now numbering around 60 000). In 1988

Japanese financial support amounted to $2.5 billion, or approximately 40 per cent of the total annual cost of maintaining the US military presence in Japan.[98]

How then might one interpret the evolution of Japanese security policy? At one level, the increased allocation of resources to the defence effort can be read as evidence of Japan's intention to build a closer strategic partnership with the United States. Certainly, the period from the mid-1970s onwards is characterized by higher levels of defence co-operation, including the development of joint operational plans, more joint training and more extensive exchanges of technology and intelligence. Japanese perceptions of a Soviet military build-up in Asia Pacific may well have been a contributing factor. At another level, however, Japan's decision to assume a higher military profile may be understood as one element in the gradual reassertion of Japanese nationalism. In other words, the evolution of Japanese security policy may be considerably more ambiguous than appears at first sight. Nowhere is this ambiguity perhaps better expressed than in the tensions which bedevilled US–Japanese co-operation in defence technology.

Despite a series of agreements concluded during the 1980s, including the November 1983 Exchange of Notes on the Transfer of Japanese Military Technologies, negotiations regarding the transfer of advanced defence technology proved difficult, and at times acrimonious. US concerns included Japan's possible emergence as a competitor in the international arms trade, the degree to which Japan could be trusted with classified technologies, the wish to retain superiority in advanced civil and military technologies, and the related expectation that Japan should look to the United States as its major source of sophisticated military hardware. The illegal sales of sensitive technology to the Soviet Union by the Toshiba Machinery Company in March 1987 and congressional misgivings following the signing of a contract allowing Japan to produce Aegis anti-aircraft cruisers were indicative of the delicacy of the defence relationship. Even more damaging was the dispute surrounding Japan's projected procurement of a new support fighter, known as the FSX. The Pentagon had consistently argued that, on grounds of cost effectiveness, interoperability and the large trade imbalance between the two countries, US technology was Japan's most compelling option. The Japanese Defense Agency (JDA), for its part, responding to powerful industrial and bureaucratic pressures at home, advocated the development of indigenous technology. A compromise agreement was reached in October 1987 to build an advanced aircraft based on the F-16 model produced by General Dynamics, but with substantial Japanese modifications. It took another year of difficult negotiations before the agreement could be signed in November 1988, and even then its future remained uncertain following vociferous criticism of the sharing scheme by the US

Congress and the Department of Commerce.[99] The Bush Administration's subsequent decision to review the agreement and then to add additional 'clarifications' to it served to highlight the formidable obstacles in the path of US–Japanese collaboration in advanced defence technology.

The tensions associated with issues of burden-sharing and the transfer of sensitive technologies, though they did not call into question the US–Japan security relationship, did nevertheless indicate the profound changes which had occurred in the domestic and external environment of both countries. Geoeconomic and geopolitical considerations were inextricably entwined in the shaping of defence policy. The FSX controversy was itself the symbol of 'an intense policy debate within Japan over the best strategy to maximize the country's economic, technological and foreign policy objectives'.[100] Perceptions and attitudes within the policy-making elites were far from uniform, but there was an emerging consensus that the defence industry and defence research and development would play a key role in Japan's future security and commercial competitiveness. The major employer federations (*keidanren*), individual defence contractors, and in particular industrial associations specializing in military production (for example, Japan's Weapons Industry Association)[101] were now strongly wedded to the principle of increasing self-reliance in defence. Co-development arrangements with US firms and the transfer of US technology were seen as provisional but necessary expedients, given the current technological supremacy of the United States, the continuing usefulness of the alliance relationship with the United States, and not least the new opportunities for entering the international weapons market. There were, however, more fundamental factors at work in the rapidly evolving bilateral security relationship. Japan's emergence as a major trading and financial power could not but modify the relative bargaining strengths of the two sides.

During the 1980s the Reagan Administration's Cold War posture may have successfully reasserted the global projection of US military power, but it also contributed in tandem with tax reduction policies to steeply rising budget deficits, which in turn resulted in a massive federal debt (in 1986 these were estimated at $201.1 billion and $2.05 trillion respectively).[102] The increasing dependence of the United States on Japanese capital to finance its trade and current account deficits – a theme to which we shall return in later chapters – reflected a substantial shift in the balance of economic power which would sooner or later rebound on the security component of the relationship. US demands for more equitable burden-sharing flowed directly from the realization that in the vastly altered circumstances of the 1970s and 1980s the United States could no longer afford to underwrite, virtually single-handedly, the enormous costs associated with the maintenance of the elaborate western alliance system. Europe and especially Japan were expected to make financial contributions more in keeping with their newly acquired wealth. To put it differently, the United States was intent on securing a redistribution of the costs of collective defence. Faced with such a prospect, US allies could hardly avoid a reappraisal of the costs and benefits, indeed of the underlying purposes, of the policy of alignment. These were highly complex and delicate questions, for none more so than for Japan.

Japanese governments were strongly committed to the retention of the US nuclear and conventional umbrella, but numerous voices in Japan were now questioning the effectiveness of US leadership. A report commissioned by Prime Minister Ohira reported in 1980:

> In considering Japan's security, the most fundamental change that took place in the international situation in the 1970s is that the clear US superiority, in both military and economic dimensions, came to an end.[103]

The marked expansion of military outlays during the Reagan years and the corresponding decline of Soviet power prompted a more nuanced but essentially unchanged assessment of the international situation. Japan's 1988 Diplomatic Blue Book referred specifically to the steadily increasing weight of Japan, Western Europe and China, and to the decline, at least in economic terms, of the position of the United States.[104] While the policy implications of this redistribution of power were as yet only dimly perceived, Japan, under Nakasone and Takeshita, developed an increasingly activist bilateral and multilateral diplomacy, with a strong focus on expanded development assistance, promotion of cultural exchanges and greater involvement in issues of regional and global security.

Japanese interests could no longer be as easily satisfied within the bilateral edifice of Japan–US relations built on the foundations of Japanese military defeat and US post-1945 hegemony. Whether in relation to the Soviet Union, China or Southeast Asia, Japanese perceptions and priorities could not be assumed to coincide with US policy. The 'Nixon shocks' had delivered to Japan a rude diplomatic awakening, but the divergence of interests did not become fully apparent until the Carter and Reagan years. By the early 1980s the strains in the US–Japan relationship had become a fact of geopolitical life which neither the periodic fluctuations between Cold War and détente nor the changing chemistry of the personal relationship between leaders of the two countries could obscure or reverse.

Both sides, while reaffirming the centrality of the alliance, brought to it a new critical perspective born of the realization that the US–Japan relationship had 'shifted from that of patron–client to that of competitive peers'.[105] Washington's decision to pressure Tokyo into shouldering a greater share of the 'burden' was a perfectly understandable reaction given Japan's greatly expanded capabilities, but it did have equally understandable though perhaps unforeseen consequences. When a senior ally, particularly one which has occupied a hegemonic position, asks a junior ally to carry more of the burden, what might the latter's reaction be? Assuming a positive response to such pressure, as was Japan's inclination, there will be a natural, even if not clearly articulated, expectation on the part of the junior ally that greater burden-sharing will mean more effective participation in the decision-making process. This, however, may be an expectation which the senior ally is either reluctant or poorly equipped to accommodate. The call for greater burden-sharing may at the same time provoke a different and almost conflicting reaction: the junior ally may begin to wonder whether the desire on the part of the senior ally to shed some of the burden is but the first sign in the long-term process of disengagement. Either response – elements of both were discernible in Japan's case – is likely to engender new tensions or uncertainties in the relationship. The United States might regularly reaffirm its strategic commitment to the region, but such reassurances could not be guaranteed to have the desired effect.

There was in the case of the US–Japan alliance a further complication, namely Japan's peace constitution and public sensitivities on issues of peace and war. Tokyo could and often did argue that it was precluded by domestic political constraints from acceding to many of Washington's demands, especially those requiring Japan to develop a higher strategic profile. However, as already indicated, Japanese governments and their advisers were not all of one mind. For important elements of Japanese industry, the bureaucracy and the Liberal Democratic Party, US pressure for a greater Japanese defence effort was an opportunity to expand Japan's Self-Defense Forces. Even greater defence co-operation with the United States, though a financially costly exercise, might prove a worthwhile investment in the consolidation of Japan's defence industry and associated research and development infrastructure. Collaborative projects with US industry and even the purchase of US technology might be the short-term price that Japan would have to pay in the long-term drive for greater defence autonomy. In other words, for a number of strategically placed interests in Japanese society, the US alliance was not an alternative to greater national self-assertion but the indispensable instrument which would facilitate and legitimize an expanded strategic and diplomatic role for Japan. Quite apart from its potential military value in relation to external threats, the US umbrella had a political and psychological function in helping to shield Japanese policy-makers from adverse domestic and international opinion, thereby making Japan's transition to great power status more palatable than it might otherwise be. Regardless of short-term policy fluctuations, usually reflecting the immediate exigencies of Japanese or US domestic politics, the alliance was by the late 1980s undergoing profound mutation, mirroring and reinforcing changing power relationships and corresponding attempts by national policy-making elites and non-state actors to reposition themselves in what was a rapidly evolving regional and global geopolitical landscape.

Lesser Alliances

The shifts in the US–Japan relationship were exceptional only in their subtlety and long-term significance. While the pace and intensity of the response varied markedly from case to case, no US alliance in the region remained impervious to the winds of change. A few brief observations will suffice to provide the necessary backdrop for the later and more detailed analysis of contemporary trends. At one end of the spectrum was the final phasing out of SEATO's activities in September 1975 after cosmetic changes in the functions of the organization introduced during the last two years of its existence had failed to bring the corpse back to life. Established primarily as a legitimating instrument for US intervention in Southeast Asia, the organization had always lacked the clarity of purpose or commonality of interests it needed to function as a workable alliance. Once the whole of Indochina came under communist rule and the United States lost its appetite for military engagement on the Asian mainland, SEATO was effectively deprived of any meaningful role. While the Manila Pact on which SEATO rested remained legally in force, this chapter in the history of collective security had clearly come to a close.

More durable were the security arrangements the United States had concluded with South Korea and Taiwan. In both instances the ostensible rationale for the military presence was to deter North Korea and China respectively from using force in pursuit of their reunification plans. Such a presence, however, also served the wider US purpose of extending force projection capabilities, gaining access to strategic sea lanes and enhancing the overall credibility of the policy of containment. Yet both alliances would be subjected to considerable pressure during the 1970s and 1980s. As already noted, the shift in US priorities was evidenced in the Carter Administration's declared intention to withdraw some 33 000 ground troops from South Korea. These plans were subsequently abandoned, but the thinking which had inspired them continued to manifest itself in other ways.

During the Reagan years, US support for South Korean military modernization was enhanced, with the US Congress approving foreign military sales credits and the sale of US military equipment worth some $8 billion. In May 1984, the United States announced plans to deploy another 2000–2500 military personnel to South Korea by 1985. Yet these moves, prompted in large measure by tensions on the Korean peninsula, could not altogether conceal several other influences bearing on the relationship, notably anti-American sentiment within South Korea, US concerns about the slow pace of South Korean democratization, and increasing US pressure on South Korea to open up its domestic market to foreign imports of manufactured goods and to contribute more to the cost of maintaining US forces in Korea. More significant still, at least in the longer term, were the growing signs of movement in US–North Korea relations, which, though they did not imply any immediate lessening of the US security commitment to South Korea, reflected a heightened desire on Washington's part to reduce tensions on the peninsula and pave the way for a negotiated settlement of the conflict. By the late 1980s North Korea might still qualify in American eyes as a rogue state but no longer as a proxy of Soviet or Chinese interests. The bipolar prism through which international reality had been perceived for the best part of three decades had lost much of its potency.

In the case of Taiwan, the shift in US policy was far more explicit and came much earlier. It was clearly evident in the Shanghai communiqué issued at the conclusion of Nixon's historic visit to China in February 1972. Given the sensitivities of the issue the two parties found it necessary to present separate statements of their respective positions. Whereas China simply restated its traditional demands – 'Taiwan is a province of China ... the liberation of Taiwan is China's internal affair ... all US forces and military installations must be withdrawn from Taiwan' – the United States, in a striking departure from previously established policy, acknowledged that 'there is but one China and that Taiwan is part of China', and affirmed 'the ultimate objective of the withdrawal of all US forces and military installations in Taiwan'.[106] The next important step did not come until December 1978 when Beijing and Washington announced the normalization of their relations as from 1 January 1979. As part of a diplomatic compromise, the United States accepted China's three principal conditions: diplomatic ties with Taiwan were to be severed; the US–Taiwan mutual defence treaty abrogated; and the 700 remaining US troops (down from almost 10 000 at the height of the Vietnam War) withdrawn from the island.[107] To demonstrate its continuing commitment to Taiwan's security and to cushion the shock of US disengagement, Washington declared unilaterally that it reserved the right to continue supplying Taipei with defensive weapons. An agreement was also reached for the establishment of offices which would provide the necessary framework for the continuation of bilateral trade, US arms sales and various loan arrangements. US military support for Taiwan inevitably became a source of intermittent tension in Sino-American relations. In response to sustained Chinese pressure Washington agreed to place limits on the amount and kind of military aid with which it would furnish Taiwan, and even foreshadowed an eventual end to such aid. The agreement, left deliberately ambiguous on both counts, was nevertheless further evidence that for the United States the residual security commitment to Taiwan would be increasingly subordinated to the priorities of its China policy.

In Southeast Asia the Philippines, and in particular the air base at Clark Field (with nearly 8000 air force personnel) and the naval base at Subic Bay (the largest naval supply depot outside the United States), had played a pivotal role in US military planning in the western Pacific since the Second World War. These bases provided essential support for US operations in the Korean and Vietnam wars and helped to guard crucial sea lanes extending from the Pacific to the Indian Ocean.[108] Though the Marcos government had consistently sought to use the bases as a lever to extract maximum economic advantage from the United States, it was not until the collapse of the Marcos regime in 1985 that the future of the bases became a bone of contention. On assuming office President Aquino indicated that she would respect the US–Philippines bases agreement until its expiry in 1991, but would thereafter keep her options open. The political climate inside the Philippines had nevertheless become much less hospitable to the US military presence.[109] Moreover, the new constitution had made the retention of foreign military bases, troops and facilities conditional on a bilateral treaty to be ratified by a two-thirds vote in the Senate and then endorsed by popular referendum. In October 1988, the United States signed a two-year agreement with the Philippines, which provided for US payments of $481 million a year in economic, military and development aid in return for continued use of the bases. Faced with ever-increasing financial and political costs, the US Administration's enthusiasm for the retention of its bases in the Philippines was visibly declining even before the final collapse of the negotiations. The geopolitical order and the security calculus which accompanied it were visibly transformed under the mounting pressure of domestic politics.

While Thailand did not feature as prominently in US strategic planning as the Philippines, the US–Thai military relationship had played an important part in the US policy of containing Southeast Asian communism. Indeed, Thailand was often portrayed as one of the dominoes that might eventually fall if communist subversion in Indochina were not effectively resisted.[110] Between 1950 and 1980 about 18 000 Thai officers received training in the United States and the Thai armed forces were supplied with substantial quantities of US military equipment. Thailand sent combat units to fight alongside US troops in both the Korean and Vietnam Wars. In the joint statement of March 1962, which subsequent US administrations reaffirmed more than once, the United States declared 'the preservation of the independence and integrity of Thailand as vital to the national interests of the United States'. In 1966 US forces in Thailand were significantly augmented, but force reductions began immediately after the ceasefire in Vietnam in June 1973, and by early 1976 all US air force personnel had been withdrawn. The US–Thai security relationship remained generally close during the 1980s, as evidenced by joint military training exercises in Thailand, a number of US military assistance programmes and the prepositioning in Thailand of US military resupply facilities.[111] Yet the bilateral relationship could not but be affected by profound changes in the regional and global environment. The normalization of Sino-American relations, the subsequent easing of tensions between China and the Soviet Union, Vietnam's stated intention to withdraw its forces from Cambodia, the emergence of Japan as the largest contributor of development assistance in Southeast Asia, Thailand's closer links with China (which had now become a useful source of military hardware) and, perhaps most importantly, ASEAN's increasing cohesion and maturity, had all contributed to the diversification of Bangkok's diplomatic and security arrangements and a corresponding decline in the centrality of the US relationship.

It remains to say a word about the ANZUS alliance, which Australia and New Zealand had regarded since its inception as constituting the bedrock of their security. Though differences of view might periodically emerge in their relationship with the United States, most frequently and vehemently expressed on issues of trade, the ANZUS Treaty had consistently enjoyed widespread public approval in New Zealand as much as in Australia. Yet the meaning and context of the alliance would undergo considerable change as the junior allies sought to internalize the lessons of the Vietnam War and the implications of the Nixon Doctrine. With the election of the Whitlam government in December 1972 Australia would begin to place greater emphasis on the defence of continental Australia and on bilateral and multilateral co-operation with the states of Southeast Asia – a process which steadily gained momentum under both conservative and Labor governments. This trend was partially obscured during the Fraser period largely because of the prime minister's preoccupation with the threat posed by Soviet interventionism and rapidly expanding Soviet military capabilities. Significantly, however, it was this globalist perspective rather than the value of the alliance for the direct defence of Australia which served as the primary justification for strengthening Australia's diplomatic and military alignment with the United States. Accordingly, the 1976 defence White Paper made it clear that Australia's security policy would no longer be based on the expectation that its armed forces would 'be sent abroad to fight as part of some other nation's force, supported by it'.[112] The policy of self-reliance, and the implicit abandonment of the forward defence strategy would assume even greater importance under the Hawke government. The review of the ANZUS Treaty conducted in 1983, while reaffirming the coincidence of strategic interests between the ANZUS parties, the deterrent value of the alliance and the mutual benefits of defence cooperation, argued that Australia was not totally dependent on ANZUS for its security, that each partner carried primary responsibility for its own defence, that ANZUS did not provide an automatic guarantee of military support in the event of attack or major threat, and that diversity of opinion within the alliance was both desirable and possible.

Australia's attempted redefinition of its defence and regional policies, the ramifications of which will be explored in a subsequent chapter, had effectively displaced the ANZUS alliance from the centre stage of Australian diplomacy. Policy developments in New Zealand would have even more radical consequences. As late as 1983 the New Zealand Defence Review had reaffirmed the country's commitment to ANZUS and acceptance of deterrence as the foundation stone of a stable global balance of power. Less than two years later, following the election of the Lange government in July 1984, New Zealand adopted a nuclear-free policy, subsequently entrenched in legislation, which effectively barred nuclear-armed and nuclear-powered ships from visiting New Zealand ports.

The US response was both immediate and unambiguous. The US Navy's right of access to New Zealand ports was declared to be non-negotiable: the 'neither confirm nor deny' policy was essential to deterrence and to the operational effectiveness of US ships and aircraft; without unfettered port access the strategic utility of ANZUS would be dramatically undermined. Prime Minister Lange responded by arguing that New Zealand's anti-nuclear initiative was not aimed against the ANZUS alliance or the United States, but intended as a gesture against the insanity of the nuclear arms race. New Zealand did n ot, in any case, have any obligation under the Treaty to host nuclear weapons on its territory. Notwithstanding Lange's protestations of good faith, there is no denying that New Zealand's attempt to denuclearize the alliance was a direct challenge to the American definition of obligations under ANZUS, which perhaps helps to explain Washington's decision to retaliate by curtailing defence and intelligence links with New Zealand and 'suspending its security obligations to New Zealand under the ANZUS Treaty pending adequate corrective measures'.[113] The severity of America's punitive response, intended in part to dissuade other allies from emulating the Lange initiative, failed to bring New Zealand back into the fold and effectively transformed ANZUS from a trilateral to a bilateral alliance.[114]

Enough has been said to indicate that the alliance system the United States had constructed in Asia Pacific between 1945 and 1955 had by the end of the 1980s acquired a rather different geopolitical complexion. The United States remained the world's pre-eminent military power, and in Asia Pacific the US Navy, particularly in the wake of the Reagan Administration's procurement and deployment programmes, had acquired a strong offensive capability. The increasing scale and frequency of naval exercises – many of them conducted in close proximity to Soviet waters and involving B-52 bombers, AWACS planes, P-3 Orion ASW aircraft and attack submarines – were designed to demonstrate the US navy's capacity to sustain even in remote areas major and protracted military operations.[115] Yet this awesome display of military power, though it might have had the desired effect of intimidating Soviet planners, did not necessarily inspire confidence on the part of US allies that such power would be readily available to support their respective interests.

Nor could Washington readily convert its military arsenal into effective political influence, particularly when it came to managing complex tensions and conflicts, whether in Northeast or Southeast Asia. To liken the decline of US power to that of post-imperial Britain would be misleading,[116] but the increasing emphasis of successive US administrations on the need for more effective burden-sharing was evidence of America's diminishing capacity or willingness to underwrite the rising costs of maintaining its far-flung security system. Indeed, it is arguable that the Reagan presidency, precisely because it devoted so much of America's energies and resources to confronting its principal military adversary, the Soviet Union, was insufficiently attuned to the more serious economic challenges emanating from Europe and Japan, or to the emerging political and cultural undercurrents that would significantly transform the structure and psychology of alliance relationships, and more generally the Asia-Pacific geopolitical landscape.

SOVIET POWER IN DECLINE

In sharp contrast to the dismal failure of US military intervention in Vietnam and the consequent decline of US military strength on the Asian mainland, Soviet power at that time appeared to many observers to be rapidly expanding. The latter half of the 1970s witnessed the conclusion of the 1978 Treaty of Friendship and Co-operation with Vietnam, the invasion of Afghanistan, support for Vietnam's military intervention in Cambodia, the establishment of new military facilities on the disputed Kurile islands (or Northern Territories), and a sustained military build-up in Soviet Asia. By the mid-1980s Soviet strategic capabilities in the region included SS-18 land-based ICBMs and SS-N-18 SLBMs, complementing some 50 long-range Bear and Bison strategic bombers. The number of ballistic missile submarines had tripled since 1966. Soviet theatre nuclear forces included more than 135 SS-20 launchers and about 80 Backfire and 120 Badger bombers. Over a period of 20 years the strength of Soviet ground forces had risen from 17 to 52 divisions, and the Pacific fleet, previously confined to coastal defence, was now the largest and most active of the four Soviet fleets. The Soviet military presence in Vietnam had been considerably upgraded with the establishment of major naval facilities, intelligence collection bases and rotational airfields.[117]

At one level, it seemed as if Soviet military forces had acquired a much greater capacity to project power in both the Indian and the Pacific Oceans. At another level, however, those forces, concentrated largely around coastal cities, notably Vladivostok and Petropavlosk, were subject to multiple constraints, including poor weather conditions, long supply lines and major transportation problems. According to one official US estimate, 90 per cent of Soviet ground forces were in any case directed against China and, in particular, its growing nuclear arsenal.[118] Moreover, Soviet naval forces tended to be separated from the open seas by narrow straits over which US military planes could, in conjunction with Japan and South Korea, exercise effective control. Unlike US forces, which were capable of attacking Soviet bases, troop concentrations and nuclear installations, only a few Soviet combat divisions or aircraft could be deployed outside the Soviet Union. A number of Soviet bombers and naval forces could be assigned to long-range missions, but the Soviet Pacific fleet was primarily designed 'to protect the Pacific flank of the Soviet Union, to help secure the Delta SSBN launch areas and provide limited interdiction'.[119] Extensive though it was, the Soviet military build-up did not endow Moscow with a capacity to control the sea lines of communication. It may arguably have provided Soviet allies with a degree of reassurance, but it is doubtful whether it succeeded in intimidating US allies. Perhaps its more lasting effect was to contribute to the general but growing regional unease about the long-term security implications of Cold War politics and the escalating nuclear arms race in the Pacific.

As for Soviet alliances, their military reach and political effectiveness were limited, to say the least. China, once Moscow's principal ally, had become its arch enemy. Throughout the 1970s and well into the 1980s, Beijing was intent on establishing a new united front comprising the Third World, the Second World (principally Western Europe and Japan) and the United States as a deterrent to 'Soviet hegemonism'. By 1978 the most important Soviet ally was Vietnam. Not only did it give Soviet policy in Africa its full support, but it openly echoed Moscow's criticism of China and branded Beijing's 'three worlds theory' as 'reactionary'. The Soviet Union for its part facilitated Vietnam's membership of the Council for Mutual Economic Assistance (COMECON) and provided Hanoi with significant quantities of arms. In November 1978 the two countries signed a 25-year treaty of friendship and co-operation, in which they pledged that in the event of attack or threat of attack they would 'immediately consult each other with a view to eliminating that threat'. According to western estimates, Soviet military and economic aid to Vietnam increased dramatically after 1978, reaching $1.1 billion in 1979 and $2.2 billion in 1980, with Soviet military advisers in Vietnam now numbering well in excess of 5000, as against 1000 during the Vietnam War.[120] Almost immediately after the outbreak of Sino-Vietnamese hostilities in February 1979 the Soviet Union had deployed Tu95 Bear reconnaissance aircraft in the South China Sea, with a view to monitoring Chinese troop movements along the Vietnamese border. This action and the subsequent despatch of Soviet ships to the area, including a missile destroyer, were presumably designed to deter or at least restrain Chinese military action. For the Soviet Union the principal strategic benefit of the alliance was enhanced access to military facilities, in particular at Cam Ranh Bay, which now hosted MiG 23s as well as Soviet ships and other aircraft.

Yet as early as 1980 strains began to appear in the relationship. The Soviet Union would periodically decline to make new aid commitments as a way of expressing its displeasure with certain aspects of Vietnam's domestic and foreign policies. Hanoi for its part would from time to time suggest that its close relationship with Moscow was more a matter of strategic necessity than political choice. Vietnamese unease visibly intensified in 1982 when, for the first time, Moscow signalled its interest in improved relations with Beijing. Soviet assurances that such an improvement would not be to 'the detriment of third countries' was less than comforting to Vietnamese leaders, for whom the principal value of the alliance with the Soviet Union was its deterrent effect on China. Hanoi's initial response was to stress 'the identity of strategic interests' between Vietnam and the Soviet Union, presumably as a reminder to Moscow of the strategic benefits of continued access to Vietnamese air and naval facilities. It soon became apparent, however, especially after Gorbachev became Soviet leader, that a comprehensive reappraisal of Soviet foreign policies in Asia Pacific was under way. Gorbachev's Vladivostok speech of 28 July 1986 made it clear that improved Sino-Soviet relations – and as a corollary the resolution of the Kampuchean conflict – was now one of Moscow's high priorities.[121] Indicative of the new direction of Soviet policy was Moscow's non-committal response to Sino-Vietnamese tensions in the contested Spratly Islands. There were also increasing signs that the Soviet Union, beset by serious economic difficulties of its own, might not be willing to sustain levels of assistance to Vietnam on the scale provided in previous years.

The combined impact of changes in Vietnam's domestic and external environment would inevitably compel a reassessment of its security policies. Accordingly, the Vietnamese leadership proceeded, at first in small steps that were not immediately apparent, to reduce the country's reliance on the Soviet Union, to improve Sino-Vietnamese relations, reduce defence expenditure and lessen Vietnam's international isolation, in part by revising its Indochina policy and broadening its commercial and financial relations with the outside world. In 1985 Hanoi indicated its intention to withdraw all its troops from Kampuchea by 1990. Though at first Vietnamese claims of troop withdrawals were treated with suspicion, particularly by China and the United States, a decisive stage was reached in 1988 with Hanoi announcing in May that a further 50 000 troops together with the Vietnamese high command in

Kampuchea were to be withdrawn by December, and then in July that all remaining troops would be withdrawn by the end of 1989.

The evolving geopolitical configuration, which had so profoundly transformed the Soviet–Vietnamese relationship, would also affect, though in less drastic fashion, the Soviet alliance with North Korea. During the greater part of the 1970s the polarization of relations within the communist world had seen Pyongyang move decisively closer to Beijing. Kim Il Sung's consistently pro-Chinese declarations did not, however, interrupt the flow of Soviet economic and military aid. In 1979, with North Korea's debt to the Soviet Union estimated at $750 million, Moscow signed a new trade protocol with Pyongyang, offered the North Koreans observer status at a COMECON conference and reportedly sent more than 100 pilots for training on MiG 23s. This did not prevent Pyongyang from clearly siding with Beijing in the Kampuchean conflict and supporting the ASEAN demand for the withdrawal of all Vietnamese troops from Kampuchea. China, which had since the mid-1970s become North Korea's main supplier of military equipment, was now seen as having placed North Korea in the frontline of its security perimeter.

Yet the diplomatic fallout from the North Korean bombing in Rangoon in October 1983, which killed several South Korean ministers and high-ranking officials, only a month after the Soviets had shot down a South Korean airliner killing all 269 passengers and crew, set the stage for a significant improvement in Soviet–North Korean relations. The escalating tensions of the Second Cold War and the emergence of an informal anti-Soviet coalition comprised of the United States, China and Japan were no doubt contributing factors. Even after Gorbachev's accession to the Soviet leadership, the signing of border-transit, consular and economic assistance agreements in 1985 followed by the delivery of SA3 surface-to-air missiles and the first shipment of some 50 MiG 23 supersonic fighters, which Moscow had long denied to Pyongyang, not to mention a series of reciprocal high-level visits, military exchanges and strong public manifestations of mutual solidarity, gave every indication of a close and expanding long-term relationship.[122]

These indicators were nevertheless misleading, or at least ambiguous, and would soon be overtaken by the spill-over effects of the thaw in Soviet–American relations and the increasing attraction which the rapidly industrializing South Korean economy now had for the Soviet Union and Eastern Europe. In developing contacts with South Korea the East Europeans had, at least initially, more diplomatic room for manoeuvre than either Beijing or Moscow. During 1988 Hungary and Yugoslavia exchanged trade officers with South Korea, and Bulgaria and Poland began moving in the same direction. In February 1989, the Hungarian government established full diplomatic relations with Seoul. The Soviet Union, too, was now engaged in negotiations on trade representation. In keeping with Gorbachev's Krasnoyarsk speech of September 1988, in which he explicitly referred to the development of economic relations with South Korea, the two countries soon established their first joint venture.[123] Though continuing to provide North Korea with economic and military aid, Moscow was exerting increasing pressure on Pyongyang to improve its relations with the West. The Soviet–North Korea relationship was simply marking time. The improvement in Sino-Soviet relations was itself a significant factor in lessening the competition between Moscow and Beijing for influence in Pyongyang and accelerating their economic links with Seoul. By the end of 1987 changing economic and diplomatic circumstances were beginning to have a visibly corrosive effect on the framework of Soviet–North Korean relations.

Though it was not immediately apparent, Gorbachev's objective was to extricate Soviet foreign policy from the unproductive and debilitating straitjacket imposed by the Second Cold War, which compounded the social and economic malaise now gripping the Soviet system. This strategic reorientation, itself part of the larger political programme of *Perestroika,* signalled a drastic readjustment of geopolitical imagination. The Soviet leadership had concluded that the vastly expanded military capabilities at its disposal could not be readily converted into political and economic gains. Military intervention as in Afghanistan, support for allies involved in intractable conflicts, notably Vietnam and North Korea, and continuation of the technological arms race with the United States entailed diverse but cumulative diplomatic and financial costs, which were subjecting the Soviet polity and Soviet economy to severe and perhaps irreparable damage.

The Soviet Union may have established a strategic presence in the north Pacific and to a lesser extent in Southeast Asia, but such a presence had not enhanced its capacity to influence events or establish rewarding friendships in either region. Nowhere was this more apparent than in relations with Japan, where historical animosities, the lingering territorial dispute and the build-up of the Soviet Pacific fleet had accentuated Japanese perceptions of a Soviet threat, strengthened the hand of those in the Japanese establishment arguing for an expanded military role for Japan and aborted repeated Soviet efforts to attract Japanese capital and technology in the development of Siberian resources. In Southeast Asia, Moscow's close if nuanced identification with Hanoi's diplomatic posture, whatever its strategic benefits, negated any prospect of developing a more effective dialogue with the ASEAN countries. As for the south Pacific, and Oceania more generally, the Soviet Union remained largely a fringe player. In John Dorrance's words, 'the Soviets have offered little in the way of aid or trade of interest to the region, have failed to win over any government, and continue to have a lower level of presence, dialogue and influence than in any other global region'.[124] The reappraisal of Soviet policies initiated by Gorbachev may to this extent be seen as a belated response to the increasing evidence of Soviet economic and diplomatic weakness.

There was, however, more to Gorbachev's attempts to bring 'new political thinking' to bear on Soviet foreign policy than this simple formula would suggest. In a sense, Moscow was now intent on making virtue out of necessity, that is, on bringing Soviet policies more clearly into line with emerging trends in global and regional geopolitics, and extracting at least relative advantage from an accurate reading, and perhaps dexterous management, of these trends. While the effectiveness of this strategy would be significantly diminished by the Soviet Union's internal political and economic difficulties, the analysis underlying Soviet initiatives and pronouncements is highly instructive in that it sheds considerable light not only on Soviet policy but on changing interpretations of the geopolitical equation in Asia Pacific. In this context, it is worth examining three speeches in which Gorbachev would gradually develop and refine a number of key themes: the Vladivostok speech of July 1986, the Krasnoyarsk speech of September 1988 and the May 1989 speech delivered after the first Sino-Soviet summit in 30 years.

At Vladivostok Gorbachev singled out China and Japan, the two new centres of power in Asia, as countries with which the Soviet Union wished to establish a co-operative relationship. With China he foreshadowed the expansion of economic ties and a more accommodating Soviet attitude which would facilitate the settlement of their long-standing border dispute. With Japan he proposed intensified co-operation, notably in space research, but stressed the need for 'an atmosphere of calm unburdened by the problems of the past', presumably because he saw little prospect of an early resolution of their territorial dispute.[125] Gorbachev was intent on exploiting the geopolitical fluidity characteristic of an increasingly multipolar world. Equally illuminating was the proposal to apply the Helsinki process to Asia, which many observers interpreted, somewhat crudely, as an attempt to freeze the territorial status quo in Asia.[126] The Soviet leader was no doubt interested in promoting a regional framework which would preserve Soviet strategic assets in the region, weaken US alliances (in part through the establishment of nuclear weapons-free zones) and integrate Soviet Asia with the dynamic economies of Asia Pacific. The noteworthy aspect of the proposal, however, was not so much its self-serving character as its emphasis on multilateral diplomacy, based presumably on an understanding that new forms of regional co-operation in both the security and economic arenas would increasingly coexist with, cut across and eventually supplant the institutional arrangements created in the era of ideological and strategic bipolarity.[127]

The Krasnoyarsk speech returned to the same themes, but with a number of new perspectives and proposals, partly in response to the rapidly evolving domestic and international environment.[128] One of the distinctive features of Gorbachev's analysis was indeed the emphasis on change, on what he took to be promising trends in international relations, which had to be sustained and even accelerated.[129] In the Asia-Pacific context he referred specifically to the impending resolution of the Afghan problem, which he implicitly attributed to Moscow's firm commitment to complete the withdrawal of Soviet troops by February 1989. He also pointed to the serious headway being made in diplomatic efforts towards a negotiated settlement of the Kampuchean conflict. He could even discern early signs of progress in the establishment of a process of dialogue on the Korean peninsula. As for Soviet regional policy, the primary objective was the full normalization of relations with China, though high priority was also given to greater co-operation with the ASEAN countries. The importance of the Soviet–Japanese relationship was underlined, but so were Soviet misgivings about the steady build-up of Japan's military potential. For Gorbachev, the thaw in East–West relations offered a unique opportunity to resolve regional conflicts and to reduce or at least limit military arsenals. To this end, he offered to abandon Soviet military facilities in Vietnam in exchange for the closure of US bases in the Philippines. The accent, however, was very much on multilateral initiatives. Gorbachev's proposals included discussions for a freeze followed by reduction in naval and air forces in Northeast Asia (widely interpreted as an attempt to limit the activity of the US Seventh Fleet); a negotiated agreement on measures to promote the safety of sea lanes and air communications of the region; and the establishment of a forum to consider proposals relating to security in the Asia-Pacific region, starting with discussions between the Soviet Union, the United States and China as permanent members of the Security Council. The regional response to the Gorbachev programme was less than enthusiastic. The United States, for its part, saw little merit in any new arrangement which might erode its strategic pre-eminence in the region; others remained suspicious of Soviet motives; while others still were reluctant to allow the Soviet Union to exercise a leadership role in the development of multilateral processes and institutions. The Soviet Union, lacking the necessary legitimacy and diplomatic muscle, could not give institutional impetus to the multilateral agenda, yet its proposals, to the extent that they articulated trends already under way, helped to raise the profile of scholarly and policy debate on the scope and limitations of multilateral approaches to regional security.

It remains to say a word about Gorbachev's public address in Beijing, which, ranging as it did over diplomatic, bilateral and international issues, lacked the focus of the earlier two speeches but nevertheless conveyed three important messages.[130] First, Gorbachev expressed his satisfaction with the pace of Sino-Soviet rapprochement, laying particular emphasis on the progressive demilitarization of the Sino-Soviet border and the expansion of trade and economic ties. Second, he highlighted the paradox of an increasingly interdependent yet still politically fragmented world. The only viable response to this paradox, particularly in the context of Asia's cultural diversity, uneven economic development and unresolved conflicts, was a collaborative approach to common tasks that excluded 'hegemonism' and 'interference' in internal affairs. Bilateral co-operation based on the principles of equality and mutual benefit had much to contribute but was not enough. It was now time to introduce into Asia Pacific mechanisms for regular multilateral consultation – the Cambodian peace process was cited as a sign of things to come. Third, Gorbachev foreshadowed a special role for the Soviet Union. Given that Asia could not be isolated from other continents, the Soviet Union was uniquely placed, by reason of geography and history, to act as a kind of connecting link between Asia and Europe. Whether this unique role would be readily accepted by the rest of Asia or Europe and whether the Soviet Union had the capacity to perform such a role were highly debatable propositions. Whatever the Soviet Union's future place in Asia, which would soon be further complicated by the formation of the independent Central Asian republics, Gorbachev had nevertheless placed several important issues on the regional agenda, not least the contribution of multilateral institutions to Asia-Pacific security, and the relationship between regions and between regionalism and globalism.

CHINA'S GRADUAL RESURGENCE

The communist leadership that came to power in 1949 had set itself the task of erasing the humiliation China had suffered at the hands of foreign powers throughout the nineteenth and a good part of the twentieth century. In a major speech in September 1949, Mao left no doubt of his view of China's vocation as a great power and civilization: 'Our nation will never again be an insulted nation. We have stood up ... The era in which the Chinese were regarded as uncivilised is now over'.[131] Twenty years later China still lacked sufficient economic and military resources to conduct a global diplomacy on the scale of either superpower, yet its assertive independence, its influence in the Third World and above all its geopolitical weight in Asia had forced the United States and the Soviet Union into a triangular relationship. The Sino-Soviet dispute had become a significant factor in the Soviet–American equation; which, at least in part, explains Nixon's opening to China. For the Maoist leadership skilful management of the triangular relationship held the prospect of weakening Soviet primacy within the communist world, undermining the bipolar structure of international relations and enhancing China's diplomatic standing in Asia. As argued elsewhere, Beijing's principal objective in playing the triangular game was 'to reduce

Soviet–American collusion to a minimum, mount opposition to the two superpowers by highlighting such collusion, and contain Soviet expansion by threatening collusion with the United States'.[132] Having guided China's external relations during the greater part of the 1970s, this strategy would eventually be modified to take account of significant changes in its domestic and external environment.

Under Deng Xiaoping's leadership, China embarked on a modernization programme designed to bring the country by the end of the century to the front ranks of the world's great powers. The accent was now on high-speed industrialization, to be facilitated by the transfusion of capital and technology on a scale which only the industrialized West could provide. The requirements of economic and even military modernization coupled with the intensification of the Sino-Soviet conflict prompted the Chinese leadership to adopt a more co-operative approach to the capitalist West, and in particular the United States. An equidistant relationship with the two superpowers was no longer deemed feasible or desirable, at least for the time being. China's decision to open up its economy had considerable implications for its diplomacy and its growing linkages with the global system. Chinese membership of international governmental organizations increased from 1 to 21 in the period 1966–77 and from 21 to 37 during 1977–88. Apart from its participation in the UN system, Beijing joined several international financial and monetary institutions, including the IMF and the World Bank, and applied for membership of GATT. Equally striking was China's increasing adherence to international conventions. By 1987 China was a signatory to 126 multilateral treaties, up from 23 in 1976; during the same period, its membership of international non-governmental organizations had risen from 71 to 574.[133] Increased Chinese activism in the institutional processes of world politics was motivated principally by a perceived need to harness every possible resource which the international capitalist system could offer in support of China's modernization drive. By the mid-1980s the twin notions of global interdependence and a single world market had been adopted as an integral part of Chinese political theory and practice.

China's progressive incorporation into the global political economy raised a number of complex questions, the full implications of which were not immediately apparent. What would the impact be on the rapidly expanding and deepening linkages between China and international institutions? To what extent would such linkages impose new constraints on China's domestic and foreign policies, indeed on the very structure of its political system? To put it differently, would Chinese leaders be able to make selective use of these linkages, taking full advantage of transactions, processes and resources they deemed consistent with the objectives of their modernization programme, yet effectively resisting or excluding those influences which they considered injurious to Chinese national interests or to the viability of Chinese political institutions, and more specifically to the continued primacy of the Chinese Communist

Party? These questions will be explored more fully in subsequent chapters, particularly in the context of the 1990s. Suffice it to say here that the Chinese geopolitical imagination underwent considerable change during the 1980s, which is not to say that such change was uniform or unidirectional or that it did not generate tensions within the party machine and the bureaucratic apparatus or between the state and civil society.

In one sense, China's membership of international institutions was perhaps least contentious when it came to issues of peace and security. Raising China's profile within the UN Security Council, assuming a more accommodating attitude to peacekeeping operations and even playing a more active role in arms control and disarmament negotiations were unlikely to provoke much heated debate, except within a relatively small circle of experts and officials. On the other hand, policy formulation on questions of free trade, foreign investment and technology transfer was to prove more problematic. Allowing the World Bank to become the most important source of concessionary aid and technological expertise on development issues was novel enough, but even more revolutionary was the decision to transform coastal China into an export-launching platform for labour-intensive industries. The ensuing decentralization of economic decision-making, with provincial governments acquiring much greater commercial authority to deal with foreign firms, was to prove a delicate and often highly contested political operation. Nowhere were the dilemmas posed by China's increasing participation in international institutions more acute than in the field of human rights. On the one hand, the Chinese leadership wished to establish its international credentials, hence its greater involvement in UN human rights fora, its readiness to pay lip service to a number of human rights principles and norms and its more positive public pronouncements, particularly in the late 1980s, on the value of international covenants. On the other hand, there was a clearly discernible fear that any relaxation of political controls would weaken the party's political authority and derail the modernization programme.

China's adaptation to the rapidly changing international situation – variously referred to as the 'opening up to the outside world'[134] or 'global learning'[135] – was therefore both complex and highly selective. Though external environmental factors, not least the changing complexion of Soviet–American relations, were conducive to a reorientation of Chinese perceptions, China's domestic political and economic circumstances, and in particular Deng Xiaoping's reform priorities, provided the lens through which outside influences would be carefully filtered and strategically applied. The long-standing Maoist position on the inevitability of war was abandoned in favour of a more relaxed interpretation. In Deng's words, 'as long as the forces for peace continue to expand, it is possible that world war will not break out for a fairly long time to come, and there is hope of maintaining world peace'.[136] Peace and development, rather than war and revolution, became the dominant themes of Chinese political discourse. The five principles of peaceful coexistence, which were originally conceived as an important element in the international struggle against imperialism, were now used to facilitate and justify co-operative relations with any government, regardless of its ideological complexion.

Greater Chinese involvement in the world economy and participation in international economic institutions must therefore be seen as both cause and effect of the readjustment in China's security perceptions. The preoccupation with economic objectives could not but moderate China's interest in pursuing geopolitical rivalries, whether at the regional or the global level. Conversely, the Sino-American rapprochement of the 1970s followed by steady progress in Sino-Soviet reconciliation a decade later had helped to create a new triangular relationship, which privileged co-operative rather than conflictual behaviour and economic rather than strategic considerations. Beijing's decision to improve relations with Moscow was in part a response to a series of initiatives by the Soviet Union, including the withdrawal of its forces from Afghanistan, the promise to reduce its military presence in Mongolia and along the Sino-Soviet border and its willingness to encourage the withdrawal of Vietnamese troops from Kampuchea. By 1988 Moscow had gone a long way towards removing all three obstacles which in Beijing's view had stood in the way of improved Sino-Soviet relations.

There were, however, several other elements in China's reassessment of the structure of the international system. By 1989, the decline of the Soviet Union's 'national strength' coupled with the collapse of the Soviet bloc in Eastern Europe and the impending reunification of Germany, seemed to leave the United States as the only effective superpower. To that extent there had been a shift from bipolarity to unipolarity. On the other hand, the United States was now locked in fierce economic competition with Europe and Japan. Chinese scholars and commentators now preferred to describe the world as moving towards 'multiple polarization',[137] a trend which they considered to have particular relevance for Asia Pacific. Its principal manifestations were said to be the emergence of a complex quadrilateral relationship (involving the United States, the Soviet Union, China and Japan), the rise of regional powers (such as Japan and Indonesia), the rapid growth of the East Asian economies, the deepening economic tensions between the United States and Japan, and the gradual resolution of regional conflicts (for example, Afghanistan, Cambodia). Generally, these were seen as positive developments which enhanced China's security and freedom of action and should therefore be encouraged and accelerated.

Chinese perceptions of a relatively benign security environment, both internationally and around China's periphery, made it possible for defence modernization to be given a relatively low priority. Between 1979 and 1988 China's defence expenditure as a proportion of its national budget was steadily reduced from 17.5 per cent to 8.2 per cent. Under the restructuring of the People's Liberation Army (PLA), announced in 1985, one million soldiers were demobilized and the eleven greater military regions reduced to seven. Specialized armed services were expanded to deal with conventional threats, including hijacking, terrorism and rioting, although a number of rapid reaction units were also formed to enhance China's special warfare capabilities. The Chinese navy was moderately upgraded with the acquisition of new weaponry, including missile destroyers, landing ships, and conventional and nuclear submarines. For its part, the air force acquired fighters, bombers, attack planes, helicopters, and ground-to-air and air-to-air missiles. The result was a leaner, better trained and technologically more sophisticated military force, whose primary objectives were to preserve China's territorial integrity, protect its maritime interests, and consolidate a secure and stable environment for economic construction.

With Sino-Soviet reconciliation well under way and the progressive withdrawal of Vietnamese forces from Kampuchea, it was no longer necessary for China to make anti-Sovietism the centrepiece of its Asia policy. Perhaps for the first time since 1949, it was possible for China to base its bilateral relations with the other three major Pacific powers (the United States, Russia and Japan) on the principle of equidistance. From Beijing's strategic perspective, such a balanced approach neatly dovetailed with two closely related objectives: maintaining a relatively stable equilibrium and preventing any one of the great powers from establishing a hegemonic position. In this more fluid and less predictable geopolitical environment, Chinese diplomacy, it is true, would face a formidable challenge: how to attain great power status and all the benefits that it confers and at the same time successfully allay regional suspicions and anxieties about China's future course. In the minds of Chinese policy-makers, as indeed of many observers, establishing the framework for a workable relationship with Southeast Asia generally and ASEAN in particular would be decisive in the resolution of this dilemma.

The delicate task of defining China's future place in the world led the post-Maoist leadership to place increasing emphasis on the economic dimension of power and concepts of comprehensive national strength. The view that 'in the future a nation's standing in the world would not be determined by a military war but by a "major war" in the economic and technological fields'[138] became a recurring theme in Chinese expert opinion on international affairs. Comprehensive national strength was defined in terms of 'the ability to survive, potential for development, and co-ordinative ability',[139] attributes which in turn derived from multiple factors, including resources, economic strength, scientific and technological power, cultural and educational levels, defence capabilities and diplomatic skills. One attempt to quantify this composite concept concluded that China had over the past 40 years risen steadily on the world ladder of comprehensive national strength from thirteenth place in 1949 to tenth place in the early 1960s and to sixth place at the end of the 1980s.[140] Whatever its actual status in the international pecking order, China was already acting as if it had become a great power, or at least deserved to be treated as such.

As the Chinese leadership gained in confidence, notions of national stability and national strength became closely associated with the internationally more contentious issues of sovereignty and national unity, especially in relation to Hong Kong, Macao and Taiwan. From Beijing's perspective, a major breakthrough came with the signing on 19 December 1984 of an agreement with Britain on the future status of Hong Kong. Though the British government had hoped to retain administrative control over the colony even after sovereignty had been returned to China, Beijing was adamant that administration and law were inseparable from sovereignty and had to be transferred to China. After two years of painstaking negotiations, it was agreed that on 1 July 1997, following the transfer of sovereignty, Hong Kong would become a special administrative zone of China but administered separately from the rest of the country. In line with the concept of 'one country, two systems', Hong Kong would remain a capitalist enclave with its own currency, a special judicial system and legislative and executive autonomy.[141] The terms of the agreement had been carefully crafted to reinforce China's growing sense of 'national pride' and 'national identity',[142] but also to demonstrate its commitment to regional stability and political pragmatism. Integral to Chinese thinking was the hope that a relatively smooth transition in Hong Kong could serve as an example that might be followed in resolving the more intractable problem of Taiwan. Throughout the 1980s Chinese leaders had envisaged a gradual expansion of China–Taiwan contacts and trade culminating in negotiations under which Taiwan would accept the concept of 'one country, two systems' in return for a high degree of autonomy. Beijing took strong exception to US arms sales to Taiwan and in particular to technology transfers which the United States now used to circumvent the limitations imposed by the Shanghai communiqué of 17 August 1982, precisely because they were perceived as a symbol of Washington's persistent refusal to support the Chinese strategy and the principle of unification on which it rested.

The growing preoccupation with national unity and national strength was a measure of China's newly found self-confidence, yet it was also a sign of the continuing search for a new national identity.[143] What, after all, were the distinctive cultural and political foundations of the modern China? Were they to be found in the primordial attachment to the Confucian tradition and the notion of the 'middle kingdom' long regarded as the hallmark of China's civilizational greatness, or in some national reconstruction of socialist ideology, or again in the internationalism of the globalizing capitalist market? There is, of course, no simple answer to such a complex question. Suffice it to say that in the China of the 1980s competing symbols and multiple identities were feeding an on-going and profound normative transformation. Coastal China and inland China, ethnocentric Han China and the non-Han minorities (comprising more than 80 million people), state-centric China and a rapidly emerging civil society were all competing for political space in which to articulate and legitimize their preferred vision of China's political future. Placed in this context, the Tiananmen events of June 1989 may be seen as another stage in the unfolding process of national self-definition. The clash between authoritarian institutions and democratic tendencies was but one element of this process. The conflicting imperatives of national self-assertion and global interdependence, of centralized political control and economic liberalization, of modernization and rediscovery of the past had yet to be reconciled. These unresolved contradictions were bound to have profound but troublesome implications for China's relations with the outside world.

IMPLICATIONS FOR REGIONAL SECURITY

During the 1970s and 1980s the political complexion of the Asia-Pacific region had undergone profound and probably irreversible change. While few events were as dramatic as the end of the Vietnam War, the 20-year period witnessed the end of the Soviet–American ideological and strategic confrontation, the relative failure of Soviet and US interventionism, most spectacularly in Afghanistan and Vietnam respectively, the slow but steady decline of US and more particularly Soviet influence, and the corresponding rise of Japan and China as significant actors on the international stage. What was the cumulative impact of these geopolitical trends on regional security? In grappling with this multidimensional question Buzan's 'security complex' model, briefly outlined at the beginning of this chapter, provides a useful starting point.

To assess the impact of geopolitical change on a security complex Buzan suggests four structural options: *maintenance of the status quo* (the distribution of power and pattern of conflict co-operation within the complex remain fundamentally intact); *internal transformation* (significant shifts in the distribution of power or pattern of conflict/co-operation occur within the existing outer boundaries of the complex); *external transformation* (the essential structure of a complex is altered by either expansion or contraction of its existing outer boundary); and *overlay* (the indigenous security dynamic of the complex is suppressed by the intervention of one or more external powers).[144] Two important refinements to this analytical framework would seem necessary before it can be fruitfully applied to the geopolitical evolution of Asia

Pacific during the 1970s and 1980s. First, there is a case for widening the scope of external transformation to allow for the intervention of an external power in addition to the expansion or contraction of the existing outer boundary, since such intervention could also radically alter the context and structure of the security complex. Second, it may be worth clarifying the meaning of overlay so as to distinguish it more clearly from external transformation. Central to the concept of overlay is not the intervention of an external power *per se* but the imposition of an external security dynamic. Understood in this sense, great power intervention, and alliances for that matter, are relevant to overlay only in so far as they are a conduit for the intrusion of an external axis of conflict. Overlay may therefore be said to have occurred in Northeast and Southeast Asia to the extent that the logic of the Cold War came to dominate the security dynamic of either local complex.

If, for the moment, we think of Asia Pacific as comprising three regional subsystems (Northeast Asia, Southeast Asia and Oceania), each with its distinctive security complex, it is difficult to avoid the conclusion that all three complexes experienced significant structural change through the progressive removal of overlay and varying degrees of internal and external transformation. During the Cold War, particularly in periods of high tension, regional and even domestic rivalries became in Bloomfield's phrase 'surrogates for systemic war'.[145] The three security complexes under discussion were no exception, although in the case of Oceania the Soviet presence was negligible. By internalizing the logic of international bipolarity, the Korean conflict, the Vietnam War, the Taiwan dispute and even the Cambodian conflict tended to rebound on each other even when the connections between issues and protagonists were at best indirect. The East–West confrontation, and more specifically the opposing alliance systems which underpinned it, served as a transmission belt, with friction and instability in one regional subsystem militating against the resolution of conflict in another. By the end of the 1980s the Cold War overlay, and the geopolitical bifurcation of space which it expressed, was entirely absent from Oceania, barely visible in Southeast Asia and rapidly diminishing in significance on the Korean peninsula and in Soviet–Japanese relations.

Yet the decline of Cold War rivalries (that is, the removal of Cold War overlay) did not mean that all local or regional conflicts would as a consequence be amenable to quick resolution. To begin with, it is worth remembering that even at its height the Cold War had not entirely suppressed the security dynamic of each local complex. Tensions, for example between Japan and Korea or between Malaysia and Singapore, persisted even though they did not accord with the logic of the Cold War. Second, the Cold War overlay had in several instances merely served to reinforce already existing conflicts rather than introduce altogether new fault lines. The long-standing animosities between Japan and the Soviet Union, the unfinished business of the Chinese civil war and numerous other internal conflicts, whether in Korea, Vietnam, Laos, Cambodia or the Philippines, would over time assume a high Cold War profile, with opposing parties (for example, China/Taiwan, North Korea/South Korea, North Vietnam/South Vietnam) establishing a close ideological identification with one or other of the superpowers, at times virtually acting as proxies for them. By the same token these local conflicts usually had a logic and dynamic of their own, which could not be reduced to the vagaries of the East–West conflict. Third, the early breakdown of the Sino-Soviet alliance and the considerable geopolitical weight which China carried in Asia by virtue of its history, geography and demography meant that Beijing's strategic and diplomatic position – its border disputes with the Soviet Union and Vietnam, its support at various times for North Korea and the Khmer Rouge or its hostility to Japanese rearmament – could not be attributed solely or even primarily to the imperatives of geopolitical bipolarity.

There is no denying, however, that the steadily improving US–Soviet relationship from 1985 onwards had contributed to the loosening, transformation or even disintegration of of great many alliance arrangements (for example, US–Philippines, US–New Zealand, US–South Korea, USSR–Vietnam, USSR–North Korea). The net effect of this sustained but uneven and far from universal trend was to create a psychological climate far more conducive to the alleviation of tensions (for example, in the Korean peninsula), withdrawal of military forces (notably in Afghanistan) and at least partial resolution of regional conflicts (for example in Cambodia). The removal of Cold War overlay was mirrored and reinforced by various forms of external transformation, including the withdrawal of international forces, the partial demilitarization of borders and the growing impetus for nuclear disarmament and arms control. In the Cambodian case, several factors – the progressive reduction of the Vietnamese military presence, strongly encouraged by Moscow; the slow but steady improvement in Sino-Vietnamese and ASEAN– Indochinese relations;[146] ASEAN's and Australia's readiness to play a limited mediating role; and last but not least, the growing signs that the United States itself wished to alter its Cambodian policy and engage in dialogue with Vietnam[147] – would combine in the space of a few years to create the conditions for a negotiated, internationally brokered settlement of the conflict.[148] The 16-point statement adopted at the Paris Conference on 16 January 1990 by the five permanent members of the Security Council was indicative of the much greater fluidity in Asia-Pacific diplomacy and, more generally, the enhanced opportunities for international mediation and UN peacekeeping.

Even where conflicts were not susceptible to resolution (for example, Northern Territories, Korea, Taiwan, Spratlys), there were promising signs that they would be contained below the threshold of violence. These possibilities were no doubt attributable to a new geopolitical configuration, to what Mackinder or Spykman may have characterized as the decline of the heartland and the reorganization of the World Island. Neither the United States nor the Soviet Union, nor indeed China or Japan, now considered its physical or political security seriously threatened by any of the others. There was, however, more to it than crude geopolitics. As we have already noted, and will explore at greater length in the next chapter, domestic and economic considerations would also prompt both external and regional parties to practise the politics of accommodation. A good deal of internal transformation, evidenced in the increasing importance attached to trade and economic growth as national priorities and in the deepening interdependence between the national economies of the region, had substantially raised the stake of most states in a stable and secure regional environment. A separate but closely related development was the gradual emergence of broader conceptions of security, which emphasized the linkages between the domestic and international environment and reduced the salience of military threats and responses by directing attention to the social, political and environmental as well as economic dimensions of security. Though ASEAN states had for some time subscribed to the notion of comprehensive security, all four great powers were in varying degrees also beginning to show interest in the concept.

The mid-1980s had ushered in a transitional period of uncertain duration, but with far-reaching implications for regional security. Notwithstanding the continuing salience of the strategic ties binding the United States and a number of its allies, notably Japan, South Korea and Australia, Cold War alliances had themselves undergone profound change and even those that survived the end of the Cold War were likely to perform an increasingly ambiguous role. It was doubtful that they would have the cohesion or coherence characteristic of the bipolar era or perform the same co-ordinating or stabilizing functions. To return to the geopolitical categories of an earlier era, the rimlands of Asia were much less disposed to accept or rely on the primacy of either the heartland or the World-Island. On the other hand, the policies of the great powers gave only the vaguest indication as to what other mechanisms or institutions might underpin any new geopolitical arrangement, either regionally or subregionally.[149] The United States, for its part, had little interest in initiating change, fearing that any departure from the status quo would adversely affect its highly privileged strategic position. Successive US administrations had reaffirmed in general terms the policy of continued engagement in Asia Pacific, but considerable doubt remained as to the priorities such engagement would pursue, the forms it would take and the institutional arrangements it would promote.

As for China, the triangular relationship with the United States and the Soviet Union, which had served it relatively well during the greater part of the 1970s and 1980s, had lost much of its former relevance. Multipolarity might be here to stay and might well have positive spin-offs for regional stability, but it remained to be seen how multipolarity could be translated into a durable security framework and what part, if any, China might play in such a process. Uncertainty also characterized Japan's security policy. The commitment to maintain the security relationship with the United States while at the same time developing a wider regional role left many questions unanswered, not least the norms that would guide such an expanded role, the balance to be struck between bilateralism and multilateralism and the relationship that would emerge between economic and military power. The Soviet Union, preoccupied with the disintegration of its empire and its internal economic and political difficulties, lacked the status and resources to pursue the Gorbachev agenda with any confidence or prospect of success.

The collapse of the Berlin Wall symbolized for Asia Pacific no less than for Europe the end of an era. What would follow it was far from clear. A good many concepts – multipolarity, complex interdependence, the diffusion of power, multilateralism, to name a few – were advanced as important clues to the future. But they did not, singly or collectively, constitute a plausible logic, certainly not a coherent architectural design that would replace that of the Cold War. Nor did it seem as if any one of the great powers or any combination of them had the incentive and capacity to develop, let alone apply, such a logic. Both scholars and policy-makers would often refer to new windows of opportunity, but it was not readily apparent who would seize such opportunities, or the method and agency by which initiatives could be co-ordinated and diverging interests and perceptions reconciled. The emerging geopolitical uncertainties testified to the fact that the geographical determinants of power had to be placed in historical and sociological context. The discourse of statecraft could not be fashioned independently of domestic political circumstances or of economic currents operating both within and across national boundaries. Nor could new approaches to the security dilemma overlook the powerful religious, cultural and other normative impulses that would help to shape the geopolitical imagination and new patterns of regional conflict and co-operation.

NOTES

1. Friedrich Ratzel, 'The Territorial Growth of States', *Scottish Geographical Magazine,* 12(7), July 1896, 351–60; also Friedrich Ratzel, 'The Laws of the Spatial Growth of States', in Roger Kasperson and Julian Minghi (eds), *The Structure of Political Geography*, Chicago:

Aldine, 1969, pp. 17–28.

2. See Sven Holdat, 'The Ideal State and the Power of Geography: The Life-world of Rudolf Kjellén', *Political Geography,* 11, May 1992, 307–23.

3. Cited in Henning Heske, 'Karl Haushofer', in John O'Loughlin (ed.), *Dictionary of Geopolitics*, Westport, Conn.: Greenwood Press, 1994, pp. 112–13.

4. Karl Haushofer, 'Defence of German Geopolitics', in Edmund Walsh, *Total Power: A Footnote to History*, New York: Doubleday, 1948, p. 345.

5. Gearóid ÓTuathail, *Critical Geopolitics*, London: Routledge, 1996, pp. 23–4.

6. Ibid., p. 33.

7. Simon Dalby, 'Critical Geopolitics: Discourse, Difference and Dissent', *Environment and Planning: Society and Space,* 9, 1991, 274; see also R.B.J Walker, *Inside/Outside: International Relations as Political Theory*, Cambridge: Cambridge University Press, 1993, pp.176–83.

8. ÓTuathail, *Critical Geopolitics,* p. 53.

9. See Geoffrey Parker, *Geopolitics: Past, Present and Future,* London: Frances Pinter, 1993, p. 5.

10. See Harold and Margaret Sprout, *Foundations of International Politics*, Princeton, N.J.: D. van Nostrand, 1962, p. 319.

11. J. Gooch, 'Maritime Command: Mahan and Corbett', in C.S. Gray and R.W. Barnett (eds), *Seapower and Strategy: Spatial Variations in Politics*, London: Sage, 1989, p. 3.

12. Alfred Thayer Mahan, *The Influence of Sea Power upon History 1660–1783*, London: Sampson Low, Marston, 1890, p. 88.

13. Ibid. pp. 24–8.

14. Alfred Thayer Mahan, *Armaments and Arbitration*, Port Washington: Kennikat Press, 1973, pp. 15–19, 57–60 (first published Harper, 1911).

15. Halford J. Mackinder, *Distant Lands*, London: George Philip, 1910, p. 126.

16. Halford J. Mackinder, *Britain and the British Seas*, Westport, Conn.: Greenwood Press, 1969, p. 358 (first published D. Appleton, 1902).

17. Halford J. Mackinder, 'The Geographical Pivot of History', *Geographical Journal*, 23(4), April 1904, 421–37.

18. Ibid. p. 436.

19. Halford J. Mackinder, *Nations of the Modern World*, vol. 1, London: George Philip, 1911, p. 290.

20. Halford J. Mackinder, *Democratic Ideals and Reality: A Study in the Politics of Reconstruction*, New York: H. Holt, 1950 pp.152–4 (first published 1919).

21. Mackinder, *Nations of the Modern World*, vol. 2, London: George Philip, 1924, p. 252.

22. Mackinder, *Democratic Ideas and Reality*, pp. 202–5.

23. Mackinder, 'The Geographical Pivot of History', pp. 421–2.

24. Halford J. Mackinder, 'The Round World and the Winning of the Peace', *Foreign Affairs*, 21(4) July 1943, 601–4.

25. Nicholas John Spykman, *The Geography of the Peace*, edited by Helen R.Nicholl, New York: Harcourt, Brace & Co, 1944, p. 24.

26. D.W. Meinig, 'Heartland and Rimland in Eurasian History', *Western Political Quarterly*, 9, 1956, 553–69.

27. Parker, *Geopolitics*, p. 70.

28. The 'geopolitical gaze' is a useful term coined by ÓTuathail to describe the complex intellectual prism through which geopolitical analysis endows the observed world with an aura of permanence and durability (*Critical Geopolitics*, pp. 33–5 , 50–3).

29. John Agnew and Stuart Corbridge, *Mastering Space: Hegemony, Territory and International Political Economy*, London: Routledge, 1995, p. 15.

30. R.W. Cox, *Production, Power and World Order*, New York: Columbia University Press, 1987, pp. 151–210. For a useful summary of these approaches, see Agnew and Corbridge, *Mastering Space*, pp. 23–5.

31. I. Wallerstein, *The Politics of the World-Economy*, Cambridge: Cambridge University Press, 1987, pp. 37–46.

32. G. Modelski, *Long Cycles in World Politics*, Seattle, Wash: University of Washington Press, 1987, pp. 217–33.

33. P.J. Taylor, 'Geopolitical World Orders', in P.J. Taylor (ed.), *The Political Geography of the Twentieth Century*, London: Belhaven Press, 1993, pp. 31–62.

34. Agnew, *Geopolitics*, pp. 86–124.

35. We shall have occasion to refer more than once to what is now an extensive though uneven body of literature on theories of hegemony, hegemonic stability and hegemonic succession. For a useful *tour d'horizon*, see Paul Kennedy, *The Rise and Fall of the Great Powers: Economic Change and Military Conflict from 1500 to 2000*, New York: Random House, 1987; R. Gilpin, *The Political Economy of International Relations*, Princeton, N.J.: Princeton University Press, 1987; Charles Kindleberger, 'Dominance and Leadership in the World Economy', *International Studies Quarterly*, 25(3), June 1981, 242–54.

36. See Agnew, *Geopolitics*, pp. 20–30.

37. Of particular interest is Simon Dalby's conceptualization of self and other, and of the linguistic, epistemological and political differences which underlie the construction of space, and which have been central to the construction of a formidable and expensive, nuclear-armed 'security state'. See S. Dalby, 'Geopolitical Discourse: The Soviet Union as Other', *Alternatives*, 13, 1988, 415–42; also *Creating the Second Cold War*, New York: Guildford, 1990.

38. Yves Lacoste, *La Géographie, ça sert, d'abord à faire la guerre*, Paris: Maspero, 1976.

39. Agnew, *Geopolitics*, p. 7.

40. Parker, *Geopolitics*, p. 6.

41. For a fuller examination of the relationship between systemic analysis and spatial forms, see Joseph A. Camilleri and Jim Falk, *The End of Sovereignty? Politics in a Shrinking and Fragmented World*, Aldershot, Hants.: Edward Elgar, 1992, pp. 246–51.

42. The constraints on collective human action imposed by the natural environment is one of the recurring themes of the 'new' geopolitics. See W. Bunge, 'Our Planet Is Big Enough for Peace but Too Small for War', in R.J. Johnson and P. Taylor (eds), *A World in Crisis: Geopolitical Perspectives*, 2nd edn, Oxford: Basil Blackwell, 1989; also S. Dalby, 'Ecopolitical Discourse: "Environmental Security" and Political Geography', *Progress in Human Geography*, 16, 1992, 503–22; T. Homer-Dixon, 'On the Threshold: Environment Changes as Causes of Acute Conflict', *International Security*, 16, 1991, 76–116.

43. Barry Buzan, *People, States and Fear: The National Security Problem in International Relations*, Brighton, Sussex: Wheatsheaf Books, 1983, pp. 104–6.

44. Ibid., pp. 107–10.

45.   For a fuller elaboration of the need for such conceptual distinctions, see Joseph A. Camilleri, 'Security, Old Dilemmas and New Challenges in the Post-Cold War Environment', *GeoJournal*, 34(2), 1994, 136–9; also F. Kratochwil, 'The Challenge of Security in a Changing World', *Journal of International Affairs*, 43(1), 1989, 119–41.

46.   The theoretical connection between geopolitics and geoeconomics is developed by among others, Albert Bergesen, 'Cycles of War in the Reproduction of the World Economy', in Paul H. Johnson and William R. Thompson (eds), *Rhythms in Politics and Economics*, New York: Praeger, 1985. For an empirical application with particular reference to the armaments industry, see Trevor Taylor, 'Defence Industries in International Relations', *Review of International Studies*, 16(1), January 1990, 59–73.

47.   See also Camilleri and Falk, *The End of Sovereignty?*, pp. 153–7.

48.   Ibid. pp. 146–8.

49.   See Stephen E. Ambrose, *Rise to Globalism: American Foreign Policy since 1938*, 6th rev. edn, Harmondsworth, Middlesex: Penguin Books, 1991, pp. 97–109; J.P.D. Dunbabin, *The Cold War: The Great Powers and their Allies*, London: Longman, 1994, pp. 96–100.

50.   See statement by US Secretary of State Dean Acheson on 18 May 1949 in US *Department of State Bulletin* (hereafter referred to as *DOSB*), 29 May 1949, p. 696. Much has been made in the literature of the distinctive features of the Cold War in Asia as compared to Europe. The undeniable differences must not, however, be allowed to obscure the geopolitical rationale that underpinned what was essentially a global confrontation. See Michael Schaller, *The American Occupation of Japan: The Origins of the Cold War in Asia*, Oxford: Oxford University Press, 1985; Marc S. Gallichio, *The Cold War Begins in Asia: American East Asian Policy and the Fall of the Japanese Empire*, New York: Columbia University Press, 1988.

51.   See Sir Percy Spender, *Exercises in Diplomacy: The ANZUS Treaty and the Colombo Plan*, Sydney: Sydney University Press, 1969, p. 54.

52.   Spender, *Exercises in Diplomacy*, p. 66.

53.   See Dulles's remarks at the San Francisco Conference, reported in *Official Record of the Proceedings*, US Department of State Publication 4392, p. 302.

54.   Dunbabin, *The Cold War*, p. 101.

55.   Ambrose, *Rise to Globalism*, p. 116.

56.   See Robert E. Harkavy, *Great Power Competition for Overseas Bases: The Geopolitics of Access Diplomacy*, New York: Pergamon Press, 1982, p. 141; also William M. Arkin and Richard W. Fieldhouse, *Nuclear Battlefields: Global Links in the Arms Race*, Cambridge, Mass: Ballinger, 1985, pp. 231–2.

57.   For a more detailed outline of the development of the US alliance system in the western Pacific, see Fred Greene, *U.S. Policy and the Security of Asia*, New York: McGraw-Hill, 1968, pp. 71–83.

58.   The economic foundations of America's geopolitical expansion into Asia are subjected to probing analysis in Carl Oglesby and Richard Shaull, *Containment and Change*, New York: Macmillan, 1967, pp. 51–71.

59.   Franz Schurman, *The Logic of World Power: An Inquiry into the Origins, Currents and Contradictions of World Politics*, New York: Pantheon Books, 1974, p. 205.

60.   See J. Camilleri, *Chinese Foreign Policy: The Maoist Era and Its Aftermath*, Oxford: Martin Robertson, 1980, pp. 47–50; for a fuller analysis of the uneasy relationship between the Russian and Chinese Communist leaderships during this period, see Robert C. North,

Moscow and the Chinese Communists, Stanford, Cal: Stanford University Press, 1953.

61. The Soviet government made no secret of its support for the Chinese side. See the official Soviet account in B. Ponomaryov, A. Gromyko and V. Khostov (eds), *History of Soviet Foreign Policy 1945–1970*, Moscow: Progress Publishers, 1973, p. 196; also *Khrushchev Remembers*, vol. 1, trans. and ed. by Strobe Talbot, Harmondsworth, Middlesex: Penguin Books, pp. 393–9; see also I.F. Stone, *The Hidden History of the Cold War*, New York: Monthly Review Press, 1952; Sergei N. Goncharov, John W. Lewis and Xuei Litai, *Uncertain Partners: Stalin, Mao and the Korean War*, Stanford, Cal: Stanford University Press, 1993, pp. 187–205.

62. For a detailed analysis of this relationship, see Donald S. Zagoria, *Vietnam Triangle: Moscow, Peking, Hanoi*, New York: Pegasus, 1967.

63. See P.J. Honey, *Communism in North Vietnam*, Cambridge, Mass. MIT Press, 1963, ch. 3; also Stephen J. Hood, *Dragons Entangled: Indochina and the China–Vietnam War*, Armonk, NY: M.E. Sharpe, 1992, pp. 3–30.

64. See Robert Harkavy, *Bases Abroad: The Global Foreign Military Frame*, Oxford: Oxford University Press, 1989; Roland Paul, *American Military Commitments Abroad*, New Brunswick, N.J.: Rutgers University Press, 1973.

65. See William J. Barnds, 'Changing Power Relationships in East Asia', in Hedley Bull (ed.), *Asia and the Western Pacific: Towards a New International Order*, Melbourne: Nelson in association with the Australian Institute of International Affairs, 1975, pp. 12–16.

66. For an instructive account of the dominance of alliance politics by a proponent of neutrality and non-alignment, see Noordin Sopiee, 'The "Neutralisation" of South-East Asia', in Bull (ed.), *Asia and the Western Pacific*, pp. 132–60.

67. See, for example, Paul Nitze, 'Coalition Policy and the Concepts of World Order', in Arnold Wolfers (ed.), *Alliance Policy in the Cold War*, Baltimore, Md: Johns Hopkins Press, 1959, pp. 15–30.

68. See Philip B. Davidson, *Vietnam at War: The History, 1946–1975*, London: Sidgwick & Jackson, 1988, pp. 587–622.

69. *US Foreign Policy for the 1970s: Building for Peace. A Report to the Congress by Richard Nixon*, 25 February 1971, in *DOSB*, 64(1656), 22 March 1971, 379.

70. *US Foreign Policy for the 1970s: A Report to the Congress by Richard Nixon*, 28 February 1970, in *DOSB*, 62(1602), 9 March 1970.

71. Ibid.

72. For an early critical assessment of the Nixon Doctrine, see Earl C. Ravenal, 'The Nixon Doctrine and our Asian Commitments', *Foreign Affairs*, 49(2), January 1971, 201–17.

73. See Ole R. Holsti and James N. Rosenau, *American Leadership in World Affairs: Vietnam and the Breakdown of Consensus*, Boston, Mass.: Allen & Unwin, 1984, pp. 47–58, 238–40; Richard A. Melauson, *American Foreign Policy since the Vietnam War: The Search for Consensus from Nixon to Clinton*, Armonk, NY: M.E. Sharpe, 1996 pp. 111–13, 190–96.

74. See speech by Richard Holbrooke, Assistant Secretary for East Asian and Pacific Affairs, 16 June 1978, *DOSB*, 78(2017), August 1978, 2.

75. These remarks were part of a briefing given to US businessmen, and are reproduced in *DOSB*, 79(2023), February 1979, 20.

76. See statement by (Deputy Secretary of State) Walter J. Stoessel, Jr before the Senate Foreign Relations Committee on 10 June 1982, *DOSB*, 82(2065), August 1982, 55.

77. See Fred Halliday, *The Making of the Second Cold War*, London: Verso, 1984, pp. 234–42.

78. The most notable official publication was *Soviet Military Power*, published by the US Department of Defense (1st edition, September 1981; 2nd edition, March 1983).

79. See Bernard K. Gordon, 'Asian Angst and American Policy', *Foreign Policy*, no. 47, Summer 1982, 52–3.

80. See Neil Renwick, 'Ending the US–Japan Alliance: The Search for Stable Peace in NE Asia after the Cold War', *Interdisciplinary Peace Research*, October/November 1992, 16–17; also Michael Schaller, *Altered States: The United States and Japan since the Occupation*, Oxford: Oxford University Press, 1997, pp. 7–46.

81. Shigeru Yoshida, *The Yoshida Memoirs: The Story of Japan in Crisis,* translated by Kenichi Yoshida, Westport, Conn.: Greenwood Press, 1973.

82. See Hiroyuki Umetsu, 'Dulles's Second Visit to Japan: The Tokyo Talks of 1951', *Journal of Northeast Asian Studies,* 14(4), Winter 1995, 59–80.

83. For a revealing account of the racial divide that characterized the years of occupation, see Yukiko Koshiro, 'The U.S. Occupation of Japan as a Mutual Racial Experience', *Journal of American East Asian Relations*, 3(4), Winter 1994, 299–323.

84. John Dower, 'The Eye of the Beholder', *Bulletin of Concerned Asian Scholars*, 2(1), October 1969, 16–25.

85. For contrasting interpretations of the underlying thrust of US occupation policy, see Justin Williams Sr, 'American Democratization Policy for Occupied Japan: Correcting the Revisionist Version' (followed by rejoinders from John W. Dower and Howard Schonberger), *Pacific Historical Review*, 57(2), May 1988, 179–208; also Sodei Rinjiro, 'No More Pearl Harbours', *Japan Quarterly*, 4, October–December 1991, 399–406.

86. 'Eisaku Sato, Prime Minister Heralds the New Pacific Age', *Japan Report*, 15(22), 1 December 1969, 5–8.

87. J. Welfield, *An Empire in Eclipse: Japan and the Postwar American Alliance System*, London: Athlone Press, 1988, p. 61.

88. See Toshiyuki Toyoda, 'Japan's Policies since 1945', *Bulletin of the Atomic Scientists*, 41, August 1985, 57–62.

89. US pressure on allies to bear a greater share of the financial costs arising from the overseas deployment of US forces steadily increased through the 1980s. See Pat Towell, 'Seeking to Redress Burden Sharing Imbalance', *Congressional Quarterly Weekly Report*, 46(27), 2 July 1988, 1822; 'On Burden-sharing: A Softening of the Blow', *Congressional Quarterly Weekly Report*, 46(33), 13 August 1988, 2293.

90. Renwick, 'Ending the US–Japan Alliance', p. 20.

91. Japan's gradualist approach is emphasised in Suzan J. Pharr, 'Japan's Defensive Foreign Policy and the Politics of Burden Sharing', in Gerald L. Curtis (ed.), *Japan's Foreign Policy after the Cold War: Coping with Change,* Armonk, NY: M.E. Sharpe, 1993, pp. 235–62.

92. Sheldon W. Simon, 'Is There a Japanese Regional Security Role?', *Journal of Northeast Asian Studies*, 5, Summer 1986, 38.

93. Gregory P. Corning, 'US–Japan Security Co-operation in the 1990s: The Promise of High-tech Defence', *Asian Survey*, 29(3), March 1989, 274.

94. Cited in Nathaniel B. Thayer, 'Japanese Foreign Policy in the Nakasone Years', in Curtis (ed.), *Japan's Foreign Policy*, pp. 90–104.

95. 'Joint Statement Read by Secretary Schultz, May 29, 1983', *DOSB*, 83(2076), July 1983, p. 4.

96. See *Strategic Survey 1987–1988,* London: International Institute for Strategic Studies, 1988, p. 123, and *Strategic Survey 1988–89,* p. 163.

97. Reinhard Drifte, *Japan's Foreign Policy,* London: Routledge, 1990, p. 35.

98. Ibid., p. 38.

99. See Debora Spar, 'Co-developing the FSX Fighter: The Domestic Calculus of International Co-operation', *International Journal,* 67, Spring 1992, 265–92.

100. Richard P. Cronin, *Japan, the United States and the Prospects for the Asia-Pacific Century: Three Scenarios for the Future,* New York: St Martin's Press, 1992, p. 99.

101. Welfield, *An Empire in Eclipse,* pp. 434–41.

102. *Financial Accounts of OECD Countries 1976–1991, OECD Financial Statistics,* Part 2, Paris: OECD, 1993, pp. 41–3.

103. Cited in Tsuneo Akaha, 'Japan's Security Policy after US Hegemony', in Kathleen Newland (ed.), *The International Relations of Japan,* London: Macmillan, 1990, p. 153.

104. *Diplomatic Blue Book 1988: Japan's Diplomatic Activities,* Tokyo, Japanese Ministry of Foreign Affairs, pp. 1–3.

105. Takashi Inoguchi, *Japan's International Relations,* London: Frances Pinter, 1991, p. 43.

106. The full text of the communiqué will be found in *United States Foreign Policy 1972: A Report of the Secretary of State,* Washington, DC: Department of State,1972, p. 642.

107. *DOSB,* 79(2022), January 1979, 25–6.

108. See James Fallows, 'The Bases Dilemma', *Atlantic Monthly,* 261(2), February 1988, 18–27.

109. See Peter Bacho, 'US–Philippines Relations in Transition: The Issue of the Bases', *Asian Survey,* 28(6), June 1988, 650–61.

110. See R. Sean Randolph, *The United States and Thailand: Alliance Dynamics, 1950–1985,* Berkeley, Cal: University of California Press, 1986.

111. See Robert J. Muscat, *Thailand and the United States: Development, Security and Foreign Aid,* New York: Columbia University Press, 1990, pp. 20–29.

112. *Australian Defence,* presented to Parliament by the Minister for Defence, November 1976, Canberra: AGPS, 1976, p. 10.

113. *Age* (Melbourne), 13 August 1986, p. 6.

114. For a further discussion of the implications of New Zealand's redefinition of alliance obligations, see Joseph A. Camilleri, *The Australia–New Zealand Alliance: Regional SecurityintheNuclearAge,*Seattle,Wash:UniversityofWashingtonPress,1987,pp.140–47.

115. William M. Arkin and David Chappell, 'Forward Offensive Strategy: Raising the Stakes in the Pacific', *World Policy Journal,* Summer 1985, p. 490.

116. Joseph S. Nye, Jr, 'The Misleading Metaphor of Decline', *Atlantic Monthly,* March 1990, 86–94.

117. See Arkin and Fieldhouse, *Nuclear Battlefields,* pp. 117–18, 122, 124, 126.

118. US Pacific Command, 'Pacific Area Update', 17 February 1984, no. P4080.1, pp. 1–4.

119. This assessment, offered to the Congressional Subcommittee on Asian and Pacific Affairs in July 1982 by the Defense Intelligence Agency, is cited by Arkin and Fieldhouse, *Nuclear Battlefields,* p. 122.

120. *Asia 1982 Yearbook,* Hong Kong: Far Eastern Economic Review, 1982, p. 27.

121. See Leszek Buszynski, 'The Soviet Union and Vietnamese Withdrawal from Cambodia', in Gary Klintworth, *Vietnam's Withdrawal from Cambodia: Regional Issues and Realignments*, Canberra: Australian National University, Strategic and Defence Studies Centre, 1990, pp. 32–47.

122. Suh Dae-Sook, 'North Korea in 1986: Strengthening the Soviet Connection', *Asian Survey*, 27(1), January 1987, pp.56–63.

123. See Kyongsoo Lho, 'Seoul–Moscow Relations: Looking to the 1990s', *Asian Survey*, 29(12), December 1989, 1153–66; Shim Jae, 'Kremlin Connection', *Far Eastern Economic Review*, 30 August 1990, pp. 27–8; Seung Ho Joo, 'Soviet Policy toward the Two Koreas, 1985–1991: The New Political Thinking and Power', *Journal of Northeast Asian Studies*, 14(2), Summer 1995, 23–46.

124. John C. Dorrance, *Strategic Cooperation and Competition in the Pacific Islands: An American Assessment*, Canberra: Australian National University, Strategic and Defence Studies Centre, Working Paper no. 203, January 1990, p. 10.

125. The full text of Gorbachev's Vladivostok speech of 28 July 1986 was reproduced in *Soviet News*, 30 July 1986, 337–43.

126. See Hiroshi Kimura, 'Gorbachev's Agenda for Asia', *Pacific Review*, 1(3), 215–26; also Peter Berton, 'Russia and Japan in the Post-Cold War Era', in James C. Hsiung (ed.), *Asia Pacific in the New World Politics*, Boulder, Col.: Lynne Rienner, 1993, pp. 24–30.

127. Bilveer Singh, 'Gorbachev and a "Pacific Community"', *Pacific Review*, 1(3), 232–34.

128. See V. P. Lukin, 'The USSR and the Asia-Pacific Region', *Adelphi Paper 248*, Winter 1989–90, 17–32.

129. *The Current Digest of the Soviet Press*, XL(38), 19 October 1998, 5–7.

130. Speech by M.S. Gorbachev at the Great Hall of the People, Beijing, 17 May 1989, Foreign Broadcasting Information Service daily report, China (hereafter referred to as FBIS-CHI)-89-095, 18 May 1989, pp. 12–18.

131. *Mao Tse-tung and Lin Piao: Post Revolutionary Writings*, ed. K. Fa, Garden City, NY: Anchor Books, 1972, pp. 91–2.

132. Camilleri, *Chinese Foreign Policy*, p. 148.

133. For a more detailed analysis of the globalization of China's international relations, see Samuel S. Kim, 'Thinking Globally in Post-Mao China', *Journal of Peace Research*, 27(2), 1990, 193.

134. Xu Xin, *Changing Chinese Security Perceptions*, North Pacific Co-operative Security Dialogue (hereafter referred to as NPCSD), Working paper no. 27, Ontario: York University, April 1993.

135. Kim, *Thinking Globally in Post-Mao China*, p. 194.

136. Deng Xiaoping, *Fundamental Issues in Present Day China*, Beijing: Foreign Language Press, 1987, p. 116.

137. Yao Yun, 'How to Look at the Changes in the World Structure at Present', in FBIS-CHI-90-227, 26 November 1990, pp. 3–9.

138. See article by Huan Xiang in *People's Daily*, 5 January 1989, 7.

139. See interview with Huang Shoufeng, in FBIS-CHI-90-057-S, 23 March 1990, p. 41.

140. Ibid, p. 42.

141. See Roda Mushkat, 'The International Legal Status of Hong Kong under Post-Transitional Rule', *Houston Journal of International Law,* 10(1), Autumn 1987, 1–24; David M. Corwin, 'China's Choices: The 1984 Sino-British Declaration and Its Aftermath', *Law and Policy in International Business,* 19(3), Summer 1987, 505–36.

142. See Andrew Nathan and Robert S. Ross, *The Great Wall and the Empty Fortress: China's Search for Security,* New York: W.W. Norton, 1997, 193–211; also Michael Yahuda, 'Hong Kong and China's Integration into the International Community', in Warren J. Cohen and Li Zhao (eds), *Hong Kong Under Chinese Rule,* Cambridge: Cambridge University Press, 1997, pp. 198–212.

143. For a useful analysis of the evolution of Chinese nationalist sentiment and the competing interpretations of national identity by the Chinese and Taiwanese governments, see Christopher Hughes, *Taiwan and Chinese Nationalism: National Identity and Status in International Society,* London: Routledge, 1997. For a more sharply focused examination of the interplay of identity, interest and power in Chinese foreign policy, which incidentally challenges prevailing western attitudes to and perceptions of Chinese nationalism, see Yongnian Zhong, *Discovering Chinese Nationalism in China: Modernization, Identity, and International Relations,* Cambridge: Cambridge University Press, 1999, especially pp. 111–59.

144. Barry Buzan, 'The Post-Cold War Asia-Pacific Security Order: Conflict or Cooperation', in Andrew Mack and John Ravenhill (eds), *Pacific Cooperation: Building Economic and Security Regimes in the Asia-Pacific Region,* Boulder, Col.: Westview Press, 1995, pp. 130–51.

145. Lincoln P. Bloomfield, 'Coping with Conflict in the Late Twentieth Century', *International Journal,* 44(4), Autumn 1989, p. 777.

146. See Nayan Chanda, 'Taking a Soft Line: Vietnam Signals China that It Wants Improved Relations', *Far Eastern Economic Review* (hereafter referred to as *FEER*), 8 December 1988, 27–8; Charles McGregor, 'China, Vietnam, and the Cambodian Conflict: Beijing's End Game Strategy', *Asian Survey,* 30(3), March 1990, pp. 266–83.

147. The progression in Washington's attitude to the conflict is highlighted in the following official statements: Secretary Schultz's statement to the ASEAN Post-Ministerial Conference, 7 July 1988, *DOSB,* 88(2139), February 1989, 65–7; Secretary Baker's statement to the International Conference on Cambodia, 30 July 1989, *DOSB,* 89, October 1989, pp. 25–6.

148. See Michael Leifer, 'Power-sharing and Peacemaking in Cambodia?', *SAIS Review,* 12(1), Winter–Spring 1992, 139–53; MacAlister Brown and Joseph J. Zalsoff, *Cambodia Confounds the Peacemakers 1979–1998,* Ithaca, N.Y.: Cornell University Press, 1998, pp. 9–42.

149. The persistence of the basic structure of the Cold War, and more specifically of the network of US alliances known as the San Francisco system, is rightly underlined, though without the necessary qualifications, in Kimie Hara, 'Rethinking the "Cold War" in the Asia-Pacific', *Pacific Review,* 12(4), 1999, 515–36.

2. East Asia's economic transformation

The end of the Cold War may have meant the end of an era in geostrategic confrontation, but the changes it ushered in were overshadowed by the profound transformation of the regional economy that unfolded in the relatively short space of three decades. The rise of Japan as a major centre of economic power, the ensuing frictions in the US–Japan trading relationship, the remarkable performance of the newly industrializing economies (South Korea, Taiwan, Hong Kong and Singapore), the subsequent take-off of the ASEAN economies and the rapid pace of China's economic modernization were but the most striking features of a rapidly changing geoeconomic landscape.

DYNAMICS OF COMPETITIVENESS

Underlying these trends is a complex dynamic that is central to the analysis of economic change and sheds considerable light on the linkage between economic and geopolitical trends and between economic and security policy. A clearer understanding of this dynamic is necessary if we are to make sense of the changing pattern of regional institution-building in economic and strategic relations, and the emerging forms of interaction between the Asia-Pacific region and its subregions, between the subregions themselves, and between the region and the rest of the world. For purposes of analytical convenience the dynamic in question may be described in terms of five distinct but closely interconnected elements: *economic competitiveness, structural reorganization, shift in the balance of productive capacity, rise of transnational actors* and *social dislocation.*

Economic competitiveness refers to the policy actively pursued by states seeking to enhance the performance of their export sector by establishing and maintaining a foothold in certain international markets.[1] The products to be exported may remain relatively constant over time or undergo considerable variation over time, depending on judgements of shifting comparative advantage. In either case, the policy aims to maximize export performance, in large part by increasing productivity and minimizing the costs of production, thereby undercutting likely competitors. A similar competitive approach may be applied to the attraction of foreign investment, where the emphasis is on creating the fiscal, financial, industrial and regulatory conditions most likely to appeal to potential international investors. Economic competitiveness, evident as much in the policies of advanced industrial states and newly industrializing countries as in those of communist or post-communist states, has been instrumental in accelerating the interpenetration and integration of national economies.

Implicit in the principle of economic competitiveness is the need for national economies to undergo periodic structural reorganization in order to adapt to changing market conditions, and hence to shifts in the international division of labour and changing notions of comparative advantage.[2] Such reorganization may entail the abandonment of certain product lines in favour of others or, more significantly, the dismantling of entire industries and establishment of new ones, with all that this implies for employment, education and training, infrastructure, taxation, social welfare and financial flows. Structural reorganization will normally involve a shift in the balance between the primary, secondary and tertiary sectors of the economy, or at least changes in the composition of one or more sectors. In the case of developing economies, it is likely to be associated with rapid urbanization and a marked growth in the manufacturing sector of the economy.

The competitive dynamic, precisely because it gives rise to shifting patterns in the international division of labour, inevitably means a geographical redistribution of productive capacity, which may be global or regional in scale.[3] While such redistribution may assume a variety of forms, two are especially noteworthy. First, there may be a rearrangement of productive capacity within the core, in the sense that major centres of economic power may decline and new centres emerge, with the result that relations between core economies, particularly as mediated by trade, may become both more complex and more contentious. Second, there may be a considerable degree of mobility – here again with trade as the primary instrument – between the core and peripheral sectors of the world economy. To capture something of the structure and functional characteristics of that mobility, Wallerstein postulates the existence of a *semi-periphery,* which he describes as the intermediate link in 'the surplus extraction chain'.[4] Though Wallerstein's characterization of the world economy as comprising a core, a periphery and a semi-periphery may not fully reflect its complexity or the subtle fluctuations in global stratification and integration, it does nevertheless clarify the way in which state power combines with efficient production to achieve a competitive advantage on the world market. As a consequence, the delicate balance within the hegemonic centre (relationships between core states) may be altered, or alternatively a new cluster of upwardly mobile producers may develop, which entails at least the partial redistribution of economic benefits from the core to the semi-periphery. Both mechanisms have particular relevance for Asia Pacific, given Japan's re-emergence as a core state and a core economy and the rise of a more productive and assertive semi-periphery in the rest of East Asia.

The emphasis on the geographical dimensions of a rapidly evolving international division of labour may, however, be seriously misleading if it concentrates attention on state actors and state boundaries while neglecting the increasingly important role of transnational actors and the far-reaching implications of the transnationalization of trade, production and finance. Partly as a result of increased mobility across state boundaries, made possible by technological innovation but also by trade liberalization and financial deregulation, firms have acquired much greater strategic freedom to operate in international markets, whether by producing in the home state and exporting, by producing in a host state for local consumption or by producing in a host state for export either back to the domestic market or to regional and global markets. Firms can exercise similar freedom when obtaining the requisite resources and other inputs for production, whether by producing at home and importing from abroad or by producing abroad and gaining access to local resources.

Increasingly attuned to these possibilities, firms with an eye on regional and global markets are intent on

> organizing or reorganizing their cross-border production activities in an efficiency-oriented, integrated fashion, capitalizing on the tangible and intangible assets available throughout the corporate system. In the resu¹ting international division of labour within firms, any part of the value added chain can be located wherever it contributes most to a company's overall performance.[5]

The greater international division of labour within transnational corporations, evidenced in increasing intra-firm trade and investment flows, shows how the engine of industrial restructuring is increasingly driven by transnational objectives and strategies. States will no doubt continue to perform a number of important administrative and legitimizing functions in the management of economic activity, but their ability to control, let alone plan, the industrial restructuring process is diminishing. More and more their principal function is to adapt to changing patterns of comparative advantage shaped largely by integrated international production systems.

Our analysis of the dynamic underlying the economic transformation of East Asia has thus far concentrated on the structural implications of economic competitiveness. There is, however, more to this dynamic than economics. Reference has already been made more than once to the role of the state in policy formulation and implementation. Beyond that, individual states – and the state system as a whole – must contend with the social dislocation arising from the structural reorganization of the economy.[6] The liberalization of rules and regulations governing trade, investment, finance and technology flows may help to deliver higher levels of aggregate economic growth, but to the extent that it also creates winners and losers it may deepen social and economic divisions, not least in multi-ethnic societies, and add further strain on the already delicate fabric of existing political systems. For the state it may well be a case of expanding responsibilities and diminishing capabilities. The widening gap between promise and performance may become particularly acute in periods of economic downturn. Equally relevant in this context is the environmental impact of rapid industrialization, evident in the mounting pressures associated with the depletion of scarce renewable resources, pollution and waste disposal, often compounded by the absence of effective environmental regulatory procedures and institutions. Though economic, social and environmental disruption may be most strikingly evident in the domestic political process, there is also an important external dimension, which has considerable bearing on political and strategic relationships.[7] The policy of economic competitiveness, as we shall see in later chapters, imposes on the state the difficult task of reconciling national and transnational interests with the requirements of national and regional security. This chapter will restrict itself to an examination of the scope and limitations of the East Asian 'economic miracle'. Particular emphasis will be placed on the interplay between the principle of economic competitiveness and shifts in the balance of productive capacity, on the one hand, and between the state-mediated policies of structural reorganization and the production and marketing strategies of transnational enterprises on the other.

JAPAN'S RISE AS A MAJOR ECONOMIC POWER

Over several decades East Asia experienced faster economic growth than any other region of the world. Indeed, this sustained rate of growth, encompassing such a large fraction of humanity, has few parallels in modern history. During the 1960–85 period annual output per capita increased on average by 5.5 per cent in Japan, 6.2 per cent in Taiwan, 5.7 per cent in South Korea, 5.9 per cent in Singapore and 5.9 per cent in Hong Kong.[8] During 1980–7 Asia's annual GNP growth rate averaged 8.5 per cent compared with 3.0 per cent for the European Community and 3.3 per cent for North America. Asia's export growth rate recorded similarly impressive results.[9] In Ross Garnaut's words, East Asia had by the 1990s joined 'Western Europe and North America as one of the three main centres of global production and trade', and become 'the world's largest source of surplus savings for international investment and the world's most voracious importer of foodstuffs and raw materials'.[10] While the magnitude of this economic transformation is not open to doubt, the factors which have made it possible and its regional and global implications are complex and contentious questions. In any case, despite important commonalities, East Asia cannot be treated as a single entity. The analysis will therefore focus first on Japan – the country where the whole process was set in motion – before turning our attention to the four tiger economies, the ASEAN countries and China.

Japan's meteoric economic expansion during the 1960s and 1970s hardly needs restating. While its annual growth rate after the oil price increases of the early 1970s fell well below the 10 per cent average growth of the 1960s, Japan continued right through to the end of the 1980s to outperform both Europe and the United States. In the period 1984–9 it recorded a growth rate of 4.5 per cent compared with 3.2 per cent for Europe and 3.1 per cent for the United States.[11] Between 1965 and 1990 Japan's industrial production increased fivefold whereas it only doubled in the United States and the leading economies of Western Europe. By 1980, the Japanese economy represented 44 per cent of the US economy; by 1990 the proportion had risen to 62 per cent.[12]

The remarkable impact of Japan's industrialization was clearly reflected in its export performance and especially its favourable current account balance, which rose from $4.8 billion in 1980 to a peak of $87 billion in 1987. Although it declined in subsequent years because of rising imports, in 1991 it still stood at $72.6 billion.[13] This large surplus coincided with the export of capital on an unprecedented scale. Following the liberalization of capital controls in the first half of the 1980s, the net outflow of capital climbed to $136.5 billion in 1987. The external assets of Japanese banks passed those of the United States in 1987, and by 1990 had reached more than $950 billion.[14] Between 1985 and 1989 Japan's contribution to international financial markets had risen from 8.0 per cent to 24.7 per cent. By the end of 1990, the net credit position was estimated at $328 billion, effectively making Japan the world's largest creditor nation.

Perhaps the single most revealing indicator of Japan's global economic presence was the scale of its foreign direct investment (FDI), which rose in value from $15 billion in 1986 to $48 billion in 1990. By 1992 Japan's accumulated FDI outflow was estimated at $248 billion,[15] representing an average annual growth rate estimated at between 24 and 26 per cent over the preceding decade.[16] While it is true that the greater part of these investments was directed to Europe and North America (nearly two-thirds of the total for the period 1981– 93), Asia was also a substantial recipient (approximately 17 per cent of the total). Japanese FDI flows to Asia assume even greater importance when it is remembered that for the same period Asia accounted for one-quarter of Japan's direct investment outflows in the manufacturing sector.[17] By 1985 Japan had become the leading investing nation in Asia (Indonesia and Hong Kong being the principal recipients), with US capital retaining its dominant position only in the Philippines, Taiwan and Singapore. Much the same pattern emerged in Japan's overseas development assistance (ODA) programme, which exceeded that of the United States in 1990 and reached $10 billion in 1991.[18] Significantly, the largest portion of Japanese aid (almost two-thirds) was allocated to Asia; by 1995 Japan was by far the leading source of development aid for several Asian countries, including China (54.5 per cent of total), Indonesia (68.5 per cent), Malaysia (60.7 per cent), Myanmar (90.5 per cent), the Philippines (55.6 per cent) and Thailand (80.7 per cent).[19]

One of the keys to Japan's economic expansion and rapid technological development was the ability of Japanese firms to commit themselves to large investments in new plant and equipment. In this they were greatly assisted by secure access to credit, made possible by their close connections with the leading Japanese banks and by the state's readiness to guarantee the loans secured from these banks. The banks themselves had a strong incentive to lend because the sheer size and technical sophistication of the firms in question greatly minimized the risk of bad debts. The intimate relationship between the large banks and major industrial corporations produced, as Rob Steven has aptly described it, 'a qualitatively greater measure of power than each could achieve on its own'.[20] The resulting technical, financial and industrial capacity of Japanese firms provided them with an effective platform from which to develop their marketing, trading and investment strategies. The outward projection of Japanese industrial and financial power, particularly in the Asian context, followed an evolutionary process, which for analytical purposes maybe divided into three principal phases: late 1960s to early 1970s, mid-1970s to mid-1980s, and mid-1980s to mid-1990s.

The first phase (1968–73), during which Japan's cumulative FDI rose from $2.0 billion to $10.3 billion, was largely driven by an offshore production strategy intent on circumventing rising labour costs at home and the restrictions imposed by environmental legislation and other forms of state regulation. The emphasis during this period was on the development of low-level manufacturing capacities, including textile industries, primarily in East Asia's newly industrializing economies (NIEs). During the second phase (1974–84), Japan's cumulative FDI rose to $71.4 billion,[21] with . investments focusing more on the manufacture of capital-intensive and technology-intensive goods. Japanese firms were now developing through subsidiaries and subcontracting arrangements a more elaborate division of labour, whereby the technological capacity to manufacture parts and components was progressively devolved to host economies in East Asia.[22]

By 1985 the relatively easy first steps in the offshore expansion of Japanese capital had been completed. The strategies to be developed in the third phase would be less clearly defined and more subject to tension and ambiguity. Following the September 1985 Plaza agreement and the revaluation of the yen, Japan had available to it, at least hypothetically, three options if it were to stem the likely loss of international competitiveness. It could try to restructure its industries and so make them less dependent on the export market; or it might keep its own production costs down and so to some degree nullify the impact of the realignment of the world's major currencies; or it could relocate part of its industrial production offshore, thereby taking advantage of lower costs and gaining better access to foreign markets.[23] Though efforts were made in all three directions, the continued penetration of export markets and the greatly expanded outflow of capital became the centrepiece of Japan's strategy. Given relatively low wages – as compared with the United States – and consistently high levels of domestic savings, there was a limit to how much and for how long Japan's economic growth could rely on increased domestic consumption. The annual rate of growth in domestic demand did rise from 4.0 per cent in 1985 to 7.4 per cent in 1988, only to fall again to 2.7 per cent in 1991 and 0.6 per cent in 1992. As in the past Japan's natural response was to export its way out of stagnation, with the result that, despite the yen's revaluation, export volumes rose: the period 1985–90 registered an average annual compound growth rate of 10.2 per cent compared with 6.3 percent in 1980–5.[24] Greatly assisted by a relatively stable import bill, even when measured in dollar terms, Japan's favourable trade balance, which stood at $56.0 billion in 1985, had risen to $96.4 billion in 1987 and to $124.6 billion in 1992.[25]

The growth in the volume and dollar value of exports played, however, a subordinate role to the export of capital. Whereas between 1981 and 1985 Japanese FDI was estimated to average $9.4 billion per year, it rose to $32.3 billion in 1986 and peaked at $67.5 billion in 1989. Japan's cumulative FDI rose from $83.7 billion in 1985 to $310.8 billion in 1990, with the greater part of this extraordinary outflow directed to North America (where the annual flow ranged between 46.0 and 50.2 per cent of Japan's total FDI) and Europe (where the proportion increased from 15.5 per cent in 1986 to 25.1 per cent in 1990).[26] The flow of Japanese FDI to Asia increased at a much slower rate, from $2.3 billion in 1986 to $7.1 billion in 1990. Although the volume of FDI directed to the NIEs rose in absolute terms from $1.5 billion in 1986 to $3.4 billion in 1990, it fell as a proportion of Japan's total FDI from 6.9 per cent in 1986 to 5.9 per cent in 1990. In the case of the ASEAN economies, Japanese direct investment increased in both absolute and relative terms (rising from $553 million in 1986 to $3.2 billion in 1990).[27] FDI flows to East Asia were particularly significant because of their heavy concentration in manufacturing. In 1991 there were 2680 Japanese companies with manufacturing operations in East Asia, well in excess of the corresponding number of companies in North America (1186) or Europe (595).[28]

Southeast Asia was of particular interest to Japan because the availability of cheap labour made it one of the main sites of low-cost production in the world. In 1988 annual manufacturing wages in Japan were estimated to be ten times higher than in Malaysia and thirty-five times higher than in Indonesia. In shifting its unprofitable industries to Southeast Asia, Japan was pursuing a familiar path. Having already relocated productive capacity in shipbuilding, non-ferrous metals, textiles and other labour-intensive industries, and even steel, it was now turning to cars and electronics; having already targeted the tiger economies, it was now giving greater attention to the ASEAN region. The expanded manufacturing capacity of the East Asian economies was inevitably reflected in increased manufacturing exports to Japan. The proportion of manufacturing output which Japanese subsidiaries operating in Southeast Asia were shipping back to Japan had increased from 11 per cent in 1983 to 16 per cent in 1989. Yet Japan soon developed a healthy trading surplus with the four main ASEAN economies (other than Singapore), estimated at $3.7 billion in 1993.[29] The trading surplus with the NIEs was even greater, amounting to $30.8 billion in 1990, whereas in the same year the United States recorded a trade deficit of $22.4 billion.[30]

What, then, can we conclude about Japan's role in East Asia's regional economy? At one level, it is arguable, in line with several indicators, that Japan had achieved a strikingly dominant position although, as we shall see, the scope, function and coherence of Japan's leadership posed difficult and as yet unanswered questions. By the mid-1980s most East Asian economies had developed high levels of export dependence on Japan, high levels of import dependence, particularly in the areas of capital and intermediate goods as well as parts and components, and a marked dependence on the transfer of Japanese capital and technology. As a broad generalization, East Asia had become economically more dependent on Japan than on the United States. Of course, as Chung-in Moon and others have observed, the creation of a Japanese economic sphere of influence is not without historical precedent.[31] After its military victories against China in 1895 and against Russia in 1904 Japan set out to establish an East Asian 'co-prosperity sphere' with a view to securing guaranteed access to the region's markets and raw materials. While this grand design was brought to an abrupt halt by Japan's defeat in the Second World War, important elements of the strategy were revived beginning in the 1960s, with the obvious important difference that during this period Japan's expanding influence did not rest on the use of armed force and enjoyed substantial support from the United States.

Japan clearly played a key role in East Asia's rapid industrialization. That role is perhaps best understood by dividing East Asia into three tiers: the NIEs, the ASEAN-4 and China. The NIEs may be regarded as the first tier in a chronological sense, but also by virtue of the scale of their commercial and financial transactions with Japan. Between 1951 and 1988 Japanese FDI flows to Hong Kong amounted to $6.2 billion, followed by Singapore ($3.8 billion), South Korea ($3.2 billion) and Taiwan ($1.8 billion).[32] Japan was also a significant destination for NIE exports ($9.9 billion in 1985), but it was an even greater source of NIE imports ($22.7 billion in 1985).[33] Through the transfusion of technology and capital, Japan had been a useful though perhaps not decisive catalyst in the development of export-oriented light, labour-intensive industries in the 1960s, but a crucial factor in the growth of technologically sophisticated industries in the 1970s.

As already indicated, Japan's early interest in Southeast Asia was confined largely to securing access to vital energy resources and other raw materials – an interest understandably accentuated by the two oil crises in the early and late 1970s. The obvious beneficiary was Indonesia, whose exports to Japan rose from $640 million in 1970 to $13.2 billion in 1980 before falling back to $10.1 billion in 1985. Malaysia too as a significant exporter of primary commodities developed a healthy trade surplus with Japan. This steadily rose from $420 million in 1970 to $4.3 billion in 1985. By contrast, Singapore, Thailand and to a lesser extent the Philippines had less to offer the Japanese economy and were by 1985 recording sizeable trade deficits.[34] By the mid-1980s, however, Japan was well on the way to incorporating Southeast Asia into its regional and global economic strategy. Given the added incentives provided by the revaluation of the yen, the protectionist tendencies of the US and West European economies and the greater competitiveness of the NIE economies, Southeast Asia became increasingly attractive to Japanese firms wishing to relocate part of their operations offshore and to use these as a platform for exporting to third parties and even back to Japan, as well as for capturing a large slice of the domestic market. Within the ASEAN countries a degree of sectoral and geographical specialization soon emerged, with Japanese investment focusing on advanced electronics in Malaysia, foodstuffs, electronics and intermediate goods in Thailand, heavy industry in Indonesia, and electronics, petrochemicals, banking and other services in Singapore.[35] By the late 1980s ASEAN had become Japan's second trading partner, accounting for 25 per cent of its imports and 26 per cent of its exports.

Trade, Investment and Aid

With this brief survey in mind, it is now possible to examine more closely the respective roles of trade, FDI, technology transfer and development assistance in the strategic partnership which Japan was painstakingly constructing with the main East Asian economies. Trade and investment were closely connected. In becoming the main supplier of capital and intermediate products to the NIEs and the ASEAN-4 economies, Japan had, by strengthening their technical and commercial capabilities, enabled them to make substantial inroads into the American market. Heizo Tanaka has described this triangular relationship as one in which 'Japan fills the role of supplier, while the United States fills that of an export absorber'.[36] Significantly, in 1987 East Asia accounted for 65 per cent of the US trade deficit, with 40 per cent attributable to Japan, 20 per cent to the NIEs, and 5 per cent to ASEAN. Japan, on the other hand, recorded in the same year a trade surplus of $20.7 billion with the NIEs, a trade deficit of $6.8 billion with the other ASEAN countries, and a trade surplus of $52.1 billion with the United States. In 1993 this three-way trade relationship yielded Japan an overall surplus of $107.4 billion compared with an overall deficit for the United States of $74.1 billion.[37] Several factors had contributed to Japan's success in securing this privileged trading position: the enormous technological and financial resources at its disposal, its geographical and cultural proximity to the region, the aggressive export promotion policies of the NIEs, the relatively open market for East Asian manufactures in the United States and Western Europe, and the relative difficulty which the advanced industrial economies, NIEs and ASEAN had all experienced in penetrating the qualitative barriers to Japanese markets in the manufacturing sector.[38]

The triangular trade relationship between the United States, Japan and the NIEs had one other dimension which pointed to the increasing integration of the Pacific economy, but also to the scope and limitations of Japan's productive capacity. The East Asian NIEs increased their share of total world manufactured exports from 1.7 per cent in 1965 to 8.8 per cent in 1984. Japan's share during this period also increased, from 8.0 per cent to 15.7 per cent.[39] As a result of the yen's revaluation the NIEs gained a competitive edge, thereby restricting Japan's further expansion into these markets, particularly in such industries as integrated circuits, television picture tubes, pocket calculators, video cassette recorders, steel and machine tools. NIE exports to Japan also rose substantially between 1985 and 1989: a trend which, as we have already noted, was more than offset by the dependence of NIE export-oriented manufacturing on Japanese capital and intermediate goods and components.[40]

There was, however, more to Japan's economic stake in East Asia than trade. Frequent reference has already been made to the scale and strategic importance of

Japanese investment flows to the region. In search of skilled workforces and lower labour costs, Japanese capital partially relocated from the NIEs to the ASEAN economies, and increasingly to China and Vietnam. The NIEs, ASEAN and China taken together had increased their share of total world exports from 9 per cent in 1982 to 14 per cent in 1992.[41] The tendency in the 1980s was for Japanese investment in NIEs to concentrate on general and electric machinery and transport equipment, but by the end of the 1980s the focus shifted to human capital-intensive and technology-intensive manufactures. In the case of ASEAN a comparable shift occurred from raw materials to labour-intensive industries.[42] It is worth noting that, while Japanese FDI flows to the NIEs fell by 50 per cent from $4.8 billion in 1989 to $2.4 billion in 1992, the corresponding decline in FDI flows to the ASEAN-4 economies was less than 20 per cent, from $4.8 billion to $3.9 billion. Allowing for time lags and understandable variations from one country to another, a striking correlation emerged between the export of Japanese capital to East Asia and Japan's favourable trade balance with the region. Japan's trade surplus with the NIEs rose from $12.6 billion in 1985 to $53.5 billion in 1993. During the same period Japan's trade with ASEAN moved from a deficit of $9.4 billion to a surplus of $3.7 billion.[43]

Mirroring and helping to sustain the expansion of East Asia's production capacity and Japan's stake in it was the growth of both private and public financial flows from Japan to the region. By the end of 1992 Japanese banks had lent some $75 billion to Asian borrowers, and contributed about 60 per cent of the funds being funnelled to the Hong Kong and Singapore financial markets. In addition, Japan had a cumulative investment of $59.9 billion in real estate, $46.6 billion in services, $40.3 billion in commerce and $21.7 billion in the transport sector.[44] The big four Japanese security firms, Nomura, Daiwa, Nikko and Yamaichi, had penetrated the region's financial markets and helped to establish a number of funds, some operating nationally and others regionally.[45] To ensure the profitability of its investments, Japan had a vested interest in promoting East Asia's economic and political stability. Official development assistance became a key instrument in this strategy, providing avenues for technical co-operation (critical to the development of industrial infrastructure) as well as grant aid, loans and contributions to multilateral organizations – all of which helped Japan to influence both political processes and development policies in recipient countries. Having topped the $10 billion mark in 1991, Japan's ODA programme surpassed the $14 billion mark in 1995. Throughout this period Japan remained by far the largest contributor to Asian and especially East Asian development. Although Japan's ODA in 1996 would fall substantially (by 35 per cent from the previous year, reflecting in part the reduced dollar-denominated value of the yen), the amount disbursed to East Asian countries, with the exception of China, remained relatively unchanged. Eight of the top ten recipients of Japan's bilateral assistance were Asian countries (Indonesia, China, Thailand, India, the Philippines, Pakistan, Bangladesh, Sri Lanka). Japan was the main donor for virtually the whole of East Asia, contributing more than half of all the aid received by China, Indonesia, Laos, Malaysia, Myanmar, the Philippines and Thailand.[46]

While the 1990 ODA White Paper and the 1992 ODA charter considerably widened the philosophical underpinning of Japan's aid policies, there can be little doubt that the primary objective was to maximize complementarity between developing Asian economies and the Japanese economy. The establishment of the Japan–ASEAN Investment Corporation in 1981 and the ASEAN–Japan Development Fund in 1987 was designed to promote in Southeast Asia the instruments and practices characteristic of Japanese industrial policy. Japan's Ministry of International Trade and Industry (MITI) was itself actively seeking the participation of the private sector in targeted industries in ASEAN countries. Particularly significant was the role of the Japan Overseas Development Corporation which, supported by both private and public funds, provided concessional finance and technical expertise for numerous projects in East Asia. The Association for Overseas Technical Scholarships and the Japan International Co-operation Agency also played an important part in supplying East Asian countries with the technical training needed to service the textile, electrical, machinery, chemical and other manufacturing industries in which Japanese capital had heavily invested.[47]

Over and above its technical and financial rationale, Japan's aid policy also served a useful psychological function, helping to endow Japan's large and growing economic presence in East Asia with a human face, thereby enhancing its legitimacy. Central to this strategy was the increasing attention paid to environmental concerns. To give one example, in 1992 Japan and China agreed to make environmental co-operation one of ODA's future priorities. The establishment of the Japan–China Comprehensive Forum on Environmental Co-operation in April 1996 was followed in September 1997 with an in-principle agreement to launch a new scheme, Japan–China Environmental Cooperation Toward the Twenty-first Century, consisting of two projects: the establishment of an Environmental Information Network and the creation of environmental model cities.[48] Notwithstanding the increasing attention paid to the quality of aid, in practice both MITI and increasingly the Ministry of Foreign Affairs saw ODA as a useful instrument for enhancing the competitiveness of Japanese business.[49]

By the late 1980s it appeared as if the extensive trade, aid, investment and technology networks linking the Japanese and East Asian economies had firmly consolidated Japan's regional leadership. Reinforcing these economic foundations were ideological or ideational linkages facilitated by 'geographic proximity, linguistic and cultural similarities, personal networks, and a proven record of economic performance'.[50] Singapore's 'Learn from Japan' campaign in 1978 and Malaysia's 'Look East' policy launched in 1982 were indicative of Japan's newly found prestige. Even in South Korea, where serious reservations persisted about Japanese cultural influence, there were those who acknowledged that useful lessons could be learnt from the coalition politics of the Japanese Liberal Democratic Party and the strategic orientation of large Japanese corporations. Some East Asians admired the stability and effectiveness of Japan's system of government, others felt a strong affinity with its Confucian cultural tradition, while still others were impressed by its economic and technological prowess.[51] The Japanese model of economic development, it seemed, had become a major pole of attraction.

Leadership Role

Any discussion of leadership inevitably raises difficult questions not only about the form, function and effectiveness of leadership – of which more later – but about its source. In the case of Japan, who or what could be said to exercise leadership? Here we approach one of the most contested areas of inquiry in political economy: the relationship between the state and the private sector, between the bureaucracy and the economy. The issues are especially complex when it comes to Japan because of the highly polarized state of the debate between those who subscribe to the notion of the 'strong state'[52] and the neo-classical view with its emphasis on the twin principles of free trade and comparative advantage.[53] Over time, the debate has become somewhat more sophisticated and given rise to a third position which takes issue with both the traditional view of the Japanese economy as dominated by a well-oiled and monolithic bureaucratic machine and the image of the Japanese state as a fragmented, rudderless, often paralysed polity that is vulnerable to powerful domestic interests, on the one hand, and external pressures, on the other. According to this third perspective, Japan is led by a coalition of political and economic elites, variously described as 'a government–business network', a 'bureaucratic–industrial complex' or a partnership based on 'reciprocal consent'.[54] A good deal of evidence does, indeed, point to a network of interlocking interests guiding the allocation of public resources, the development of industry policy and the distribution of benefits. This partnership, it is argued, has, despite factional tensions between and within elites, been able to take strong and decisive action and is credited with having constructed, admittedly through a series of *ad hoc* responses, a vision of East and Southeast Asia as integral parts of a steadily expanding Japan-centred production and exporting alliance.

This third hypothesis, theoretically sophisticated and empirically grounded though it may be, does not however fully answer the question of leadership. To postulate the emergence of an Asian division of labour, in which Japan, the NIEs and ASEAN act as 'upper-, middle-and lower-grade economies'[55] is one thing; to identify and explain the sources of Japanese leadership is quite another. To begin with, it is not at all clear whether, or to what extent, the interests of Japan's 'government–business network' coincide with the 'national interest'. There is no denying that several of Japan's bureaucratic institutions, notably MITI, the Ministry of Finance (MOF) and the Economic Planning Agency (EPA), performed important functions in integrating Japan more closely with the globalizing world economy. The Japanese state used a number of aid, trade and investment policy instruments to extract advantage from the rapidly changing international environment in which both natural and policy-based barriers to the movement of goods, services, capital, technology and labour were progressively reduced.[56] But the question remains: did such state intervention serve national interests or, to be more exact, the interests of the national economy, in which case these interests and objectives have to be given concrete meaning and content? Or did it merely perform an instrumental role, serving primarily corporate strategies and interests?

Though Japanese corporations have traditionally prided themselves on their Japanese identity, in assuming an increasingly global posture they nevertheless developed interests, perspectives, strategies and operations which did not necessarily benefit the national economy, whether in terms of GNP growth, employment, financial stability or consumer confidence. The restructuring in which they were engaged was in many respects an exogenous process, in which traditional patterns of trade and investment gave way to new international business alliances, including a wide range of mergers, acquisitions, joint production ventures and technology co-operation arrangements. It may be argued that Japanese corporations contributed much to Japan's 'ability to restructure its manufacturing sector continuously from labour-intensive industries through resource-based heavy industries and assembly-oriented industries towards high technology industries'.[57] Each wave of Japanese FDI may be said to have enhanced Japanese competitiveness, whether by gaining access abroad to resources lacking at home, utilizing cheap unskilled labour, overcoming the protective barriers of other countries, off-loading or reducing the mounting costs of pollution control, circumventing the disadvantages of an appreciating yen or simply finding a profitable outlet for Japan's consistent surplus of savings over domestic investment.[58] Yet these strategies were not entirely successful. More to the point, the increased profitability of individual firms or business networks did not necessarily work to the advantage of the Japanese economy as a whole.

The production plans devised by Japanese corporations, precisely because they were regional and global in scope, conferred considerable importance on their offshore operations, not only in manufacturing, but in design, parts procurement and even in marketing and finance. The aim was no longer merely to capture export markets but to meet the import requirements of domestic operations. The regional strategy pursued by Japanese corporations was to have their Asian subsidiaries import sophisticated plant, machinery and parts from Japan and the head office in Japan import supplies which had become too expensive to produce at home. What was once a series of domestic transactions within a company or business network (*keiretsu*) was transformed into a complex web of cross-border transactions, with the important caveat that these were still contained within the boundaries of a single transnational firm or the *keiretsu* to which it belonged.[59] Initially, these Japanese networks had a stronger presence in the NIEs, but by the mid-1980s their foothold in the ASEAN region was just as robust. By the early 1990s intra-firm trade was said to account for as much as 40 per cent of Japan's total trade with ASEAN.[60] The overwhelming proportion of high-technology products (for example, electrical and precision machinery) exported to Japan by Japanese manufactures in Asia went to parent companies. Similarly, the bulk of sophisticated manufacturers imported from Japan by Japanese subsidiaries in Asia came from parent companies.[61] These were the outward manifestations of a vertically integrated production network, which could well deliver Japan a continuing stranglehold on high-technology and knowledge-intensive industries; but was this enough to avert the substantial deindustrialization of the Japanese economy or to create the domestic conditions necessary for high levels of consumer demand?

In the early 1990s, when Japan became for the first time a net importer of television sets, video recorders and other electrical appliances, and when production of 1 megabyte and 4 megabyte chips was shifted to overseas affiliates, the deindustrialization argument gained ground, but many economists and policy-makers remained unconvinced. They pointed to 'Japan's concentration on the production of value-added inputs', which they saw not only as benefiting high-tech corporations but as retooling and revitalizing the Japanese economy as a whole.[62] The proposition, however, that corporate profitability and the health of the national economy were closely connected tended to be asserted rather than demonstrated. Japanese capital, it is true, now had a vastly increased productive capacity. The question is: how would such capacity be used? Perceiving that the Japanese domestic market could not be relied upon to absorb much of this expanded capacity,

Japanese corporations and *keiretsu* developed regional strategies for producing and exporting more and more, thereby accumulating ever increasing trade surpluses with both the United States and East Asia.

Whether such an export strategy was ultimately sustainable, economically or diplomatically, was open to question. Even more doubtful was the assumption that Japan's regional leadership could rest upon such a strategy. There were also domestic considerations which might in due course impinge on Japan's future leadership capabilities. Partly in response to the relocation of Japanese manufacturing capacity to East Asia, the Japanese government, prodded by the United States and other governments, pursued expansionary fiscal and monetary policies. Though the intention was to increase Japanese consumption, and indirectly Japan's capacity to absorb imports, the unintended consequence of such a strategy, to which other factors also contributed, was excess liquidity in the economy. The net effect was to encourage speculative behaviour by both firms and individuals, thereby inflating the value of land, stock and other assets. In 1988 residential land prices rose by about 70 per cent; between early 1987 and December 1990 the Nikkei stock average index had nearly doubled.[63] The 'bubble economy' had served to fuel the unprecedented outflow of capital in the late 1980s.

Recession

When the bubble eventually burst, a recession set in despite the rapid expansion of the information and communications industry and positive developments in a number of service industries. The recession continued throughout most of the decade with continued hollowing out of existing industries, added pressures for asset deflation and sustained falls in both consumer and investment demand, which no amount of government spending seemed able to arrest or offset. Given the large investments made during the boom, the emphasis was now on contracting productive capacity, but attempts to reduce plant and equipment inevitably meant increased unemployment, which in turn compounded the problem of weak consumer demand. Japan's official unemployment rate rose from 2.1 per cent in 1991 to 3.1 per cent in 1995 and 4.8 per cent in March 1999.[64] These figures significantly understated the extent of company retrenchments and other 'adjustment measures', including substantial reductions in overtime work, enforced holidays and increased recourse to contract work. Another important factor contributing to Japan's economic woes was the precariousness of the financial sector resulting from the mounting volume of bad debts, which was itself a direct legacy of the excessive lending associated with the bubble economy. According to official figures released in September 1997, non-performing loans (estimated at 21 trillion yen) accounted for 3.48 per cent of outstanding gross bank loans, but within less than a year, in line with government attempts at greater financial transparency, the figure was revised upwards to 87.5 trillion yen; that is, more than 13 per cent of outstanding loans.[65] The closure of a number of high-profile banks and financial institutions, including the Hokkaido Dakushoku Bank and Yamaichi Securities, the collapse of countless small and medium-sized firms and the steady depreciation of the Japanese currency were all indicative of the depth of Japan's financial crisis.

With banks and other enterprises struggling to remain solvent and continuing pressure on an already depressed stock market, business confidence was severely shaken. Real GDP, which had grown annually by an average of 5.0 per cent during the boom years 1988–91, increased by a mere 0.7 per cent in the ensuing four-year period.[66] The return to a respectable rate of growth in 1996 (3.9 per cent) proved short-lived, with GDP in 1997 rising by 0.8 per cent and contracting by nearly 2 per cent in 1998.[67] Stock prices in 1997 had fallen to 42.7 per cent of their 1987 value, while real estate prices had depreciated by 42 per cent between 1990 and 1997.[68]

To lift the economy out of recession the Hashimoto and Obuchi governments were compelled to launch a succession of fiscal and financial initiatives. These included a structural policy package in November 1997 designed to facilitate land transactions and promote investment; a financial stabilization programme in January 1998 which committed 30 trillion yen (6 per cent of GDP) of public funds to strengthen the deposit insurance and banking systems; a supplementary budget in February 1998, with an allocation of 2 trillion yen for income tax cuts and public works; a comprehensive economic package in April 1998 of over 16 trillion yen, half of which was earmarked for social infrastructure investment and the other half for a range of tax reductions; new legislation passed by the Diet and associated measures to prepare for bank failures and infuse additional public funds into banks still struggling with bad debts; yet another stimulus package in November 1998 committing 24 trillion yen, much of it to fund public construction works; the introduction in October 1998 of a 20 trillion yen special credit guarantee scheme for small firms designed to curb corporate bankruptcy growth; and a raft of measures announced in June 1999 with the stated aims of creating 700 000 new jobs, extending government assistance programmes to another 100 000 job seekers, and helping private firms to restructure their businesses and tackle the problems of excessive debt and excessive production capacity.[69]

That so many attempts should have been made in such a short space of time was evidence enough of the intractability of Japan's economic and financial difficulties. Why had the Japanese economic miracle come to such a seemingly abrupt halt? Was this a transient condition or one with deep structural roots? Were its origins primarily endogenous or exogenous? While no thorough analysis of this complex set of questions can be attempted here, a few observations may prove helpful. Of the numerous interpretations offered one is especially deserving of attention. For Moon and Rhyu policy failure holds the key to the answer.[70] Japan's protracted recession is attributed primarily to the failure of the state to introduce appropriate fiscal as well as banking and financial reforms, and underlying this failure is said to be 'waning executive dominance'. More specifically, the political limitations of the Hashimoto cabinet, imposed by the new era of electoral realignments and coalition politics, are identified as having undermined the leadership function of the chief executive.

Compounding this new political volatility was the structural rigidity in policy formulation associated with a bureaucratic system known for its inertia, its jealously guarded autonomy and its predilection for secrecy in decision-making. The mismanagement, or at least poor management, of the economy on the part of the political and administrative arms of government did no doubt contribute to the problem. But this can hardly be the whole or even a major part of the explanation. If we are to account for Japan's economic crisis by reference to the shortcomings of the executive–bureaucratic nexus, how are we to explain the timing of the problem? If the state apparatus had somehow managed to preside over a prolonged period of economic success, why should its defects become so critical in the mid to late 1990s? In any case, if policy failure is to be blamed for the crisis, it cannot be confined to the Hashimoto period, since the economic downturn dates back to 1992. Indeed, the economic boom of the late 1980s and the speculative spiral that accompanied it could also be ascribed to policy failure, namely an excessively expansionary monetary policy.

A contrary interpretation favoured by Richard Katz traces the unravelling of the Japanese economic miracle to two long-standing structural deficiencies, namely the unproductive use of capital and the inability of private domestic demand to consume all that Japan produces.[71] The late-1980s bubble is thus depicted as 'a futile attempt to make up for that deficiency', a symptom rather than a cause of Japan's systemic problems. Here again, the analysis rightly draws attention to key dimensions of Japan's political economy, but is less than convincing in its emphasis on the decline of Japanese productivity and the failure to innovate or on the linkages between returns on investment and underconsumption. Equally, the time lag between the initial appearance of these deficiencies and the onset of economic crisis is not adequately explored. The analysis does, however, point to a distinguishing structural feature of the economy, namely its in-built tendency to offset relatively low levels of domestic demand with large trade surpluses – Japan's visible trade surplus during the twelve months to February 2000 had risen to $124.1 billion, and its current-account surplus to $109.6 billion.[72] For success on this front begets new problems. Trade surpluses are sustainable only so long as other economies are prepared to tolerate trade deficits, an issue to which we return in the next chapter. Moreover, a strategy which makes the trade surplus its engine of growth is likely to confront the periodic appreciation of its currency, which will in turn reduce the competitiveness of its exports and to that extent reduce its capacity to compensate for excess savings and insufficient consumption. Nor was the financial leverage which Japan had secured, in part through the profitability of its export strategy in the 1960s and 1970s, likely to be preserved in the increasingly deregulated global financial markets of the 1990s without comprehensive reorganization of its financial institutions and their economic underpinnings. Here again we encounter the pivotal but elusive duality of the state's function as both agent of macroeconomic regulation and the arena for the transnational organization of production and finance.

By 1999, the Japanese economy was witnessing the first tentative signs of recovery. Industrial production was rising as inventories fell, household spending was increasing with the help of government loan guarantees, bankruptcies were declining, and government loan and tax incentives were boosting housing construction.[73] At the same, time legislative and administrative arrangements for the prudential regulation of Japanese financial markets were being greatly strengthened. Yet the road ahead remained at best uncertain. Unemployment was still at record levels and could rise still further in the wake of continued industrial restructuring as firms closed or downsized unprofitable units. Financial institutions had still to overcome the problem of non-performing loans, and the yen was beginning to appreciate sharply against the US dollar, rising from a low of about 145 yen per US$ in June 1997 to just over 102 yen in November 1999.[74] In other words, it remained to be seen whether higher rates of growth would be self-sustaining or dependent on the continual use of fiscal stimulus. With the added constraint of an ageing population and a declining labour force, Japan's medium-term potential growth rate was considered unlikely to exceed an annual average of 2 per cent over the coming decade.

By the end of the 1990s the Japanese state was still trying to adapt to the radically altered economic and political environment resulting from the mutually reinforcing but contradictory effects of globalization and regionalization. Instructive in this regard was the sharp increase in foreign participation in the Japanese economy. Traditional business relationships were opening up; regulations were being dismantled or revised; and foreign direct investment into Japan was rising sharply, admittedly starting from an extremely low base.[75] It was, however, too early to tell whether these limited attempts at liberalization were a sign of Japan's renewed confidence in its economic competitiveness or of grudging compliance with powerful external pressures. Against this backdrop, it is not altogether surprising that Japan should have found it difficult to formulate a response to the East Asian financial crisis that was equal to the task or that in any sense matched the expectations of East Asian governments.

We shall return to the financial turmoil that swept East Asia in 1997–8 and to Japan's response in the concluding section of this chapter. Suffice it here to say that by the late 1990s notions of Japanese regional leadership, let alone hegemony, had lost the plausibility they had acquired a decade earlier. This is not to say that Japan did not still exercise a pervasive economic presence in the region. Such a presence, however, did not readily translate into effective political or even economic leadership. Japanese corporate and financial muscle, as reflected in the regional division of labour, was the result not so much of a grand design as of a combination of disparate yet interconnected corporate interests and decisions. The Japanese state may have attempted to play a supportive role, but it lacked the confidence, internal cohesion, popular legitimacy or degree of regional acceptance to enable it to exercise the sustained and multifaceted leadership needed for the development and management of regional strategies and institutions.

EXPORT-ORIENTED INDUSTRIALIZATION

The East Asian 'economic miracle' has given rise to a voluminous, though not always illuminating, literature which variously seeks to describe, explain, commend or criticize this unique phenomenon. The following few pages do not purport to offer a comprehensive historical survey or an original explanatory model. The more modest aim is to highlight key features of the phenomenon and to identify the complex conditions which gave rise to it, in order to situate it *vis-à-vis* the larger currents which are presently shaping the economic and geopolitical landscape of the region.

The rapid and sustained economic growth that different parts of East Asia experienced at different times over the last several decades transformed the region into one of the three major centres of global economic activity. Contemporary East Asia has rightly been described as 'the world's largest source of surplus savings for international investment, and the world's most voracious importer of foodstuffs and new materials'.[76] During the 1960–85 period the average annual increase in output per capita was estimated at 5.5 per cent for Japan and just under 6.0 per cent for the four tiger economies.[77] Even if one excludes Japan, East Asia's average annual economic growth, measured in terms of output per worker, during 1960–92 was 4.1 per cent compared with 2.4 per cent for the advanced industrial countries.[78]

These indices of growth must, of course, be treated with caution. In many cases growth emerged from a rather low base, and even by the end of the 1990s less than 15 per cent of East Asia's population enjoyed per capita incomes or rates of industrial productivity comparable to those of the leading western economies. Moreover, growth rates were not uniform across the region, either in magnitude or timescale; there were considerable variations both within and between subregions. For purposes of analytical convenience, East Asia may be divided into five zones: Japan, the NIEs, the ASEAN-4 economies (comprising Thailand, Malaysia, Indonesia and the Philippines), China, and Indochina, in particular Vietnam. The order in which these five zones is listed reflects the chronological sequence they followed in terms of the rapid growth of manufacturing industry, with Japan having established a substantial industrial base by the turn of the century and Vietnam having only just embarked on the path of industrialization. In the remainder of this chapter, the focus will be on three zones: the NIEs, the ASEAN-4 economies and China, where the drive for export-oriented industrialization got under way in the 1960s, 1970s and 1980s respectively.

Newly Industrializing Economies

Turning to the NIEs first, though considerable differences are discernible between their respective industrializing paths since the early 1960s, they all achieved impressive economic growth rates for the best part of three decades. As Table 2.1 indicates, all four economies registered average annual GDP growth rates of between 8 per cent and 10 per cent during 1965–80. These rates declined somewhat during 1980–92 but they still ranged between 6.7 per cent and 9.4 per cent, far surpassing the performance of any other economic region or subregion in the world. There were several dips in the growth curve, notably those associated with major recessionary currents in the world economy in 1974–5 and again in 1982–3. While sensitive to disturbances in the international trading system, the NIEs were able on both occasions to adjust rather quickly to the new environment and by the mid-1980s had markedly improved their export competitiveness.

Taiwan is widely regarded as East Asia's greatest success story. By the early 1990s, with a population of under 21 million, Taiwan had become the world's thirteenth largest trading nation and had acquired foreign-exchange reserves in excess of $80 billion. Its exports had grown from $450 million in 1965 to $5.3 billion in 1975, $55.5 billion in 1987 and $85.1 billion in 1993.[79] They averaged an annual growth rate of 11.6 per cent during 1980–90 and 5.9 per cent during 1990–5. Even more remarkable was the changing composition of its exports, with manufactured goods as a proportion of total exports rising from 8.1 per cent in 1952 to 50.5 per cent in 1962, 83.3 per cent in 1972 and 96.2 per cent in 1990.[80] Equally striking was the steady shift from labour-intensive to capital-intensive and technology-intensive manufactures. The export of electrical machinery had risen from $5.8 billion in 1986 to $13.8 billion in 1992; during the same period office and computing equipment exports had risen from $2.2 billion to $11.6 billion.[81] As a proportion of total manufactured exports, machinery exports had increased from 3.9 per cent in 1980 to 22.3 per cent in 1992.[82]

Table 2.1: Growth indicators, 1965–92

	Average annual real GDP growth		Average annual growth rate of GNP per capita (%)	GDP per capita[a] ($US)	
	1965–80	1980–92	1965–90	1965	1992
Korea	9.9	9.4	7.1	1046	7235[a]
Taiwan	9.8	7.8	7.1	1651	8067[a]
Hong Kong	8.6	6.7	6.2	3498	16461
Singapore	10.0	6.7	6.2	1845	12633

Note: [a] Indicates data for 1991.
Source: Heather Smith, ' "Western" versus "Asian" Capitalism: Is There Anything New under the Sun?', paper presented at Northeast Asia Program Workshop, Australian National University, 11–13 December 1995

Contributing to the rising volume and changing pattern of trade were FDI inflows and outflows. Though relatively small in volume in the early period of Taiwanese industrialization, FDI nevertheless played a strategic role in the development of the more advanced manufacturing industries. During the period 1952–85, FDI, largely of US and Japanese origin, was concentrated in the electronic, electrical and chemical industries. In subsequent years the volume of FDI increased substantially (reaching $15.2 billion during 1986–95), with Japan providing the largest proportion of the total (29.3 per cent) and the chemical, banking, insurance and other service industries attracting by far the largest investments.[83] Significantly, in this more recent period FDI outflows assumed increased importance, rising from a total of $215 million during 1952–85 to $9.4 billion during 1986–95, to which should be added the amount flowing to China (estimated by Taiwan authorities at $5.1 billion for the period 1991–5). China aside, the three major destinations of Taiwanese direct investment during 1986–95 were North America ($3.4 billion), Southeast Asia ($2.7 billion) and Hong Kong ($668 million).[84] Outward investments to Southeast Asia, China and Hong Kong were concentrated in the manufacturing sector, especially electronics, electrical appliances, food and beverages, plastics, precision instruments, chemicals, textiles, and basic metals and products, and contributed to the rapid expansion of Taiwanese exports (especially industrial chemicals and electrical machinery) to these countries.

Table 2.2 Sectoral share of GDP (%)

	Newly Industrializing Economies			Southeast Asia				China (PRC)
	Hong Kong	South Korea	Singapore	Taiwan	Indonesia	Malaysia	Philippines	Thailand	
Agriculture									
1970	-	29.8	2.2	-	35.0	-	28.2	30.2	42.2
1980	0.9	14.2	1.1	7.9	24.4	22.9	23.5	20.2	25.6
1998	-	6.1	-	2.3	17.2	11.3	19.4	12.0	16.3
Industry									
1970	-	23.8	36.4	-	28.0	-	33.7	25.7	44.6
1980	32.0	37.8	38.8	46.0	41.3	35.8	40.5	30.1	51.7
1998	-	43.2	-	34.7	42.3	45.8	35.5	40.4	55.4
Services									
1970	-	46.4	61.4	-	37.0	-	38.1	44.1	13.2
1980	67.2	48.1	60.0	46.1	34.3	41.3	36.0	49.7	22.7
1998	-	50.6	-	62.9	40.5	42.9	45.1	47.6	28.3

Source: Asian Development Outlook 1999, New York, Oxford University Press for the Asian Development Bank, 1999, p. 247.

Compared to Taiwan, South Korea's growth rates were less even, its per capita income lower and its external debt much higher. Nevertheless its economic performance was in other key respects remarkably similar. Apart from a few short-lived downturns, economic growth was consistently high from the early 1960s to the mid-1990s. Its annual GDP growth rate averaged 6.2 per cent during 1960–5, 7.4 per cent during 1973–84, 9.8 per cent during 1984–9 and 7.2 per cent during 1984–94.[85] As with Taiwan, the internal structure of the Korean economy shifted substantially from agriculture to manufacturing (see Table 2.2). As a proportion of total output the agricultural sector fell drastically from 17 per cent in 1970 to 7.7 per cent in 1985, its contribution to employment falling from 48 per cent in 1971 to only 20 per cent in 1990.[86] By contrast, the share of the manufacturing sector rose from 40.3 per cent in 1970 to 50.4 per cent in 1975. Although the relative contribution of manufacturing declined thereafter in favour of the services sector, manufacturing exports continued to rise, accounting for 91.6 per cent of total exports in 1984 and 93.8 per cent in 1990.[87] The value of total exports rose sharply from $17 billion in 1980 to $82.2 billion in 1993,[88] as did the ratio of exports (and imports) to GNP. By the mid-1980s, South Korea had become one of the leading trading nations in the world, but also one of the most trade-dependent economies, the ratio of total trade to GNP steadily rising from the early 1960s and reaching a peak of 85.4 per cent in 1984. In subsequent years the ratio declined appreciably but remained relatively high (52.7 per cent in 1995), though much lower than in the case of Taiwan, Malaysia, Hong Kong or Singapore.

The other important feature of South Korea's trade was a fluctuating trade balance, recording for example a surplus of $11.4 billion in 1988 but deficits of $7.1 billion in 1991 and $5.6 billion in 1994. These periodic imbalances, coupled with the government's ambitious investment plans, were reflected in relatively high levels of external public debt (estimated at $45.3 billion in 1984). In the ensuing decade, this external debt stabilized and even declined, particularly when measured as a proportion of exports, from well in excess of 100 per cent in the early 1980s to just under 50 per cent in 1995.[89] By contrast, FDI inflows were relatively small in volume in the early phases of industrialization, averaging much less than $1 billion per year through the 1980s, and rising appreciably only in later years to reach $5.5 billion in 1991 and $8.7 billion in 1993.[90] At the crucial stage of its industrial development, South Korea preferred to take advantage of the increasing liquidity in the international financial system by subscribing to large foreign loans than by encouraging foreign investment.

When compared to Taiwan and South Korea, Singapore's and Hong Kong's experiences indicate striking differences, particularly with regard to the FDI and trade linkages in the manufacturing sector. Singapore's GNP real growth averaged 9.4 per cent in 1970–9, 7.5 per cent in 1980–9, and 5.0 per cent in 1990–6,[91] but its exports rose at an even faster rate. The average annual growth rate for 1980–93 was estimated at 12.7 per cent.[92] Throughout the 1970s and 1980s Singapore's exports in any one year far exceeded its GDP. In 1994 they amounted to $69 billion or 140.4 per cent of GDP.[93] Official export figures in any case greatly underestimated the extent of Singapore's trade with the rest of East Asia. For example, in 1986–93 Singapore's domestic exports of manufactures represented only 60 per cent of its total manufacturing exports. If Singapore's important entrepôt role is taken into account, then total exports of manufactures assume even greater dimensions, rising from $29.4 billion in 1986 to $94.8 billion in 1993.[94] In Singapore's case export-oriented industrialization was closely linked to large FDI inflows. Cumulative foreign investment in gross fixed assets in the manufacturing sector nearly doubled between 1986 ($20.9 billion) and 1992 ($39.1 billion).[95] By 1990 firms which relied on foreign sources for more than 50 per cent of their capital accounted for 58.9 per cent of the workforce in the manufacturing industry, 75.9 per cent of its output and 85.8 per cent of its exports.[96] Foreign capital had greatly accelerated Singapore's transformation into an export-manufacturing economy, and helped to move its product cycle to highly automated operations, especially in the electronics, chemicals, machinery and transport industries. In due course, foreign investment would also play a part in the development of the services sector, particularly in the areas of design, research, product development, and marketing. The involvement of international business was now seen as playing a crucial role in developing Singapore as a global city and a hub for regional business operations, notably in finance, shipping, air transport, telecommunications and information.

Foreign direct investment was equally prominent in the development of Hong Kong's manufacturing industries. As a proportion of total exports manufactures rose from 78 per cent in 1984 to 87 per cent in 1988, and to 95 per cent in 1994. In absolute terms manufacturing exports rose from $17.2 billion in 1984 to $55.0 billion in 1988 and to $143.8 billion in 1994.[97] These growth rates far exceeded the annual growth in GDP, which averaged 9.2 per cent in 1970–9, 7.5 per cent in 1980–9 and 5.0 per cent in 1990–6.[98] However, as labour costs started rising in the 1980s, and as China became more hospitable to foreign investment, manufacturing firms based in Hong Kong sought to improve their competitiveness by relocating their productive capacity to the Chinese mainland. As of 1997, Hong Kong investors in Guangdong province alone employed some 3.5 million people, a number larger than Hong Kong's own labour force. As a consequence the contribution of the manufacturing sector to GDP had fallen from 17.6 per cent in 1990 to 9.3 per cent in 1994.[99] By contrast the services sector had risen from 69 per cent of GDP in 1980 to nearly 83 per cent in 1995,[100] with tourism, transport and financial services among the major sources of foreign exchange. The rise in manufacturing exports was closely parallelled by increasing FDI inflows: the average annual growth rate during 1986–92 was about 10.9 per cent, directed largely to the electronics, textiles and garment industries and originating primarily from the United Sates, Japan and China.[101] Despite disagreement as to whether official trade figures overstated the trade intensity between Hong Kong and China, there is little doubt that China supplied an increasing proportion of Hong Kong's manufacturing imports, particularly in textiles and electrical machinery, or that the regional headquarters and international procurement offices which foreign affiliates had established in Hong Kong provided China with access to a number of services, including sourcing of raw materials and components, technical support, financing, marketing and sales promotion.

ASEAN

In this brief overview of East Asian industrialization, it remains to highlight a few key trends in ASEAN's economic development before turning to the more complex questions central to our analysis. As with the NIEs, though starting later and from a lower base, the ASEAN-4 economies with the exception of the Philippines experienced substantial economic growth after the early 1970s. During 1980–5,

Table 2.3 East Asian export growth

Export Performance	Average Annual Growth 1980-93%	Average Annual Growth 1990-4%
Taiwan	11.9	5.9
South Korea	12.3	7.4
Hong Kong	15.8	15.5
Singapore	12.7	16.1
Indonesia	6.7	21.3
Malaysia	12.6	17.8
Thailand	15.5	21.6
Phillippines	3.4	10.2

Source: Asia Yearbook 1996, 1997.

Indonesia's real GDP increased at an annual average of 3.5 per cent, compared to 5.5 per cent and 5.6 per cent for Malaysia and Thailand respectively. For the period 1980–93, GDP growth rates were even higher: 5.8 per cent for Indonesia, 6.2 per cent for Malaysia, 8.2 per cent for Thailand, with the Philippines lagging well behind with 1.4 per cent.[102] It is worth noting, however, that in the post-Marcos era the Philippines too would experience an economic resurgence, its GNP rising from $52.5 billion in 1992 to $64.2 billion in 1994.[103] The same upward trend continued for another three years (1994–6), with Indonesia's GDP growing at an average annual rate of 7.9 per cent, compared with 9.1 per cent for Malaysia, 7.6 per cent for Thailand, and even the Philippines registering a healthy growth rate of 5.0 per cent.[104] Taking Southeast Asia as a whole, the industrial sector's share of GDP had risen from 24 per cent in 1970 to 35 per cent in 1985, whereas during the same period, the agricultural sector's share had fallen from 36 per cent to 24 per cent.[105] In the case of Indonesia, the decline in agriculture's share of total production was even steeper, falling from 45 per cent in 1970 to 19 per cent in 1991 (during the same period manufacturing grew from 10 per cent to 21 per cent).[106] Perhaps the most revealing aspect of the changing structure of production in the ASEAN economies was the progressive shift within the manufacturing sector to higher levels of processing (for example, textiles, apparel, electrical and electronic equipment), which was itself mirrored in and sustained by the growth in manufacturing exports.

In pursuing this path, often referred to as 'outward-looking industrialization', ASEAN countries benefited, especially during the 1970s, from favourable prices for their main exports, notably petroleum and other energy and agricultural products. However, with the onset of a worldwide recession in the early 1980s, export earnings fell sharply, with a corresponding rise in the size of their trade deficits. Most affected were Indonesia and Malaysia. In 1985, all ASEAN-4 economies experienced negative growth in their annual exports. It was only with the expansion of domestic demand in the advanced industrial countries and adjustments in their trading policies that new opportunities emerged for an increase in ASEAN exports (see Table 2.3). Between 1982 and 1993 ASEAN exports rose from $71.1 billion to $211.8 billion, with the United Sates and the European Union (EU) absorbing a very substantial part of this increase (see Table 2.4). Whereas the US share of ASEAN's exports rose from 14.8 to 19.9 per cent and the EU share from 10.2 per cent to 15.0 per cent, Japan's share fell from 29.0 per cent to 15.7 per cent.[107] As already noted, this period also witnessed a dramatic shift in the composition of ASEAN merchandise exports: between 1970 and 1993 the proportion accounted for by textiles and clothing rose from 4.0 per cent to 10.0 per cent; the corresponding increase for machinery and transport equipment was from 7.0 per cent[108] to 30.0 per cent and for other manufactures from 9.0 per cent to 40.0 per cent.

The general trend described above was far from uniform. There were significant national variations in GNP and export growth, composition of trade, volume and direction of capital flows and policy orientation. A few of these variations are worth noting. Partly in response to the second oil crisis of the late 1970s Thailand and Malaysia had moved rapidly to enhance their industrial development and export performance. Between 1980 and 1993 Thailand's manufacturing output per capita had increased from $206 to $831 and Malaysia's from $628 to $1357. While the growth of manufacturing exports as a proportion of total exports was common to all four economies, Malaysia accounted for 23.8 per cent of ASEAN's manufacturing exports and Thailand for 19.0 per cent, compared with 14.1 per cent for Indonesia and 6.4 per cent for the Philippines.[109] The disparity was all the greater given that in 1993 Indonesia's population (189 million) was ten times that of Malaysia (19 million) and more than three times that of Thailand (59 million). In terms of per capita manufacturing exports the performance of the Philippines (with a population of 67 million) was roughly comparable to that of Indonesia.

Table 2.4 Direction of East Asian exports (% share)

	Newly Industrializing Economies				Southeast Asia				
	Hong Kong	South Korea	Singapore	Taiwan	Indonesia	Malaysia	Philippines	Thailand	China (PRC)
DMCs[a]									
1985	35.6	12.9	36.7	15.6	17.2	38.1	19.5	27.1	38.2
1997	46.6	39.2	50.1	-	34.8	46.0	23.9	36.0	39.4
Japan									
1985	4.2	15.0	9.4	11.3	46.2	24.6	19.0	13.4	22.3
1997	6.1	10.9	7.1	-	24.4	12.5	16.0	15.2	17.4
USA									
1985	30.8	35.6	21.2	15.5	21.7	12.8	35.9	19.7	8.5
1997	21.8	15.9	18.5	-	14.4	18.6	34.4	19.4	17.9
EU									
1985	11.8	10.4	10.1	5.5	6.0	13.6	13.8	17.8	7.8
1997	14.7	11.2	13.9	-	14.9	14.4	16.0	15.9	13.0
Aus/NZ									
1985	2.3	1.3	4.4	2.4	1.2	1.9	2.1	1.9	0.8
1997	1.5	1.6	2.7	-	3.2	2.0	1.1	1.8	1.3
Other									
1985	15.3	24.7	18.1	49.7	7.6	9.1	9.7	20.1	22.5
1997	9.3	21.3	7.8	-	8.3	6.5	8.5	11.7	11.0

Note: [a] developing member countries.
Source: Asian Development Outlook 1999, p. 253.

It was not until the mid-1980s, with oil prices plummeting from $30 a barrel in 1986 to less than $10 in 1984, that Indonesia embarked in earnest on the path of export-oriented industrialization. Economic policy nevertheless retained a complex blend of mercantilist planning and trade liberalization measures. In 1988 foreign investment procedures were streamlined, inter-island shipping deregulated, and the oligopolistic structure of the steel and plastics industries substantially loosened. Between 1980 and 1993 manufacturing exports as a proportion of total exports rose dramatically from 4 per cent to 54 per cent; this amounted to an annual average growth rate of 30 per cent. A slowdown in the rate of growth was clearly discernible in 1992–4, owing primarily to the decline of two key sectors (textiles and clothing and wood and cork manufactures), which was itself a reflection of increasing competition from China and other emerging low-cost production countries.[110] Generally speaking, export growth during this period coincided with substantial increases in foreign investment, net FDI rising from $180 million in 1980 to $2.0 billion in 1993[111] and $7.9 billion in 1996, bringing total FDI stocks to $58.6 billion.[112] From the mid-1960s to the mid-1980s Japan had been the principal source of foreign investment, accounting for 33.1 per cent of the total, but was replaced in the following decade by the Asian NIEs, which contributed 29.1 per cent of total approved foreign investment.

Two other features of Indonesia's political economy are especially pertinent to this analysis. The development of domestic industries often rested on the creation of state-owned enterprises, some of these operating as monopolies which used their dominant position in the domestic market to secure access to capital. These monopoly interests often owed their position to political influence, which helps to explain the pivotal role assumed by members of the Suharto family and by a small group of Chinese Indonesian businesses in several large state-sponsored industries. As a consequence, the Suharto family acquired a large stake in the clove trade and in the telecommunications, broadcasting, car production, construction and shipping industries. For their part, leading businessmen of Chinese extraction gained control of several key industries (such as steel and forestry) in exchange for infrastructural investment.[113]

Of the ASEAN-4 economies, Malaysia is often cited as the most impressive success story, its per capita income having risen from $1875 in 1987 to $4425 in 1996, its GDP by an annual average of 8.7 per cent during 1990–6, and its manufacturing exports (in current US dollars) at an annual compound rate of 35 per cent during 1980–96, and as a proportion of total exports from 10 per cent to 80 per cent.[114] Malaysia was now one of the world's leading exporters of semiconductors, room air conditioners and video recorders. The emphasis on export-oriented industrialization dates back to the second Malaysia Plan 1971–5, which also provided for greater Malay participation in the ownership of capital and business management. The fourth five-year plan (1981–5) took the strategy a step further by targeting the development of heavy industries, in part through joint ventures with foreign companies. In tandem with the rapid increase in FDI inflows (from $0.4 billion in 1987 to $5.2 billion in 1992 and a rise in FDI stocks of $28 billion between 1990 and 1996),[115] a series of market-oriented policy reforms geared to the privatization of state-owned enterprises, tariff reductions and deregulation of the labour market provided added stimulus to GDP growth, and in particular to the manufacturing sector, which expanded at an average annual rate of 15 per cent. As a consequence, by 1996 unemployment had declined to 2.6 per cent, real wages had risen substantially, and a large and growing number of migrant workers, primarily from Indonesia, the Philippines and southern Thailand, were entering the Malaysian labour market.

By contrast, the Philippines economy recorded much lower levels of growth. During 1973–84 its GDP increased by 4.8 per cent, giving it a per capita annual growth rate of little over 2 per cent. During the same period the value of its exports rose by 5.6 per cent a year – a growth rate which, in fact, declined during the second half of the 1980s and early 1990s. GDP average annual growth during 1980–93 was estimated at 1.4 per cent.[116] Though it does not fully explain the relatively poor performance of the economy, unresolved political conflict and debilitating insurgencies, especially in the latter part of the Marcos period, were contributing factors. By 1993, however, there was evidence of a marked improvement in GNP growth, coupled with an expanding export capacity and rising levels of foreign investment. In 1994 GDP grew by 18.6 per cent and exports by 20.0 per cent;[117] and FDI inflows from $0.8 billion in 1993 to $1.7 billion in 1994 and $1.8 billion in 1995.[118]

Notwithstanding the differences in scale and timing between the industrialization trajectories of the ASEAN-4 economies, and the even greater differences separating them from the NIEs, it is nevertheless possible to discern a certain commonality of experience. The first common characteristic, which we have already highlighted, is three-dimensional growth: increase in the export of manufactures, increasing ratio of manufacturing exports to total merchandise exports, and growth of the manufacturing sector as a proportion of GDP. In this sense all eight societies may be said to have undergone a rapid and radical – and in most instances still unfolding – economic transformation. A second important characteristic is the concentration, particularly in the early stages of industrialization, on labour-intensive manufactures, with East Asian economies capturing market share, first from Japan and other advanced industrial countries, and subsequently from one another. East Asia's net export of labour-intensive goods rose from $20 billion in 1970 to more than $80 billion in 1993.

It is worth noting, however, that the strong export orientation of the East Asian economies was normally preceded by import substitution policies. In his industrialization typology Chen postulates four possible stages of industrial development: import substitution 1 (IS1) designed to groom infant consumer industries; import substitution 2 (IS2) aimed at producing selected capital goods; export orientation 1 (EO1) where the emphasis is on labour-intensive, light–manufactured goods; and export orientation 2 (EO2) where the economy is capable of producing technology/capital/knowledge-intensive industries.[119] He rightly reminds us that, while some of the NIEs may have bypassed the second stage of import substitution, the foundations for industrialization in most East Asian economies were laid by protecting a number of infant manufacturing industries.

The first stage of import substitution may, in fact, be regarded as the third distinguishing characteristic of the East Asian experience. Hong Kong and Singapore, where a relatively small domestic market limited the scope for import substitution, represent only partial exceptions to the rule. In this instance, a period of prolonged involvement in entrepôt trade helped to establish the necessary preconditions for the development of a competitive manufacturing sector. Indonesia's industrialization, on the other hand, was dominated by import substitution until the mid-1980s, with a number of highly protected firms capturing a large share of the domestic market. Thailand's experience was similar, with tariff protection and fiscal measures used to promote the domestic production of finished goods, both durable and non-durable, including assembly of motor vehicles, electrical appliances and electronic products, spinning and weaving of textiles, and the development of chemical, paper and tyre industries.[120] In Taiwan's case imports continued to rise right through the 1960s to the 1980s, as many of its industries depended on the import of capital goods, energy fuels and industrial raw materials. A conscious policy of import substitution was nevertheless pursued, with the specific aim of discouraging the importation of consumer goods. It was only when Taiwan's domestic market could no longer absorb the expanding capacity of its manufacturing industries that export promoting measures were introduced, although even then these were intended to complement rather than replace the import substitution regime.

There is another dimension to East Asian industrialization which requires careful examination. It relates to the export of manufactured commodities and the penetration of fringe markets. One study, for example, has analysed East Asia's penetration of the markets of industrially advanced economies (IAEs), which increased substantially from 1.2 per cent in 1980 to 3.7 per cent in 1993. This growing penetration of IAE markets indicates that East Asia's exports significantly outpaced the growth of apparent consumption in these economies. The magnitude of market penetration may be illustrated with reference to Korea and Indonesia. Korean exports of manufactures to the IAEs during 1980–93 registered a four-fold increase from $9.99 billion to $38.73 billion, and in Indonesia's case almost a six-fold increase from $2.25 billion to $12.7 billion. These increases far exceeded the overall growth of IAE consumption during this period and, after allowing for other factors contributing to this gap, represented an increased market share of 95.3 per cent for Korea and 97.8 per cent for Indonesia.[121] East Asian exports had increased as a proportion not only of the total imports of IAEs but of their overall domestic consumption.

Two other findings are worth noting: the increased penetration of East Asian exports applied to all major centres in the advanced industrial world (though it was far more pronounced for Europe and the United States than for Japan) and to the large majority of manufactured commodity groups (most strikingly evident in the textile and apparel industries, but also in electrical appliances, fabricated metal products, machinery and equipment). As a generalization, the East Asian economies exported relatively more primary commodities to Japan than to the United States and Western Europe, but the converse was true for the export of manufactures. Whereas 60 per cent of East Asian exports to the United States consisted of technology-intensive products, the comparable figures for Japan were 18.2 per cent (NIEs) and 4.8 per cent (ASEAN).[122]

Two final observations are needed to complete this brief overview of East Asia's export orientation. While the United States and Europe were the principal recipients of East Asian manufactures, Japan was the principal source of East Asian imports of capital-intensive and technology-intensive commodities. To illustrate, in 1989 Japan, with a GNP less than one-third the combined GNP of the United States and the European Community, supplied 41.3 per cent of all capital-intensive and technology-intensive manufactures imported by NIEs. The corresponding figure for ASEAN was 42.7 per cent.[123] This pattern persisted well into the 1990s, but with a few modifications, the most important of these being the diminishing proportion of NIE exports destined for the United States and the marked increase in intra-regional trade within East Asia (see Table 2.4). While it did not necessarily, or at least immediately, diminish the critical financial, economic, technological and organizational role of the United States in regional affairs, the trend was unmistakable. During 1985–95 Korean exports to North America increased by $13.9 billion, but exports to ASEAN and to the Chinese economies increased by $14.9 billion and $20.7 billion respectively. During the same period, Taiwan's exports to North America rose by $14.7 billion, to ASEAN by $10.7 billion and to the Chinese economies by $23.5 billion.[124] As for ASEAN's exports, the proportion absorbed by the United States had continued to rise (from 16.4 per cent in 1980 to 20.3 per cent in 1994), but the corresponding increase in exports to the NIEs was much greater (from 5.9 per cent to 14.7 per cent).[125]

Explaining the East Asian 'economic miracle'

Though sketched with a rather broad brush, the preceding survey of East Asia's export-oriented industrialization nevertheless indicates something of the magnitude and wide-ranging ramifications of the phenomenon, which is all the more dramatic given the relatively short timespan over which it unfolded. Multiple attempts have been made to explain it but most have suffered from varying degrees of oversimplification. The aim here is not to add to the already long list of explanations but to draw attention to the diverse and interacting variables which form part of what is a complex and still fluid equation. In this sense, Clark and Chan are right to argue that East Asia's 'political economies cannot be adequately conceptualized in terms of any single theoretical paradigm . . . or the prescriptions for developmental strategy that can be derived from them'.[126] Numerous studies have sought to explain the dynamics of economic growth by reference to trade liberalization, resource allocation and the mix of incentives offered by government policy.[127] Often the emphasis is placed, in line with neoclassical orthodoxy, on the role of the market, that is, on the ability of East Asian economies to specialize on the basis of comparative advantage. Having allowed market signals to guide resource allocation, these economies, it is argued, had got their prices right and were as a result able to use the market mechanism to maintain the momentum of growth.

While still set within a neo-classical framework, the analysis sometimes draws attention to the soundness of macroeconomic management and to the fiscal, monetary, financial, trade, labour and infrastructure policies pursued by East Asian governments.[128] For others the role of government was the key to success – a perspective which, despite significant differences in emphasis and vocabulary, characterizes a substantial body of literature. Hofheinz and Calder, for example, attribute the impressive performance of East Asian economies to institutions generally, and to political systems in particular, which they see as enshrining a high degree of respect for authority and helping to create the conditions for political stability and flexible decision-making.[129] Various other formulations have been offered which focus on the interventionist role of the state and on its ability to prevent sectional interests from dictating national economic policy. Chalmers Johnson, who formulated one of the earliest versions of the developmental state, sought to interpret Japan's strong industrial performance by reference to MITI's role in influencing and co-ordinating decision-making.[130] Subsequent versions of the developmental state have pointed to the close linkages between the public and private sectors, and to the control mechanisms (for example, financial, taxation, foreign exchange and R&D policies) which states have used to set and implement strategic goals.[131]

These perspectives, to which we return in Chapter 5, are no doubt helpful in so far as they isolate an important variable in the equation, but they do not, either individually or collectively, offer an adequate explanation of the phenomenon. The Korean state, and more specifically the highly centralized administrations of the 1960s and 1970s, may be credited with having identified long-term investment opportunities, encouraged the development of key industries, established an extensive educational system, ensured that wage increases did not exceed productivity growth, and facilitated the growth of the large conglomerates (*chaebol*). None of this, however, explains why Korean governments acted as they did, the extent to which their policies determined outcomes, or the degree to which these policies were successful. Arguments which stress the importance of the market and the related notions of free trade and comparative advantage, or openness to foreign capital and foreign technology, or high rates of savings and investment, or rapid changes in industrial structure, are likely to encounter similar difficulties. To list these conditions is one thing, to demonstrate that they were the necessary and sufficient conditions of East Asia's economic success is quite another. Such an approach in any case begs a larger question: how did these favourable economic conditions emerge in the first place?

Economic conditions favouring industrialization

To overcome the shortcomings that inevitably beset monocausal explanatory models, in this case those predicated on the primacy of either state or market, a good many studies have adopted a more nuanced position, eclectically combining a range of political and economic factors. Krause, for example, offers the following list: 'the societal commitment to growth in each country', the propensity to hard work, high savings rates and high domestic investment rates, the market-conforming policies of governments, and the contagious spread of success.[132] A dualistic framework, based on the close interaction of state and market, enables Krause to argue that East Asian governments consciously pursued high rates of personal savings as part of a wider strategy to raise national savings. Similarly, it is claimed that, through a carefully crafted policy of export-oriented industrialization, these governments took advantage of the trade liberalization policies of other countries while continuing to protect their own markets from foreign competition. However, as these economies became larger and more complex, governments found it increasingly difficult to make well-informed allocative decisions, hence the later trend towards trade liberalization and financial deregulation, and the general tendency for public policy to become less interventionist and for the players in the marketplace to be given a freer rein to pursue their own investment and production strategies.[133]

A more sophisticated version of the same analytical approach, offered by Clark and Chan, places particular emphasis on the dichotomous nature of East Asian capitalist development:

> They [East Asian states] have thus encouraged private entrepreneurship and at the same time insisted on governmental economic tutelage. Vigorous market competition has accompanied active statist intervention, and private firms have coexisted and indeed developed a symbiotic relationship with public enterprises.[134]

For them this 'pragmatic flexibility' or 'eclecticism' lies at the heart of East Asian economic success. By incorporating elements of both the neo-classical and statist models, these writers have developed an explanatory framework which more accurately reflects the ambiguities of East Asia's political economy. Others have drawn attention to the importance of yet another variable, namely culture. Though the language in which it is couched is by no means uniform, the argument almost invariably refers to the function of Confucianist culture in providing a strong stimulus to East Asian innovation and entrepreneurship. Reference is usually made to such Confucian values as the attachment to kinship ties and loyalty to family, the stress on education, hard work and investment, respect for authority (as embodied in both government and business), and the strong preference for personalized business networks and relationships.[135] Some have gone so far as to describe the Confucian ethic as the missing link which effectively connects Japan's economic performance with that of the four tigers.[136]

There is much to be said for each of the preceding explanations, yet none of them is entirely convincing. This is not to deny the analytical relevance of market, state and culture, but merely to question the way these variables and their interaction have been conceptualized and applied to the concrete experience of East Asian industrialization. Chen's argument that in this case 'the key to success [was] that the measures of intervention [were] market-conforming rather than market-distorting'[137] sheds considerable light on the seemingly contradictory relationship between state and market. He is no doubt right to point to the close connection 'between economic (gradual market-conforming policies) and institutional (Confucian values and development-oriented authoritarianism) factors'.[138] There is also a good deal of evidence to support the implicit argument that it is the market which has been driving the engine of East Asian industrialization and that state and culture have played a largely supportive or instrumental role. Helpful though they are, these insights still leave unanswered a number of difficult questions.

The first question has to do with timing and sequence. Why is it that some economies embarked upon the course of export-oriented industrialization before others? To put it differently, how are we to explain the progression from Japan to the

NIEs, to the ASEAN-4 economies, to China, and more recently to Vietnam? The second question derives from East Asia's political and cultural diversity. Despite certain outward similarities, political institutions have varied considerably from one country to another. Whereas Japan generally had weak executive leadership, Korea and Taiwan tended to operate under strong presidential authority. The bureaucracy, while relatively monolithic in Korea, developed competing centres of power in Japan. The bureaucratic elites servicing the Northeast Asian economies were on balance more disciplined and better trained than their Southeast Asian counterparts. Even if it could be argued that the Confucian ethic held sway in Japan, Korea and Taiwan, it did not exercise a decisive influence in Malaysia, Indonesia or the Philippines. Quite apart from these and other variations in the institutional and cultural environment prevailing in different countries – China and Vietnam, after all, retained centralized models of state economic planning – there were substantial differences in economic performance, in the rate of GNP growth, in the ratio of exports to GNP, and in the size of the external debt. How could any explanatory model focusing on a single domestic variable, expressed in terms of policy, institutional framework or political culture, or some combination of these, supposedly common to all East Asian societies, be reconciled with the political, cultural and economic diversity of the region?

Conscious of the need to explain commonality of trends in the face of contextual difference, some have sought the answer in some kind of demonstration effect or a gradual learning process, with Japan serving as principal role model, and each economy also learning from the experiences of other relatively more advanced regional economies. Just as Taiwan and Korea learnt from the Japanese experience, so did China benefit from Taiwan's and Hong Kong's development strategy, and Southeast Asia from Northeast Asia.[139] This argument is a step in the right direction in that it adds an international dimension to the analysis, but it hardly does justice to the external environment's multiple functions or structural characteristics.

Role of core economies

The first and most obvious external factor contributing to the rise of a semi-periphery in East Asia has been the role of core states and core economies, in particular the United States and Japan, although the role of European markets and European capital has not been insignificant. As indicated in the previous chapter, US aid, capital, training and technology played an important part in the post-1945 reconstruction of several East Asian economies, not least Japan, South Korea, Taiwan, Thailand and the Philippines. To give one example, US aid to Taiwan, including grants, loans and military equipment, from 1951 to 1965 is estimated at $4 billion. Apart from offsetting Taiwan's cumulative trade deficit during that period, the aid programme, particularly in the early stages, was instrumental in containing the high rate of inflation and in developing Taiwan's technical and industrial infrastructure.[140] Even more decisive was the ability of the US market to absorb large quantities of imported manufactures produced by these economies. To cite another example, the United States was South Korea's largest single customer from the early stages of its industrial development in the 1960s, accounting for one-third of its total exports. Indeed, the size of South Korea's trade surplus with the United States assumed such proportions ($9.5 billion in 1987) as to provoke serious trade frictions between the two countries. Over and above these explicitly economic mechanisms, the United States provided the overarching institutional framework (including GATT and the Bretton Woods institutions) which actively encouraged the rapid expansion of trade, as well as the elaborate strategic system which helped to stabilize the newly formed economic and political arrangements.

While the United States continued to sustain many of the conditions which favoured the rapid growth of East Asian exports market, Japan over time came to play an increasingly important part in the process. To cite the South Korean example again, Japan became its largest market for primary commodities and light manufactures, and main supplier of technology, expertise, machinery, components and parts for its export industries. However, Japan's single most important contribution to East Asian industrialization was the export of capital. The substantial relocation of Japanese production facilities, first in Northeast Asia and then in Southeast Asia, gave rise to increasingly complex Japanese corporate networks comprising multiple sources of supply and multiple sales outlets and closely linking the local economy with the Japanese and other regional economies. Whether or not one accepts the argument which sees the FDI–trade nexus as the key to greater industrial competitiveness and to 'a self- sustained high rate of economic growth',[141] there is no denying that FDI inflows contributed to the restructuring of key East Asian industries. As Table 2.5 indicates, FDI flows reached unprecedented levels during 1992-97. Investment patterns were nevertheless far from static. By the late 1980s the NIEs had displaced Japan as the principal source of FDI flows to the ASEAN-4 economies. By 1988 NIE investment in Indonesia, which accounted for 34.1 per cent of the total, had significantly outstripped that of Japan.[142] Rising wage levels and appreciating currencies had prompted the NIEs, as in Japan's case, to relocate production activities in Southeast Asia, thereby paralleling and reinforcing the third phase in Japan's FDI flows and in particular its increasing emphasis on intermediate and even high-tech manufacturing.

The accelerated upgrading of ASEAN's and, as we shall see, China's technological capabilities led a number of writers to postulate the 'consolidation of

an East Asian regional production network with Japan at its core'.[143] Leaving aside
for the moment scenarios of a fourth phase which envisage either the formation of

Table 2.5   Foreign direct investment ($ million)

Economy	1992	1993	1994	1995	1996	1997
Newly industrializing economies	5861	7858	12552	13645	16129	17189
Hong Kong	2051	1667	2000	2100	2500	2600
South Korea	727	588	809	1776	2325	2341
Singapore	2204	4686	8368	8210	9440	10000
Taiwan	879	917	1375	1559	1864	2248
ASEAN-4	9302	10052	9364	11941	14654	13951
Indonesia	1777	2004	2109	4348	6194	5350
Malaysia	5183	5006	4342	4132	4672	3754
Philippines	228	1238	1591	1459	1520	1253
Thailand	2114	1804	1322	2002	2268	3600
China (PRC)	11156	27515	33787	35849	40800	45300

Source: *Asian Development Outlook 1999*, p. 258.

a second regional production network centred on 'Greater China' or of a single but
more complex network based on extensive linkages between Japanese and Chinese
capital, it is clear that an East Asian economic sphere had emerged, characterized by
a constantly evolving but at any given moment distinctive division of labour.

Division of labour and the 'flying geese' model

This East Asian division of labour was the outcome of a competitive dynamic, whose
logic becomes apparent when placed in the context of a rapidly globalizing world
economy. For some this dynamic entails a continuing wave of catch-up
industrialization, in which the tiger economies followed on the heels of Japan, only
to see themselves in turn chased up the industrial ladder by the ASEAN-4 countries,

with China and Vietnam now engaged in the same race.[144] The shifting pattern of trade that we have observed in terms of the composition and destination of East Asian exports is perhaps the most obvious manifestation of the changing division of labour and of the competitive dynamic on which it rests. The conventional economic explanation of this process is predicated on the notion of comparative advantage, which attributes changes in trade flows to changes in a country's factor endowment (availability of cheap inputs) or stage of industrial development (level of technology).

Applied to East Asia, shifting patterns of comparative advantage and the related process of catch-up industrialization have been conceptualized in terms of the 'flying geese' model.[145] Drawing in part on the product cycle theory of trade, the proponents of this model have argued that Japan, as the most advanced and innovative economy in the region, first created new products for its domestic market, but, once supply exceeded demand, inevitably turned its attention to export markets. In time, countries (in this case other East Asian economies) which had imported those products from Japan learned how to produce them in order to meet their own domestic requirements. When these markets were in turn saturated, they themselves started exporting these products, first making inroads into Japan's export markets (in particular, ASEAN) and eventually penetrating the Japanese market itself.[146] In the formulation proposed by Chen and Kwan, each industry passes through five stages: establishment of the industry, import substitution, export of surplus capacity, decline of production and exports, resumption of imports.[147] Diagrammatically represented, the rise and fall of imports, domestic production and exports in any given industry (for example, textiles, steel) appear as overlapping inverted V-shaped curves, hence the 'flying geese' designation. The East Asian phenomenon has a closely related dimension, namely the relocation of industries from a higher to a lower tier (for example, from the United States to Japan, from Japan to the NIEs, from the NIEs to the ASEAN-4), which again takes the form of inverted V-shaped curves.

It is worth noting that in the 'flying geese' model foreign direct investment is as important a mechanism as trade in the ongoing transformation of comparative advantage. The relocation of declining industries, it is argued, enabled both home and host economies to upgrade their industrial structures. In the former case, the closing down of certain industries released resources which could then be directed to the development of technologically more sophisticated industries, while in the latter case the inflow of foreign capital provided the financial, technological and managerial infrastructure for more capital-intensive and technology-intensive industries. The evolution of the textile and apparel industry in the NIEs is often used to illustrate this process. One study distinguishes four phases: in phase I Japanese trading and textile companies started relocating their production bases, taking advantage of an abundant low-wage labour force; in phase II, with the growth of local trading firms capable of sustaining the export drive, the local apparel industry moved upstream, gradually taking up the spinning, weaving and dyeing of synthetic fibres; in phase III the industry underwent further restructuring, moving further upstream into synthetic textiles, hence the need for more capital and more advanced technology, much of it supplied by Japan; in phase IV these economies introduce new upstream operations, including the production of petrochemicals for synthetic fibres but also for plastics, again relying on transnational corporations (TNCs) as technology licensees and participants in joint ventures. The evolution of the electronics industry in South Korea reveals a similar progression from the production of radios and black and white television sets for domestic consumption in the 1960s to videorecorders, cassette players, computers and telecommunications equipment in the 1980s. This progression is paralleled by the changing role of TNCs and FDI: the assembly of imported parts and components by foreign affiliates in the 1960s gives way in the 1970s to greater licensing of foreign technology, and in the 1980s to strategic alliances with foreign TNCs and the shifting of production facilities to China and Southeast Asia. By the 1990s, Korean companies, though still dependent on Japanese and US TNCs for marketing, were producing domestically a much larger proportion of electronic components.[148]

What emerges from this account of East Asian industrialization is that what drives the process forward is not so much comparative advantage – understood as some more or less constant natural endowment – as competitive advantage based on a favourable but quite possibly short-lived combination of factors. Whereas cheap labour was initially crucial to East Asian competitiveness, by the early 1990s real wage rates had risen sharply, both in absolute terms and relative to wage rates in Europe and the United States. The shifting basis of competitiveness thus required flexible production strategies to capture specific market niches, which meant a continuous upgrading of products and production processes wedded to aggressive marketing strategies.[149] To ensure that they retained the necessary competitive edge firms felt compelled to anticipate future economic conditions, hence the decision to build excess manufacturing capacity designed to achieve world-scale efficiencies, and the development of regional and global strategies through both intra-firm integration (that is, increasing linkage of material, capital, labour, technology and information flows) and inter-firm co-ordination (that is, the formation of strategic alliances with suppliers, customers and even competitors).[150] In this sense, the initiative for defining and achieving competitive advantage rested first and foremost with the strategic behaviour of individual firms. Governments performed an important but subsidiary function, which was to promote a fiscal, financial, industrial relations and educational environment conducive to the attainment of these strategic goals.

In the light of these observations the 'flying geese' model, at least as initially conceived, appears deficient on at least two counts. First, it does not adequately characterize the role of TNCs and of firms more generally in shaping competitive advantage and the continuous reorganization of industry which it implies. Second, it overstates the sequential character of industrial development; that is, the supposed time lag between a production curve and an export curve for producer goods, or for that matter between a production curve for consumer goods and a production curve for producer goods. It is largely in order to remedy this second deficiency that Chen has proposed the 'aerobatics' model, which emphasizes technological rather than product life-cycles, thereby making technology the key to industrial specialization and the ensuing division of labour. The intention here is to allow, as in an aerobatic display, for the formation of different patterns and different roles in the division of labour, which need not be preordained, and may be specific to particular industries rather than to national economies as a whole.[151]

When it comes to conceptualizing the recent trajectory of East Asian industrialization, aerobatics as a metaphor may be preferable to flying geese. It certainly injects a greater degree of variety and complexity and, at least implicitly, frees us from the straitjacket which insists on treating the national state and the national economy as the key units of analysis. The aerobatics model remains nevertheless highly ambiguous: if the patterns formed by aeroplanes in an air display are meant to reflect the signals sent by the commander, we have to ask who performs the commander's function when it comes to industrial restructuring. Is it the state, or the system of states, individual firms, or production networks engaged in varying degrees of co-operation and competition, or more abstractly the financial markets, or multilateral institutions be they global or regional? The question is not merely one of agency, but of the relationship of agency to structure. It is becoming increasingly apparent that countries, national economies and even states, in East Asia as elsewhere, are from an analytical point of view most usefully represented not just as actors but also as the stage on which a multiplicity of other actors – subnational, transnational, supranational and international – compete for the maximization of their respective value-systems. This is not to say that the governments of Japan, Taiwan, South Korea, Malaysia or even the Philippines are powerless or deprived of agency, but rather that the way they exercise that power and agency can be understood only in the context of a multidimensional structure that is increasingly regional and global in scope.

By the end of the 1980s a vertical division of labour had emerged in East Asia, with economies at different stages of industrialization performing different functions. The primary engine driving this regional division of labour – and the product cycles and associated diffusion of activities which gave it its distinctive structure – were the needs of capital. The regional patterns of trade and investment were shaped in no small measure by the restructuring of Japanese capital, itself dictated by the reorganization of the global economy.[152] To put it crudely but not inaccurately, Japanese industrial and financial firms were at the core of the regional economy, with ASEAN and NIE firms occupying the periphery and semi-periphery respectively. Expressed a little differently, regional integration did not mean regional interdependence. To give but one example, the diminishing capacity of Korean and Taiwanese electronic industries to penetrate the Japanese market in the late 1980s was the direct result of Japanese enterprises establishing production facilities in Southeast Asia. By combining their technological, financial and marketing dominance with cheap Southeast Asian labour, they were able to gain a competitive edge over their NIE competitors, thereby substantially eroding their share of the Japanese market.[153]

As others have argued, it is the shifts in the regional production and investment strategies of Japanese capital which largely shaped the environment within which NIE and ASEAN enterprises had to operate. At times the net effect was to intensify competition, but more often than not, by using the array of carrots and sticks at its disposal, Japanese capital was able to integrate potential competitors 'into a regional production structure that is supportive of Japanese interests'.[154] NIE firms may have retained a certain margin of manouevre, but their profitability – and at least indirectly the capacity of NIE governments to manage the national economy – was ultimately constrained by the requirements of the Japan-centred regional production structure. The dependence of ASEAN economies was even more pronounced. Their export manufacturing sector was characterized by high levels of foreign ownership and control and heavy reliance on Japan for procurement of machinery, components and parts. Increasingly, Japanese capital was using the ASEAN region as a production platform not only to serve the Japanese market, but to penetrate a great many other core markets (the United States and Europe) and semi-peripheral markets (principally in East Asia). The relocation of export industries from Japan to Southeast Asia had three other important structural features, namely the displacement of environmental pollution and associated health hazards from the core to the periphery, the accelerated population shift in the periphery from the countryside to the cities, designed in part to increase the pool of available labour to service the export manufacturing and sex-tourist industries; and continuing pressure on ASEAN governments to increase export capacity and at the same time maintain a relatively low labour cost structure in order to maximize market share.

The foregoing representation of the East Asian political economy is an advance on the flying geese model, but a number of important variables have still to be factored into the equation. First, it cannot be stressed enough that the structures of regional integration we have just outlined are not static. As our discussion of the East Asian financial crisis will suggest, they are subject to constant readjustment in response to pressures exerted by a wide range of actors, both within and outside the region. Second, as we shall see in this and subsequent chapters, the analysis has to be widened to take account of China's rise as a major centre of economic activity and the residual but still crucial role of American capital and the American state. Finally, an adequate interpretation of East Asia's emerging structures of production and investment must give due regard to the evolution of regional institutions and subregional economic zones, a task undertaken in the companion volume, *Regionalism in the New Asia-Pacific Order.*

EMERGING GREATER CHINA

At this point it is necessary to refer, however briefly, to the profound transformation of the Chinese economy, the far-reaching impact of which on both China and the region is only now beginning to emerge. This section will confine itself to a general outline of China's recent economic growth, touching on trade and investment linkages with the core economies and the regional economy, but leaving a detailed analysis of geoeconomic and geopolitical implications to later chapters. It is worth stressing at the outset that China's economy had not stood still during the Maoist era. Despite two severe troughs associated with the Great Leap Forward and the Cultural Revolution, its GDP grew by an annual average of 5.8 per cent during 1950–73, and by 6.85 per cent during 1973–84.[155] The modernization policies first introduced in the late 1970s did nevertheless give rise to unprecedented rates of economic growth. The size of China's economy more than doubled between 1978 and 1989, its GNP rising from 392.76 billion yuan to 987.24 billion yuan (measured in constant 1980 prices).[156] During 1990–4 GDP registered an annual average growth rate of 12.9 per cent,[157] and in parts of China, including Guangdong province, well in excess of 25 per cent.

Economic expansion began to lose momentum in 1995 with GDP growth for that year estimated at 10.5 per cent, and falling back to 9.6 per cent in 1996, 8.8 per cent in 1997 and 7.8 per cent in 1998.[158] Even for the earlier period there is evidence to suggest that official Chinese figures may have overestimated the actual rate of growth. A number of studies in the early 1990s indicate that discrepancies in the treatment of new products and the failure of state firms to measure output in constant prices had resulted in an upward bias of 2–3 per cent.[159] Two later studies suggest that official deflators used to convert nominal into real GDP may have substantially underestimated price increases. Using alternative price indices, a 1997

World Bank study indicated a GDP per capita annual growth rate of 7.4 per cent for 1978–86 and 6.6 per cent for 1986–95.[160] A 1998 OECD study estimated the average annual growth role for 1978–95 to be 7.5 per cent compared with the official figure of 9.5 per cent.[161] Regardless of the method of calculation, China's GDP growth during this 20-year period remains comfortably among the highest in the world.

This 20-year period of high and sustained economic growth was underpinned by an even higher rate of growth in China's external trade. Measured in 1990 constant prices, the value of its merchandise exports during 1978–95 rose from $16.1 billion to $138.4 billion. Chinese export volume rose eightfold from 1978 to 1995 at an annual average compound rate of 13.5 per cent. In 1995 China's exports were 2.9 per cent of the world total, compared to 0.8 per cent in 1978. Commodity exports as a proportion of GDP had, according to official figures, grown from 4.6 per cent in 1978 to 18.3 per cent in 1996.[162] Two important features of the changing pattern of China's trade are worth noting here. In 1959 the Soviet Union and other communist countries accounted for 72.4 per cent of China's commodity exports; by 1996 that proportion had collapsed to 2.1 per cent. By contrast, Japan, the United States and Western Europe received 25.6 per cent of Chinese exports in 1965; by 1996 that share had risen to 51.8 per cent.[163] To put it simply, the trade dependence of China's economy had risen markedly since the late 1970s and much of that trade was directed to the major centres of the international capitalist economy. One of the consequences of the dramatic increase of Chinese exports was the succession of favourable trade balances achieved by China during the 1990s, which translated into much greater holdings of foreign exchange, with gross reserves rising from $18.5 billion in 1989 to $108.3 in 1996 and $140 billion in 1997.[164]

Closely linked to China's export performance were high rates of investment (the investment/GDP ratio rising to 34.8 per cent in 1990 and reaching a peak of 42.8 per cent in 1993).[165] An important contributing factor was the large inflow of foreign direct investment, which grew by an annual average of 16 per cent during the second half of the 1980s and by nearly 30 per cent during the early part of the 1990s.[166] FDI inflows, which had averaged $718 million per year during 1980–5, rose to $1.9 billion in 1986, $3.5 billion in 1990, $31.8 billion in 1994 and $41.7 billion in 1997, making China the second largest recipient of FDI flows worldwide.[167] Between 1979 and 1995 total FDI entering China had amounted to $133 billion.[168] The import of capital tended to be trade promoting, as much of it was directed to manufacturing industries in which China had a competitive advantage. Exports by firms dependent on foreign investment had grown from $300 million in 1990 to $43.7 billion in 1994.[169] The exports of foreign-owned enterprises as a proportion of total exports had grown from 0.3 per cent in 1984 to 42.3 per cent in 1995.[170] According to official estimates released in December 1999, the exports of foreign-funded enterprises totalled $80.96 billion in 1998, representing 44.1 per cent of the national total.[171] While China's total exports trebled between 1986 ($30.9 billion) and 1993 ($91.8 billion), the proportion accounted for by foreign firms had risen during the same period from 1.6 per cent to 27.5 per cent.[172] By 1993 manufactures accounted for 81 per cent of China's total exports.[173] By 1995 the proportion had risen still further, to 85.6 per cent. Exports of machinery and transport equipment had risen in value from $772 million in 1985 to $31.4 billion in 1995.[174]

The inescapable impression that emerges from this brief overview is of a rapidly expanding economy, with trade and capital flows as the two principal mechanisms integrating China's manufacturing into the regional and global division of labour. This impressive growth must nevertheless be set in context: as of 1994 Japan's GNP was still nine times larger than China's and Japanese exports more than three times greater than Chinese exports. On the other hand, to gain an accurate measure of China's economic weight account must be taken of the regional ties linking the more advanced regions of the Chinese economy with Hong Kong and Taiwan, and even other economic actors in East and Southeast Asia. The notion of a 'Greater China' is in part an attempt to synthesize or at least aggregate linkages, and to that extent is a useful reminder of the limitations of a state-centric analysis.

Paradoxically, these integrative tendencies coexisted with and to a large extent contributed to the structural fragmentation of the Chinese economy, which was the inevitable result of the concentration of capital-intensive and technology-intensive industries in special economic zones (SEZs), open coastal provinces (OCPs) and open coastal cities (OCCs).[175] The development of industrial, export-oriented enclaves, and the economic dualism which it implies, was compounded by the differential productivity of the state-owned, privately-owned and foreign-owned sectors. We shall consider the implications of these asymmetries in Chapter 5, but for the moment suffice it to say that regions such as Guangdong and Fujian benefited disproportionately from industrial restructuring and transnational linkages. Guangdong was especially favoured, having gained three of the four SEZs, and developed a privileged relationship with Hong Kong which accounted for 80 per cent of its exports and imports and more than 90 per cent of its foreign investment.[176]

The steady shift from state controlled or directed economies to market economies, which we have already observed in other parts of East Asia, was now also discernible in China. An important contributing factor in this instance was the development of a loosely structured but extensive Chinese network in which the China–Hong Kong connection played a pivotal role. By the mid-1990s Chinese state-owned companies controlled some 1000 Hong Kong businesses, while 25 000 Hong Kong companies employed close to 3.5 million Chinese in China.[177] By the early 1990s, Hong Kong accounted for nearly 45 per cent of China's exports and more than 26 per cent of its imports,[178] making China by far Hong Kong's largest trading partner. In this sense, economic interdependence, not to say integration, was an established fact of life well before Hong Kong was formally restored to China's sovereign jurisdiction. Indeed, Hong Kong was to play a crucial intermediary role in the developing symbiosis between China and Taiwan.

Reference has already been made to the phenomenal increase in China's bilateral trade with Taiwan (from $77 million in 1979 to $14.3 billion in 1993). Even more telling was the growth of Taiwan's exports to China (from $384.8 million in 1981 to $22.4 billion in 1997), which now accounted for 18.4 per cent of its total exports. During this same period Taiwan's trade dependence on China rose from 1.05 to 11.15 and Chinese trade dependence on Taiwan from 1.04 to 8.11.[179] Equally significant was the share of Taiwan's total exports absorbed by Hong Kong, which rose from 7.7 per cent in 1987 to 21.2 per cent in 1993 – close to 50 per cent of those exports were destined for China,[180] and some 30 per cent of Taiwan's imports from Hong Kong actually originated in the PRC.[181] The trilateral connection between the three Chinese economies was also reflected in the large proportion (in excess of 25 per cent) of Taiwanese visitors to Hong Kong whose eventual destination was China. However, investment flows constituted the most significant linkage between the three economies. By 1991, some 2600 Taiwanese firms were established in Hong Kong, and of these 99 per cent traded with or invested in China through Hong Kong. As of 1994 investments flowing from Taiwan to China, both directly and indirectly, were said to range between $14 billion and $20 billion. Chinese investments in Hong Kong totalled $30 billion, with some $20 billion directed to banking and real estate. Hong Kong and Macao entrepreneurs had established some 30 000 firms in the province of Guangdong alone, which accounted for 80 per cent of its foreign capital.[182] The Bank of China was said to control 10 per cent of Hong Kong's banking assets and 25 per cent of its currency deposits.

The interdependent commercial and economic ties between China, Hong Kong and Taiwan rested on a well-integrated division of labour, in which Hong Kong provided China with capital as well as financial and marketing expertise; Taiwan, using Hong Kong as an intermediary, supplied China with capital and technology; and Guangdong and Fujian supplied the relatively cheap labour for Hong Kong's and Taiwan's sunset industries. No discussion of Greater China would be complete without reference to the strategically placed Chinese business communities of Southeast Asia. Overseas Chinese held majority ownership of 50 per cent of listed companies in the Philippines, 61 per cent in Malaysia, 73 per cent in Indonesia and 81 per cent in both Thailand and Singapore.[183] Taken as a whole, Hong Kong, Macao, Taiwan and the Chinese in Southeast Asia accounted in 1992–3 for nearly four-fifths of FDI in the PRC.[184] Cultural and linguistic affinities, geographical proximity and shifts in the regional division of labour had encouraged the consolidation of elaborate business networks connecting different parts of the 'Chinese Economic Area'.

Even if 'Greater China' is defined more narrowly to include only China, Hong Kong, Macao and Taiwan, its 1991 GDP was estimated at $0.6 trillion at market prices. Both the United States and Japan, it is true, had a much higher GDP ($5.5 trillion and $3.4 trillion respectively), but most forecasts expected a significant narrowing of the gap. With adjustments made for differences in purchasing power, the World Bank had forecast, perhaps a little prematurely, that Greater China's GDP would by 2002 overtake that of the United States and be double that of Japan.[185] Even by 1995 Greater China's two-way trade (in excess of $800 billion) and foreign exchange reserves (in excess of $200 billion) compared favourably with those of Japan. Impressive though they may be, these figures are nevertheless misleading if they are read as indicators of the economic leverage at the disposal of some monolithic Chinese entity, let alone of China's central government. The 'borderless economy' may have become somewhat of a cliché but it did accurately describe two key dimensions of Greater China's economic structure, namely its internal fragmentation and external interdependence. The asymmetries and divisions between different sectors of the Chinese economy were, paradoxically enough, compounded by Hong Kong's return to China, since the financial, investment and technological linkages between Hong Kong and the rest of China's economy were concentrated in those sectors and regions, notably the SEZs and OCCs of southern China, which were already more productive and had pronounced export orientation. The principle of 'two systems, one country' which underpinned Hong Kong's formal incorporation into China was itself suggestive of the regionalization of the Chinese economy. When Taiwan is included in the Chinese Economic Area, then the fault lines between regions and sectors become even deeper and assume a distinctly political as well as an economic profile.

It remains to say a word about China's interaction with the core industrial economies and the wider regional economy. US and Japanese capital performed a more strategic role, concentrating on highly productive industries and bringing with it the technology and financial sophistication available to the large US and Japanese corporations. Whereas NIE investment was targeted largely at services and light manufacturing, Japanese FDI was primarily focused on raw materials and machinery, but encompassed a wide range of activities, including procurement, assembly, distribution and marketing. Large transnational corporations were quick to exploit the willingness of the Chinese authorities to depart from previously declared policy, which required foreign investors to enter into joint venture arrangements, and allow the establishment of wholly foreign-owned enterprises. Significantly, by 1995 the volume of FDI inflows in the form of wholly foreign-owned ventures was rising sharply, while other types of investment were stabilizing or even beginning to decline.[186] Trade linkages with Japan, the United States and Western Europe had assumed particular importance, although, as we shall see in the following chapter, there was a tendency for two-way trade with Japan to decline in favour of bilateral trade with the United States.[187] Official Chinese statistics substantially understated Chinese exports to the United States, in part by failing to include the re-export of Chinese goods through Hong Kong, which were estimated in 1992 to total close to $18 billion. While the full extent of the US trade deficit was in contention, there is little doubt that it had risen sharply since the late 1980s,[188] as a direct consequence of China's accelerating penetration of US markets.

China's increasing integration with the regional economy was closely connected with, but by no means confined to, the emergence of Greater China. Highly revealing in this context was the rapid growth of South Korean investment in China, which in 1993 represented nearly 60 per cent of South Korea's export of capital. Even the Philippines, Thailand and Indonesia were contributing a higher share of FDI flows into China. The expansion of China's regional economic role was also reflected in China's FDI outflows, which averaged $2.4 billion annually during the period 1992–4, with 61 per cent directed to Hong Kong and Macao and another 13 per cent to Asia and Oceania.[189] A similar pattern was evident in the growth of China's trade, with East Asia accounting for 57.1 per cent (that is, $69.0 billion) of the total increase in the value of Chinese exports during 1985–95 (estimated at $121.0 billion). If the Chinese economies are taken as a whole, their exports during the same period increased by a total of $339.2 billion, of which $110.6 billion represented trade among themselves and $74.3 billion in exports to the other East Asian economies. By the early 1990s the dynamism of Chinese industrialization had become a significant factor in the continuing growth of other regional economies.

The pace of economic growth began to falter in the latter part of the 1990s. The steady decline of GDP growth between 1993 and 1998 was symptomatic of the fall in domestic demand which export growth could not offset, particularly in the context of recessionary economic conditions in much of East Asia. Price deflation, declining freight volumes and increasing pressure on state-sector profitability were the outward manifestations of as yet unresolved structural problems. Of these, perhaps the most intractable was the industrial sector's excessive capacity. According to one estimate, the utilization of productive capacity in several key industries, notably those producing machine tools, motor vehicles and colour television sets, in 1995 was less than 50 per cent.[190] To varying degrees the same trend now beset a number of other industries, including steel, paper and petrochemicals. Other obstacles militating against sustainable high growth included increasing competition in world markets and resulting trade frictions; financial instability associated with a poorly regulated banking sector that had amassed a dangerously high proportion of non-performing loans (variously estimated at between 20 per cent and 40 per cent of all loans made by the four major state banks); the restructuring of inefficient state-owned enterprises, which was bound to compound the problem of unemployment; high and rising income inequalities and regional disparities, in particular between the southeast coastal region and the biggest cities, on the one hand, and the central and western regions, on the other; and the diminishing tax collecting capabilities of central government, with tax revenues as a proportion of GDP estimated to have declined from 30 per cent in 1989 to 12 per cent in 1998.[191] By the end of the 1990s the Chinese economy seemed poised to resume its upward curve, with official estimates indicating that GDP growth would rise from 7.1 per cent in 1999 to 7.5 per cent in 2000.[192] Several factors were contributing to the quickening pace of economic growth, notably the substantial rise in industrial output, the marked increase in exports, and the easing of there recent decline in foreign direct investment. Yet, neither these factors nor the Chinese government's determination to persevere with state-funded pump-priming of the economy could conceal, let alone remedy, the deep-seated structural problems facing China's economic planners.

To the long list of obstacles already mentioned must be added a sharply deteriorating energy trade balance, itself the by-product of high rates of economic growth. By 1996 Chinese imports of oil had reached 600 000 barrels a day, and were expected to exceed 1 million barrels by 2000 and close to 3 million barrels by 2010.[193] Despite gains in energy efficiency, which enabled China to hold the growth in energy consumption to half the level of economic growth, break-neck industrialization exacted a heavy toll on the environment. By the end of the 1990s air and water pollution had reached alarming levels, with concentrations of total suspended particulates and sulphur dioxide in urban areas among the world's highest, and few Chinese cities equipped to treat the 20 billion tons of sewage annually discharged into rivers, lakes and seas.[194] The economic costs of China's air and water pollution were calculated at 3.8 per cent of GDP a year.[195] China's rise as a major centre of economic activity was beyond dispute as was its increasing integration with the world economy. Less easily discernible but equally far-reaching were the social, political and ecological implications of the unprecedented levels of economic growth, and the geopolitical and geoeconomic repercussions for the region and beyond.

FINANCIAL CRISIS AND THE LIMITS OF EAST ASIAN INDUSTRIALIZATION

The preceding survey has consciously emphasized the remarkable success of the East Asian economies, at least as measured by such indicators as GNP, manufacturing capacity and export performance. Yet this image of success, which gained wide currency in the West as much as in Asia, obscured important drawbacks to the East Asian experience. It took the financial crisis of 1997 for these drawbacks to become apparent, although even then the tendency was to focus on the symptoms rather than the causes of East Asia's predicament.

Table 2.6   Currency depreciation (Currency units per US$)

Dates	Indonesia (rupiah)	Thailand (baht)	Malaysia (ringgit)	Philippines (peso)	Hong Kong (dollar)	Taiwan (dollar)	Korea (won)	Singapore (dollar)
June 96 (average for month)	2333	25.4	2.50	26.2	7.74	27.8	787	1.41
4 June 97	2428	24.7	2.52	26.4	7.74	27.9	891	1.43
30 July 97	2575	31.7	2.63	29.8	7.74	28.6	892	1.47
15 October 97	3575	37.0	3.15	33.9	7.74	28.5	915	1.55
28 January 98	11800	53.7	4.36	42.2	7.74	34.0	1680	1.72
22 April 98	7950	39.3	3.77	38.3	7.75	33.0	1375	1.59

Source: *The Economist* (various issues).

The most obvious aspect of the crisis was the rapid depreciation of several currencies, set off by the decision of the Central Bank of Thailand on 2 July 1997 to allow the baht to float against the dollar after numerous but vain attempts to stabilize the currency. Within days, the baht lost 20 per cent of its value and stock prices fell by 25 per cent. The Philippines, Malaysia and Indonesia soon followed suit. Within six months, the depreciating currencies and collapsing stock prices affected, though much less severely, even Singapore and Taiwan, and eventually engulfed South Korea. As Table 2.6 indicates, currency depreciation was most dramatic in the case of Indonesia, South Korea and Thailand, with the rupiah losing

80.2 per cent of its value in relation to the US dollar, the won 53.2 per cent and the baht 52.7 per cent. Hong Kong's currency which, with China's support, remained pegged to the US dollar, escaped devaluation, but during the same period the stock market index suffered a fall of 42.1 per cent.

Of the NIEs and ASEAN-4 economies, only Taiwan remained relatively unscathed. Both its currency and stock exchange experienced a slump of between 15 per cent and 20 per cent, but by April 1998 appeared relatively well positioned for full recovery (see Table 2.7). The short-term prospects for the other economies were less encouraging. By early 1998 Korea was in the midst of a severe recession, with real GDP in the first half of 1998 contracting by 5.2 per cent and official unemployment rising from 2.5 per cent in mid-1997 to 7.6 per cent in August 1998. Productive capacity utilization was estimated to have dropped from 81 per cent in mid-1997 to 63.7 per cent in mid-1998.[196] Hong Kong's GDP in the first half of 1998 experienced its first negative growth in 13 years, contracting by 4 per cent compared to a year earlier. Even Singapore's growth rate was decelerating, reaching a low of 3.8 per cent in the first half of 1998.

The sudden end of East Asia's economic boom, which, like the end of the Cold War, few theorists or policy-makers had anticipated, was not the gradual or modest downturn resulting from a conventional currency crisis. Even Paul Krugman, whose analysis was critical of the Panglossian accounts of the East Asian 'economic miracle',[197] had not explained, let alone predicted, the collapse in domestic asset markets or the succession of bank failures and business bankruptcies which were to afflict most East Asian economies. With the crisis in full swing, the general tendency was to ascribe it to cyclical factors. Some pointed to the tight monetary policies pursued by the Chinese, Malaysian and Thai governments as they sought to moderate the overheating of their economies. More frequently, and somewhat more persuasively, reference was made to the appreciation of the US dollar, which had risen by 50 per cent against the yen from its low point in April 1995. Given that East Asia's currencies were in practical terms pegged to the dollar, this trend, it was argued, had enhanced the competitiveness of Japanese producers at the expense of their East Asian competitors. The consequent fall in export revenue effectively meant an increase in foreign debt.[198] Similarly, the rising value of the US stock market was said to have adversely affected the 'mechanism of global credit creation' and sharply reduced the ability of the NIEs and ASEAN-4 'to sustain confidence in their dollar-linked currencies'.[199] The pegging of exchange rates, it is claimed, resulted in a growing overvaluation of East Asian currencies which squeezed exporters and forced governments to deplete their foreign exchange reserves in a futile attempt to defend the currency. The appreciating dollar and depreciating yen were no doubt contributing factors, as was the devaluation of the Chinese yuan in early 1994.

According to one assessment published by *China Analyst* in Montreal, the decision to devalue the yuan by 33 per cent in relation to the dollar, 'coupled with a 17 per cent tax rebate for exporters and a four-year austerity drive meant that the prices of China's tradable goods fell by one-quarter between October 1994 and June 1997'.[200]

Table 2.7   Stock market depreciation

	20 March 1996	4 June 1997	30 July 1997	15 Oct 1997	28 Jan 1998	22 April 1998
Indonesia	586.0	693.5	722.0	518.9	485.9	500.6
Thailand	1287.9	552.9	679.5	535.6	434.2	436.7
Malaysia	1126.9	1193.3	1024.7	801.5	569.5	619.7
Philippines	2859.8	2796.1	2595.4	2040.1	1782.1	2154.3
Hong Kong	10836.5	14831.6	15983.2	13384.2	9252.4	10977.5
Taiwan	5040.5	8282.9	9942.8	8264.4	8085.5	8636.5
Korea	870.0	763.3	726.9	604.7	518.6	431.8
Singapore	2378.3	2047.9	1966.4	1855.0	1259.9	1475.5

Source: *The Economist* (various issues).

Other explanations emphasizing cyclical factors in the form of policy failure included the investment boom, which had contributed to large and growing current account deficits; excessive lending to risky, less profitable projects, arising from a mixture of political pressure and implicit or explicit government guarantees to lenders; and deficient financial systems lacking the necessary prudential and supervisory safeguards.[201] Under-regulation of the banking system, it was argued, had created a 'moral hazard' in the sense that banks and firms could engage in dubious lending, confident nevertheless that government support would ensure repayment of loans, and hence their own profitability. Asian business practices, it was claimed, lent themselves to corruption ('crony capitalism'), thereby undermining the allocation of capital and the efficiency of the financial system. The net effect of these factors, once the credit-driven boom had subsided, was to weaken the capacity of the tiger and Southeast Asian economies to penetrate export markets, particularly in North America. These cyclical factors had no doubt served as triggers for the currency crises, but they were more the symptoms than the causes of East Asia's predicament.

Structural Factors

Causal connections are more likely to emerge if we focus on structural rather than cyclical factors. In this context we propose to examine four distinct but closely related variables: government financial policy, private financial flows, productivity, and the relationship between production and consumption. To the extent that most governments had previously embarked upon ambitious policies of financial deregulation, conditions had been created that were highly favourable to large and rapid movements of short-term foreign funds and intense speculative activity in real estate. To illustrate, between 1990 and 1994 Thai governments, hoping to turn Bangkok into a regional financial sector, initiated a major programme of financial liberalization, removing ceilings on various kinds of savings and time deposits, reducing constraints on the management of portfolio investment, relaxing rules on capital requirements applying to commercial banks and other financial institutions, effectively dismantling the system of foreign exchange controls, and establishing the Bangkok International Banking Facility which permitted the subsidiaries of foreign banks to issue dollar-denominated loans to local borrowers.[202] A similar course was followed in the Philippines which saw the lifting of most foreign exchange restrictions, enabling the unfettered flow of capital and use of foreign currency accounts, the deregulation of the insurance sector, and the opening up of the banking system to foreign banks, 12 of which had established operations by September 1996.[203] In the absence of effective government supervision and control, economies became highly vulnerable to volatile capital flows and to the rapid accumulation of non-performing loans. The radical application of neo-liberal ideology in East Asia had ushered in a process of far-reaching structural change, the implications of which were only now beginning to emerge.

Another significant factor was the willingness of Southeast Asia's central banks to keep interest rates at remarkably high levels. Apart from enticing speculative capital, this made it extremely difficult for property developers to repay their loans, for manufacturers to maintain competitive export prices and for consumers to maintain high rates of consumption. High interest rates had the added effect of encouraging financial firms to borrow large sums abroad relatively cheaply and lend domestically at far higher rates, much of this to fund investment in real estate and loans on the local market. Soaring investment in construction projects, including offices, hotels and luxury homes, eventually resulted in vast overcapacity, causing rents and prices to fall sharply and bringing even greater pressure to bear on the big banks, many of which had committed as much as 30 per cent of their lending to property development.

Once the real estate bubble burst, banks and the other lending institutions were saddled with a rapidly expanding mass of non-performing loans, causing an abrupt downturn in their liquidity. Lenient disclosure rules helped for a while to obscure the scale of the problem. In Korea, as late as June 1997 only 6.1 per cent of total loans were classified in official figures as non-performing loans, but independent sources estimated the real figure to be more than 15 per cent. With the worsening property glut a number of finance companies were forced to close or suspend operations. Central banks attempted to shore up the financial system by selling off holdings of foreign currency, but the size of foreign exchange reserves placed strict limitations on such a strategy. In the latter part of 1997 the Central Bank of Thailand may have spent as much as $2.6 billion a month to stabilize the country's finances. On 8 November the South Korean Central Bank pumped $5.1 billion to shore up the financial system. The accumulation of non-performing loans combined with the depreciating value of banking assets – a direct consequence of high interest rates – had undermined the foundations of the financial sector.[204]

During the period 1992–6 loans and portfolio investment averaged each year more than 3 per cent of GDP in Indonesia and the Philippines, between 4 and 5 per cent in South Korea and Malaysia, and more than 8 per cent in Thailand.[205] By 1995 Thailand's short-term debt had risen to $41 billion. By October 1997 South Korean firms had accumulated non-performing loans estimated at $50 billion. The leading *chaebol* were themselves indebted, with the top ten burdened by debt–equity ratios of between 359.9 per cent and 1214.7 per cent.[206]

The currency crisis assumed critical proportions precisely because of the high levels of indebtedness. With local currencies plummeting, loan repayments were insufficient to enable financial enterprises to meet their dollar liabilities. According to the Bank for International Settlements (BIS), foreign currency loans with a maturity of less than two years amounted to 120 per cent of Thailand's foreign exchange reserves and almost 200 per cent of Indonesian and Korean reserves.[207] It is worth noting in parenthesis that well before these dramatic events the ASEAN-4 economies had accumulated large external debts representing in each case a high proportion of GNP (in the case of both Indonesia and the Philippines a little under 60 per cent of GNP).[208] During the period 1980–93, Indonesia's external debt had risen from $20.9 billion to $89.5 billion, Malaysia's from $6.6 billion to $23.3 billion, and Thailand's from $8.3 billion to $45.8 billion.[209] By the end of June 1997 South Korean banks had external debts of $103.4 billion, followed by Thailand ($69.4 billion), Indonesia ($58.7 billion) and Malaysia ($28.8 billion).[210] According to Thailand's national accounts, the country's total foreign debt at the end of 1996 stood at $89 billion.[211] But even these figures often understated the size of the debt. In Indonesia's case, following a quick succession of upward revisions, foreign debt was officially placed in February 1998 at $137.4 billion.[212]

Nor was it merely a question of the size of the debt or even of the debt–service ratio (interest payments as a percentage of total exports). In South Korea's case, neither its overall debt nor its debt–service ratio had approached what were commonly regarded as dangerous or unsustainable levels. More troublesome was the accumulation of debts with very short maturity. South Korea's short-term debt (debt with less than one year's maturity) as a proportion of total debt had by the end of 1996 risen to 58.2 per cent.[213]

Financial policy and indebtedness were no doubt key contributing factors, yet they do not adequately explain either the scale or the timing of the financial meltdown. The analysis offered by Yoshitomi Masaru is helpful in this respect.[214] International lenders, conscious of the financial weakness of the East Asian economies, were no longer willing to advance new loans. Indeed, they were intent on retrieving their capital as quickly as possible, and accordingly refused to rollover their existing loans when these became due. The massive capital influx had come to an end. To make matters worse, speculators and managers of hedge funds, now anticipating currency devaluations, started selling their local currency holdings.

Here the mechanisms developed for hedge fund management played a critical role. Large institutional investors who placed tens of billions of dollars of portfolio capital in emerging capital markets entrusted the task to a relatively small number of emerging market fund managers (EMFMs). Though under intense pressure to succeed in a highly competitive environment, these fund managers had to rely on at best imperfect information. Uncertain as to the financial strength of the economies in which they had invested, but with an eye to the behaviour of other investors, individual managers rushed to sell their shares in the hope of escaping before their portfolio investments drastically depreciated in value.[215] The foreign exchange reserves available to the central banks might provide adequate protection against adverse shifts in the current account balance, but they were simply unable to withstand the dual pressure exerted by non-performing foreign loans and speculative sales of local currency driven by a self-fulfilling creditor panic. Paul Krugman took the argument a step further, linking the financial crisis to the collapse of asset values.[216] In what he described as 'a circular process in reverse', the excessively risky lending of financial institutions had contributed to substantial overpricing of assets, with the result that these institutions appeared much healthier than was actually the case. Conversely, when the bubble burst and asset prices started falling, the financial system's vulnerability was suddenly exposed, forcing a number of banks and financial companies to suspend operations, thus provoking even greater asset deflation. Diminishing asset prices in turn had a contagious effect on capital outflows, thereby greatly accelerating the trend. Within the space of a year net capital flows to Thailand, Korea, Indonesia, Malaysia and the Philippines had reversed from a positive flow of $97.1 billion in 1996 to a negative flow of $11.9 billion in 1997.[217]

The conjunction between financial crisis and currency crisis no doubt offers important clues to East Asia's abrupt economic downturn, but still falls well short of a full explanation. More substantial and long-term factors appear to have been at work. The rising US dollar, as we have seen, made it difficult for many of East Asia's economies to retain their export competitiveness while continuing to anchor their currencies on the US dollar. Without such anchorage the incentives needed to attract large capital inflows   gradually diminished. This was the debilitating contradiction most of the economies were unable to resolve. By 1996 their current account deficits were beginning to assume troubling proportions. Thai merchandise exports registered 0.1 per cent growth in 1996 compared to 22.2 per cent growth in 1994 and 24.7 per cent in 1995. A comparable trend occurred in Malaysia, which saw its export growth decline from 29.4 per cent in 1995 to 1.3 per cent in 1996. Though Philippine exports as a whole continued to rise in 1996, exports of apparel fell by 27 per cent, a sign of troubled times ahead.[218] Export growth in Indonesia was down to 8.8 per cent and in Malaysia the current account deficit reached 4.1 per cent of GDP, with the month of June registering the country's largest trade deficit in 17 years.[219] In 1996 South Korea recorded a massive trade deficit with both Japan ($15.3 billion) and the United States ($11.5 billion), which contributed to an overall trade deficit of $20.6 billion.[220] Here, it is worth noting that the United States had over the preceding few years brought fierce pressure to bear on South Korea with a view to erasing its large deficit in bilateral trade ($9.6 billion in 1987). By 1992 the deficit had been converted to a surplus of $159 million, with the upward curve continuing over the next four years to rise sharply in favour of the United States. Contributing to the slowdown in South Korean exports was the decline in world prices for a number of products, notably semiconductors, which fell by 20 per cent between 1995 and 1997.[221] East Asia's deteriorating trade performance, whether attributable to declining export prices or to sluggish volume performance, was a signal to the financial markets that its currencies were overvalued.

The East Asia export slowdown was itself the result of several factors, including the NAFTA-induced shift in US textile imports from East Asia to Mexico and Canada and the relatively stagnant economic conditions prevailing in Japan and Western Europe. There was, however, one other contributing factor, which received less attention than it deserved. Krugman, one of the few economists to question the solidity of the East Asian 'miracle', attributed the region's growth to quantitative inputs (that is, heavy investment and the shift from agriculture to manufacturing) rather than to productivity gains associated with technological or organizational inputs.[222] As in the case of the Soviet Union, he expected that with declining inputs capital-to-output ratios would rise and growth rates sharply diminish. This conclusion drew considerable criticism from other economists, who argued that Krugman had underestimated the rates of total factor productivity achieved by East Asian countries and that high rates of investment in the context of an open economy – low taxes and government spending, flexible labour markets and openness to trade – were much more likely to yield productivity improvements than in centrally planned economies.[223] Krugman may well have overstated his case, but he had identified another important variable in this complex equation.

By the mid-1990s it had become apparent that the productivity of East Asian enterprises was not keeping pace with that of their competitors. Thailand's labour-intensive exports lost their competitiveness in part because of rising labour costs. The very pace of industrialization had helped to raise wage scales, most strikingly in Hong Kong, Singapore, Taiwan and South Korea, but also in the ASEAN countries. In South Korea wages more than doubled between 1987 and 1991. In many East Asian economies, wages for skilled jobs were rising even faster. Rising wages, reflecting in part labour shortages, were in some cases outpacing productivity increases, and helping to make labour-intensive export industries less competitive than their Chinese counterparts, which could rely on a vast pool of cheap labour.

There was, however, more to East Asia's rising trade deficits than higher labour costs. Another contributing factor was inadequate investment in secondary and tertiary education as well as in research and development.[224] To protect their profit margins NIE enterprises often tended to relocate their low-tech, labour-intensive, manufacturing industries to low-wage countries rather than upgrade their manufacturing capacities at home. Even where governments sought to develop technologically more advanced industries, they often discovered that they lacked the necessary infrastructure (for example, an adequate supply of electricity, sophisticated transport and telecommunications facilities) or the supporting industries needed for the reliable and timely supply of high-quality parts and components.[225] These deficiencies in industrial capability help to explain declining export performance and high and rising levels of dependence on manufacturing imports, both factors contributing to high and rising trade deficits. It is instructive that Taiwan, which fared much better than the other economies, had a smaller external debt, a better regulated banking system and, more importantly, a tougher approach to business efficiency. The continuous entry of new firms into key industries (in particular, chemical manufacturing, metal fabrication, textiles and clothing, plastics) at the expense of more established but less efficient ones may have been a major factor in raising productivity across the economy.[226]

Table 2.8 Financial conditions of top 15 Korean chaebol at the end of 1996 (in hundred million won and %)

Chaebol	Total assets	Debts	Sales	Net profit	Debt–equity ratio
Samsung	508.6	370.4	601.0	1.8	268.2
Hyundai	531.8	433.2	680.1	1.8	439.1
Daewoo	342.1	263.8	382.5	3.6	337.3
LG	370.7	287.7	466.7	3.6	346.5
Hanjin	139.0	117.9	87.0	-1.9	556.9
Kia	141.6	118.9	121.0	-1.3	523.6
Ssangyong	158.1	127.0	194.5	-1.0	409.0
Sunkyong	227.3	180.4	266.1	2.9	385.0
Hanhwa	109.7	97.2	96.9	-1.8	778.2
Daelim	57.9	45.9	48.3	0.1	380.1
Kumho	74.0	61.2	44.4	-0.2	477.9
Doosan	64.0	55.9	40.5	-1.1	692.3
Halla	66.3	63.2	52.9	0.2	2067.6
Sammi	25.2	25.9	14.9	-2.5	3245.0
Hyosung	41.2	32.5	54.8	0.4	373.2

Source: *Chosun Ilbo*, 29 November 1997.

East Asia's financial crisis owes, then, a good deal to the poor productivity performance of its industries. A study by international management consultants McKinsey & Co. found that eight key South Korean industries were on average only 51 per cent as productive as their American counterparts. The leading manufacturing firm, Hyundai, 'produced 27.9 cars per employee in 1996, compared with 44.7 per cent by Toyota in 1974 when Japanese industry was at a similar stage of development'.[227] Paradoxically, major industrial groups in Korea and elsewhere had overinvested in plant and equipment, most obviously in semiconductors. They had sought, in other words, to offset low productivity by high levels of investment (financed by massive international borrowing), hoping that economies of scale would yield the desired profit margins. In South Korea's case, the result was excess capacity in such industries as steel, motor vehicles, semiconductors and petrochemicals. To make matters worse, the *chaebol* conglomerates had diversified into areas where they had little expertise. The top five embraced on average 140 businesses each. The top four (Hyundai, Samsung, Daewoo and LG) accounted for more than half the country's exports. Yet profits remained low.[228] Not surprisingly, many firms went bankrupt: some 14 000 firms in 1997, including eight large *chaebol* with an estimated combined debt of $21 billion (see Table 2.8).[229]

Notwithstanding national variations, reflecting differences of political culture and different stages of industrialization, the crisis assumed remarkably similar features in each country. While referring specifically to Thailand, Rosenberger graphically describes the general pattern:

> The huge capital inflows left Thai banks awash in cash . . . using this cheap money borrowed overseas, Thai companies over-invested in redundant manufacturing plants. The private sector, used to growing simply by investing, gave little or no thought to the actual demand for the new capacity. In fact, other Asian governments were already struggling with a serious problem of excess manufacturing capacity. And yet, Thailand kept building more factories. The country became burdened with a surplus of virtually idle steel mills and petrochemical plants.[230]

Excess investment resulting in excess capacity simply became a recipe for low return on investment. Viewed from a neo-liberal perspective, East Asian firms had not tackled the fundamental issue of global competiveness. In this they were said to have been hampered by over-reliance on government protection, the structure of family businesses, which limited their capacity to attract managerial talent and raise capital, and the failure of East Asian firms, in particular South Korea's *chaebol*, to upgrade the technological sophistication of their industrial capabilities.[231]

International Environment

The strategic choices of East Asia's corporate sector must, however, be placed in a larger context. Our analysis has thus far concentrated on influences deriving in large measure from the interaction between state and market or, expressed a little differently, between government policies and corporate strategies. Consideration of domestic influences cannot, however, be divorced from the international environment. While the state could hypothetically help to fashion new forms of competitive advantage, the range of options was in practice greatly circumscribed not only by the prevailing political culture and various forms of clientelism and cronyism, but also by the powerful and in many respects homogenizing pressures exerted by other states, transnational corporations, financial markets and international organizations.

Core states, in particular the United States, would not easily reconcile themselves to high and rising trade deficits with the Asian NIEs or the new wave of industrializing economies. Not surprisingly, US Administrations used the considerable leverage at their disposal, including threatened use of Super-301 legislation, to pressure South Korea, Taiwan and others to open up their markets faster and wider to US products. As a consequence trade restrictions on thousands of NIE services and commodities were wholly or partially lifted. As part of its concerted trade offensive the United States also moved to limit penetration of its own markets. It terminated the tariff-free entry of selected NIE imports, introduced Voluntary Export Restraints (VERs) and restrictive quotas on NIE products, and forced the revaluation of the Taiwan dollar and Korean won. Placed in this larger context, the East Asian financial and currency crisis can be seen as symptomatic of the periodic restructuring of competitive advantage in the world trading system. This was one of the mechanisms which enabled the system to eliminate excess capacity, thereby re-establishing at least a temporary equilibrium between production and consumption.[232] There was nothing unusual in such restructuring, mediated as it was by powerful states and international institutions reflecting primarily the interests of the core rather than the periphery or semi-periphery of the world economy.

We are now better placed to examine the regional dimensions of the East Asian financial crisis and the rationale and significance of IMF intervention. As we have already seen, East Asia's financial predicament was not so much a series of isolated or discrete national crises as the outward manifestation of a deeper ailment which now afflicted most, if not all, of the economies that had embarked upon the road of export-oriented industrialization. There were a number of connecting mechanisms which collectively constituted a powerful transmission belt, helping to spread the disease from one country to another and its effects from one region to another. These mechanisms may be seen as the bridge connecting general trends in the region's political economy with the specific circumstances of each national economy.

The first of these mechanisms was the international financial system itself, in particular the vast capital flows between Japan, the NIEs and the ASEAN countries and the mutually reinforcing impact of non-performing loans. Within the space of a few months South Korean, Indonesian and other banks and finance companies were repeatedly forced to revise upwards the extent of their external obligations. The mass of debts incurred by the private sector in most of these countries involved a long and intricate chain of lending and borrowing arrangements whose solidity rested on the precarious solvency of its participants. The foundations of this elaborate financial edifice were all the more tenuous given the radical programme of financial deregulation which governments had diligently pursued in the preceding years. The ensuing lack of transparency, and the ideology of market self-regulation which sustained it, made it difficult for governments and international institutions to detect at an early stage the severity of the crisis. A process of reciprocal vulnerability had now taken root, as was graphically illustrated by the collapse of a major Hong Kong bank, Peregrine Investment, attributable in large measure to the failure of a $200 million loan to the Indonesian transport company, Steady Safe.[233] The impact on Japanese banks was particularly severe given that they were the single largest source of lending to the region, accounting in Korea's case for nearly 35 per cent of its external debt.

The second mechanism was the almost instantaneous linkage between national stock exchanges. Widely shared perceptions of financial turmoil, rapidly mounting external debts and declining export prospects led foreign investors to scale down their commitments across the region, precipitating an abrupt downward plunge in most stock markets. A third and closely related mechanism operated within the industrial sector, where firms beset by liquidity shortages and diminishing sales had little option but to curtail their activities and shed a substantial fraction of their workforce. Regional trade constituted a less direct but no less important mechanism. Intra-regional exports among East Asian economies accounted for nearly 40 per cent of total exports (50 per cent if Japan is included). This concentration of trade, reflecting the evolving regional division of labour and the outsourcing of activities from higher-income to lower-income countries in the region, had helped to fuel rapid regional growth in the heyday of the 'Asian Miracle' but was now 'a perfect channel for the contagion to spread swiftly throughout Southeast Asia'.[234] The subsequent intervention of the IMF (of which more later) merely served to accelerate the deflationary spiral, which, given the extensive trade links between the various economies, soon acquired a regional dynamic.

Accentuating the crisis was the absence of a timely or coherent regional response. The role of regional institutions and the constraints on efficacious action are examined at length in the companion volume. Suffice it here to say that the ASEAN countries could not easily jettison the dollar umbrella even though it had left their currencies exposed to external developments over which they had little or no control. The Malaysian government was the most vocal in calling for the establishment of an Asian fund specifically designed to meet the needs of Asian economies and currencies. In the wake of vehement US opposition, in December 1997 ASEAN adopted a substantially diluted proposal, which provided for the creation of a fund mobilized from private capital and subjected to market principles and to IMF regulations.[235] In February 1998 ASEAN reached agreement on two other initiatives: a trade arrangement which would allow regional currencies to be used for trade within the group, thereby reducing current reliance on the US dollar; and the establishment of a regional surveillance agency to provide early warning of deteriorating economic or financial conditions, which would initially be run within the Asian Development Bank before being handed over to the ASEAN secretariat.[236] These tentative steps were, however, late in coming and would take considerable time to implement. They were more an attempt to project an image of continuing relevance and cohesion than an effective remedy for the crisis at hand.

If regional leadership were to have been exercised in response to the crisis, the only possible candidate would have been Japan. It certainly had the incentive, given the exposure of its manufacturing firms and its banks to the ill winds blowing across East Asia's economies. Although it accounted for only a small fraction of total Japanese production, Asia absorbed some 44 per cent of Japan's exports (compared with 30 per cent for the United States and 9 per cent for the European Union). More significantly, Japanese companies specializing in the manufacture of cars and electrical machinery had a particularly high stake in Southeast Asia: according to one estimate these sectors were to generate more than one-third of the growth in Japanese corporate profits in 1997.[237] The threat to Japanese exports was not in any case confined to Asian markets directly affected by the crisis. With the drastic devaluation of the South Korean won, Japanese firms now faced the prospect of fierce competition from South Korean exporters of cars, electrical appliances and semiconductors. Shrinking export markets would make Japan's prospects of economic growth more dependent on increased domestic demand at a time when its economy was bordering on recession. Equally troublesome was the extent to which Japanese banks had financed East Asia's mounting external private debt. According to one calculation Japan accounted for $69.3 billion in outstanding loans to the ASEAN-4, or 46 per cent of their combined debts.[238] The Bank for International Settlements estimated that more than half of Thailand's – and more than 40 per cent of Indonesia's – foreign currency debts were owed to Japanese banks,[239] and this at a time when the Japanese financial system was itself under enormous pressure.

It was in Japan's interest for East Asia's financial and economic health to be restored as quickly as possible. Yet incentive did not easily translate into capability, which is not to say that the Hashimoto government was inactive during the crisis. Of the $17.2 billion loan to Thailand coordinated by the IMF in early August, Japan's Export–Import (EXIM) Bank had contributed $4 billion. In response to external criticism, Tokyo claimed that its financial support for Indonesia, Thailand and Korea amounted to $19 billion compared to $8 billion offered by the Untied States and $6.2 billion by the EU. In addition, Japan provided flexible application of trade insurance to facilitate private sector activities, emergency grant aid valued at 4 billion yen, as well as assistance to Asian students in Japan.[240] Yet, to judge from a succession of public statements, Asian governments remained deeply dissatisfied. Though they appreciated Japan's financial support and took some encouragement from Japan's belated attempt to pump-prime its stagnant economy through tax cuts and increased public spending, what they wanted first and foremost was greater access to Japanese markets and the continuing flow of Japanese investments.[241] Tokyo's response, constrained by domestic political considerations, fell short of Asian expectations.

At the height of the financial crisis the weakness of demand in Japan was severely restricting its capacity to absorb East Asian exports. Japan's imports from ASEAN countries in April 1998 compared to a year earlier had fallen by 26 per cent.[2,2] East Asian economies were also adversely affected by the financial weakness of the yen and the fragility of the Japanese banking system, both of which to varying degrees accentuated the problems posed by the sudden outflow of capital. Japanese banks were certainly not well placed to entertain requests even for a temporary moratorium on loan repayments. In late 1997 Japan proposed the creation of an Asian Monetary Fund which, capitalized initially at $100 billion, would extend emergency support to regional economies. It would operate with greater flexibility and sensitivity than the IMF, and its membership would be confined to East Asia. For Japan this was an opportunity to take a major policy initiative independently of the United States and perhaps lay the groundwork for the emergence of a yen-dominated regional monetary bloc. For the United States, it was a mechanism bound to weaken its influence in Asia and severely dent the IMF's institutional primacy in overseeing adjustments to the international financial system.

Japan's failure to withstand US pressure and insist on the establishment of an Asian fund independent of the IMF provoked deep disappointment. In October 1998 Finance Minister Kiichi Miyazawa cautiously launched the Joint Recovery Initiative, which envisaged a $30 billion collective aid package involving the other G7 countries as well as the World Bank and the IMF. It was only at the summit of Asian leaders in Hanoi in December 1998 that Prime Minister Obuchi finally declared Japan's readiness to play a leading role in East Asia's economic recovery, obliquely criticizing the IMF approach and unveiling more details of Japan's financial aid initiative.[243] Significantly, however, many of the funds were to be channelled through co-financing arrangements tied to World Bank and Asian Development Bank projects.[244] Even then, domestic political infighting and the weakened Japanese economy made progress painfully slow. Japan, it seemed, lacked the institutional and economic muscle needed to initiate and coordinate a comprehensive recovery plan.

IMF Intervention

In the absence of more palatable alternatives, particularly in the critical months immediately following the financial meltdown, the worst-hit economies turned for assistance to the IMF. Their most immediate need was to stem the seemingly unstoppable outflow of dollars which had so weakened their currencies, and to have their short-term debts rolled over and rescheduled. In return for such assistance, the IMF exacted a heavy price, arguing that drastic measures were required to remedy what were deeply flawed financial systems. The IMF rescue packages were contingent on Asian governments agreeing to implement 'programs of rigorous fiscal stringency, regulatory system improvements, greater transparency of financial information in both the public and private sectors, and the opening of the financial sectors in each country to foreign investors'.[245] As was widely observed at the time, the IMF at first appeared to have great confidence in its prescriptions, although its diagnosis, at least until the eve of the crisis, had not been particularly perceptive. Its 1997 annual report described South Korea's fiscal policy as 'enviable' and Thailand's macroeconomic policy as 'sound'.[246] It had especially kind words for Indonesia's 'prudent macro-economic policy, its high rates of savings and investment and its reforms for the opening up of its markets'.[247]

The IMF's assessments, it must be said, were widely shared by international banks and credit rating agencies. Presumably, the IMF had been prepared to turn a blind eye to the danger signals because these governments had on the essentials of macroeconomic policy acted within IMF guidelines. They had pursued a policy of export-oriented industrialization predicated on financial liberalization, increased privatization and avoidance of budget deficits. High current account deficits were acceptable to the extent that they were financed by foreign investment. IMF intervention must therefore be seen as an attempt not so much to bring about a radical change of economic direction, but to accelerate the twin processes of financial deregulation and trade liberalization. The preferred strategy, however, was for this to be done in ways which did not privilege domestic private interests *vis-à-vis* their foreign competitors; hence the call for transparency and an end to political cronyism.

In return for a rescue package valued at $17.2 billion, Thailand agreed to a stabilization programme aimed at reducing the current account deficit (by maintaining high interest rates) and achieving a budget surplus (by increasing taxes and reducing public spending). The reform of the financial sector envisaged the restructuring or suspension of unviable institutions and the recapitalization of other financial enterprises through a policy of mergers and foreign capital injection.[248] The negotiations with Indonesia were protracted and less conclusive, in part because they became closely entwined with the domestic political crisis which, in the wake of rapidly deteriorating economic conditions, led to widespread student and public unrest and culminated in President Suharto's resignation in May 1998. With the rupiah in free fall, the Suharto government had agreed in October 1997 to a $43 billion loan agreement, including $23 billion of first line financing to which the IMF contributed $10 billion, the World Bank $4.5 billion and the Asian Development Bank $3.5 billion.

The policies dictated by the IMF agreement were substantially the same as those that had been imposed on Thailand: tight monetary policy (including high interest rates to attract foreign investment); the closing of unviable financial institutions; trade liberalization (including tariff reduction in specific industries); investment liberalization; and privatization of public enterprises.[249] The IMF rescue strategy failed, however, to restore public confidence in Indonesia's banking system. With the Indonesian Central Bank in disarray and the rupiah losing half its value in the space of a few days, the IMF drew up in January 1998 a new $43 billion package tied to an even more restrictive set of requirements, including the lifting of subsidies on a number of basic necessities and the ending of state support for a range of strategic industries. In his speech to the Indonesian Parliament on 1 March, Suharto made it clear that, despite implementing the IMF's austerity package, Indonesia saw no prospect of relief from its financial woes, and called on the IMF to devise 'a more appropriate alternative'.[250] With the outbreak of riots across Indonesia, the IMF felt it necessary in April 1998 to produce yet another agreement, this time relaxing some of its previous conditions and agreeing to an indefinite delay in the lifting of food and fuel subsidies.[251]

The wider ramifications of Indonesia's social and political crisis will be examined in Chapter 4. The primary focus here is the underlying rationale of IMF policy and its implications for the region's political economy. It is therefore necessary to refer, however briefly, to the Korean experience. As in the other two cases, the immediate objective of the IMF rescue package concluded on 3 December 1997 was to prevent South Korea defaulting on its short-term foreign debt, estimated at $66 billion. Out of the total package of $57 billion, the largest ever put together by the IMF, $35 billion would be available as a first line of credit, with the IMF, the World Bank and the Asian Development Bank contributing $21 billion, $10 billion and $4 billion respectively. Seven OECD countries (the United States, Japan, Canada, Australia, Britain, France and Germany) would offer $22 billion as a second line of credit, while the lending banks would enter into separate negotiations with a view to reaching agreement on the rescheduling of debts, bridging finance and the future of South Korea's financial system. The IMF reform formula was once again remarkably familiar: tight fiscal and monetary policy; labour market reforms; faster liberalization and greater transparency of financial transactions; the opening up of Korean markets; a review of all remaining restrictions on foreign corporate borrowing; and relaxation of foreign investment controls to allow for majority foreign ownership of Korean enterprises. The IMF document had set as targets a current account deficit for 1998 and 1999 of less than 1 per cent of GDP, a maximum inflation rate of 5 per cent, and 3 per cent real economic growth in 1998 leading to substantial recovery the following year.[252]

The IMF's intervention in the East Asian financial crisis proved to be one of the most controversial in its history. The sheer scale of the rescue packages, the uncertain prospects of East Asian economic recovery, sensitive issues of leadership succession in all three countries and, above all, the diverging interests of the main protagonists dramatized the IMF's strategic role in the crisis and the far-reaching political ramifications of its actions. Many questioned the appropriateness of IMF remedies. Highly conservative Republican voices in the US Senate took exception to massive international rescue operations which impeded the free play of market forces, serving only to encourage high-risk investments and dubious financial transactions. More sophisticated arguments pointed to the likelihood that the IMF's insistence on budget surpluses, high interest rates and reduced government spending would accelerate the economic downturn and exacerbate social and political tensions. Evidence in support of this view was not hard to find. Within a few months of being prescribed, the IMF medicine had contributed to the doubling of Thailand's and Indonesia's unemployment rates. South Korea's rose from 2.3 per cent in October 1997 to 6.7 per cent in March 1998.[253] A preliminary analysis of social indicators in Thailand indicated that the economic downturn had compounded the country's social problems, in particular the incidence of suicide and child drug abuse, and the numbers of children in orphanages.[254]

Wittingly or otherwise, the IMF had misdiagnosed the East Asian crisis as 'a crisis of excess consumption rather than excess investment'.[255] As for the suspension or closure of financial enterprises, though it may have helped to contain unproductive speculation in real estate, it also deprived small and medium-sized businesses of access to much-needed funds, thereby provoking further bankruptcies. Economies in receipt of IMF largesse – but also others by dint of the spill-over effect – had, if anything, been made more vulnerable to the downward spiral of slowing growth, failing banks and contracting credit. It is perhaps significant that even the World Bank felt it necessary to distance itself from IMF positions, warning that, without a change of direction, the number of poor in Southeast Asia could more than double to 90 million by 2001.[256] Both the World Bank and the Asian Development Bank were now intent on assisting governments to expand public spending, in part by guaranteeing government and semi-government borrowing programmes.[257]

To the extent that IMF-sponsored reforms did not offer a break from, but an acceleration of, the market-integration strategies of the recent past, dissatisfaction with these reforms helped to spark the beginnings of a debate on the future direction of economic policy. In this sense, the East Asian financial crisis and the emerging critique of the efficiency and underlying rationale of the IMF's response represented the first serious challenge to the assumptions which had hitherto governed the commitment to export-oriented industrialization. The negative reactions to IMF intervention had another, perhaps politically more sensitive consequence, in that they drew attention as much to the structure and ideological complexion of the organization as to its policy recommendations. The two main elements in this critique went to the heart of contemporary geopolitics and geoeconomics.

More than the myth of the Asian economic miracle, the IMF's strictures had, at least temporarily, punctured East Asia's self-confidence and sense of achievement. The IMF, it is true, could be portrayed as simply responding to a crisis which was not of its making, and seeking to correct it by substituting market discipline for cronyism and government–business collusion as the principal mechanism shaping investment decisions.[258] It is even arguable that the IMF's intervention   hastened Suharto's departure and assisted Kim Dae Jung's early presidency, thereby weakening the foundations of authoritarian rule and accelerating the trend towards democratic politics. Yet it is also clear that the humiliating dependence on international financial institutions had exposed the weaknesses of East Asia's political economy and reinforced the supremacy of western-dominated global markets. In South Korea's case, it was openly acknowledged that compliance with the IMF's requirements would see a significant fraction of Korean assets being sold to foreign investors. As one analyst put it, 'only the best Korean companies that become more focused and can compete with foreigners will survive'.[259] The clear message was that while a number of domestic companies would be energized by the new financial regime, a good many others would not be able to withstand the pressure of competition and would be forced to dispose of their assets at bargain prices.

The IMF's intervention brought to light another contradiction. It was graphically symbolized on the occasion of the second agreement between Indonesia and the IMF by a photo of President Suharto appending his signature with Michael Camdessus, the IMF's Managing Director, imperiously looking over his shoulder. The same symbolism came to light in the IMF's demand that the agreement negotiated with the South Korean government be formally endorsed by all three candidates in the December 1997 presidential elections. Even Malaysia, which pointedly refrained from seeking IMF assistance, nevertheless implemented a programme of reforms strikingly similar to those imposed by the IMF on other East Asian economies. Michael Camdessus is reported to have advised Deputy Prime Minister Anwar Ibrahim that Malaysia needed to tone down its 'political rhetoric' and implement painful measures to restore confidence 'as soon as possible'.[260]

The unmistakable lesson of the crisis was that East Asian governments had much less room in which to manoeuvre in setting national economic goals and strategies than had often been assumed. For critics in the West, the IMF's secrecy militated against sustained professional and public scrutiny of its operations. For many in Asia, the issue was one of global power and authority. To quote a leading article in the *New Straits Times*:

Yet this world government in all but name is not accountable to the people it says are the beneficiaries of its policies, and operates behind tightly closed doors. Democracy and transparency might be global watchwords . . . but they are not the concern of the priesthood that runs the IMF.[261]

Democracy, it was argued, was deemed acceptable, indeed desirable by the West so long as it was applied within the narrow confines of domestic politics and did not endanger western economic or geopolitical interests. It had little or no place in international institutions even though their decisions would largely shape what could or could not be done at the national level, in relation not just to financial policy and corporate governance, but even competition and social policies.[262] Rightly or wrongly, the IMF was increasingly perceived as an intermediary whose primary task was to establish an international framework tailored to the needs and priorities of core states and core producers in the western world.

A CONCLUDING NOTE

The preceding analysis indicates that the confident predictions of the 1980s and early 1990s about the Asian or Pacific century may have been a little premature. While the sheer volume of economic activity in East Asia, measured in domestic productivity, trade and financial flows, rose sharply both relatively and absolutely over the preceding 30 years, the shift in the global balance of economic power was less pronounced than these indicators would suggest. The NIEs and the ASEAN-4 may have established for a time a competitive export sector in consumer and industrial products, but their competitive advantage rested on an international division of labour and an international financial system over which they still had limited influence. A semi-periphery had well and truly emerged in East Asia, but it was in no position yet to challenge the core. Dependence on foreign capital and technology remained a distinguishing feature of export-oriented industrialization.

It would be equally misleading, however, to interpret the 1997 financial crisis as having reduced East Asia's governments to powerless pawns compelled to do the bidding of foreign creditors. The crisis was an important moment in an ongoing transitional process in which the United States – here we are referring both to the American state and to US-based financial and industrial capital – having lost the hegemony it once exercised, was nevertheless able to protect its interests by using the array of bilateral and multilateral levers at its disposal. The Clinton Administration derailed the Japanese proposal for an Asian monetary fund and at the same time refused to take prompt action of its own to assist East Asia's ailing economies.[263] It preferred to leave the initiative to the IMF, since the institution, by projecting the image of an independent multilateral agency committed to the principles of sound financial management, could spare the United States the widespread backlash which its policies were bound to provoke. Yet those policies, often inspired by or at least congenial to the US Treasury, clearly reflected the interests of US exporters, investors and fund managers.[264] Equally significant was Washington's relative success in securing the opening up of East Asian markets.

There were, however, limits to US power. True enough, Japan, its principal competitor in Asia Pacific, was experiencing economic and financial difficulties of its own, which, as we have seen, narrowed the scope for effective Japanese leadership. China attempted to demonstrate its Asian credentials by contributing $1 billion to the IMF rescue package (in addition to the $1 billion pledged by Hong Kong). It expressed its readiness to explore investment opportunities in Southeast Asia and, more importantly, pledged support for ASEAN currencies. Yet China too, preoccupied with its troubled state sector, manufacturing overcapacity and weakening demand, could offer only limited assistance. The economic and strategic implications of the complex triangular relationship between the United States, Japan and China will be the subject of detailed analysis in the next chapter. Suffice it to say that the United States, while in no danger of having its commanding position usurped in the immediate future by either China or Japan, could not itself remain indefinitely immune to the East Asian virus, should it remain unchecked. With Asian producers attempting to offset weak domestic demand by increased exports, greatly facilitated by weaker currencies, it would be difficult to bring the US current account deficit down to more acceptable proportions. If the East Asian crisis were to continue to spread or intensify, the long-term net effect might be slower economic growth and increased unemployment in the United States, compounded by downward pressure on corporate profits and a probable fall in stock prices. Adding to this pressure were the troubled circumstances of Japanese financial institutions. Having acquired large quantities of US treasury bonds during the preceding decade, they might now have to sell these bonds to cover their financial losses at home and in East Asia. The ensuing fall in US stock and bond prices could adversely affect US consumption, which could in turn accelerate the downward pressure on share prices and provoke a deflationary spiral both in the domestic and international markets. Large and dynamic though it was, the US economy could not insulate itself from the consequences of globalization.

By mid-1998 it was possible to discern tentative signs of economic recovery in much of East Asia. Most currencies had stabilized, and the Korean won and Indonesian rupiah appreciated by some 10 per cent during the course of 1999. Stockmarket prices were still well below their pre-June 1997 levels, but they had made a partial though uneven recovery, regaining considerable ground in Indonesia,

South Korea and Singapore. More instructive perhaps were the higher growth rates registered in 1999 (see Table 2.9), with GDP in the 12 months to June rising by 1.8 per cent in Indonesia, 3.5 per cent in Thailand, 4.1 per cent in Malaysia, 6.5 per cent in Taiwan, 6.7 per cent in Singapore and 9.8 per cent in South Korea. Hong Kong recorded by far the most disappointing result, with a growth rate of only 0.7 per cent. In industrial production, for the 12 months to September 1999 South Korea and Malaysia registered the best performances with growth rates of 18.1 per cent and 19.3 per cent respectively.[265] The expansion of economic activity was translated into higher export volumes, rising in several cases to 20–30 per cent during 1998, although measured in dollar terms exports tended to stagnate or even fall. None the less, partial export recovery combined with a marked decline in imports brought a significant improvement to the current - account balances of several economies, with corresponding increases in their foreign reserves.[266] South Korea's reserves rose to $50 billion in January 1999 from just $3 billion in November 1997. Similar improvements in Thailand prompted a government announcement to forgo the last $3.7 billion of the IMF's $17.2 billion assistance package.[267]

Table 2.9   Growth rate of GDP (% per annum)

Economy	1996	1997	1998	1999[a]
Newly industrializing economies	6.3	6.0	-1.6	5.2
Hong Kong	4.5	5.3	-5.1	-0.5
Korea, Rep. of	7.1	5.5	-5.8	8.0
Singapore	6.9	7.8	1.5	5.0
Taipei, China	5.7	6.8	4.8	5.5
People's Rep. of China	9.6	8.8	7.8	6.8
Southeast Asia	7.0	3.7	-7.4	2.6
Indonesia	7.8	4.9	-13.2	2.0
Malaysia	8.6	7.7	-7.5	2.0
Philippines	5.8	5.2	-0.5	3.0
Thailand	5.5	-1.3	-9.4	3.0
Vietnam	9.3	8.2	4.4	4.0

Note: [a]Based on data available up to 25 August 1999.
Source: *Asian Development Outlook 1999 Update*, p. 47.

East Asia's economies had, it seemed, weathered the worst of the storm, but medium- to long-term prospects remained uncertain. As of August 1999, Thailand's financial system was still afflicted by non-performing loans, representing some 47 per cent of total outstanding loans.[268] In South Korea, unemployment in early 1999 was officially estimated at 9 per cent of the workforce and still rising. Government plans for the restructuring of the financial and corporate sectors were not guaranteed success. It was not at all clear that the closure of some banks and the restructuring of others, whether through the injection of public funds or through recapitalization by way of mergers and foreign capital flows, would resolve the problem of non-performing loans. The proposed reform of the *chaebol*, in part by requiring them to lower their debt–equity ratios to 200 per cent, might have the beneficial effect of streamlining their core business lines, but it might also mean further concentration and monopolization of key sectors, including motor vehicles, semiconductors and electronics.[269] In 1998 the *chaebol*'s share of the economy had continued to grow, with the combined sales of the five largest accounting for 37 per cent of South Korea's gross output and 44 per cent of its total exports in 1997.[270] In Indonesia, the government, despite signs of economic improvement, including lower inflation rates and lower interest rates, was dependent on soft loans to cover its high and still rising budget deficits. As of mid-1999, it was still struggling with $65 billion in overdue corporate foreign debt. The Indonesian Bank Restructuring Agency had closed 68 banks, recapitalized nine banks, merged twelve banks into one, sold another, and placed four banks under supervision, but only 5 per cent of non-performing loans had thus far been effectively restructured.[271] The net cost to taxpayers of recapitalizing Indonesian banks was estimated at $67 billion, or 41 per cent of GDP, equivalent to more than four times the total amount of loans promised by the IMF.[272]

East Asian confidence in future economic recovery was gaining pace,[273] but neither the national basis for that recovery nor the regional and global framework which would sustain it had yet been clearly articulated.[274] Numerous voices both in Asia and beyond had, in response to recurring financial crises in Mexico, East Asia and Russia, advocated greater levels of international regulation. Referring to the instability engendered by the uncontrolled development of financial markets, French Prime Minister Lionel Jospin called for the operation of capital markets to be reformed, the world's financial architecture to be strengthened and the international monetary system to be rebuilt.[275] Ian Macfarlane, Governor of the Australian Reserve Bank, took issue with the western policy establishment for presenting inadequate financial infrastructure and governance as the root cause of the East Asian crisis, and argued for changes to the international financial system to prevent capital flight by raising the costs of currency speculation.[276] Within Asia, capital account liberalization came under increasingly critical scrutiny. China, it was argued, had escaped the direct impact of the crisis largely because its currency was non-convertible, thereby preventing speculative flows of money in or out of the country. Malaysia's decision to introduce capital controls in August 1998, in defiance of IMF prescriptions, was explicitly based on the Chinese model. A wide range of regulations, including the requirement that payments for imports and debt servicing be made through the central bank, effectively halted the buying of foreign exchange for speculative purposes. These controls were aimed specifically at short-term flows but did not cover foreign direct investment or the repatriation of interests, dividends and profits.[277] Though the IMF chose to stress Malaysia's willingness to restructure its financial system in much the same way as other East Asian economies, there was no concealing the significance of Malaysia's challenge to financial orthodoxy. The new interventionist mood was also evident in the purchase by Hong Kong's central bank of $15 billion of equities in a successful bid to fend off an attack by hedge funds on its exchange rate. Taiwan, for its part, closed the door on short-term capital inflows and virtually halted the trade in futures instruments, which it viewed as a threat to the New Taiwan dollar.

These diverse but limited attempts to challenge IMF orthodoxy hardly amounted to a concerted assault on neo-liberalism. East Asia's policy-makers simply lacked the institutional and financial muscle to mount such a campaign. On the other hand, the erratic behaviour of the hedge funds, the sudden offensive on 'crony capitalism' and the IMF's undisguised paternalism had provoked profound resentment among political and business elites, the media and even the wider public. The financial crisis had radicalized East Asian opinion by laying bare the wide gulf separating Asian ambitions and aspirations from dominant western – more specifically, American – economic and financial interests. It had at the very least called into question popular representations of globalization as the necessary path to economic success, and provoked more critical reflection on how East Asian societies would in future relate to the twin processes of global integration and global governance. The future of export-oriented industrialization and the direction of East Asia's developmental strategies would be shaped by a dynamic that was as much cultural and geopolitical as economic. It was therefore premature to assume that East Asian polities would readily adopt the Anglo-Saxon neo-liberal model or fully implement IMF policies and strictures.

The most probable outcome of the East Asian crisis was a subtle, gradual, at times ambiguous repositioning within the Asia-Pacific region and between the region and the rest of the world. Criticism of the relentless march of international economic liberalization was not in any case confined to East Asia. The OECD's abortive bid to secure swift passage of the Multilateral Agreement on Investment, the failure of the WTO meeting in Seattle in November 1999 to launch a new round of trade negotiations, and mounting international pressure for a more radical approach to Third World debt were themselves indicative of the emerging crisis of globalization. As we shall see in later chapters, most East Asian polities were finding it difficult to formulate economic policies capable of reconciling sharply diverging domestic and regional interests and perceptions. Success on this front would depend on the resilience of the state and the strength of civil society, but also on the pace and form of regional integration, itself closely linked to the prospects for regional leadership. China's and Japan's respective roles within the regional political economy were in that sense likely to exert a decisive influence over the still fluid relationship between states and markets, and perhaps more importantly on the future of neo-liberalism as the dominant form of economic organization. A critical element in this process would be the shifting balance of initiative between the national, regional and global tiers of governance in every major area of policy, be it energy, environment, trade or finance.

NOTES

1. Though it has become one of the buzz words of economic globalization, competitiveness remains an elusive concept, in part because of the changing patterns of international competition and the need to distinguish between the micro and macro applications of the term. See OECD, *Globalisation of Industrial Activities: Four Case Studies: Autoparts, Chemicals, Construction and Semiconductors*, Paris: OECD, 1992, pp. 11–25; James R. Markusen, *Productivity, Competitiveness, Trade Performance and Real Income: The Nexus among Four Concepts*, Ottawa: Canada Communication Group, 1992, pp. 5–9, 130– 38; D. Malana (ed.), *Critical Technologies and Economic Competitiveness*, NY: Nova Science, 1993, pp. 2–17; Franz Peter Lang and Renate Ehr (eds), *International Economic Integration*, Heidelberg; Physica-Verlag, 1995, pp. 23–48.

2. See B. Stuckey, 'The Division of Labour and the Dynamic of the World Economy', in Herman Muegge and Walter B. Stohr, *International Economic Restructuring and the Regional Community*, Aldershot, Hants: Avebury, 1987, pp. 13–29; Paul R. Krugman and Maurice Obstfeld, *International Economics: Theory and Policy*, Reading, Mass.: Addison-Wesley, 1997, pp. 14–32. For a more critical perspective, see F. Frobel, J. Heinrich and O. Kreye, *The New International Division of Labour*, Cambridge: Cambridge University Press, 1980.

3. See Gijsbert van Liemt (ed.), *Industry on the Move: Causes and Consequences of International Relocation in the Manufacturing Industry*, Geneva: ILO, 1992, pp. 136–48, 219–22, 309–13; Gary Gereffi and Miguel Koreniewicz (eds), *Commodity Chains and Global Capitalism*, Westport, Conn.: Greenwood Press, 1994, pp. 163–224; Kurt Hoffman and Raphael Kaplinsky, *Driving Force: The Global Restructuring of Technology, Labour and Investment in the Automobile and Components Industries*, Boulder Col.: Westview Press, 1998, pp. 287–93, 332–54; Ed Rhodes, David Wield and Noeleen Heyzer, *Clothing the World: First World Masters, Third World Labour*, Milton Keynes: Open University Press, 1983, pp. 9–19.

4. Immanuel Wallerstein, 'Semi-peripheral Countries and the Contemporary World Crisis', *Theory and State*, 3(4), Winter 1976, 461–84.

5. UNCTAD, *World Investment Report 1996: Investment, Trade and International Policy Agreements: Overview*, New York: United Nations, 1996, p. 13.

6. See Bob Jessop, 'Changing Forms and Functions of the State in an Era of Globalization and Regionalization', in Robert Delorme and Kurt Dopfar (eds), *The Political Economy of Diversity: Evolutionary Perspectives on Economic Order*, Aldershot, Hants: Edward Elgar, 1994, pp. 102–25; Tang Banuri and Martina Jagerhorn, 'Social Costs of Economic Restructuring: A Regional Overview', in Economic and Social Commission for Asia and the Pacific, *Social Costs of Economic Restructuring in Asia and the Pacific*, Bangkok, 1992; Nicholas Spulber, *Redefining the State: Privatization and Welfare Reform in Industrial and Transitional Economies*, New York: Cambridge University Press, 1997, pp. 162–88.

7. For a detailed analysis of these linkages in the Asia-Pacific context, see Alan Dupont, *The Environment and Security in Pacific Asia*, Adelphi Paper 319 (Oxford: Oxford University Press/International Institute for Strategic Studies, 1998); the implications of unregulated population flows, which are driven as much by economic as by political factors, are discussed by Myron Weiner, 'Security, Stability and International Migration', *International Security*, 17(3), Winter 1992–3, 91–126.

8. Figures based on R. Summers and A. Heston, 'The Penn World Table (Mark 5): An Expanded Set of International Comparisons 1950–88', *Quarterly Journal of Economics*, 106, 1991, 327–68.

9. *Economic Bulletin for Asia and the Pacific*, XLIII(2), December 1992, Table 2, p. 47.

10. Ross Garnaut, *Open Regionalism and Trade Liberalization: An Asia-Pacific Contribution to the World Trade System*, Singapore: Institute of Southeast Asian Studies (ISEAS), 1996, p. 122.

11. See Chia Siow Yue and Joseph L. H. Tan (eds), *ASEAN and EU: Forging New Linkages and Strategic Alliances*, Singapore: Institute of Southeast Asian Studies, 1997, p. 138, Table 7.1.

12. Cited in Jean-Pierre Lehmann, 'L'économie japonaise en mutation: perspectives et implications pour l'économie mondiale', *Politique étrangère*, 57(3), Autumn 1992, 529.

13. Bank of Japan, International Department, *Balance of Payments Monthly*, Tokyo: Bank of Japan, January and December 1991, pp. 7–8, 29–30.

14. See Philip J. Meeks, 'Japan and Global Economic Hegemony', in Tsuneo Akaha and Frank Langdon (eds), *Japan in the Posthegemonic World*, Boulder, Col.: Lynne Rienner, 1993, pp. 48–58.

15. Rob Steven, *Japan and the New World Order: Global Investments, Trade and Finance*, London: Macmillan, 1996, p. 85, Table 3.5.

16. See Edward J. Lincoln, 'Japanese Trade and Investment Issues', in Danny Unger and Paul Blackburn (eds), *Japan's Emerging Global Role*, Boulder, Col.: Lynne Rienner, 1993, pp. 136, 151.

17. Steven, *Japan and the New World Order*, p. 79.

18. *Japan's Official Development Assistance: Summary 1997*, Tokyo: Japan Ministry of Foreign Affairs, 1997, p. 3.

19. Ibid., p. 43.

20. Steven, *Japan and the New World Order*, p. 9.

21. Kit G. Machado, 'Japanese Foreign Direct Investment in East Asia: The Expanding Division of Labour and the Future of Regionalism', in Steve Chan (ed.), *Foreign Direct Investment in a Changing Global Political Economy*, London: Macmillan, 1996, p. 44.

22. These two phases are succinctly outlined in Chung-in Moon, 'Managing Regional Challenges: Japan, the East Asian NICs and New Patterns of Economic Rivalry', *Pacific Focus*, VI(2), Fall 1991, 28–30.

23.   The argument developed here draws extensively on the analysis of Japanese options and strategies offered by Steven, *Japan and the New World Order*, pp. 41–69.

24.   ESCAP, *Economic and Social Survey of Asia and the Pacific 1992*, New York: UN, 1993, p. 8.

25.   *OECD Economic Outlook*, 59, June 1996, A50.

26.   ESCAP, *Economic and Social Survey of Asia and the Pacific 1992*, p. 19; see also Machado, 'Japanese Foreign Direct Investment in Asia', p. 44.

27.   ESCAP, *Economic and Social Survey and the Pacific 1992*, p. 19.

28.   Machado, 'Japanese Foreign Direct Investment in Asia', p. 44.

29.   IMF, *Direction of Trade Statistics Yearbook 1998*, Washington, DC: International Monetary Fund, 1998, p. 272.

30.   See John Ravenhill, 'The Japan Problem in Pacific Trade', in R. Higgott, R. Leaver and J. Ravenhill (eds), *Pacific Economic Relations in the 1990s: Cooperation or Conflict?*, Sydney: Allen &Unwin, 1993, p. 127, Table 6.10.

31.   Chung-in Moon, 'Managing Regional Challenges', pp. 25–6.

32.   *Far Eastern Economic Review* (hereafter referred to as *FEER*), 3 May 1990, 48.

33.   IMF, *Direction of Trade Statistics Yearbook 1991*, Washington, DC: International Monetary Fund, 1991, pp. 158–59.

34.   Ruperto P. Alonzo, 'Japan's Economic Impact on ASEAN Countries', *Indonesia Quarterly*, XV(3), July 1987, 476.

35.   See Sophie Boisseau du Rocher, 'Le Japan et l'Asie du Sud-Est: un nouveau partenariat', *Politique étrangère*, 57(3), Autumn 1992, 542–3.

36.   Heizo Takenaka, 'The Japanese Economy and Pacific Development', in Mohamed Ariff (ed.), *The Pacific Economy: Growth and External Stability*, Sydney: Allen & Unwin, 1991, p. 63.

37.   IMF, *Direction of Trade Statistics 1993*, pp. 456–7.

38.   See *Economic Bulletin of Asia and the Pacific*, XLIII(2), December 1992, 36.

39.   Cited in Chung-in Moon, 'Managing Regional Challenges', p. 37.

40.   See Dilip K. Das, *The Yen Appreciation and the International Economy*, New York: New York University Press, 1993, p. 60.

41.   Steven, *Japan and the New World Order*, p. 168.

42.   *Economic Bulletin of Asia and the Pacific,* December 1992, 39.

43.   These figures are based on Tables 3.12 and 3.13 in Steven, *Japan and the New World Order*, pp. 96–7.

44.   See Tomomitsu Oba, 'Japan's Role in East Asian Investment and Finance', *Japan Review of International Affairs*, 9(3), Summer 1995, 249; also Machado, 'Japanese Foreign Direct Investment in Asia', p. 44.

45.   *FEER*, 29 March 1990, 59.

46.   *Japan's Official Development Assistance Summary 1997,* pp. 42–3.

47.   For a more detailed exposition of Japan's ODA policy, see Danny Unger, 'Japan's Capital Exports: Molding East Asia', in Unger and Blackburn (eds), *Japan's Emerging Role*, pp. 156–66; also Bruce M. Koppel and Robert M. Orr Jr (eds), *Japan's Foreign Aid: Power and Policy in a New Era*, Boulder, Col.: Westview Press, 1993; Dennis T. Yasutomo, 'Why Aid? Japan as an Aid Great Power', *Pacific Affairs*, 62, Winter 1990, 1–40.

48.   *Japan's ODA Summary 1997*, pp. 14–6.

49.   See Steven Hook and Guang Zhang, 'Japan's Aid Policy since the Cold War: Rhetoric and Reality', *Asian Survey,* 38(11), November 1998, 1051–66.

50.   Chung-in Moon, 'Managing Regional Challenges', p. 31.

51. See Lee Poh-Ping, 'Japan and the Asia-Pacific Region: A Southeast Asian Perspective', in C. Garby and M.B. Bullock (eds), *Japan: A New Kind of Superpower?*, Baltimore, Md.: Johns Hopkins University Press, 1994, pp. 134–5.

52. The classical exposition of this view is provided by Chalmers Johnson, *MITI and the Japanese Miracle: The Growth of Industrial Policy 1925–1975,* Stanford Cal.: Stanford University Press, 1992, although the author's position has become increasingly nuanced (see Chalmers Johnson, 'MITI, MPT and the Telecom Wars: How Japan Makes Policy for High Technology', in Chalmers Johnson, Laura D'Andrea Tyson and John Zysman (eds), *Politics and Productivity: The Real Story Why Japan Works*, Madison: University of Wisconsin Press, 1989).

53. See Henry Wai-chung Yeung, 'State Intervention and Neoliberalism in the Globalizing World Economy: Lessons from Singapore's Regionalization Programme', *Pacific Review*, 13(1), 2000, 133–62.

54. See Walter Hatch and Kozo Yamamura, *Asia in Japan's Embrace: Building a Regional Production Alliance,* Cambridge: Cambridge University Press, 1996, p. 116; also Richard J. Samuels, *The Business of the Japanese State: Energy Markets in Comparative and Historical Perspective*, Ithaca, N.Y.: Cornell University Press, 1987, p. 9.

55. Hatch and Yamamura, *Asia in Japan's Embrace*, p. 119.

56. The tendency towards international production networks in the globalizing economy is analysed by Karl P. Sauvant, 'International Trade and Investment Trends', keynote address to the First Annual Australian Conference on International Trade, Education and Research, University of Melbourne, 5–6 December 1996.

57. UNCTAD, *World Investment Report 1995: Transnational Corporations and Competitiveness – Overview*, New York: United Nations, 1995, p. 29.

58. Machado, 'Japanese FDI in East Asia', pp. 44–5.

59. For a fuller account of the structure and mode of operation of the *keiretsu* networks and their relationship to regional or 'zone strategies' see Steven, *Japan and the New World Order*, pp. 80–3, 171–9; Hatch and Yamamura, *Asia in Japan's Embrace*, pp. 62–72; Michael Gerlach, 'Twilight of the Keiretsu? A Critical Assessment', *Journal of Japanese Studies*, 18(1), Winter 1992, 79–118.

60. *FEER*, 3 June 1993, 48.

61. Hatch and Yamamura, *Asia in Japan's Embrace*, p. 185.

62. Ibid, p. 188.

63. Steven, *Japan and the New World Order*, p. 60.

64. *OECD Economic* Outlook, June 1996, p. A.25; *Asia Financial Markets, Second Quarter 1999*, Tokyo: J.P. Morgan Economic Research, 30 April 1999, p. 30.

65. Cited in Chung-in Moon and Sang-young Rhyu, 'The State, Structural Rigidity and the End of Asian Capitalism: A Comparative Study of Japan and South Korea', paper presented at the Conference *From Miracle to Meltdown: The End of Asian Capitalism*, Murdoch University, Fremantle, Australia, 20–22 August 1999, pp. 3–4.

66. *OECD Economic Outlook,* June 1996, p. A4.

67. *FEER*, 2 September 1998, 37.

68. Chung-in Moon and Sang-young Rhyu, 'The State, Structural Rigidity and the End of Asian Capitalism', p. 3.

69. *1998 APEC Economic Outlook: Economic Trends and Prospects in the APEC Region*, Singapore: APEC Secretariat, 1998, p. 161; J.P. Morgan, *Asian Financial Markets*, 30 April 1999, p. 31.

70. Moon and Rhyu, 'The State, Structural Rigidity, and the End of Asian Capitalism', pp. 7–16.

71. Richard Katz, *Japan: The System that Soured. The Rise and Fall of the Japanese Economic Miracle,* New York: M.E. Sharpe, 1998, pp. 55–74, 197–217.

72. See *The Economist*, 15 April 2000, p. 117.

73. Chester Dawson, 'Buying Again', *FEER*, 2 September 1999, 36–8.

74. D. Sanger, 'US Intervenes in Currency Markets to Support the Yen', *New York Times*, 18 June 1998; *The Age* (Melbourne), 1 December 1999, p. 1 (Business).

75. See Peter Drysdale, Toshi Naito, Ray Trewin and Dominic Wilson, *The Changing Climate for Foreign Direct Investment into Japan*, Pacific Economic Paper No. 293, Australian Japan Research Centre, Australian National University, Canberra, 1999.

76. Garnaut, *Open Regionalism and Trade Liberalization*, p. 122.

77. A. Young, 'Lessons from the East Asian NICs: A Contrarian View', *European Economic Review*, 38, 1994, 964–73.

78. These figures, which cover South Korea, Taiwan, Hong Kong, Singapore, Indonesia, Malaysia and Thailand, are based on B. Bosworth, S.M. Collens and Yu-chin Chen, 'Accounting for Differences in Economy Growth', paper presented to the Conference on *Structural Adjustment Policies in the 1990s: Experience and Prospects*, Institute of Developing Economics, 5–6 November 1995.

79. Lim Chong-Yah, 'Taiwan's Economic Miracle: A Singaporean Perspective', in Seiji Naya and Akira Takayama (eds), *Economic Development in East and Southeast Asia: Essays in Honor of Professor Shinichi Ichimura*, Singapore: ISEAS, 1990, p. 46; *Asia 1996 Yearbook*, p. 14.

80. Ibid., p. 39; *Industry of Free China*, April 1991.

81. Tu Jenn-Rwa, 'Taiwan: A Solid Manufacturing Base and Emerging Regional Sources of Investment', in Wendy Dobson and Chia Siow Yue (eds), *Multinationals and East Asian Integration*, Singapore: ISEAS, 1997, p. 66.

82. World Bank, *World Development Report 1997*, New York: Oxford University Press, 1997, pp. 242–3.

83. Tu Jenn-Rwa, 'Taiwan: A Solid Manufacturing Base', p. 68, Table 3.3.

84. Ibid., pp. 69–71, Tables 3.4, 3.5; the author argues that official figures seriously underestimate FDI flows to Southeast Asia: if account were taken of investments for which approval was not required, the total volume would be considerably (perhaps several times) higher.

85. *Korea to the Year 2000: Implications for Australia*, Report by the Australian National Korean Studies Centre, Canberra: Department of Foreign Affairs and Trade, 1992, p. 127, Table 1.1; Heather Smith, ' "Western" vs "Asian" Capitalism', p. 33, Table 3(b); Chia Siow Yue and Joseph L.H. Tan (eds), *ASEAN and EU: Forging New Linkages and Strategic Alliances*, Singapore: ISEAS, 1997, p. 138, Table 7.1.

86. *Korea to the Year 2000*, p. 20.

87. Bank of Korea, *Monthly Statistical Bulletin*, April 1991.

88. ESCAP, *Economic and Social Survey of Asia and the Pacific 1995*, p. 70, Table lll.1.

89. These figures and those relating to the current account balance are drawn from *Asia 1986 Yearbook*, pp. 6–9 ; *Asia 1990 Yearbook*, pp. 6–9; *Asia 1995 Yearbook*, pp. 14–7; *Asia 1997 Yearbook*, pp. 14–9.

90. Yue and Tan (eds), *ASEAN & EU*, p. 63, Table 4.2.

91. *The Economist*, 1 March 1997, 23.

92. *Asia 1997 Yearbook*, p. 15.

93. *Asia 1995 Yearbook*, p. 15.

94. Chia Siow Yue, 'Singapore: Advanced Production Base and Smart Hub of the Electronics Industry', in Dobson and Chia (eds), *Multinationals and East Asian Integration*, p. 35, Table 2.1.

95. Ibid., p. 38.
96. These figures are based on data provided by Steven, *Japan and the New World Order*, p. 252, Table 7.2.
97. *Asia 1986 Yearbook*, p. 8; *Asia 1990 Yearbook*, p. 8; *Asia Yearbook 1997*, p. 14.
98. *The Economist*, March 1997, 23.
99. *Hong Kong: The Transfer of Sovereignty,* report of the Joint Standing Committee on Foreign Affairs, Defence and Trade, Australian Parliament, May 1997, p. 85.
100. BIS Schrapnel, *East Economic Outlook*; 1997–2007, p. 41.
101. Edward K.Y. Chen and Teresa Y.C. Wong, 'Hong Kong: Foreign Direct Investment and Trade Linkages in Manufacturing', in Dobson and Chia (eds), *Multinationals and East Asian Integration*, p. 84.
102. See Lawrence B. Krause, 'Change in the International System: The Pacific Basin', *Annals, AAPSS*, no. 505, September 1989, p. 107, Table 2.
103. *Asia 1994 Yearbook*, p. 14; *Asia 1997 Yearbook*, p. 15.
104. See Chia Siow Yue, 'Trade, Foreign Direct Investment and Economic Development of Southeast Asia', *Pacific Review,* 12(2), 1999, 251.
105. Malcolm Dowling, 'Structural Change and Economic Development in Developing Asia in the 1990s', in Naya and Takayama (eds), *Economic Development in East and Southeast Asia*, p. 4.
106. Shujiro Urata, 'Obstacles to Further Growth in East Asia and Japan's Economic Assistance', *Japan Review of International Affairs,* 7(4), Fall 1993, 302.
107. *ASEAN Statistical Indicators*, Singapore: ISEAS, 1997, p. 35.
108. Ibid, p. 25.
109. Ibid., p. 28.
110. Mari Pangestu, 'Indonesia: Trade and Foreign Investment Linkages', in Dobson and Chia (eds), *Multinationals and East Asian Integration*, p. 195.
111. *ASEAN Statistical Indicators*, p. 65.
112. See Chia Siow Yue, 'Trade, Foreign Direct Investment and Economic Development of Southeast Asia', p. 259.
113. For a more detailed account, see Anthony Smith, 'Indonesia's Economy: Conglomerates, the Soeharto Family and Free Trade', *New Zealand International Review*, XXII(1), January/February 1998, 9–13; also Michael Backman, *Asian Eclipse: Exposing the Dark Side of Business in Asia,* Singapore, John Wiley & Sons (Asia) Pte Ltd, 1999, 288–99.
114. Prema-chandra Athukorala, 'Poverty, Ethnicity and Economics: Malaysia's Challenges and Achievements', *Asia Pacific Magazine*, 8, 1997, 7–12; Asian Development Bank, *Asian Development Outlook 1997* and *1998,* New York: Oxford University Press, 1997, p. 88.
115. Garnaut, *Open Regionalism*, p. 136; Chia Siow Yue, 'Trade, Foreign Direct Investment and Development of Southeast Asia', p. 259.
116. World Bank, *World Development* Report, 1986; *Asia 1996 Yearbook,* p. 14; Chia Siow Yue, 'Trade, Foreign Direct Investment and Development of Southeast Asia', p. 259.
117. *Asia 1997 Yearbook,* p. 15.
118. Garnaut, *Open Regionalism*, p. 136.
119. Edward K.Y. Chen, 'Dynamic Asian Economies: Retrospect and Prospect', in Chan Heng Chee (ed.), *The New Asia-Pacific Order,* Singapore: ISEAS, 1997, p. 6.
120. See Narongchai Akrasanee and Somsak Tambunlertchai, 'Transition from Import Substitution to Export Expansion: The Thai Experience', in Naya and Takayama (eds), *Economic Development in East and Southeast Asia*, pp. 113–4.

121. P.J. Lloyd and Hisako Toguchi, 'East Asian Export Competitiveness: New Measures and Policy Implications', Asian Business Centre, Institute of Applied Economic and Social Research, University of Melbourne, Working Paper Series, 6/96, September 1996, p. 8.

122. *Economic Bulletin for Asia and the Pacific*, December 1992, p. 33.

123. Ibid.

124. Garnaut, *Open Regionalism*, p. 126, Table 7.1.

125. East Asia Analytical Unit, Department of Foreign Affairs and Trade, *Growth Triangles of Southeast Asia*, Canberra, 1995, p. 21, Table 2.4.

126. Clark and Chan, 'Lessons from East Asia', p. 207.

127. See, for example, Bela Balassa, *The Newly Industrializing Economies in the World Economy*, New York: Pergamon Press, 1981; Anne O. Krueger, *Alternative Trade Strategies and Employment: Synthesis and Conclusions*, Chicago: Chicago University Press, 1983; Louis Turner and Neil McMullen, *The Newly Industrializing Countries: Trade and Investment*, London: George Allen and Unwin, 1982.

128. See Helen Hughes, 'Why Have East Asian Countries Led Economic Development?', *Economic Record*, 71(212), March 1995, 88–104.

129. Roy Hofheinz, Jr and Kent Calder, *The Eastasia Edge*, New York: Basic Books, 1982, pp. 248–9.

130. Johnson, *MITI and the Japanese Miracle*, pp. 157–97.

131. See C. Frederic Deyo (ed.), *The Political Economy of New Asia Industrialism*, Ithaca, N.Y.: Cornell University Press, 1987.

132. Krause, 'Changes in the International System', pp. 106–8.

133. Ibid., pp. 109–13.

134. Clark and Chan, 'Lessons from East Asia', p. 207.

135. See Hung-Chao Tai, 'The Oriental Alternative: A Hypothesis on East Asian Culture and Autonomy', *Issues and Studies*, 25, March 1989, 10–36.

136. See Herman Kahn, *World Economic Development: 1979 and Beyond*, London: Croom Helm, 1979.

137. Chen, 'Dynamic Asian Economies', p. 7.

138. Ibid., pp. 8–9.

139. Garnaut, *Open Regionalism*, p. 131.

140. See Fred Robins, 'Taiwan's Economic Success', in Kyoko Sheridan, *Emerging Economic Systems in Asia: A Political and Economic Survey*, Sydney: Allen & Unwin, 1998, pp. 49–50.

141. Garnaut, *Open Regionalism*, p. 12.

142. See Dilip K. Das, *The Yen Appreciation and the International Economy*, New York: New York University Press, 1993, p. 182.

143. Hadi Soesastro, 'Economic Development and Security in the Asia Pacific Context', *Indonesian Quarterly*, 25(1), 1997, 63–4.

144. Toru Nakakita, 'The Takeoff of the East Asian Economic Sphere', *Japan Review of International Affairs*, 5(1), Spring/Summer 1991, 72.

145. One of the earliest versions of the model was put forward by K. Akamatsu in the 1930s. See 'A Historical Pattern of Economic Growth in Developing Countries', *Developing Economies*, 1, March–August 1962; also K.S Jomo et al., *Southeast Asia's Misunderstood Miracle: Industrial Policy and Economic Development in Thailand, Malaysia and Indonesia*, Boulder, Col.: Westview Press, 1997, pp. 27–55.

146. For this simple exposition of the model, see *Economic Bulletin for Asia and the Pacific*, December 1992, 41.

147. Edward K.Y. Chen and C.H. Kwan, 'The Emergence of Subregional Economic Zones in Asia', in Edward K.Y. Chen and C.H. Kwan (eds), *Asia's Borderless Economy: The Emergence of Subregional Economic Zones*, Sydney: Allen & Unwin, 1997, p. 6.

148. The evolution of these two industries is described in UNCTAD, *World Investment Report 1995*, pp. 246–53, and based in part on a study by Terutomo Ozawa, 'The Flying Geese Paradigm of Tandem Growth: TNCs' Involvement and Agglomeration Economies in Asia's Industrial Dynamism', paper presented at the AIB Annual Meeting in Seoul, 15–18 November 1995.

149. For a discussion of 'flexibility' as a key feature of East Asian development, see Clark and Chan, 'Lessons from East Asia', p. 208.

150. See Norma Harrison and Lambros Karavis, 'The Impact of Globalization on Operations in the Asia-Pacific Region', in *Asia Pacific International Business: Proceedings of the Academy of International Business–Southeast Asia Regional Conference*, 20–23 June 1995, Murdoch University, pp. 15–6.

151. Chen, 'Dynamic Asian Economies', pp. 17–9.

152. See Martin Hart-Landsberg and Paul Burkett, 'Contradictions of Capitalist Industrialisation in East Asia: A Critique of "Flying Geese" Theories of Development', *Economic Geography*, 47(2), 1998, 97.

153. M. Bernard and J. Ravenhill, 'Beyond Product Cycles and Flying Geese: Regionalisation, Hierarchy, and the Industralisation of East Asia', *World Politics*, 47(2), January 1995, 171–209.

154. Hart-Lansberg and Burkett, 'Contradictions of Capitalist Industrialization in East Asia', p. 99.

155. Smith, ' "Western" versus "Asian" Capitalism', pp. 32–3, Table 3(a), 3(b).

156. Cited in Yasheng Huang, 'China's Economic Development: Implications for Its Political and Security Roles', *Adelphi Paper 275*, March 1993, 54.

157. *Asia 1997 Yearbook*, p. 14.

158. *1998 APEC Economic Outlook*, p. 141.

159. Cited in Nicholas R. Lardy, 'China's Economic Growth', *Pacific Review*, 12(2), 1999, 164.

160. World Bank, *China 2020: Development Challenges in the New Century*, Washington D.C.: World Bank, 1997, p. 3.

161. Angus Maddeson, *Chinese Economic Performance in the Long Run*, Paris: OECD, 1998, p. 151.

162. Ibid., pp. 85, 87.

163. Ibid., p. 89.

164. *China 2020*, p. 128.

165. UN, *Economic and Social Survey of Asia and the Pacific 1995*, p. 60.

166. These figures are cited by Robert F. Ash, 'Mainland China's Emerging Role in the World Economy: Implications and Future Prospects', in *Issues and Studies*, 31(1), January 1995, 7.

167. UN, *Economic and Social Survey of Asia and the Pacific 1992*, p. 17; UN, *World Investment Report 1995*, p. 54.

168. Allen Y. Tso, 'Foreign Direct Investment and China's Economic Development', *Issues and Studies*, 34(2), February 1998, 3.

169. The figures are drawn form *Asian Wall Street Journal*, 7–8 April 1995, and cited in Jawono Sudarsono, 'China as an Economic Power: A Regional View', in Chan (ed.), *The New Asia-Pacific Order*, p. 97.

170. Tso, 'FDI and China's Economic Development', p. 28.

171. *Beijing Review*, 6 December 1999, p. 22.

172. See Zhang Zhaoyong and Chen Kang, 'China: A Rapidly Emerging Light Manufacturing Base in Guangdong Province', in Dobson and Yue (eds), *Multinationals and East Asian Integration*, p. 154.
173. *Asia 1997 Yearbook*, p. 14.
174. *China 2020*, p. 129.
175. This classification is developed at some length in Y.Y. Kuch, 'Foreign Investment and Economic Change in China', *China Quarterly*, 131, September 1992, 637–90.
176. Zhang and Chen, 'China: A Rapidly Emerging Light-Manufacturing Base in Guangdong Province', p. 153.
177. These figures are cited in Naisbitt, *Megatrends Asia*, p. 18.
178. See Ash, 'Mainland China's Emerging Role', p. 8.
179. See Chu-tien Hu, 'Challenges to Economic Co-operation in the Asia-Pacific Region', *Issues and Studies*, 35(1), January–February 1999, 135. Here trade dependence is defined as the ratio of one country's exports to imports from another country over the first country's total exports and imports.
180. Maria Hsia Chang, 'Greater China and the Chinese Global Tribe', *Asian Survey*, 35(10), October 1995, 962.
181. Robert F. Ash and Y.Y. Kuch, 'Economic Integration within Greater China', *China Quarterly*, 136, December 1993, 713.
182. Chang, 'Greater China', pp. 960–61.
183. Naisbitt, *Megatrends Asia*, pp. 19–20.
184. Chung-Tong Wu, 'Globalization of the Chinese Countryside', in Peter J. Rimmer (ed.), *Pacific Rim Development: Integration and Globalization in the Asia-Pacific Economy*, Sydney: Allen & Unwin, 1997, p. 59, Table 4.1, based on data from *Statistical Yearbook of China* – various years.
185. World Bank, *Global Economic Prospects and the Developing Countries*, April 1993, pp. 66–8.
186. See *The Economist*, 19 April 1997, 72–3.
187. Notwithstanding this decline, Japan continued to be a major source of China's capital-intensive manufactures (estimated at 64.4 per cent in 1989). See *Economic Bulletin for Asia and the Pacific*, December 1992, 33.
188. During the early and mid-1990s considerable discrepancies existed between Chinese and US official estimates of the Sino–US balance of trade. Whereas PRC figures for 1992 suggested a US trade deficit of $0.3 billion, the comparable US figure placed the deficit at $16.7 billion. A more reliable estimate is provided by an independent study which indicates a deficit of $12.6 billion (see Nicholas R. Lardy, *China in the World Economy*, Washington, D.C.: Institute for International Economics, 1994, p. 76).
189. UNCTAD, *World Investment Report 1995*, pp. 56–7.
190. See Renhong Wu, 'China's Macroeconomy: Review and Perspective', *Journal of Contemporary China*, 7(19), 455.
191. See Yolanda Fernandez Lommen and Plamen Tonchev, *China in East Asia: From Isolation to a Regional Superpower Status*, Athens: Institute of International Economic Relations, November 1998; *The Economist*, 24 October 1998, 21; *FEER*, 9 September 1999, 74.
192. *FEER*, 27 April 2000, p. 24.
193. See Kent Calder, 'Asia's Empty Tank', *Foreign Affairs*, 75(2), March/April 1996, 56.
194. Changhua Wu, 'The Price of Growth', *Bulletin of the Atomic Scientists*, 55(5), September/October 1999, 58–66.
195. *China 2020*, p. 71.

196. These figures are cited in Ha-Joan Chang, 'South Korea: Anatomy of a Crisis', *Current History*, 97(623), December 1998, 437.

197. Paul Krugman, 'The Myth of the Asian Miracle', *Foreign Affairs*, 73(6), November–December 1994, 62–78.

198. *The Economist,* 1 March 1998, 24.

199. Twu Jaw-Yann, 'The Yen and East Asia's Currency Turmoil', *Japan Echo*, 24(5), December 1995, 12.

200. *The Economist*, 6 September 1997, 70.

201. See G.P. Corsetti, P. Pesenti and N. Roubini, 'What Caused the Asian Currency and Financial Crisis?', Cambridge, Mass.: National Bureau of Economic Research, 1998.

202. See Nicola Ballard (with Walden Bello and Kamal Malhotra), 'Taming the Tigers: The IMF and the Asian Crisis', unpublished paper, March 1998, p. 3.

203. See Walden Bello, 'Addicted to Capital: The Ten-year High and Present-day Withdrawal Trauma of Southeast Asia's Economies', *Focus Papers* (published by Focus on the Global South), November 1997, pp. 14, 26.

204. Leif Roderick Rosenberg, 'Southeast Asia's Currency Crisis: A Diagnosis and Prescription', *Contemporary Southeast Asia*, 19(3), December 1997, 229.

205. *The Economist,* 24 January 1998, 72.

206. *The Economist,* 30 April 1998, 12

207. *The Economist,* 15 November 1997, 20.

208. Chia and Tan (eds), *ASEAN and EU*, p. 72.

209. *ASEAN Statistical Indicators*, p. 60.

210. These figures are based on BIS calculations (reproduced in *The Economist*, 4 April 1998, 30).

211. Cited in Bello, 'Addicted to Capital', p. 19.

212. *The Age*, 7 February 1998, 22.

213. Chang, 'South Korea: Anatomy of a Crisis', p. 438.

214. See Yoshitomi Masaru, 'The Asian Crisis and the IMF's Medicine', *Japan Echo*, 25(2), April 1998.

215. For a detailed outline of the psychology of hedge fund management, see Jeffrey Winters, 'The Financial Crisis in Southeast Asia", paper presented to the Conference 'From Miracle to Meltdown: The End of Asian Capitalism', Murdoch University, August 1998, pp. 12–16.

216. Paul Krugman, 'What Happened to Asia?', on Paul Krugman's website at http://www.mit.edu/Krugman/WWW?DISINTER.html.

217. World Bank, *East Asia: The Road to Recovery*, Washington, D.C.: World Bank, 1998, p. 10.

218. *Asian Development Outlook 1997 and 1998*, pp. 79, 88, 102.

219. *The Economist*, 9 August 1997, 23.

220. IMF, *Direction of Trade Statistics Yearbook 1998*, p. 280.

221. See Steven Radelet and Jeffrey Sacks, 'What Have We Learned, So Far, from the Asian Financial Crisis?', 4 January 1989, 6.

222. Krugman, 'The Myth of the Asian Miracle', pp. 69–72, 76–8.

223. These arguments are conveniently summarized in 'The Asian Miracle: Is It Over?', *The Economist*, 1 March 1997, 23–5; for a more detailed analysis see 'Asian Economic Miracle', *UBS International Finance*, Issue 29, Autumn 1996.

224. Kamal Malhotra, 'East and Southeast Asia Revisited: Miracles, Myths and Mirages', *Focus Papers*, November 1997, p. 21.

225. See Urata, 'Obstacles to Further Growth', pp. 304–8.

226. See 'The Flexible Tiger, *The Economist*, 3 January 1998, 73.
227. The study's conclusions were reported in *FEER*, 30 April 1998, 13.
228. *The Economist*, 29 November 1997, 23.
229. *The Economist*, 24 January 1998, 75.
230. Rosenberger, 'Southeast Asia's Currency Crisis', p. 230.
231. The neo-liberal argument is developed at some length by Ku-Hyun Jung, 'Foreign Direct Investment and Corporate Restructuring in East-Asia', *Pacific Review*, 12(2), 1999, 271–90.
232. For a fascinating insight into the thinking of senior corporate executives, see 'How the Experts See It', *FEER*, 8 January 1998, 38–43.
233. *The Australian*, 13 January 1998, 1
234. *East Asia: The Road to Recovery*, p. 27.
235. BBC, *SWB*, 4 December 1997, FE/3093 B/3-4.
236. *The Australian*, 2 March 1998, 6.
237. *The Economist*, 11 October 1997, 97.
238. Cited in Twu Jaw-Yann, 'The Yen and East Asia's Currency Turmoil', p. 14.
239. *The Economist*, 11 October 1997, 97.
240. Letter by Japanese Foreign Affairs Ministry official published in *The Age*, 31 March 1998, 12.
241. See speech by the Malaysian Prime Minister to the Fifth Symposium of the Institute for International Monetary Affairs, Tokyo, 2 June 1998 (http://www.kln.gov.my /KLN/ statemen.nsf/146dd58e48c825661a002310f02?OpenDocument).
242. *FEER*, 20 June 1998, 85.
243. *Business Asia*, 18 January 1999, 16. This was followed in May 1999 with a further pledge of up to $17 billion to guarantee Asian government bonds, thereby reducing the risk of bad loans and attracting investors back to Asia (*Business Asia*, 31 May 1999, 22).
244. *FEER*, 31 December 1998/7 January 1999, 12–3.
245. *Beyond the Asian Financial Crisis*, A Special Report of the United States Institute of Peace, Washington, D.C.: April 1998, p. 5.
246. IMF, *1997 Annual Report*, International Monetary Fund, 1997, pp. 91–2, 58–60.
247. Ibid., pp. 80–1.
248. *The Economist*, 9 August 1997, 21–3.
249. See *Indonesia Letter of Intent*, addressed to IMF Director, Michael Camdessus, 31 October 1997 (http://www.imf.org/external/np/loi/103197.HTM), which was followed during 1998–99 by a succession of similar letters and memoranda setting out the Indonesian government's intended compliance with the IMF's economic and financial prescriptions.
250. BBC, *SWB*, 3 March 1998, FE/3165 S2/3.
251. See *FEER*, 16 April 1998, 18–20, 59; also David Bourchier, 'Suharto vs the IMF', *Asia View*, 8(1), April 1998, 1, 4.
252. Ibrahim Wade, 'Les remèdes absurdes de FMI', *Le Monde Diplomatique*, February 1998, 18.
253. *The Economist*, 25 April 1998, 79.
254. *The Economist*, 22 January 2000, 28.
255. Wade, 'The Asian Crisis and the Global Economy', p. 366.
256. *The Age* (Melbourne), 30 September 1998, 14.
257. *The Australian*, 10 November 1998, 8.
258. For a version of the IMF's defence of its policies, see Stanley Fischer, 'Lessons from a Crisis', *The Economist*, 3 October 1998, 19–23.
259. *FEER*, 30 April 1998, 11.

260. *FEER*, 18 December 1997, 15.

261. *New Straits Times* (hereafter referred to as *NST*), 17 January 1998, 11.

262. See J. Hamann and M. Schulze-Ghattas, 'Structural Reforms', in T. Lane *et al.*, *IMF-Supported Programmes in Indonesia, Korea and Thailand: A Preliminary Assessment*, IMF Occasional Papers No. 178, International Monetary Fund, 1999.

263. It was only late in the piece and after repeated criticisms by Southeast Asian governments that the Clinton Administration offered Thai Prime Minister Chuan Leekpai, during his visit to Washington in March 1998, up to $1 billion in Export–Import Bank credits and agreed to the deferment of a major defence contract for the purchase of F/A-18s.

264. Max Conden, *The Asian Crisis: Is There a Way Out?*, Singapore: ISEAS, pp. 50–51. For a clear statement of US attitudes and priorities, see Deputy Treasury Secretary Lawrence Summers, 'Policy Challenges for Asia in 1999', remarks before the American Chamber of Commerce, Seoul, 25 February 1999.

265. *The Economist*, 13 November 1999, 122.

266. *The Economist*, 29 August 1998, 70.

267. *FEER*, 4 November 1999, 11.

268. *The Economist*, 9 October 1999, 95.

269. Heather Smith, 'Structural Reform and Macroeconomic Policy in Korea', *APEC Economies Newsletter*, 3(2), February 1999; see also Danny M. Leipziger, 'Global Standards and Korea's Economic Reforms', *Journal International and Area Studies*, 6(2), 1999, 1–18.

270. *The Economist*, 14 November 1998, 69–70.

271. *FEER*, 19 August 1999.

272. George Fane, 'Indonesia's Economy Makes a Slow Recovery', *APEC Economic Newsletter*, 4 (4), April 2000.

273. A survey of Asian executives in October 1999 found that nearly two–thirds (62.9 per cent) of respondents saw concrete signs of recovery in their industry, while 55.4 per cent considered Asia likely to provide the strongest momentum for growth in their industry, followed a long way behind by the United States (27.4 per cent) and Europe (17.3 per cent). See *FEER*, 21 October 1999, 34.

274. While the financial crisis did not signify a process of collapse and disintegration, it certainly amounted to something more than "transient disruption", as suggested by Peter W. Preston, 'Reading the Asian Crisis: History, Culture and Institutional Truths', *Contemporary Southeast Asia*, 20(3), December 1998, 247.

275. *New Straits Times*, 16 September 1998, 12.

276. *The Australian*, 15 October 1998, 1.

277. Wade, *The Asian Crisis and the Global Economy*, pp. 367–8.

3. From hegemony to competitive interdependence

From the mid-1980s to the end of the 1990s the international security system was in a state of flux. It was possible to identify the features of the Cold War system which had disappeared – some gradually, others more abruptly – but difficult to specify what exactly had replaced them. This was a transitional period when the old was dying, but the new had yet to be born. The inescapable impression was of a mosaic of relatively fluid arrangements, a complex architecture of competing yet overlapping global and regional designs.[1]

On the one hand, several indicators pointed in the direction of enhanced US dominance, notably the break-up of the Soviet Union and the collapse of its remaining alliances, the preservation of the more important US security partnerships, including those with Europe and Japan, the relative success of the US-led coalition in the Gulf War, and America's strategic pre-eminence, especially in the Asia-Pacific region. On the other hand, other perhaps more durable factors signalled the development of a polycentric system, in which Western Europe, Japan and China were beginning to play a more prominent role in defining and executing preferred security outcomes. Russia, by virtue of its size and military capabilities, and in the longer term India and even some Islamic coalition were also likely to contribute to the growing diffusion of power. In the space of little more than a decade, strategic bipolarity had given way to two closely interacting but contradictory trends, unipolarity and quasi-multipolarity.

CONCEPTS AND DISTINCTIONS

We have stated more than once that the United States, by virtue of its productive, commercial and financial dominance, not to mention its vast military power, was able to exercise hegemonic leadership in the organization of the post-1945 world economy. Hegemony, however, is an elusive concept. Not only have different theories assigned different weights to the economic, military and ideological components of hegemony, they have also diverged considerably on its function within the world system.[2] Kindleberger, an early exponent of 'hegemonic stability' theory, contends that hegemony performs three specific functions in a liberal economic order: it promotes the expansion of trade by offering an outlet for surplus production; it acts as a lender of last resort, thereby ensuring financial stability; and it exports the large quantities of capital and technology needed to stimulate production and productivity in other economies. The performance of all three functions is said to be critically important to the stability of the international market system, which would otherwise be vulnerable to prolonged recession and even depression. Britain, it is argued, performed this role in the second half of the nineteenth and early part of the twentieth centuries, and the United States in the period immediately following the Second World War.[3] This reading is largely consistent with Gilpin's interpretation of the evolution of 'liberal economic orders', although in his case the hegemon's capacity to stabilize the system is said to decline as a result of diminishing rates of profit and rising exports of capital.[4] Gilpin, in other words, distinguishes the interests of the US economy from the interests of US corporations. Though the latter may profit by exporting capital and technology, the former may as a consequence lose its competitive edge.[5]

These and other attempts to elucidate the concept of hegemony and the historical trajectory of hegemonic leadership were in large measure a response to the perceived erosion of US hegemony in the 1970s. The official abandonment of gold convertibility by the United States in August 1971 and its humiliating defeat in Vietnam in April 1975 were psychologically potent symbols of decline. Quantitatively more precise indicators of America's diminishing influence usually included the loss of its nuclear superiority, the fall in its GNP as a proportion of world GNP, the even greater fall in its share of global manufacturing capacity, and the accompanying decline of its share of world trade. The United States, which for more than four decades had been the world's largest creditor nation, was by 1988 burdened with a foreign debt of $532.5 billion. The military and economic resources at its disposal, though still formidable, were no longer sufficient, it seemed, to preserve the post-1945 hegemonic order. With the rise of Western Europe and Japan as major trading and financial centres, the world economy was rapidly acquiring a multipolar complexion.

What, then, are we to make of these two complementary yet conflicting tendencies, namely the collapse of strategic bipolarity and the decline (which is not to say disappearance) of US hegemony? The contradiction is potentially resolvable if we postulate a global geopolitical system that is unipolar in structure but is rapidly developing multipolar characteristics, and a geoeconomic system that is essentially multipolar but retains some of the earlier features of US hegemony. While analytically useful, such a resolution still requires considerable conceptual refinement. Key categories must be sharply distinguished but at the same time their interconnections clearly established. First, a distinction must be drawn between regional and global systems. Whereas the effects of economic multipolarity may be global in scope, the structure of each region need not be multipolar. A case in point is the Asia-Pacific community which, at least until recently, revolved around two major poles of attraction, the United States and Japan, and where Europe, though a key variable in the global economic equation, has been a less visible or influential actor. Regional systems interact with each other and with the world system, but such interaction does not thereby produce a homogeneous world economy, nor does it imply that the internal dynamic of a regional system will simply replicate that of the world system.

Second, the geopolitics/geoeconomics distinction must be treated with caution for the two sets of processes and policies cannot be separated in practice. Indeed, the two are closely intertwined: military power cannot be divorced from economic power since one can serve as an instrument for the attainment of the other, and economic conflict can provoke and even shape military conflict. In any case, hegemony does not rest purely on material capabilities, that is on economic, technological or military prowess. John Ikenberry identifies three sources of hegemonic control, which he labels structural leadership (based on the distribution of material capabilities), institutional leadership (based on institutionalized rules and mutual expectations) and situational leadership (derived from diplomatic skill, or more generally the effective use of rhetoric, ideas and imagination).[6] Situational leadership is itself highly relational, for rhetoric, ideas and imagination to be effective must resonate with the intended audience, they must enjoy legitimacy, that is, they must be grounded in norms and purposes whose acceptance rests on consent rather than coercion.[7]

Third, to think in terms of polarity, whether unipolarity, bipolarity or multipolarity, is to assume the existence of poles, which almost automatically become the key units of analysis. It is then but a small step to depict these poles as states, or to put it differently, to reduce all polarities to the interests and capabilities of states. Yet the reality is likely to be far more complex. Given that leadership and hegemony invariably have a strong economic dimension, economic actors are likely to perform a critical function in shaping the distribution and exercise of power. States are no doubt economic actors in their own right, but they are not the only ones, or necessarily the most powerful ones. A range of other economic players, whose interests and strategies are not reducible to the objectives and priorities of any given state, in particular large industrial, commercial and financial enterprises but also leading international organizations, exercise substantial economic, political and ideological leverage, both nationally and internationally. Notions of polarity must therefore be substantially qualified and take into account not only a range of economic actors but also the complex interactions between them, and between states and the national, regional and global markets which define the framework of economic decision-making.

Bearing in mind this conceptual backdrop, we shall argue that three competing yet overlapping tendencies best encapsulate the recent evolution of the political economy of Asia Pacific:

- *Residual US hegemony*   Despite the relative decline of American power, measured primarily in material and more specifically economic terms, the American state, when working in conjunction with the managerial elites of transnational corporations and financial enterprises but also the bureaucratic elites which administer international governmental organizations, was still able, at least intermittently, to exercise a moderately effective form of hegemony. US hegemonic control, to the extent that it relied less on material and more on institutional capabilities, was more subtle, and less statist, centralized or predictable than in the past.
- *Increasing interdependence*   The interpenetration of national economies and the transnationalization of markets, mirroring and reinforcing the erosion of 'extreme hegemony', made it necessary for states to pursue shared or complementary interests by engaging in various forms of bilateral and multilateral negotiation, in which non-state actors, in particular business interests, now played an increasingly important though often informal role; even institutional arrangements established and maintained under US leadership were now subject to review and renegotiation.
- *Intensifying competition*   Economic interdependence does not presuppose or translate into the harmonization of interests. Indeed, competitiveness was the defining principle structuring the production and marketing strategies of the most powerful economic players; it was equally at work in the complex interaction between national economies vying for competitive advantage, and between states intent on maximizing their power and security within a hierarchical but anarchic system, and between states on the one hand and a multiplicity of ethnic and social movements on the other, with the former attempting to redraw political boundaries and the latter to redefine the priorities and modalities of international decision-making.

This chapter will examine how these three tendencies impacted on the region's geopolitical and geoeconomic landscape. The analytical focus will be on the United

States, partly because of its residual hegemonic role, but also because US markets and corporations play a crucial mediating role in the changing structure of regional economies. Particular attention will centre on the changing complexion of US relations with the two major centres of power in East Asia, Japan and China, both of which, in different ways and to different degrees, pose a challenge to US hegemony in Asia Pacific.[8] It is worth stressing, however, that, strategically and economically significant as the decisions of states may be, this analysis would be deficient if it neglected the role of economic actors other than states. The United States, Japan and China are therefore used as convenient geographical entities which encompass within their boundaries a wide range of state and non-state actors. In so far as states receive greater attention, it is because they serve a dual function: a state is both an actor in its own right and an arena in which a great many other actors – subnational, transnational and international – compete and co-operate as part of their value-maximization strategies.

Situated within this multidimensional framework, an examination of the three bilateral relationships (that is, US–Japan, US–China, China–Japan) should clarify the changing balance of interests which they represent and the complex web of perceptions and policies which characterize the triangular relationship. As we shall see, the range of options open to all actors is simultaneously enhanced and circumscribed by the dynamics of this triangular constellation of threats and inducements, affinities and disparities. Environmental challenges and constraints are not, of course, located exclusively within this triangle. Russia will also be considered, especially in terms of its influence on the triangular balance or, to be more precise, on the triangular encounter of competing values, interests and capabilities. Russia may no longer be a major centre of power but it remains a significant variable that is bound to affect the shape of the triangular equation. It goes without saying that in any geometric approximation of geopolitical and geoeconomic reality, account must be taken of exogenous as well as endogenous factors. The not inconsiderable role of peripheral and semi-peripheral actors will be examined in the next chapter.

US POLICY IN THE ERA OF COMPETITIVE INTERDEPENDENCE

One of the recurring themes in official US discourse during both the Bush and the Clinton years was 'leadership'. A stream of public pronouncements described the United States as 'a Pacific power with enduring economic, political and security interests in the Asia-Pacific and Indian Ocean region'.[9] By virtue of history and geography, it was argued, the United States had to maintain commercial access to the region, ensure freedom of navigation and prevent the rise of any hegemonic power or coalition. Validating these interests were said to be the magnitude of America's trans-Pacific trade (estimated in 1988 at $271 billion, compared with $186 billion in trans-Atlantic trade), the scale of its investments in the region ($33 billion in 1988) and the substantial profits accruing to US corporations (23 per cent of their total overseas profits). The post-Cold War period was seen as requiring the United States to exercise leadership no less than in the Cold War era, in the Pacific no less than in Europe.

The imperative of US global leadership was graphically expressed by the Pentagon's draft *Defense Planning Guidance* for 1994–9. The United States would have to prevent other states

> from challenging our leadership or seeking to overturn the established political and economic order. We must maintain the mechanisms for deterring potential competitors from even aspiring to a larger regional or global role.[10]

In the Pacific the structure of US engagement was visualised in the following terms:

> imagine a fan spread wide, with its base in North America and radiating westward. Its central support is the alliance partnership between the United States and Japan. To the north, one spoke represents our alliance with the Republic of Korea. To the south another line extends to our ASEAN colleagues. Further south a spoke reaches Australia . . . Connecting these spokes is the fabric of shared economic interests now given form by the . . . APEC process.[11]

The question immediately arises: Were the perceptions and aspirations of US administrations, which, it should be noted, were not universally shared by Congress, consonant with the geopolitical and geoeconomic trends characteristic of this period of transition and adjustment? Did the American polity have the will, the resources or even the need to exercise the kind of global and regional dominance envisaged by US policy-makers?

Under Bush the United States proceeded to reduce and reconfigure its military capabilities, but without prejudicing its key objective, which was to prevent any other power from assuming a dominant role in either Europe or Asia Pacific. Two reports published by the Department of Defense under the title *A Strategic Framework for the Asia-Pacific Rim* (the first in April 1990 and the second in July 1992) assumed that threats to Japanese and South Korean security were the contingencies most likely to require a military response, hence the emphasis on tactical naval and air deployments. The plan envisaged a Pacific Base Force of 100 000 by the year 2000 (down from 135 000 in 1990), and a more evenly distributed presence in Southeast Asia following the closure of US bases in the Philippines. These force levels were deemed sufficient to demonstrate US resolve to retain military predominance in the region and a credible role as 'regional balancer' capable of managing future crises.[12] However, there was in all of this no authoritative statement of America's purpose in the region, no substitute offered for the role which the Soviet or communist threat had played during the Cold War years, except for periodic reaffirmations of the importance of democracy and human rights. The closest the Administration came to enunciating a strategic purpose was its acknowledgement that, especially in the case of Japan, there would be 'a certain degree of friction and frustration as well as friendship and cooperation in the relationship', and that a new partnership might need to be forged between the two countries.[13]

It was left to the Clinton presidency to flesh out these ideas, although it was often difficult to distinguish between substance and rhetoric. Under the slogan 'cooperative engagement' many of the earlier themes of US security policy were preserved: strong bilateral alliances, respect for international norms, forward presence, and crisis response. US withdrawal was rejected on the grounds that it would create an unhealthy vacuum, kindle arms races in East Asia, encourage the spread of weapons of mass destruction and slow the momentum of Asian democracy and economic growth.[14] US engagement, on the other hand, was needed to eliminate the nuclear threat on the Korean peninsula, strengthen APEC and foster greater co-operation in response to global challenges (for example, the environment, refugees, narcotics, non-proliferation).[15] The creation of a 'New Pacific Community' became the focal point of the Clinton Administration's strategic thinking, with the emphasis on linking economy, security and democracy.[16] At face value, this was a significant departure from the conceptual framework that underpinned the first *Strategic Framework report*. In practice, not a great deal had changed.

In 1998 a fourth report reaffirmed the commitment to retain a military presence of approximately 100 000 in the region, the importance of strengthening the alliance with Japan and Australia, and the need to expand security co-operation and military access in Southeast Asia. Reference was also made to progress in working with friends and allies to develop new regional mechanisms for transparency and confidence-building, and in pursuing the policy of comprehensive engagement with China. The report went on to outline the formidable capabilities of US force projection in the Asia-Pacific region, which included the Eighth Army and Seventh Air Force in Korea, the Third Marine Expeditionary Force and Fifth Air Force in Japan, and the US Seventh Fleet. Under new access arrangements US aircraft carriers and other vessels would have use of the Changi Naval Station in Singapore, and the Visiting Forces Agreement with the Philippines would permit routine combined exercises and training and ship visits. In addition to the benefits deriving from the 'Revolution in Military Affairs', US forces in the region were expected to take advantage of interoperability with allied and friendly forces. To this end, the focus would be on joint research and development, combined doctrine formation and training, and compatibility of systems.[17] It was not altogether clear, however, how alliances and security ties designed to serve Cold War objectives would be reshaped to meet the priorities of a 'New Pacific Community'. Significantly, the *Bottom-Up Review* placed considerable stress on rapid force deployment and mobile amphibious combat capabilities as an appropriate response to both actual and potential regional crises.[18] It was as if alliances, despite the high priority ascribed to them, could not be relied upon to prevent such crises or effectively manage them once they occurred.

Paradoxically, the end of the Cold War and the collapse of Soviet power had presented US security policy with a complex and unforeseen challenge. In the absence of a common and clearly identifiable external threat, how would the rationale and structure of existing and projected alliance arrangements be adapted to the new realities? Compounding the difficulties of readjustment was the desire of the United States to have its allies upgrade their defence capabilities and share more of the defence burden. Alliances, in other words, were now expected to operate differently from before – allies would no longer be given a 'free ride'. The United States, it seemed, was offering its allies, and in particular Japan, a new partnership which promised greater defence responsibilities but possibly fewer, or at least less tangible, security guarantees. Diplomatic and strategic uncertainty was also accentuated by the fact that America's China policy was still very much in the balance, with relations regularly oscillating between friction and co-operation. The notion of a global partnership with Japan and the policy of engagement with China were, as we shall see, an attempt as much to obscure as to resolve the dilemmas and ambiguities confronting US diplomacy in the post-Cold War period.

At one level it is arguable that US military capabilities in the region had never been more potent and any challenge to US military preponderance weaker. At another level, the political circumstances or strategic priorities which would provoke the application of US military force were far from clear. While the United States continued to exercise enormous military leverage in the region, its political profile was widely perceived to be diminishing. These perceptions were influenced not so much by a conscious shift in US strategy as by the changing realities of power, the shifting priorities of the United States, and the powerful constraints exerted by budgetary imperatives and domestic politics. In a remarkably frank assessment of

US policy, Lee Kuan Yew merely said aloud what many Asians had been thinking:

> Nobody believes that an American government that could not sustain its mission in
> Somalia because of an ambush and one television snippet of a dead American pulled
> through the streets of Mogadishu could contemplate a strike on North Korean nuclear
> facilities like the Israeli strike on Iraq.[19]

Emerging Asian uncertainty about the reliability of US declaratory policy prompted
the Clinton Administration to operationalize a number of policy commitments but
regional responses were far from universally favourable. To make matters worse,
America's politico-strategic orientation remained stubbornly ambiguous.

Weighing heavily on US diplomacy were not only a number of unresolved
geopolitical dilemmas but rapidly changing economic circumstances. The United
States could no longer exercise exclusive dominance over East Asian markets and
capital. As indicated in the previous chapter, Japan had by the late 1980s become
a larger provider of aid than the United States, the principal source of foreign
investment for most Asia-Pacific economies (with the exception of the Philippines,
Canada and New Zealand) and an increasingly important trading partner for many
of them. To this should be added the growth and consolidation of the other East
Asian economies and the emergence of an elaborate regional division of labour less
dependent on US leadership and more conducive to economic competition and
strategic uncertainty. As Richard Solomon, Assistant Secretary for East Asian and
Pacific Affairs, acknowledged:

> Our allies and friends in Asia . . . have now become robust competitors . . . Their success
> requires them to assume the responsibilities necessary to sustain and expand the global
> trading system that has nurtured their growth . . . Yet many of our relationships in the
> region are beset with trade tensions as economic issues move center stage. The asymmetry
> in the easy access which our Asian trading partners have to our markets, but with our
> limited access to them, *must be remedied.* (italics added).[20]

Solomon's observations are highly instructive in that they foreshadow the Clinton
Administration's hard-nosed pursuit of US economic interests in Asia Pacific and
make it plain that the United States could no longer disperse the economic largesse
associated with the heyday of *Pax Americana.* The changing balance of economic
power had constrained the United States to adopt a much tougher bargaining
position with 'allies and friends in Asia'.

The new orientation, though formally articulated by the executive and legislative
arms of the state, was to a large extent driven by the perceived needs of US
business. In a major address to the American business community on 27 July 1993,

Secretary of State Warren Christopher was remarkably explicit on the linkage between business interests and US diplomacy:

> One of the key pillars of America's foreign policy today is the promotion of America's economic security . . . I recently sent a message to all ambassadors making it clear that I expect each of them to take personal charge of promoting our commercial interests – and to engage their embassies in a sustained effort to help the American business community. On a policy level the Clinton Administration is working to eliminate unfair obstacles to American business here in the Pacific rim and around the world.[21]

Economic imperatives had, if anything, reinforced America's commitment to remain a Pacific power, but that commitment was conducive as much to tension as to co-operation. The United States invested considerable energy in promoting rules and norms favourable to regional stability, but that investment was made on the assumption that the existing highly advantageous structures of power would be preserved. Nowhere, as we shall see, was the complex task of managing the nexus between co-operation and conflict and between economy and security likely to prove more demanding than in America's attempts to forge a new relationship with China and Japan.

JAPAN AND THE UNITED STATES: A FLUID AND CONTRADICTORY RELATIONSHIP

US–Japan relations, particularly since the early 1980s, have given rise to numerous and often conflicting interpretations, which is not altogether surprising given the speed and intensity of change in their respective domestic and external environments. It is nevertheless a relationship which, precisely because it consumed the energies of both governments, sheds much needed light on their hesitant adjustment to post-Cold War geopolitical and geoeconomic realities. The Bush Administration sought at first to emphasize the positive features of the relationship, expressing satisfaction with 'the mutually agreed division of defense roles and missions' in bilateral security arrangements, and appreciation of Japan's increasing contribution to the cost of maintaining US forces in Japan.[22] Even the uneasy compromise on the joint development of the FSX fighter plane was portrayed as a highly beneficial flowback of Japanese technology to the United States. Yet so much water had flowed under the bilateral bridge that a process of adjustment had become virtually unavoidable.

In June 1989, Secretary of State Baker, in calling for a new 'global partnership', outlined a vision of a closer relationship serving the economic interests of both parties, promoting regional peace and security, and permitting greater co-operation on transnational issues (for example, the environment, narcotics control, refugees and terrorism).[23] The notion of partnership was substantially extended or refined to encompass the strengthening of the GATT multilateral trading system, macroeconomic policy co-ordination, UN reform, nuclear non-proliferation, as well as bilateral economic and trade relations.[24] It soon became apparent that the United States, while mindful of the need to recognize Japan's claim to a greater role in regional and international decision-making, was primarily concerned to remedy what it regarded as the shortcomings of the relationship.

First, Japan had to carry a greater share of the defence burden, by which was meant not merely greater financial support for US forces, but the build-up of Japanese military capabilities, greater use of Japanese development assistance to advance commonly agreed diplomatic and security objectives (such as the Philippines Multilateral Aid Initiative), more effective bilateral defence co-operation and technology-sharing arrangements, and greater Japanese involvement in international peace operations. Second, and perhaps more importantly, Japan was expected to play a greater part in the development of an open global economic system, by which was meant significant liberalization of Japanese trade and investment policies. To drive the point home, unflattering comparisons were drawn between the German and Japanese economies. Germany, which produced some of the finest cars in the world, imported 30 per cent of the cars sold on its domestic market, whereas Japan imported only 4 per cent of its cars. Foreign direct investment in Germany accounted for 17 per cent of its national assets but in Japan's case the corresponding figure was only 1 per cent.[25] Japan's failure to reciprocate the openness of other economies was said to explain its never-ending accumulation of trade surpluses and the consequent accumulation of trade deficits by the United States, estimated at $500 billion at the end of 1992. The United States was now demanding immediate remedial action. It is to this major source of friction that we first turn our attention.

Economic Dimensions of Conflict

The strategy adopted by the Bush Administration revolved largely around the Structural Impediments Initiative (SII), a framework of action explicitly designed to correct unacceptable asymmetries in the economic relationship. The ensuing discussions identified six broad structural impediments which in the view of the United States restricted market forces and hindered access by foreign firms and products in the Japanese economy: the savings/investment imbalance; the distribution system; land use policies; *keiretsu* and related foreign direct investment issues; exclusionary business practices; and pricing mechanisms. The United States sought to make the bitter pill a little more palatable for the Japanese by allowing the discussion to consider also structural impediments in the US economy, including savings and investment patterns, corporate behaviour, government regulation, export promotion, and education and training of the workforce. An interim report presented to the two governments in April 1990 was cautiously optimistic, pointing to policy commitments made by Japan in each of the six policy areas and implementation steps for at least some of these commitments. These encouraging signs could not, however, obscure the magnitude and complexity of the reform agenda or the long lead times needed to deliver meaningful change. Negotiations on specific market access problems in such areas as satellites, wood products and supercomputers might prove more successful, but here too tensions were inevitable and US expectations of quick results collided with the Japanese bureaucracy's skilful resistance to change.

The suspicion and mistrust that now characterized the bilateral relationship were not confined to governments. By the end of the 1980s American public sentiment had become more hostile to Japan than to the Soviet Union, while the Japanese public was sharply critical of American high-handedness in economic negotiations. Much of the friction between the two countries was attributable to the shifting balance of economic power. The fact that one was an ascending power and the other in slow but visible decline meant that the premises which had guided co-operation in the past were less likely to apply in the future. The different structures of the two economies (for example, the relationship between capital and labour, corporate governance, the relative emphasis on production and consumption), their vastly different policy-making processes (for example, business–government relations) and the conflicting business interests which they reflected were likely to perpetuate or even exacerbate existing macro-economic imbalances.[26]

In line with the analysis offered by Japanese economist Iwao Nakatani, Chalmers Johnson characterized these differences by distinguishing Japan's 'network capitalism' from the Anglo-American version of liberal capitalism. Far from being a market economy in the liberal mould, Japan was a 'cartelized (*keiretsuka*) economy ... conducive to so-called lean manufacturing, where corporate decisions based on interlocking shareholding were virtually free of the influence of owners'.[27] Johnson went on to refer to the widely held view, shared by Akio Morita, author of *The Japan That Can Say No*, that Japan's management philosophy had created a pricing structure with which western firms could not compete.[28] Placed in this context, the Bush Administration's SII strategy may be interpreted as a concerted attempt to compel Japan to jettison business practices and structural features of its economy which gave it a competitive edge over the US economy. Japan's participation in bilateral trade negotiations on the other hand could be read as a ploy to distract or appease the United States rather than a genuine commitment to the US reform agenda. In the absence of quick and tangible results an American counterattack seemed inevitable, particularly against the backdrop of Clinton's 1992 election victory, coming as it did in the wake of an election campaign that had single-mindedly focused on the need to restore US economic competitiveness.

On coming to office the new Administration acknowledged the improvement in the US–Japan trade balance, US exports having risen by 70 per cent in the 1987–92 period, as against an increase of 15 per cent for Japanese exports. The bilateral trade imbalance had as a result shrunk from a high of $57 billion in 1987 to $49 billion in 1992. In American eyes, however, the 1992 deficit was still unacceptably high, and all the more so as it resumed its upward curve after reaching a low of $41 billion in 1990.[29] Japan's global current account surplus, which had grown sharply in previous years to reach an estimated $118 billion in 1992, was characterized by US officials as applying a brake on world growth and hindering efforts to strengthen the international trading system. Japan, it was argued, despite improved access to its markets in sections covered by negotiated agreements, imported a disproportionately small share of manufactured goods. Whereas Europe and the United States imported 7.4 per cent and 6.5 per cent respectively of their GDP in manufactured goods, Japan's share was only about 3 per cent and falling.[30] Even where trade agreements had been negotiated (over 30 such agreements between 1980 and 1993), these had generally failed to produce the desired result. In the glass sector, despite commitments made in 1992, the foreign share of Japan's consumption of flat glass had fallen from 5.1 per cent in 1991 to 3.5 per cent in 1993. Similarly foreign share in Japan's $32 billion market for primary paper and card products had remained stagnant (rising slightly from 3.7 per cent in 1991 to about 4 per cent in 1990). As for Japanese government procurement of computer products and services, foreign share of that market had fallen from 4 per cent in 1991 to 3.7 per cent in 1992. Even in the Semiconductor Arrangement, often described as a success story, the 20 per cent market share achieved at the end of 1992 was followed by a decline in 1993.[31]

The US–Japan Framework for Economic Partnership was to be the centrepiece of Clinton's strategic response to the imbalances and frustrations in the bilateral trade relationship. Under the framework agreement, announced in July 1993, Japan undertook to promote domestic demand-level growth and increasing market access for foreign goods in order to bring about a substantial reduction of its current account surplus. The market access issues to be addressed were divided into five separate 'baskets': government procurement; cars/car parts; regulatory reform; economic harmonization (with a view to increasing foreign business activity in Japan, foreign access to Japanese technology and buyer–supplier networks, and increased intellectual protection); and implementation of existing agreements. The framework agreement also contained a 'Common Agenda for Cooperation in Global Perspective', which served as an umbrella for 15 joint programmes relating to such issues as the environment, AIDS and population growth.[32] The US plan was to establish a structure for an ongoing set of consultations and biannual summit meetings which would yield a series of agreements for greater penetration of the Japanese market, geared to specific areas of the economy, specific timetables and objective criteria for measuring success.[33]

During 1994 and 1995 there were clear signs of improvement in the trade relationship, at least as viewed by the United States, with US exports to Japan rising by 20.3 per cent in 1995 following increases of 11 per cent in 1994 and 20 per cent in 1993, and a corresponding reduction in the US trade deficit from $54.9 billion in 1994 to $45.6 billion in 1995.[34] Japan's current account surplus had declined to 2.2 per cent of GDP in 1995, down from 3.2 per cent in 1994 and 3.5 per cent in 1993. Yet the negotiating process remained difficult, at times acrimonious and often inconclusive, with the United States periodically threatening unilateral action. Although not directly associated with the framework negotiations, the Clinton Administration determined in February 1994 that Japan had not complied with the 1989 agreement requiring it to open its cellular telephone market to US manufacturers of cellular equipment. A few days prior to a list of sanctions being published on 17 March, Japan agreed to a series of measures that it would introduce over the following 21 months ensuring US access to the Japanese cellular market.[35] However, success on one front merely displaced the friction to another front.

During 1995 tensions came to a head in the areas of aviation and motor vehicles. US car manufacturers had pressed the Clinton Administration to stand firm on its results-based approach and to terminate participation in the Framework process should the Japanese refuse to give ground.[36] The Japanese rejected the US demand for numerical targets in the foreign share of the Japanese market for motor vehicle parts and for the number of foreign dealerships. In May 1995, the United States announced that it would unilaterally place a 100 per cent tariff on imports of Japanese luxury cars under Section 301 of the Trade Act, and actually suspended the elimination of tariffs on these luxury cars. Japan responded by requesting consultations under Article XXXII of the 1994 General Agreement on Tariffs and Trade, and insisted on settling the dispute within WTO regulations. Significantly, the settlement that was reached immediately prior to the 28 June deadline set by the United States for retaliatory action against Japan provided for the deregulation of the Japanese market in replacement parts, but excluded the application of numerical targets or government intervention in the private sector.

At their June summit, Japan and the United States decided to extend the Framework agreement, but the strains in the relationship were seldom far from the surface. Even in the case of the successful semiconductors agreement, which helped to lift the foreign share of the Japanese market from 19.4 per cent in 1993 to 25.4 per cent in 1995, the United States was intent on extracting additional concessions, including greater access to the automotive, telecommunications and video games sectors, and increased sales to small and medium-sized Japanese companies.[37] Similar battles were raging on other fronts. The Clinton Administration charged Japan with failing to implement the insurance agreement and to proceed with deregulation of the primary life and non-life sectors, which together comprised some 95 per cent of its insurance market, estimated at over $380 billion in total premiums in 1994.[38]

In the second half of the 1990s the focus of bilateral exchanges would shift in response to changing domestic and international circumstances. Whereas the Japanese economy was in serious difficulty, the US economy had recovered enormous ground, registering persistently high levels of GDP growth, falling unemployment and rising productivity associated with a renewed information-driven technological dynamism. Trade frictions were less conspicuous, but acrimony, never far below the surface, would soon rebound with the onset of the East Asian crisis. Tokyo's proposal for the creation of an Asian Monetary Fund floated at a G-7 meeting in Hong Kong in September 1997 met with a decidedly negative response from Washington. Envisaging a pool of up to $100 billion to assist East Asian economies with balance of payments difficulties, the initiative was clearly intended to offer them a financial lifeline that would reduce their dependence on the IMF and its inflexible prescriptions.[39] US officials immediately condemned the initiative, precisely because it would weaken the force of IMF conditionality, hinting that this was little more than an attempt to protect the interests of Japanese banks.[40] Tokyo's relatively meek surrender on the issue, far from placating the US administration, merely prompted a barrage of criticism of Japan's alleged failure to undertake appropriate economic reforms. US demands may have changed in emphasis, but the underlying message remained essentially the same: Japan had to stimulate its economy, increase domestic demand, open up its markets and liberalize its financial system. As US criticism escalated, so did Japanese official and private resentment. US actions were described in the pages of *Asahi Shimbun* as designed 'to prop up the economic side of the [US-dominated] unipolar world – especially through steps that continue to finance the US current account deficit'.[41] For many in Japan, the East Asian turmoil was attributable largely to capricious short-term capital flows causing hovoc in what were essentially sound economies. The scale of Japan's financial contribution was contrasted with the meagreness of US offerings, and Japan's financially sensitive approach with the bluntness of IMF instruments.

At every opportunity and using the vast array of unilateral, bilateral and multilateral levers at its disposal, the United States had launched a ferocious and multifaceted campaign to compel Japan to adopt macroeconomic, structural and sectoral policies designed to hasten the liberalization of its markets and deregulation of its industries. Japanese political leaders, be it Hosokawa, Muryama, Hashimoto or Obuchi, regardless of differences in outlook or power base, could not ignore the interests of powerful Japanese constituencies or the growing public resentment and distrust provoked by the unilateralist thrust of US policy. US economic interests may have profited from the Administration's aggressive diplomacy, but the debit side of the ledger, though more subtle and less easily quantifiable, was none the less real. The judgement that the trade frictions of the 1990s presaged a return to the 1930s was no doubt ill-founded or at best premature. Yet, official rhetoric aside, the cohesion of the US–Japan partnership and the mutual confidence on which it rested had been dealt a severe blow, precisely at a time when perceptions of the Soviet/Russian threat had largely dissipated. The single-minded pursuit of economic advantage by the US Commerce Department, acting on behalf of influential business lobbies, and the implicit demotion of the political and security dimensions of the relationship prodded the State and Defense Departments into taking remedial action, but whether such action would prove timely or efficacious was far from certain.

The Security Relationship

It has become commonplace to contrast the recurrent tensions in US–Japan economic relations with the stability and closeness of the security partnership. Such a reading, though plausible at first sight, is nevertheless misleading on two counts: it underestimates the underlying divergence of interests and perceptions even in the diplomatic and strategic arenas, and it fails to take account of the complex interaction between economic and security policy. Official discourse on both sides, it is true, tended to concentrate on the benefits conferred by bilateral security arrangements. The 1992 Japanese Defense White Paper, for example, stressed the direct contribution these arrangements made to Japan's security (thereby relieving Japan of an excessive economic burden), to the effectiveness of its diplomacy, particularly in times of strategic uncertainty, to regional peace and stability, and to bilateral co-operation.[42]

Yet the complex motivation underlying these broadly stated objectives could not be entirely obscured from view. Indeed, the need to prevent a rearmed or resurgent Japan was not infrequently advanced by senior US military officers as justification for the continued presence of US forces in Japan. The 1990 Pentagon report *A*

Strategic Framework for the Asian Pacific Rim: Looking toward the 21st Century
openly acknowledged that a key US strategic objective was to discourage the
destabilizing development of power projection capabilities. The American interest
in keeping Japan denuclearized and defensively postured might be music to Korean
and Southeast Asian ears, but was unlikely to elicit universal approval inside Japan.
For the Japanese body politic, the core issue was ultimately as much psychological
as strategic. The alliance with the United States might be beneficial to Japanese
security, but was this sufficient reason for perpetuating Japan's subordination to the
United States? Was strategic and diplomatic dependence the price Japan had to pay
for continued prosperity and stability? Though Japan's political, bureaucratic and
intellectual elites were far from united in their response to these questions, they were
increasingly conscious of their complexity and wide-ranging ramifications. To
illuminate the gradual evolution of official Japanese thinking on this issue, it is
worth examining, however briefly, four main areas of contention in the bilateral
security relationship: the size and form of the US military presence in Japan; the
requirements of burden-sharing; defence co-operation; and the direction of Japanese
foreign policy.

The stationing of US forces in Japan has always confronted Japanese
governments with a delicate balancing act between internal and external
considerations. As was dramatically evidenced in the Vietnam War, access to these
military facilities enabled the United States to use Japan as a forward base in Asia.
It is estimated that between 1965 and 1973 the Kadena air base in Okinawa handled
more than a million flights and Tokyo's civilian airport at Haneda more than 2000
military flights in 1967 alone. In Washington's view, use of these facilities was
sanctioned by Article 6 of the Security Treaty even though Vietnam was not strictly
speaking part of the 'Far East' region explicitly designated as coming under the
purview of the treaty.[43] US troops stationed in Japan would in any case be deployed
outside of Asia, notably in the Gulf War. The argument that Japanese consent is not
legally required for US forces to participate in such military engagements, because
Japan is not directly involved, may be technically valid, but it does not alter the fact
that the US–Japan security treaty has acquired a global function and may involve the
application of US force without the prior approval of, or even adequate consultation
with, the Japanese government.

The external ramifications of the US military presence in Japan were
compounded by even more troublesome domestic difficulties which arose from the
geographical concentration of these forces in Okinawa, Japan's smallest and poorest
prefecture. Housing three-quarters of the US military facilities and two-thirds of the
45 000 US troops in Japan, Okinawa was especially vulnerable to the disruption of
everyday life caused by artillery firings, low-flying aircraft, military exercises and
the not-infrequent misbehaviour of US soldiers. The rape of a 12-year old Japanese

girl by US servicemen in September 1995 served to exacerbate tensions in Okinawa, prompting some 85 000 Okinawans to protest against US military bases and more than half a million to call for changes in the US–Japan security arrangements.[44] To appease Okinawan sentiment, the Clinton Administration agreed to have US military personnel who were accused of murder, rape or other serious crimes turned over to Japanese custody, and to consider changes to the disposition of US forces stationed on the island. In line with the recommendations of a committee established for the purpose by the US and Japanese governments, the United States announced in April 1996 that it would return some 20 per cent of the land currently used by US facilities in Okinawa to local landowners and introduce a number of noise reduction initiatives and adjustments to operational procedures. However, these measures were unlikely to address the deeper reservations of Okinawans (and the wider Japanese public) about the US presence in Japan. With Okinawa's governor still demanding the closure of all bases on the island by the year 2015 and the local government's refusal to renew land leases for the US bases, Prime Minister Hashimoto was compelled to take emergency legislative action to enable US forces to remain in Okinawa.

In a significant address delivered in Washington, former Prime Minister Hosokawa voiced growing Japanese disquiet about the scale and function of US military facilities:

> [I]n the last fifty years Japan, so far as we know, has not seriously discussed the level of forces deployed on Japanese territory or even the need of them with the United States of America, its security partner. If there has been any such discussion the people have not been told. How much will Japan be involved in the global strategy of US forces in our country? . . . Why are 47 000 US troops necessary in Japan? What specific usefulness is served by the Yokota and Kadena air bases? . . . [M]ore than ever before, convincing explanations must be provided if the present security system is to be maintained.[45]

Hosokawa went on to recommend the relocation of the US marine corps based in Okinawa to Hawaii or Guam, though he was careful to present his proposal as enhancing the viability of the existing security system. Japanese public support for the US military presence was in decline. An *Asahi Shimbun* survey conducted in October 1995 found that 76 per cent of Japanese favoured a gradual reduction of US facilities in Okinawa. More surprisingly perhaps, only 7 per cent supported the status quo, and 58 per cent opposed the transfer of US bases from Okinawa to the main islands. Another poll in April 1995 found that for the first time less than 50 per cent of Japanese surveyed felt 'they could count on the United States to come to Japan's aid if attacked', and 38 per cent felt that they 'definitely couldn't'.[46] The rape incident had certainly contributed to increasing Japanese ambivalence about the alliance, but all the indications were of a trend with deeper and more durable roots.

While less sensitive an issue and less immediate in its impact, burden-sharing also had a corrosive effect on the bilateral relationship. Japan's host-nation support for US forces, which had steadily increased after the late 1970s, reached $5.6 billion in 1994 or just under half the total cost of maintaining the US presence in Japan. The proportion rose to over 70 per cent if the salaries of US military personnel were not included in the calculation of cost. While the United States saw Japan's increasing share of the financial burden as a valuable contribution to a strengthened security partnership, Japan itself had yet to determine what benefits, other than US goodwill, might accrue in return for its greater generosity. As for defence co-operation, the co-development of the FSX had already demonstrated how difficult it would be to reconcile strategic and diplomatic interests on the one hand and trade, industry and technology policies on the other, and at the same time ensure mutual benefit.[47] Did these new arrangements merely rectify the one-way flow of benefits from the United States to Japan, or did they signify a new imbalance in the relationship with Japan carrying an increasing share of the costs but without a corresponding share of benefits?

These irritants or festering ambiguities were bound to affect both American and Japanese perceptions of the alliance, particularly in the absence of Cold War rivalries and shared strategic goals. Articulating a new and compelling rationale for the alliance was all the more difficult for, unlike Germany, Japan's political elites had yet to acknowledge the legacy of the Second World War, to fashion a coherent strategy for regional integration, or to assume diplomatic responsibilities commensurate with Japan's newly acquired economic influence. Conversely, whenever Japan made tentative steps in this direction US Administrations, while welcoming such steps, were not entirely convinced that a more assertive Japanese diplomacy would always dovetail with US security objectives and priorities. US declaratory policy was predicated on Japan assuming 'the role and responsibilities of an equal and globally oriented partner',[48] but it was far from clear whether the emphasis would fall on burden-sharing or power-sharing.

The extension of Japan's diplomatic and strategic influence was a gradual, complex, even contradictory process in which internationalization, Asianization and nationalism all played a part, although in varying degrees and with variable outcomes depending on time and circumstance. Perhaps the earliest and most striking application of the internationalization strategy was in the formulation and execution of Japan's ODA policy. In line with the 1980 *Report on Comprehensive Security Policy* prepared for Prime Minister Ohira Masayoshi, which provided the framework for a number of political and security initiatives, Japan substantially increased its overseas aid in Asia and elsewhere, and made it an integral part of its cultural exchange programme and engagement with a range of transnational issues (such as the environment, population control, AIDS, narcotics, refugee resettlement).

It also supported a number of UN-related conflict prevention and conflict resolution activities: for example, by dispatching civilian personnel to UN peacekeeping operations in Afghanistan, the Iran–Iraq conflict and election observer groups in Namibia and Nicaragua, as well as by extending financial support for these and other UN activities,[49] and for refugee and reconstruction programmes in post-conflict situations.

Something of a watershed was reached in August 1990 with Iraq's annexation of Kuwait. Prime Minister Toshiki Kaifu described the crisis as 'a major time of testing for Japan . . . and the most severe trial we have faced since the end of the war'.[50] Japan's initial response involved support for UN sanctions on Iraq and a pledge of $4 billion to assist developing economies hardest hit by the crisis, more than half of which was earmarked for such frontline countries as Egypt and Turkey. Washington's request for Japanese minesweepers and tanks to be sent to the Gulf was refused on the grounds that such deployments carried the risk of involvement in armed hostilities. In the wake of increasing US pressure, the Kaifu government introduced legislation in October 1990 for the establishment of a United Nations Peace Co-operation Corps which would include military as well as civilian personnel but would not perform any military functions. In the face of widespread public and parliamentary opposition, the legislation was not even put to the vote, and the government had to content itself with making a hefty financial contribution to the war effort, estimated at some $13 billion.[51]

A new law was eventually enacted in June 1992, enabling Japan to commit its Self-Defense Forces to peacekeeping (PKO) and humanitarian operations in Cambodia, Mozambique, Zaire and the Golan Heights[52]. However, in response to widespread opposition within Japan to the forward projection of military power, a number of important limitations were placed on the scale and modalities of such involvement. The five PKO principles, as they came to be known, made Japanese participation conditional on agreement on a cease-fire, consent of the parties to the deployment of the UN force, impartiality, rights of withdrawal, and limitations on the use of weapons to self-defence.[53] The government's resolve to press ahead with some form of participation in UN peacekeeping reflected its appreciation that the world body offered the least contentious forum within which it could pursue the reinvigoration of its security policy. The military dimensions of the new security outlook will be examined shortly. Suffice it here to say that Japan now wished to be more directly and visibly engaged in international decision-making. Active involvement in the debate on UN reform and vigorous lobbying for a permanent seat on the Security Council were intended to signal to the rest of the world a new maturity in Japan's global and regional diplomacy.

Though still in its formative stages, the new Japanese internationalism as practised in the 1990s served two complementary yet potentially conflicting objectives. On the one hand, it enabled Japan to claim, especially with the United States in mind, that it was ready to assume greater responsibility for the maintenance of international order and regional security. On the other hand, the new internationalism was a codeword for Japan's resolve but also increased capacity to promote or defend, as the case may be, the economic and political conditions on which depended its continuing stability and prosperity. There was no reason, however, to suppose that Japanese diplomatic self-assertion would always coexist with, let alone reinforce, the long-standing security relationship with the United States. The geopolitical, not to mention economic, interests of these two centres of power were, at least on some key issues, as likely to diverge as to converge.

Significantly, the policy of internationalization was accompanied and to some extent nurtured by a more forceful expression of Japanese nationalism than at any time since the end of the Second World War. Though mainstream academic and political opinion was still wedded to the Yoshida doctrine, increasingly influential voices within and outside the LDP were calling for an expansion of the Self-Defense Forces, greater participation in UN peace operations and, if necessary, changes to the Japanese constitution. Even Kato Koichi, LDP Secretary General from 1995 to 1998, widely regarded as a dove on security and related constitutional issues, was prepared to entertain future Japanese participation in a regional collective security system. Though opposed to 'rear-area support' for the United States which might involve combat, he strongly supported Japanese engagement in peacekeeping operations even if it meant Japanese military personnel being placed 'in harm's way'.[54] Ozawa Ichiro, head of the Liberal Party, was willing to make a more radical break with the past, advocating active and ongoing participation by Japanese forces in UN peacekeeping, even if this required amending the constitution.[55] Indicative of the new political climate was the law passed by the Diet in July 1999 authorizing the establishment of constitutional 'research councils' which were expected to provide a forum for discussing, among other things, Article 9 of the Constitution.[56] Equally instructive were the legislative measures designed to grant official status to the Hinomaru flag and Kimigayo anthem, despite the close association of these symbols with Japan's military past.[57] Such views, it is true, had been expressed before, but not with the same degree of confidence and public visibility or comparable levels of public support.[58]

Asianization, the third important dimension in Japan's evolving security policy, had its origins in the Fukuda doctrine of August 1977 but was given considerable impetus by the end of the Cold War and the consequent need to redefine Japanese security interests. Indicative of this trend were the high priority assigned to the Asian region in Japan's ODA programmes, Tokyo's active participation in the Cambodian peace process and in the nuclear negotiations with North Korea, increasing interest in the development of regional multilateral institutions, and persistent efforts to forge closer ties with ASEAN. These culminated in December 1997 in a joint statement paving the way for enhanced political and security dialogues and exchanges between the two sides. Many of these initiatives could be interpreted as consistent with, indeed supportive of, US interests in the region. Japan was in any case careful not to exceed the limits of US tolerance, hence its refusal to align itself with Malaysia's proposal for an East Asian Economic Caucus (EAEC). Japan's rediscovery of Asia indicated a greater willingness on its part to assume a leadership role in the region, which in part reflected the growing strains in its relationship with the United States.

The notion of 'partnership', it is true, had assumed great prominence in Japan's official rhetoric, but the meaning or content attached to the notion was ambiguous to say the least. Was it to be understood as a widening of Tokyo's international security agenda and a willingness to lend more effective support to US strategic interests, or was it a new codeword for the old policy of economic self-interest and risk minimization? If Japan was now ready to flex more diplomatic muscle, would this be at the service of common or more narrowly defined national objectives?

This ambiguity in Japan's security policy was also apparent in the steady development of its military capabilities and gradual evolution of its defence policy. Measured in yen, Japanese military spending during the 1980s recorded an average annual growth of 5 per cent, enabling Japan to purchase 'more US weapons under the Foreign Military Sales program than any other nation, and more than Italy, Britain, France, and Germany combined'.[59] Measured in constant dollars, Japan's defence budget rose from $37.6 billion in 1985 to $50.2 billion in 1995. By the mid-1990s Japan had a potent conventional force which included 64 major surface combatants, 16 attack submarines, 100 long-range patrol aircraft, 200 F-15 fighters, AWAC systems and advanced anti-submarine warfare capabilities. It planned to instal the Aegis ship-defence system on four new destroyers to be built in Japan (the first of which was completed in 1993), co-produce the new FSX surface attack fighter, and acquire a new array of missiles and over-the-horizon radar systems. At the same time the Japanese Defense Agency was intent on achieving an advanced and comprehensive defence research programme and higher levels of self-reliance in defence production.

There was more, however, to the evolution of Japanese defence policy than the acquisition of military hardware. The gradual relaxation of the formal and informal restrictions on the role and capabilities of the SDF was itself indicative of emerging trends. As Chalmers Johnson observed, by 1992 the Three Non-Nuclear Principles – the ban on the export of arms, the limitation on military expenditures to 1 per cent of GNP, and the refusal to despatch Japanese forces outside the country – had all been breached.[60] Article 9 of the Japanese Constitution, it is true, still exercised a powerful constraining influence on the future direction of Japanese strategic planning, which helps to explain why a number of prominent figures keen to see an expanded security role for Japan were openly advocating revision or at least reinterpretation of Article 9. Yet the constitution was not an insuperable barrier to change.

Japanese governments had traditionally reconciled the development of the Self-Defense Forces with constitutional requirements by arguing that these forces would not be used for any purpose other than the defence of Japanese territory. This right of self-defence was confined to 'the minimum necessary level for the defence of the nation'. As a consequence, successive official statements described the exercise of the right of 'collective self-defence' as exceeding that limit and therefore as 'constitutionally not permissible'.[61] In line with this interpretation Japan, it was argued, could not despatch military personnel to foreign territories, seas or airspace for the purpose of using force. These limitations did not, however, preclude Japan from expanding its military capabilities or widening the purposes to which they could be put.

The review process was given considerable impetus with the establishment in June 1993 of the Forum for Discussing Defense in a New Era and the Advisory Group on Defense Issues in February 1994. Appointed by Prime Minister Hosokawa, the Advisory Group presented its conclusions to Prime Minister Murayama in August 1994. It proposed a comprehensive security policy comprised of three prongs:

> First, promotion of multilateral security cooperation on a global and regional scale; secondly, enhancement of the functions of the Japan–US security relationship; and thirdly, possession of a highly reliable and efficient defense capability based on a strengthened information capability and a prompt crisis-management capability.[62]

The third prong (the upgrading of the SDF) was justified partly in terms of its relevance to the other two prongs (the US–Japan alliance and multilateral security co-operation). The report, however, left no doubt that 'possession of a reliable self-defense capability' was considered the ultimate guarantee of national independence. The potentially threatening situations identified included 'interference in the safety of maritime traffic, violation of territorial air space, limited missile attack, illegal occupation of a part of the country, terrorist acts, and influx of armed refugees',[63] thereby making it clear that what was envisaged was a highly sophisticated and potent military capability.

The Advisory Group's thinking was reflected in the National Defense Program Outline (NDPO) issued in December 1995, replacing the 1976 NDPO which had adopted the 'Concept of Basic and Standard Defense Capability'. While many features of the concept were preserved, emphasis was placed on 'enhancing necessary functions and making qualitative improvements' in order to enable the SDF to respond flexibly and effectively to a variety of circumstances.[64] The evolution in Japanese strategic thinking continued to unfold with the publication of *Defense of Japan 1996*. It was no longer deemed appropriate for the SDF 'to focus solely on aggression against Japan'. In addition to preventing and responding to aggression, defence capability was now expected to deal with 'indirect aggression or any unlawful military activity that might lead to aggression'. Disturbances on Japanese territory instigated or supported by foreign governments and organized intrusions by foreign personnel aimed at overthrowing the Japanese government were cited as examples of indirect aggression. Other situations were said to include conflicts in Japan's surrounding region which could seriously affect Japan's peace and security and might require the SDF to engage in search and rescue operations; evacuation of Japanese nationals; or removal and disposal of mines.[65] References to these contingencies did not constitute a comprehensive list of threat scenarios, but it did signal a widening security agenda and a commitment to enhanced military capabilities. NDPO 1995 envisaged that the Maritime Self- Defense Forces (MSDF) would be equipped with a mobile escort force and substantial surveillance, patrol and minesweeping capabilities, and the Air Self-Defense Force (ASDF) with advanced control and warning capabilities, air transportation and air reconnaissance, fighter units, ground-to-air missile units, and a capacity to interdict airborne or amphibious invasions.

It remains to say a word about one other element of Japan's potential military capability, namely the nuclear option. Two sources of evidence are worth considering here: the initial reluctance of the Japanese government to endorse the indefinite extension of the Non-Proliferation Treaty (NPT), and the steady accumulation of a large stockpile of separated plutonium. Though Japan eventually agreed to sign the unconditional extension of the NPT, the prospect of nuclear proliferation in the Korean peninsula, and perhaps more importantly the increasing sophistication of China's nuclear arsenal and the Indian and Pakistani nuclear tests in May 1998, probably strengthened the hand of Japanese policy-makers who questioned the wisdom of accepting a position of permanent nuclear inferiority.[66] This is not to say that Japan had already resolved, or would soon resolve, to proceed with the development of a nuclear arsenal. On the other hand, Japan clearly possessed both the materials and the technology needed to detonate a nuclear device at very short notice. The unirradiated separated plutonium inventory, which grew from 6 tons at the end of 1992 to 20 tons in 1995 and 24 tons in 1997,[67] was generally regarded as far exceeding the requirements of Japan's civil nuclear power programme. There was, moreover, little indication that Japan was about to cease plutonium production at its fuel fabrication plants or halt reprocessing of its spent fuel in France and Britain. The inescapable conclusion was that Japan, while avoiding the domestic and international hostility to declared nuclear capability, would pursue a policy of 'denial and ambiguity' and effectively retain the option of joining the nuclear weapons club at an unspecified future date.[68]

If ambiguity was a distinguishing feature of Japan's defence policy, it was by no means confined to the scope and function of its conventional capabilities or nuclear options. A lingering ambivalence, if not studied ambiguity, also characterized the security relationship with the United States, which in a sense mirrored the unresolved tensions between burden-sharing and power-sharing in US policy towards Japan. At the level of declaratory policy Japanese governments would consistently endorse the principle of close military co-operation with the United States and the need for joint action in the event of a direct military threat to Japanese security. Yet important questions remained as to the direction of Japan's long-term strategic thinking.

Maintaining and even enhancing security links with the United States served a number of immediate Japanese objectives. It obviated the need for Japan to develop a fully independent military and nuclear weapons option, which would have aroused widespread opposition both at home and abroad. To that extent the alliance with the United States helped to allay regional fears and suspicions about Japanese intentions and endowed Japanese security policy with a legitimacy it would not otherwise have possessed. At the same time, defence collaboration with the United States provided the SDF with a number of practical benefits, including privileged access to advanced US military equipment, opportunities to exercise with armed forces equipped with the most sophisticated technology, collaboration in defence research development, and a window on US military planning. It is, however, possible to interpret Japan's commitment to the US alliance as a provisional investment, as a strategy which sought to take advantage of the returns likely to be derived in the short to medium term, but with the intention of using, or at least reserving the option to use, this capital to develop over time a more independent defence posture. This possible interpretation should be borne in mind as we turn our attention to the extensive review of the 'security partnership' undertaken in 1995 and the agreements which ensued.

According to Joseph Nye, the then Assistant Secretary of Defense for International Security Affairs, the aim of the bilateral security dialogue[69] was to bring about a closer alignment of the post-Cold War thinking of the two countries. Three main issues were identified: the defence of the Japanese homeland, including such questions as the Okinawa bases and host-nation support; the likely evolution of the regional security environment; and the global implications of US and Japanese involvement in peacekeeping and humanitarian operations.[70] The first practical outcome of the dialogue was the Special Measures Agreement of September 1995 which set cost-sharing guidelines for the next five years, with Japan agreeing to provide direct financial support for US forces stationed on its territory equivalent to 70 per cent of the total cost – an arrangement which made it less expensive for the United States to maintain its forces in Japan than at home.[71] This was followed a few weeks later by changes to the criminal jurisdiction procedures under the bilateral Status of Forces Agreement. Under this agreement the United States undertook to give sympathetic consideration to Japanese requests for transfer of custody of criminal suspects prior to indictment in specific cases of murder or rape.

The Japan–US summit meeting of April 1996 produced the next major development in the form of two documents: 'Message to the Peoples of Japan and the United States' and 'Japan–US Joint Declaration on Security'. Whereas the first document focused on the importance of democracy, freedom and other shared values, the second document reaffirmed the importance of the Japan–US security relationship, and in particular the US commitment to the continued deployment of about 100 000 military personnel in the region, Japan's readiness to continue appropriate support for the maintenance of US forces in Japan, and the need to base Japan's defence on a combination of appropriate SDF capabilities and the Japan–US security arrangements, notably US deterrence as the ultimate guarantee of Japanese security. More specifically, the Joint Declaration envisaged enhanced bilateral consultation on defence policies, a review of the Guidelines for Japan–US Defense Co-operation, studies on bilateral responses to situations that might emerge in areas surrounding Japan, exchanges in the areas of technology and equipment, and co-operation in on-going research on ballistic missile defence. Clinton's visit to Japan also saw the signing of an acquisition and cross-servicing agreement which provided for reciprocal exchanges of supplies and services between the armed forces of the two countries to facilitate joint training and exercises, and the conduct of peacekeeping and humanitarian missions. Perhaps the most revealing feature of this agreement was Japan's willingness to waive the existing ban on the export of arms production-related equipment, at least so far as the United States was concerned.

The report on defence co-operation guidelines, which duly followed in September 1997, sought to enhance the level of defence co-operation across a range of functions (for example, intelligence, command and control, communications/electronics, logistic activities). In responding to potentially adverse contingencies in the areas surrounding Japan, the two governments undertook to establish at an early stage a bilateral co-ordination mechanism. Contingencies identified included humanitarian relief operations (such as refugee flows), search and rescue, economic sanctions, evacuation of nationals, and Japanese support for US military activities. In the event of such contingencies arising, Japan would provide US forces with temporary use of military and civilian facilities and with rear-area support which might require the involvement of Japanese government agencies and the allocation of both public and private resources.

On first reading these measures do suggest a substantial tightening of the security relationship, greater Japanese integration with US military doctrines, planning, operations and capabilities, and a greater readiness on Japan's part to commit its military and civilian assets to the defence of US strategic interests even on the high seas and in international airspace.[72] On closer inspection, it emerges that the contingencies that would trigger these responses were defined only in the most general terms, and that co-ordinated responses were subject to common assessment of the situation and joint agreement on the measures and mechanisms to be adopted. The package of bills for implementing the guidelines were passed by the House of Representatives in May 1999, but with three key amendments: Japanese forces would not be able to conduct operations outside Japan without prior Diet approval; emergencies in areas surrounding Japan were defined as 'situations which, if not acted upon, may bring about a direct armed attack against Japan'; the most contentions issue – high-sea inspections of unidentified ships by the SDF to enforce economic santions – was removed from the bill package and left to separate legislation.[73] This is not to say that the strengthening of bilateral defence ties was not sufficiently concrete to provoke, as we shall see, a sharply critical Chinese response or to circumscribe the range of strategic options available to Japanese defence planners. On the other hand, the guidelines also provided the Japanese armed forces with the political shield they still needed if they were to expand their fire power and forward projection capabilities.

The Pentagon's strategy was clear enough: to lock the Japanese Self-Defense Forces into strategic technological and psychological dependence on the United States. In this, US planners were assisted by a series of provocative North Korean actions. In August 1998 Japan accused North Korea of launching a ballistic missile into Japanese airspace, though Pyongyang insisted it was a rocket designed to put a satellite into orbit. In March 1999 suspected North Korean ships entered Japanese territorial waters, prompting Japanese ships to fire live rounds as warning shots before the two unmarked vessels retreated into North Korean waters.[74] These intrusions coupled with the alleged abduction of Japanese nationals by North Korean agents created a higher level of security consciousness among Japanese policy-makers and gave added impetus to the passage of legislation to implement the defence guidelines. They also accelerated Japan's decision to commit up to $250 million in joint research with the United States on a new theatre missile defence (TMD) programme with particular emphasis on the Navy Theater–Wide Defense System (NTWD). It could not be assumed, however, that Japan's rapidly changing domestic and international environment would permit its past subordination to US strategic interests to shape the future direction of its global and regional diplomacy.

US–Japan security links were part of a larger and more complex relationship, in which economic, political and geostrategic influences were closely interwoven. During the 1980s and early 1990s it appeared as if Japan was well on the way to translating economic power into diplomatic influence, especially in a regional setting. Its status, it was argued, as the leading East Asian capitalist developmental state, with its successful blend of state intervention and growth of corporate power, provided Japan with 'the capacity to plan and implement the construction of a regional division of labour'.[75] The sheer scale of Japanese investments in Asia (estimated in 1994 at $65.5 billion compared with $37.8 billion for the United States)[76] added weight to the argument that Japan was assuming a regional leadership role. By contrast the US economy seemed to lose its competitive edge, unable to rectify its large and chronic balance of payments deficit or to match Japan's higher rate of savings and investment. At the same time, the United States could no longer underwrite the viability of East Asian industrialization, nor, without considerable financial assistance, could it afford to shoulder the heavy cost associated with the forward projection of military power. The end of the Cold War and the implicit loss of ideological hegemony were likely to compound the effects of economic decline.

The new distribution of power was nevertheless subject to considerable flux. Japan had emerged as a major centre of economic power, but its position, even regionally, was far from hegemonic, ideologically, politically or structurally. Having chosen after 1945 to fashion its national identity with the West as its standard, it became a virtual outsider in Asia. Dependent largely on the United States for international recognition and legitimacy, its symbolic diplomacy did not resonate with those societies, in Asia and elsewhere, which had only just emerged from their colonial past. The only other alternatives available to Japan's political elites were either to retreat into uniqueness, which might simply arouse lingering regional suspicions, or to assume a new cosmopolitan identity, for which task they were not psychologically equipped. Cosmopolitanism was a particularly difficult option given Japan's cultural insularity, its reluctance to articulate an overarching statement of moral purpose or, to put it simply, its apparent inability to define foreign policy goals in terms of any distinctive set of transcendent values.

The experiment with 'internationalization' in the 1980s coupled with the hesitant attempts at 'Asianization' were indicative of a country conscious of its economic and technological prowess, but still searching for its rightful place in the world, still struggling to overcome the cultural confusion and lack of self-confidence engendered by defeat in war and subsequent military occupation.[77] Not surprisingly, Asia, long dominated by the West, was unlikely to find in Japanese culture and politics 'the language and psychology of self-assertion',[78] much less the vehicle for a compelling vision of regional order. The limitations on Japan's prestige and influence, mirrored and reinforced by continuing self-doubts and steadily increasing factionalism and new corruption within the political leadership, made it difficult to project coherent power on a regional, let alone global, scale.

Compounding these difficulties was Japan's prolonged economic downturn during the greater part of the 1990s and an unprecedented crisis in its banking system.[79] Virtually every sector of the economy was affected, not least the profitability of the car industry (Mitsubishi's and Nissan's profit margins per car produced having fallen to $700 and $100 respectively, well below the levels recorded by their American competitors).[80] The response of Japanese governments was to introduce one stimulus package after another, but it was by no means certain that these measures would enable Japanese industry to find market outlets capable of absorbing the vast excess it had accumulated over two decades. To make matters worse Japanese politics had entered a period of drift and mounting public scepticism, reflected in an increasingly fragmented Liberal Democratic Party (LDP), the absence of a politically cohesive opposition capable of articulating coherent policy alternatives, powerful interest groups intent on blocking any policies likely to affect them adversely, and a bureaucracy deeply compromised by its close association with vested interests and seemingly uncertain about how to navigate the Japanese ship across the turbulent seas of economic globalization.

The United States, on the other hand, continued to enjoy a residual primacy in world affairs, nowhere more evident than in Asia Pacific where it continued to hold unchallenged military sway through the awesome power of its navy, the technological sophistication of its military system generally and an elaborate network of bases, alliances and related security agreements. The collapse of the Soviet Union, the isolation of North Korea and the eagerness of both Beijing and now Hanoi to cultivate closer ties with Washington had effectively eliminated any serious obstacle to US strategic pre-eminence. To this must be added the pervasive influence of American culture and the continued though reduced dependence of many regional economies, not least Japan, on the large US market. Moreover, by the mid-1990s there were clear indications of a significant improvement in US productivity and export performance in the manufacturing sector. Finally, the United States continued to exercise enormous structural power by virtue of its organizational and co-ordinating capacity, evident as much in the economic as in the diplomatic arenas. Not only did it retain a key role in existing regional and international organizations, but, as the abortive proposal for the establishment of a regional fund clearly indicated, its support and participation appeared indispensable to the success of any enduring multilateral initiative.

Yet these manifestations or symptoms of American power on the one hand and a faltering Japanese economy on the other were also misleading, for they told only part of the story. By the end of the 1990s Japan was beginning to recover from its prolonged economic recession. To this end the many stimulus packages introduced by the government had necessitated a vast public sector borrowing programme, which saw Japan's budget deficit in 1999 rise to 8 per cent of GDP and gross public sector debt to 128 per cent of GDP (and perhaps as much as 150 per cent of GDP if hidden debts were included). Unsustainable as these high levels of government debt might be in the long term, Japan remained the world's largest creditor nation and did not therefore depend on foreign capital to finance its deficit. By contrast, the United States, while successfully eliminating the soaring budget deficit associated with heavy borrowing in the 1980s, had accumulated a massive private sector (firms and households) debt estimated in 1999 at an unprecedented 132 per cent of GDP.[81] With much of the borrowing used to finance share buying at a time of rising share prices, firms and households had become highly vulnerable to a future downturn, whether expressed in an economic slowdown, higher interest rates or a fall in asset prices. Private sector debt had also stimulated a large and growing import bill resulting in correspondingly large current account deficits. High levels of foreign debt had in turn made the US economy dependent on the willingness of foreigners to hold mounting volumes of dollar-denominated assets. It was after all Japanese lending (that is, the recycling of Japan's trade surplus into US Treasury bonds) which in part had enabled Americans to buy Japanese goods and at least indirectly had helped to sustain the US boom of the 1990s.[82]

The role performed by the United States, both regionally and globally, was qualitatively different from what it had been in the heyday of *Pax Americana*. The US policy of burden-sharing, to which we have referred more than once, was not confined to defence expenditure. Washington was now vigorously pressing its allies and friends to share the burden in such areas as development and humanitarian aid, support for multilateral institutions, liberalization of world trade, expanded use of bases and other facilities, and the establishment of *ad hoc* coalitions for purposes of peacekeeping and peace enforcement. In other words, US Administrations were seeking to strengthen or at least prevent any further decline of the hegemonic order, largely through increasing reliance on collective action. In exchange for enjoying the fruits of stability, security and prosperity, junior members of the hegemonic system had to accept the establishment or maintenance of international regimes over which the United States would retain effective control but for which it was prepared to shoulder a diminishing proportion of the cost.

Our analysis, then, of US–Japan relations suggests that the preconditions for the continued viability of US hegemony were only partially satisfied. Japanese governments, it is true, still generally deferred to US diplomatic and strategic leadership, but such deference could not be mistaken for subservience or complete identity of interests. Japan's political and bureaucratic elites were pursuing an incremental though complex and at times contradictory strategy designed to widen

Japanese freedom of action while retaining the valuable mantle of respectability conferred by the US alliance. In any case, in the economic arena, Japan's policy-making institutions and important elements of Japanese capital were not at all disposed to comply with US priorities or directives. There was certainly little prospect that Japanese capitalism or Japanese society more generally was about to adopt the Anglo-American neo-liberal model, or jettison the intimate links between government, bureaucracy and business or the *keiretsu* structure of its economy.[83] Japan's faltering economic performance in the 1990s may have blunted its economic assertiveness, but there was little reason to think that trade, fiscal policy and financial flows would not remain a source of considerable and growing friction in the bilateral relationship. Japan might for some time to come continue to bear the costs of US hegemony, but such a role was likely to give rise to increasing ambiguity in its external relations and profound ambivalence within its body politic.

CHINA AND THE UNITED STATES: COMPREHENSIVE OR CONDITIONAL ENGAGEMENT?

With the dissipation of Cold War rivalries and the decline of Soviet power, the United States saw itself as the sole superpower, the only state with the capacity and moral authority to construct a 'new world order'. In Asia Pacific the only potential challenge to continued US preponderance appeared to be China. US policy-makers might profess that they did not consider China a threat to US interests, but both public and elite opinion was visibly disconcerted by the prospect of China's rise as a world power.[84] Exponents of the 'China threat' thesis were struck by the incompatibility of US and Chinese objectives.[85] In the view of two leading US commentators, 'China's sheer size and inherent strength, its conception of itself as a center of global civilization, and its eagerness to redeem centuries of humiliating weakness were propelling it toward Asian hegemony'.[86] Beijing, it was argued, was intent on controlling the South China and East China Seas and the region's essential sea lanes. Chinese military expenditures were rising appreciably year in, year out (by 14.6 per cent in 1995 and 11.3 per cent in 1996) and therefore, regardless of the exact figures (vastly understated by official estimates), the unavoidable conclusion was that China had embarked upon 'one of the most extensive and rapid military buildups in the world'.[87]

At no stage was the 'China threat' thesis[88] adopted as official US policy. On the other hand, both the Bush and Clinton Administrations were aware that the thesis was shared by a substantial and often vocal minority in Congress and by a wide cross-section of the US media.[89] These sentiments, coupled with the constant pressure mounted by the highly organized Taiwan lobby, could not but influence or at least constrain the formulation and execution of policy. For Beijing the China threat argument was disquieting, not because it was likely to precipitate, at least in the short term, a major clash with the United States, but rather because it was likely to fuel the suspicions of regional neighbours and more generally complicate the already difficult task of establishing the legitimacy of China's claims to several disputed territories, notably Taiwan. The Chinese leadership was therefore at pains to emphasize the defensive character of China's military modernization and the high priority it attached to the development of its domestic economy, hence its strong interest in promoting a peaceful international environment.[90]

There was, however, a more subtle but perhaps more significant dimension to China's response. In a lengthy analysis of what it labelled as 'the strategy of containment by US hegemonism and the West towards China', the Chinese Communist Party (CCP) fired a broadside against the United States, accusing it of attempting to thwart China's growth as a prosperous and powerful country, of obstructing its entry into the World Trade Organization and of engaging in interference in China's internal situation.[91] Implicit in this accusatory language, echoed in numerous official and semi-official statements, were two important messages: first, that committed though it was to co-operative relations with the United States, China would never be intimidated into retreating on issues of sovereignty; and second, that, despite America's determination to preserve its superpower status, the international system was inexorably moving towards a multipolar structure. There were, of course, differences of emphasis, but the widely shared view was that the international system had entered a period of transition in which US dominance would decline, in part as a result of the diminishing utility of military power and the global redistribution of economic and technological capabilities. Just as the United States stood to lose in this 'power transition', so China stood to gain.

These conflicting perceptions of the future would profoundly influence the Sino-American relationship,[92] which is not to argue that conflict was the inevitable outcome either in the short or longer term. Chinese leaders remained throughout the 1990s conscious of the immensely powerful levers still at the disposal of the United States, hence the perceived need for accommodation. Not surprisingly, this phase of the relationship gave rise to both tension and co-operation, with conflicting signals becoming a distinguishing feature of both US and Chinese policy.

To flesh out this analysis we begin with the Bush presidency, which was in many respects a dress rehearsal for the fluctuating fortunes of Sino-American relations during the Clinton years. In response to the Tiananmen events of June 1989, the US Administration responded with appropriate outrage to Chinese government actions and imposed a range of sanctions, including a ban on US military sales to China and high-level military exchanges between the two countries, suspension of all high-level government contacts, prohibitions on Export–Import Bank programmes, withholding of development funds, opposition to loans from multilateral development banks, and suspension of export licences for advanced civilian end-use technologies. Yet behind the severity of the US retaliatory measures was a more carefully modulated diplomatic response. Barely three weeks after the suspension of the Chinese democracy movement, US Secretary of State Baker cautioned against 'the hasty dismantling of a constructive US–Chinese relationship', and counselled a 'measured' response as the most effective way of stimulating the process of democratization.[93] By February 1990, the US State Department, while conceding widespread human rights abuses in China, was also drawing attention to positive signs of normalization. These included the lifting of martial law in Beijing, assurances on M-9 missile sales, the release of 573 detainees, and progress towards resumption of the Fulbright programme. It was now openly acknowledged that US policy towards China – a blend of sanctions and continuing economic, cultural and other contacts – reflected 'a balance of competing objectives', which embraced support for political reform in China but also the need for dialogue with Beijing on regional conflicts (for example, in Korea, Cambodia), conventional and nuclear arms control and other global issues.[94]

Within weeks of the imposition of sanctions, the Bush Administration had authorized the delivery to China of four Boeing 757-200 commercial jetliners valued at $200 million. A few months later export licences were issued for US-built Aussat and Asiasat satellites to be launched on Chinese vehicles. In the course of the next three years Congressional pressure for additional sanctions was firmly resisted; and substantial shipments to China of satellites, satellite components and high-speed computers[95] were authorized through a succession of presidential waivers. The United States was using technology-transfer policy to punish the Chinese government for its human rights violations but also to reward it for co-operation with US endeavours to prevent the proliferation of weapons of mass destruction. This is not to argue that, aside from the question of human rights, US and Chinese interests largely coincided or even converged. Far from it. The argument rather is that serious differences would periodically emerge across the policy spectrum – human rights, economic practices, China's missile and nuclear exports – and that as a consequence US policy-makers could not allow the question of human rights to shape the entire relationship.

In any case, there was convergence as well as divergence of interests. In the economic arena, Deng Xiaoping's policies of openness and reform offered the prospect of a rapidly growing market-oriented economy and enormous opportunities, which the United States could not easily ignore. For its part, the Bush Administration preferred to treat each issue on its merits, applying pressure at various points of the relationship, but refraining from making progress in one area of negotiation conditional on progress in other areas. Though it eventually bowed to Congressional pressure for a tougher negotiating stance with China, it nevertheless continued to veto legislation which attached human rights conditions to the retention of China's MFN status. This approach was seen as instrumental in securing a number of concessions from China, including the opening up of its markets to US exports, its pledge to ban the export of the products of prison labour, ratification of the Nuclear Non-Proliferation Treaty, and agreement to comply with the provisions of the Missile Technology Control Regime (MTCR).

Despite these successes, Congress remained critical of the policy engagement and sought to restrict the President's freedom of action by considering, and in several instances enacting, legislation designed to reinforce US leverage over China's human rights performance. In 1992, for example, Congress responded to continued Chinese jamming of Voice of America (VOA) broadcasts by creating the Commission on Broadcasting to the People's Republic of China with a view to exploring the establishment of a separate broadcasting service to China. Also in 1992, Congress enacted the US Hong Kong Policy Act, which provided for a number of punitive measures to be applied in the event that China did not adhere to the Joint Declaration on Hong Kong.[96]

Though the dilemmas and tensions underlying America's China policy became more acute under the Bush Administration, the differences in diplomatic perspective between the two countries did not fully emerge and the options available to US policy-makers did not fully crystallise until halfway through Clinton's presidency. There were, of course, any number of disagreements or grievances, which both sides would express with monotonous regularity. For Washington matters of particular concern – other than human rights issues, which inevitably raised questions about the future of Tibet and Hong Kong – included the openness of China's military budget and strategic planning, its willingness to sell technologies related to mass destruction and missile delivery systems, its apparent support for the Iranian and Pakistani nuclear programmes, its extensive claims in the South China Sea, PLA exercises and missile tests in the Taiwan Strait, and the rapidly growing US trade deficit.[97]

For Beijing the list was equally long: US obstructionism preventing China from joining the World Trade Organization (WTO) as a founding member; the decision to supply Taiwan with 150 F-16 fighter planes; the visa granted to Taiwan's President Lee Teng-hui to visit the United States in 1995; the human rights conditions attached to the extension of China's most favoured nation status; US willingness to host, fund and honour Chinese dissidents; the shadowing and interception of a Chinese freighter, the *Yinhe*; US opposition to China's bid to host the 2000 Olympic Games; the embargo on high-technology exports to China.[98] Considered in isolation, none of these skirmishes appeared substantial enough to provoke an irreparable fracture in the relationship. Yet, taken together, they diminished the prospects for a durable *modus vivendi*. To understand the full implications of the gap separating the two sides, it is necessary to investigate more closely some of the key areas of contention before placing them in a wider geopolitical, economic and socio-cultural context.

In the strategic arena two issues merit special attention: diverging attitudes on arms control and the conflict over Taiwan. Of particular concern to the United States was the possible transfer of nuclear materials and equipment to nuclear threshold countries. Iran, though a party to the NPT, had long been regarded by Washington as harbouring nuclear ambitions. It reacted therefore with predictable hostility to intelligence reports that China might be assisting Iran to build a uranium hexafluoride plant and supplying it with missile production technology and missile component transfers as well as shorter-range ballistic and anti-ship cruise missiles.[99] However, by 1995 China had cancelled the projected sale of a nuclear power plant to Iran, curtailed its assistance to Iran's chemical weapons programme and refrained from exporting the M-9 missile to any country in the region. Whether in response to the threat of US sanctions or not, the simple fact is that China, with the partial exception of its strategic relationship with Pakistan, had not exported raw materials, equipment or technology in violation of any arms control agreement. While the US Congress in May 1997 imposed sanctions on Chinese firms for exporting chemical weapons material to Iran, these exports were not in breach of the Chemical Weapons Convention.[100]

The fluctuating fortunes of the Sino-American arms control dialogue stemmed from conflicting interests and priorities as much within as between the two polities. Since the end of the Cold War US export control policy had set itself the primary objective of preventing the proliferation of weapons of mass destruction. To this end it sought to deny China access to dual-use technologies, either in retaliation for alleged non-proliferation violations or to restrict China's capacity to develop sensitive technologies which might be diverted to third countries. In 1991 the United States accused China of violating the MTCR guidelines by selling M-9 and M-11 missiles to Pakistan. It retaliated by blocking export licences for satellite parts and other advanced technologies, while still engaging the Chinese in non-proliferation negotiations. In the course of the following year, the sanctions were lifted and highly lucrative export licences issued for US-built satellites, satellite parts and high-speed computers. In August 1993, sanctions were again imposed, this time by the Clinton Administration, following a determination that China had transferred to Pakistan M-11 missile-related components and technologies. A few months later, the ban was partially lifted and the sale of two sophisticated US-built satellites permitted in exchange for an undertaking by China not to allow future missile sales. In October 1994, the two countries concluded an agreement which provided for an end to all US sanctions imposed the previous year, a Chinese pledge to halt further M-series missile transfers in contravention of MTCR guidelines, and a joint undertaking to co-operate on missile and nuclear non-proliferation. China also committed itself to the conclusion of a multilateral convention banning production of fissile materials.[101]

Significantly, when new intelligence reports indicated that in 1995 and 1996 China had supplied Pakistan with M-11 components and assistance for the construction of a missile production facility, the Clinton Administration refrained from taking punitive action. Clearly, non-proliferation and more generally strategic objectives constituted only one of the variables shaping US policy. At least as influential were economic considerations, notably the large and growing Chinese market for advanced technologies (not just satellites and computers, but telecommunications equipment, machine tools and commercial jet liners) and the political pressure exerted by business groups which stood to gain from unfettered access to this market. Not surprisingly China policy became highly contested territory for the various bureaucratic arms of government, in particular the State, Commerce, Defense and Energy Departments, each of which reflected the interests and perceptions of disparate constituencies. Though less transparent, similar divisions emerged in the Chinese decision-making process, with the commercial and strategic gains arising from the sale of military technologies to Pakistan, Iran, Algeria, Syria and others having to be balanced against the risks of proliferation, the possible loss of access to US technology, and the potential for regional instability, which might in turn prejudice China's ambitious plans for economic modernization.

By the mid-1990s, China had many reasons for wishing to promote a more effective global non-proliferation regime, not all of which could be ascribed to the Clinton strategy of 'comprehensive engagement'.[102] Its accession to the Non-Proliferation Treaty in March 1992, followed by its active participation in the negotiation of the Comprehensive Test Ban Treaty and ratification of the Chemical Weapons Convention, indicated a conscious desire to assume a higher profile on arms control issues and to project an image as a responsible great power and permanent member of the Security Council. It was, in effect, the slow pragmatic convergence of US and Chinese interests which eventually paved the way for the implementation of the 1985 US–China Agreement for Peaceful Nuclear Co-operation. Secretary of State Warren Christopher's visit to Beijing in November 1996 marked an important step in this direction. China reaffirmed its previously stated commitment not to provide assistance to unsafeguarded nuclear facilities, and indicated an interest in joining the Zangger NPT Suppliers Committee.

A year later, on the occasion of Clinton's visit to China, the two sides agreed to take additional steps to implement the nuclear co-operation agreement and to collaborate at the UN Conference on Disarmament for an early start to negotiations on a treaty to prohibit the production of fissile materials.[103] China for its part undertook to strengthen dual-use export controls over nuclear-related technology.

The way had thus been opened for the US Congress to lift the 12-year ban on the sale of US nuclear technology to China and for US corporations to gain access, whether through trade or investment, to the Chinese nuclear energy market, now expected to generate capital investment opportunities of the order of $60 billion. For the US nuclear industry, this meant the likelihood of contracts worth in excess of $1.5 billion per year,[104] which was welcome news given the depressed state of the nuclear market in most advanced capitalist economies.

If arms control policy indicated the feasibility of a Sino-American *modus vivendi* based on converging, if not exactly common, interests, other facets of the strategic relationship were less encouraging. The situation on the Korean peninsula, it is true, had given both Beijing and Washington the opportunity to engage in parallel and even collaborative diplomacy with a view to managing or at least containing the conflict within acceptable levels of risk and tension. Yet, as we shall see in a later chapter, even here the interests of the two countries were far from identical. However, when it came to Taiwan, the clash of perspectives was deep-seated and undisguised. For the United States, Taiwan, strategically located between Northeast and Southeast Asia, was an ideal launching pad for the regional projection of military force. The competitiveness of Taiwan's economy, its extensive links with US business interests, the US Congress and US educational and cultural institutions, and the slow but steady democratization of its polity made it a doubly attractive partner for the United States as it attempted to cement its economic and strategic stake in the Pacific.[105] Not surprisingly, the US commitment to Taiwan, enshrined in the Taiwan Relations Act (TRA) of 1979, was both extensive and explicit, envisaging the defence of Taiwan 'against any resort to force or other forms of coercion' that would jeopardise the security or social or economic system of the people of Taiwan.[106]

For China, on the other hand, Taiwan was central to the goal of national reunification. Deng Xiaoping and other Chinese leaders made it clear that the particular form that reunification might take was a matter of negotiation, and that under the principle of 'one country, two systems' Taiwan would be free to retain its preferred economic and political institutions, including an independent judiciary and even its own army. However, the proposition that the People's Republic of China alone could represent China internationally was itself non-negotiable.[107] China's resumption of sovereignty over Hong Kong in June 1997 and over Macao in December 1999 was seen as the necessary prelude to reunification with Taiwan. After so many decades of humiliation at western hands, Taiwan's return to the fold was to be the pre-eminent symbol of China's reassertion of its unity and sovereignty. More importantly, it was a test of the legitimacy of China's governing party. With the collapse of Marxist ideology, economic modernization and national reunification were now the only two ideals capable of serving as a unifying force and providing a plausible psychological and intellectual foundation for the continuation of communist rule.

There were none the less subsidiary considerations which also reinforced Beijing's bid for unification with Taiwan, not least the likely synergy between the mainland's large resource and demographic base and Taiwan's technological and entrepreneurial dynamism.[108] Two-way trade between China and Taiwan increased from less than $50 million in 1978 to $7.4 billion in 1992 and some $25 billion in 1999. By 1993, some five million Taiwanese had visited China, and between 6000 and 7000 small and medium-sized firms had investments in China worth between $5 billion and $10 billion.[109]

This complex blend of geoeconomic, geocultural and geopolitical factors had made the future of Taiwan a central Chinese preoccupation, all the more so as the governing elite in Taipei and its supporters in Washington seemed intent on frustrating Beijing's objectives and priorities. Chinese leaders were particularly irritated by Taiwan's increasingly assertive and generously funded bilateral and multilateral diplomacy. Even more troubling was the growing popularity of Taiwanese political parties advocating notions of Taiwanese independence, which, Beijing suspected, had the sympathy, if not overt support, of the ruling Nationalist Party. If Taiwanese President Lee Teng-hui's private visit to the United States in June 1995 provoked a vitriolic Chinese response, it was precisely because in Chinese eyes the Clinton Administration's decision to allow the Taiwanese leader to set foot on US soil symbolized American support for Taiwan's international diplomacy. In retaliation Beijing recalled its ambassador from Washington, postponed talks on the MTCR regime, suspended cross-strait negotiations, and intensified military exercises in the East China and South China Seas.

In March 1996, China conducted a series of missile launching exercises in waters 30 miles off Taiwan's port cities of Jilong and Gaoxiong, and completed these with two rounds of live-ammunition naval and air force manoeuvres, the first in the vicinity of the Taiwan-controlled Jinmen and Penghu islands, and the second off Fujian province near the Taiwan-controlled islands of Mazu and Wuchiu.[110] The US Administration immediately condemned China's provocative actions and sent two aircraft carriers, *Independence* and *Nimitz*, to the area. Yet both Beijing and Washington conveyed clear signals that they would not allow the crisis to escalate into military hostilities. China made it known that it did not intend to invade or attack Taiwan and the US Administration accepted those assurances, distancing itself from Congressional committee resolutions pledging support for Taiwan against invasion or missile attack. With the ending of PLA exercises on 20 March, three days prior to elections in Taiwan, the crisis was effectively defused.

What, then, are we to make of this particular skirmish in the protracted Taiwan dispute? The Chinese strategy, it seems, was not to attack but to apply pressure on

Taiwan and indirectly on the United States. The show of strength did not imply that China had either the will or the capacity to achieve reunification by force. Rather the intended message was that, unless Taiwan came to the negotiating table, it could in future expect continuing harassment of a kind which, though it may not pose a direct military threat, could nevertheless cause serious economic and financial uncertainty and in the process acute social and political tension. Judging from the severe downward pressure the March 1996 military exercises had exerted on the Taiwanese stock market, a prolonged war of nerves could lead to a massive flight of capital and people from Taiwan and the general demoralisation of the population.[111] While the exact mix of military actions China might unleash would depend on prevailing circumstances, missile tests, a sea blockade, combined forces drill and large movements of PLA units into offensive positions could all be attempted without a single shot having to be fired.[112] That the PLA might be incapable of mounting an amphibious invasion of Taiwan was in this sense peripheral to Beijing's strategy.

Diplomatic subtlety and military ambiguity were not, however, exclusive to Chinese policy. The US position on Taiwan was itself a carefully crafted amalgam of competing priorities. On the one hand, the United States had an interest in maintaining Taiwan's *de facto* independence and the benefits derived from that relationship. On the other hand, it did not wish to see its support for Taiwan precipitate a conflict likely to endanger its own relationship with China. To resolve this dilemma US policy-makers had opted for a 'no-war, no-peace' strategy designed to keep the China–Taiwan dispute simmering without actually coming to the boil (which carried the risk of US involvement in a military conflict in China) or allowing the temperature to fall (to such a point that a negotiated settlement might become feasible).

To maintain the dispute in this delicate state of limbo, the United States was prepared to reaffirm periodically the principles enunciated in the three joint communiqués with the PRC, notably recognition of the PRC government as 'the sole legal Government of China'; acknowledgement of the Chinese position that 'there is but one China and Taiwan is part of China'; and Taiwan's exclusion from international organizations where membership was based on sovereign statehood.[113] The clear implication of these three principles, which Clinton verbally restated during his visit to China in 1998, was that the United States was opposed to the creation of a sovereign Taiwan, and that, should political forces on the island proceed along this path, they could count on no external assistance.[114]

Having effectively excluded the independence option, the United States was none the less intent on maintaining the integrity of a separate Taiwan. Despite the long-standing ban on official contact between the US and Taiwanese armed forces, Washington had managed to maintain extensive military ties with Taiwan as if it were a separate state. The same strategy was evident in the annual allocation of US visas to Taiwanese nationals and in US support for Taipei's participation in a range of international conferences and organizations. To lend credibility to its extended deterrence strategy, the United States was prepared to support the development of a potent Taiwanese military arsenal and to threaten US intervention should Beijing seek reunification through force. In line with this policy, arms sales to Taipei increased sharply during the early 1990s; these included F-16 fighters, Hawkeye 2-ET early-warning aircraft, MK-46 torpedoes, M60A3 tanks, Knox-class frigates, harpoon anti-ship missiles and a version of the Patriot missile air-defence system.[115]

Chinese leaders took obvious comfort from America's refusal to encourage formal Taiwanese independence, but they could not accept US support for the *status quo*, which they interpreted as a legacy of the old containment policy, or to be more precise, a key element in a new policy of 'conditional engagement'. If reunification, therefore, were to become a reality, a more feasible approach might be to strike some arrangement directly with the authorities in Taiwan, thereby circumventing Washington's preference for the *status quo*. With this end in mind, Beijing pursued a carrot-and-stick strategy. The function of the stick was to deter Taiwanese independence, that is, to persuade both political elites and public opinion in Taiwan that this was a high-risk plan which China would never allow to succeed. The carrot, on the other hand, consisted of incentives – extensive legal and political autonomy within a unified China and a major stake in China's future economic growth – which Beijing hoped the Taiwanese could not refuse. In this sense, Beijing and Washington were engaged in a competition for hearts and minds, with both players using a complex mix of political, economic and military instruments, but with each player careful not to allow the competition to degenerate into outright conflict.

The visit to China by the Chairman of Taiwan's semi-official Straits Exchange Foundation, Koo Chen-fu, in October 1998 graphically demonstrated the scope and limitations of Chinese diplomacy.[116] On one hand, this was the highest-level contact between the two sides – Koo Chen-fu had talks with President Jiang Zemin and other senior officials, including Vice-Premier Qian Qichen – which, coming soon after the 1996 crisis, indicated how quickly and effectively Chinese strategy could oscillate between stick and carrot. On the other hand, it illustrated the enormous psychological as much as political gap separating the two sides, and how difficult it would be to bridge that gap in the foreseeable future. Rightly or wrongly, Beijing's calculation was that, with Hong Kong's successful incorporation and the rapidly developing trade, investment, professional and cultural ties between Taiwan and the mainland,[117] finding an acceptable formula for political association was only a matter of time.

The increasing breadth and intensity of economic linkages were certainly one of the most valuable cards in China's hand. Between 1995 and 1998 the proportion of computer-related products which Taiwanese companies made in mainland China had risen from14.1 per cent to 28.9 per cent; approved Taiwanese investments in China had surged from just over $3 billion during 1994–6 to well over $6 billion during 1997–8.[118] Conscious of the risks of increased economic dependence on China, Taipei was nevertheless compelled to allow limited shipping links with the mainland and increased commercial flights using Macao as a detour. Important elements of the Taiwanese business community were becoming influential advocates of improved cross-strait relations. Taipei's only option was to take advantage of any countervailing trends. The most potent of these was the emergence of a Taiwanese identity separate from that of China and closely associated with the gradual institutionalization of democratic politics. A number of surveys – some of them government-inspired – indicated that in the course of the 1990s the proportion of the population identifying themselves as Taiwanese had more than doubled to nearly 40 per cent, whereas those identifying themselves as Chinese had declined to 16 per cent from a high of 50 per cent in 1993.[119] Riding on the wave of Taiwan's economic success and a new sense of national identity, President Lee Teng-hui's Administration embarked upon an intense battle for greater international recognition. Yet attempts at financial largesse, including plans for substantial aid to Kosovo and the Balkans and enticements offered to PNG and Fiji, yielded few diplomatic successes.[120]

Possibly with an eye to breaking the diplomatic logjam, but also as a way of capturing political ground from the pro-independence opposition in the lead-up to a presidential election scheduled for March 2000, Lee Teng-hui launched a new offensive in July 1999. Describing himself as the leader of a sovereign state, he argued that his government deserved equal standing with the government in Beijing, and that henceforth relations between Taiwan and the mainland should be placed on a state-to-state footing.[121] China's response was predictably vitriolic in its rhetoric, yet carefully measured in its execution. Lee was vilified as a traitor, the PLA reiterated its readiness 'to safeguard the territorial integrity of China and smash any attempt to separate the country',[122] and at the ASEAN Regional Forum meeting in late July 1999, Chinese Foreign Minister, Tang Jiaxuan, counselled the United States 'not to say anything or do anything that may fan the flames of Taiwan's independence or Lee Teng-hui's separatist remarks or activities'.[123]

The first concrete action came on 31 July when the Chinese customs police seized a civilian freighter transporting supplies to the estimated 10 000 troops on the Taiwan-occupied island chain of Matsu.[124] On 2 August, China announced it had successfully conducted a launching test of a new type of long-range missile, known as the Dong Feng-31 intercontinental missile, that could carry a nuclear warhead over a range of about 8000 kilometres. Capable of reaching targets in the western part of the United States and likely to be fired from a mobile launcher that would be difficult to detect or intercept, the missile was clearly designed to weaken the credibility of Washington's extended deterrence posture. In November 1999 the *Washington Times* reported that US spy satellites had photographed construction of a missile site at Yangang in Southern China, about 440 km from Taiwan.[125] It was expected that China would deploy advanced CSS-7 missiles – also known as advanced M-11s – capable of carrying different types of warheads over a range of 500 km. Anxious to prevent an outbreak of hostilities, the US State Department signalled to Taipei that it had overstepped the threshold of prudent diplomacy in cross-strait relations.

The next major development came on the eve of Taiwan's presidential election in March 2000. Possibly with a view to influencing the outcome – or perhaps the policy of the incoming administration - Beijing issued on 21 February a White Paper entitled *The One-China Principle and the Taiwan Issue*. The document, which set out China's proposals for negotiations on reunification, also formulated a new criterion for the use of force against Taiwan:

> If the Taiwan authorities refuse, indefinitely, the peaceful settlement of cross-Straits reunification through negotiations, then the Chinese government will only be forced to adopt all drastic measures possible, including the use of force to safeguard China's sovereignty and territorial integrity . . .[126]

Taipei's political elites were not, however, the only intended audience. The White Paper was also meant as a signal to the United States that arming and protecting Taiwan would constitute a threat to one of China's primary interests, namely its national sovereignty. Any move which strengthened military ties between Washington and Taipei would incur Beijing's implacable hostility, precisely because it was likely to erode Taiwan's incentive to negotiate. In other words, the White Paper carried a clear message for US policy-makers: greater military support for Taiwan would have a double effect: it would strengthen the hand of China's military and political hardliners, and it would increase the probability that China would use force against Taiwan as the only way to break the impasse.

Significantly, Chen Shui-bian, the successful opposition candidate in Taiwan's presidential election, lost little time in distancing himself from his own Democratic Progressive Party's constitution, which still advocated a formal declaration of Taiwanese independence. In his victory speech, he expressed his willingness to negotiate with mainland China 'in every aspect . . . including direct links, investment, a peace agreement'.[127] In his inauguration speech in May 2000 he went even further, pledging not the declare independence during his presidency so long as China did not use military force, and to proceed jointly with Beijing 'with wisdom and creativity' in addressing 'the question of a future One China'.[128] Though these early signs indicated a promising thaw in cross-strait relations, resolution of the Taiwan dispute was still a distant prospect, and one likely to remain a major irritant in Sino-American relations.

While Taiwan loomed as the single most intractable problem in Sino-American relations, the conceptually distinct but often politically connected issues of trade and human rights proved more immediate and just as controversial. In a sense, the dramatic events of June 1989, coupled with saturation coverage in the western media and the peculiarities of US Congressional politics, made it almost inevitable that human rights would occupy diplomatic centre stage. The PRC's White Paper on Human Rights issued in 1991, largely in response to western pressure, was viewed as a step in the right direction but not as an accurate account of the human rights situation in China. The paper enumerated the many rights granted by the Constitution of the PRC, but was virtually silent on questions of legality and due process, judicial independence or the numerous abuses surrounding the detention, trial, conviction and punishment of those charged with either criminal or political offences.[129]

In a bid to exercise greater leverage over US policy, Congress began to use the President's annual request for renewal of China's MFN status – routinely extended since 1979 - as a vehicle for registering US disapproval of China's human rights record. In the 1991 and 1992 MFN debates, Congress passed legislation requiring China to satisfy demands in the areas of trade and proliferation as well as human rights if it was to retain its MFN status. Though Bush vetoed the resolution, his Administration now sought to apply greater pressure on China.[130] An agreement was signed in August 1992 prohibiting Chinese prison labour exports to the United States and providing for regular formal talks on human rights issues. A year later, Clinton, having pledged during his 1992 campaign that he would use US economic leverage to promote democracy in China, agreed to extend China's MFN status for another year while placing conditions on future extensions. To secure renewal of its MFN status in 1994, China would have to demonstrate compliance with the 1992 agreement and significant overall progress in its human rights performance, including treatment of political prisoners and protection of Tibet's religious and cultural heritage.

Although Beijing's immediate response was relatively muted – presumably because the presidential initiative deflected even stronger action by Congress – the following few months saw a marked deterioration of the relationship. Chinese protests against US actions and intentions became noticeably harsher. Following the Administration's reassessment of US–China relations, US policy entered a new phase in September 1993 with the adoption of an expanded strategy of 'comprehensive engagement'.[131] A series of high-level exchanges between the two countries in October 1993 paved the way for the liberalization of US licensing procedures for high-tech exports to China and the resumption of high-level military contacts suspended since June 1989. Human rights remained nevertheless a highly sensitive issue. Repeated US statements impressing on China the need for rapid progress on human rights were met with equally forceful declarations by China that it would not allow human rights policies to be dictated by the United States. To break the impasse Clinton announced on 26 May 1994 that China's MFN status would be renewed despite its failure to satisfy the human rights conditions he had set out in his 1993 Executive Order. The decision was part of a general softening of the US position, hence Clinton's abandonment of 'linkage' politics. While trade and human rights would now be treated as separate issues, the pressure on China to improve its human rights policies would be maintained. Accordingly, there was to be some tightening of US sanctions, increased broadcasts by Radio Free Asia and Voice of America, increased support for NGO activities concerned with human rights in China, and an attempt to develop a voluntary code of conduct for US firms operating in China.

The official rationale for the strategic shift in US policy was that it offered the best available tools 'to advance core American interests'. Speaking in May 1996, Clinton claimed that the policy of engagement had already delivered results: in the area of nuclear non-proliferation; in the attempts to freeze North Korea's nuclear weapons programme; and in arms control negotiations generally. Similarly, in the economic arena, China's elimination of quotas and licensing requirements had helped to double US exports of telecommunications equipment in little more than four years. US total exports to China had risen by nearly 30 per cent in 1995, making it America's fastest-growing export market. Had the United States revoked China's MFN status, it would have jettisoned these gains and curtailed the opportunities for human contact between the two countries, yet done little to strengthen China's respect for human rights.[132] The emphasis now was on establishing an intensive human rights dialogue with China at ministerial and senior official level. Washington would continue to speak out on human rights violations, especially in multilateral fora, and pursue formal or informal initiatives (regular State Department reports on human rights conditions in Hong Kong, pressure on Beijing to resume negotiations with the Dalai Lama) designed to keep China's judicial and political practices under the international spotlight. Put simply, the Clinton Administration portrayed its new policy as an attempt to influence China's behaviour, including its human rights policies, by presenting it with a new set of opportunities and constraints.

The Administration's case for the strategic reorientation of its China policy was not received with universal acclaim. Sections of Congress and a great many public interest organizations, both inside and outside the United States, remained sceptical either of the sincerity or efficacy of the policy. The Lawyers Committee for Human Rights had consistently argued that the sanctions imposed after the Tiananmen

Square crackdown had been instrumental in extracting concessions from China and would have been even more effective had they been applied with the necessary rigour and clarity of purpose.[133] In the minds of many, Administration policy had yielded to powerful industrial and financial interests. By contrast, the US–China Business Council made no secret of its view that withdrawal of MFN status would destroy the framework of the bilateral commercial relationship. It identified US business interests most likely to be hurt as wheat and cotton farmers, producers of fertiliser, textiles, and commercial aircraft, and US investors in China. The same message was relentlessly delivered by other business associations, notably the National Association of Manufacturers, and individual companies, not least Boeing and General Motors.

The notion that 'an expanded presence in China' was central to 'the long-term global marketing strategies' of major firms in leading US export sectors would soon become commonplace in official speeches and testimony before Congress.[134] By 1997, the Administration's position had become firmly entrenched:

> Today we have annual exports to China of $12 billion, directly responsible for 170 000 American jobs. Those exports and those jobs would be at risk from China's certain retaliation to revocation of MFN. . . The World Bank estimates that China will invest $750 billion in infrastructure in the next decade. Without a normal trading relationship, American firms would be frozen out of this market, to the delight of our competitors.[135]

In March 2000, President Clinton, with the support of the Business Roundtable and the Chamber of Commerce but in the face of sustained opposition from labour, human rights, environmental and other organizations, would send legislation to a hostile Congress granting China Permanent Normal Trade Relations (PNTR) status.[136] Two months later the US House of Representatives voted 237 to 197 to pass the bill, thereby ending the annual ritual of reviewing China's trade status. None of this is to suggest that bilateral trade would henceforth be devoid of friction. On the contrary, trade and human rights had been delinked precisely in order to allow the Administration to give US trade interests its undivided attention, unencumbered by the exigencies of human rights policy.

As with Japan so with China, the US deficit had over a number of years emerged as the principal irritant in the bilateral trade relationship. According to the US Department of Commerce, the deficit in merchandise trade had risen from $71 million in 1983 to $22.8 billion in 1993, $33.9 billion in 1995[137] and $49.8 billion in 1998.[138] Here it is worth noting the significant disparity between US and Chinese trade statistics. Whereas the Chinese government recorded many goods that it shipped through Hong Kong as Chinese exports to Hong Kong, US official figures recorded these as Chinese exports to the United States.[139] Similarly, the US

Department of Commerce insisted on designating US sales to China via Hong Kong middlemen as exports to Hong Kong. The net effect of US calculations was to inflate the extent of the US deficit just as Chinese calculations had significantly understated it. According to US statistics, Chinese exports to the United States in 1994 amounted to $38.78 billion and accounted for 32.05 per cent of China's total exports, whereas the corresponding Chinese statistics showed $21.46 billion and 17.74 per cent.[140] Regardless of the intricacies of the methodological dispute, there was no denying the rather healthy surplus China enjoyed in its trade with the United States. This large and growing trade balance would now be used by the Clinton Administration as powerful ammunition with which to press American commercial interests.

Apart from stressing the sheer magnitude of the US trade deficit, influential US business and trade union organizations drew attention to the composition of US–China trade. Of the 20 American industries running the largest trade surplus with China, only one, aerospace, produced high-value, sophisticated products that generated highly paid jobs. The rest, it was argued, consisted of raw materials and lower value-added products (for example, fertilisers, cereals, food residue and pulp wood). By contrast, the United States incurred its largest deficit in electrical machinery, appliances and parts.[141] The reality was much less ominous than this stark representation would suggest. As we noted in the previous chapter, China was now the beneficiary of an intra-Asian geographic shift of manufacturing capacity. Companies from Hong Kong, Taiwan, South Korea, Singapore and Japan that had been unable to upgrade their technological and organizational infrastructure were forced by competition to move their export production base offshore. China, by virtue of its abundant supply of cheap labour and potentially huge market, was a favourite destination. As a consequence, much of the apparel, footwear, luggage and electronic equipment that the United States once imported from East Asia's newly industrializing economies – and earlier from Japan – now came from China.[142]

Significant voices from industry and organized labour were nevertheless intent on contrasting America's open market policies with China's restrictive practices. These were said to include violations of intellectual property rights, failure to honour textile agreements and strict local content rules designed to limit motor vehicle imports. Through a combination of high tariffs, import quotas, discriminatory standards, lack of transparency and foreign exchange requirements China was pursuing an export-led growth strategy sharply at odds with any notion of free trade. The transfer of US capital and technology to China was also criticized by unions on the grounds that it made possible the employment of 'low-cost oppressed cheap labour', thereby establishing manufacturing export centres which priced US products out of the market.

In response to these grievances, the United States sought, and through the Memorandum of Understanding (MOU) of October 1992 secured, China's agreement to increase the transparency of its trade regime, by openly publishing all trade-related laws, regulations and decrees; removing a number of non-tariff barriers; and significantly reducing selected tariffs. Three years later, the General Accounting Office reported that, though China had generally complied with the provisions of the agreement, US companies were still experiencing market access problems. According to the 1996 US Trade Representative (USTR) report on foreign trade barriers, China continued to impose a large number of non-tariff barriers, its tariffs remained prohibitively high in some areas, and its market for services was still severely restricted. Of particular concern was China's failure to halt intellectual property piracy at its source. In May 1996, the Administration announced that in retaliation it would target Chinese exports to match the approximate value of damage inflicted on US industries – estimated at $2 billion. The following month, China moved to close over 15 factories producing pirated compact disks, offered protection against the import and export of pirated intellectual property, and took steps to open its market to US software and audio-visual companies.[143]

The Clinton Administration was clearly intent on opening up Chinese markets by applying sustained pressure on several fronts, both in relation to specific industries and across a range of broader policy issues. Yet, behind this façade of diplomatic robustness one could discern a profound strategic ambivalence. For the American business community was itself deeply divided between winners and losers in what had become a rapidly expanding but acutely unbalanced trade relationship. Firms or industries that were already doing well or hoping to do well in the near future (such as the aerospace and the communications and power industries) preferred to emphasize the enormous opportunities for US exporters in China, whereas those in other manufacturing sectors (for example, electrical machinery, toys, footwear, apparel, furniture and plastics) sought to stem the Chinese onslaught on their industries by advocating a punitive policy designed to redress the existing trade imbalance. Caught between conflicting pressures and perspectives, the Administration oscillated between firmness and accommodation.

A complex overlay soon emerged between the tangled web of influences underlying the MFN controversy and those which shaped the World Trade Organization dispute. In both instances US policy was subjected to powerful but sharply diverging domestic pressures. On the one hand, US interests stood to benefit from China's membership of WTO, that is, from Beijing's compliance with the standards built into the structure of the established international trading system. US firms interested in supplying the Chinese telecommunications economy with capital goods, advanced technologies and a range of financial and other services were attracted by the greater predictability and stability which China's accession to the WTO system would bring to the Sino-American economic relationship. On the other hand, there were also advantages in driving a hard bargain and making China's membership conditional on modifications to its international trading policies. In line with this latter strategy the Clinton Administration set a long list of conditions, notably the substantial reduction of tariffs, including duties on over 2000 'priority' items; the elimination of remaining import quotas on several hundred products; the abolition of the licensing system on imports and exports, which Chinese authorities could use to negate the effect of tariff reductions; the phasing out of laws and regulations discriminating against foreign goods and services; the liberalization of foreign investment rules, including domestic content and export performance requirements; and the introduction of a fully transparent system for the publication of trade rules and regulations.

The problem with such a strategy was that the list of conditions was too demanding and its likely effects on the Chinese economy too severe for Beijing to be able to accept them.[144] Given the traumatic effects of these and other structural changes on the Chinese economy and the difficulties encountered after 1997 in maintaining high rates of growth, to accede to US demands would have been to fan the flames of social and political discontent, possibly to destabilize the Chinese government and even to undermine the dominant position of the Chinese Communist Party. Faced with the prospect of declining support in China for WTO membership, the Clinton Administration began to soften its position. The joint statement issued at the end of President Jiang Zemin's visit to the United States in October 1997 envisaged intensified negotiations with a view to China acceding to the WTO 'on a commercially meaningful basis at the earliest possible date'.[145] A year later, amid reports of slow progress, Clinton acknowledged during his visit to China in the summer of 1998 the need for 'an individual agreement that recognizes the transitions China must undertake'.[146] The gap between the two governments was narrowed further when Zhu Rongji made major concessions, especially on agricultural issues, during his visit to the United States in April 1999. Having refused the Chinese offer in the hope of extracting an even better outcome, the US Administration was now under increasing pressure from an influential cross-section of the US business community to conclude an agreement. An intense lobbying effort led by the Beijing and Shanghai branches of the American Chamber of Commerce and supported among others by General Motors, General Electric, IBM, CIGNA, Boeing and Unison, coupled with mounting criticism of Zhu Rongji by ministry officials and industry leaders in China for having given too much ground, finally persuaded Washington to bring the negotiations to a close. A bilateral trade agreement signed on 15 November 1999 effectively removed the biggest obstacle to China's 13-year efforts to join the WTO.[147]

Under the agreement US investors could own up to 49 per cent of all joint ventures in telecommunications and up to 50 per cent two years after entry. Manufacturers would be able to distribute their products directly, and import and export without relying on Chinese middlemen. Foreign banks would be permitted to offer local currency services to businesses two years after entry and to individuals five years after entry. China undertook to reduce tariffs on cars by 2006 to 26 per cent of their current levels and on agricultural products to 14.5 per cent, with all export subsidies eliminated and the Multi-Fibre Arrangement phased out by 2005. Chinese concessions, significant though they were, still left Beijing with a good deal of room for manoeuvre. In practice the Chinese government could be expected to use the panoply of regulatory levers at its disposal to protect fragile state industries and control levels of foreign investment. The Chinese leadership would presumably pursue a phased approach in dismantling China's trade barriers, stretching out over a longer period the substantial costs of adjusting to international competition and making them socially and politically more palatable It remained to be seen whether the WTO agreement would sufficiently accommodate the conflicting pressures bearing upon the Chinese and American policy-making processes, and how durable the agreement would prove should the bilateral relationship come under additional strain.

The Vicissitudes of Engagement

Enough has been said to indicate that at the end of the 1990s, with trade, human rights and Taiwan still the subject of contention, Sino-American relations remained delicately poised. The Clinton Administration had, it is true, moved relatively quickly to embrace a policy of engagement, yet a good deal of ambiguity persisted in relation to both ends and means. Though the policy was officially labelled 'comprehensive engagement', it was by no mean clear how open-ended or conditional such engagement would prove. To put it simply, was engagement an attempt to construct a durable relationship between two major centres of power and civilizations in the expectation that conflicts of interest and perception would henceforth be resolved through negotiation and compromise? Or was the Clinton strategy premised on the notion that engagement was the carrot that Washington would offer Beijing to persuade it to accept US geopolitical and geoeconomic primacy? In the event that persuasion failed, would Washington then be driven to a more coercive or punitive strategy, with precisely the same end in mind: to steer China into accepting the norms, laws and rules governing the prevailing international liberal order? There is reason to think that US policy-makers were leaning towards the first option but were somehow unwilling or unable to make a clear break with the second option, partly because they had yet to formulate US long-term interests with any degree of precision, but also because they were still wedded to notions of American global and regional leadership.

In his address at Fudan University in November 1996, Secretary of State Warren Christopher went as far as any senior US policy-maker in indicating a clear preference for the first option. Rather than 'engagement' he spoke of 'intensive dialogue' conducted bilaterally as well as at the regional and global levels, leading to co-operation across the spectrum of issues likely to dominate the international agenda of the twenty-first century: environment, non-proliferation, terrorism, international law enforcement and narcotics.[148] His successor, Madeleine Albright, returned to the same theme the following year, referring to 'a record of cooperation on agreements to enhance international nuclear safeguards, ban nuclear tests, and make illegal the possession and production of chemical arms'.[149] Reference was also make to the good working relationship at the UN Security Council, regular consultations on Korea, and on-going negotiations on avoidance of military incidents at sea and halting the practice of smuggling illegal aliens. In all of this, however, there was a clear strategic goal: 'greater interaction, *based on China's acceptance of international norms'*[150] (italics added).

Much the same interpretation could be put on Clinton's visit to China in 1998, during which the two parties engaged in a positive dialogue on a number of regional issues, including the Asian financial crisis, the revival of tensions on the Korean peninsula, and nuclear testing by India and Pakistan. In their joint statement, Jiang and Clinton pledged 'to prevent the export of equipment, materials or technology that would in any way assist programmes in India or Pakistan for nuclear weapons or for ballistic missiles capable of delivering such weapons'.[151] They also agreed to work together to develop an enforcement mechanism for the Biological Weapons Convention. American satisfaction with progress on these various fronts was attributable in no small measure to Beijing's increasingly co-operative attitude in multilateral forums, which in turn reflected a conscious effort on China's part to portray itself as a responsible and reliable partner in the construction of a stable post-Cold War international order.

Clinton's policies were predicated on the assumption that, in 'opening up to the outside world', China had no option but to conform with existing global rules and disciplines. This was very much the drift of the statement he delivered during a brief visit to Canberra in November 1996:

> The direction that China takes in the years to come, the way it defines its greatness in the future, will help to decide whether the next century is one of conflict or cooperation. The emergence of a stable, an open, a prosperous China, a strong China confident of its place in the world and willing to assume its responsibilities as a great nation is in our deepest interest.[152]

Though the President's carefully crafted language conveyed a desire, no doubt genuine, for a constructive relationship with China, there was no mistaking its underlying message: co-operation would depend largely on China's willingness to play a responsible role in international affairs, with the United States presumably reserving the right to pass judgement on China's performance.

The future, then, of the Sino-American relationship would centre on China's response to American expectations. Increasingly, interaction or even more extensive 'engagement' offered no guarantee of harmony. Indeed, it was likely to generate more friction should the Chinese polity decide at a given moment to assert Chinese perspectives and priorities and expect these to be treated with the respect and attention to which the United States had long been accustomed. This scenario had yet to materialize primarily because of a peculiar combination of domestic and external factors. On the other hand, the Chinese leadership had for the best part of two decades embarked upon a modernization programme which required China to open up its economy and participate in a range of international regimes (for example, trade regime, non-proliferation regime, environmental regimes, human rights regime) whose norms and structures had been shaped by western centres of power, notably the United States. On the other hand, Chinese leaders were acutely aware of the constraints imposed by China's economic and political circumstances.

The leadership itself was struggling to overcome a domestic and international legitimation deficit which the Tiananmen upheaval had greatly exacerbated. The modernization of China's economy was generating much new wealth but also profound social and economic inequalities which were severely testing the viability of its political institutions. The increasing incidence of crime, drug use, smuggling and prostitution, the slow but steady fracturing of the nuclear family, and the widespread alienation of youth and intellectuals were but the most visible symptoms of the erosion of the state's authority and the Party's prestige. The recourse to nationalist themes and symbols was in part intended to paper over the cracks in China's social and political edifice. Though the devolution of government functions from the centre to the regions had not visibly weakened the central management of foreign and defence policy, the emergence of powerful economic regions around major metropolitan centres was reflected in the decentralization of international economic transactions, cultural and educational exchanges, and even arms transfers.[153]

The economy itself had made remarkable progress, but it was not without its vulnerabilities. China did not altogether escape the spillover effects of the Asian financial crisis, and the Chinese government's attempts to counter powerful deflationary pressures through large stimulatory packages were only partially successful. The declining rates of growth in gross domestic production, exports and foreign investments, which became quite noticeable in 1997–8, would not be easily reversed.[154] Premier Li Peng's report to the Ninth National People's Congress in March 1998 and that of his successor Zhu Rongji in March 1999 presented a stark picture of China's economy: low productivity in many state-owned enterprises, rising unemployment, a fragile agricultural system, investments that were often speculative and unproductive, inadequate financial supervision, uneven regional development, corruption, and extravagant and wasteful practices.[155] For some time to come China would not have the economic muscle to engage in a sustained or comprehensive confrontation with the United States.

As for China's military capabilities, to which exponents of the 'China threat' thesis invariably referred, these remained modest. Its efforts to modernize its armed forces involved a good deal of reorganization: fewer military regions; the number of military personnel reduced by one million during the 1980s and a further reduction of 500 000 announced in September 1997; retirement of elderly officers; greater emphasis on technical skills in the training of young officers; and the development of a legal system for the PLA, its administration, discipline and operations. The military modernization programme, it is true, also entailed the acquisition and deployment of advanced weapons systems, but the objective was to make limited improvements in a few areas. For the navy the emphasis was on developing anti-submarine warfare, ship-borne air defence and amphibious warfare capabilities. In practice this meant the addition of locally built destroyers, frigates, supply ships, landing ships and other smaller vessels and the purchase of a number of Russian-built kilo-class submarines, as well as a few modern systems from western sources.[156] In December 1996, China announced its intention to purchase two Russian Sovremennyi-class guided missile destroyers, thereby providing the PLA Navy with a more lethal and less vulnerable platform. Increased arms purchases, notably from Russia, were designed not so much to improve naval combat capability as to enhance access to, and familiarity with, advanced technology.[157]

The priorities for the air force, particularly in the wake of intensive studies of both the Gulf War and the air campaign in Kosovo, were to acquire a lift capability, a ground attack capability, a greater capacity for air refuelling and a new generation of fighter aircraft. China purchased 48 Russian-built Su-27 multirole fighters, and in 1996 concluded an agreement to co-produce more Su-27s and possibly upgraded versions of the fighter. There were also plans for the production of the Chinese J-10 aircraft and the purchase of an AWAC system from Israel. It was also buying Russian RD-33 engines to upgrade its indigenously produced F-7 fighter.[158] The ground forces, which received a smaller share of the advanced equipment budget, focused on improving mobility and logistical support, air defence capabilities and command and control facilities. To achieve higher levels of combat readiness, a number of rapid reaction units were established and provided with modern equipment and additional funds for training. However, as one informed observer put it, 'despite these improvements, the PLA is not capable of *sustained* force projection at any distance from China's borders. Moreover, it is at least a decade away, and probably more, from achieving such capabilities'.[159] Even if all the acquisitions planned for the three services were to be realized, pockets of technological sophistication would still co-exist with a number of obsolete systems and inadequate infrastructure, particularly in training and maintenance. As for its ballistic missile forces, improvements in the 1990s had concentrated on the deployment of medium- and shorter-range mobile, conventional (or dual-capable) ballistic missiles. China was also proceeding with development of a new generation of long-range nuclear-armed ICBMs (DF-31, DF-41) and a submarine-launched ballistic missile (JL-2).[160]

By the end of the 1990s the PLA had at its disposal a leaner and more potent force, which would no doubt gain still greater potency in the coming decade.[161] Yet the improvements in China's military capabilities could not be viewed in isolation; they had to be compared with those of its actual or potential adversaries. While Beijing may have improved its capacity to conduct long-range operations across the Taiwan Strait, Taipei had also made significant investment in the modernization of its armed forces, sufficient at any rate to make a PLA assault on the island a rather costly and improbable exercise. The comparison with the United States and Japan was even less flattering. In a highly illuminating analysis of China's military capabilities, Avery Goldstein concluded:

> Compared with the current, and especially anticipated future, modernized air and naval forces of Japan or the United States, the PLA will remain outclassed well into the next century even if China's current round of modernization proceeds smoothly.[162]

There was certainly little evidence to suggest that the development of Chinese military capabilities was part of a grand strategic design on China's part to provoke a military confrontation with a major adversary, or to use the threat of force to impose its will on its neighbours.[163]

Much the same conclusion emerges from an examination of China's military budget. Chinese official figures indicate that military spending rose from 20.1 billion yuan in 1986 to 63.2 billion yuan in 1995. This 314.2 per cent increase over a ten-year period is, however, much less impressive when it is remembered that an increase of 266 per cent was needed merely to keep up with inflation. As a proportion of the state budget, military expenditures tended to fluctuate from one year to the next, rising modestly from 8.8 per cent in 1986 to 9.9 per cent in 1995. Calculated as a proportion of GNP – a more revealing indicator of national priorities

– the percentage had in fact steadily declined, from 2.07 per cent in 1986 to 1.32 per cent in 1995.[164]

The PLA, it is true, supplemented its official defence budget with funds derived from other budget accounts as well as from unofficial revenues, notably earnings from arms exports – the cash value of these exports fell appreciably in the first half of the 1990s – and from commercial activities. Estimates of annual unofficial revenues were difficult to verify, ranging from $1.2 billion to $20 billion.[165] The overall trend, however, did not seem in dispute. The US Arms Control and Disarmament Agency calculated that Chinese military expenditures expressed in constant dollars had fallen from $53.1 billion in 1983 to $43.8 billion in 1988, and risen only slightly from $51.3 in 1989 to $56.2 billion in 1993. Despite budgetary increases in the early 1990s, military spending as a proportion of GNP was estimated to have declined from 6.8 per cent in 1983 to 2.7 per cent in 1993.[166] Military spending continued to increase in the second half of the 1990s, and the budgetary outlay for 2001–5 was expected to double that of 1996–2000, but did not represent a marked increase as a proportion of GNP.

It is difficult, then, to avoid the conclusion that China's military modernization was designed to achieve limited objectives. It was largely defensive in orientation, although, as the 1998 Defence White Paper put it, China's armed forces had the task of defending the nation's 'sovereignty, unity, territorial integrity and security'.[167] This meant in practice the maintenance of a limited nuclear deterrent, but with a clear emphasis on improving its range, accuracy and survivability.[168] At the same time the development of conventional forces was intended to achieve higher levels of training, equipment, mobility and co-ordination with a view to enhancing China's force projection capability. Here again the aim was not crude expansion but the subtle and controlled application of military leverage, in Taiwan as in the South China Sea, to achieve what were essentially political objectives. To put it simply, the Chinese leadership was confident that time was on China's side. They expected that the US resolve to shoulder the burden of its extensive military presence in the Pacific rim and fully maintain wide-ranging security guarantees extended to friends and allies in the region would slowly but steadily diminish. Moreover the US economic stake in the region would assume increasing importance, and for this if no other reason the United States would need to be more attentive to Chinese interests and sensitivities. To this extent China could afford to be more assertive, at least in the pursuit of certain objectives, two of which were assigned the highest priority: resolution of the Taiwan dispute in a manner respectful of Beijing's moral authority; and acknowledgement of China's central role in the shaping of the region's security architecture.

It remained to be seen whether US and Chinese political elites could successfully manage the tensions likely to result from their conflicting perceptions and expectations. Former Australian Prime Minister Malcolm Fraser succinctly encapsulated the dangers posed by this difficult transitional period:

> [T]he time-scale in which America will remain supreme economically and militarily is already strictly limited. The US will not want to be pushed off its pinnacle, no great power ever does. A danger time between nations arises when one country seeks to challenge the dominance of another or when a country growing in power believes itself to be unreasonably thwarted by an older power. Events develop until they feel a need to test each other's respective strengths.[169]

Disagreements which surfaced in the 1980s and 1990s on issues of trade, human rights, Taiwan, arms control and regional security, though they each had different origins and different rationales, could all be placed within this larger geopolitical context.

Complicating still further the already complex task of conflict management were the domestic cleavages which were a feature of the political landscape of both countries. The Sino-American relationship was to some extent hostage to opposing factions within the Chinese Communist Party, policy divisions between the White House and Congress, and perhaps more importantly the differential impact of globalization on different industries and competing bureaucratic interests. In the United States, no sooner had Jiang Zemin completed his 1997 visit than the US House of Representatives passed a raft of bills, which among other things tightened import bans on products made by forced labour in China, urged sanctions against China unless it ceased missile exports to Iran, promoted a ballistic missile defence system for Taiwan, opposed subsidized World Bank loans to China, and proposed direct military contacts with Taiwan.[170] In February 2000, the House of Representatives passed by an overwhelming majority the Taiwan Security Enhancement Act, which promised more extensive and more explicit military assistance for Taiwan. Though the bills themselves might not become law or pose an immediate obstacle to the implementation of executive policy, they made it more difficult for both sides to pursue a policy of accommodation. If nothing else, they made it easier for the Pentagon to paint a bleaker picture of Chinese intentions and capabilities.

In a report to Congress in September 1998, the Defense Department argued that China could attain its primary national goal, which was to gain respect as 'a great power in the world . . . and the pre-eminent power in Asia,' only through 'the weakening of US political influence in the region'. The November 1998 *East Asian Security Report* was even blunter, referring to China's rise as a major power as presenting 'an array of challenges', of which the most serious was the 'gap in strategic visions' – codewords for Chinese opposition to the US military presence in the region.[171] Responding in part to these pressures, the White House announced in February 1999 that the Hughes Electronics Corporation would be denied a licence to export a satellite to China on the grounds that the buyer, a Singapore-based consortium in which China had a 51 per cent stake, had partners with links to the PLA, and that the technology, regardless of its commercial applications, would help Beijing improve the accuracy of its nuclear missiles.[172]

A few months later a declassified version of the Congressional report, better known as the Cox report, was published, with almost hysterical claims that China had over the best part of three decades steadfastly stolen US nuclear secrets. That Beijing had over the years acquired by both licit and illicit means an array of US commercial and military technologies was plausible enough. But the evidence offered in support of the report's dramatic claims, including theft of warhead designs, was at best meagre and at worst non-existent. Equally lacking in credibility was the Cox assertion that nuclear espionage had enabled China to 'fabricate and successfully test strategic thermonuclear weapons'. Most of the technology transfers to China are likely to have occurred through access to unclassified publications, study at US universities (60 000 Chinese nationals were estimated to be studying in the United States in 1999) and the conscious decisions of at least four presidents and their advisers. The gradual relaxation of export controls on a wide range of dual-use technologies, including satellites, computers, machine tools and high-end electronics, was also the result of sustained pressure by some of America's most influential corporations, including Hughes, Loral, McDonnell Douglas and Motorola, which stood to profit handsomely from China's lucrative market. To put it simply, overestimation of the Chinese threat stemmed largely from the marriage of political convenience between elements of the military establishment intent on optimizing defence budget allocations and sections of Congress out to embarrass the President. Unintended though the consequences might be, such domestic power play could not but influence the direction of US policy, including levels of military spending, arms sales to Taiwan and deployment of missile defence systems.

The impact of domestic influences was in any case likely to extend beyond the explicitly military dimensions of policy. Whereas the policy priorities of the President, Congress and the Pentagon were bound to bear the imprint of their respective interests and perceptions, these could not be divorced from the deeper currents sweeping American civil society. Bankers, industrialists, trade unionists, educators, scientists, journalists, religious agitators and human rights activists were all seeking to steer US policy, as much in the diplomatic, economic and cultural as in the military sphere. To this extent US–China policy could be likened to a ship cast adrift with conflicting officers vying for ascendancy. The frequent swings of the pendulum from comprehensive to conditional engagement and from covert to overt containment reflected deep-seated societal tensions, originating in part in, and at the same time compounding, the uncertainties and vulnerabilities generated by rapid and often unexpected economic and geopolitical change. Much the same could be said of China's rapidly transforming polity. Its external policies, especially its relations with the United States, would be profoundly affected by the already substantial and still widening economic and social disparities between provinces and between the cities and the countryside. Mirroring and reinforcing these trends were the diverging interests and attitudes of the political, bureaucratic, entrepreneurial and intellectual elites, which were themselves far from monolithic. The complex interaction of these two seemingly cohesive yet deeply fractured civil societies had yet to give rise to a clearly defined geopolitical equation. At the end of the 1990s, the extent to which the political leadership of either country would safely navigate these uncharted waters and develop a durable *modus vivendi* remained delicately in the balance.

SINO-JAPANESE RELATIONS:
ECONOMIC PARTNERSHIP AND STRATEGIC STAND-OFF

China and the United States were in the throes of constructing arguably the single most important bilateral relationship in Asia Pacific, certainly the one that would most sharply define the contours of the region's geopolitical landscape in the coming decades. Yet it would be a serious mistake to underestimate Japan's function in what was in effect a multidimensional, complex and still rapidly unfolding triangular relationship. Though America's ties with China and Japan constituted the sturdier and more conspicuous sides of the triangle, the China–Japan relationship offered perhaps the more revealing litmus test of the solidity of the emerging regional security system. These were after all the two major Asian powers and natural rivals for regional leadership and influence. They had both exercised a profound influence over the course of Asia's modern history and both had claims to great power status. They were on the other hand endowed with vastly different resources; they had pursued a vastly different path to modernization; and their relationship with the United States pointed to strikingly different assumptions, expectations and rationales. These differences and similarities made for a degree of complementarity, but also for a heavy dose of mutual antagonism.

The co-operative aspects of the relationship were most apparent in the economic arena, notably in the area of trade. Under the Long-Term Trade Agreement signed in 1978 Japan committed itself to Chinese coal and oil worth $10 billion in return for purchase of Japanese capital goods. In the ensuing decade bilateral trade flourished, rising from barely $5 billion in 1978 to $19.3 billion in 1988, which is not to say that the trade relationship was entirely free of tension. The sheer scale of the agreements negotiated and the consequent drain on China's foreign exchange reserves placed it under enormous financial strain, eventually forcing it to cancel or suspend a number of contracts. China's chronic trade deficit with Japan, fuelled in large measure by highly unfavourable terms of trade, surpassed $6 billion in 1986.[173] To avert an inflationary spiral and the overheating of its economy, Beijing reduced its imports from Japan and exerted greater pressure on Tokyo to open up its markets and facilitate Chinese exports. These efforts were not, however, immediately successful. The inherent qualitative asymmetry in Sino-Japanese trade remained essentially unchanged, with China still exporting primarily foodstuffs and raw materials and Japan supplying the steel, machinery, chemical products and technology on which China depended for its industrial modernization.[174]

The first signs of radical change in the quantitative trends of previous years emerged in 1988. China recorded a trade surplus of $383 million, which steadily rose thereafter, reaching $14 billion in 1995.[175] Economic contraction in China and the appreciation of the yen had both contributed to the declining performance of Japanese exports. The five-year trade agreement concluded in December 1990 had, it is true, envisaged little change to the composition of trade. China committed itself to supplying 8.8–9.3 million tons of crude oil and 3.7–5.3 million tons of coal in exchange for Japanese delivery of construction equipment, machinery and technology valued at $8 billion.[176] Several factors, including rising levels of Japanese FDI and improvements in China's productive capacity, would soon combine to produce a marked increase in the export of Chinese manufactures, in particular chemical products, metals and metal products, machinery and equipment and textile products. With Sino-Japanese trade rising from $16.6 billion in 1990 to $63.9 billion in 1997,[177] Japan had become China's largest trading partner, and China Japan's second largest trading partner after the United States.

Both investment and aid were important elements of the economic relationship, fuelling both the increasing volume and changing composition of bilateral trade.[178] Japanese FDI rose from $100 million in 1985 to $1127 million in 1987, reached a new low of $349 million in 1990 (in the aftermath of Tiananmen) but rose sharply again to reach $2565 million in 1994, with textiles, electrical machinery and transport equipment absorbing the bulk of the more recent flows.[179] By June 1995 the cumulative contract value of Japanese direct investment amounted to $16.4 billion, involving 11 466 approved projects, with the average value of each project rising steadily during the 1990s and reaching close to $2.5 million in 1995.[180] Complementing these investment flows was a substantial aid programme, comprised largely of concessional loans, which in 1993 amounted to 138.7 billion yen, compared with 0.98 billion yen in grants and 0.75 billion yen in technical co-operation.[181] The volume of Japanese lending rose from an annual average of 82.7 billion yen during 1979–83 to more than $190 billion yen during 1996–8.[182] Though late in coming, substantial transfers of Japanese technology now became an integral part of the bilateral economic relationship and by 1993 accounted for 28 per cent of China's total technology imports.[183]

Notwithstanding the scale or intensity of these trade, investment and financial links, friction was never far below the surface. During the 1980s Chinese complaints were directed principally at the meagreness of Japanese capital and technology exports; a decade later the focus had shifted to the qualitative aspects of these transfers. In Beijing's view, Japan was reluctant to transfer advanced technology for fear of enhancing Chinese competitiveness at the expense of Japanese exports (the so-called 'boomerang effect'), and was exacting too high a price for what was essentially outdated technology. The Japanese on the other hand argued that more sophisticated technology was ill-suited to China's lower level of development, that the Chinese lacked the experience to form appropriate judgements on the cost of technology, and that inadequate bureaucratic and economic conditions within China were themselves an impediment to larger or more effective technology transfers.

The advantages which both sides derived from their economic links did nevertheless endow the relationship with a rationale and a robustness which it would otherwise have lacked. That is precisely the significance of the Long-Term Trade Agreement which the two countries concluded in February 1978 and which laid the basis for the subsequent proliferation of bilateral economic projects and exchanges. Yet economics was inseparable from politics. The year 1978 was also marked by the signing of the Peace and Friendship Treaty. Taken together, these two documents did more than just reconcile economic interests or encourage a wide range of collaborative activities. They provided the framework for a diplomatic dialogue which kept lines of communication open even during moments of high tension.

Significantly, when it came to relations with China, Japan sought to distinguish itself from the United States and Western Europe, and became the first to lift sanctions against China. Japanese governments of different political complexion advocated a closer political dialogue, with a view to identifying and sustaining common ground. Prime Minister Kaifu spoke of Japan's wish to engage China and encourage it to become 'an integral part of the regional framework of peace and prosperity'.[184] The stability of Japan's own regional environment, it seemed, and the efficacy of regional institutions more generally depended in part on China's active participation. There was, however, another consideration in Japanese thinking, namely a wish to offset dependence on the United States, especially in the area of security, by maintaining a *modus vivendi* with Beijing, by serving as a bridge-builder between China and the West, and on occasions by keeping its distance from US policy, at least on issues which did not directly impinge on the US–Japan strategic alliance (for example, in relation to sanctions and human rights). In becoming the first of the Group of Seven industrialized countries to reach agreement in July 1999 on China's bid to join the global trading forum, Japan had symbolically reaffirmed its bilateral relationship with China.

In the three decades that followed normalization the bilateral relationship assumed a much higher profile in the respective diplomacies of the two countries and in the political economy of the Asia-Pacific region. The emergence of Japan as one of the engines of regional and global economic growth and the vast scope of China's modernization programme pointed to the complementarity of the two economies and to the unique role which the two polities would play in the region's geopolitical and economic transformation. Economically, diplomatically and even culturally China and Japan had a strong incentive to develop a closer, more extensive, multidimensional relationship, which is not to say that conflict and competition would not remain important features of that relationship.

To begin with, the tendency towards complementarity could not be considered either permanent or all-embracing. Second, significant historical and contemporary animosities coloured the geopolitical imagination of both countries. China, which had been the target of Japanese military expansion in the 1930s, remained deeply allergic to any signs of Japanese remilitarization. Since the early 1980s, albeit intermittently, the Chinese leadership had voiced its concern at Japan's rising military expenditures. It was particularly critical of the Nakasone government's decision in 1987 to allow the defence budget to exceed 1 per cent of GNP, which it interpreted as symbolic of Japan's renewed desire to exercise strategic influence in the region. The upgrading of Japanese defence capabilities was now said to be far in excess of the requirements of territorial defence.[185] Coupled with the gradual strategic redeployment of Japan's Self-Defense Forces, the acquisition of state-of-the-art defensive and offensive air and naval weaponry was portrayed by Chinese commentators as an attempt to expand Japan's sphere of influence through military means. Pointing to unresolved territorial disputes between Japan and its neighbours, Beijing was not loath to raise the possibility of a regional conflict which might in due course involve Japan's powerful navy and air force.[186]

What made Japan's acquisition of sophisticated military hardware so contentious was not so much its immediate consequences as its historical context. The failure of successive Japanese governments to offer a convincing public apology for Japanese conduct during the Second World War had a double effect: it provided China with disquieting evidence of Japan's future intentions, but also with additional ammunition which it could use with great effect more than half a century after the event to embarrass and constrain Japanese policy-makers. There was, of course, more to Chinese leverage than Japan's persistent refusal to acknowledge its past aggression. Particularly troublesome were the periodic actions or pronouncements of senior political figures. The repeated attempts of educational authorities to dilute references in school texts to Japan's invasion and occupation of China in the 1930s served only to rekindle bitter Chinese memories. As Deng Ziaoping put it in May 1989, 'If we want to settle the historical account, Japan owes China the largest debt'.[187] Equally provocative were the periodic visits by cabinet ministers to shrines honouring Japanese soldiers, which invariably attracted vociferous Chinese condemnation and, on occasions, anti-Japanese demonstrations. Beijing was also quick to take advantage of incidents involving attempts by senior Japanese ministers to rewrite history. Public statements attributing nobler motives to Japanese military expansion or suggesting that such expansion did not legally constitute aggression were especially damaging to Japan's regional standing, and more often than not ended with the relevant ministers resigning or withdrawing their statements.[188]

Expressions of regret by Prime Ministers Hosokawa and Murayama went further than those offered by any of their predecessors but still fell short of Chinese or South Korean expectations. Indicative of the emotional and political potency of the issue was the prominence given to it by Chinese leaders in discussions with their Japanese counterparts.[189] In his visit to Japan, in November 1998, the first by a Chinese head of state in decades, President Jiang Zemin made China's historical grievances about Japanese war crimes a central theme of his diplomacy. Referring time and again to history as 'a mirror for the future', he warned his Japanese hosts that any long-term improvement in bilateral relations would depend on Japan's readiness to come to terms with its past. The matter came to a head when Prime Minister Keizo Obuchi refused to include in their joint declaration a written apology for Japanese war crimes. The Chinese President responded by refusing to sign it. The promised new era of closer diplomatic, economic and environmental co-operation had got off to an inauspicious start.[190]

The Chinese preoccupation with the historical record was not mere indulgence in rhetorical symbolism; it was a pragmatic and carefully designed signal to Japan that its security policies were under close scrutiny. To put it differently, history was not simply a mirror for the future but a barometer of the present state of Sino-Japanese relations. In a sense, the dispute over the Diaoyutai Islands (known in Japanese as Senkaku) performed the same function. Administered by Tokyo since they were handed over by Washington together with Okinawa in 1971 but claimed by Beijing and Taipei, the islands were an intermittent source of friction. Although periodically reaffirming its claim to sovereignty, China expressed its willingness after an incident in September 1990 to shelve the issue, advocating instead that resources in the waters surrounding the island be jointly developed and fishing resources opened to the outside world.[191] With both countries increasing their oceanographic activity in the area, partly with a view to bolstering their respective claims to the continental shelf, the dispute assumed both symbolic and practical significance.

Ratification of the Law of the Sea Convention gave Japan, China and South Korea the incentive and the opportunity to proceed with continental shelf claims extending 200 nautical miles from their coastlines. Given overlapping claims, China and Japan entered complex negotiations which resulted in September 1997 in the establishment of a joint control zone in the central part of the East China Sea.[192] Though the zone did not include the Diaoyutai, the two countries were also engaged in ongoing negotiations about the commercial development of fishing and oil resources, making it clear that the sovereignty dispute would not be allowed to obstruct commercial co-operation. By the same token, such co-operation did not mean that the dispute would be quickly or amicably resolved. Periodic incidents, provided they did not escalate, might even prove diplomatically useful. The episode in July–August 1996 is particularly instructive in this regard.[193] Beijing described official and unofficial Japanese activities as 'a series of provocations' and 'an inevitable manifestation of the rightist deviation of Japanese domestic politics and the display of its strength to the outside world'.[194] Japan's conduct in the dispute was portrayed as symptomatic of a more general drive towards 'outward expansion'. The obvious intent was to contrast China's moderation with Japan's pugnacity, and to bring even greater pressure to bear on those elements of Japan's security policy which, in Beijing's view, were especially objectionable. These elements were not hard to discover. They were Japan's more forceful military posture and its readiness to act at the behest of the United States, or at least to allow its territory and military assets to be integrated into a bilateral or multilateral framework which Beijing considered inimical to its core strategic interests.

Beijing's anxieties about the future direction of Japanese policy were paralleled by Tokyo's ambivalence towards China. The slow but steady development of China's nuclear deterrent – notwithstanding the cessation of its nuclear testing – and its military modernization programme, in particular the prospect of greater naval force projection, combined with the rise of nationalist sentiment and diplomatic self-assertion to create a deepening sense of disquiet about China's future role.[195] For Japanese policy-makers the issue was not so much the direct threat China posed to Japan's military security, but rather the implications of a more assertive China for regional stability, at least as understood by Japanese political and military elites. Were, for example, the exercises China conducted at the time of the March 1996 Taiwan presidential election merely a taste of things to come? Was the dynamism of the Chinese economy generating a renewed political and diplomatic self-confidence which might in turn lead to heightened military tension in the Taiwan Strait, and in due course to other sovereignty disputes, perhaps over the Spratlys or even the Senkaku Islands? Would the US–Japan military alliance itself become the target of increasing Chinese hostility?

Aside from these larger strategic concerns were more concrete yet not altogether unconnected considerations to do with future energy supplies, control of the sea lanes, and diplomatic rivalry in Southeast Asia. For one informed commentator at least, energy was rapidly emerging as a key factor in Sino-Japanese competition for power and influence:

> Japan has long been a huge energy importer. And China, despite its large domestic reserves, is rapidly moving in that direction. A generation hence, each should command roughly a third of Asia's oil imports. In tight global and regional energy markets, the two could easily become active and determined competitors.[196]

For Japan secure access to energy supplies was closely linked to freedom of navigation since 70 per cent of Japan oil imports flow through a number of choke points, including the Tsushima Strait and the strategic straits of Malacca and Lombok. To this must be added the prospect of military confrontation in the Taiwan Strait and the possible escalation of the Spratlys dispute. By the late 1990s Tokyo and Beijing were engaged in a significant though still fragile bilateral security dialogue, involving discussions between senior ministers and defence chiefs, more frequent exchanges between high-level defence officials and reciprocal visits by the two navies. Issues discussed included Korea and Taiwan, but also energy, security and the prospects for bilateral and multilateral confidence- and security-building.

The Sino-Japanese relationship represented, then, a subtle blend of conflict and co-operation, with each side needing what the other could offer, yet both suspicious of each other and competing for regional leadership and legitimacy. Japanese ambivalence towards China was in part the expression of a more profound and still unresolved self-questioning about its Asian identity, which Samuel Kim has aptly described as the 'pendulum swings . . . between escaping and conquering Asia'.[197] The contradictory pressures underlying Tokyo's policies were strikingly evident in its 'apology diplomacy' (wanting to put an end to the historical legacy of mutual mistrust and hostility, yet somehow unwilling or unable to accept responsibility for past aggression) and its foreign investment strategy (wanting to take full advantage of the opportunities offered by China's rapidly expanding economy, yet nervous of the competitive edge which Japanese capital and technology might confer on Chinese industry). These ambiguities to a degree reflected the emotional experience of Japanese policy-makers and public alike. They were also indicative of the serious fractures emerging within the ruling LDP and the highly influential industrial and financial communities, and increasingly within civil society itself.

China, for its part, could not easily overcome the painful experience of invasion and occupation; and, though it valued the contribution Japan could make to its modernization drive, it was not convinced that greater economic interaction could of itself heal the wounds of past enmities. During the late 1980s and early 1990s Beijing's criticism of Japan's security policies, including the decision to participate in UN peacekeeping operations and the continued upgrading of Japan's military capabilities, was certainly more muted than might have been the case in an earlier period. Yet by the late 1990s, there was evidence of growing anxiety, which China's impressive economic success for more than a decade and Japan's faltering economic performance could only partially obscure.[198] Growing economic interdependence may have strengthened in both cases the hand of pragmatic self-interest, but it also engendered among both Chinese and Japanese political elites a new self-confidence and a readiness to challenge each other's policies when these were deemed inimical to their interests.

TOWARDS A NEW TRIANGULAR BALANCE

To shed more light on the ambiguities, not to say contradictions, of the Sino-Japanese connection, it is necessary to situate it within the triangular relationship in which the United States continued to play a pivotal role. Gradually at first but with accelerating speed after the demise of the Cold War, the triangle, as much geoeconomic as geopolitical in character, assumed increasing importance for all three parties as well as for the region and the international system as a whole. The dynamics of the triangular balance was such that it favoured certain outcomes and impeded others. Precisely because the United Sates remained central to the Asia-Pacific economy and to regional security, the possibility of constructing an East Asian bloc under Chinese, Japanese or joint leadership was effectively precluded. For different reasons and to different degrees Japan and China lacked the capacity but also the incentive to pursue external policies that would bring them into direct conflict with the United States. Secure access to the US market was critical to both economies. The security alliance with the United States left Japan with limited room for diplomatic manoeuvre, and even China was less than enthusiastic about the termination of the alliance if that would mean a substantially rearmed Japan and perhaps the development of a Japanese nuclear deterrent.

It would be misleading, however, to suggest that the triangular balance was set in concrete, or that the three sides of the triangle were in any sense equal or symmetrical. On the contrary, each of the three bilateral relationships was in a state of considerable flux attributable in large measure to changing relativities of power, the far-reaching impact of economic restructuring, and associated changes to the international division of labour and the ensuing political volatility and social discontent in all three countries. Strains in the US–Japan economic relationship had magnified in intensity, and even the security partnership had, despite the façade of close co-operation, become increasingly fragile and its precise function and *modus operandi* in time of crisis less clearly defined.[199] In this period of transition, the emerging ambiguities in US–Japan defence arrangements were as likely to discomfort as to reassure China.

Viewed from Beijing, the Security Declaration issued by Tokyo and Washington, the revised defence co-operation guidelines and the proposed joint development of a theatre missile defence system all had disturbing if contradictory implications. One possible reading of American intentions was that these measures were part of a larger strategy designed to contain China, thereby neutralizing the greatest challenge to US strategic dominance in the region.[200] Placed in this context, expanded US–Japan defence co-operation raised the possibility of the two allies taking concerted action in the event of a new crisis in the Taiwan Strait. The revised US–Japan defence co-operation guidelines committed Japan to extending its support to US forces in 'areas surrounding Japan', a geographic concept vague enough to permit Japanese evasiveness as to its intended content, but clear enough to cause discomfort in Beijing.[201] US–Japanese co-operation in the development of a ship–based TMD system was equally disturbing because, it could, by virtue of its high mobility, be extended to cover the island of Taiwan. Though Chinese analysts remained unconvinced of the system's ultimate effectiveness they were troubled by its political and psychological implications, in particular by its likely impact on US–China relations and the added pressures it would generate for the accelerated development of Chinese missile capabilities.[202]

Another possible reading was that the US containment strategy was directed primarily at Japan. In other words, Japan's closer integration with US global and regional military planning[203] was intended to circumscribe Tokyo's freedom of action while strengthening Washington's leverage *vis-à-vis* Japan as much in the economic as in the politico-military arena. If this second reading of US intentions was at all accurate, would it not effectively dispel Beijing's anxieties? Was US policy not the most effective brake on the renewal of Japanese militarism? Though such a scenario might at first sight seem favourable to Chinese interests, difficult questions remained about its implications for Japan's future strategic posture.

China's response to the revamping of Japan–US security relations had to concern itself with the Japanese as much as with the American side of the equation. As already noted, Japanese motives, viewed from China's vantage point, were not entirely transparent, which in itself was hardly reassuring. In any case, two highly plausible interpretations, though sharply at odds with each other, had equally disturbing implications for Beijing. The first inferred from Japanese actions and pronouncements a willingness on Tokyo's part to give wholehearted support to the US policy of containing China, even on the highly sensitive issue of Taiwan. The second treated Japan's compliance with US strategic priorities as a conscious attempt on its part to camouflage its actual policy, which was to upgrade its military capabilities and expand its sphere of influence. The alliance arrangements were simply a convenient way of legitimizing its actions by making it appear as if they were largely a response to US pressure and in keeping with US strategic requirements. Chinese official and unofficial statements gave credence to both interpretations, although the emphasis tended to shift from one to the other depending on the period, the setting or the intended audience. Beijing was in a sense hedging its bets, either because it was unsure of the real intent of Japanese policy or because it believed that Tokyo itself had yet to make up its mind and was keeping both options alive for as long as possible.

A third possibility was equally plausible, namely that Japanese economic and political elites were themselves deeply divided on how best to handle the triangular relationship with China and the United States. Hence the tendency of the Japanese government to speak with many voices, as much on the scope of the revised defence guidelines as on the relationship of theatre missile defence to the ABM treaty on the one hand and Japan's defence on the other, a possibility which would not have escaped the Chinese leadership and one they could exploit with considerable skill. For Beijing the preferred outcome was the gradual demotion of the US–Japan alliance as the geostrategic fulcrum of the Asia-Pacific region and its replacement by greater symmetry between the three bilateral relationships. Integral to this vision was China's newly found sense of its own geoeconomic and geopolitical importance and its expectation that both Washington and Tokyo, increasingly alarmed by the drift of each other's policies, would turn to Beijing as a useful counterweight.[204]

China's reading of the emerging trilateral relationship, as rendered in the writings of Chinese scholars and the publications of leading think-tanks and research institutes, was far from monolithic.[205] Yet a number of key assumptions constituted a common interpretative core:

1. the international political system and the world economy were closely interlinked;
2. none of the three poles in the tripolar balance constituted a military threat to the other two;
3. while both Japan and the United States were keen to take advantage of China's expanding market, they remained ambivalent about China's economic success;
4. because of competing economic interests, they would find it nevertheless difficult to co-ordinate the containment of China;

5. however determined the United States might be to retain its leadership in Asia Pacific, Japan would be less and less willing to live in the shadow of the United States;
6. these tensions would in the long run adversely affect the US-Japanese alliance.[206]

The cumulative impact of these tendencies would be to make China's involvement indispensable to the resolution of any regional conflict.

Yet Chinese leaders were realistic enough to know that the American hand would continue to hold several important cards. US engagement would remain crucial to the success of China's economic and technological modernization and at least tacit US consent vital to China's reunification plans. To secure these two objectives Beijing would periodically make concessions to the American position, whether on human rights, nuclear proliferation, conventional arms sales or the trade deficit. These were viewed by the Chinese leadership as tactical or strategic adjustments which did not require any substantial deviation from the policy direction set by Deng Xiaoping. They were premised on the understanding, clearly in evidence at the Clinton–Jiang Zemin summits in 1997 and 1998, that for a time at least America's capacity to manipulate the China–Japan relationship to its advantage would exceed the capacity of the two countries to use their relationship to gain greater leverage *vis-à-vis* the United States.

From this analysis of the triangular balance emerge three main conclusions. First, while *Pax Americana* might be in decline, it was not about to be replaced by *Pax Nipponica* or *Pax Sinica*. Japan's rise in the 1980s as a global centre of economic and financial power, notwithstanding the difficulties encountered in the 1990s, had propelled Japanese corporations, Japanese banks and the Japanese state to the centre stage of the Asia-Pacific economy. Yet Tokyo's capacity for regional leadership remained uncertain. The East Asian crisis of the late 1990s had, if anything, confirmed the limits of Japan's financial strength and diplomatic influence. China had undoubtedly become a regional power of the first magnitude, but its understandable preoccupation with the economic, social and political pressures generated by its modernization policies severely curtailed its diplomatic freedom of action. The United States, by virtue of its military preponderance and the greatly improved performance of its economy during the 1990s, was still well placed to protect its interests and capabilities as a global and regional economic actor. On the other hand, the projection of American military power, whether in relation to Korea, Taiwan or the Spratlys, could not of itself resolve these conflicts or even guarantee the outcomes favoured by US diplomacy. In an increasingly multipolar and interdependent world economy, whose features were closely replicated in the Asia-Pacific economy, the United States still had enormous capacity to cajole, persuade and resist, but it could no longer perform the co-ordinating and legitimating functions characteristic of the Cold War period. Its leadership role was now one of *residual hegemony*.

We come, then, to our second conclusion. This was a transitional period marked not only by the diminished authority of the hegemon, but by structural instability. The institutional framework which the hegemon had largely created and subsequently managed was in a state of advanced degeneration. Rising tensions in trade relations, in the regulation of financial flows, in the management of sovereignty disputes and in the maintenance of the non-proliferation regime were indicative of a fractured and highly competitive system of economic and geopolitical relations. What made the emerging triangular balance between the United States, China and Japan so instructive was precisely the fact that none of the three centres of power was in a position to dictate institutional terms to the other two. Regime formation and regime change could now occur only in the context of negotiation; which brings us to the third conclusion.

To manage their complex diplomatic, strategic and economic interdependence these three centres of power – and the multiple, often conflicting interests which they subsumed – found it necessary to 'engage' and communicate with each other. Even in the case of the US–Japan security partnership, a bilateral arrangement *par excellence*, the two partners, in agreeing to new defence co-operation guidelines, had no option but to draw China into a consultative process, if for no other reason than to defuse the intensity of China's hostile reaction. Similarly, in responding to the East Asian financial crisis, the United States, China and Japan had no alternative but to engage in complex and protracted discussions which, even when they were conducted bilaterally, were in practice trilateral in both intent and consequence. Similar tendencies were in evidence around such issues as non-proliferation, environment and the Korean conflict. This is not to suggest that the triangular balance was on its way to becoming a *ménage à trois*. Elements of co-operation would continue to co-exist with conflict and competition, but regional stability would increasingly depend on a trilateral dialogue complementing and nurturing the three bilateral relationships. It remained to be seen what institutional forms such a dialogue would assume, how resilient they would prove in the face of contradictory interests and perceptions, and what specific roles governments, economic players and other non-state actors would perform in the institutionalization of the dialogue.

THE RUSSIAN CONNECTION

That our analysis of the US–China–Japan triangle should have proceeded as far as it has without reference to Russia is testament to the dramatic decline of Russian

(Soviet) power that occurred in the space of little more than a decade. Even before the end of the Cold War, the normalization of Sino-Soviet relations under Gorbachev and the Soviet policy of reducing the economic and political burden of international commitments had meant a reduced Soviet military presence in Southeast Asia and much lower levels of economic and military assistance to friends and allies, including Vietnam.[207] Cam Ranh Bay, once regarded as a strategic platform for Soviet power projection into the Indian and Pacific oceans, was drastically downgraded with the withdrawal in late 1989 of TU-16s and the squadron of MiG-23s and the subsequent reduction in naval vessels.

A comparable scaling down of Russian military activity had taken place in Northeast Asia with a substantial reduction in naval and aircraft operations as well as in the number of large-scale exercises involving ground forces.[208] Naval exercises and training operations were increasingly confined to home waters; Russian forces were withdrawn from Mongolia in 1992; and border agreements were signed with China in 1991 and 1994. These developments were, in fact, part of a comprehensive contraction of Russian military capabilities. Russian armed forces were reduced from three million at the time of the breakup of the Soviet Union at the end of 1991 to 2.3 million in 1993 and 2.1 million by the end of 1994.[209] The weakness of the Russian economy, its increasing dependence on western infusions of capital, industrial stagnation bordering in some sectors on paralysis, the consequent contraction of the defence budget, not to mention the lack of strategic direction in foreign policy, had all contributed to a greatly diminished Russian military presence in Asia Pacific.

With the disintegration of the Soviet Union, the institutional and procedural infrastructure for the formulation of foreign and defence policy had been grievously damaged. Perennial tensions between the President and the legislature, conflict between rival ministries, corruption in high places, serious questions about Yeltsin's physical health and political acumen, combined with the fracturing of the Soviet empire, had severely weakened Moscow's capacity to adjust to the geopolitical realities of the post-Cold War period. In these difficult circumstances Russian diplomacy had little option but to devote its scarce energies and resources to handling the most pressing issues on its agenda, notably relations with the United States and NATO and its place in the new Europe. It was only in 1994 that Russia's approach to Asia Pacific regained a degree of intellectual coherence.[210]

As Foreign Minister Andrei Kozyrev indicated in January 1994, the economic dynamism of the Asia-Pacific region coupled with the increasing economic importance of the Asian part of Russia and its corollary, the increasing volume of Russia's trade with Asia, had of necessity raised Asia's profile in Russian thinking. He went on to highlight several considerations that would govern Moscow's policy, notably the need for great power co-operation in the era of multipolarity, the absence of any 'irreconcilable contradictions' between Russia and other powers, the low probability of military conflict despite unresolved border disputes and other outstanding problems, including access to seabed resources, and the contribution that economic progress could make to the advancement of human rights.[211] This highly positive reading of Asia's prospects had been carefully crafted to portray Russia as a constructive player in the region. To the extent that its relative weakness and peripheral role in many of the most pressing regional conflicts made it less threatening to others, Russia sought to make virtue out of necessity, and to suggest that it was uniquely placed to facilitate negotiations and other conflict resolution processes.

While Moscow was keen to retain its links with North Korea and at the same time develop its economic and diplomatic relations with South Korea (in 1995 two-way trade soared to a record $3.3 billion), its actual capacity to influence the course of events on the Korean peninsula remained strictly limited.[212] In a bid to buttress its diplomatic relevance Moscow proposed in early 1994 the convening of an eight-power conference to discuss a comprehensive solution to the crisis, based in part on security guarantees for the two Koreas and international verification of the denuclearization of the peninsula. Thought-provoking though they were, these ideas attracted little support, presumably because of Russia's negligible political and economic leverage, which current or projected arms sales to Pyongyang and Seoul could do little to offset. Similarly, though it might wish to develop a closer relationship with ASEAN and rebuild its links with Vietnam, Russia's diplomatic relevance in Northeast Asia as much as in Southeast Asia would in large measure depend on the substance of its relations with the United States, Japan and China. At issue were not only the scope and content of three bilateral relationships, but their interaction or, to put it differently, Russia's connection with the triangular balance.

In the post-Cold War period US policy towards Russia continued to be predicated on naval pre-eminence in the region, but US objectives were pursued more through diplomatic and economic instruments than through military containment. Washington's principal concerns were to promote market reform and political stability in Russia, an acceptable limit on Russian military capabilities and more centralized control of Commonwealth of Independent States (CIS) nuclear capabilities. In sharp contrast to the 1970s and 1980s, East Asia was not a major arena of Russian–American geopolitical rivalry. The end of the East–West strategic confrontation in Europe, in particular the intermediate-range nuclear forces (INF) treaty negotiations of the late 1980s and the subsequent Conventional Armed Forces in Europe (CFE), Strategic Arms Reduction Talks (START) and Confidence- and Security-Building Measures (CSBM) agreements, had significant flow-on effects in East Asia. The reductions in nuclear and conventional forces, even in the absence of any explicitly Asian agreements, had helped stabilize the Asia-Pacific theatre. The

United States remained nevertheless resistant to proposals for naval arms control, claiming that any constraints on the US naval presence would be damaging to the 'logistical lifelines' of the United States and its allies, and create 'uncertainty and "empty spaces" that other major powers would be tempted or compelled to fill'.[213] The preferred US strategy was to expand the programme of multilateral military contacts and complex combined operations with Pacific Russia as an incentive for additional downsizing and restructuring of Russia's Asia-Pacific forces.[214] Moscow, for its part, was prepared to accept this consolation prize, which it hoped would enhance its standing in the region and facilitate military-to-military contacts with China, South Korea and even Japan.

In the case of Japan several obstacles continued to impede any significant rapprochement. Historical enmity and lingering Japanese suspicions of Soviet intentions meant that Japan took longer to adjust to the new post-Cold War climate. Gorbachev's diplomacy had consistently stressed the need to break with military approaches to security and extolled the virtues of arms control, but Tokyo's reaction was generally unenthusiastic. Moscow's willingness to eliminate its intermediate- and short-range nuclear weapons from Asia, its withdrawal from Afghanistan, its active support for the Cambodian peace process and the removal of Soviet troops from the Mongolian People's Republic had little immediate impact on Japanese perceptions.[215] Gorbachev's proposals, which had as their underlying objective the elimination of military alliances and removal of foreign bases, may well have alarmed Japanese policy-makers intent on preserving the security relationship with the United States and building up Japan's military preparedness, particularly the capacity to protect its sea lines of communication.

The Northern Territories dispute remained, however, the single most intractable problem in the bilateral relationship. For its part, Japan was unwilling to make any gesture which could be construed as acceptance of the territorial *status quo*. The Soviet Union, on the other hand, was unwilling to offer any compromise in the absence of corresponding concessions from Japan. In the view of some analysts, the Soviet negotiating position was in any case constrained by 'the strategic significance of the Northern Territories as the southern segment of the defensive barrier provided by the Kuriles'.[216] Moscow may have been willing to entertain the possibility of transferring the two smaller islands, Shikotan and Habomai, to Japan following the conclusion of a Soviet–Japanese peace treaty, but it is doubtful that Tokyo would have found the proposition at all attractive. Gorbachev's visit to Japan in April 1991 did little to overcome this impasse, though it kept open the channels of communication.

With Gorbachev's departure from centre stage, the collapse of the Soviet Union and its consequent retreat from superpower status, the Yeltsin Administration became increasingly interested in developing closer relations with Japan. Conscious of Russia's parlous economic condition, it revived long-standing Russian hopes of attracting substantial Japanese economic aid and investment. The Russian Foreign Ministry's already difficult task was, however, further complicated by outspoken opposition within the country to any territorial concessions. Valentin Fedorov, governor of the Sakhalin region and fierce opponent of any transfer of sovereignty to Japan, openly challenged Moscow's handling of the issue and threatened a 'nationalist' political campaign should any attempt be made 'to sell ancient Russian land'.[217] Despite these domestic difficulties, but amid signs of greater Japanese flexibility, Moscow pursued a policy of dialogue with Tokyo, which Yeltsin's visit to Japan in October 1993 helped to consolidate. The joint declaration issued by Yeltsin and Prime Minister Hosokawa at the end of the visit promised the continuation of talks with a view to the early conclusion of a peace treaty linked to the resolution of the territorial dispute on the basis of 'the principles of law and justice'.

The following few years saw no major new developments, particularly as significant voices in the military as well as in the Russian Duma and even Prime Minister Chernomydin distanced themselves from Yeltsin's more conciliatory line.[218] The fluidity, not to say instability, of Russian and Japanese politics had a doubly negative effect on the relationship, exacerbated by periodic clashes between Japanese fishing vessels and Russian border patrols around the disputed islands.[219] The two foreign ministries nevertheless maintained close contact on a range of issues, including negotiations for a bilateral agreement on fishing in the South Kurils area and the mutual expansion of consular representation.[220] The visit to Tokyo by Russian Foreign Minister Evgenii Primakov in November 1996 maintained the more accommodating tone of Russia's recent diplomacy. In line with the 1993 Declaration, it reaffirmed recognition of the dispute, favoured the continued reduction of military troops on the disputed island, proposed joint economic development of the Northern Territories, and paved the way for high-level contacts aimed at substantially improving the bilateral relationship.

The Japanese response was at best ambivalent. Tokyo did not accept the Russian proposals for fear of appearing to recognize Russian sovereignty over the four islands. Yet it did not reject them for to do so would have been to jettison any prospect of a breakthrough in the dispute. Though Japanese policy continued to uphold the inseparability of politics and economics, there were indications that Tokyo might now be willing 'to offer humanitarian, intellectual, technological, and financial aid in proportion to the amount of progress made in the territorial dispute'.[221] By 1997, with the withdrawal of Russian troops stationed on Kunashiri and Shikotan islands and increased bilateral military contacts, the Hashimoto government was ready to announce a multidimensional policy towards Moscow, involving support for Russia's market reforms, more active economic co-operation and financial aid, and the promotion of political and security dialogue.[222]

The momentum was maintained in the Yeltsin–Hashimoto unofficial summit held in Krasnoyarsk in November 1997. At the meeting the two sides agreed to strive for a peace treaty by 2000 in line with the 1993 Tokyo Declaration, which had envisaged the conclusion of a peace treaty following resolution of the territorial dispute. At their subsequent meeting in April 1998 both leaders expressed satisfaction with the development of co-operative relations, but acknowledged that the bilateral commission working on the peace treaty had made slow progress.[223] Agreements were concluded to initiate feasibility studies on some 20 new Japanese projects in Russia and launch a new bilateral committee to promote co-operation in outer space. On the more delicate but closely related issues of the peace treaty and the Northern Territories dispute both leaders came to the meeting with new ideas. Yeltsin proposed that Moscow and Tokyo jointly build facilities for processing marine products and much-needed infrastructure such as roads and ports on the disputed islands. Hashimoto's preference was to consider these proposals 'in parallel with negotiations for a peace treaty'. As an added incentive for the Russians to accept this proposal, Hashimoto offered to oversee visa-free visits to the Northern Territories and extend humanitarian aid to Russian residents on the islands. A broad range of other fields were identified as deserving of upgraded bilateral co-operation, including cultural exchanges and joint disaster prevention drills in the Sea of Japan between Japan's Self-Defense Forces and the Russian Navy.

The Japanese accepted in principle the Yeltsin proposal for a treaty of peace, friendship and co-operation but insisted that such a pact should be signed only after the settlement of the territorial question. Agreement was also reached on staging joint exercises later in the year to practice search and rescue operations in the event of natural and other disasters. These exercises, which were to take place in the northern part of the Sea of Japan, would constitute the first example of large-scale co-operation between the Russian and Japanese armed forces. Trilateral exercises, involving the United States, Russia and Japan, were planned for May to mop up oil pollution near Sakhalin in preparation for the multilateral development of oil and gas fields on the Sakhalin shelf. Finally, consideration was given to the establishment of a four-party security dialogue between Russia, Japan, China and the United States.

Russia's loss of superpower status, its transition to a market economy and the more co-operative Russian–American relationship had helped to create a more favourable climate for the normalization of relations with Japan. The same factors had contributed to a marked improvement in Sino-Russian relations, although in this case additional factors peculiar to the changing geopolitical context of the two countries also played an important part. The collapse of communism in the Soviet

Union and throughout Eastern Europe had left China exposed as the last major communist state. Both Moscow and Beijing now had a shared sense of vulnerability, which sharpened the perceived advantages of co-operation while substantially allaying mutual fears and mistrust. Closer links were seen to be in the interests of both countries, not least because they could serve as a useful counterweight to US geopolitical dominance both regionally and globally.[224] The poor condition of Russia's armed forces was itself a powerful incentive for greater strategic collaboration. With the collapse of internal discipline and morale, the accelerating obsolescence of equipment (much of it in serious disrepair) and above all the drastic fall in income and consequent cutbacks in weapons acquisitions – only two combat aircraft were purchased in 1995, compared with 585 in 1991[225] – Russian military capabilities seemed nowhere near as threatening as in previous decades. On the contrary, the relative sophistication of Russia's scientific, technological and military base was now viewed by China as an asset which it could use to facilitate its own military modernization.

The transformation of the Sino-Russian relationship from fierce ideological hostility to 'strategic partnership' did not occur overnight. As already noted in Chapter 1, the repositioning of Soviet foreign policy under Gorbachev was only the first stage in a decade-long transitional period. An important barometer of the mending of fences was the long-standing border dispute. Following Gorbachev's 1986 Vladivostok speech, border talks resumed in February 1987, with the two sides agreeing to review the border in its entirety and to proceed section by section. The appreciable growth of trade along the border was itself a powerful inducement for a negotiated settlement. Agreements signed in 1988 greatly expanded border areas designated for trade exchanges as well as increasing joint production ventures.[226] The decision to construct a joint hydroelectric facility to help control flooding in the Amur and Ussuri river valleys and joint efforts to improve navigation conditions and safety along the rivers pointed to a rapidly improving bilateral relationship. The agreement in 1990 for the mutual reduction of military forces along the border areas gave added impetus to the negotiations, although periodic incidents, including detention of fishing boats by the PLA navy, highlighted the volatility of the situation. An agreement on the demarcation of the eastern section of the border (about 4200 km) in May 1991 was followed in November 1997 by an announcement that all issues dealing with the implementation of the agreement had been finalized and that work was proceeding on the demarcation of the western sector of the border.[227] Demarcation of the entire common border was now seen by both governments as a feasible objective and a litmus test of their improved relationship.

Complementing and facilitating progress in border talks was the steady expansion of bilateral trade. With local governments and individual companies playing a prominent role in trade agreements and cash transactions complementing barter arrangements, Russia's trade with China increased from $3 billion in 1991 to $5 billion in 1992 and $7.7 billion in 1993, making China its second most important trading partner after Germany. Much of this increase was accounted for by vigorous border trade, particularly with the northeastern Chinese provinces of Heilongjiang and Jilin. There were nevertheless significant limitations on continued expansion, attributable largely to inadequate transportation and other infrastructural facilities, the weakness in the legal and contractual framework for bilateral trade, Russia's financial difficulties and the poor quality of products being traded.[228] As a consequence the volume of trade fell abruptly in 1994 and for the rest the decade fluctuated between $5 billion and $7 billion. Having set the unrealistic target of $20 billion by 2000, the two governments were now seeking to co-operate on large projects in the areas of energy, machine construction, aerospace, aviation and transportation.

Gorbachev's visit to China in 1989 had certainly given a badly needed boost to bilateral trade and border negotiations. However, it did more than that; it established the foundations for a larger co-operative framework which Li Peng's return visit to Moscow in 1990 helped to solidify. Six agreements were signed, covering such diverse fields as science and technology, the peaceful use of space, mutual force reductions along the Sino-Soviet border, and consultation between the two foreign ministries.[229] Reciprocal visits by ministers and senior officials culminated in Yeltsin's visit to China at the end of 1992 and the signing of some 24 accords. More important than the content of any single agreement was the emerging commonality of interests and perceptions. Especially significant for Beijing were the clear signals given by Russia that it would not join the West in its condemnation of China's domestic policies. Particularly pleasing to Moscow was China's recognition of the contribution that Moscow could make to the maintenance of stability in Asia Pacific, not least in Central Asia. The new Sino-Russian understanding was codified in a 21-point joint declaration which, *inter alia*, committed both sides to resolving all disputes by peaceful means and precluded either side joining military or political alliances against the other, or allowing its territory to be used by a third party to violate the sovereignty or security interests of the other. Despite the noticeable similarity of language, the declaration was in no sense a replica of the 1950 treaty; it had, on the other hand, all the hallmarks of a mutual non-aggression pact.[230]

A spate of other agreements soon followed, including those on border management, marine transport and natural resources protection, which coincided with Chernomydin's visit to China in May 1994. Military co-operation was also gathering pace. In 1992 Moscow announced plans to sell to China SU-27s, Il-76 air freighters and other air defence weapons valued at $1.8 billion. In subsequent years Russian arms sales to China were estimated at around $1 billion per annum, including a licence for the production of another 36 SU-27s and delivery of four Sovremenny-class guided missile destroyers, each armed with supersonic SS-N-22 anti-carrier missile systems.[231] For Chinese military planners, defence co-operation with Russia, by building on links established during the 1950s, was the most cost-effective way of achieving military modernization. Moscow's willingness, reportedly conveyed during Yeltsin's visit in 1992, to transfer military technology to China and provide it with parts on barter terms was especially attractive to the Chinese, not least because it enhanced their capacity to produce arms for export.[232] Not surprisingly, the decision to strengthen ties with Russia was taken at the highest levels, with Deng Xiaoping's blessing and extensive support in the party and the military. By the mid-1990s military co-operation included an extensive programme of reciprocal visits by senior military officers, substantial transfers of equipment and technology, and ongoing dialogue on a range of security issues.[233]

The newly found warmth in the relationship was nevertheless tempered by a good dose of realism on each side. In addition to the powerful constraints exerted by their economic circumstances, both Moscow and Beijing were acutely aware of the limitations of their diplomatic influence, be it on the global or the regional stage. Even in the case of the Korean conflict, where by virtue of proximity and long-standing connections with Pyongyang the leverage available to Moscow and Beijing had at different times proved decisive, neither was currently in a position to perform such a role. Power considerations aside, the possibilities of a Sino-Russian entente were also constrained by lingering suspicion and mistrust. Reports of large numbers of Chinese moving into the Russian Far East in search of jobs and business opportunities and fears of future mass migration from China's overpopulated northern provinces tended to fuel alarmist accounts of the 'Chinese threat'.[234] The bilateral relationship was also vulnerable to the progressive estrangement of Russia's eastern provinces from the European part of the country and from Moscow in particular. The tendency towards regionalization, with local authorities increasingly impervious to Moscow's directives – a trend not without parallel in China's outer provinces – threatened to curtail the capacity of the centre to pursue coherent and sustained policies, notably on the sensitive and closely related issues of border demarcation, population movements, economic exchanges and military deployments.

Yet the balance of domestic and international pressures predisposed the political leadership in both countries to pursue a policy of rapprochement beyond the normalization of relations achieved during the Gorbachev years. In Chinese declaratory policy three distinct phases marked this evolutionary process: 'good neighbourliness' (beginning with Yeltsin's visit to China in December 1992); 'constructive partnership' (launched during Jiang Zemin's visit to Russia in September 1994); and 'strategic partnership' (set in train with Yeltsin's second visit to China in April 1996). This third phase, though it was built upon the groundwork of the preceding phases, represented a significant threshold. Complementing the proliferation of reciprocal visits and other exchanges between governments, parliaments and military forces, as well as between academic groups and regional representatives, were a number of qualitative developments: progress in the demarcation of the Russian–Chinese border; enhanced military ties; the creation of a legal contractual base for trade; investment and scientific co-operation; and the initiation of major joint projects in gas, oil and nuclear energy development.[235] Both Moscow and Beijing now openly expressed support for each other's positions on issues which they deemed central to their security interests. Just as Russia expressed sympathy for China's stance on Taiwan, Tibet and human rights, so China supported Russian efforts 'to maintain national sovereignty, unity and integrity', opposed NATO's enlargement, and encouraged Moscow's bid to join APEC. Chinese commentators went so far as to describe the current phase as 'the best period in the history of Sino-Russian relations'.[236]

There was clearly more to the relationship than the economic, military, scientific and other practical advantages which both sides derived from it. The crucial element was its geopolitical and geoeconomic context. Both sides opted for closer ties as a way of functioning more effectively in the emerging multipolar system. Like many others, Beijing and Moscow were busily repositioning themselves in order to circumvent the strictures of unipolarity. However, neither China, the ascending power, nor Russia, the former superpower, constituted a sufficient counterweight to American military and diplomatic muscle. Sino-Russian co-operation was therefore a co-ordinated response to the perception of relative weakness.[237] Even jointly, China and Russia could not hope to match America's capacity to project power on a global scale, but they could at least reinforce each other's policy preferences, widen the margin of manoeuvre at their disposal, and create a political space which might allow other players, including allies of the United States, to pursue a more independent policy than might otherwise be the case.

More specifically, the 'strategic partnership' offered useful leverage *vis-à-vis* Japan and the United States. On the one hand, both Moscow and Beijing needed to extract every possible advantage from the two economic giants, whether it be a steady flow of capital and technology, access to the American and Japanese markets or favourable treatment by the world's leading international trade and financial institutions. On the other hand, they wished to minimize the costs involved, or to put it differently, to strengthen their capacity to resist the pressures to which Tokyo or Washington would subject them (for example, Japan's demands that it resume sovereignty over the Northern Territories; American insistence that China take appropriate action to reduce its trade surplus with the United States or improve its domestic human rights record). The Sino-Russian partnership was clearly designed to blunt the force of these pressures. It was meant to erode the effectiveness of the policy of conditional engagement to which, for different reasons and to different degrees, Japan and the United States had committed themselves in their relations with both Russia and China.

For Beijing the strategic partnership was intended to enhance its position within the China–US–Japan triangle which, as we have already seen, constituted the key variable (or set of variables) shaping the geopolitical equation in Asia Pacific. These were the three centres of power whose reach, by virtue of geography, demography, economy, military capability or some combination of these, extended, unevenly perhaps, but across the entire region. Only the United States enjoyed virtual omnipresence. China and Japan tended to focus their influence in Northeast and Southeast Asia, although in Japan's case an expanding network of aid and investment projects extended that influence to several Pacific Island states. Russia's stake, on the other hand, was very much confined to Northeast and Central Asia and was primarily a function of its residual military capabilities and the as yet largely untapped resources of its Far Eastern provinces. For Beijing the Russian connection served notice on the other two powers that a policy of containment would result in even closer ties with Moscow and jeopardize the relaxation of tensions in Asia Pacific. It was a useful way of signalling to Washington and Tokyo the risks associated with a revamped policy of containment, whether latent or overt. The fact that on certain issues, notably the projected joint US–Japanese development of theatre missile defence systems, China and Russia could speak vigorously and in unison added an important new dimension to the decision-making process in both Tokyo and Washington. In determining whether or not to proceed with development and possible deployment, the United States and Japan now had to take into account its implications for the still evolving Sino-Russian connection.

For Moscow the rapprochement with China was less likely to pay immediate dividends in the Asia-Pacific arena. So far as its own triangular relationship with the United States and Japan was concerned, it could conceivably strengthen its credentials as a Pacific power, marginally lift its profile in the security dialogue with both countries and make its voice in regional fora a little louder. At least for the foreseeable future, Russia was likely to find collaboration with China more rewarding at the global level. In a number of international fora, especially the UN Security Council, a degree of policy co-ordination could, as in the case of the UN's role in Iraq and NATO's bombing of Serbia, either negate or at least complicate US priorities and initiatives. It might also provide other states, including friends or allies of the United States, with greater freedom of action which Russian diplomacy could again use to its advantage.

A CONCLUDING NOTE

Our analysis of the emerging triangular relationship between the United States, China and Japan and the briefer discussion of the Russian connection with the triangle should not be seen as an argument for the contemporary relevance of balance of power theory. This is not to say that the four states involved were not conscious of the utility of power, not least military power, or that they were not engaged in some kind of balancing. What emerges, however, from our analysis is that during this period of transition neither competition nor co-operation could be understood exclusively, or even primarily, in a bilateral context. Interaction among any three actors can be reduced to three bilateral relationships, and to six bilateral relationships in the case of four actors. However, it is also possible to visualize these interactive processes in trilateral terms. In post-Cold War Asia Pacific, the evidence suggests that three crucial bilateral relationships (US–Japan, US–China, China–Japan) were themselves closely connected by an intricate web of reciprocal influences as if they constituted different sides of the same triangle, which is not to say that each side (that is, bilateral relationship) was identical in character or importance, or that all points of the triangle were equidistant from one another. Clearly, the US–Japan relationship had greater economic and strategic breadth and depth than the other two. The Sino-Japanese relationship, on the other hand, despite a much longer history, subtler and more profound cultural affinities and extensive contacts, was in material terms the least developed of the three.

In order that our geometric representation approximate geopolitical reality a little more closely, we introduced a fourth actor, Russia, which, despite its greatly diminished power, could still, by virtue of its size, strategic position, resource potential, permanent membership of the UN Security Council and above all its subjective expectations, visibly affect the dynamic of the triangular relationship. Theoretically at least, interaction between the four powers can be depicted in terms of one quadrangle or four triangles. In practical terms, it is analytically simpler and more instructive to examine Russia's role in terms of its two principal bilateral relationships in the region (that is, with Japan and China), and to situate these in the wider context of the US–Japan–China triangle.

Both the triangle taken as a whole and each of the three sides that comprise it embraced, as much in the security as in the economic arena, elements of conflict and co-operation, of competition and interdependence. Economic growth – and the rapid expansion of trade, capital flows and technology transfers on which it rested – may have contributed to regional integration but it also unleashed a competitive dynamic which existing institutions could not easily contain. Much less could it resolve regional conflicts, whether in Korea, Taiwan or the Spratlys, or prevent great power rivalries, whether in relation to trade, military postures or spheres of influence. Even while continuing to rely on the United States for markets and protection, powerful Japanese interests were fiercely resisting US economic and diplomatic domination. Chinese leaders, while conscious of China's dependence on US markets and Japanese capital, were not prepared to abandon their sovereignty claims or their drive for great power status. Gone were the days when a clear line could be drawn between friend and foe. In the words of one Chinese commentator, post-Cold War great power relationships in Asia Pacific were 'more complicated and characterized by a condition in which one [was] neither friend nor foe or both friend and foe'.[238]

In many respects China's conduct was the key new variable in the geopolitical equation. Many of the axes of conflict and co-operation revolved around China's expectations regarding its future place in the region and beyond, and the way these expectations were perceived by others. In this fundamental sense it is arguable that China, even when it seemed to be reacting to the initiatives of others (for example, China's decision to sign the Comprehensive Test Ban Treaty), was in fact the proactive power. The other major players, on the other hand, even when they seemed to be taking the initiative, (as with US efforts to influence China's human rights policies), were largely responding to a new phenomenon: China's actual, imagined or anticipated advance to a leading role on the world stage.

During this transitional period Beijing was, where possible, mending fences with Southeast Asian neighbours, developing closer economic links with other major centres of power, notably Western Europe, and normalizing relations with former enemies, in particular Russia and to a lesser extent Japan, as a prelude to reining in American power. But for all that, Chinese strategy was not unilinear. It did not involve surrendering long-standing positions, whether in relation to Taiwan, the Spratlys, the Paracels or the Diaoyutai. Nor did it mean forsaking the advantages of a workable relationship with the United States. It was more a case of consolidating China's cultural, diplomatic, economic and strategic assets to a point where the international community, the region and above all the United States would have little option but to recognize the pre-eminent place in Asia to which China aspired.

The strategy was, of course, riddled with unanswered questions. Could this transitional period be so managed as to prevent potential rivalry with India or Japan from derailing the strategy? Could regional conflicts be contained so as not to fuel regional anxieties about Chinese intentions? Would Washington be prepared to accommodate Beijing's ambitions? Should the answer to these questions be in the negative, most importantly should the United States take advantage of the contradictions inherent in China's position, how would the Chinese political leadership respond? To pose these questions is to demonstrate the need for a multidimensional analytical framework. The competitive interdependence we have surveyed in this chapter cannot be divorced from the policies and priorities of other regional actors, be it India, the Koreas or ASEAN, nor indeed from the influence of extra-regional actors, not least the European Union.

The full complexity of competitive interdependence cannot be grasped without reference to its interregional dimension, and more specifically to the triangular relationship that connects the three metropolitan centres of global economic activity, the European Union, the US-led North American Free Trade Area and the Japan-centred East Asian region. Less pervasive in its effects but no less revealing in its structure is the strategic triangle linking Western Europe, Russia and North America. Here, one other crucial dimension needs to be injected into the analysis. To speak of bilateral and trilateral relationships is useful and unavoidable, but care must be taken not to oversimplify or distort by assuming that states are the only relevant actors or interstate relations the only appropriate level of analysis. As we have been at pains to stress more than once, the state itself is not a monolithic institution but an area in which diverse interests compete for legitimation and the allocation of scarce resources. Nor is their locus of action necessarily co-extensive with the boundaries of the state. More often than not these interests are subnational, international or transnational in their scope and mode of operation. In that sense, the competitive dynamic which engulfed both states and national economies in the Asia-Pacific region reflects simultaneously a globalizing imperative and multiple disintegrative tendencies. Though it assumed different forms and produced different effects in different places, this dualism was evident as much in China as in Japan or the United States, and was a distinguishing feature of their triangular relationship. The analysis must now be widened to incorporate the region's periphery and semi-periphery, for the logic of competitive interdependence was also at work both within and between these societies, as indeed it was in their relations with the core.

NOTES

1. In the early 1990s we identified four competing security models: *unipolar security, balance of power, concert of powers, and universal security*. See J.A. Camilleri, 'Alliances and the Post-Cold War Security System', in R. Leaver and J.L. Richardson (eds), *Charting the Post-Cold War Order*, Boulder, CO: Westview Press, 1993, pp. 81–94.

2. A number of writers argue that imperial states owe their hegemonic position principally to military power and the manipulation of alliances, hence the sequential dominance of international relations since the sixteenth century by Portugal, the Netherlands, Britain and the United States (See G. Modelski, 'The Long Cycle of Global Politics and the Nation-State', *Comparative Studies in Society and History,* 20, April 1978, 214–35; W.R. Thompson, 'Uneven Growth, Systemic Challenges and Global Wars', *International Studies Quarterly,* 27(3), September 1983, 341–55). Wallerstein, on the other hand, equates hegemony with productive, commercial and financial dominance, although political and military power is seen as a necessary instrument in establishing and maintaining the domestic and external conditions conducive to such dominance (see Immanuel Wallerstein,

The Modern World System: Mercantilism and the Consolidation of the European World Economy, 1600–1750, New York: Academic Press, 1980, p. 38). Yet there is more to hegemonic leadership than the military and economic dimensions of power. Drawing on the Gramscian interpretation of hegemony, Robert W. Cox conceives of a hegemonic order as one in which the dominant state has been able to establish the ideological framework on which rests the legitimacy of its dominance (see Robert W. Cox, 'Labor and Hegemony', *International Organization,* 31(3), Summer 1977, 387; also 'Social Forces, States and World Orders: Beyond International Relations Theory', *Millenium: Journal of International Studies,* 10(2), Summer 1981, 126–55.

3. Charles Kindleberger, *The World in Depression 1929–1939,* Berkeley, CA: University of California Press, 1973; see also his 'Dominance and Leadership in the International Economy', *International Studies Quarterly,* 25(3), June 1981, 242–54.

4. See Robert Gilpin, *War and Change in World Politics,* Cambridge: Cambridge University Press, 1981, p. 156.

5. For a variation of this theme, see Paul Kennedy, *The Rise and Fall of the Great Powers: Economic Change and Military Conflict from 1500 to 2000,* New York: Random House, 1987, pp. 413–37.

6. G. John Ikenberry, 'The Future of International Leadership', *Political Science Quarterly,* 111(3), Fall, 1996, 388–95.

7. Ibid., pp. 396–98.

8. Useful in this regional context is Bobrow's notion of 'hegemony management' involving the complex interactions between the current and two potential hegemons, and between them and other states intent on thwarting their hegemonic ambitions. See Davis B. Bobrow, 'Hegemony Management: The US the Asia-Pacific', *Pacific Review,* 12(2), 1999, 173–97.

9. United States Pacific Command, *Posture Statement, 1993,* p. 1.

10. The draft (which was leaked to the *New York Times,* 8 March 1992, pp. 1, A14) was subsequently qualified in response to criticism from within Congress and from a number of allies, but the commitment to preserving US preponderance remained essentially unchanged (see *Report of the Secretary of Defense to the President and Congress,* Washington, DC: US Government Printing Office, 1993, p. 3).

11. *US Department of State Dispatch* (hereafter referred to as *Dispatch*), 2(46), 18 November 1991, 841.

12. See Douglas Stuart and William T. Tow, 'A US Strategy for the Asia-Pacific', *Adelphi Paper* no. 299, December 1995, pp. 8–11.

13. See Secretary Baker's message to the Japanese people (12 January 1991), *Dispatch,* 2(3), 21 January 1991, 46.

14. See Anthony Lake, 'The Enduring Importance of American Engagement in the Asia-Pacific Region', *Dispatch,* 7(7), February 1996, 545.

15. For a fuller list of US objectives, see Winston Lord's statement before the Senate Foreign Relations Committee, 31 March 1993, *Dispatch,* 4(14), 5 April 1993, 217.

16. See President Clinton's Address to the Korean National Assembly, Seoul, 10 July 1993, in *Regional Security Asia Pacific Defense Forum,* 18(3), 1994, 15; William J. Clinton, *A National Security Strategy of Engagement and Enlargement 1995-1996,* Washington, DC: US Government Printing Office, July 1994, p. 28.

17. Department of Defense, Office of International Security Affairs, *The United States Security Strategy for the East Asia-Pacific Region 1998,* Washington, DC: Department of Defense, 1998, p. 270.

18. *The Bottom-Up-Review: Forces for a New Era,* Washington, DC: Department of Defense, 1993.

19. Fareed Zakaria, 'Culture is Destiny: A Conversation with Lee Kuan Yew', *Foreign Affairs,* 73(4), March 1994, 124.

20. 'America and East Asian Security in an Era of Geoeconomics', *DOSB*, 3(21), 25 May 1992, 411.
21. 'Supporting US Business in Asia and Around the World', *Dispatch*, 4(31), August 1993, 551.
22. *DOSB*, 89(2146), May 1989, 9.
23. James Baker Jr, 'A New Pacific Relationship: Framework for the Future', *Current Policy*, no. 1185, 26 June 1989.
24. See 'The Tokyo Declaration on the US–Japan Global Partnership', *Dispatch*, 3(3), 20 January 1992, 44–5.
25. See 'US and Japan: An Evolving Partnership', address by Richard Solomon, Assistant Secretary for East Asian and Pacific Affairs, 10 April 1990, *Current Policy*, no. 1268, 3.
26. See Stephen W. Bosworth, 'The United States and Asia', *Foreign Affairs*, 71(1), Winter 1991–2, 125; Kenneth Dam, John Deutch, Joseph S. Nye Jr and David M. Rowe, 'Harnessing Japan: A US Strategy for Managing Japan's Rise as a Global Power', *Washington Quarterly*, 16(2), 1993, 35.
27. Chalmers Johnson, 'Japan in Search of a Normal Role', *Daedalus*, 121(4), 1992, 8.
28. Ibid., 9.
29. 'Fact Sheet: US–Japan Relations', *Dispatch*, 4(28), 12 July 1993, 495.
30. See statement of Charlene Barshevsky, Deputy US Trade Representative, to a joint hearing of the Subcommittees on Economic Policy, Trade and Environment, and Asia and the Pacific of the House of Representatives Committee on Foreign Affairs, 5 October 1993, Washington, DC: US Government Printing Office, 1994, p. 12.
31. See testimony by Michael Kantor, US Trade Representative, to the Subcommittee on Trade, Committee on Ways and Means, House of Representatives, 15 March 1994, Washington, DC: US Government Printing Office, 1994, pp. 14–16.
32. See 'US–Japan Framework for a New Economic Partnership', *Dispatch*, 4(28), 12 July 1993, 495–6; also Winston Lord, 'US Policy on Japan and the New Japanese Government', *Dispatch*, 4(42), 18 October 1993, 733.
33. See Clinton's Statement, 10 July 1993, *Dispatch*, 4(28), 12 July 1993, 493.
34. These are Japan Ministry of Finance statistics. See *Diplomatic Bluebook 1996*, p. 32.
35. See statement of Charlene Barshevsky, Deputy US Trade Representative, to the Hearing before the Commerce, Consumer and Monetary Affairs Subcommittee of the Committee of Government Operations, House of Representatives, 23 March 1994, Washington DC: US Government Printing Office, 1994, p. 134.
36. See testimony of Andrew H. Carr, Jr, president and chief executive of the American Automobile Manufacturers Association (AAMA) to the Commerce, Consumer and Monetary Affairs Subcommittee of the Committee of Government Operations, House of Representatives, 24 February 1994, Washington DC: US Government Printing Office, 1994, pp. 54–6.
37. Statement by Ira Shapiro, Office of the US Trade Representative to the Subcommittee on Trade of the Committee of Ways and Means, House of Representatives, 28 March 1996, Washington, DC: US Government Printing Office, 1996, pp. 13–14.
38. Ibid., pp. 14–15.
39. See Eric Altbach, 'The Asian Monetary Fund Proposal: A Case Study of Japanese Regional Leadership', *JEI Report*, 47A, 19 December 1997.
40. See Christopher B. Johnstone, 'Strained Alliance: US–Japan Diplomacy in the Asian Financial Crisis', *Survival*, 41(2), 1999, 126–8.
41. Yoichi Funabashi, 'A US-Led Unipolar World Negative for Japan', *Asahi Evening News*, 16 June 1998.
42. See *White Papers of Japan*, Tokyo: Institute of International Affairs, 1992 pp. 75–6.
43. See Peter J. Katzenstein and Nobuo Okawara, 'Japan's National Security: Structures, Norms, and Policies', *International Security*, 17(4), 1993, 111–12.
44. Mike Mochizuki and Michael O'Hanlon, 'The Marines Should Come Home: Adapting the US–Japan Alliance to a New Security Era', *Brookings Review*, 14(2), 1996, 10–13.

45. Morihiro Hosokawa, 'Restructuring the Japan–US Alliance', address to Council on Foreign Relations in Washington, DC, 12 March 1996 (H-ASIA US Okinawa Forces.htm, 19 March 1996).

46. Cited in 'Japanese See US as Unfair, Unreliable and – in the Long Run – Unimportant', *Japan Digest,* 25 April 1995.

47. See Anthony DeFilippo, *Cracks in the Alliance: Science, Technology, and the Evolution of US–Japan Relations,* Aldershot, Hants.: Ashgate, 1997, pp. 164–85.

48. Richard Solomon, 'US and Japan: An Evolving Partnership', *Current Policy,* no. 1268, April 1990, 4.

49. See *Diplomatic Bluebook 1992,* p. 53.

50. Speech to the National Diet, 12 October 1991, *Diplomatic Bluebook 1991,* p. 360.

51. *White Papers of Japan,* Tokyo: Japan Institute of International Affairs, 1993, p. 31.

52. See *Defense of Japan 1999,* Tokyo: Urban Connections, 1999, pp. 97–102.

53. *Defense of Japan,* Tokyo: Defense Agency of Japan, 1993, pp. 178–206.

54. 'Kato Koichi Interviewed by Tahara Soichiro', *Japan Echo,* 26(3), June 1999, 36.

55. Ozawa Ichiro, 'Japan's Crisis of Politics', *Japan Echo,* 26(3), June 1999, 40.

56. *FEER,* 12 August 1999, 18.

57. A poll of Asian executives conducted in August 1999 found that this initiative, widely interpreted as a sign of rising nationalism, was supported by 76.2 per cent of Japanese respondents (*FEER,* 2 September 1999, 29).

58. The striking shift in official and unofficial Japanese perceptions is discussed in David Arase, 'Japan's Evolving Security Policy after the Cold War', *Journal of East Asian, Affairs,* 8(2), 1994, 369–418; see also Seizaburo Sato, 'Japanese Perceptions of the New Security Situation', in Trevor Taylor (ed.), *The Collapse of the Soviet Empire: Managing the Regional Fallout,* London: Royal Institute of International Affairs, 1992.

59. Reinhard Drifte, 'Japanese Defence Policy and the Security of the Korean Peninsula in the 1990s', *Journal of East Asian Affairs,* 6(1), 1992, 88–9.

60. Johnson, 'Japan in Search of a Normal Role', p. 20.

61. Japan Defense Agency, *Defense of Japan,* 1996, p. 58.

62. Advisory Group on Defense Issues, *The Modality of the Security and Defense Capability of Japan: The Outlook of the 21st Century,* 12 August 1994, p. 7.

63. Ibid, p. 18.

64. *National Defense Program Outline in and after FY 1996,* Ministry of Foreign Affairs, December 1995.

65. *Defense of Japan,* 1996, pp. 71–2, 76–7.

66. See Arase, 'Japan's Evolving Security Policy after the Cold War', pp. 413–14.

67. *Nuke Info Tokyo,* no. 63, January–February 1998, p. 9; Jinzaburo Takagi, 'Japan's Plutonium Program', in Selig S. Harrison, (ed.), *Japan's Nuclear Future,* Washington, DC: Carnegie Endowment for International Peace, 1996, pp. 69–83; Peter Hayes, 'Japan's Plutonium Overhang and Regional Insecurity', Canberra: Australian National University, Peace Research Centre, 1993.

68. See Walden Bello, 'The Triple Threat of Japan's Plutonium Programme', *The Nation,* 18 March 1997.

69. Joseph Nye had been a strong advocate of the need to review the security relationship. The 'Nye Initiative' as it came to be known had as its centrepiece the *United States Security Strategy for the East Asia Region,* issued in February 1995.

70. Joseph S. Nye Jr, 'The Case for Deep Engagement', *Foreign Affairs,* 74(4), 1995, 97.

71. Winston Lord, testimony before the House International Relations Committee, Subcommittees on Asia and the Pacific and International Economic Policy and Trade, 25 October 1995, Washington, DC: US Government Printing Office, 1996, p. 6.

72. See Tsuneo Akaha, 'Beyond Self-defense: Japan's Elusive Security Role under the New Guidelines for US–Japan Defense Cooperation', *Pacific Review,* 11(4), 1998. 472–3.

73.   BBC, *SWB*, 5 May 1999 FE/3526 E3.
74.   *FEER*, 12 August 1999, 19.
75.   David Arase, 'Japan in East Asia', in Akaha and Langdon (eds), *Japan in the Posthegemonic World*, p. 130.
76.   Cited in Calder, *Pacific Defense*, p. 161.
77.   For an instructive, though different, interpretation of Japan's identity crisis, see Masaru Tamamoto, 'The Japan that Wants to Be Liked: Society and International Participation', in Danny Unger and Paul Blackburn (eds), *Japan's Emerging Global Role,* Boulder, CO: Lynne Rienner, 1993, pp. 44–7.
78.   Jung-en Woo, 'East Asia's American Problem', *World Policy Journal*, 8(3), 1991, 472.
79.   *The Economist,* 9 May 1998, 29–31; 'Japan, danger immédiat', 'Dérive de la Maison Japan', *Le Monde Diplomatique,* no. 535, 45e année, Octobre 1998, pp. 1, 25; *International Herald Tribune,* 31 July 1998.
80.   *The Economist,* 26 September 1998, 21–3.
81.   For a more detailed comparative survey, see 'Debt in Japan and America: Into the Whirlwind', *The Economist,* 22 January 2000, pp. 22–4.
82.   See Murray Sayle, 'The Social Contradictions of Japanese Capitalism', *The Atlantic Monthly,* June 1998, 90.
83.   For an incisive analysis of the implicit contestation between these two versions of capitalism (and by implication the competing interests which they represent), see Simon Reich, 'Miraculous or Mired? Contrasting Japanese and American Perspectives on Japan's Economic Problems', *Pacific Review*, 13(1), 2000, 163–93.
84.   According to one survey, 57 per cent of the public and 46 per cent of leaders believed that China's rise as a great power posed a threat to vital US interests (cited in Hon E. Reilly, 'The Public Mood at Mid-decade', *Foreign Policy,* no. 98, Spring 1995, 86). A *Time*/CNN poll conducted in May 1999 found that China was perceived as the greatest threat to the United States, well ahead of Iraq, Russia or Yugoslavia; and that 46 per cent of respondents considered China to be a 'very serious' threat, with 54 per cent expressing an 'unfavourable opinion' of China (*Time*, 7 June 1999, 32.).
85.   For an outline of this hawkish view of China, see Nigel Holloway, 'Making an Enemy', *FEER*, 20 March 1997, 14–16.
86.   Richard Bernstein and Ross H. Munro, 'The Coming Conflict with America', *Foreign Affairs*, 76(2), 1997, 19.
87.   Ibid., 21.
88.   See Jing-dong Yuan, 'United States Technology Transfer Policy toward China: Post-Cold War Objectives and Strategies', *International Journal*, LI, Spring 1996, 314–24.
89.   According to one survey, 51 per cent of the American 'general public' regarded China as a threat and a challenge to US security interests, and therefore in need of containment (see the analysis of a public opinion survey 'Americans Look at Asia' by William Watts, Henry Luce Foundation Project, October 1999, p. 36).
90.   See Qian Qichen's speech to the US Council on Foreign Relations (29 April 1997), reproduced in *Beijing Review*, 19–25 May 1997, 7.
91.   See, for example, He Fang, 'The International Situation in Transition', *Foreign Affairs Journal* (Beijing), no. 24, June 1992, 11; Li Qinggong, 'Bush's "State of the Union" Address and the New US Global Strategy', *Shijie Zhishi*, 1 March 1991, *FBIS-CH-*91-065, 4 April 1991, 5–8.
92.   See William J. Murphy, 'Power Transition in Northeast Asia: US–China Security Perceptions and the Challenges of Systemic Adjustment and Stability', *Journal of Northeast Asian Studies,* Winter 1994, 61–84.
93.   James Baker, Jr, 'A New Pacific Partnership: Framework for the Future', *Current Policy,* no. 1185 (US Department of State), 26 June 1989, p. 3.

94. Richard H. Solomon, 'Sustaining the Dynamic Balance in East Asia and the Pacific', *Current Policy*, no. 1255 (US Department of State), 22 February 1990, p. 3.

95. Jing-dong Yuan, 'United States Technology Transfer Policy toward China', pp. 314–24.

96. See Robert G. Sutter and Kerry Dambaugh, *China–US Relations: Issue Brief*, Congressional Research Service, Washington, DC: Government Printing Office, 1995, p. 198.

97. See Winston Lord's statement before the Senate Foreign Relations Committee, 31 March 1993, *Dispatch*, 4(14), 5 April 1993, 218; and his statement before the Subcommittee on East Asian and Pacific Affairs, 11 October 1995, *Dispatch*, 6(43), 23 October 1995, 774.

98. See article by He Chong published in *Zhong quo Tongxun she,* Hong Kong, 18 November 1993, in *FBIS-CHI-93-223,* 22 November 1993, 3.

99. See Leonard Spector's testimony in the Hearing before the House of Representatives Committee on International Relations, 12 September 1996, *Consequences of China's Military Sales to Iran*, p. 14.

100. See Robert S. Ross, 'Why Our Hardliners Are Wrong', *National Interest*, Fall 1997, 44.

101. For details of the agreement, see *US Policy Information and Texts*, 6 October 1994, p. 16; also Jing-dong Yuan, 'US Technology Transfer Policy toward China', pp. 326–7.

102. The claims made for 'comprehensive engagement' are clearly set out in testimony by Kent Wiedemann, Deputy Assistant Secretary of State for East Asia and Pacific Affairs, before the Senate Foreign Relations Committee, Subcommittee on East Asia and Pacific Affairs, 25 July 1995.

103. For a complete text of the joint statement, see *China Daily*, 31 October 1997, 4–5.

104. Xiaobo Hu, 'A Milestone as well as Millstone: The Jiang–Clinton Summit', *Issues and Studies*, 33(2), December 1997, 6–7.

105. Ronald Montaperto and Ming Zhang, 'The Taiwan Issue: A Test of Sino-US Relations', *Journal of Contemporary China*, no. 9, Summer 1995, 8–11.

106. Winston Lord, 'The United States and the Security of Taiwan', *Dispatch*, 7(6), February 1996, 30.

107. Deng Xiaoping, 'An Idea for the Peaceful Reunification of the Chinese Mainland and Taiwan' (26 June 1983), in *Selected Works of Deng Xiaoping, Vol. III, 1982–1992*, Beijing: Foreign Language Press, 1994, pp. 40–41.

108. James C. Hsiung makes this point but does not develop it beyond alluding to the size of a reunited China's GNP. See 'China in the Twenty-first Century', in S. Chan and G. Clark (eds), *The Evolving Pacific Basin in the Global Political Economy: Domestic and International Linkages*, Boulder, CO: Lynne Rienner, 1992, pp. 76–7.

109. Randall S. Jones, Robert E. King and Michael Klein, 'Economic Integration between Hong Kong, Taiwan and the Coastal Provinces of China', *OECD Economic Studies*, no. 20, Spring 1993, 123, 126; *Xinhua News Agency*, 7 March 1998, in FE/3170 S1/6.

110. Ming Zhang, 'The Emerging Asia-Pacific Triangle', *Australian Journal of International Affairs*, 52(1), 1998, 48.

111. This scenario is canvassed by Bruce Gilley, 'Operation Mind Games', *FEER*, 28 May 1998, 31–2.

112. Much of the literature has unduly emphasized the scope and limitations of Chinese military capabilities, in particular the logistical and transport difficulties that would beset any attempt by the PLA Navy and Air Force to embark on the physical conquest of Taiwan. Yet, more feasible Chinese strategies are likely to rely on the application of low-level military pressure and various forms of economic coercion. For a useful discussion of Chinese strategic options see Denny Roy, 'Tensions in the Taiwan Strait', *Survival*, 42(1), Spring 2000, 76–96

113. Winston Lord, 'The United States and the Security of Taiwan', *Dispatch*, 7(6), February 1996, 30.

114. That this is an accurate reading of the message intended by Washington was confirmed by these reactions from Taiwan (*FEER*, 9 July 1998, 14).

115. See Dennis Van Vranken Hickey, 'The Taiwan Strait Crisis of 1996: Implications for US Security Policy', *Journal of Contemporary China*, 7(19), 411.
116. See 'Breaking the Ice' *FEER*, 15 October 1998, 24–6; *The Age* (Melbourne), 20 October 1998, 12.
117. For a useful overview of Taiwan's economic prospects and political options, see 'Taiwan Survey', *The Economist*, 7 November 1998, 1–22; see also the book written by PLA Air Force Senior Colonels Qiao Liang and Wang Xiang Sui, *Unrestricted Warfare* (a translation appeared on the US Embassy Beijing website at http://www.usembassy-china. org.ch/english/sandt/WEBRES4.htm, sighted 10 April 2000, 9).
118. *FEER*, 25 March 1999, 11–12.
119. *FEER*, 4 March 1999, 22.
120. Julian Baum, 'Marshalling Friends', *FEER*, 19 August 1999, 25–6.
121. Julian Baum, Shaun W. Crispin and Lorien Holland, 'Upping the Ante', *FEER*, 22 July 1999, 18.
122. *The Age* (Melbourne), 16 July 1999, 11.
123. *The Age* (Melbourne), 27 July 1999, 9.
124. *FEER*, 12 August 1999, 22.
125. *Washington Times*, 23 November 1999.
126. *White Paper – The One-China Principle and the Taiwan Issue*, published by the PRC's Taiwan Affairs Office and the Information Office of the State Council, 21 February 2000 (reproduced on the website of the Chinese Embassy in the United States at http://www.china-embassy.org/papers/taiwan00.htm, sighted 7 July 2000, p. 7)
127. *FEER*, 30 March 2000, p. 19; also *FEER*, 13 April 2000, 18.
128. *Australian*, 22 May 2000, 19.
129. Tao-tai Hsia and Wendy I. Zeldin, 'China's White Paper on Human Rights,' Foreign Law Issue Brief, Washington, DC: Library of Congress, April 1993. See also Department of State, *Country Reports on Human Rights Practices for 1993*, Washington, DC: US Government Printing Office, 1994, pp. 80–95.
130. For a useful account of the twists and turns of US attempts to link human rights and MFN status, see Sutter and Dumbaugh, *China–US Relations: Issue Brief.*
131. The underlying rationale for Clinton's attempt to develop a broader and more sustained dialogue with China was elaborated by Winston Lord in Testimony to a Joint Hearing of Four Subcommittees of the House of Representatives Committee on Foreign Relations, 24 March 1994, pp. 13–14.
132. Address to the Pacific Basin Economic Council, Washington, DC, 20 May 1996, *Dispatch*, 7(22), 27 May 1996, 262–63.
133. See statement by the Lawyers Committee on Human Rights submitted to the Joint Hearing of the House of Representatives Committee on Foreign Affairs, 29 May 1991, Washington, DC: US Government Printing Office, 1992, pp. 239–240.
134. See testimony by Kent Wiedemann, Deputy Assistant Secretary of State for East Asian and Pacific Affairs before Senate Foreign Relations Committee, Subcommittee on East Asian and Pacific Affairs, 25 July 1995, *Dispatch*, 6(30), 24 July 1995, 587–90.
135. Stuart Eizenstat, 'United States Trade with Asia,' *Dispatch*, 8(6), July 1997, 17.
136. See *The Age*, 10 March 2000, p. 15; also *FEER*, 24 February 2000, pp. 22–3.
137. See Statement of Jay Etta Z. Hecker, US General Accounting Office, before House of Representatives Committee on Banking and Financial Services, 29 July 1996, 64.
138. See Statement of Jay Etta Z. Hecker, 29 July 1996, pp. 71–2. Fact sheet released by Bureau of East Asian and Pacific Affairs, US Department of State, 26 October 1998.
139. For an explanation of the differences in calculation, see *International Trade: US Government Policy Issues Affecting US Business Activities in China* (GAO/GGD 1993–1994, 4 May 1994); also Jialin Zhang, 'US–China Relations in the Post-Cold War Period: A Chinese Perspective', *Journal of Northeast Asian Studies*, 24(2), Summer 1995, 54–7.

140. 'Economic Relations with US, Japan Reviewed, *International Trade Journal* (Beijing), 19 May 1995 (translated in FBIS-CHI-95-147, 1 August 1995, p. 43).

141. See statement by Richard L. Trumka, AFL-CIO Secretary-Treasurer, to Senate Select Committee on Foreign Relations, 6 June 1996, p. 17.

142. This emerged as one of the key points in a speech by Chinese Premier Zhu Rongji, delivered at MIT during his visit to the United States in April 1999. While the deficit with China may have increased over the preceding decade, the overall US deficit still represented only 2 per cent of its GDP. Morever, Chinese exports to the United States, primarily 'labor or resource-intense, low-value added consumer goods' posed no threat to US enterprises (see *Beijing Review*, 10 May 1999, 19–20).

143. See Statement of Jay Etta Z. Hecker, 29 July 1996, pp. 71–2 .

144. As part of the liberalization of its economy, China had, in a relatively short space of time, already drastically reduced its trade barriers. China's tariffs in 1997 were at an average level of 17 per cent, from 23 per cent in 1996 and 44 per cent in 1993.

145. *China Daily*, 31 October 1997, 4.

146. 'Remarks by the President to US Business Leaders and Leaders of the Shanghai Business Community', issued by the White House Office of the Press Secretary, 1 July 1998.

147. See Brenda Zhen Huang, 'China and the WTO: Towards Accession', *New Zealand International Review*, XXV(3), May–June 2000, 11–15.

148. Warren Christopher, 'The United States and China: Building a New Era of Cooperation for a New Century', remarks made at Fudan University, Shanghai, 21 November 1996.

149. Madeleine Albright, 'American Principle and Purpose in East Asia', *Dispatch*, 8(3), March–April 1997, 23.

150. Ibid.

151. *FEER*, 9 July 1998, 13.

152. Clinton's Address to the Australian Parliament, 20 November 1996, *Dispatch*, 7(48), 25 November 1996, 577.

153. For an examination of these trends attempting a balanced account of the centrifugal and centripetal forces bearing upon the Chinese political system, see David Shambaugh, 'Containment or Engagement of China', *International Security*, 21(2) Fall 1996, 180–209. For two opposing views of the durability of China's political fabric, see Jack Goldstone, 'The Coming Chinese Collapse', and Huang Yasheng, 'Why China Will Not Collapse', *Foreign Policy*, no. 99, Summer 1995, 35–68.

154. *The Economist*, 2 May 1998, 69–71.

155. The texts of the two reports are reproduced in BBC, *SWB*, 6 March 1998, FE/3168S1/2-16 and BBC, *SWB*, 9 March 1999, FE/3478 SI/I.

156. See *Impact of China's Military Modernization in the Pacific Region*, Report by US General Accounting Office to Congressional Committees, June 1995, p. 20.

157. See Mark Farrer, 'Chinese Submarine Force in Change', *Asia-Pacific Defence Reporter*, 24(6), October/November 1998, 12–15.

158. See Mark Farrer, 'China's Air Force – Kosovo Spurs a Race to Change', *Asia-Pacific Defence Reporter*, 25(6), October/November 1999, 20–21.

159. Testimony by Ron Montaperto before the Subcommittee on East Asian and Pacific Affairs of the Senate Committee on Foreign Relations, 11 October 1995, p. 50.

160. For a fuller description of China's ballistic missile capabilities see David Shambaugh, 'Sino-American Strategic Relations: From Partners to Competitors', *Survival*, 42(1), Spring 2000, 105.

161. The PLA's attempts to learn the lessons of the Gulf War and embrace the 'revolution in military affairs' are highlighted in You Ji, *The Armed Forces of China*, Sydney: Allen & Unwin, 1999, pp. 1–27.

162. See Jing-Dong Yuan, 'Studying Chinese Security Policy: Toward an Analytic Framework', *Journal of East Asian Affairs*, 13(1), Spring/Summer 1999, 131–97.

163. See testimony by Alfred D. Wilhelm, Jr, Executive Vice-President of the Atlantic Council of the United States before US Senate Committee on Foreign Relations, Subcommittee on East Asian and Pacific Affairs, 11 October 1995, p. 55.
164. See Goldstein, 'Great Expectations', p. 42; also see Tai Ming Cheung, 'China's Entrepreneurial Army: The Structure, Activities, and Economic Returns of the Military Business Complex', in C. Dennison Lane, Mark Weisenbloom and Diman Liu (eds), *Chinese Military Modernization*, New York: Kegan Paul International, 1996, pp. 184–7; Solomon M. Karmel, 'The Chinese Military's Hunt for Profits', *Foreign Policy*, no. 107, Summer 1997, 106.
165. US Arms Control and Disarmament Agency, *World Military Expenditures and Arms Transfers 1993–1994*, Washington, DC: US Government Printing Office, 1995, p. 58.
166. *China's National Defense*, issued by the Information Office of the National State Council of the People's Republic of China, July 1998, *Beijing Review*, 10–16 August 1998, 16.
167. Ming Zhang, 'What Threat?', *Bulletin of the Atomic Scientists*, 55(5), September–October 1999, 52–7; See also Evan A. Feigenbaum, 'China's Military Posture and the New Geoeconomics', *Survival*, 41, Summer 1999, 81–3.
168. *The Australian*, 2 August 1996, 11.
169. *FEER*, 27 November 1997, 18–19.
170. *FEER*, 10 December 1998, 28–9; *The Age* (Melbourne), 4 February 2000, 7.
171. For a Chinese response, see BBC, *SWB*, 10 March 1999, FE/3749 G/R-3.
172. See US Congress, *Report of the Select Committee on US National Security and Military/Commercial Concerns with the People's Republic of China*, Washington, DC: US Government Printing Office, 1999. The overview of its findings appears on pp. I-XXXVI.
173. See Walter Arnold, 'Political and Economic Influences in Japan's Relations with China since 1978', *Journal of International Studies*, 18(3), 1989, 419.
174. See Allen S. Whiting, 'China and Japan: Politics versus Economics', *Annals of the American Academy of Political and Social Science*, no. 519, January 1992, 41.
175. See Joseph Y.S. Cheng, 'China's Japan Policy in the 1990s: Adjusting to the Evolving Multipolar World', *Pacifica Review*, 8(2), 1996, 21.
176. *FBIS-CHI*, 19 December 1990, 8.
177. *FEER*, 26 November 1998 (according to Japan External Trade Organization [JETRO] estimates). This compares with a total of $60.8 billion cited in *Beijing Review*, 2–8 November 1998, 9.
178. For an examination of these linkages and the shift in the structure of trade between the two countries, see Hoichi Yokoi, 'Major Developments in Japan–China Economic Interdependence in 1990–1994', in Christopher Howe (ed), *China and Japan: History, Trends, and Prospects*, Oxford: Oxford University Press, 1996, pp. 147–54.
179. *Asia's Global Powers: China--Japan Relations in the 21st Century*, Canberra: Department of Foreign Affairs and Trade, East Asia Analytical Unit, 1996, pp. 43, 50.
180. Cheng, 'China's Japan Policy in the 1990s', p. 26.
181. Harvey W. Nelsen, 'Japan Eyes China' *Journal of Northeast Asian Studies*, Winter 1995, 86.
182. Yong Deng, 'Chinese Relations with Japan: Implications for Asia-Pacific Regionalism', *Pacific Affairs*, 70(3), Fall 1997, 379; *Kyodo News Service*, 22 September 1998.
183. For a useful overview of Japanese FDI flows and technology transfers to China, See Robert Taylor, 'Sino-Japanese Economic Cooperation since 1978', in Peter Drysdale and Dong Dong Zhang (eds), *Japan and China: Rivalry or Cooperation with East Asia*, Canberra: Australian National University, Australia–Japan Research Centre, 2000, pp. 71–91.
184. Toshiki Kaifu, 'Japan's Vision', *Foreign Policy*, no. 80, Fall 1990.
185. See, for example, Li Genan, 'A Great Change in Japan's Stance on Asian Security Measures', *Waiguo wenti yanju* [*Studies of Foreign Affairs*], February 1993, 26.
186. See Chen Lineng, 'The Japanese Self-defence Forces Are Marching toward the 21st Century', *Guoji Zhangwang* [*World Outlook*], in FBIS-CHI-96-085, 9–12.

187. *Selected Works of Deng Xiaoping*, vol. 3, Beijing: Renmin Chubanshe, 1993, p. 293.
188. See Cheng, "China's Japan Policy in the Mid-1990s', pp. 11–13.
189. See Xinhua News Agency report (4 September 1997) of talks between Premier Li Peng and Prime Minister Ryutaro Hashimoto, in FE/3017/G/-2, 6 September 1997.
190. *The Age* (Melbourne), 28 November 1998.
191. See comments by Vice Foreign Minister Qi Huaiyan reported in *Renmin Ribao*, 29 October 1990, p. 1.
192. Greg Austin and Michael Tomas, 'Geo-economics and Sovereignty in the East China Sea', *Asia-Pacific Magazine*, no. 13, December 1998, 30–3.
193. For a detailed examination of the dispute see Erica Strecker Downs and Philip C. Saunders, 'Legitimacy and the Limits of nationalism: China and the Diaoyu Islands', *International Security*, 23(3), Winter 1998-99, 124–38.
194. *Xinhua News Agency*, 30 August 1996, in FE/2706g/2–3, 2 September 1996.
195. Such disquiet was made explicit in *Defense of Japan*, 1996, pp. 42–7.
196. Kent E. Calder, *Pacific Defense: Arms, Energy and America's Future in Asia*, New York: William Morrow, 1996, p. 137.
197. Samuel S. Kim, 'China's Pacific Policy: Reconciling the Irreconcilable', *International Journal*, 50, Summer 1995, 470.
198. This shift is alluded to in a highly nuanced analysis by Stuart Harris, 'The China–Japan Relationship and Asia-Pacific Regional Security', Canberra: Australian National University, Department of International Relations, Working Paper no. 1996/7, pp. 4–5.
199. See 'Refocusing in Asia', *US News and World Report*, 22 April 1996, 48–9; also Aurelia George Mulgan, 'The Japan–US Security Relationship', paper presented to the IISS/SDSC Conference on 'The New Security Agenda in the Asia-Pacific Region', Canberra, 1–3 May 1996.
200. See Ni Feng, 'Enhanced US–Japanese Security Alliance: Cause for Concern', *Beijing Review*, 16–22 June 1997, 7.
201. See Chinese Foreign Minister Qian Qichen's criticism of Japan, reported in *Kyodo News Service*, 29 September 1997, in FE/3038 G/01.
202. See Thomas J. Christensen, 'China, the US–Japan Alliance, and the Security Dilemma in East Asia', *international Security*, 23(4), Spring 1999, 64–9.
203. Chen Zhijiang, 'Japan–US Joint Declaration on Security: Dangerous Signal', *Guangming Ribao*, 18 April 1996, in *FBIS-CHI* -96-079, 23 April 1996, 2.
204. For a forthright exposition of this view, see article by Chang Xin, 'Inherent Contradiction and Future of America's Asia-Pacific Strategy', *Shijie Jingli* [*World Economy*], no. 10, 1 October 1994, reproduced in *FBIS-CHI*-95-037, 24 February 1995, 6–11.
205. For a comprehensive compilation of Chinese expert assessments, see Rex Li, 'Unipolar Aspirations in a Multipolar Reality: China's Perceptions of US Ambitions and Capabilities in the Post-Cold War World', *Pacifica Review*, 11(2), June 1999, 115–50. For a nuanced Chinese exposition of the triangular relationship, but with the accent on opportunities for co-operation, see Liu Jiangyong, 'Clinton's China Visit and the New Trends in Sino–US–Japanese Relations', *Contemporary International Relations* (China Institute of Contemporary International Relations), 8(7), July 1998, 1–13.
206. Duang Tang, 'China–Japan–US Triangle: A Critical Relationship', *Beijing Review*, 7–13 April 1997, 7.
207. Multhiah Alagappa, 'Soviet Policy in Southeast Asia: Towards Constructive Engagement', *Pacific Affairs*, 63(3), 1990, 329–35.
208. Leszek Buszynski, 'Russia and the Asia-Pacific Region', *Pacific Affairs*, 65(4), 1992–3, 487.
209. Shulong Chu, 'The Russian–US Military Balance in the Post-Cold War Asia-Pacific Region and the "China Threat", *Journal of Northeast Asian Studies*, XIII(1), 1994, 78–9.

210. The tendency, however, in much of the literature to focus on Russian weakness reflected an excessive preoccupation with the unique conjuncture of the late 1980s and early 1990s and a questionable reinterpretation of the more enduring dimensions of Russia's geopolitical condition and imagination. A clear illustration of this tendency is the analysis offered by Robert Ross, 'The Geography of the Peace: East Asia in the Twentieth-first Century', *International security*, 23(4), Spring 1999, 86–90.
211. *FBIS, Daily Report, Central Eurasia*, 7 February 1994, 10–11.
212. See Sharif M. Shuja, 'Russia's Foreign Policy in Asia: Continuities, Changes and Challenges', *Journal of International and Area Studies*, 6(1), May 1999, 85–96.
213. Richard H. Solmon, 'Asian Security in the 1990s: Integration in Economics, Diversity in Defense', *Dispatch*, 5 November 1990, 243.
214. See statement by Admiral Joseph W. Prucher to Senate Armed Services Committee, 28 March 1996, p. 828.
215. The divergence in security perceptions is examined in Peggy Falkenheim, 'The Soviet Union, Japan, and East Asia: The Security Dimension', *Journal of Northern Asian Studies*, Winter 1989, 43–50.
216. Rajan Menon and Daniel Abele, 'Security Dimensions of Soviet Territorial Disputes with China and Japan', *Journal of Northeast Asian Studies*, Winter 1989, 14.
217. Buszynski, 'Russia and the Asia-Pacific Region', pp. 493–4.
218. Tsuneo Akaha, 'Russia in Asia in 1994: An Emerging East Asian Power', *Asian Survey*, XXXV(1), 1995, 104–5.
219. A more detailed analysis of the impact of domestic politics is offered by Konstantin Sarkisov, 'The Northern Territories Issue after Yeltsin's Re-election: Obstacles to a Resolution from a Russian Perspective', *Communist and Post-Communist Studies*, 30(4), 1997, 353–7; see also Roger E. Karet and Susanne M. Birgesson, 'The Domestic Foreign Policy Linkage in Russian Politics: Nationalist Influences on Russian Foreign Policy', *Communist and Post-Communist Studies,* 30(4), 1997, 335–44.
220. *BBC, SWB* 25 September 1997 FE/3033 E/11–12.
221. Hiroshi Kimura, 'Primakov's Offensive: A Catalyst in Stalemated Russo-Japanese Relations?', *Communist and Post-Communist Studies*, 30(4), 1997, 366.
222. See *Yomiuri Shimbun,* 4, 20, 21, 22 January 1997.
223. For a comprehensive account of the summit and agreements reached, see BBC *SWB*, 20 April 1998, FE/3205 E/1-6.
224. This strategic perspective was reflected in a good many Chinese writings, for example in Jen Hui-wen, 'China's Strategic Considerations in Developing Sino-Russian Relations', *Hsin Pao*, reproduced in *FBIS-CHI-94-105,* 1 June 1994, 10–11.
225. See Dale R. Herspring, 'Russia's Crumbling Military', *Current History*, October 1998, 325–8.
226. *FBIS-SOV*, 11 April 1989, 18–19.
227. See text of Russian–Chinese Joint Declaration in BBC, 11 November 1997, FE/3073 G-2.
228. Akaha, 'Russia in Asia in 1994', p. 103.
229. Gu Guanfu and Chun-tu Hsueh, 'Sino-Soviet Ties Grow Steadily' *Beijing Review*, 3–9 September 1990, 9–12.
230. 'Joint Declaration on the Basis of Relations between the People's Republic of China and the Russian Republic', *People's Daily*, 19 December 1992, 1.
231. Gary Klintworth, 'Regional Defense Budgets Down, Russian Arms Selling Well', *Asia-Pacific Defence Reporter*, January 2000, p. 23.
232. See Ya-Chun Chang, 'Peking–Moscow Relations in the Post-Soviet Era', *Issues and Studies*, January 1994, 91–3.
233. Jen Hui-Wen, 'China's Strategic Considerations', p. 11.
234. See Vladimir Shlapentokh, 'Russia, China, and the Far East: Old Geopolitics or a New Peaceful Cooperation', *Communist and Post-Communist Studies*, 28(3), 1995, 310–11, 315–16.

235. See text of Russian–Chinese joint declaration released on 10 November 1997 on the occasion of Yeltsin's third visit to China, BBC, *SWB*, 11 November 1997, FE/3073 G-2/3; also 'In Beijing, The Signs of a New Strategic Partnership', STRATFOR.COM Global Intelligence Update, 3 March 2000.

236. Xia Yishan, 'Sino-Russian Partnership Marching into 21st Century', *Beijing Review*, 5–11 May 1997, 10.

237. See Jennifer Anderson, *The Limits of Sino-Russian Strategic Partnership*, Adelphi Paper 315, 1997, pp. 61–72.

238. See column article by Gu Ping in *Renmin Ribao*, 4 June 1994, 6, in *FBIS-CHI-94-110*, 8 June 1994, 3.

4. Periphery and semi-periphery: in search of a new equilibrium

Our discussion of the United States–China–Japan triangle was predicated on the assumption that these were three core states, though their bilateral relationships were as much conflictual as co-operative and their respective economic, military and diplomatic circumstances characterized by enormous disparities in wealth, power and influence. The notion of 'core' state was used to denote the dominant role which these three poles occupied within the political economy of Asia Pacific, and above all the centrality of their triangular relationship for the region's evolving geopolitical and geoeconomic landscape.

CORE, PERIPHERY AND SEMI-PERIPHERY

There is more, however, to postulating the existence of a core, and by implication that of a periphery, than the conventional classification of states as great, middle and small powers. Given that this chapter focuses on the conduct of a number of smaller states in the region, it may be useful to delve more closely into questions of structure and hierarchy. Viewed in terms of the now familiar core–periphery or dominant–dependent dichotomies which gained currency in the late 1960s and 1970s,[1] particularly in the heyday of dependency theory, China's position is anomalous. Its effective subordination in the second half of the nineteenth century to the will of European colonial powers and the relatively underdeveloped state of its economy which persisted well into the second half of the twentieth century are compelling reasons for categorizing China as a dependent society. Yet, by virtue of its demographic weight, the size and location of its territory, the regional pre-eminence of its culture, the extent of its military capabilities and the rapid growth of its economy, China could now be described as enjoying, at least regionally, metropolitan or core status. Clearly, notions of dominance and dependence are highly abstract concepts which, when applied to the complex and often contradictory tendencies of historical reality, must be treated with a good deal of caution.

The explanation of underdevelopment proposed by the *dependistas*, and the historical narratives on which they are based, have been subjected to numerous and telling criticisms.[2] There is nevertheless one relatively simple insight, highly relevant to our analysis, which lies at the heart of dependency theory, namely its emphasis on the complex linkages that connect dominant and dependent systems or, to put it more succinctly, the centre (or core) and the periphery. Implicit in this approach is the contention, substantially refined and elaborated by world-system theory, that the dividing line which separates national and international processes, and for that matter the political, economic, military and ideological dimensions of social interaction, is at best tenuous and at worst illusory.[3] To concede this point is not to accept the specific characterization of the twin notions of underdevelopment and unequal exchange favoured by different dependency theories.[4] It is to recognize that the web of 'hidden or subtle financial, economic, technical and cultural mechanisms' operating both within and between states is an integral part of the equation which connects the accumulation of privilege with the continued reproduction of a marginal class. Essentially, the dependency model postulates a pattern of asymmetric relationships such that it consistently advantages one party at the expense of the other, or at least favours one more than the other. The outcome is said to be economic development, military ascendancy, technological sophistication and cultural dominance for the centre, and economic underdevelopment (or less development), military inferiority, technological backwardness and cultural emulation for the periphery.

In the contemporary international system dependence is said to have been institutionalized through a diverse network of private and governmental economic, political and military structures and agencies.[5] For most Third World countries, it is argued, these institutional processes have neutralized the anticipated benefits of political independence and sustained the widening gap in productive performance between advanced and underdeveloped economic systems. In the Asia-Pacific context, dependency theory can no doubt shed useful light on the political and economic circumstances of much of Southeast Asia as well as the small island nations of the South Pacific. Yet, analytically instructive though it may be, the model is nevertheless deficient on several counts. The notion of a global order pacified and integrated under the unchallenged supremacy of global capital is not easily reconciled with the reality of a sharply fragmented world. Dependency theory does not appear able to identify with any clarity, much less explain, shifts in the international division of labour, the geographic relocation of industries, the rise of new centres of power, or the emergence of new political movements, new demands and new institutions, which cumulatively shape the prevalent pattern of stratification. It is not sufficiently attuned to the *politics of disorder,*[6] which endows the constituent units and sub-units of the international system with a greater degree of autonomy, manoeuvrability and resistance to external constraints.

Though Wallerstein's analysis of the world economy is a much larger intellectual project than dependency theory, it can be interpreted in part as an attempt to overcome some of its limitations. Concerned as he is with the overall expansion of global capitalism, he is able to situate the mechanisms of unequal exchange within a global setting. Both states and economic producers are said to operate within a world market, whose structure and logic largely shape their respective positions and strategies. Two features of world-system theory, as developed by Wallerstein and his associates, are worth noting here. First, a crucial function is assigned to the system of states in developing and maintaining a pattern of global stratification. It is states which institutionalize and legitimize the core–periphery division of labour, and concretize through a dense network of legal, diplomatic and military instruments the distribution of power within the core. Second, Wallerstein's analytical framework introduces a new category, the 'semi-periphery', which acts as an intermediate link in the 'surplus-extraction chain'[7] and to that extent allows for a degree of mobility within the system. Semi-peripheral status is in a sense a point of transition for core states and economies in decline but also for peripheral actors on the rise.

These two features of world-system theory have important implications for our analysis. Most obviously, it offers a category which, at least at face value, neatly applies to the newly industrializing economies of East Asia. More importantly, it opens up new possibilities for clarifying the role of the East Asian state at various stages of economic development, and in particular its dual function as the provider of security and manager of the fragile relationship between capital and labour. In this sense, a study of the semi-periphery in Asia Pacific should yield useful insights into the strategies of industrial and financial enterprises and the way they can mobilize the resources of the state to enhance their position *vis-à-vis* their competitors. To put it differently and perhaps more accurately, the analysis of export-oriented industrialization in the Asia-Pacific context, when approached from a world-system perspective, can help to explain how the legal and political apparatus of the state has combined with the operations of domestic and foreign capital to achieve a degree of efficiency in production capable of yielding greater market share for a number of manufacturing industries.

Equally significant is the historical perspective which imbues Wallerstein's reading of the world system. Stressing the evolving character of the world-economy, he postulates a number of phases: the emergence of the European world-economy, that is, the transition from feudalism to capitalism (1450–1650); the establishment of British hegemony; the shift from agricultural to industrial capitalism; and the subsequent consolidation of industrial capitalism under American hegemony.[8] The particulars of this attempted periodization are no doubt open to dispute, but what clearly emerges from Wallerstein's historical account is the relentless evolution of the global political economy. Its trajectory is punctuated by a series of thresholds, each ushering in a new phase characterized by a distinctive structure connecting the process of capital accumulation with the geopolitical rivalries of the state system. To the extent that the most recent period is marked by the decline (which is not to say disappearance) of US hegemony, hence our notion of residual hegemony, both peripheral and semi-peripheral economies and states are likely to experience profound changes in their internal structure as well as external relations.

The pace and intensity of adaptive change are likely to be all the more pronounced given the steady rise of multipolarity or, to put it more starkly, the progressive fracturing of the core. It is here that the Wallerstein model is in need of revision or qualification. Its conceptualization of the international division of labour is still too rigid, its portrayal of the world system too functionally integrated. Despite the role ascribed to semi-peripheral states and producers, the pattern of global stratification remains relatively immune to contradictions. History is not simply a succession of hegemonic states presiding over different stages of the world-economy. Nor is each stage characterized by an unbroken chain of political, economic and cultural domination. Individual states, and the state system as a whole, do not serve a purely instrumental or functional role. They retain a degree of autonomy and give rise to multiple alliances and coalitions both within and across state boundaries whose logic cannot be reduced to the core–periphery division of labour.

Such autonomy must not, of course, be confused with the anachronistic notion of sovereignty with its connotations of absolute and indivisible authority and the rigid demarcation of boundaries implicit in a system made up of exclusive sovereign jurisdictions.[9] Rather the state is envisaged here as an arena of conflict, giving expression to and institutionalizing the tension between competing values, interests and organizational principles, which are likely to be as much transnational as national in origin and form. Where a given state is unable to mediate or contain these tensions, the natural tendency will be to experiment with new institutional arrangements. As numerous writers have observed, the state is both agent and victim of the twin processes of integration and fragmentation.[10] Obliged to adapt to an inescapable yet fragile global environment and to the often unpredictable terrain of social and political conflict, the state is spawning a proliferation of subnational, international and supranational structures, which is not to say that the trend is regular or uniform across time or space. The ensuing delegation of tasks and resources to new organizational forms and agencies does nevertheless point to a steady institutional outgrowth which, even when directly instigated and monitored by states, is bound to give rise to an even more complex pattern of competition and co-operation.

Therefore in making a number of states the focus of this chapter, there is no prior assumption that the state, let alone the sovereign state, is the sole or even primary agency shaping the political economy or geostrategic complexion of the region. As previous chapters have already indicated and subsequent ones will further elucidate, the conduct of states must be set against a backdrop of accelerating globalization and regionalization. Our analysis of peripheral and semi-peripheral states in the Asia-Pacific region, while informed by some of the insights of dependency and world system theory, is in fact intended to problematize three key relationships: notably those between structure and agency, between security and economy, and between domestic politics and foreign policy.

At first sight, it may seem as if the international system of the 1990s was less constrained by great power rivalries and more responsive to the interests and priorities of smaller powers. Even the United States, despite its awesome military power, was unable to exercise decisive political control over intractable local and regional conflicts, whether in Somalia, Rwanda, Bosnia, Korea or Cambodia. It did not automatically follow, however, that the periphery and semi-periphery were better able to shape the international political agenda. Much less did it mean that they were all equipped or inclined to play a more constructive role in peacekeeping, peace making or crisis prevention. The conclusion that agency in post-Cold War international relations was steadily gaining ground at the expense of structure is largely unsubstantiated. The new trends point rather to several important but still unanswered questions: were some states better placed than others to exercise leadership either in agenda setting or in institution building? How and to what extent were these differential capabilities to be explained by differences in their resource and demographic base, political culture, stage of economic development or external environment? What organizational forms did leadership assume? What strategic options were pursued, and with what success? Central to all these questions is the function of the state and its capacity to manage the national economy.

A second and closely related dimension of this problématique is the national–international dichotomy. The dividing line between a state's internal and external environment and between its domestic and foreign policies has become rather blurred. The interpenetration of national economies – and the increasing porosity of national boundaries of which it is the most striking outward manifestation – has significantly circumscribed the hegemonic influence which any one state can exercise. It is by no means clear, however, that the same trend can be used by less powerful or dependent states to widen their own freedom of action. The evidence adduced by Stanley Hoffman in support of the notion that 'games of skill' were replacing 'tests of will' in the 1990s[11] was far from conclusive. The increased salience of economic, environmental and human rights issues in the changing structure of the global order could not easily or automatically be translated into greater leverage for so-called middle or small powers.[12] Regardless of geographical location or normative preference, the capacity of states to pursue multilateral solutions to security, to use their good offices to help resolve international conflicts, or more generally embrace notions of good international citizenship, was subject to multiple constraints, including military alliances, financial and trading arrangements, and dependence on global information and communication networks.

Logically connected with, and to some extent consequent upon, the ambiguities of the structure/agency dynamic and the internal/external divide is the fluid relationship between security and economy. That states, markets and societies – their structure, *modus operandi* and underlying rationale – can no longer be understood in isolation from one another is plain enough. Much less clear was the impact of economic globalization and regionalization, in particular shifting patterns of trade, capital flows, aid and technology transfers, on the security dilemma, that is, on the perception of threats or on the formulation and execution of policy responses. There is no denying that a clearly discernible trend had emerged in the 1980s and 1990s: the security agenda was being steadily widened to encompass such notions as 'economic', 'environmental', 'societal' and even 'human' security.[13] At the same time states appeared increasingly willing to explore multilateral approaches to security to complement, though not replace, the more traditional practices of bilateral diplomacy. The implications of all this for the incidence and intensity of violence, or conversely for the peaceful settlement of disputes, were not, however, immediately apparent, and were often contradictory.

This chapter examines how these three interacting dualities (structure–agency, national–international, economy–security) have manifested themselves in the circumstances and policies of five semi-peripheral states (South Korea, Indonesia, Malaysia, Canada, Australia) and more generally the peripheral island states of the South Pacific. Three criteria have guided the selection of states to be considered: geography; political culture; status and power. The countries chosen are meant to represent all three sub-regions, reflect the region's cultural and ideological diversity, and take account of the disparities between the capabilities of different states. Whether some states should be labelled peripheral or semi-peripheral is ultimately an arbitrary exercise. By virtue of its size, population, strategic location and pre-eminent role in ASEAN, Indonesia can be assigned semi-peripheral status. On the other hand, the size and structure of its economy and its vulnerability to externally and internally induced political crises suggest that Indonesia might be more aptly situated in the periphery. Attributing semi-peripheral status to Indonesia is, it seems, as problematic as attributing core status to China. To acknowledge these ambiguities is not to question the relevance of these categories but to caution against treating them as a rigid classification system or a self-contained explanatory model. On the other hand, by placing them within the larger analytical framework just outlined, they can become useful tools enabling us to explore the scope and limitations of state autonomy and diplomatic initiative. To be more specific, they can help us to delineate the political space within which these states operate, and assess their capacity to formulate and execute policy, define axes of conflict and initiate conflict resolution processes, establish and sustain coalitions, and more generally engage in discursive practices, independently of the major centres of power, be they core states, core economies, transnational corporations, financial markets or international financial institutions.

SOUTH KOREA

Korea's painful historical experience, as victim of periodic Chinese incursions and later Japanese colonial domination, and more recently as one of the enduring casualties of the Cold War, has helped to produce a profound sense of vulnerability. In South Korea both rulers and ruled have had to contend not only with the continuing uncertainties of Korean division but also with prolonged dependence on the United States, uneasy coexistence with Japan and, at least until recently, a peripheral role in regional and international diplomacy. For the best part of four decades South Korea's political and military elites sought refuge in authoritarian rule. The assassination of President Park Chung Hee in 1979 raised hopes of democratic reform, but these proved short-lived with the brutal suppression of dissent in Kwangju and declaration of full martial law in May 1980. General Chun Doo Hwan's regime disbanded all independent political parties, placed a ban on most political activity, and continued to strengthen the principal instruments of state power and control, notably the security and intelligence apparatus, in particular the National Security Planning Agency and the Korean military, whose ranks were increasingly filled by the graduates of the Korean military academy.[14] In a real sense, Korean security had come to be understood as equivalent to state security or, to be more precise, to regime security.

The first signs of regime transition did not emerge until 1985 when limited attempts at liberalization by the Chun government led to the formation of an opposition alliance, the New Korea Democratic Party.[15] The subsequent debate on constitutional reform, protracted and often acrimonious, did not bear fruit until massive protests in the first half of 1987 compelled the government to accept the principle of a popularly elected president. With the presidential election of December 1987 and the National Assembly elections of April 1988, South Korea acquired the institutional trappings of a democracy. Divisions within the democratic opposition enabled Roh Tae Woo, the Democratic-Justice Party's presidential candidate and Chun's handpicked successor, to win the election by gaining a plurality of votes (36.6 per cent of votes cast). Predictably his administration was initially dominated by former military personnel, but subsequent reshuffling steadily lowered the military profile of his government. Yet neither these incremental steps nor the more radical break associated with the inauguration of Kim Young Sam's presidency in February 1993 decisively changed South Korea's security culture and the peculiar blend of anti-communism, nationalism and *buguk gangbyong* ('rich nation, strong army') which it embodied.[16]

The ideology of national security, so assiduously cultivated to maintain the cohesion of civil society and the legitimacy of the state apparatus, could not be quickly or easily dismantled. The task was all the more difficult given that rapid economic growth had enabled the state to present itself as the architect of a thriving economy, built on the solid foundations of effective national security management. The other critical element in the armoury of the security establishment was the Cold War itself – and the associated threat from the North – which endowed it not only with the necessary legitimacy, but with the justification for unusually high levels of military spending (averaging more than 30 per cent of the national budget during the 1960s and 1970s). At the same time, security planning, including strategic doctrine, procurement decisions, links with the industrial sector and the domestic application of security laws and procedures, was effectively insulated from political, let alone public, scrutiny and control.

This elaborate national security edifice was not, however, a purely home-grown project. The US military connection was indispensable to its internal and external legitimation, and to its construction and subsequent maintenance. The Republic of Korea (ROK)–US security relationship, built on the foundations of the Korean War and the ensuing Mutual Defense Treaty of 1953–4, provided the basis for the stationing of US forces in South Korea and for substantial US oversight of South Korea's armed forces. While the US military presence gave rise to periodic protests, the wider public was generally persuaded that the alliance and associated defence arrangements were essential for the preservation of South Korean security. The close support offered by US administrations to successive authoritarian regimes had, on the other hand, provoked widespread public misgivings, which explains why both US and South Korean policy-makers became increasingly interested in, or at least amenable to, notions of democratic reform. Though their political calculus differed, they both concluded that the partial liberalization of state control was unavoidable if key elements of the security framework they had painstakingly created were to be salvaged. Modest democratization now seemed the only viable strategy likely to stave off future demands for more radical change.

For South Korea the relationship with the North may be considered the linchpin of its overall security policy and the most accurate barometer of its diplomatic freedom of action. On coming to office Roh adopted a more conciliatory profile on ROK–Democratic People's Republic of Korea (DPRK) relations, with promises of greater diplomatic, economic and human contacts between the two sides. These efforts proved largely unavailing, partly because of North Korea's unwillingness to reciprocate, but also because of his own administration's inability to loosen internal security controls, which Pyongyang was only too willing to exploit by emphasizing the value of people-to-people as against government-to-government contacts. For its part the South Korean security establishment saw the ensuing visits to the North by radicals and dissenters as an opportunity to discredit the Party for Peace and Democracy (PPD) and its leader Kim Dae-jung. Against this backdrop, liberal and other critics of the security apparatus intensified their demands for comprehensive institutional reform, in particular the repeal of the National Security Law, the Anticommunist Law and the Military Secrecy Act. They also called for the abolition of the Agency for National Security Planning and other security organizations, and pressed for a fundamental shift in Seoul's strategic posture, including the withdrawal of US forces from the South and the establishment of a co-operative relationship between the two Koreas. Despite periodic bursts of diplomatic activity, and even after Kim Young Sam's electoral victory, South Korean governments remained impervious to calls for radical change.

To clarify the domestic and external constraints bearing upon South Korea's security policy-making process, it may be useful to concentrate on its handling of two crucial and closely related issues: relations with the North and the possible nuclearization of the peninsula. At first, the agreement concluded at the end of 1991 (the Agreement on Reconciliation, Non-aggression, Co-operation and Exchanges between South and North) signalled a substantial breakthrough, with both sides committing themselves to developing a wide range of bilateral contacts and confidence- and security-building measures. However, it soon became apparent that few, if any, of the exchanges and mechanisms envisaged by the agreement would materialize.[17] Once established, the inter-Korean Military Commission could not agree on its method of operation, and failed to introduce any measures in military transparency. On assuming office, the Kim government sought to breathe new life into inter-Korean relations with a number of proposals and incentives, including the possible exchange of special envoys. Though Pyongyang responded favourably, the initiative once again faltered, with conservative ideologues and obdurate bureaucratic elements combining forces to stem what they branded as the rising influence of liberal ideology. Official pronouncements maintained a strong rhetorical commitment to the twin principles of reconciliation and reunification, but the departure of leading liberal intellectual Han Wan-sang as deputy prime minister of national unification made it clear that the political wind was now blowing in a different direction.[18] Compounding the loss of impetus in inter-Korean dialogue was the vitriol intermittently exchanged between the two sides and Kim Il Sung's death on 8 July 1994, which effectively cut short plans for an historical presidential summit meeting to be held later that month.[19]

The 'agreed framework' signed by the United States and North Korea in October 1994 (about which more shortly) did envisage the resumption of North–South Korean contacts and negotiations, but made no mention of specific measures or timetable. The next significant development did not come until April 1996, when Clinton and Kim Young Sam offered to enter peace talks with North Korea without preconditions, without deadlines and without a predetermined agenda. The proposal preserved the principle that the two Korean parties would need to take the lead in any settlement of the conflict. On the other hand, the proposal for a four-party format, which would include China and the United States, went part of the way towards accommodating North Korean preferences. It also brought China directly into the equation in the hope that this would encourage Pyongyang to adopt a more conciliatory attitude.[20] Washington, for its part, while still unwilling to accede to Pyongyang's desires for bilateral negotiations, had now offered direct US participation throughout the process. In April 1997, after a series of briefing sessions and preliminary meetings at which South Korea made it known that it would be prepared to discuss the question of food aid to North Korea in the context of tension-reduction and confidence-building measures, Pyongyang accepted 'in principle' the four-party talks proposal. The first meeting of the four parties occurred in December 1997 with the specific aim of developing appropriate confidence-building measures as a prelude to a more comprehensive dialogue. A second session in March 1998, however, concluded without tangible result.

Kim Dae-jung's victory in the December 1997 presidential elections, though narrow, had raised hopes of faster progress in North–South relations. The immediate issue facing the incoming administration was whether to deliver food aid to the North without political concessions in return. Official North–South talks in April 1998 foundered on this very question, the only practical result being an in-principle agreement by the two sides to help millions of separated families exchange letters and to set up a meeting place, possibly at the border village of Panmunjom.[21]

Despite this early setback, Kim Dae-jung's 'sunshine' policy represented the most determined attempt yet to implement the 1991 agreement. In his inaugural address Kim announced three key principles that would govern his administration's approach to North–South relations: the South would actively pursue a policy of reconciliation and co-operation; it would not seek to undermine or absorb North Korea; it would not tolerate armed provocation.[22]

Kim's 'sunshine' policy was committed to building a 'social-democratic, grass-roots bridge to the North' and pursuing a more flexible negotiating strategy. It favoured putting an end to rhetorical warfare against the North and widening the channels of communication. In this latter context, it expressed support for the creation of a '2 + 2 + 2' framework (North plus South, United States plus China, and Russia plus Japan) to complement bilateral negotiations and the four-party talks. Finally, it was willing to entertain the possibility of other states developing bilateral relations with the DPRK.[23] This marked shift in declaratory policy coupled with several goodwill gestures, including the proposal to exchange special envoys, the removal of restrictions on the allowable amount of investment by South Korean companies in North Korea, and moves to open North Korean airspace to South Korean commercial flights,[24] helped to create an unusually propitious climate for both bilateral and multilateral dialogue. Other promising developments included the initiative of the Hyundai group to stage tourist visits to the scenic Kumkang mountain resort in the North, continuing efforts by the two sides to negotiate an agreement that would regulate fishing in their waters, and support for international efforts to fund the renewal of North Korea's agricultural infrastructure.[25]

Perhaps the most distinctive feature of Kim's 'sunshine' policy was its emphasis on the need to eliminate the polemical tone of previous attempts at dialogue. This ideologically less rigid approach was aimed as much at the South Korean polity as at the North. Domestic opposition to Kim's policy was widespread. Both opposition parties and the media described it as 'ineffective, even dangerous',[26] and even his coalition partner Kim Jong Pil, whose support had ensured victory in the presidential election, was less than co-operative. Kim Dae-jung was no doubt relying on substantial public support to overcome the deep resistance and inertia which could still be mobilized in favour of the old national security ideology. In addition, his more progressive policy had to contend with the powerful constraints imposed by the country's social and economic difficulties, the misgivings of a conservative US Congress, and the limited room for manoeuvre available to the North Korean regime. In order to break the impasse, the South Korean President proposed in February 1999 a 'package deal' which would simultaneously resolve all outstanding political, security and economic differences with North Korea. In exchange for Pyongyang's agreement to curb its nuclear weapons and missile programme, Kim promised the North substantial food and economic aid, an end to US trade sanctions, and the normalization of relations with Japan and the United States as well as with the South. Predictably, the 'sunshine' policy was easier to articulate than to execute.

Of the many impediments none was more disconcerting than the eccentricity, not to say obstructionism, of Pyongyang's diplomacy. The DPRK's decision to test the Taepo-Dong I missile, a multistage variant of the Soviet SCUD missile, in the Western Pacific in August 1998 greatly complicated Seoul's strategic calculations and gave added ammunition to those elements of the South Korean security establishment already critical of the opening to the North. Even more troubling was the nine-day North–South naval clash near Yongpyong Island in June 1999. According to South Korean military accounts, the intrusion of North Korean patrol boats prompted South Korean ships to be dispatched to the area. Northern vessels responded by opening fire, and in the ensuing exchange one North Korean torpedo boat was reportedly sunk and another five seriously damaged. With each side accusing the other of intruding into its territorial waters, the incident raised new questions about Pyongyang's motives and subjected Kim's policy of engagement to even sharper criticism at home.[27] Yet, while offering a public apology for mishandling the situation, his Administration was intent on salvaging the delicate process of confidence-building. Significantly, Samsung continued to explore investment possibilities in the North; the Hyundai business group persevered with its organized tours of Kumkang; some 200 South Korean engineers and technicians remained at work at the nuclear reactor site in the northern port of Sinpo; bilateral discussions on the reunion of families divided since the war went ahead as scheduled; and Seoul promised new shipments of food and fertilizer.[28]

By early 2000 several signs pointed to a new thaw in inter-Korean relations: two-way trade in 1999 ran to a record of $200 million in 1999; Seoul offered to ship another 100 000 tonnes of fertilizer if the North agreed to facilitate family reunions; and Kim Jong Il had personally approved plans for two Hyundai projects (a light industry complex north of the border and a large export centre west of Pyongyang that would rely on the North's cheap labour costs), Pyongyang was exploring normalization of diplomatic relations with several western countries (including Italy, Australia, Japan and the United States, presumably with South Korea's tacit support);[29] and Seoul proposed at an APEC meeting that Pyongyang be allowed to join a regional economic organization to enable it to receive financial assistance. In April 2000 the two Korean governments announced simultaneously that Kim Dae-jung and Kim Jong Il would hold a summit in Pyongyang in June, the first such meeting since the Korean War. For North Korea the historic summit would be an opportunity to press for a much larger injection of South Korean capital to help restore its shattered economy. Indicative of Kim Dae-jung's thinking was his declared willingness to strengthen economics ties with the North by adding a public sector layer to the developing private sector framework.

The summit, hailed as the most important breakthrough in inter-Korean relations since the bipolar division of the peninsula, ended with a decision to establish a symbolic cross-border link and a declaration committing the two countries to a path of reconciliation and co-operation. Its centrepiece was an agreement on family reunions, envisaging an 'institutional process' which would allow both sides unfettered access to relatives. The South was estimated to have more than 7 million Koreans with severed family links, including 1.2 million 'first-generation citizens' – elderly people denied contact with relatives since the Korean War. The first family exchange was scheduled to take place on 15 August – a day of national celebration to mark Korea's liberation from Japanese occupation. In return for this major concession by the North, Kim Dae-jung was expected to review his efforts to reform South Korea's National Security Law which defined North Korea as an 'anti-state entity', made it illegal for South Korean citizens to support or praise it in any manner, and had been used to jail thousands of North Korean sympathisers. From Pyongyang's perspective perhaps the most important provision of the Declaration was the undertaking to promote the 'balanced development of the national economy', although little detail was given as to the scale of any financial commitment by the South [30] With an economy nearly 25 times larger and a per capita income of $6823 compared with North Korea's $573, South Korea was expected to provided a generous and sustained infusion of funds.[31] Though the practical consequences of the summit would not become fully apparent for months and possibly years, enough had been accomplished to make, for the first time, reunification, or at least some form of loose association, a feasible subject of political discussion.

South Korea's ability to reconstruct its relationship with the North was clearly dependent on the latter's responsiveness to such overtures, but other factors were just as important, notably the internal dynamics of its political culture, the state of its economy, and the pressures emanating from its alliance with the United States. Nowhere was the combined impact of these interacting influences more strikingly evident than in the nuclear arena. Here, it is worth recounting that South Korea had itself toyed more than once with the nuclear option. In the early 1970s, the Park Chung Hee government, partly in response to the projected withdrawal of the 7th US Infantry Division from South Korea, began planning, in collaboration with France, for the reprocessing of spent nuclear fuel. Under strong pressure from the United States, the French and South Korean governments eventually agreed to cancel the reprocessing deal. Whereas during the 1970s Seoul was still focused on the dangers posed by the North's military superiority, within a matter of ten years roles were almost completely reversed. It was now South Korea's turn to feel increasingly threatened by what it claimed was the North's clandestine nuclear programme.

Though Pyongyang signed the Non-Proliferation Treaty (NPT) in 1985, it was not until 1992 that it finally concluded a nuclear safeguards agreement with the International Atomic Energy Agency (IAEA), thereby allowing its declared nuclear facilities to be subjected to regular IAEA inspections.[32] This more accommodating approach on the North's part followed quickly on the heels of a joint North–South Declaration in December 1991, in which both sides agreed not to test, produce, receive, process, store, deploy or use nuclear weapons, or acquire nuclear reprocessing or uranium enrichment facilities whereby their ostensibly civilian programmes could be diverted to military weapons. A contributing factor had been Washington's decision to withdraw its land-based nuclear weapons from South Korea, itself a byproduct of substantial progress in Soviet–American nuclear disarmament and arms control negotiations.

These welcome developments, however, soon lost momentum. The two Korean states could not reach agreement on the mechanisms that would monitor their respective nuclear activities, an impasse which acquired even more ominous implications when IAEA inspection of North Korean facilities appeared to suggest that Pyongyang was pursuing a covert nuclear weapons programme. The ensuing crisis, accentuated by persistent North Korean objections to IAEA procedures, came to a head when the IAEA formally demanded that the suspected sites at the Yongbyon nuclear complex be subjected to a 'special inspection'.[33] The North's refusal to accede to IAEA demands prompted the IAEA Board of Governors to issue an ultimatum threatening 'further measures', to which Pyongyang responded by announcing its withdrawal from the Nuclear Non-Proliferation Treaty. Incensed by international condemnation of its actions and the Team Spirit military exercise the United States and South Korea were jointly conducting at the time, North Korea closed its borders and placed its forces on alert.

On receiving a report from the IAEA, the UN Security Council adopted a resolution on 11 May 1993 requesting North Korea to rescind its decision, at which point the main protagonists chose to retreat from the brink. Pyongyang 'suspended' its decision to withdraw from the NPT, thereby paving the way for tortuous negotiations with the United States and the IAEA. The eventual outcome, facilitated by former President Carter's intervention, including direct talks with Kim Il-Sung, was the Agreed Framework which the United States and the DPRK concluded in Geneva on 21 October 1994. Both during and after the negotiations South Korea was very much an interested party, but its influence on Washington's strategy was less than decisive.[34] The Clinton Administration, now pursuing the more limited objective of containing rather than completely eliminating North Korea's nuclear programme, was able to persuade Pyongyang to proceed to the implementation stage of the denuclearization agreement with South Korea. More importantly perhaps, the United States now operated on the assumption that North Korea was playing the nuclear card to achieve economic as much as strategic or political advantage. Accordingly, it was to be compensated for freezing its nuclear programme and placing it under international inspection. An international consortium would be established to provide North Korea with light-water reactors (LWR) to replace its graphite-moderated reactors, and the United States would arrange supplies of heavy oil for electricity production. The two sides also agreed to remove barriers to mutual trade and contracts and to work towards full diplomatic normalization. In return for US guarantees against nuclear attack North Korea agreed to reactivate its dialogue with South Korea, to remain a party to the NPT and, on condition that all other elements of the agreement were implemented, to allow full IAEA inspections of its nuclear facilities.

The Agreed Framework was a compromise document whose ambiguity was designed to bridge the inevitable gap between diverging expectations.[35] Not surprisingly much confusion surrounded the practical arrangements and exact timetable needed to give effect to the LWR project. The first significant step came with the creation of the Korean Peninsula Energy Development Organization (KEDO) in March 1995, with the United States, Japan and South Korea making up its Executive Board, but with the terms for Japanese and especially South Korean participation in the project set largely by Washington. Seoul was to be the prime supplier of reactors to North Korea as compensation for providing the bulk of the financing. As one might have expected, tensions arose with regard to the choice of light-water reactor, the privileged role conferred on South Korea and the level of financial support for KEDO, on which depended its capacity to supply North Korea each year with 500 000 tons of heavy fuel oil. Uncertainty, if not contradiction, also surrounded the safeguard obligations which the Agreed Framework had imposed on North Korea. Was Pyongyang required to accept IAEA 'special inspections' of all its nuclear activities or only of those which it had designated as non-military? If it insisted on the latter interpretation, thereby excluding the two disputed underground sites, then the same deadlock that had developed in March 1993 would presumably return to haunt relations with both Seoul and Washington.

By 1999 the ambiguities of the Agreed Framework were fully exposed. Though the United States was able to maintain oil supplies to North Korea and work was under way for the construction of the Kumho nuclear reactors, raising the required levels of funding for both operations had become increasingly problematic. Annual oil delivery costs were now estimated at $65 million, while the cost of the LWR project was expected to exceed $5 billion.[36] The US and South Korean governments faced a difficult dilemma: to fully honour the commitments they had made or to hand Pyongyang the perfect excuse for not honouring its own undertakings. North Korea's nuclear activities were in any case overshadowed by its missile testing programme, intended, at least in part, to secure even greater concessions from Washington and Seoul. If the United States and its allies, Japan and South Korea, attached a high priority to 'the cessation of North Korean flight-testing, production, deployment, and export of missiles and related material and technology',[37] then presumably they would be willing to pay a reasonably high price to achieve the desired outcome, namely the cost of meeting the North's energy and food requirements. In March 1999 Pyongyang announced after protracted negotiations that it would give the United States access to the suspected nuclear construction site in Kumchang-ri without, however, specifying for how long such access would be given, what it would entail in practice or how it related to the North's missile capabilities, the wider talks or North Korea's worsening economic situation.

Pyongyang favoured the piecemeal approach to negotiations because it enabled it to keep the other side guessing as to its true intentions while extracting maximum advantage from each small concession it was prepared to make. For exactly the same reasons Washington came to prefer a comprehensive solution, which Seoul had long advocated in the hope of minimizing the likelihood of differences emerging between the US and South Korean negotiating positions or of South Korea being marginalized in the negotiating process. To give added impetus to the search for a comprehensive approach, Clinton asked former Secretary of Defense William Perry to oversee the co-ordination of US policies on North Korea. In the course of extensive discussions in Pyongyang in late May 1999, Perry laid out a plan whereby the United States would lift economic sanctions gradually in return for undertakings by North Korea to stop testing missiles and exporting missile technology and solidify the freeze on nuclear weapons development.[38] The prospect that Pyongyang might soon test a Taepo-Dong 2 missile with an estimated range of 3500–6000 km prompted Perry, with the support of the Japanese and South Korean governments but in the face of profound misgivings on the part of the Republican-dominated Congress, to pursue his plan with renewed urgency.

At talks convened in Berlin in September, US and North Korean negotiators reached a tentative agreement. Pending further discussions, the two sides agreed not to do anything which would interfere with the positive atmosphere that existed in the talks. In essence, Pyongyang had agreed to postpone testing any long-range missile so long as the two governments continued to negotiate. In return, the United States would ease 'non-sensitive' sanctions against North Korea as would Japan and South

Korea.[39] As part of an integrated accommodation with North Korea on all major outstanding problems, the United States could also offer to release North Korean assets held in the United States, and eventually to normalize relations with the North, an initiative likely to be emulated by Japan. It could not be taken for granted that these incentives were sufficient for Pyongyang to accede to the requirements of US non-proliferation policy. Nor was it clear that the Clinton Administration or its successor would be able to deliver fully on the promises it had made without the effective support of Congress and its Northeast Asian allies. Nevertheless, the inter-Korean declaration of June 2000, though it did not directly address Pyongyang's nuclear and missile capabilities, had sufficiently altered the political climate to induce Washington to lift a range of economic sanctions on North Korea.

Scope for Leadership and Initiative

Enough has been said to indicate the complex constraints bearing upon South Korea's diplomatic freedom of action, which is not to say that the profound changes in its domestic and international milieu had not created a new window of opportunity. The enhanced political space associated with democratization was mirrored and facilitated by the development of closer links with communist or post-communist states. China and the Soviet Union were no longer perceived as threats to its security. Full diplomatic relations were established with both countries as well as with the majority of East European states. Meetings between Gorbachev and both Kim Young Sam and Roh Tae Woo paved the way for steady growth in bilateral exchanges. Following diplomatic normalization with China in October 1992, economic ties blossomed, with annual bilateral trade rising from virtually nothing in the mid-1980s to $3 billion in 1992 and $20 billion in 1996. Equally dramatic was the flow of South Korean FDI, which reached $4.2 billion in 1996, and the steady rise of exchanges – tourists from South Korea and legal and illegal workers from China – estimated at 700 000 in 1996.[40]

Another important dimension to Seoul's steadily expanding diplomatic presence, itself a reflection of its deepening integration into the world economy, was its burgeoning trade with ASEAN, especially after achieving full dialogue partnership in 1991, its admission to the UN in 1992 and accession to the OECD in 1996. Indicative of the same trend was the establishment of the Economic Development Co-operation Fund in 1987, which substantially boosted the ROK's assistance programme to less developed countries; its increasing participation in UN peacekeeping operations beginning with Somalia in 1993; its contribution to the UN's rapid deployment capability; and the renewed emphasis, at least at the declaratory level, on the 'universal values of democracy and human rights'.[41] Even closer to home, where diplomatic initiative was circumscribed by the sharply competing interests of the great powers, South Korea was paying greater attention to the requirements of regional security. In October 1989 Roh Tae Woo proposed the creation of a six-country consultative forum for East Asian security, and in July 1994 Han Sung-joo, ROK Minister of Foreign Affairs, canvassed the idea of a Northeast Asian multilateral security dialogue to parallel and complement the ASEAN Regional Forum. Seoul was now openly advocating a range of confidence-building measures, including exchange of defence white papers, exchanges of military personnel and joint participation in UN peacekeeping operations, as a way of strengthening strategic transparency and predictability in the region. In the first year of his presidency, Kim Dae-jung urged the establishment of a regional co-operative system for the resolution of conflicts

In defining and executing their policy preferences during the 1990s South Korean governments had progressively set themselves a larger agenda and a more assertive role, both regionally and internationally. Yet the constraints arising from the strategic connection with the United States and from the internationalization of the South Korean economy had, if anything, become more inhibiting. This is not to say that South Korean military and political elites were wedded to radically different positions from those favoured by their American counterparts. Such differences as did periodically emerge, especially on the sensitive issue of North Korea, were not indicative of a sharp ideological or geopolitical divide between the two sides. They did, however, point to the enormous power differentials between them and to the relatively narrow margin for manoeuvre available to Seoul.

The dynamic of the US–South Korea relationship was largely governed by the scale and function of the US military presence in South Korea and the Western Pacific more generally. In the late 1980s, in response to tensions within the South Korean polity and the vastly improved climate in Soviet–American relations, the United States was considering a scaling down of the annual Team Spirit military exercises, the closure of several secondary military facilities, and the withdrawal of some 7000 troops from Korea by 1993, as the first of three stages in what was to be a gradual but substantial reduction of US forces in Korea. The first stage of the withdrawal was in fact completed by 1991, but the process was brought to an abrupt halt by the Pentagon, which cited North Korean nuclear ambitions and the inadequate preparedness of its forces in Korea as justifying a number of reinforcement measures. By 1995 the United States had introduced an additional heavy artillery division, mine sweepers, amphibious landing ships, AH-64 Apache helicopters, 130 M-IAI Abrams tanks, Bradley armoured personnel carriers, Patriot missiles and a mobile ground satellite station.[42] In 1994, just as the Team Spirit exercise was cancelled, US and South Korean forces participated in a new series of joint exercises in which they rehearsed the actions needed to receive forces, stage them, move them into forward assembly areas, and then integrate them into combined forces. The net effect of expanded pre-position capabilities, joint military exercises and increased co-ordination of operational procedures was to integrate the South Korean military even more firmly into US strategic planning.

Taking advantage of nearly two decades of rapid industrialization, the South Korean armed forces embarked upon a massive programme of military modernization. Expressed as a proportion of government expenditure or of GNP, defence spending had steadily declined after 1980. Yet, precisely because of the pace of economic growth, it rose dramatically from \$8.27 billion in 1985 to \$13.15 billion in 1994.[43] The same trend was evident in the rise of a large armaments industry that now produced an impressive array of ground weapons, including machine guns, howitzers, mortars, canons, rifles and tanks. Complementing these production arrangements was the purchase of state-of-the-art technology, including fighter planes, reconnaissance planes and advanced surveillance and intelligence gathering systems.[44] Much of this technology was acquired from the United States, with South Korean arms imports totalling \$1909 million in 1995 and \$1727 million in 1996.[45] A report released by the South Korean Defence Ministry in July 1995 envisaged a vastly expanded military budget of \$113 billion to be spent over a five-year period (1997–2001), with a further increase authorized the following year, which brought projected total spending for the period 1998–2002 to \$120.7 billion. Though the 1997 financial crisis would subsequently force these ambitious plans to be pruned back and legislative and bureaucratic intervention would expose the defence sector to increasing public scrutiny, there was no denying that the South Korean armed forces had acquired a sizeable military machine.

The number or potency of weapons systems is not, however, synonymous with political influence, let alone political independence. The South Korean military remained, by virtue of arms procurement, access to technology and intelligence, training and above all the dominance of the US strategic presence in Korea, closely tied to the priorities of US military planning. In that sense, the alliance with the United States remained central to the management of South Korea's external relations. A kind of strategic interdependence now coloured the bilateral relationship, yet such interdependence was essentially asymmetrical. For South Korea, the perception of threat from the North revolved around issues of state and regime survival. For the United States, on the other hand, North Korea was not just a local or regional security concern. Viewed as the leading rogue state in the world, with both the motive and the capacity to develop a nuclear arsenal, North Korea posed a serious challenge to US non-proliferation policy, to the stability of US–China and US–Japan relations, and perhaps most importantly to the US conception of world order. In pursuing its global interests and global strategies, the United States would approach the Korean problem with varying degrees of diplomatic and military assertiveness, prompting its junior ally to oscillate between the fear of 'entrapment' and that of 'abandonment'.[46]

Frequent affirmations to the contrary notwithstanding, policy co-ordination between the two allies was, especially after the onset of the nuclear crisis, often erratic and at times noticeably absent. At first, Seoul, fearing that the crisis might provoke a punitive US response in which it would be automatically involved, tended to counsel caution. After the Geneva Agreed Framework, when the Clinton Administration adopted a strategy of direct bilateral contacts and a soft-landing approach to the problem, Seoul's apprehensions intensified; its primary concern was now that of diplomatic marginalization. In neither case does the evidence suggest decisive South Korean influence on the bilateral consultative process. Kim Dae-jung's 'sunshine' policy may be interpreted in part as an attempt to wrest the initiative from the United States, and to make North–South dialogue an integral part of any conflict-management strategy. How consistently or effectively the policy would be pursued depended on a number of factors, over which Seoul was likely to have only limited control.

Quite apart from the unpredictability of North Korean diplomacy, South Korean governments would have to contend with the underlying imperatives of US policy. In return for its military presence in South Korea the United States expected its ally to assume a high and rising share of the costs of maintaining that presence and the continued interoperability of US and South Korean forces. But US and South Korean strategic interests were not necessarily identical. Whereas Seoul wished to develop a 500 km short-range missile to target military bases in North Korea, the United States was adamantly opposed to any extension of South Korea's missile capability beyond its current 300 km-range missile. Similarly, whereas Washington was seeking to involve South Korea in its theatre missile defence programme, Seoul was concerned not to give undue offence to Beijing, and was interested in exploring the advantages of a cheaper Russian air-defence system and a number of advanced Israeli early warning systems and ballistic missile defence systems.[47] In any case, the US commitment to South Korea formed part of a larger and more complex strategic framework, in which the primary preoccupation for Washington would continue to be its bilateral relationships with China and Japan.

The revised US–Japan Defense Co-operation Guidelines were bound to have far-reaching implications and to accentuate Seoul's ambivalent attitude to Japan.[48] On the one hand, closer US–Japan defence co-operation could help reinforce Washington's commitment to South Korea and even entrench the deployment of US forces at their current level. On the other hand, the Guidelines also meant an expanded regional security role for Japan, hence a continued Japanese arms build-up which, set against the backdrop of Japan's oppressive colonial rule during 1911–45, might easily rekindle Korea's lingering mistrust and suspicion of Japanese intentions. During his visit to Japan in October 1998 Kim Dae-jung reminded his host that 'there are many people in Asia, including Korea, who still cannot discard their suspicions of Japan . . . they believe Japan has not done enough on its own to understand correctly and reflect humbly on its past'.[49] The joint Korea–Japan Declaration issued on the same day went some of the way towards soothing South Korean sensitivities. The subsequent expansion of diplomatic dialogue, the decision to hold regular bilateral summit meetings and negotiations for an investment agreement were all signs of a more co-operative relationship. On the other hand, South Korea could not neglect the psychological and diplomatic implications of Japan's evolving security posture as much for the future of inter-Korean dialogue as for its relations with China and the wider region.

The ambiguities surrounding the strategic dimension of US–ROK relations were compounded by South Korea's new economic circumstances. Since the early 1980s the balance of economic and military power on the Korean peninsula had shifted markedly in favour of the South. By the early 1990s the DPRK was spending 22 per cent of its GNP on defence, yet this represented only half of the South's military budget.[50] According to another estimate, by 1994 the South was outspending the North by a 2.3 to 1 ratio.[51] Yet the widening gap in the performance of the two economies, increasingly reflected in their respective patterns of military spending, was a double-edged sword. The precipitous decline of the DPRK economy during the 1990s was attributable to three structural bottlenecks, namely inadequate supplies of energy, food and capital, although severe floods in 1995 and 1996 and reduced levels of Chinese and especially Russian aid were no doubt contributing factors.[52] The dramatic fall in North Korea's agricultural and industrial production – estimates of the decline ranged from 5 per cent to 10 per cent per year since 1990 – and the accompanying depreciation of its currency on the black market were but the most visible symptoms of an acute economic illness[53] for which North Korea's political leadership seemed unable to offer a quick or effective remedy

Paradoxically, for Seoul the economic trials and tribulations of the North were at best a mixed blessing. South Korea could have taken advantage of the North's economic weakness and sought to extract concessions by threatening or applying a range of sanctions. However, such a punitive strategy may have simply produced economic collapse and political disintegration of the kind experienced by the former Soviet Union and several East European countries, with serious destabilizing consequences for the South Korean polity and economy. In these circumstances, the only viable option for the ROK would have been the German strategy of 'reunification by absorption', which would entail financial costs variously estimated at between $200 billion and $300 billion. Even if performing at its peak, the South Korean economy would have had great difficulty carrying a burden of such magnitude. Once the financial crisis hit the South in the middle of 1997, such an option became virtually unthinkable.[54] The traumatic impact of the crisis, as much social as economic, had undermined the South's self-confidence and deprived it of the psychological advantage it once enjoyed. Negative economic growth coupled with a steady stream of financial bankruptcies and sharply rising unemployment also sidelined the hardliners, who had advocated a punitive strategy aimed at Pyongyang's capitulation and Korean reunification on southern terms.[55] In this sense, there was little alternative to Kim Dae-jung's policy of 'peaceful co-existence'.

To complete this brief overview of the powerful economic constraints on Seoul's diplomatic freedom of action two further observations may be in order. The financial upheaval which gripped South Korea in the late 1990s was no accident. Though a complex phenomenon, it was, as indicated in Chapter 2, a logical outcome of the policy of export-oriented industrialization. The inadequacies of prudential management in the finance sector coupled with corruption in high places had exacerbated the structural weaknesses of East Asia's economies, particularly in the harsh environment of increasingly deregulated markets. South Korea's economic weight, both regionally and internationally, had grown enormously over the space of two decades. The downturn of the late 1990s was unlikely to reverse the general trend, but it did signal the structural limitations of semi-peripheral states, with respect both to managing their national economies and translating increased productive capacity into political influence. The steady relaxation of controls on capital movements in and out of the country, in particular the new Foreign Investment Promotion Act, the Foreign Exchange Transaction Act and the Bilateral Investment Treaty with the United States, were indicative of Seoul's determination to create an economic climate favourable to foreign investors. Complicating Kim Dae-jung's task was the need to reconcile the neoliberal demands of the global market with the demands of his popular constituency.[56] How to resolve that dilemma would be central not only to the success of his own presidency, but to the stability of future governments. For their part US Administrations, under pressure from strategically placed corporate interests, had committed themselves to prising open East Asian markets and were using to this end the strategic levers at their disposal.

US dominance of South Korea's foreign military procurement was another graphic illustration of leverage politics. The United States accounted for 73 per cent of Seoul's military imports in 1992, and the figure rose to 90 per cent in 1995.[57] Conversely, the transfers of US technology provided the United States with an effective power of veto over the export of South Korean military hardware. According to one report, during 1992–96 the United States approved only 0.39 per cent of the total amount of planned exports of ROK-produced weapons systems.[58] Given these distinct but closely integrating pressures, South Korean governments had little option but to fall in behind the US policy of engagement which, at least after 1994, envisaged trading diplomatic and economic concessions in exchange for the North's moderation of its military ambitions and capabilities. The United States might at some future date, in the light of changed circumstances or perceptions, choose to modify or altogether abandon its current strategic priorities. Regardless, however, of the twists and turns of US policy, there was little reason to expect that the ROK and the DPRK, individually or jointly, could soon offset or displace the pre-eminent role which the United States had occupied in the peninsula for close to half a century.

INDONESIA

In turning our attention from Northeast to Southeast Asia we discern a striking change of scenery. Whereas the Northeast Asian region generally, and the Korean peninsula in particular, continued to experience the full weight of great power interests and rivalries and high levels of tension and militarization, Southeast Asia, especially after the Vietnam War, was far less militarized, less prone to external conflict and less amenable to great power intervention. Though most Southeast Asian states in various ways and to varying degrees contributed to this outcome, none played a more important role than Indonesia and Malaysia. Neither could boast South Korea's economic performance or level of technological sophistication, but each had achieved a distinctive and influential diplomatic profile and wielded considerable influence both within Southeast Asia and beyond.

Indonesia's regional and international standing was a function of demography, geography and history. With a population of over 200 million it was by far the largest Southeast Asian country. As an archipelagic state strategically located between the Indian and Pacific oceans, it encompassed many of the vital choke points leading to major sea lines of communications (SLOCs). Just as valuable was the protection from external threat afforded by the surrounding seas which, by virtue of the application of 'archipelagic state' and territorial sea principles, had seen Indonesia's marine territory expand to some 5 million sq km. In addition, Indonesian jurisdiction over its 200-mile exclusive economic zone and continental shelf meant effective control of natural resource development, environmental management, marine scientific research and establishment of artificial islands and installations over an area covering some 3 million sq km. Such control meant, however, added responsibility for the defence and protection of this vastly extended marine and air space. The advantages of geographic location, though facilitating the projection of influence, were offset by the difficulties of maintaining the cohesion and unity of an ethnically disparate state comprising some 16 000 islands. In other words, Indonesia's relatively benign external environment had to be set against the multiple challenges to internal security. Compounding separatist tendencies in East Timor and West Irian were widespread animosities towards the numerically small but economically successful Chinese community.[59]

Faced with these multiple challenges and conscious of the deeply divisive circumstances in which it assumed power, the Suharto regime made political stability one of its highest priorities. The 'New Order' established after 1965 had ushered in a period of severe political repression, in particular a violent onslaught against the Communist Party of Indonesia, resulting in some 500 000 deaths[60] and the jailing of 1.35 million people. To paper over these deep cracks in the Indonesian body politic, the new government launched the concept of 'national resilience', understood as the national strength needed to cope with the complex domestic and external challenges capable of endangering national identity, national security and the national economy.[61] Central to this notion of comprehensive security was the maintenance of social and political order in the face of the perceived threat posed by communism, Muslim fundamentalism and democratic movements, as well as the threat to territorial integrity posed by secessionist tendencies. There was more, however, to the theory and practice of 'national resilience' than the commitment to state security or nation-building. The one constant in the equation of New Order politics was the preoccupation with the regime's survival, with the need to enhance its power, authority and legitimacy.[62] Legislative and administrative measures designed to depoliticize society, restrict civil rights and the freedom of the media, and establish Golkar as the political organ of the government, though justified in the name of development, were in reality driven by this overriding calculation.

The impact of domestic politics on Indonesia's external relations during the Suharto years was pronounced but not entirely predictable. Precisely because of the high priority accorded to internal security, the level of energy and resources devoted to external threats appreciably declined. Suharto was, in any case, much less inclined ideologically or strategically to pursue the radical policies of his predecessor, a tendency reflected in the New Order's vehement anti-communism, its dependence on the United States and Japan for aid and foreign investment and, as time went on, the loss of revolutionary momentum in both China's and Vietnam's foreign policy orientation. The anxiety about internal security may also account for the Indonesian government's emphasis on economic development, which it regarded as the most effective instrument for defusing ethnic and religious disaffection and solidifying the cohesion of the Indonesian state.

This peculiar combination of factors helps to explain why the Suharto regime, notwithstanding the enormous political influence exercised by the Armed Forces of the Republic of Indonesia (ABRI), should have presided over a substantial and prolonged decline in defence spending. Though military expenditure did rise from $1.3 billion in 1975 to $2.8 billion in 1982, a sharp decline in both absolute and relative terms ensued thereafter. The official defence budget fell steadily over the following eight years, reaching $1.7 billion in 1990, and did not recover its 1982 level until 1995. Measured as a proportion of GNP, military expenditure had fallen from 4.2 per cent in 1982 to 1.5 per cent in 1990, and remained at this low level throughout the 1990s.[63] Official figures no doubt underestimate the actual level of defence spending, since they do not include allocations from the budgets of other departments, the core of presidential discretionary funds or contributions by government corporations and ABRI business enterprises.[64] On the other hand, these estimates include the budget of the Indonesian police force and the navy's coast guard, costs which do not usually feature in the defence budgets of other countries. Such increases in military spending as did occur in the late 1980s and early 1990s were intended to equip the Indonesian navy and air force with more sophisticated weapons systems, but these acquisitions remained remarkably modest when compared to the general pattern of military spending by other Northeast and Southeast Asian countries. By the late 1990s Indonesia had little power projection capability and still had to contend with serious maintenance problems, shortages of technically qualified personnel and an inadequate logistics system.[65]

Given the constraints imposed by military and economic considerations – and more broadly by its domestic political environment – it is not surprising that the scope for diplomatic manoeuvre available to Jakarta should have been severely circumscribed. The policy of non-alignment, of which Sukarno was one of the principal architects, remained, at least rhetorically, the centrepiece of Indonesian foreign policy. Certainly, options of military alignment, with either major or smaller regional powers, were effectively excluded. Indonesian defence policy continued to promote a policy of self-reliance based on the strategy of 'layered stability', which encompassed the economic and political as well as military security of the whole archipelagic state. The search for self-sufficiency envisaged an increased production and maintenance capability and contingency planning for the mobilization of reserves of personnel, civil logistic services and other defence-related infrastructure. National defence assets were to be supplemented by a number of bilateral co-operative arrangements with neighbouring countries, especially Malaysia and Singapore, but also with the United States. Participation by Indonesian military officers in US training courses, combined military exercises and a significant US military assistance programme were indicative of a much closer strategic and diplomatic relationship between the two countries. Indonesian anxieties about the possible resurgence of Chinese power was no doubt an important motivating factor. Indicative of the same reasoning was Jakarta's change of attitude to the Five Power Defence Arrangements, which had traditionally been perceived as designed to contain Indonesia's regional influence. In deciding to sign an Agreement on Maintaining Security with Australia in December 1995, Suharto merely took that trend to its logical conclusion. In that sense, Indonesian non-alignment under the New Order had become a far more ambiguous policy; which is not to say that Jakarta was ready to emulate Singapore in making maintenance and other military facilities available to the United States, or that it was prepared to abandon the long-established commitment to an 'independent and active foreign policy'.[66]

To balance its close links with the West generally and the United States in particular, Indonesia sought to widen the scope of its diplomacy through its membership of multilateral institutions, including the United Nations, the Group of 77 and the Non-Aligned Movement (NAM). For the Suharto regime, the non-aligned club had several attractions. First, it provided an important element of continuity in Indonesian foreign policy, and could to that extent be used to enhance the legitimacy of the New Order. Second, it offered Jakarta a stage on which it could perform a leading role within the Third World, at least one commensurate with the size of its population, its strategic location, the performance of its economy and its capacity to project an image of moderation. This was precisely the opportunity which was presented to Indonesia when it assumed the NAM's chairmanship for three years after the Tenth NAM Summit Conference in Jakarta in September 1992. The occasion was all the more significant as the Non-Aligned Movement now confronted the difficult task of redefining its purpose and function in the radically altered circumstances of the post-Cold War era. Third, NAM support might be used to deflect UN criticism of Indonesia's handling of the East Timor situation. Though Jakarta could not expect to persuade the UN General Assembly to recognize Indonesian sovereignty over the territory, it was rather successful in stifling UN discussion of the dispute during the greater part of the 1980s.

Notwithstanding these opportunities, there were significant limitations to the diplomatic leverage offered by NAM membership. The collapse of Soviet power had effectively put an end to the bipolar system and substantially eroded the NAM's capacity to play a balancing or moderating role between the two superpowers. Nor could NAM continue to portray itself as the authentic voice of the United Nations or as the only effective vehicle for the establishment of a new international order. The fragility of many Third World states, their propensity to domestic instability, political repression, economic crisis and varying degrees of militarization, had largely robbed the NAM of the prestige and moral authority on which it had previously built its influence.

As for repositioning the NAM in the post-Cold War environment, that was easier said than done. What new role could NAM assume? What strategic options were available to it? How would it relate to the only remaining superpower? These were just a few of the troublesome questions for which there were no obvious or immediate answers: certainly none that Indonesia's chairmanship could deliver. In his capacity as NAM chairman, Suharto was able for three years to occupy diplomatic centre stage, but his appeal to the industrialized world for increased economic assistance and for more effective debt relief policies could not, any more than his calls for the revitalization and democratization of the UN system, endow the NAM with the sense of purpose or strategic direction it clearly needed. Such exhortations in a sense highlighted the NAM's relative weakness and its diminishing capacity to capture the attention of the great powers or shape the global multilateral agenda

Not surprisingly, Southeast Asia became the focus of Indonesia's multilateral diplomacy, for here its interests were more immediate and its voice likely to carry greater weight. Indeed, it is arguable that ASEAN constituted the cornerstone of Indonesian foreign policy, in that it provided a useful umbrella for bilateral co-operation with neighbours, for negotiation with dialogue partners and for a more innovative but also more stable regional security framework. In December 1996, Foreign Affairs Minister Ali Alatas described the ASEAN approach to security as comprising two concepts: the first geared to the comprehensive security of each member state, and the other aimed at providing a basis for regional peace and co-operation. The two principles were said to be closely connected in that the first, with its emphasis on national resilience, envisaged the development of political, economic and socio-cultural strengths which could best be achieved 'not through military alliances [or] arms build up but through regional cooperation'.[67] The second principle, encapsulated in the notion of a Zone of Peace, Freedom and Neutrality (ZOPFAN) and enshrined in the 1976 Treaty of Amity and Co-operation (TAC), served as a code of conduct for relations within ASEAN as well as between its members and external powers. ASEAN's unique contribution to regional security, as well as its fluctuating fortunes in performing the diverse functions assigned to it, will be the subject of detailed discussion in *Regionalism in the New Asia-Pacific Order*. Suffice it to say for the moment that the ASEAN umbrella, though it offered no guarantee of protection against external threat, provided Indonesia with an arena for quiet diplomacy within which it could pursue its leadership aspirations without running the risk of antagonizing neighbours or great powers. It also laid the foundations for other multilateral initiatives – to be examined at some length in the companion volume – notably the ASEAN Regional Forum, in which Indonesia would perform an active and at times decisive role.

One facet of Indonesia's approach to regional multilateralism merits a few preliminary observations, however. Taking full advantage of the diplomatic informality that had become an integral part of ASEAN practice, Jakarta began in the late 1980s to offer its good offices, first to facilitate resolution of the Cambodian conflict and subsequently to promote security dialogue in the South China Sea. In the case of Cambodia, ASEAN, as a consequence of the clearly discernible shift in Vietnamese policy and increasing regional concern about China's role, became a strong advocate of the internationalization of the conflict. In July–August and October 1989 Indonesia joined France in co-sponsoring the Paris International Conference on Cambodia, which paved the way for the UN's direct involvement in the peace process, with the Security Council authorizing the Secretary-General through Resolution 718 (3 October 1991) to designate a Special Representative for Cambodia and establishing the UN Transition Authority in Cambodia. It is worth noting that well before this diplomatic breakthrough Indonesia's low-key involvement had prepared the ground by hosting informal meetings in 1988–9,[68] helping to create a climate conducive to dialogue and to identify, at least in broad outline, the contours of a possible dispute settlement strategy.

Indonesia's role in initiating and steering the Workshops on Managing Potential Conflicts in the South China Sea is equally instructive. Though originally intended to discuss all territorial disputes in the region, the spotlight soon fell on the Spratlys.[69] In his address to the first Workshop held in Bali in 1990, Ali Alatas described the initiative's principal objective as transforming potential sources of conflict in the South China Sea into constructive forms of co-operation for mutual benefit.[70] Whereas the workshops had over the years explored a range of ideas with eventual resolution of the conflict in mind, their primary function was to serve as a confidence-building measure.[71] The Suharto government gave political, moral and material support to the workshop process, with the Ministry of Foreign Affairs hosting all meetings, Ali Alatas delivering the opening address on each occasion, and Indonesia's Agency of Research and Development and its Director General Hasjim Dalae providing much of its initial inspiration and continuing momentum. Even at the height of the financial crisis, Ali Alatas was pressing participating governments to contribute the necessary resources for the successful implementation of projects approved by the workshop process.[72] For Jakarta this high-profile initiative was a valuable investment of diplomatic energy and resources, for it promised to demonstrate and at the same time strengthen ASEAN unity and confirm Indonesia's intermediary, even leadership role within ASEAN. The workshops were also a convenient instrument for internationalizing the Spratlys dispute and allowing it to intrude into the ASEAN–China dialogue and the deliberations of the ASEAN Regional Forum.

Over more than 30 years the Suharto regime had sought to pursue a subtle, at times ambiguous, but patient and generally low-key diplomacy, designed to restore Indonesia's former international standing, while at the same time enhancing the regime's own legitimacy and survival. The success of such a strategy, driven in large measure by domestic imperatives, was itself dependent on continued economic growth and relative political stability, conditions which no longer obtained in the wake of the 1997 East Asian crisis. As we saw in Chapter 2, the policy of export-oriented industrialization and the accelerating integration with the world economy which it implied did result in substantial economic growth, a greatly expanded manufacturing sector and a sharp decline in the proportion of the labour force employed in agriculture. However, the policy rested on less secure foundations than Indonesian policy-makers and experts of various kinds were willing to concede.[73] When the Asian currency crisis spread to the Indonesian financial sector the impact was rapid and calamitous. The sharp fall in the value of the rupiah, coupled with heavy exposure to foreign debt, huge rises in interest rates and restrictions on credit; resulted in virtual bankruptcy for most large Indonesian firms. Although the construction industry was the most severely hit, dropping by 43 per cent from mid-1997 to mid-1998, the spillover effect soon spread to other industries, with machinery production falling by 72 per cent in the 12 months, and the iron and steel, cement, retail and transport industries also registering a drastic decline. The economic, not to mention social and political, consequences of the crisis and the difficulties in recapitalizing and restructuring the finance sector would prove more intractable for Indonesia than for any other East Asian country.

Early estimates of the social dimensions of the crisis may have been overestimated, but there is no denying the severity of its impact on the livelihood of millions of people. Most dramatic was the rise in unemployment, which official figures seriously obscured – in part because they did not show that many families, in particular women and young people over the age of ten, were forced to increase their participation rate in the workforce in order to maintain their incomes. Nor did they reveal the full extent of underemployment in all sectors of the economy. Aggregate estimates of the levels of poverty and unemployment were misleading given substantial income and employment disparities both within and between provinces. Indonesia's economic downturn could not in any case be reduced to its immediate social effects. Even after the economy resumed its upward curve, there was no guarantee that such growth would be reflected in higher levels of employment, or that the 2.8 million children who had to drop out of primary and secondary schooling[74] would be adequately compensated. It would be several years before the adverse impact of the crisis on education, health and housing, and more generally on the sense of economic security, could be accurately assessed.

By virtue of the uncertainties it had unleashed, the crisis was bound to have far-reaching political as well as social implications. With the New Order regime unable to maintain the living standards and aspirations not just of Indonesia's working class but of its rapidly expanding middle class, Suharto's grip on the presidency was irreparably weakened. More importantly, perhaps, the sense that the New Order had finally set Indonesia on a long-term path to prosperity had been dealt a fatal blow. Widespread popular discontent, fuelled by corruption in public life, the concentration of wealth in the hands of a small elite, and in particular the personal fortunes amassed by members of the president's family, was now given a much sharper political focus. The outbreak of riots in several regional towns, particularly in response to steep price rises in January 1998, were soon followed by indiscriminate attacks on ethnic Chinese-owned businesses, widely perceived as the principal beneficiaries of Suharto's largesse. By the early months of 1998, student demonstrations had become large and vociferous. Given rapidly diminishing confidence in his capacity to govern, not least on the part of influential elements in ABRI and the political elite, Suharto announced his resignation on 21 May 1998. He had presumably calculated that to have his protégé, Vice-President Habibie, assume the presidency was the most effective damage-limitation strategy; that is, the option that afforded him, his family and his close friends and associates the best possible financial and political protection. While it was not immediately apparent how well-founded the strategy would prove, one thing was clear: Indonesia was undergoing a period of profound social, economic and political transformation, a transition of uncertain duration that called into question the authority of existing institutions, including the dual administrative and military function performed by the armed forces.

Habibie's first year in office set in train a process of democratization, in part through the reform of electoral laws and new elections for a reconstituted House of Representatives (DPR). Substantially weakened by the June 1999 elections, Golkar nevertheless secured 20.9 per cent of the national vote and 120 out of the 462 contested seats. On the other hand, the Indonesian Democratic Party of Struggle (PDI-Perjuangan) led by Megawati Sukarnoputri gained the largest share of the national vote (37.4 per cent) but only 154 seats.

The subsequent tensions between presidential aspirants, political parties and ideological currents were themselves symptomatic of the deeper cleavage between those pressing for more radical political reform and those intent on preserving the wealth, influence and status they had acquired under the New Order. The dramatic events leading up to the presidential election on 20 October 1999 crushed President Habibie's re-election chances and demonstrated the fragility and unpredictability of the new experiment in democratic politics. The historic 373–313 vote in the People's Consultative Council (MPR)[75] confirmed Abdurrahman Abdurrahman as Indonesia's new president. Beset by problems on all fronts, including the East Timor débâcle, the Bank Bali scandal and the stigma of his close association with former President Suharto, Habibie withdrew from the presidential contest only hours before the vote. Though widely regarded as the most likely candidate, by virtue of the electoral success of her party and her pedigree as the daughter of Sukarno and upholder of Indonesia's secular nationalist traditions, Megawati was thwarted by an effective Muslim coalition which instead placed its faith in Abdurrahman Wahid (affectionately known as Gus Dur), long-standing moderate Islamic intellectual and former leader of the mass Islamic organization, Nahdlatul Ulama. In keeping with his stated aim of reintegrating a badly fractured polity, Abdurrahman ensured Megawati's election as Vice-President, presenting their political leadership as a partnership or 'duality' (*dwitunggal*) of Islamic identity and secularist orientation. Similarly, to accommodate the wide range of interests represented in the new parliament, Abdurrahman's cabinet was expanded from the initially intended 25 to an eventual 35 portfolios.[76] Amien Rais, leader of the other mass Islamic organization (Muhammadiyah), had obtained only modest support in the June election but was elected chairman of the MPR. General Wiranto, former Defence Minister and commander of the armed forces, was effectively demoted but given a cabinet portfolio as Co-ordinating Minister for Political Affairs and Security. Ministerial status was also conferred on five other active or retired military officers.

Compounding the difficulties of leadership succession and political renewal were long-standing ethnic and religious resentments which the policy of national resilience had never fully defused, and in some cases had aggravated. Reference has already been made to the violence directed against the Sino-Indonesian community during the events of May 1998. The enormous wealth accumulated by a relatively small number of Chinese families had made the whole Chinese population, estimated at between four and six million, a convenient scapegoat for the country's economic and social ills. Though the violence subsided, many Sino-Indonesians remained anxious about the future and were inclined to shift their capital offshore, a trend which, if not reversed, would seriously handicap the Indonesian economy's prospects of recovery.

Even more serious outbreaks of communal violence occurred in the eastern provinces of Maluku, especially in the provincial capital of Ambon, where the Christian Maluku people became increasingly resentful of Muslim migrants from South Sulawesi. Fuelling the animosity was the perception that the government sector now favoured Muslims both in the availability of jobs and the enforcement of religious practices. Here the animosities were compounded by the fact that local Ambonese military and police personnel tended to side with one or other of the opposing groups. In the wake of Indonesia's retreat from East Timor, the arrival of new forces from Java in the early part of 2000, which effectively doubled the number of security personnel in the office,[77] helped to reduce but certainly not eliminate the intensity of the violence which had claimed more than 3000 lives since January 1999. Jakarta's decision to decline a state of civil emergency in the provinces of North and South Maluka in June 2000 provided further evidence of the intractability of the conflict. Similarly, in the province of West Kalimantan indigenous Christian Dayaks clashed with Muslim transmigrants from the island of Madura. In both cases the tensions generated by an accelerated programme of transmigration were accentuated by sharpened competition over diminishing economic opportunities. To this must be added the secessionist movements in Aceh, Irian Jaya (West Papua) and East Timor, each of which had its own unique features, but all of which involved the deployment of ABRI forces and widespread human rights abuses.

In Aceh, where separatist sentiment predated Indonesian independence, popular discontent with rule from Jakarta was fuelled by military excesses and a perception that the region was not adequately compensated for the exploitation of its rich oil and gas reserves. The Free Aceh movement, benefiting from the fall of Suharto and unprecedented freedom of speech, revived its political network and initiated a mass recruitment campaign.[78] Despite Jakarta's promises of greater autonomy and more equitable allocation of resources, in November 1999 some 750 000 people – close to half of the province's eligible voters – rallied in the capital of Aceh demanding a referendum on independence. Abdurrahman's response to these demands represented a blend of sensitivity and studied ambiguity. While a referendum on the implementation of Islamic law was at least negotiable, the possibility of independence was firmly rejected. Following contact with separatist leaders, the agreement reached in May 2000 calling for a 'humanitarian pause' in hostilities offered the necessary impetus for further talks,[79] without, however, any guarantee that this breathing space would lead to a durable resolution of the conflict or an end to the violence which had already killed at least 300 people since the beginning of the year.

In Irian Jaya, Jakarta had to confront opposition to its authority from the moment the territory became part of Indonesia in 1962 after a UN-supervised 'Act of Free Choice'. Despite repeated assaults, ABRI forces were unable to destroy the Free Papua Movement (OPM), in part because of the mountainous terrain but also because of the deep resentment provoked by a sustained policy of transmigration.

The large number of new settlers from Java and South Sulawesi who now constituted approximately half of the total population, inevitably generated grievances relating to almost every facet of daily life, including culture, economy and environment. By late 1999 the clamour for independence had spread to previously quiescent parts of the country, including Riau and South Sulawesi. Here again Jakarta's response was to keep open its lines of communication with Papuan leaders, but to question the legitimacy of any call for independence.[80]

Despite the severity of the multiple challenges to Indonesian political stability, it could not be assumed that the integrity of the state had been irreparably shattered. The rapidly unfolding drama of Indonesian politics had yet to reach its climax. The powerful domestic constraints bearing upon the policy-making process had in the meantime diminished the capacity of the Indonesian state to project power and influence beyond its borders.[81] By the end of 1999 it was as yet unclear what would replace the disintegrating power structure established in the heyday of the new order, or what new equilibrium might emerge between the institutions of central and provincial government. Even if the Abdurrahman presidency could produce a conceptual blueprint capable of holding together the fractured Indonesian state, it was by no means certain that the Indonesian president would be able to impose his will on the armed forces, the legislature (DPR) or the country's supreme constitutional authority (MPR).

The proposed devolution of authority and resources to some or all the provinces, already foreshadowed in the Habibie government's legislative reforms, was tantamount to creating a federal state, which would be contrary to the ideological inclinations and national interests of powerful constituencies, not least key elements of the Indonesian military. At stake was the decentralization of authority in such diverse policy areas as health, education, agriculture, communications, industry and trade, environment and land, but also the election of regional heads of government. Barely two months after assuming office Abdurrahman had to contend with increasing resistance from senior generals, with some desperately trying to evade responsibility for grave human rights violations in East Timor, Aceh and other parts of Indonesia, and others sharply critical of his refusal to impose martial law in Aceh or to curb the investigations of Indonesia's Commission of Inquiry into Human Rights Violations in East Timor. Several of Abdurrahman's military appointments, including Admiral Widodo Adisucipto as chief commander of the armed forces, Tyasno Sudarto as army chief of staff, Craito Usodo as military spokesman, Ian Halim Perdanakusma as head of military intelligence and Agus Wirahadikusumah as head of the country's main combat force, but most importantly his decision on 15 February to suspend General Wiranto from his cabinet post, indicated a concerted effort on his part to strengthen the authority of the civilian presidency and those elements within the armed forces reconciled to the need for political reform.[82]

Military resistance to the civilianization of power was not, however, the only obstacle to Abdurrahman's vision of Indonesia as a nation united yet multi-ethnic, and secular yet multi-religious. Despite the advantages of personal charisma and the legitimacy conferred by a democratic presidential election, the new president had to contend with opposition on many fronts. His campaign against ministerial corruption, his support for Attorney-General Marzuki Darusman's efforts to bring the force of law to bear on widespread human rights abuses and the unlawful accumulation of wealth during the Suharto years,[83] and his stated desire to lift the long-standing ban on communism[84] had already provoked the hostility of significant elements of his support base.

The reorganization, not to say fragmentation, of the Indonesian state was pregnant with both dangers and opportunities as much for the country's domestic politics as for its external relations. The East Timor conflict, which had plagued the Suharto government since the annexation of the territory in December 1975, had already demonstrated how effective management of ethnic discontent would be crucial to Jakarta's future standing, both regionally and internationally. East Timor had, it is true, a unique status in Indonesian political life, and this primarily for two reasons: the refusal of the international community to recognize Indonesian sovereignty over East Timor, in particular the UN's long-standing though not immediately tangible support for East Timorese self-determination; and the ability of the East Timorese cause to capture the attention and imagination of international civil society. These factors combined with Suharto's departure and the accompanying economic and political turmoil to force President Habibie's hand. There was, however, one other important lesson to be drawn from the East Timor experience. Excessive and persistent use of force as a way of handling intercommunal conflict or ethnic separatism, and the abuse of human rights which it invariably entailed, was likely to subject the conflict to intense international scrutiny, widen political divisions at home and diminish the effectiveness of the state's regional diplomacy.

In responding to the East Timor crisis, both Habibie and to a lesser extent Abdurrahman were victims of the Suharto legacy. It was only in the latter part of 1998 that the Indonesian government began to express interest in a solution that would give East Timor 'a special status with wide-ranging autonomy', but even as late as February 1999 Ali Alatas readily conceded that alternatives were still subject to consideration and that he did not know 'exactly how to go about' assessing East Timorese approval or disapproval of any Indonesian proposal.[85] Jakarta's main preoccupation at the time, even while engaged in UN-sponsored negotiations with

Portugal, was to minimize or delay international intervention in the crisis and continue to obfuscate the indiscriminate use of force by the Indonesian military against supporters of East Timorese independence and their direct role in training and arming pro-integration militia forces.[86]

In May 1999 the Habibie government, partly in response to increasing international pressure, reached an agreement with Portugal which effectively allowed East Timor to choose between autonomy and independence, thereby conceding the possibility of an outcome his predecessor had steadfastly refused to entertain. Habibie had probably calculated that force would be needed to keep East Timor under Indonesian rule for as long as one could see into the future. The existing policy based on fear and intimidation was unlikely to succeed, but likely to prove financially costly, distract the government's attention away from more pressing economic and political problems and tarnish Indonesia's international reputation, regionally and at the United Nations. The policy shift by the presidential office did not, however, mean that the Indonesian National Army (TNI) – the new name for ABRI after the police were separated from it on 1 April 1999 – was reconciled to 'losing' East Timor. Hence, the continuing campaign of intimidation conducted by elements of the Indonesian military in conjunction with the East Timorese armed militia which it had organized and funded, with the aim of thwarting the UN-supervised *de facto* referendum on autonomy or independence. In the wake of widespread violence, the ballot, initially scheduled for 8 August 1999, was postponed by the UN Secretary-General by three weeks to allow for a more favourable security environment. The United Nations was clearly intent on preventing a repetition of the 'act of free choice' it had supervised in West Papua more than three decades earlier and now widely regarded as a fraudulent exercise intended simply to legitimize Indonesia's annexation of the territory.

Under Security Council Resolution 1246, UNAMET was established on 11 June 1999 to administer the referendum that would determine whether the East Timorese accepted or rejected proposed autonomy. With more than 98 per cent of the 451 792 registered voters casting a vote and 78.5 per cent voting for independence and against integration, the referendum of 30 August produced a decisive result.[87] But no sooner had UNAMET announced the outcome of the referendum than Indonesian military trucks rumbled through Dili emptying interrogation and intelligence centres of information and setting them on fire. On 6 September the home of Bishop Belo was razed and many of the 6000 refugees sheltering in it were taken away at gunpoint. With the imposition of martial law on 7 September, the militia with the close co-operation of Indonesian soldiers embarked upon 'an apparently orchestrated campaign of mass destruction'.[88] Dili was set on fire; university, telecommunications and government buildings destroyed; entire towns emptied of their populations; and tens of thousands of refugees moved across the border to West Timor.

With Habibie seemingly unable or unwilling to act, Alatas accused the UN mission of bias in favour of independence and the foreign media of misreporting the situation. The military, for their part, continued to depict the violence as fighting between rival factions. By the time the UN Security Council authorized the formation of the International Force on East Timor (INTERFET) on 15 September 1999, some 300 000 East Timorese had been internally displaced, more than 250 000 refugees were encamped in West Timor and many, willingly or otherwise, had been progressively resettled to other parts of Indonesia. Though subjected to fierce international criticism, particularly from western governments, the IMF and the World Bank, the Habibie presidency was now in virtual paralysis. All it could do to extricate itself from the East Timor tragedy was to accept, however grudgingly, the establishment of an international peace enforcement operation. On 26 October 1999, the Abdurrahman government officially terminated Indonesian control over East Timor, and responsibility for the administration of the territory was handed over to the UN Transitional Authority in East Timor (UNTAET). Its mandate would run until 31 January 2001 but was widely expected to be extended by one or two years.[89] The signing of a joint Indonesia–UNTAET memorandum in April 2000, which provided for regular liaison meetings between UN and Indonesian commanders, was expected to facilitate the resolution of border disputes and the return of East Timorese refugees.

The enormous political and economic pressures to which Indonesia had been subjected in the late 1990s were especially severe but by no means unique. In the context of increasing economic interdependence, associated with unfettered expansion of trade and capital flows, the range of policy options available to the Indonesian state had greatly diminished. The state's predicament had become all the more acute in the wake of competing claims over its limited resources and the deepening contradiction between its coercive and legitimating functions. The mutually reinforcing effects of fragmentation and globalization had left the state with less room for manoeuvre and fewer opportunities to manage crises through short-term bargaining strategies. It remained to be seen whether the Abdurrahman presidency or any alternative political coalition could successfully reconcile the conflicting interests of Indonesian society and maintain the organizational and territorial integrity of the Indonesian state. At issue were two conceptually distinct yet politically inseparable questions: would the post-Suharto political order be able to construct a more democratic yet cohesive framework of national governance? Would it pursue policies conducive to a stable system of regional governance? Though success or failure on one front would not necessarily be replicated on the other, Indonesia's capacity to pursue an assertive but effective regional diplomacy would in large measure depend on the solidity of its political institutions and the performance of its economy. These were themselves highly dependent variables, with both globalization and regionalization likely to exert a decisive influence if not on the actual choices that Indonesian political elites were likely to make, then certainly on the range of options available to them.

Even in the first few months of the Abdurrahman presidency, Washington attempted to influence the outcome, expressing its support for the President and his commitment to political democratization and economic liberalization, and warning Indonesian generals against staging a military coup. It was doubtful, however, whether such diplomatic forays on the part of the United States would be efficacious or even welcomed by those they were meant to assist. The bruising experience of the financial crisis and East Timor had left a wide cross-section of the Indonesian polity sceptical of the sincerity of western motives.

In a symbolically significant initiative, Abdurrahman began his presidency with an extensive tour of Asian capitals. His public comments gave an early indication of the likely direction of his foreign policy:

> There have been signals that Indonesia's foreign policies have been shifting from Western countries to Asian countries . . . Political hegemony has been used by superpower countries in the international community . . . To overcome that, we need Asian strength from countries like China, India, Singapore and Thailand. With an Asian force we can protect our own Asian interests in the global community.[90]

Indeed, the president went so far as to identify the PRC as one of Indonesia's most important partners, no doubt with a view to gaining better access to the Chinese market and encouraging Chinese Indonesian business people to return home with their financial assets.[91] Any improvement in Sino-Indonesian relations had, of course, to contend with several unresolved issues, including competing territorial claims over the waters surrounding the Natuna Islands, the tensions generated by the treatment of the ethnic Chinese community in Indonesia, and Indonesian uncertainty as to China's future intentions in Southeast Asia. Yet, counterbalancing these impediments was an emerging sense that the diplomatic support which China could offer, in part through its permanent membership of the Security Council, might be one of the few effective constraints on the kind of western intervention displayed in Kosovo and East Timor. The challenge, then, facing Indonesia was not simply the development of a more stable and democratic framework of national governance, but the kind of contribution it might make to the creation of an effective system of regional governance, without which any hope of domestic stability and cohesion might well prove illusory.

MALAYSIA

With a population only one-tenth that of Indonesia, Malaysia was nevertheless the only other Southeast Asian state with serious leadership aspirations during the 1980s and 1990s. This period, which neatly coincides with Mahathir's ascendancy in Malaysian politics, was marked by unprecedented ambition – and appreciable achievement – in domestic as much as foreign policy. A central feature of the Malaysian experiment was its stress on multidimensional or comprehensive security, which no doubt owed a considerable debt to the Indonesian concept of national resilience. In March 1984, Deputy Prime Minister Musa Hitam described the doctrine of comprehensive security in the following terms:

> Reduced to basics, there are three pillars in Malaysia's doctrine of comprehensive security. The first is the need to ensure a secure Southeast Asia. The second is to ensure a strong and effective ASEAN community. The third, and most basic, is the necessity to ensure that Malaysia is sound, secure and strong within.[92]

This inner strength, or national resilience, was tied to the pursuit of four objectives: to remove the incentive on the part of other states to threaten or intervene in Malaysia; to cope with real or potential external threats; to respond to security threats, whether internally or externally instigated; and to eradicate internal conflicts and contradictions, thereby denying outside powers an opportunity for intervention or interference.[93] Internal security was, in other words, inseparable from external security.

In the Malaysian environment of the early 1980s internal security had two crucial dimensions, intercommunal harmony and economic development, both of which were seen as crucial to nation-building and the integrity of the state. The Malaysian political system, particularly after the May 1969 racial riots, had been constructed on ethnically based political institutions, with the Barisan Nasional (BN) coalition providing the vehicle for interethnic negotiation and resource allocation, but with the United Malays National Organization (UMNO) as the dominant partner. UMNO projected itself as the principal instrument for the expression of Malay ethnicity and the achievement of Malay economic security. Indeed, Malay political supremacy was viewed as the *sine qua non* of Malaysian stability,[94] an approach which underwent significant refinement during the Mahathir period,[95] with the accent increasingly on the development of a pan-ethnic Malaysian identity. Complementing the drive for stable multiethnic political and constitutional arrangements had been the 'federalist notion of national security', which was vigorously applied to deny any state government the possibility of rupturing 'the political or territorial unity of the federation'.[96]

Crucial, however, to the success of the whole enterprise of nation-building, itself a prerequisite for the development of a strong and cohesive state, was the priority given to economic development. Unless the state was able to deliver improved material conditions, the already fragile political edifice would presumably have crumbled under the weight of unfulfilled expectations. In the immediate aftermath of the 1969 riots, the New Economic Policy (NEP) was launched with the specific objective of overcoming deep-seated Malay insecurity through an affirmative action programme in support of Malay interests. State intervention in the economy, a distinguishing characteristic of the early phase of NEP, was gradually replaced by privatization and deregulation policies, but without abandoning the key objective of strengthening the *bumiputra* (ethnic Malay) stake in the Malaysian economy. Though economic growth during the NEP period (1970–90) was uneven, it was substantial, registering an average annual increase of 6.7 per cent, and was accompanied, as we saw in Chapter 2, by a striking expansion of the manufacturing sector, much of it directed to the export market. By 1990 the Malaysian Prime Minister was ready to announce his vision of an economy that was 'competitive, dynamic, robust and resilient'.[97] Riding on a crest of economic and political self-confidence, the 'Wawasan 2020' (Vision 2020) policy, as it came to be known, envisaged an average annual growth rate of 7 per cent over the next 30 years, with Malaysia achieving the status of a developed economy by 2020.

Relative political stability and rapid industrialization, which became the two key ingredients of comprehensive security policy under Mahathir, also made it possible to assign a higher priority to military modernization. Measured at constant 1995 prices and exchange rates, Malaysia's defence budget had risen from $1.17 billion in 1988 to 2.44 billion in 1995.[98] Before the onset of the 1997 financial crisis, the seventh Malaysian Five-year Plan (1996–2001) had envisaged a military procurement programme estimated at $2.8 billion.[99] The Royal Malaysian Navy was the principal beneficiary, partly because of the greater demands on naval assets arising from the declaration of Malaysia's Exclusive Economic Zone in 1980. Two British-built guided missile frigates, four Italian-built Assad-class corvettes and up to 30 patrol boats were to be among the Navy's most important acquisitions. After a review conducted soon after the Gulf War, the Royal Malaysian Air Force (RMAF), having made a strong case for catching up with the modernization plans of neighbouring air forces, was to have its own capability substantially upgraded with contracts for the purchase of 18 MiG-29 Fulcrum and eight McDonald-Douglas F-18 aircraft. Malaysia's surveillance capability was to be enhanced with the acquisition of two sophisticated radars and a state-of-the-art command, control, communications and intelligence system.[100]

While economic factors – greater purchasing power and more extensive maritime interests to protect – were crucially important in shaping Malaysian defence policy, they were not unconnected to geopolitical considerations. Threat perceptions had certainly not evaporated but they differed markedly in tone and substance from those of the 1960s and 1970s. The threat posed by communist insurgency had virtually disappeared by the late 1980s. An agreement signed between the Communist Party of Malaya (CPM) and the Malaysian government (as well as a separate agreement between the CPM and the Thai government) on 2 December 1989,[101] followed by a similar agreement in 1990 with the North Kalimantan Communist Party, ended the communist armed struggle in Malaysia and effectively removed counterinsurgency as a high priority for Malaysian defence planning. Similarly, the external threat associated with the notion of an expansionist Vietnam had subsided even before Vietnamese troops had completed their withdrawal from Cambodia in September 1989. Malaysia, together with Indonesia, was instrumental in modifying ASEAN's previously hardline anti-Vietnam position, and by the early 1990s was actively seeking to establish 'close and positive relations' with both Cambodia and Vietnam and to facilitate their membership of ASEAN and endorsement of the Treaty of Amity and Co-operation.[102]

Even China, which had traditionally loomed large in Malaysian defence thinking, did not appear, at least officially, to inspire the same degree of suspicion or apprehension. Mahathir's explanation of this shift is worth quoting at some length:

> The perception that China is a threat is a popular one. Malaysia itself once nursed this view, but then those were the days when the Communist Party of Malaya drew inspiration and support from the Chinese Communist Party and when fears of a Chinese fifth column in Southeast Asia were strong . . . But times have changed dramatically . . . *We no longer regard China as a threat* . . . [T]o perceive China as a threat and to fashion our security order around this perspective would not only be wrong policy, but . . . a bad and dangerous one . . . We prefer to see China as a friend and partner in the pursuit of peace and prosperity for ourselves as well as for the region.[103] (italics added).

The repudiation of the China threat thesis was no doubt motivated by any number of pragmatic considerations. Malaysia hoped to do business with the rapidly expanding Chinese economy. It saw a constructive relationship with Beijing as helping to maintain the delicate balance between the Malay and Chinese communities within Malaysia. More generally, it realized that China was an ascending power and that its Southeast Asian neighbours had little option but to accommodate this new reality as best they could. Yet there was, as we shall see, more to Malaysia's China policy than sheer pragmatism. Kuala Lumpur perceived China as a power intent on establishing its credentials as a responsible and legitimate member of the East Asian community, a useful counterweight to US power and dominance and a stabilizing influence in both Northeast and Southeast Asia.

None of this is to suggest that Malaysian policy was oblivious to the possible conflict of Chinese and Malaysian interests. The dispute over the Spratlys Islands was a case in point. Consisting of numerous but small and uninhabited islands, reefs and atolls, the Spratlys archipelago had become a source of regional tension, with all or parts of it the subject of competing sovereignty claims by China, Vietnam, the Philippines, Taiwan, Malaysia and Brunei. The implications of the dispute and the difficulties standing in the way of a peaceful settlement are examined in the companion volume. Suffice it to say here that, like the other claimants, Malaysia wished to establish a strategic presence and gain access to what was, at least potentially, an area rich in fisheries and oil and gas deposits. Even if not directly involved at this stage, Malaysia could not but take note of the confrontations that had already occurred between China and Vietnam and China and the Philippines. Yet, in formulating its response, with respect both to its own jurisdictional claims and the challenge posed for ASEAN as a whole, the Mahathir government was careful not to allow the dispute to jeopardize the development of bilateral or multilateral ties with China.

Maritime threats to Malaysian security were not in any case confined to, or even primarily centred on, Chinese actions. By virtue of its long coastline and the scale of its territorial waters and exclusive economic zone, the Malaysian navy was expected to deal with a range of lower-level but more likely threats associated with piracy, smuggling, illegal fishing, illegal immigration[104] and a range of navigational issues, not least in the Malacca Strait. The difficulties experienced during the exodus of boat people from Vietnam in the 1970s and Indonesia in the 1990s offered striking evidence of the multiple tasks which would increasingly occupy the attention of regional navies.

In deciding to upgrade Malaysia's military capabilities, the 'Singapore' factor was never far from the minds of Malaysian military and political leaders. Both ethnicity and economy are once again relevant to the analysis. The perennial tensions between Malaysia and Singapore have a long history, dating back to Singapore's merger with Malaysia in 1963 and its expulsion from the Federation two year later. Singapore's original inclusion was widely seen by Malays as giving the Chinese community, both numerically and economically, the upper hand in the Federation, and accentuating the Malay sense of insecurity. After partition, a range of agreements and confidence-building measures, joint participation in the SIJORI development project and common membership of ASEAN and the Five Power Defence Arrangement (FPDA) helped to create a more positive climate, although frictions grounded in history and ethnicity were never far below the surface. Conflict over access to water supply from Johor, the competitiveness of two rapidly industrializing economies, overlapping territorial claims and Singapore's military posture – its large citizen army, forward defence policy, sophisticated weapon acquisitions, and the July 1989 memorandum of understanding with the United States under which Singapore would host the Logistics Command of the US Seventh Fleet – all tended to fuel Malaysian anxieties and mistrust.[105]

It would be misleading, however, to suggest, that Malaysian policy was driven by a heightened sense of insecurity or a predisposition to military responses. On the contrary, both its comprehensive security policy and the initiatives that stemmed from it were predicated on the assumption that the post-Cold War environment offered a unique opportunity to construct a more effective regional security framework. To this task the Mahathir government brought a strong dose of assertiveness reflecting the personality of its leader and the country's newly found self-confidence. The trend, which perhaps dates back to 1970 and Britain's military withdrawal east of Suez, points to Malaysia's increasing independence in the formulation of its foreign policy, and in particular the definition of its security environment. During the Cold War years the emphasis in declaratory policy was on preventing great power intervention in Southeast Asia through neutralization of the region and avoidance of military alliances. The neutralization principle formed part of the wider Zone of Peace, Freedom and Neutrality (ZOPFAN) concept, which did not mean that theory was closely matched by practice.

There was no disputing ASEAN's pro-western bias: two of its members were allies of the United States, Singapore was sympathetically disposed to its strategic presence, and even Malaysia was, by virtue of its membership of FPDA, at least indirectly connected with ANZUS. For Malaysia, however, ZOPFAN was seen more as a signpost towards the goal of greater diplomatic independence than a disruption of current practice. There was, in any case, more to ZOPFAN than neutrality between the two blocs. Southeast Asian states were expected to conduct their relations according to certain norms, notably non-interference in one another's internal affairs, mutual respect for the territorial integrity and independence of all the countries of the region, and pacific settlement of disputes. These ZOPFAN principles were steadfastly, if not always consistently, applied to the construction of the second pillar of Malaysia's comprehensive security doctrine, namely the development of 'a strong, secure and effective ASEAN community'.[106] Even before the end of the Cold War, Malaysia saw itself as one of the main engines driving the new regionalism in Asia Pacific.

With the disintegration of the Soviet bloc, Malaysian diplomacy adopted an increasingly anti-American, even anti-western, tone, stressing the dangers of unipolarity, which it equated with 'a return to the old dominance of the powerful over the weak'. Mahathir was unsparing in his condemnation of the 'new world order' envisaged by US policy, portraying it as an attempt 'to legitimize interference in the affairs of independent nations', as 'the forceful spread of the religion of Democracy and the Free Market'.[107] He took particular exception to the formation of trade blocs in the North, the application of extra-territorial laws, and the discriminatory recourse to trade restrictions. In these new geoeconomic and geopolitical conditions, it was necessary for the non-aligned movement to redefine itself, reassert the independence of states to determine their own economic policies, and take issue with powerful interests in the North that had turned the environment, human rights and democracy into instruments of economic domination.[108] Much the same theme coloured Foreign Minister Badawi's intervention at the Vienna World Conference on Human Rights in June 1993. Emphasizing the practical linkages between development and democracy, he cautioned against the introduction of conditionalities in development assistance programmes 'which encourage political prejudices and selectivity and victimize the poor twice over'.[109] The targets of Malaysia's diplomatic vitriol were selective yet wide-ranging. At the receiving end were an assortment of western governments, financial institutions, money markets, western media, and even western non-governmental organizations. They were perceived as agencies of 'western domination' or, as Mahathir would put it, the self-proclaimed prophets of democracy and the free market.

The principles underlying Malaysia's experiment in diplomatic self-assertion, though they found expression in a number of bilateral relationships, notably the 'Look East' policy and its portrayal of Japan and Japanese economic success as a role model for the rest of East Asia, were primarily concerned with multilateral diplomacy. Even in the case of Japan, which occupied a unique place in Malaysia's economic development by virtue of trade and investment links, the preoccupation was very much with the wider economic, diplomatic and symbolic role that Japan might play in East Asia's resurgence. Kuala Lumpur's approach to multilateralism is perhaps best understood in terms of four concentric circles, with the inner circle centring on ASEAN and the three progressively larger circles on East Asia, the non-aligned movement (overlapping but not necessarily coinciding with two other frequently cited categories in the Malaysian lexicon, the 'South' and the 'developing world'), and the global system.

ASEAN's central role in Malaysia's comprehensive security policy was based in part on the perceived interconnection between national and regional resilience. It is partly this perception which accounts for Malaysia's insistence on the need to encompass within ASEAN every Southeast Asian state, notwithstanding the political difficulties such a strategy entailed, most glaringly in the case of Burma and Cambodia. For Malaysia, ASEAN's effectiveness as a security community depended on its inclusiveness, that is, on its capacity to establish a code of state conduct applicable to the whole of Southeast Asia. The Treaty of Amity and Co-operation, ZOPFAN itself, the Southeast Asian Nuclear Weapons Free Zone (SEANWFZ) and the various economic, functional and technical agreements spawned by ASEAN had the same instrumental role. They helped to establish the necessary scaffolding for an emergent security community, on the one hand restricting great power intervention and on the other containing, if not resolving, regional rivalries and animosities. For Mahathir's Malaysia, ASEAN provided its member states with an enhanced stage on which to conduct their extra-regional diplomacy. The dialogue partnerships, the ASEAN Regional Forum and the Asia–Europe Meeting were but the most striking manifestations of this process. To the extent that it was able to articulate and harness support for these principles, Malaysia appeared well placed to gain kudos and influence from ASEAN's maturation and carve for itself a niche in regional and global diplomacy.

During the Mahathir period, Malaysia sought to widen but also reinforce its ASEAN diplomacy by intruding the same though somewhat differently packaged principles into the arenas corresponding to the three other principal spheres of its diplomacy. As with ASEAN so with East Asia, Malaysia's approach stemmed from its own experience, and in particular from its blend of market-driven industrialization and centralized political authority. That in a sense was the core message of the 'Look East' policy and its two-pronged emphasis on economic modernization and East Asian consciousness.[110] The impetus and the drive for Asia's resurgence, Mahathir argued, would come from East Asia, which in the space of a few decades had become a market place 'filled with the ringing sound not of bugles and bullets but of bazaar bargaining and stock market babble, of roads and harbours and magnificent edifices, of progress and growth'.[111] The lessons for Malaysia he had spelt out at the outset of his prime ministership:

> This means emulating the rapidly developing countries of the East in the effort to develop Malaysia. Matters deserving attention are diligence and discipline in work, loyalty to the nation and to the enterprise, or business where the worker is employed, priority of group over individual interests, emphasis on productivity and high quality, upgrading efficiency, narrowing differentials and gaps between executive and workers . . .[112]

Other than economic success, two closely related features of the East Asian model were especially appealing: its Asianness and its respect for state authority.

The East Asian 'economic miracle' was culturally appealing because, in the words of Noordin Sopie, a leading Malaysian intellectual and policy adviser:

> Our program of looking East tells us that there are things in the East worthy of our learning, because previously we *only* looked West. So part of the process is to rediscover the value and the virtue of being Asian. It's part of the rediscovery of other Asians who have done well".[113]

This was a case not only of identifying but of celebrating the cultural difference between East and West, of contrasting the social-cultural decadence of the Christian West with the cultural and political revival of the East. The question here was a particularly sensitive one for Malaysia: how to give cultural or religious content to the East or to East Asia, given the diversity of civilizational influences. More specifically, what was the relative weight to be given to the Sinic or Confucian ethic on the one hand and the Islamic tradition on the other? It is worth noting in parenthesis that the frequently expressed sentiment of an Asian renaissance – and its inherent tensions in Malaysia as in other parts of East Asia – predated and may even have influenced Huntington's formulation of the 'clash of civilizations' thesis.[114] Cultural or conceptual dilemmas aside, Malaysia under Mahathir saw itself as both benefiting from and, as time went on, contributing to the articulation and development of a new Asian consciousness.[115]

East Asian prosperity, it seemed, had resulted from a unique combination of free market economics and state-centric politics. Contrasting the East Asian experience with that of Eastern Europe and the former Soviet Union, Mahathir questioned the conventional western wisdom which stressed the complementarity of democracy and free market:

> Perhaps it is the authoritarian stability which enables this [prosperity] to happen. Should we enforce democracy on people who may not be able to handle it and destroy stability? ... Democracy should come gradually. This is the East Asian way. This is culturally more East Asian.[116]

Politically convenient though it was, the East Asian model recommended itself primarily by virtue of its economic success. It was not, however, a case of Malaysia merely emulating Japan and the tiger economies, but of making full use of their, and in particular Japan's, economic strength. Japan's role was critical because it was able to transfer large volumes of development assistance, capital and technology. Moreover, Japan, by virtue of its competitive relationship with the United States and Western Europe, helped to keep down the prices of many products and services. More importantly perhaps, as Asia's only member of the G7, Japan could facilitate a process of Asian consultation, enabling it to give voice to Asia's concerns at G7 meetings and lend these added weight at multilateral trade negotiations.[117]

Japan's economic weight rendered it indispensable to the success of Malaysia's East Asian diplomacy. As he confided to an audience in Tokyo, Mahathir harboured long-term ambitions for East Asia:

> [T]he immediate need is for East Asia to do two things. First, to take advantage of the regional synergies and opportunities for cooperation in order to maximise the short, medium and long-term mutual economic advancement. Second, to build a productive coalition for the success of the Uruguay Round, for the sustenance of the open multilateral global trading system and for other non-trade goals that are productive of regional and global economic interests.[118]

This carefully crafted statement of intentions was meant to serve as the rationale for the establishment of an East Asian Economic Group (EAEG). Although invariably presented as an instrument likely to advance multilateral trade negotiations, the grouping was first and foremost intended to serve as an East Asian forum, from which the United States and its South Pacific allies would be excluded and which could therefore be critical of western policies and priorities. The EAEG proposal, its subsequent modifications and its relationship to APEC are the subject of detailed examination in *Regionalism in the New Asia-Pacific Order*. Suffice it here to say that Japan's – and for that matter South Korea's – refusal to support the Malaysian initiative was interpreted as evidence of the enormous pressure exerted by the United States on its allies and of its refusal to countenance any challenge to its conception of world order.

Japan itself was castigated for its negative response to the Malaysian proposal. Since the mid-1980s Mahathir had gently but firmly encouraged Japan to assume a leadership role in East Asia, make its vast financial resources, world-class technology and highly developed entrepreneurial and managerial skills the engine of East Asia's economic growth, open its protected markets to East Asian, not least Malaysian, manufactured goods, stop apologizing for the past, and help establish the framework for East Asian co-operation and co-ordination. Frustrated with Japan's caution, narrow definition of self-interest and concentration on APEC, Mahathir proceeded to lecture Japan with his customary bluntness:

> We are merely asking that Japan join the EAEC . . . The only Asian country with the ability to help fellow Asian countries refuses to do so, but instead demands to know why America is not included, why Australia and New Zealand are not included. The answer is obvious. They are not East Asian . . . Japan is Asian. Japan is of East Asia . . . you belong here . . . we are asking you to join us and play a leading role. You have the stature and the means.[119]

By failing to press ahead with its proposal for an 'Asian Monetary Fund' Japan was seen as having lost 'a great opportunity to help Asia and lead it through the crisis'.[120]

To give added weight to his castigations, Mahathir went so far as to deny Japan Malaysian support of its candidacy for permanent membership of the Security Council. Such support, he argued, could be extended only if Japan was prepared to act independently of the United States and speak with a strong voice on behalf of Asia. Despite Tokyo's failure to live up to Malaysia's expectations, Mahathir was intent on pressing ahead with his East Asian diplomacy. Shifting political currents and alignments inside Japan, coupled with China's economic and diplomatic resurgence, made this an opportune time for semi-peripheral states to canvass the possibilities of institutional innovation. Rather than continuing with the high-profile campaign against APEC or insisting on the specifics of its EAEC proposal, Malaysia was by the mid-1990s ready to explore new avenues for East Asian co-operation. A series of ministerial meetings beginning in July 1994 and attended by ASEAN, China, Japan and South Korea culminated in the first ASEAN-plus-three summit meeting, which Malaysia hosted in December 1997. It remained to be seen how much momentum this initiative would acquire, what concrete results it might yield and what leverage Malaysia would exercise over its future development.

Though placed far lower on the list of priorities than ASEAN or East Asia, the non-aligned movement and the developing world more generally continued to be an important focus of Malaysian diplomacy. Mahathir's high profile on North–South economic issues was a distinguishing feature of his prime ministership, as evidenced in Malaysia's strong support for the establishment of the South–South Commission at the 1986 Conference of the Non-Aligned Movement, its hosting of the inaugural summit meeting of the Group of 15 in June 1990, and its conspicuous role in helping to crystallize the South's bargaining position at the UNCED Conference in June 1992.[121] For Malaysia, the primary value of the Non-Aligned Movement, and to a lesser extent of other Third World bodies, including the Organization of the Islamic Conference, was that it offered member states the possibility of enhancing their freedom of action. By pooling their human, financial and diplomatic resources, it was argued, societies that had experienced various forms of western domination might be better placed to enhance their margin of manoeuvre. In the immediate post-independence period, bipolarity had greatly benefited Third Word countries intent on safeguarding their 'sovereignty' and independence. In the emerging unipolar system of the post-Cold War period, the solidarity of the non-aligned had become even more critical to the preservation of political freedom and territorial integrity.[122] Whereas in the earlier period external threats revolved largely around military force, they now tended to operate through economic forces, in ways that were perhaps more subtle but no less damaging. Various initiatives launched through the Group of 15 (for example, the Bilateral Payments Arrangements, the Developing Countries Payments Arrangements, the South Investment, Trade and Technology Data Exchange Centre) were seen as a modest, at times symbolic, but none the less significant effort to stem this more recent tide.

Of the four spheres of multilateral diplomacy, the global system, in particular the Bretton Woods institutions, but even the United Nations, was the one treated with greatest caution. Malaysia valued all international fora that provided it with a platform from which to project its conception of a more equitable world order. Global institutions were generally less amenable to such a strategy, hence Malaysia's repeated objections to what it considered to be their undemocratic structures and practices. The World Bank and the IMF were singled out as undemocratic institutions which, contrary to their mandate to facilitate development and regulate the international monetary system, were acting as 'debt collectors for the rich North'. As for the WTO, it was said to pose new threats to developing and newly emerging economies, forcing them to open their markets to foreign penetration but offering them little in return. The new GATT agreement had failed to protect the genetic resources of the South and allowed western biotech corporations to make huge profits by patenting genetically modified materials.[123]

In the area of security, Malaysia sharply criticized the power of veto enjoyed by the five permanent members of the Security Council, which it described as an anachronistic legacy of the Second World War. It bemoaned the increasing tendency of the great powers, notably the United States, to bypass or demote the General Assembly, to uphold resolutions they themselves favoured, and misinterpret or ignore others. It used every available opportunity to highlight the double standards of the UN's interventionist policies, and contrasted the UN's timid response to Israel's frequent use of force against Palestinians with its consistent failure to support Palestinian aspirations for a homeland and a state. Even more vitriolic was Malaysian criticism of the UN's role in Bosnia-Herzegovina, where western powers were accused of turning a blind eye to Serb atrocities and of failing to give Muslim communities the protection to which they were entitled. In Malaysia's view, structural reform of the Security Council was the only effective remedy to the UN's cumulative shortcomings in the performance of its security function.[124] To this end, it was necessary to enlarge the Council in both categories of its membership – permanent and non-permanent; to limit, if not entirely abolish, the use of the veto; and to make the UN's decision-making processes more transparent, accountable and open to the participation of all member states.

In many respects Malaysia's critical stance was not uncharacteristic of other non-aligned states conscious of the relative weakness of their position in the international system and intent on turning that weakness to their advantage. The distinctive quality of Malaysian rhetoric was its consistency and intensity and the linkages it sought to establish between the political, economic and cultural dimensions of western dominance. There was, in any case, more to Malaysia's contribution than rhetorical flourish. It played an active role in several of the UN's organs and agencies, and was closely associated with a number of initiatives and proposals. It assumed the presidency of the Twenty-fifth UNESCO General Conference, served as an alternating member of the Security Council from 1988 to 1990, chaired several international conferences (such as the International Conference on Drug Abuse and Illicit Trafficking), and in 1996 its representative, Razali Ismail, assumed the presidency of the UN General Assembly. Malaysia had also become a regular participant in UN peacekeeping missions.[125] In the case of Bosnia it made a substantial commitment to the UN Protection Force (UNPROFOR), despatching some 1500 military personnel, no doubt partly with a view to establishing its credentials both with its own Muslim population and the wider international Islamic community. In the General Assembly, it intervened on a wide range of security and economic issues, initiating or co-sponsoring resolutions on the elimination of nuclear weapons, particularly in conjunction with 'the advisory opinion of the International Court of Justice on the legality of the threat or use of nuclear weapons', and proposing closer co-ordination between the UN system and Third World organizations, notably the Organization of the Islamic Conference and its specialized institutions.

The steady growth of the Malaysian economy, the relative success in maintaining national cohesion, Mahathir's forceful leadership and the establishment of influential think-tanks and centres of research and policy advice, in particular the Institute of Strategic and International Studies,[126] all contributed to Malaysia's assertiveness. Yet as the financial crisis and its political aftermath demonstrated, there were clear limits to how far Malaysian rhetoric could be pursued, let alone implemented. As indicated in Chapter 2, the adverse impact on the Malaysian economy was substantial, yet not as disruptive as in Indonesia and other parts of East Asia. By the end of the 1990s it was still unclear whether this outcome was attributable to the relative strength of Malaysia's economy prior to the crisis, or to the policies adopted by the Mahathir government in response to the crisis, or to the fact that the long-term effects of the crisis had yet to percolate fully through the economy.

One thing was nevertheless clear: by refusing IMF intervention and applying capital and exchange controls, the Malaysian government retained a degree of leverage over economic policy and made it less likely that foreign investors would acquire or take a controlling interest in Malaysian enterprises. While GDP fell by 6.7 per cent in 1998, exports fell by less than 1 per cent in dollar terms, and grew by more than 3 per cent in 1999. By the end of 1998 unemployment had steadied at about 3.3 per cent and inflation at 5.3 per cent. The trade balance recorded a surplus of $10.8 billion. Foreign reserves had risen to $26.2 billion. To that extent at least, the Malaysian response may be said to have enhanced the appeal and legitimacy of capital controls and national regulation of the economy more generally, and to have contributed to the declining authority of IMF prescriptions. It may also have helped to strengthen the increasingly widespread perception that international financial markets lacked transparency and that the international financial architecture was in urgent need of regulatory reform. Yet none of this could conceal the precariousness of Malaysia's economy or its continuing dependence on foreign markets and foreign capital and technology.

Economic performance was in any case but one indicator of Malaysia's capacity to pursue an independent diplomacy. The political turmoil associated with the dismissal of the Malaysian Deputy Prime Minister, Anwar Ibrahim, his immensely well-attended lectures and public rallies in the ensuing three weeks, at which he highlighted the theme of social justice and the alleged prevalence of corruption and cronyism, and his subsequent arrest on charges of corruption and sexual misconduct could be viewed as the inevitable outcome of the contest for leadership succession. A more sophisticated interpretation, to be developed in the next chapter, would suggest that a significant cross-section of society, including important Islamic elements on the one hand and sections of the middle class on the other, was now much less disposed to accept the requirements of authoritarian rule. Even after the national elections of 29 November 1999, these political undercurrents, of which the *Reformasi* movement was but one, albeit dramatic, manifestation, had yet to run their course.

Although the Barisan Nasional coalition was returned with a two-thirds majority, it received only 56 per cent share of the popular vote, down 9 per cent from the previous election. The main challenge had come from Barisan Alternatif, a coalition comprised principally of Parti Islam SeMalaysia (PAS), the predominantly Chinese Democratic Action Party, and Parti Keadilan Nasional, recently formed with Anwar's wife, Wan Azizah, as its leader, and reported to have attracted some 200 000 members prior to the election.[127] The heaviest losses in the election were sustained by UMNO, which lost 20 parliamentary seats, whereas the largest gains were made by PAS, which increased its parliamentary representation from 7 to 27 seats and won control of the northeastern states of Kelantan and Terengganu. The trend was confirmed a few months later in a by-election in Sanggang which the UMNO candidate won but with a substantially reduced majority. While a significant shift had occurred in the Malay vote, no one could as yet confidently predict how the developing contest between the supporters and critics of the *status quo* would overlap with the emerging debate on economic policy or with the delicate racial balance of Malaysian politics. Nor was it clear how cohesive the coalition of opposition groups would prove. One trend, however, was unlikely to be reversed: the impact of globalization would increasingly assume political as well as economic dimensions. A new generation of leaders was likely to emerge that would find it more difficult, and be less inclined, to engage in the politics of self-assertion as practised by Mahathir. Future policy options, not least in the area of economic and social policy, would become the subject of sharper debate and division, with the potential for gradually or even suddenly eroding the carefully controlled political structure which Mahathir had used with considerable skill to cultivate the aura and rhetoric of diplomatic independence.

Even if Malaysia remained a relatively stable polity and a vibrant economy, the effectiveness of its external policies would rest in good measure on their complementarity with those of regional neighbours and on the coherence and solidarity of regional institutions. In the aftermath of the East Asian crisis neither condition could be guaranteed. Quite apart from the economic and political uncertainties facing Indonesia, ASEAN was itself vulnerable to the difficulties which member states, both old and new, were experiencing, and to the consequent disagreement, or at any rate loss of confidence, about future direction. Malaysia also had to contend with the still unfolding impact of the crisis, and globalization more generally, on Chinese and Japanese policies and with the rapidly evolving triangular balance between China, Japan and the United States. The Malaysian state might be able to continue its recent advance to semi-peripheral status, but its capacity to influence let alone control its external environment would come under increasing challenge.

CANADA

Though it appears on every map of the Asia-Pacific region – how could it be otherwise since to exclude it would also exclude the United States – Canada had until the late 1980s remarkably little visibility in regional geopolitical or geoeconomic discourse.[128] Conversely, Asia Pacific did not loom particularly large in Canadian official thinking or, with a few notable exceptions, in Canada's public consciousness. Geographically speaking, Canada is a Pacific state, yet historically it has paid little attention to the region. Despite its long Pacific coastline, long-standing trade and immigration links and substantially increased military commitments in the wake of the Korean War, Canada was content to have its diplomatic priorities set by an Atlantic agenda. During the Cold War era, its security policy was shaped largely by its close bilateral defence ties with the United States and its participation in NATO and the North American Aerospace Defence (NORAD) agreement. In so far as Canada had interests or views impinging on the Asia-Pacific region, these were invariably set in the context of bipolar politics, with due deference to US leadership, acceptance of the geopolitical centrality of the Atlantic Alliance and confidence in the security afforded by extended deterrence.[129]

Significantly, the five-fold increase in Canada's defence budget that occurred shortly after the outbreak of hostilities in Korea was earmarked almost exclusively for the defence of Western Europe, protection of the sea lines of communication between North America and Europe and the air defence of North America.[130] The 1964 and 1971 Defense White Papers, apart from references to the Korean experience, made virtually no mention of Asia. The beginnings of change emerged during Trudeau's prime ministership, which saw a gradual reduction in real defence spending. Though the implications of this change were not immediately apparent, largely because the Canadian defence establishment chose to retain the general disposition of the armed forces and their focus on the European theatre, it was only a matter of time before interacting domestic and external pressures would visibly impact on security policy.

Cautiously at first but with rapidly growing enthusiasm, a series of statements during the 1980s emanating from both parliament and government highlighted the emergence of Asia Pacific as the new centre of economic gravity in the world, and made the case for the expansion of Canada's links with the region.[131] By the late 1980s this message would be conveyed with increasing frequency by ministers with special responsibility for the Pacific, foreign ministers and even prime ministers. The new declaratory policy legitimized but also gave impetus to a number of practical developments, in particular the strengthening of bilateral relations, notably with Japan and China; efforts to complement diplomatic and economic ties with social and cultural exchanges; more strategic use of development assistance programmes;[132] avoidance of direct military involvement in the region except as part of a multilateral, preferably UN-sanctioned operation; and encouragement of immigration from Asia.[133]

Several factors had contributed to this reassessment of the Asia-Pacific region. The gradual decline of Cold War rivalries, epitomized by the Gorbachev–Reagan summits, had generated a more favourable climate for the resolution of regional conflicts. The appreciable lowering of tensions in Europe and the collapse of the Berlin Wall had at the same time substantially reduced the probability of a European war, hence the likelihood that Canada would be called upon to make major military commitments as a consequence of its NATO membership. To put it simply, threats to Canadian interests were now less likely to have a specifically military or Atlantic dimension. Conversely, Canada, like other important trading economies, had acquired a strong interest in the development of stable bilateral and multilateral trade regimes. In this context, East Asian economies had become especially relevant, given their rapid rate of expansion and their possible impact on economic growth and job creation in Canada. By the early 1990s Canadian governments were confidently pointing to a number of highly attractive possibilities: the support that Asia-Pacific markets could lend to the future development of key Canadian sectors; the size and purchasing power of the Asian middle classes and the implications for Canada of value-added products and services; Japan's rise as a major source of direct investment; and the global contribution that the Asia-Pacific region could make to industrial innovation.[134]

Nor were these expectations mere wishful thinking. As early as 1983, Canada traded more across the Pacific than the Atlantic. Within ten years, five of its top ten trading partners, excluding the United States, were in Asia: Japan, China, South Korea, Hong Kong and Taiwan. In 1994, Canadian trade with the region grew by 20 per cent, and by 30 per cent in 1995, accounting for more than half of its total non-US trade and an increasing proportion of its manufactured exports.[135] To this should be added a third factor, namely the arrival of ever-increasing numbers of Asian immigrants – as far back as 1979 Asia had overtaken Europe as a source of immigrants. By 1996, Asians accounted for over 57 per cent of Canada's annual immigration – three times the number of arrivals from Europe – with some 2 million Canadians now of Asian origin.[136] By dint of their business connections, family ties, educational affinities and bilateral and multilateral links with governments, Canada's Asian communities had provided a new incentive but also a rich resource for enhanced interaction with Asia.

Another influence at work in the much higher profile now accorded Asia Pacific was the general shift of emphasis in Canadian diplomacy. The combined impact of globalization and multipolarity had prompted a re-evaluation of security policy and greater stress on the need for 'co-operative security'. A collective approach to problem-solving was seen to be in keeping with the revitalization of the UN, the philosophy and practical recommendations of Boutros-Ghali's *Agenda for Peace* and Canada's own internationalist traditions.[137] The redefinition of Canada's place in the world was taken a step further in 1997 and 1998 by the Minister for Foreign Affairs, Lloyd Axworthy, who advocated a global concept of human security. Encompassing not just the absence of military threat but protection from economic hardship and respect for fundamental rights, security, it was argued, could not be divorced from the complexity of the human environment or the interdependence of the influences impinging on it. Canada's activist role in UN peacekeeping and its various initiatives in peace-building, disarmament and the promotion of human rights were presented as the practical expression of the commitment to human security. Security policy was reconceptualized to make it more comprehensive and better integrate its constituent elements. In the process, the role of force in the achievement of security was downgraded and the contribution of multilateral institutions correspondingly augmented.

The net effect was to enhance Canada's intellectual but also practical capacity to engage with Asia Pacific. The increasingly fashionable view was that Canada belonged to three regions: the Atlantic, the Pacific and the Americas. Added to this were Canada's links with the Commonwealth and with Francophonie, all of which suggested that Canada was more than a medium power. In Axworthy's words, 'We are a global medium power, called on to play an international role in the pursuit of global interests'.[138] Conceptually at least, the stage had been set for Canada to expand its links with Asian countries in a range of non-traditional areas, in particular governance and human rights issues, regional institutions, regional and global security initiatives and broader questions of human security. Indicative of the desire to develop the texture and complexity of its relations with Asia was Ottawa's decision to designate 1997 as Canada's Year of Asia Pacific. The ensuing year-long, countrywide programme of cultural, academic and business events with an Asia-Pacific focus was designed to showcase Canada as a Pacific nation and raise its Asian profile on both sides of the Pacific.

The question immediately arises: would words be matched by deeds? In the sensitive area of security, the first significant initiative came with the proposal in 1990 to establish a North Pacific Co-operative Security Dialogue.[139] In order to minimize the likelihood of outright rejection by the United States and Japan, both of which were still sceptical of the value of new multilateral arrangements, the Canadian government emphasized the gradualist aspects of its initiative, the desire to cultivate a 'habit of dialogue', and the possibility of beneficial spillover effects from the experience of existing regional and sub-regional institutions.[140] While the proposed dialogue might eventually entail multilateral consultations on issues of military security, care was taken to exclude naval arms control from the agenda. Conscious of the difficulties standing in the way of official acceptance of the proposed multilateral framework, Ottawa hoped that the dialogue would also be promoted on a second track, in which the main participants would be scholars and experts but with officials attending in their non-official capacity. The second track, which got under way with a series of workshops and conferences in April 1991, sought to bridge the gap between the conventional and unconventional security agenda, exploring possible arms control options and confidence- and security-building measures, but ranging also over such issues as environmental degradation, drug trafficking and energy security.[141]

The projection of Canadian multilateralism benefited from the generally positive image Canada had established in Asia Pacific. Its involvement in the region did not bring with it unpleasant historical baggage and was not therefore perceived as a threat by other states. Its internationalist credentials, including active participation in the UN system, and undoubted expertise in multilateral organizations endowed its initiatives with added respectability. Yet there were also important limitations. Despite the greater prominence given to Asia Pacific by the 1994 Defense White Paper,[142] serious doubts persisted about Canada's definition of its security interests and the extent to which changes in doctrine or strategic policy would be reflected in operational defence policy.

Beginning in 1994 with HMCS *Vancouver*'s visit to Japan and South Korea, annual naval deployments, conducted in co-ordination with the department of Foreign Affairs and Trade, alternated between Northeast and Southeast Asia.[143] Subsequent port visits included Australia, New Zealand, the Philippines, Hong Kong, Malaysia, Singapore, Thailand, Tonga and Western Samoa. As a confidence-building exercise, the navy was also engaged in developing closer links with a number of regional institutions, including the Malaysian Institute of Maritime Affairs and the Nimitz Asia-Pacific Center for Security Studies in Hawaii. Canada's security priorities continued nevertheless to be set by its North American and Atlantic connections. Apart from the defence of Canada (that is, its national territory and areas of jurisdiction), the 1998 Defense Planning Document set as the main priority the defence of North America in co-operation with the United States. In May 1996 the two governments had renewed for five years the NORAD agreement, but with a revised mandate allowing for enhanced aerospace warning and control missions. In addition, the Canada–US Basic Security Plan provided for the co-ordinated use of both countries' maritime, land and air forces in the event of hostilities against North America. It was highly unlikely that Canada would ever be called upon to activate the forces it had assigned for this purpose (a joint task force headquarters, a maritime task group on each coast, a brigade group with associated support elements, two squadrons of fighter aircraft and a squadron of transport aircraft). On the other hand, given the close integration of its defence capabilities and deployments with those of the United States and NATO, it was difficult for Canada, notwithstanding its criticism of Washington's plans to develop a National Missile Defence system, to entertain a peacekeeping or other major security involvement in Asia Pacific which did not have at least tacit US approval. Canada's presence in Asia Pacific raised, then, two closely related but distinct questions: the scale, visibility and impact of that presence, and Canada's freedom of action in formulating and implementing its strategic policy.

By the mid-1980s, the Canadian political elite certainly had both the incentive and the inclination to pursue a policy of closer engagement with Northeast as well as Southeast Asia. Yet its primary motivation had more to do with economic than with security considerations. Indeed, the endeavour to raise Canada's profile on politico-strategic issues was in no small measure driven by economic interests. By the early 1990s, it is true, Canada had developed an extensive web of bilateral relations with East Asian countries across a wide policy spectrum, including human rights, development assistance, investment and trade. The approach, however, lacked overall co-ordination. It was as if 'exports and jobs' were the engine driving the policy, with other objectives and priorities intruding where they could, but always under the shadow of economic imperatives.

The inner dynamic of Canadian policy was perhaps most apparent in relations with China. Despite the symbolic and practical importance of that relationship for an expanding Canadian involvement in the Pacific, there was little evidence of any major initiative or of an overarching strategy on Canada's part. Having steadily expanded through the 1970s and the 1980s, two-way trade in 1988 exceeded $3.5 billion. The small bilateral aid programme launched by the Canadian International Development Agency (CIDA) in 1981 devoted particular attention to agriculture, energy, forestry and human resource development. CIDA's strategy was very much based on the transfer of skills and upgrading of management programmes for the modern sector of the Chinese economy.[144] Official aid disbursements had grown tenfold from 1982–3 to 1988–9, to reach the still modest sum of Can$38.9 million, with the emphasis on Canadian capabilities and institutional linkages conducive to enhanced trade opportunities.

Events at Tiananmen Square in June 1989 posed a major challenge to Canada's China policy. On the one hand, the promotion of democracy and human rights had become a cardinal principle of Canadian diplomacy. On the other hand, a vigorous response to the abuse of human rights in this instance risked derailing the whole thrust of Ottawa's commercially driven strategy. This latter imperative ultimately prevailed, which explains why the sanctions announced on 5 and 30 June should have proved so limited in scope and duration.[145] By April 1990 the vast majority of applications by Chinese students in Canada for permanent residence status had been accepted. The special provisions for consideration of these applications were terminated in September 1990. The number of Chinese refugees granted asylum remained pitifully small. Other measures included the suspension of defence relations between the two countries and a ban on all military sales to China, but these were largely symbolic given that only one significant defence-related visit had taken place in 1988 and that the volume of Canadian arms exports to China was rather small. In any case, such exports soon resumed, yielding a substantial increase in revenue in 1990 as compared with 1988. As for the deferment of all high-level contacts between Chinese and Canadian officials, the sanction was in practice disregarded or substantially qualified. Though significant restrictions were placed on Canada's aid programme, their actual impact was marginal as the projects involved were either very near completion or reinstated within the space of a year. It is worth noting that bilateral aid to China experienced a slight fall in 1989–90 (Can$35.2 million compared to Can$38.9 million in 1988–9) only to rise sharply in the following year (to Can$72.7 million). Much the same trend was evident in credit arrangements, with the Canadian Cabinet approving two new loans to China in August and September 1989 for Can$100 million and Can$130 million respectively. Within three years of Tiananmen, Canada's Export Development Corporation had extended loans for 28 projects to the value of Can$569.3 million, an increase of more than 20 per cent over the corresponding amount for the preceding three-year period.[146]

The Tiananmen episode is highly instructive in that it points to the powerful commercial pressures bearing upon human rights policy, but also, by implication, on other facets of Canada's external conduct. Underpinning the relatively quick return to normalcy of Sino-Canadian relations was Ottawa's determination to maintain and develop Canada's stake in the modernization of the Chinese economy. The acceleration of political dialogue, culminating in visits by Premier Li Peng to Canada in 1993 and Prime Minister Jean Chrétien to China in 1994, was primarily designed to maintain the momentum in the bilateral economic relationship, with trade continuing to occupy a central place. By 1994 two-way trade had reached Can$6 billion, rising to Can$7.9 billion in 1996 and Can$10.1 billion in 1998.[147] Canada's traditional surplus to China had shifted to a trade deficit in 1992, with the imbalance rising steadily through the 1990s to reach Can$5.2 billion in 1998. But for Ottawa the priority remained greater access for Canadian companies to China's potentially vast market. Though primary commodities and resource-based products (grain/seed/fruit, woodpulp, cereals and fertilizers) made up more than half of China's exports in 1998, Canadian enterprises, including insurance companies, law firms and banks, were significant exporters of services, notably infrastructure projects.

The 'Team Canada' trade mission to China, led by Jean Chrétien and provincial premiers in November 1994, included hundreds of business leaders and yielded commercial contracts and agreements valued at more than Can$5 billion. Among the main companies participating in these business ventures were Power Corporation, Barrick Gold, Northern Telecom, Dominion Bridge, Mitel, SNC/Lavelin, Pacific Entertainment and Spar Aerospace. A Can$3.5 billion agreement was also signed by Atomic Energy Canada for the sale of two CANDU nuclear reactors to China's nuclear power corporation.[148] One could safely infer that these business interests, strongly represented in the Canada–China Business Council, exercised a decisive influence over Canada's trade policy generally and its China policy in particular.[149] China's human rights record remained on the agenda, but the ensuing low-key initiatives (for example, expressions of concern at ministerial meetings, establishment of the Canada–China Joint Committee on Human Rights, bilateral projects designed to improve management standards in Chinese jails, treatment of women and children, and enforcement of labour rights) were specifically designed to contain tensions in the political relationship and prevent any spillover effect likely to threaten the continued development of commercial opportunities.

A brief reference to Canada's other salient relationships will help to highlight key recurring themes in Canada's regional policies. Economically at least, Japan remained Canada's principal partner. Bilateral trade surpassed Can$24 billion in 1995, with Japanese exports in that year increasing by 24 per cent and bringing two-way trade almost into balance. In addition to supplying Japan with a range of raw materials, in particular cereals, wood pulp, coal and aluminium, Canada had also become a significant exporter of telecommunications equipment, executive jets and helicopters, with electronic software, building products and prefabricated housing also assuming increasing importance. Apart from pressing Japan to eliminate regulatory restrictions on market access, Canada was seeking through its Action Plan for Japan to encourage business development activities in seven expanding sectors: housing and building products, fish and seafood products, processed foods, consumer products, health care, tourism, and information technologies. A third component of the Canadian agenda was the promotion of joint partnerships between Japanese and Canadian businesses in major projects in third countries, especially in Asia Pacific.[150]

After China and Japan, South Korea was Canada's third largest export market in Asia. Following several years of uneven but substantial growth, Canadian exports in 1995 stood at Can$3.2 billion. With a significant upgrading of South Korean infrastructure in prospect, Canadian enterprises were intent on capturing a slice of the action, offering either natural resources or technology and expertise.[151] The 'special partnership' established in 1993 was followed in 1995 by an agreement on Industrial and Technological Co-operation and negotiations for an agreement on telecommunications equipment procurement. As with Japan, the possibility of joint projects in third countries was under close examination. With the opening of the Canadian Education Centre in Seoul, the number of Korean students in Canada had risen to 8000, making South Korea Canada's largest source of international students.[152] Much the same pattern emerged in the relationship with Hong Kong, Canada's fourth largest trading partner in Asia. With 12 000 Hong Kong students studying in Canada in 1996 and three Canadian universities offering courses in Hong Kong, education services had become a major export market. Equally promising was the potential for food exports, which had grown from Can$7 million in 1986 to Can$590 million in 1996.[153] Important as Hong Kong was in its own right both as a market for Canadian goods and services and a source of investment, its role as an entry point to the People's Republic of China was perhaps even more significant.

It should not be inferred from the preceding emphasis on economic ties with Northeast Asia that Canada had neglected the countries of Southeast Asia. It is nevertheless true that many Southeast Asian leaders, most openly Mahathir, remained sceptical of Canada's commitment to Southeast Asia. Reminders about Canada's participation in the Colombo Plan and CIDA's funding of several development projects were not entirely persuasive, hence the new intensity in Canada's Southeast Asian economic diplomacy. In 1990 the Canadian and Malaysian governments agreed to change the relationship from one of donor–recipient to one of partnership. Although largely symbolic at first, the initiative was followed by a series of high-level meetings, trade missions and co-operative programmes. As part of Ottawa's Asia-Pacific strategy a Team Canada mission to Malaysia and Indonesia was organized in January 1996, resulting in 44 business contracts and 54 agreements. The proposed business ventures in Indonesia were valued at Can$2.8 billion and involved a wide range of Canadian firms, including Atomic Energy of Canada, Northern Telecom, SNC/Lavelin, Sun Life Assurance, LanSer Technologies and Interprovincial Pipelines.[154] The Asia Investment Strategy released in October 1997 singled out for particular attention eight markets, which included Singapore and Malaysia. Ottawa's main priorities were to maximize participation in infrastructure projects, expand involvement in environmental programmes with promising business opportunities and strengthen the education relationship, with the specific aim of doubling the number of Malaysian students in Canada.[155] In two-way trade between the two countries, which passed the Can$1 billion threshold in 1995, Malaysia enjoyed a highly favourable balance, with a substantial flow of electronic products, clothing and textiles making its way to Canada.[156] On the other hand, a good proportion of electronic exports were manufactured by a Canadian company (Northern Telecom) operating in Malaysia. Other Canadian enterprises with a significant stake in Malaysia included Novacorp, the Bank of Nova Scotia and Bombardier, which was awarded the contract to build the Can$300 million Light Rapid Transit project in Kuala Lumpur.

This cursory survey of Canada's attempts to consolidate its presence in Asia Pacific has concentrated on a number of bilateral relations, with particular emphasis on their economic dimensions. This is not to suggest that Canada was not actively engaged in multilateral processes, in particular the ASEAN PMC, ASEAN Regional

Forum and APEC, all of which will be the subject of detailed analysis in *Regionalism in the New Asia-Pacific Order*. Indeed, as already noted, Ottawa was an energetic advocate of new multilateral security arrangements, especially in the context of Northeast Asia. Yet these forays into multilateral diplomacy did not appear to be fully integrated into the framework of Canada's external relations, with the possible exception of APEC and PECC, which, because of their close ideological commitment to trade and investment liberalization, neatly dovetailed with Canada's economic agenda. Canadian interest in issues of regional security, human rights, environment and multilateral co-ordination more generally was genuine enough, but its function was largely subordinate to, and in large part derived its operational impetus from, its economic agenda which, as we have seen, formed the bedrock of its Pacific strategy. These economic influences in turn reflected the impact of globalization on the Canadian economy, and were as much the product of corporate strategies as of government priorities. They had in any case to be placed in the context of Canada's far more extensive and deeply embedded economic links with the United States, which the North American Free Trade Agreement (NAFTA) had further privileged and solidified. Canadian initiatives in the areas of security, human rights, environment and multilateral diplomacy may therefore be interpreted as attempts to mask, or at least qualify, the effects of economic necessity by cultivating an image of national independence, policy coherence and international good citizenship.

AUSTRALIA

The Vietnam War has rightly been described as a watershed in Australia's relations with Asia. Perhaps one of its most far-reaching consequences was the abandonment of the long-established policy of forward defence which had seen Australian armed forces deployed in different parts of the world in conjunction with British forces, and after the Second World War increasingly with US forces. Australia's participation in Asian conflicts, including the Korean War, the Malayan Emergency and the Vietnam War, was intended to deal with threats along the rimlands of Asia variously identified with the policies and actions of communist governments and revolutionary movements. During the 1960s the objective was to assist in the containment of China by supporting the United States and its anti-communist allies in East Asia. As described elsewhere, the strategy was to keep 'the conflict as far away from Australia's shores as possible: by fighting there rather than here, and now rather than later'.[157] There was, however, a deeper motivation, for Australian governments perceived these defence commitments as the price that had to be paid for future

British and American protection. In that sense forward defence became inseparable from reliance on 'great and powerful friends'.

Britain's decision to withdraw its military presence east of Suez by 1971 and America's humiliating defeat in Vietnam in 1975 dealt the forward defence policy a grievous, if not fatal, blow. As leader of the new Labor government which oversaw the final stages of Australia's military withdrawal from Vietnam, Prime Minister Gough Whitlam confidently explained the break with the past:

> We are convinced that the kind of army Australia needs for her own defence and for her most effective contribution to the defence of her friends should no lo nger be structured upon the concept of fixed garrisons overseas . . . For a country like Australia the concept is unreal and unrealistic.[158]

The break was, however, far from complete. Australia maintained a residual military presence in Malaysia and Singapore under the Five Power Defence Arrangement and began to expand its defence co-operation programmes with ASEAN countries. With the decline of détente and the revival of Cold War tensions in the late 1970s and early 1980s, the Fraser government was increasingly disposed to support US military operations, particularly in the aftermath of the Afghanistan crisis. Preoccupied with what he perceived to be a deteriorating central balance, the Australian Prime Minister repeatedly called for a more cohesive western alliance system and for the reassertion of American leadership. To this end, several Australian warships were despatched to the Indian Ocean in support of US strategic requirements; Orion aircraft assisted in the tracking of Soviet submarines; authorization was given for periodic deployments of US B-52 bombers in Northern Australia; and a decision made in 1981 to participate in the US-sponsored multilateral force in Sinai.

Despite sharply contrasting perceptions and rhetoric, both the Whitlam and Fraser governments expressed a new consciousness of Australia's place in the world. Whitlam favoured a more independent Australian stance in world affairs and a more prominent role in international efforts to eliminate colonialism and racial discrimination. For the Fraser government, too, the Third World, including issues of poverty and race, had assumed considerable significance.[159] While limited in its capacity to influence events, Australia, it was argued, could make its voice heard through membership of various international fora, for example the United Nations or the Commonwealth, and by virtue of its special relationship with Southeast Asia and the South Pacific. Equally instructive was the increasing stress in public pronouncements, notably in the 1976 Defence White Paper, on defence self-reliance. Though tempered by financial and bureaucratic constraints, the new tone in declaratory policy was nevertheless indicative of Australia's new understanding of its place in the world.

It was left to the Hawke government, elected in 1983, and in particular Bill Hayden and Kim Beazley as Foreign Affairs and Defence Ministers respectively, to devise a policy that more persuasively reconciled a continuing commitment to the US alliance with a more independent international outlook. The ANZUS review, conducted by Hayden in 1983, while reaffirming the alliance's crucial contribution to Australian security, indicated that each partner carried primary responsibility for its defence, and that an excessively deferential attitude to the United States was unhealthy and diversity of opinion both possible and desirable.[160] At the same time, and somewhat paradoxically, Beazley argued that the benefits conferred by the alliance in time of peace – as distinct from its hypothetical contribution in time of war – were crucial to the development of a more effective and self-reliant Australian defence. Five benefits were normally singled out: intelligence co-operation; access to US policy-makers; privileged procurement of US military technology; joint military exercises and training; and collaboration in defence research and technology.[161] The stage was thus set for the 1986 *Review of Australia's Defence Capabilities*[162] and the 1987 White Paper[163] which, in the words of Bill Hayden's successor, Gareth Evans, 'liberated Australia's foreign policy by focussing on self-reliance rather than dependence on traditional allies'.[164]

The evolution of defence policy and the security relationship with the United States with which it was inextricably linked mirrored the vast geopolitical changes that would soon bring an end to the Cold War. In a major Ministerial Statement to the Parliament in December 1989, Gareth Evans acknowledged the transition to a multipolar world in which 'the United States and the Soviet Union [would] loom relatively less large and [would] be joined by Japan, the European Community, China and India as major global influences'.[165] Though the United States would remain the world's pre-eminent military power, its preoccupation with the economic challenge posed by Western Europe and Japan, coupled with its economic interests in Latin America and the Middle East, would mean a diminished level of security interest in Southeast Asia and the South Pacific. The stage was thus set for Australia to build on policy developments in the preceding years and define a new approach to regional security.

In the case of Southeast Asia, 'comprehensive engagement' became the catch phrase for a more extensive set of bilateral and multilateral arrangements. These were seen as fostering enhanced social and economic co-operation and a greater sense of shared security interests. 'Comprehensive engagement' was an attempt to project in the region an image of Australia 'as a confident and natural partner in a common neighbourhood of remarkable diversity, rather than as a cultural misfit trapped by geography'.[166] Here, the underlying objective was to establish the legitimacy of Australia's interests and priorities and gain acceptance for its involvement in the political life of Southeast Asia, a daunting task made all the more difficult by the traditional attachment to western alliances and spheres of influence and the painful legacy of discriminatory immigration laws, better known as the White Australia policy.

In building a more diverse and substantive array of linkages with the countries of Southeast Asia, including Vietnam, Cambodia, Laos and eventually Burma, the Australian government envisaged the retention, perhaps refinement, of existing arrangements as well as the creation of new ones. There was nevertheless a common thread that would link elements of the old and the new, namely the notion of multidimensional security. It was now envisaged that 'all components of Australia's network of relations in the region' – military and politico-military capability, diplomacy, economic links, assistance with development and so-called non-military threats, and the exchange of people and ideas[167] – were meant to help shape a more favourable security environment. Though it fell short of the more encompassing notions of 'comprehensive' or 'human' security, multidimensional security and the related strategy of comprehensive engagement represented nevertheless a significant departure from the long-established practice of interpreting security almost exclusively in terms of military threats and capabilities.

The new trends in Australia's security policy were, however, far from unidirectional. A residual commitment to forward defence was still evident in Australia's attachment to alliances and collective security mechanisms, most of which dated back to the Cold War, not least ANZUS and the Five Power Defence Arrangements. The 1987 Defence White Paper explicitly referred to circumstances in which Australia might wish to commit forces beyond the region, and to that end recommended the maintenance of military capabilities needed for the forward projection of power. As for ANZUS and the wider US military presence in Asia Pacific, the Labor government had no option but to recognize the shift in Washington's post-Cold War strategic orientation. On the other hand, it continued to argue for the stabilizing influence of such a presence, describing it as a 'balancing wheel' and seeking to reassure itself and others by claiming that foreshadowed reductions in US military capability would be 'gradual, predictable and subject to review'.[168] To put it simply, the David Lange strategy of distancing New Zealand's posture from that of the United States found little resonance in Australian diplomacy.[169] The announcement in October 1990 that command and control of the North West Communications facility would be handed over to Australia did not reflect a diminution of the Australian–US security connection but the changing technological requirements of the US navy.[170] Ministerial talks in late 1990 made it clear that the modernization of Australia's armed forces would operate within the alliance framework and contribute to 'Australia's fulfilment of its alliance responsibility'. Australia's participation in the Gulf War was a concrete application of this principle which, Gareth Evans signalled, might one day also need to be applied in the Asia-Pacific region.[171]

There was, then, a striking ambivalence in Australia's security posture, reflecting in part the post-Cold War uncertainties of Australia's regional and global environment, but also the diverging strategic perceptions of senior ministers and their respective departments, notably Foreign Affairs and Defence, and the resistance to change among the upper echelons of the defence policy community. The uneasy compromise between these various tendencies was well exposed in the 1993 Strategic Review, which defined the four pillars of Australia's security as a national defence capacity, the growth of a 'regional security community', the alliance with the United States, and a strong defence commitment to UN and other multilateral operations.[172]

The need to accommodate strongly held positions within the Defence Department presumably also accounted for the emphasis on politico-military capability in the 1989 *Ministerial Statement on Regional Security*. Such capability was needed to maintain and expand programmes of co-operative defence activities with regional armed forces; support regional security arrangements in Southeast Asia and the South Pacific; and provide various forms of military assistance. More specifically, the policy envisaged more extensive training and joint military exercises with ASEAN neighbours; comprehensive support for the PNG defence force; the Pacific Patrol Boat Project designed to equip eight Pacific Island states with effective para-military and maritime surveillance capabilities; a revitalised FPDA more attuned to Malaysian and Singaporean priorities; and a range of other peacetime activities, particularly in the South Pacific, including narcotics and fisheries surveillance, counter-terrorism operations and protection or rescue of Australians abroad. The document even entertained the possibility of a wider new regional security community or understanding which might subsume such arrangements as the FPDA.[173] Placed within a military framework, the twin policies of 'comprehensive engagement' with Southeast Asia and 'constructive commitment' to the South Pacific would re-emerge as 'strategic partnership' and 'strategic commitment' respectively.[174]

Notwithstanding ministerial differences of emphasis or tensions between and within bureaucracies, one theme consistently coloured the conduct of foreign and defence policy during the Labor years. This was the view that Australia, whether by accident or design, now had a greater margin of manoeuvre in shaping its regional relationships.[175] With the removal of Cold War 'overlay', the development of an

Asia-Pacific community had now become feasible. The concept of the 'Pacific Basin' or 'Pacific Rim' had been canvassed in academic and business circles for some years. As far back as 1976 the government-funded Crawford–Okita report on *Australia, Japan and the Western Pacific:Economic Relations* had recommended the accelerated development of regional economic links, including the formation of an Organization for Pacific Trade, Aid and Development (OPTAD). In May 1979 Fraser had indicated that the concept of a Pacific basin community had considerable potential and merited further consideration. The subsequent evolution of Asia-Pacific multilateralism will be reviewed in *Regionalism in the New Asia-Pacific Order*. Suffice it here to say that in this earlier phase the idea had limited currency and was largely confined to the economic arena. As Evans subsequently observed, the notion of a common 'Asia-Pacific' region – let alone common regional identity – transcending sub-regional identities (such as Southeast Asia, South Pacific) was a relatively recent phenomenon.[176] The Labor government of the late 1980s was thus confronted by a number of complex questions. What opportunities did this trend present to Australian diplomacy? Could Australia identify with this emerging Asia-Pacific consciousness? Might it be able to exercise a leadership role?

In addressing these questions, the Hawke and Keating governments had to overcome a difficult hurdle: the legacy of Australia's troubled relationship with Asia, widely perceived as a source of threats, and identification with western powers generally viewed as an indispensable source of protection. To this end, a conscious attempt was made to portray Australia as unequivocally part of the emerging Asia-Pacific community. There were two prongs to the strategy: getting acceptance for the notion of an Asia Pacific as distinct from a purely East Asian community; and taking full advantage of Australia's rapidly growing economic links with Asia. Gareth Evans offered the following formulation:

> [T]here has never been much doubt about our comfort with the 'Pacific' part of the equation, but nor can there now be with the 'Asian'. Australians now accept, not grudgingly but enthusiastically, the idea that the East Asian hemisphere is where we live, where we must find our security and where we can best guarantee our prosperity.[177]

The push to Asia became, at least officially, the distinguishing hallmark of what Gareth Evans labelled a 'remarkable decade of transition'. Australia, it was argued, was experiencing 'an explosion of Asia consciousness'. Australian firms were increasingly attracted by the prospect of penetrating Asia's booming markets. More extensive media coverage of the social and political life of Asian countries was complemented by significant growth in the study of Asian languages, an expanding immigrant community of Asian origin and a large stream of Asian students and tourists.

For the Labor government it was not merely a question of engaging with Asia or of establishing Australia's credentials in Asia, but of helping to shape the new Asia or, to be more exact, of setting the agenda for the new Asia-Pacific community. Within the space of a few years, numerous proposals were put forward both for confidence-building measures – including information-sharing across a range of military activities, establishment of a regional security studies centre, strategic planning exchanges, presence of observers at military exercises, a regional maritime safety and surveillance co-operation agreement, and collaborative environmental security arrangements[178] – and for more substantive agreements on such issues as the environment, chemical and nuclear weapons, multilateral trade negotiations and regional economic co-operation. The aim was clearly to set a regional agenda whereby issues could be defined and initiatives taken in ways that suited Australian interests.

However, what distinguished this period of intense diplomatic activism was the emphasis on institution-building. This is not to suggest that Australia's approach to Asia-Pacific multilateralism was based on a coherent or carefully elaborated and executed design. Gareth Evans came closest to defining the new regional architecture when referring to 'two institutional structures, dealing with economic relations and security issues, within the overarching concept of an Asia-Pacific community'.[179] In practice, however, the architecture had evolved in a much less orderly fashion and comprised a more complex mosaic of distinct yet overlapping elements than this definition would indicate. The institutional proposals and initiatives emanating from Canberra, though a recognizable pattern eventually emerged, developed principally as *ad hoc* responses to rapidly changing domestic and international circumstances.

Given the geographic and political sensitivity of the region and Australia's primary area of interest, the focus, at least initially, was on the sub-regional level. In Southeast Asia, the centrepiece of Australian policy was the Association of Southeast Asian Nations (ASEAN), which Australia had cultivated as a dialogue partner, in part through the annual discussions of the ASEAN Post-Ministerial Conference. The relationship, however, with ASEAN was far more extensive, encompassing numerous contacts and exchanges and a wide range of bilateral links with each of the member states. The same model applied to the South Pacific, where Australia's security objectives were 'to minimize opportunities for hostile external military access and influence, contain any intra-regional tensions, and promote internal stability and development'.[180] The South Pacific Forum provided the main framework for co-operation, except that in this instance Australia operated as a fully fledged member, exerting pervasive influence over both institutional arrangements and policy direction.[181]

Whereas in the case of Southeast Asia and the South Pacific, Australian policy initiatives could be channelled largely through existing institutions, the two other sub-regions of economic and strategic interest to Australia, Northeast Asia and the Indian Ocean, were less amenable to such a strategy. While lacking the necessary leverage to be a prime mover in either instance, Australia nevertheless expressed interest in institution-building, welcoming the Canadian proposal for a North Pacific security co-operation dialogue and establishing within the Department of Foreign Affairs and Trade the North-East Asian Policy Development Unit. Following a number of modest efforts to lift its profile in the Indian Ocean region, Australia proposed a triangular arrangement with India and South Africa,[182] though the form and content of such co-operation remained relatively ill-defined.

Conscious of the limited reach of its influence and of the complexity and diversity of regional issues and relationships, Australian diplomacy sought to complement existing or proposed sub-regional institutional arrangements with two other approaches to regionalization. The first, as we shall see, involved a considerable investment of diplomatic resources to the development of a region-wide architecture. The second revolved around a number of *ad hoc* institutional forms designed to handle particular problems or conflicts. In some cases, Australia's role was little more than that of an interested bystander (for example, the Southeast Asian Nuclear Weapons Free Zone), but in others it played a major initiating role (as in the Cambodian peace process) or was even the principal architect (for example, the South Pacific Nuclear Free Zone). This approach rested on the implicit assumption that multiple dialogues and organizational mechanisms could, through overlapping membership and other forms of co-ordination, make a cumulative contribution to multidimensional security.

Perhaps the most distinctive aspect of Australia's post-Cold War multilateral diplomacy was its emphasis on inclusive, overarching institutions. In the field of security, Gareth Evans made one of his boldest proposals in July 1990, advocating the establishment of an institutional framework which might parallel the Conference on Security and Co-operation in Europe (CSCE). He specifically envisaged a 'CSCA', which would address 'the apparently intractable security issues' in Asia and which, like CSCE, would comprise all the countries of the region and cut across the ideological and strategic divisions imposed by the Cold War.[183] Evans conceded that Asia was vastly different from Europe, lacking its sense of common identity and common diplomatic tradition, but did not see Asia's diversity as an obstacle to new patterns of co-operation and 'imaginative new approaches to confidence building and problem-solving'. Despite the considerable care the Australian government took to limit the scope of the proposal and obviate any inconsistency with existing alliance obligations, the response of the United States and, to a lesser extent, Japan, was generally negative. Even ASEAN governments took the view that it was preferable, in the first instance, to develop the process of dialogue at bilateral and sub-regional level. However, as we shall see in the companion volume, within three years the initial hostility of the great powers to multilateralist approaches to security in Asia Pacific had subsided, and ASEAN, anxious to maintain the initiative in its own hands, would soon propose the establishment of the ASEAN Regional Forum. Australian advocacy, while it had not succeeded in mobilizing support for its own proposal, had nevertheless fostered a more favourable climate for regional security dialogue.

By comparison, Australian efforts to promote regional economic co-operation were less carefully or clearly conceived yet, for diverse reasons, came more quickly to fruition and did not, on the whole, have to follow the same circuitous route. Having announced his intention in January 1989 to seek the attitudes of regional leaders to the creation of a 'more formal inter-governmental vehicle for regional co-operation', Hawke proceeded to mount a concerted diplomatic campaign, headed by the then Secretary of the Department of Foreign Affairs, Richard Woolcott.[184] The proposal, resting as it did on the widely shared perception of the economic dynamism of the Asia-Pacific region and an implicit commonality of interests, captured the imagination of other countries. Within ten months, the proposal was translated into a meeting of industry and foreign affairs ministers from the twelve major trading nations in the Asia-Pacific region: the United States, Canada, Japan, South Korea, the six ASEAN states, Australia and New Zealand.

The origins and subsequent evolution of APEC are subjected to detailed scrutiny in the companion volume. However, it is worth noting that both Hawke and Keating invested a good deal of time, energy and prime ministerial authority in maintaining the momentum of the APEC initiative. This large psychological and diplomatic investment stemmed in large measure from the policy of engagement with Asia and the closely related commitment of Labor governments to trade liberalization. APEC was from the outset seen as an adjunct to the GATT negotiations, accelerating the removal of regional trade barriers while at the same time contributing to the successful conclusion of the Uruguay Round.

Yet the direct economic gains to be derived from unfettered access to Asian markets do not tell the full story. Another important Australian objective throughout this period was to commit the United States to a continuing presence in the region. As Keating put it in October 1994:

[APEC] helps to lock in US economic and commercial interest in the region, which in turn helps ensure US strategic engagement. It provides a framework to help contain or manage competition between China, Japan and the United States. And it gives the smaller countries of the region a greater say in the nature and shape of the trading arrangements in the region.[185]

Though it did not feature prominently in popular or scholarly analysis, the geopolitical and geoeconomic dimensions of the APEC project were nevertheless central to Australian thinking. The aim was not simply to engage the United States, commercially and institutionally, more fully in the region, but to do it in ways which dissuaded US administrations from pursuing protectionist policies, thereby reducing the prospect of a major trade war between the United States on the one hand, and Japan, China and the newly industrializing East Asian economies on the other.

Australia's core interests were now seen as inextricably tied to the bilateral trade relationships with these economies.[186] Australia strongly favoured a central role for the United States in Asia-Pacific regionalization, but not on the basis of a hub-and-spokes model, whereby the United States could impose its economic and political will through a series of bilateral relationships which it could consistently control by virtue of superior leverage. From Australia's vantage point, the APEC process offered an avenue not only for reducing bilateral trade frictions but for discouraging the formation of regional trading blocs. This was a high-priority objective, not only because Australian export industries stood to lose from a return to protectionist policies, but also because a world of institutionalized trade rivalries would require Australia to find a bloc to join and place it in the unenviable situation of having to choose between its principal trading partner, Japan, and its 'great and powerful friend', the United States.

In the preceding survey attention has centred on Australia's multilateral diplomacy under Labor, because it was during this period that new initiatives were most enthusiastically pursued and the rationale for them most persuasively developed. With the election of a Liberal–National coalition in March 1996 after 13 years in opposition, greater stress, at least in declaratory policy, was placed on bilateral relationships. Yet the change of government represented a less radical break with the past than official rhetoric would suggest. To begin with there were constant references to the critical role performed by multilateral institutions and coalitions, both regionally and globally, in the pursuit of national interests and the strengthening of crucial bilateral relationships.[187] The Howard government, it is true, devoted much less energy to institutional innovation and concentrated instead on demonstrating the vitality of the ANZUS alliance and entrenching the US presence in East Asia. Yet it remained actively involved in all existing regional institutions, including APEC and the ASEAN Regional Forum (ARF). Indeed, it soon realized that multilateral processes and institutions could at times deliver useful, even crucial, outcomes which were beyond the reach of bilateral diplomacy. Canberra's strenuous attempts to gain ARF support for a code of conduct to manage tensions generated by rival territorial claims in the South China Sea was a case in point. So was the Howard government's use of the 1999 APEC summit to gather support for its proposed peacekeeping plan for East Timor. More remarkable still were its intense and sustained efforts to involve the United Nations in the resolution of the conflict, and in particular to maintain a close and co-operative relationship with the UN Secretary-General.

In any case, the accent on multilateralism even during the Labor years was in part designed to enhance bilateral relationships, which is not to say that execution always matched intention. Nowhere was the connection between bilateral and multilateral strategies more apparent than in the case of Japan. From the mid-1980s Australian governments made it clear that they welcomed the prospect of Japan developing a louder voice and more authoritative influence in global and regional affairs, not merely in economic but in 'political and strategic' terms,[188] including participation in UN peacekeeping and even contributions to collective security arrangements.[189] However, as with trade so with security, there was a clearly discernible desire on Australia's part to prevent a return to great power rivalries in the region. This meant cementing Japan's re-emergence as a great power within a stabilizing institutional framework. In the 1995 *Joint Declaration on the Australia–Japan Partnership*, Japan referred to Australia as 'an indispensable partner in regional affairs', while Australia expressed support for Japanese membership of the UN Security Council, and both sides pledged to strengthen their own security dialogue and co-operate in the development of the ASEAN Regional Forum.[190]

By virtue of its ANZUS connection and its close ties with both Japan and the United States, Australia seemed well placed to help smooth the friction between the two countries. Indeed, for the Howard government, maintaining the US–Japan security relationship was a precondition of regional stability.[191] Nor was this the only cementing factor: at the sub-regional level, Australia's substantial experience in defence collaboration, including co-operative air and maritime exercises with ASEAN countries, as well as in UN peacekeeping activities, was bound to be of great interest to Tokyo at a time when it was intent on raising its own regional security profile.[192] Yet none of this should obscure the limitations of the partnership, in particular the cultural and political distance separating the two societies, Tokyo's preoccupation with issues of Northeast Asian security as against Canberra's focus on Southeast Asia, and the still lingering historical sensitivities associated with the Second World War.

By the mid-1990s, for Australia as for many other countries in the region, the bilateral and multilateral strands of diplomacy were inextricably entwined. The particular combination of strands might vary in different periods or with different governments, or even on different issues and in different relationships, but their close interconnection was readily apparent. Less obvious was the effectiveness with which governments blended the different elements of their diplomacy and the particular contribution they made to the management of regional conflict. Our examination of Australia's policies *vis-à-vis* the United States and Japan has already shed some light on these two related questions. We now propose to widen the analysis by considering a few instances in which Australian governments had to handle the possibility or actuality of regional tension or conflict.

On assuming office the Hawke government was committed to pursuing a more activist policy in Indochina, and in particular to restoring relations with Vietnam. This latter policy was a source of irritation to both the United States and ASEAN, both of which were then intent on isolating Vietnam. In deference to US and ASEAN views, Canberra proceeded cautiously in its dealings with Hanoi and instead concentrated its attention on the Cambodian conflict, the resolution of which appeared to hold the key to a constructive and durable relationship between Vietnam and its neighbours. The first significant Australian initiative came with Bill Hayden's six-point peace proposal in July 1984. Though not well received at the time by Indonesia, which had been delegated by ASEAN to explore diplomatic avenues to Hanoi, the proposal gained considerable currency, and its main principles would eventually underpin the framework of the Paris comprehensive settlement.[193] However, it was not until July–August 1989 and the impasse reached at the Paris International Conference on Cambodia that Australia would be presented with another major opportunity to influence events. The stumbling block at the Paris Conference had been the composition of the proposed quadripartite transitional administration, and more specifically the role to be assigned to the Khmer Rouge. To overcome this problem Australia had proposed that the United Nations be directly involved in the administration of Cambodia during the transitional period, and in particular assume responsibility for the conduct of free and fair general elections. While preserving the main guidelines of the political settlement developed at the Paris Conference, the Australian initiative envisaged a critical role for the United Nations and a formula whereby Cambodia's seat at the United Nations would be either declared vacant or transferred to a neutral representative Cambodian body for the duration of the transitional period.[194]

Australian diplomacy proved remarkably successful, with the permanent five eventually reaching agreement on a framework document setting out the guidelines for a political settlement of the Cambodian conflict, including possible UN supervision and control of key government functions during the transitional period and the deployment of some 10 000 UN peacekeeping troops and 10 000 civilian personnel. The plan was expected to cost between \$3.6 billion and \$6 billion.[195] The breakthrough, it should be stressed, had come not simply because of the careful crafting and timeliness of the ideas put forward by Australia, but because of the intensive diplomacy which had involved a skilful blend of bilateral and multilateral mechanisms and processes. Over a period of seven weeks, during December 1989–January 1990, Michael Costello, then Deputy Secretary of the Department of Foreign Affairs and Trade (DFAT), had 30 major meetings with key players in13 countries, notably with the various Cambodian factions, all five UN permanent members, the UN Secretariat, Indonesia and Thailand (the attitudes of the last two being crucial to any prospect of a favourable ASEAN consensus). While the actual implementation of the agreements, the performance of the UN Transitional Authority in Cambodia (UNTAC) and political developments inside Cambodia in the aftermath of UNTAC's withdrawal fell short of expectations, Australia's role had at least broken the diplomatic logjam and subsequently helped at critical moments to endow the peace process with renewed momentum.

Australia's diplomatic forays into regional conflict resolution or conflict prevention were not always as dramatic, and certainly not as carefully conceived or assiduously executed as in the Cambodian case. Diplomatic inertia, powerful domestic constituencies, international pressures or a particular reading of Australia's strategic and economic interests often made it difficult to exercise comparable intellectual, tactical or organizational leadership. The East Timor conflict offers perhaps the most graphic illustration of the scope and limitations of Australian diplomacy. For reasons of space it is not possible to offer here a detailed account of Australia's role in the conflict. Suffice it to say that, following Indonesia's annexation of East Timor in December 1975, successive Australian governments of different political persuasions found it extraordinarily difficult to come to terms with the ethical or political complexities of the dispute. Though vaguely supportive of the principle of self-determination, in practice Australian governments proceeded step by step to extend *de facto*, then *de jure,* recognition to Indonesian sovereignty over East Timor, and eventually to conclude in 1989 with Jakarta the Timor Gap Zone of Co-operation Treaty. Described by Gareth Evans as 'the most substantial bilateral agreement concluded in the 40-year history of Australia–Indonesia relations', [196] the treaty purported to establish the legal basis on which Indonesia and Australia would share out the oil and gas resources in the 60 000 square miles of seabed off the coast of East Timor. Notwithstanding the consistency with which the policy was articulated from the mid-1970s to the mid-1990s, its underlying rationale underwent subtle but significant change.

During the Whitlam and Fraser periods, the survival of the Suharto regime was widely perceived as a bulwark against further communist inroads in Southeast Asia. Reflecting on the prevailing ideological mood, the principal architect of Australia's Indonesia policy at the time, Richard Woolcott, subsequently wrote:

> The Cold War was at its height. Saigon had just fallen to the Vietcong. There were real concerns . . . that East Timor could have become a 'Southeast Asian Cuba', as Indonesian Army officers put it then. The Association of South-East Asian Nations, still in its formative stages, was anxious to strengthen regional security and to avoid the emergence of a weak, leftish mini-state in the region.[197]

It seems reasonable to infer that Australia's ANZUS connections, that is to say its identification with wider western, and in particular American, interests and perceptions, exerted a decisive influence over its East Timor policy.

Though Cold War considerations gradually waned in importance during the 1980s, Australian policy remained predicated on two assumptions: first, that the association with Indonesia, and with the Suharto government in particular, was of such diplomatic, strategic and economic significance that Canberra could not allow the entire bilateral relationship to be jeopardized by an overtly pro-East Timorese policy, which might in any case prove counter-productive; second, that with the passage of time and with the benefit of low-key diplomacy on Australia's part, the conflict, even if not fully resolved, would at least subside in intensity, particularly if Jakarta could be persuaded to improve its human rights record in East Timor. Neither of these closely related assumptions was validated by subsequent events. The controversy simply refused to go away: a strong Indonesian military presence in East Timor of up to four battalions and the persistent crackdown on dissent giving rise to periodic reports of killings, arrests and torture, combined with continuing East Timor opposition to Indonesian rule to keep the issue under the international spotlight. On the other hand, Canberra's determination to cultivate close ties with Jakarta, culminating in expanded defence co-operation arrangements and the signing in December 1995 of a bilateral security agreement, did not appear to make the Indonesian government more responsive to Australian representations.

With the fall of Suharto and the escalation of violence in the territory, events began to unfold at a pace and in a direction which no Australian government had foreseen and for which the Howard government was ill prepared. To make matters worse, it soon became apparent that the Indonesian armed forces were arming and protecting pro-integration militias, an assessment subsequently corroborated by numerous sources.[198] After a prolonged period of indecision, the Australian Prime Minister wrote to Indonesian President B.J. Habibie in December 1998 urging Jakarta to engage in a negotiating process which would at least entertain the prospect of independence. Though representing a radical break from existing policy, the Australian initiative came at a time when those advising Habibie were already predisposed to extricating Indonesia from East Timor.[199] Thereafter the Australian government was unable to retain the initiative, at times giving the impression that it still preferred autonomy to independence, and that its primary concern was the call on Australian resources which East Timorese independence might imply. A clearer and more persuasive stance might have argued for a phased approach to independence, allowing for a transitional period which might lessen the likelihood and intensity of violence within post-independence East Timor, and pave the way for a continuing and constructive association with Indonesia.

At the declaratory level, Australian policy was spared the need for further improvization with the signing in May 1999 of the UN-sponsored agreement between Portugal and Indonesia. In providing for a UN-supervised ballot by the end of August 1999, in which the East Timorese would effectively be given a choice between autonomy and independence, the agreement represented the most important breakthrough in the 25-year long conflict. Several questions nevertheless remained unanswered. Would the armed militia and their Indonesian backers allow a fair and free ballot to be conducted? And if a pro-independence vote were to emerge, would they be prepared to accept it? What would Australia's response be in the event of sustained violence either before or after the ballot? Would it support and participate in a UN peacekeeping operation? Would such support, let alone participation, be conditional upon Indonesia's approval? In coming to terms with these and related questions the Australian government had to contend with highly volatile conditions in both Indonesia and East Timor. What greatly complicated and perhaps marred its diplomacy was a policy framework that was essentially reactive, and had yet to think through the consequences of an independent East Timor or the changes that might be necessary to the Australia–Indonesia relationship if such an eventuality were to be accommodated.

Right through the first eight months of 1999, Canberra attempted to downplay the seriousness of the security situation in East Timor. Yet media reports and much intelligence at its disposal clearly pointed to the complicity of the Indonesian military, notably its special forces Kopassus, in establishing, fostering, equipping and co-ordinating the militia. Their express purpose was to intimidate East Timorese against voting for independence and, should these tactics fail, to implement a 'scorch' East Timor policy. Two considerations appear to have motivated Australia's response: a reluctance to jeopardize the ties it had so assiduously cultivated with the Suharto government over the preceding three decades and a concomitant fear of playing a leading advocacy role in favour of a UN peacekeeping or peace enforcement operation. Buttressing the first consideration was the belief that, by applying discrete pressure the international community generally, and Australia in particular by virtue of its privileged access to key elements of the Indonesian military, would be able to avert the excessive use of force both before and after the plebiscite.[200] The second consideration, closely related to the first, rested on the assumption that there was little international appetite for a large-scale UN intervention, in which case Australia might have to shoulder most of the burden and in the process irreparably damage the 'special relationship' with Indonesia.

Using the military and diplomatic channels available to it, Canberra sought to dissuade Jakarta from arming and encouraging the militia, but to no avail. By April 1999, the Howard government was in possession of several intelligence assessments linking Wiranto with the militia,[201] and by June–July decided to share some of that information with UN and US officials. It continued, however, to hope against hope that UNAMET, assisted by a modest unarmed police force, would successfully oversee the conduct of the ballot and the sensitive post-ballot phase. It was only after the outbreak of frenzied militia-driven violence in the week immediately following the ballot that Foreign Minister Downer finally raised the idea of a 'coalition of the willing'. With unprecedented speed, the Security Council authorized (on 15 September 1999) the creation of a multinational force, to be known as INTERFET, with a mandate to restore peace and security in East Timor and to protect and support UNAMET in carrying out its tasks. The first contingent of the INTERFET force, made up primarily of Australian troops, arrived in Dili a week later under the leadership of an Australian commander, Major-General Peter Cosgrove. Despite the sizeable personnel contributions of two Asian countries, Thailand and the Philippines, and the more modest participation of several other countries, INTERFET was widely perceived as inspired, funded and organized by Australia. The Indonesian reaction was predictably swift and bitter. On 16 September Jakarta severed the four-year old bilateral security agreement. A few days later, amid rising anti-Australian sentiment in Indonesia, including a shooting attack on the Australian embassy, Habibie accused Australia of interference in East Timor and of having provoked a serious deterioration in relations between the two countries.[202]

Australian diplomacy was struggling to adjust to the confused and politically charged situation inside Indonesia, where the process of democratization had yet to assert itself over substantial elements of the military still intent on preserving the old order or at least derailing any policies injurious to their interests. Riding high on widespread popular support at home for the peacekeeping operation, the Australian Prime Minister chose this moment to enunciate the so-called 'Howard doctrine'. Envisaging for Australia a 'deputy' peacekeeping role in the region to complement the global policeman role of the United States, Howard foreshadowed increased defence spending and less emphasis on 'special relationships', notions which were, later enshrined in the government's defence green paper released in June 2000, but whose applicability to the so-called 'arc of instability' in Australia's near north was not entirely apparent. Australian policy had yet to come to terms with the disjuncture between defence policy geared primarily to great power alliances and inter-state conflicts and security policies equipped to deal with the spill-over effects of ethnic, religious and other internal conflicts now besetting various parts of Southeast Asia and Melanesia.

Encouraged by the apparent success of its involvement in East Timor, Howard argued that Australia was now perceived as a country

> able to do something that probably no other country could do; because of the special characteristics we have; because we occupy that special place – we are a European, Western civilisation with North America, but here we are in Asia.[203]

The new triumphalist tone in Australia's regional diplomacy, coinciding with Indonesia's extraordinary moment of weakness and ASEAN's groping efforts to regain a sense of direction, was certainly not calculated to win friends and influence people in Southeast Asia. Responding to intense and widespread regional criticism, the Howard government moved quickly to disown the intentions or implications attributed to the new doctrine without, however, offering in its place a persuasive set of principles that would govern Australia's future approach to regional security. There was certainly no clear indication as to how Canberra would handle the new triangular relationship with Dili and Jakarta. Decisions had still to be made as to the precise financial and political support Australia would offer an independent East Timor, and the steps that would be taken to re-establish a constructive and durable relationship with Indonesia.

The ambiguities and limitations of Australian diplomacy were not confined to East Timor. Despite differences of scale and context, they were also evident in its handling of the Bougainville conflict and in the bilateral relationship with Malaysia. As in East Timor, a substantial movement for independence had emerged in Bougainville, fuelled in this case by widespread local dissatisfaction with the operation of the Panguna copper mine owned by Bougainville Copper Ltd, a subsidiary of Rio Tinto. Australia's capacity to act as a moderating influence in the ensuing conflict between the Bougainville Revolutionary Army (BRA) and the PNG Defence Forces was severely constrained by its special relationship with Papua New Guinea (PNG), itself a legacy of Australian colonial rule. Here again Canberra's policy, under both Labor and Coalition governments, was premised on the notion that Bouganvillean secession would precipitate the fragmentation of PNG and the creation of small unstable states vulnerable to domination by foreign powers potentially hostile to Australia.[204]

To the extent that the Indonesian government, conscious of its own contested authority in West Irian, strongly favoured maintenance of the status quo, Australian policy-makers had an added incentive to thwart the Bouganvillean drive for self-determination. In keeping with this approach they continued to make substantial allocations to the PNG defence budget without attempting close supervision of the use that the PNG military made of the equipment, training and funding supplied to them. Retaining close ties with PNG's military and economic elites was seen as crucial to the defence of Australia's security interests. In actuality, by adopting a position so clearly at odds with Bouganvillean aspirations, the Australian government effectively deprived itself of a meaningful role in the settlement of the dispute.[205] The running was instead left to New Zealand, which brokered a series of agreements, thereby making possible the cessation of armed conflict and a gradual return to normalcy and restoration of services.[206] Australia would in due course participate in the negotiating process, assume primary responsibility for monitoring the cease-fire and commit some A$300 million over five years to the reconstruction of Bougainville. However, its ambiguous position on the future of the Panguna mine and its seeming inability to pursue a policy of equidistance between the major parties reduced its legitimacy and effectiveness as honest broker. A unitary PNG state continued to be seen as essential to the effective projection of Australia's interests and regional influence.

With Malaysia, Australia could boast a longer and more intimate association than with any other Southeast Asian country. Common membership of the British Commonwealth, Australia's military involvement in the Malayan Emergency, its participation in the Commonwealth force that would be stationed in Malaya under ANZAM, the financial and technical assistance it provided Malaysia in the 1950s and 1960s, partly through the Colombo Plan, the conclusion of the Five Power Defence Arrangement in 1971, the establishment of an RAAF base at Butterworth near Penang, had all contributed to a co-operative relationship between the two governments. Yet serious tensions were to emerge during the 1980s and 1990s, which was all the more surprising given that trade, defence ties, tourism between the two countries and the number of Malaysian students pursuing their higher education in Australia had all continued to register healthy rates of growth. These tensions revolved largely around a series of incidents, each of which seemed relatively innocuous, but which cumulatively produced a partial, and at the end of the 1990s still simmering, estrangement between the two polities and their respective governments.[207]

The most notable of the incidents were the trial and execution of two Australians (Barlow and Chambers) for possession of heroin in Malaysia (1985–6), the showing of the *Embassy* series on ABC television beginning in September 1990, the screening in March 1992 of the Australian film *Turtle Beach* based on the book of the same name, the alleged abduction of the two Gillespie children in July 1992, Prime Minister Keating's reference to his Malaysian counterpart as 'recalcitrant' on the occasion of the first APEC summit in November 1993, Canberra's noticeable irritation with Mahathir's rhetorical and policy response to the 1997 financial crisis and his handling of Anwar Ibrahim's arrest and subsequent trial (1998–9), and Mahathir's sharply critical assessment of Australia's leadership of the peace enforcement operation in East Timor.

With the possible exception of the 'recalcitrant' episode, which brought to a climax the conflicting attitudes of the two governments to APEC, none of the disagreements surrounding these incidents was initially concerned with the core of the diplomatic or economic relationship. The two governments, their senior ministers and diplomats became involved only after the event. Almost every incident, on the other hand, touched a raw cultural or psychological nerve.[208] It was as if on each occasion the aggrieved party, usually Malaysia, had taken exception to the way its culture, society, system of justice or political leadership had been (mis)represented by the other. In that sense, these episodes were but the expression of a deeper rift between an increasingly self-confident Malaysia, conscious of its newly found prosperity and political self-assertion, and an Australia committed to an ambitious yet ambivalent policy of engagement with Asia.

It was not just that the two countries, particularly under Mahathir and Keating, had different strategic objectives and styles, or even that Malaysian cultural sensitivities had been offended by Australia's arrogance, but that cultural and political currents within each country had fused in ways which could not easily be reconciled. Mahathir was, rightly or wrongly, attempting to cultivate a distinctively Asian, or at least East Asian, ethos, a set of political and cultural values or presumptions which he could use as a platform from which to challenge western, and especially US, interests and priorities. Australian protestations to the contrary, Australia was perceived as essentially European in outlook, an ally of the United States and a beneficiary of continued western dominance. Placed in this context, the friction between Kuala Lumpur and Canberra becomes less puzzling. It was a case of politics becoming the victim of cultural distance, but also of politics using culture as its instrument.[209] In all of this, a great deal was at stake for Australia: the stability of the bilateral relationship itself; the future viability of the FPDA, further complicated by unresolved tensions between Malaysia and Singapore;[210] possible membership of the Asia–Europe Meeting (ASEM) process; and most importantly the very policy of enmeshment with Asia. Whether or not Australia established a durable economic and strategic association with Southeast Asia might well depend on its ability to bridge vast and as yet relatively unexplored cultural and political distances.

It remains to say a word about China, which the 1997 review of Australia's defence policy described as 'the most important factor for change in the regional strategic environment'.[211] During the greater part of the 1970s and 1980s Australian governments entertained relatively optimistic expectations about the complementarity of Australian and Chinese economic and security interests. While that optimism was temporarily punctured by the tragic events of June 1989, Beijing calculated rightly that the volume of bilateral trade, totalling some $3 billion in 1990, and the promise of an expanding Chinese market would, despite periodic tensions on human rights issues, ensure an adequate working relationship between the two countries. When articulating Australia's China policy in 1995, Gareth Evans noted the continuing progress of trade relations – two-way trade in goods in 1994 had reached $6.2 billion – and the prospect of significant growth in the export of Australian manufactures and services, in line with increased disposable income in China. For this healthy economic relationship to prosper, it was necessary to insulate it from undue acrimony over human rights abuses in China – that was presumably the function of the institutionalized bilateral human rights dialogue – and to manage Beijing's participation 'in cooperative arrangements characterized by transparency and confidence-building'.[212] Australia, it was argued, wished to pursue a policy of constructive engagement with China, rather than a policy of containment, and to this end supported China's active involvement in the region's emerging economic and security architecture, notably APEC and ARF, and its accession to the World Trade Organization.

The Hawke and Keating governments had a keen sense of the dangers that would inevitably flow from any deterioration in Sino-American relations. As Gareth Evans put it,

> the interests of both countries . . . are best served by accommodation, promoting dialogue and understanding of each other's positions – intensified dialogue rather than rhetoric; and negotiation rather than polemics.[213]

This formulation carried with it a good measure of deliberate ambiguity. It signalled to the Chinese that Australia would use its limited influence to dissuade Washington from applying undue pressure on Beijing on any of the contentious issues, be it weapons proliferation, human rights, market access or the Taiwan dispute. It carefully avoided, however, giving any indication of the way an Australian government would respond should a crisis emerge on any one or a combination of these issues. Would Australia side with the United States, perhaps with China, or adopt some intermediate or neutral position?

The ambiguity of these signals was compounded by Labor's defeat at the March 1996 elections. Several of the Howard government's initiatives in its first few months of office were negatively received in Beijing. The axing of the soft loans scheme known as the Development Import Finance Facility (DIFF), the upgrading of Australia's defence links with the United States, unofficial ministerial visits to Taiwan, the proposed sale of uranium to Taiwan, the Dalai Lama's visit to Australia and his meetings with Howard and Downer, Australian criticism of Chinese military exercises off the coast of Taiwan, and public statements – most forcefully expressed by Defence Minister Ian McLachlan – critical of China's increasing diplomatic and strategic assertiveness, were interpreted in Beijing as evidence of a policy that was distinctly more pro-American and less comfortable with China's growing regional influence. The Howard government would eventually seek to correct this impression and reaffirm its support for a constructive Sino-American relationship as the only feasible basis for regional stability.[214]

During his visit to Beijing in May 1999 Defence Minister John Moore confirmed that the two countries had a shared commitment to a substantive bilateral defence relationship and a common interest in regional peace and security.[215] During a visit to the United States in July 1999, Howard went so far as to deliver an oblique critique of Washington's China policy, arguing that progress would depend on Australia and the United States choosing 'to engage with China in solving problems, rather than stay at a distance and lecture from the sidelines'.[216] Almost simultaneously, the Australian Foreign Minister, Alexander Downer, while visiting China, compared Washington's tariff regime unfavourably with China's willingness to open its markets, and announced that Canberra had finalized an agreement with Beijing on conditions for the latter's entry to the World Trade Organization.[217] President Jiang Zemin's successful if uneventful visit to Australia in September 1999 and John Moore's sympathetic remarks following the US bombing of the Chinese embassy in Belgrade had also contributed to a more mature Sino-Australian security dialogue. Two key questions, however, remained unanswered: would Australian governments be able to integrate economic and security issues into a coherent China policy, and how would they respond to a deterioration in the Sino-American relationship, particularly over the Taiwan dispute?

The ambiguities of Australia's China policy shed useful light on an even larger question. Did the bilateral and multilateral policies of the 1980s represent a change of direction, a greater capacity on Australia's part to influence the course of events and shape its external environment? To put it differently, did Australia's semi-peripheral status in the region undergo any discernible qualitative change? For many this was a period in which Australia made a distinctive contribution to the security and political economy of the region. Enmeshment with Asia became the dominant theme of official pronouncements, the centrepiece of numerous proposals and diplomatic initiatives, and the justification for new and often ambitious exercises in conflict prevention and conflict resolution, as well as for expanded defence co-operation programmes. More than that, the new outlook on Asia provided the rationale for a comprehensive policy of economic restructuring based on fiscal stringency, financial deregulation and trade liberalization. The stated intention was to make Australia's manufacturing and service industries more competitive, hence better equipped to take advantage of Asia's expanding markets. The increase in the proportion of Australia's output destined for export in the late 1980s and early 1990s was indeed credited by governments for the success of their structural reforms. According to one official estimate, Australia's international competitiveness had improved by as much as 30 per cent between 1983 and 1993 in contrast to the 17 per cent decline recorded during the preceding decade.[218]

If durability is taken to be the principal yardstick of success for the policy of engagement with Asia, then the overriding importance attached to economic considerations was both an asset and a liability. It was an asset in so far as it gave the policy greater ballast, providing key economic players but also the wider public with a strong incentive to identify Australia's future with Asia, while at the same time endowing the Australian economy with sufficient muscle to command the attention of actual or potential Asian partners. It was a liability in that it made Australia's commitment to Asia dependent largely on the profitability of commercial and financial transactions and the viability of existing or proposed economic arrangements. Though security issues also attracted the attention of policy-makers, it was as if the Asian focus of Australia's external relations revolved almost exclusively around the prospect of economic gain. As subsequent events would show, this was a high-risk strategy.

Nowhere was the risk factor more clearly apparent than in the zeal with which the Keating government pursued the APEC option. Much space will be devoted to an analysis of APEC in *Regionalism in the New Asia-Pacific Order*. For the moment two observations should suffice. By the late 1990s it was by no means clear that APEC would achieve the trade liberalization objectives it had set itself. Many member states, Australia included, remained hesitant about full or immediate implementation of agreements reached, particularly in the case of politically sensitive industries. More importantly perhaps, it was unlikely that either the United States or Japan would allow its trade interests and strategies to be determined by APEC. Nor was the Australian hope that APEC would serve as a forum for the resolution of US–Japan trade frictions likely to be realized. Actual or potential conflicts of economic interest aside, the assumption that the East Asian economies would continue to expand at anything like the growth rates of the 1980s and early 1990s was now open to serious challenge. Even if the financial crisis of the late 1990s were to give way to steady recovery, few economies would be able to return to the same upward trajectory. Moreover, disparities in economic performance between countries, which the crisis had exacerbated, would in all probability widen still further. How the Australian economy, notwithstanding its early ability to weather the storm, would navigate in such turbulent waters remained to be seen.

Two other limitations would seriously impact on the effectiveness of Australia's regional role. Its security policy was, as we have already noted, subject to a profound ambivalence, which the election of the Howard government in 1993 had greatly accentuated. The renewed emphasis on the US alliance, now viewed as 'a crucial element in the United States' permanent presence in the Asia Pacific region', and the revival of forward defence thinking with its implications for increased combat capabilities, could not but cast a shadow on the policy of engagement with Asia. The 1997 Strategic Review left no doubt that the planning of Australia's force structure was predicated on the possibility of 'a direct contribution to the maintenance of broader regional stability'.[219] The FFG guided-missile frigates, ANZAC-class submarines, upgraded F-111 strategic bombers and FA-18 fighters, the decision to equip many of these platforms with longer-range and more accurate weapon systems and provide the army with expanded amphibious capabilities, and the acquisition of early warning and control aircraft (AWACS) were all part of a force structure designed to defend Australian territory but also contribute to forward power projection.[220]

The fire power of Australia's defence assets was vulnerable to periodic budget restrictions, but also dependent on high levels of interoperability with US armed forces. Greater access by the Australian Defence Force (ADF) to US technologies was meant to enhance Australia's contribution 'to coalition operations, notably in the submarine, airborne early warning and control, and combat aircraft fields'.[221] The staging of large and complex joint military exercises, the ten-year extension of the Pine Gap agreement and the new arrangements that would follow the planned closure of the Nurrungar station in 2000 were additional elements of a close defence relationship, but one whose strategic priorities would be set largely, if not exclusively, by the senior partner. The disparities in power between allies and the overwhelming technological and intelligence leverage available to the United States precluded any other outcome. The absence of a competent, independent strategic assessment capability within the Australian intelligence bureaucracy compounded Canberra's dependence on the United States as much in the evaluation of the security environment as in the formulation of policy responses.[222] The constraints implicit in the ANZUS connection were likely to apply regardless of how the US presence in Asia might evolve.[223] To the extent that Australia was seen as a proxy for

US interests, the credibility of its regional diplomacy was bound to suffer. Should future US policies seriously conflict with those of China, Japan or ASEAN, whether over Taiwan, Korea, the Spratlys or Indonesia, or on issues of trade or finance, the effect on Australia could well prove debilitating.

Important as were the economic and strategic limitations on Australia's freedom of action, the salience of the cultural factor cannot be underestimated. Any society's external posture will ultimately reflect its sense of identity, its historical affinities and cultural outlook. In 1995 Gareth Evans confidently spoke of the 'explosion in "Asia consciousness"' within Australia and of its likely contribution to a 'new cross-fertilised Asia-Pacific civilisation'.[224] Speaking barely 18 months later, the new Prime Minister, John Howard, articulated a much narrower conception of Australia's place in the world, which he appropriately expressed in the form of three negative propositions: 'Australia does not claim to be Asian . . . we do not have to choose between history and geography . . . Neither do I see Australia as a bridge between Asia and the West'.[225] These words were spoken in the context of an unedifying domestic debate on issues of race, for which the rise of the Hanson phenomenon was the catalyst. The fear of Asianization, having manifested itself in more restrictive immigration and refugee policies even before the defeat of the Keating government, served as a useful reminder of the powerful psycho-social pressures bearing upon the making of Australian foreign policy. The attitudes of political leaders aside, an assertive, outward-looking Australian foreign policy premised on sustained and co-operative relationships with Asia had yet to receive the necessary levels of public support and cross-cultural acceptance.

PACIFIC ISLANDS

Its precise boundaries might be the subject of continuing debate, but Asia Pacific had by the 1980s become widely accepted as a recognizable geographical and political entity. Yet, when it came to the small island states and territories that dot the Pacific ocean, remarkably few studies of the region thought it necessary to make them an integral part of their analysis. It was as if the region consisted largely, if not exclusively, of its Asian rim, and that the Pacific basin was a 'politically empty', irrelevant expanse of water. By virtue of the size of their economy, territory and population, not to mention their geographical distance from major centres of power, the Pacific islands did indeed seem marginal to the geopolitical and geoeconomic equation. There was more, however, to the neglect of the Pacific basin than meets the eye. The relatively low political and security profile of the region was in part the byproduct of intellectual laziness, but also of a residual colonial mentality. Yet when set against the backdrop of their vast and newly established exclusive economic zones, their strategic location between East Asia and the Americas, their forced participation in the development of the British, American and French nuclear arsenals, and the enormous environmental challenges to which they were exposed, these microstates seemed destined to play a secondary but analytically illuminating role in the unfolding Asia-Pacific drama.

This brief overview is not intended to describe, let alone explain, the unique political and economic circumstances of each Pacific island state, but to highlight a number of recurring themes in their individual and collective responses to the challenges of independent statehood. The profound insecurity experienced by most of these microstates and their peripheral status at both regional and global levels constitute in a sense the overarching theme of their recent history. Almost without exception, the end of colonial rule gave rise to weak states, with relatively undeveloped institutions, high levels of economic dependence, deepseated social, economic and political tensions, acute vulnerability to pressures exerted by core and semi-peripheral states, and limited capabilities to manage or contain the impact of natural or man-made disasters. Not surprisingly, many of these states, conscious of their weaknesses, sought to disguise them or turn them to their advantage by developing mechanisms for more effective regional consultation and co-ordination.

For purposes of analytical convenience the ensuing discussion will examine these closely related themes under three headings: independence and the politics of disorder; economic dependence and insecurity; and external vulnerabilities and the politics of dependence. First, a few words by way of background. Pacific island states can be categorized into four groups: the relatively large countries of Papua New Guinea, Fiji, the Solomon Islands, New Caledonia and Vanuatu, with populations in excess of 100 000, a significant agricultural base, a range of industries (usually, forestry, fisheries, agriculture, tourism, mining) and large exclusive economic zones (EEZs); a second category comprising Tonga and Western Samoa, with small areas under agriculture, limited tourism potential, no minerals but a reasonable resource base; a third group of resource-poor countries (the Cook Islands, Kiribati, Niue, Tokelau and Tuvalu) with comparatively large EEZs but little or no capacity to develop them; and a fourth category, notably Guam, the Marshall Islands, Palau and French Polynesia, whose economic position was governed by a continuing association with the United States or France, based largely on the strategic interests of the colonial power.[226] Formal political systems varied widely, from representative democracy in Papua New Guinea to neo-traditional monarchy in Tonga, and periodic experiments with authoritarian rule as in post-coup Fiji. Substantial variations also existed with respect to the exercise of sovereignty, with the majority enjoying membership of the United Nations as fully fledged sovereign states, a few operating as quasi-sovereign, self-governing entities (for example, the Marshall Islands, Federated States of Micronesia), and quite a number still subject to various forms of colonial rule (in particular, American Samoa, Guam, the Northern Marianas, French Polynesia, New Caledonia).[227] It is also worth noting that political independence came relatively late to the region, with Nauru, Tonga and Fiji among the first to achieve independent status in 1968, June 1970 and October 1970 respectively. Of all the pacific island states only one, Vanuatu, chose to join the Non-Aligned Movement.

Independence and the Politics of Disorder

As with many of the new states of Asia and Africa, political independence, far from ushering in a new era of political stability, brought in its wake varying degrees of turmoil, lawlessness and even the prospect of secession. Though few were in any serious danger of collapse, many of these polities lacked the social cohesion or political and administrative infrastructure needed to pursue coherent domestic and external policies. Despite the many advantages it enjoyed *vis-à-vis* other island states, not least size and extensive resource base, Papua New Guinea, after an initial period of relative stability under Michael Somare's leadership, would soon experience the debilitating impact of rising levels of criminal violence and social disorder, political corruption and brittle political institutions. Endemic gang violence, often referred to as *raskolism,* social banditry in certain rural areas and tribal feuds in the highlands became major sources of personal insecurity, impediments to economic growth and contributing factors in the declining legitimacy of political leadership.[228]

The response of the state to these multiple challenges was at best inadequate and at worst counterproductive. Financial constraints on the state's policing capabilities prompted on the one hand a marked increase in the number of private security firms, and on the other frequent recourse to overt displays of force, including police raids, curfews and states of emergency. Far from countering rising levels of violence, the militarization of policing agencies served to accentuate societal insecurity and undermine public respect for the rule of law.[229] In the political arena the absence of effective administrative and legal controls enabled many politicians to gain privileged access to public funds, thereby compounding the problem of corruption. In pursuing their own narrowly defined interests, foreign companies had themselves contributed to corrupt practices. To cite one notorious case in the late 1980s, the report of the Barnett Commission of Inquiry into the Forest Industry levelled damaging criticism at Ted Diro as Minister of Forests. The scandal led to the downfall of the Paias Wingti government in July 1988. In September 1991 Ted Diro was found guilty by a special leadership tribunal of 81 charges of corruption. The Governor-General, Sir Seiro Eri, a close associate of Diro, rather than dismiss him as the law required, sought to reinstate him to his previous ministerial positions. It was only after a constitutional impasse lasting several days that Eri resigned as Governor-General and Diro resigned from Parliament.

These were not isolated instances of political misconduct nor was their impact confined to the domestic arena. Particularly instructive in this context was the Sandline affair. In January 1997 the Chan government hired the services of a private UK-based company, Sandline International, for the training of PNG security forces. In March 1997 the Commander of the PNG Defence Force, Brigadier General Singirok, announced that his forces would cease any co-operation with Sandline and accused the government of corruption in respect of the contract. Singirok was subsequently dismissed from his position, but Chan, now under strong pressure from the Australian government, suspended the Sandline project and established a commission of inquiry into the circumstances surrounding the contract. Having stepped aside for the inquiry, Chan resumed the prime ministership in early June, only to lose his seat in elections later that month. In the ensuing contractual dispute with the PNG government, Sandline sought damages plus the outstanding contract sum of $18 million. The International Arbitration Panel having ruled in favour of Sandline in October 1998, the PNG government subsequently lodged an appeal with the Queensland Supreme Court against the arbitration decision.

An even more bizarre sequence of events would see the collapse of the Bill Skate government in July 1999. Operating within a highly volatile political environment characterized by rapidly shifting political allegiances and an even more fragile economy, Skate had decided to extend diplomatic recognition to Taiwan.[230] The move was inspired by a desire to secure from Taiwan a large infusion of badly needed funds in the form of soft loans, partly with a view to servicing PNG's mounting debt obligations and meeting other urgent financial commitments. Within a matter of a few days, the see-saw in political fortunes would culminate in a dramatic parliamentary vote resulting in the formation of a new government with Mekere Morauta as Prime Minister, soon followed by an announcement that the decision to normalize relations with Taiwan had been rescinded.

No account, however brief, of the vagaries of PNG politics would be complete without reference to the Bougainville conflict, which epitomized the fragility of PNG political unity and the severe domestic and external constraints bearing upon the problem-solving capacities of the PNG state. Here, it is worth recalling that just a week prior to Papua New Guinea achieving its independence in September 1975, Bougainville leaders had proclaimed a unilateral declaration of independence. Their decision was taken following months of inconclusive negotiations with Port Moresby on the vexed question of royalty payments from the Panguna mine operated by Bougainville Cooper Ltd. With Bougainville failing to gain international support for its independence and a stand-off having been reached between the secessionists and riot police from Port Moresby, a political compromise helped to defuse the situation. In return for remaining part of PNG, Bougainville would be allowed to establish a provincial government with a sustained degree of autonomy. Over the ensuing 12 years separatist activity generally receded, but discontent with the uneven distribution of wealth from the mine continued to simmer.

The failure of the national and provincial governments to agree on terms for the review of existing arrangements rekindled Bouganvillean landowner militancy. The copper mine became the subject of sabotage in the late 1980s and was closed in 1989. Following an unsuccessful attempt to re-establish its authority by despatching riot police and military personnel, the PNG government withdrew its security forces in early 1990 and instead imposed a blockade on the island. The Bougainville Revolutionary Army, which was intent on achieving complete independence, now had effective control over a significant proportion of the territory. The violence led to the closure of most central and provincial government services, notably education and health, and the near-complete disruption of commercial activity.[231] Though Port Moresby regained partial control of parts of the island during 1992, it soon became evident that any attempt to capture the mine area or key urban centres would lead to a serious escalation of hostilities.[232] An uneasy stand-off had been reached, but by the late 1990s the Bougainville conflict had left thousands of people dead.[233] Many more thousands had been displaced or injured, or their health had been seriously impaired by virtue of the prolonged disruption to food and medical supplies.

The origins and implications of the Bougainville conflict are too complex for it to be reduced to a dispute about mining royalties. Though the landowners were profoundly dissatisfied with the inadequate compensation offered to them in return for the use of their land, several other concerns are worth noting: the alienation of the land, its physical destruction and the damage done to the environment; the disruption of cultural practices and lifestyles, including the loss of status and wealth associated with inheritance of land; continuing mistrust of Port Moresby's centralist tendencies; and the fear that Bougainville's distinctiveness and sense of identity might be eroded in the name of nation-building.[234] Similarly, for those in charge of the PNG state there was more to the dispute than the financial return on the mining operation. Precisely because their leadership role depended on the survival of the state, any attempt to reconsider or dismantle existing borders was seen as a threat to their status and power. The psychological and political gulf separating the two sides, coupled with the factional interests which developed over time on either side of the divide, helps to explain both the longevity and intractability of the dispute.

Attempts at conflict resolution, initiated by New Zealand as early as 1990, did not bear fruit until the first round of the Burnham talks, which produced the Burnham Declaration of July 1997. It would be several more months before the PNG, Australian and Solomons governments would participate directly in the second round of talks, which got under way in October 1997 and resulted in a truce. All parties agreed to a cessation of armed conflict and to the implementation of measures designed to enhance peace and reconciliation and facilitate the return of normalcy and restoration of services. A third round of talks established a Truce Monitoring Group to be led by New Zealand, with contributions from Australia, Fiji and Vanuatu. A fourth round yielded the Lincoln Agreement, which provided for 'a permanent and irrevocable cease-fire' to take effect at the end of April 1998, the election of a Bougainville Reconciliation Government by the end of 1998, and the phased demilitarization of Bougainville, including the disarming of the rebels and withdrawal of the PNG defence forces. The Loloata understanding reached between PNG and Bougainville in March 2000 envisaged continuing negotiations on a political settlement comprised of three successive stages: an interim provincial government to be established under PNG law; the election of an 'autonomous' provincial government; and at some later stage the holding of a referendum on independence.

The inevitable difficulties and delays encountered in the implementation of these agreements reflected lingering suspicion and mistrust on both sides and the profound reservations shared by the BRA and other pro-independence groups in Bougainville *vis-à-vis* the Australian government, which had now taken over New Zealand's leadership role in the peace process. Whereas New Zealand had adopted a strictly agnostic position on the issue of independence, Australia's attitude was widely interpreted as indistinguishable from that of the PNG government. Canberra committed A\$300 million over five years for the reconstruction of Bougainville, but it seemed intent on maintaining a privileged relationship with Papua New Guinea: it still provided PNG's defence forces with sustained assistance; it viewed the fragmentation of the PNG state as a threat to its long-term security interests; and, at least in the BRA's perception, Australia's hidden agenda was to re-open the copper mine. Considerable progress had been made, but the peace accords had deliberately sidestepped the two most sensitive issues: political independence for Bougainville and the future of the mine. These were the issues which went to the heart of the dispute, and over which both external and local parties were likely to exercise decisive influence.

Central as it was to Papua New Guinea's evolving political economy, the problem of internal security was also integral to the experience of several other Pacific island states and territories. In Fiji's case, ethnic divisions, which had never been far below the political surface, were the primary justification for the 1987 coups, and perhaps their driving force. Following the formation in April 1987 of a coalition government comprised of the Fiji Labour Party (FLP) and the National Federation Party (NFP), Lieutenant Colonel Rabuka, the army's third-ranking officer, initiated a military coup in May 1987, projecting himself as the defender of indigenous Fijian interests and the representative of the Fijian chiefs.[235] Once the Governor-General, Sir Ratu Penaia Ganilau, had dissolved Parliament and assumed executive authority, Rabuka launched a second coup in September 1987; he subsequently declared Fiji a Republic and abrogated the 1970 Constitution, effectively severing Fiji's links with the Crown and allowing its membership of the Commonwealth to lapse. A new constitution promulgated in July 1990 sought to guarantee political paramountcy to indigenous Fijians. Although it provided a framework for the return to parliamentary government, the new constitution entrenched communal divisions, creating significant inequalities in voting strength between groups and providing for an electoral system weighted heavily in favour of rural Fijians. Following the establishment of a Constitution Review Commission in 1994 and consideration of its recommendations by the Joint Parliamentary Select Committee in 1997, the constitution was amended to allow for more representative government in Fiji and a significant shift away from communally based politics.

The revised constitution came into effect on 27 July 1998, but it was as yet too early to evaluate the significance of the crisis unleashed by the 1987 coup.[236] Was it a mere aberration in a country where democratic institutions were the norm, or was it likely to foreshadow a prolonged period of racial tension and political instability? High levels of Indo-Fijian emigration after 1987 had altered Fiji's ethnic composition: the 1996 census indicated that Indians, who constituted a majority of the population at the time of the 1987 coups, now made up only 43.6 per cent and indigenous Fijians 51.1 per cent of the population. Notwithstanding these demographic trends, the May 1999 election gave the predominantly Indian FLP 37 of the 71 parliamentary seats. Though enjoying a parliamentary majority in its own right, the FLP, in the interests of gaining multi-racial support for its programme, formed a coalition government with three Fijian parties, the Fijian Association Party, the Party of National Unity and the newly formed Veitokani Ni Lewenivanua Vakaristo.[237] It soon became apparent that the multiracial government led by an Indian Prime Minister (Mahendra Chaudhry) would not easily withstand the strains of racial division and economic discontent, particularly as they became entangled with the vexed question of land use. The performance of Fiji's economy, influenced as much by external as by internal factors (about which more later), proved decisive both in shaping public perceptions and in determining the government's capacity to implement its programme of social and economic reform. Yet another coup, staged in May 2000 by George Speight and his supporters in the name of indigenous Fijian rights, resulted in senior members of the Chaudhry government, including the prime minister himself, being taken hostage in Suva's parliamentary compound. After two months of virtual paralysis in Fijian politics, the hostages were released, but with little prospect that the democratically elected government would be reinstated, or that the damage done to Fiji's economy, social cohesion, and diplomatic legitimacy would be easily repaired.

Numerous other examples of internal disorder can be cited. Vanuatu, which became an independent republic in July 1980, experienced several years of political stability under the leadership of the Vanua'aku Pati (VP), with Father Walter Lini as Prime Minister. However, following bitter internal divisions within the VP and the consequent fracturing of the previously secure anglophone majority, the December 1991 election saw the formation of a coalition government with the francophile Union of Moderate Parties (UMP) as the dominant partner. A succession of party splits, political realignments, cabinet reshuffles and court appeals during the 1990s mirrored and reinforced underlying societal tensions and significantly impeded the institutional cohesion of the Republic. Even more dramatic were the armed hostilities in the Solomon Islands in 1999-2000 that pitted the Malaitan Eagle Force militia against the Isatabu Freedom Movement militia and brought to the boil simmering inter-island rivalry. The recourse to violence, which soon degenerated into incipient ethnic cleansing and crude forms of political intimidation, effectively paralyzed the parliamentary process.

Though unfolding in vastly different circumstances, political tensions were equally apparent in territories which had yet to achieve full political independence. The Marshall Islands, site of 67 atomic and hydrogen bomb tests between 1946 and 1958, negotiated a Compact of Free Association with the United States in 1986. Under the Compact, the United States had undertaken to create a compensation fund for the victims of radioactive fallout. In return Marshallese claimants had to abandon cases pending in US courts, for which they were seeking payments estimated at $4 billion. It soon emerged that the $150 million grant promised by the United States would meet only a fraction of the compensation payments awarded by the Nuclear Claims Tribunal, with substantial land and environmental claims yet to be adjudicated.[238] Renegotiation of the Compact began in October 1999, with the Marshallese attempting to secure a more favourable financial package in return for guaranteeing the United States exclusive military access to their land and surrounding waters. The United States was also expected to retain the US Army Kwajalein Atoll/Kwajalein Missile Range (USAKA/KMR), now being used as a testing ground for a prototype National Missile Defence system (as well as the theatre missile defence naval programme), and considered by the US Department of Defense to be the only readily available facility suitable for full-scale testing of long-range missiles.[239] Tensions of a different kind, but again closely related to US strategic interests, also surfaced in Palau. We return to these in our discussion of external security issues.

The unresolved social and political frictions associated with residual colonial arrangements were not confined to former US trust territories in Micronesia. France's continuing presence in the Pacific, notably in French Polynesia and New Caledonia, had over the years generated a good deal of political emotion, and on occasions even political violence, both within the territories and in the region as a whole. While French Polynesia had attracted far more international attention because of France's nuclear testing programme at Mururoa, New Caledonia had in recent years experienced great political ferment as the Kanak struggle for independence gathered momentum in the 1970s and 1980s. Increasingly bitter clashes between *indépendantistes* and the loyal settler community, which resulted in significant loss of life during 1984–8, prompted the French government to initiate tripartite negotiations with the two contending parties, the pro-French Rally for New Caledonia in the Republic (PRCR) and the Kanak National Socialist Liberation Front (FLNKS). The resulting Matignon Accords of 1988 provided for greater local autonomy, but with France retaining executive responsibility in the key areas of defence, foreign affairs, health, education and telecommunications.

The carrot offered to the independence movement was the promise of a referendum on self-determination in 1998, which did not, however, materialize. With each side fearful that such a referendum might not produce its preferred outcome,[240] a new agreement was reached in May 1998 (the Noumea Accord), committing France to transferring over the next 15–20 years to New Caledonia's Territorial and Provincial Governments all powers except those pertaining to justice, public order, currency, defence and foreign affairs. Though the Kanak independence movement was far from achieving its principal objective, the agreement did at least deliver a new voting system designed to ensure its participation in any new government. The Noumea Accord was approved in a referendum by 72 per cent of New Caledonian voters and given detailed legal form by the French Parliament in February 1999.[241] A collegial government of 11 members was duly elected by proportional representation in May 1999.[242] The political compromise between Kanaks and French settlers remained nevertheless a precarious one. Persisting doubts as to how far the PRCR would co-operate in a power-sharing exercise with the FLNKS were compounded by worsening economic problems and industrial disputes, as the FLNKS sought to rectify the 'disequilibrium' in resource distribution.[243]

Economic Vulnerability

The political instability and limited freedom of action characteristic of most Pacific island states and territories were the more visible manifestations of powerful economic undercurrents. Generally speaking, these narrowly based economies suffered from extensive penetration by foreign plantations, mining operations and commercial enterprises and marked dependence 'on remittances, foreign and budget support grants for the maintenance and viability of even minimal levels of government services and infrastructural support'.[244] Economic conditions loomed large in the Pacific conception of security.[245]

Throughout the post-independence period, aid remained an essential component of the PNG government's revenue. During the 1970 and 1980s in a series of multiyear aid commitments Australia underwrote approximately 30 per cent of Papua New Guinea's budget.[246] Australia's predominance as a donor country would in due course be moderated by increases in other bilateral and multilateral contributions (primarily from Japan, the European Community and the Asian Development Bank) with the result that in the mid-1990s external financial support still accounted for some 16 per cent of Papua New Guinea's GDP. Even higher levels of dependence were recorded by the Solomon Islands (21 per cent) and Vanuatu (31 per cent).[247] The constraints imposed by such dependence were accentuated by dwindling aid budgets and increasing emphasis on conditionality. Diversifying sources of funding could cushion but not arrest, let alone reverse, the impact of the trend. Australia, for example, made continuing aid to the Pacific islands conditional on more effective conservation of natural resources. In doubling its aid to the region in 1995, France was a notable exception to the trend, but French largesse was part of a larger diplomatic strategy designed to improve its badly tarnished image. The South Pacific Forum's decision to lift its 11-month suspension of France's status as a Forum dialogue partner suggested that the strategy was working.[248]

Financial vulnerability had made most of these polities highly susceptible to external influence. Even with more intensive resource extraction, the financial position of governments remained critical. To cite a particularly striking but by no means unique example, Papua New Guinea's foreign debt rose to $4.2 billion in 1993 or 83 per cent of output, with debt-servicing costs accounting for more than 30 per cent of exports.[249] In subsequent years, the shortage of financial resources would reach critical proportions, leaving PNG governments no option but to turn to the World Bank and accept structural adjustment programmes that inevitably reduced their capacity to generate jobs or provide even minimally adequate social services.

The limited leverage available to Pacific island elites was equally apparent in the management of their resource industries, though these limitations were often exacerbated by corruption and incompetence. The logging industry in the Solomon Islands was a case in point. A confused legislative framework, inconsistent export taxes, excessive tax exemptions and poorly resourced state agencies made for windfall company profits and relatively low government revenues.[250] The proliferation of logging licences on terms highly favourable to investing companies resulted in the uncontrolled depletion of commercial forests, a trend temporarily kept in check by the Asian financial crisis. Much the same phenomenon was in evidence in Papua New Guinea, particularly in the late 1980s and early 1990s when, as a result of aggressive corporate practices (mostly by Malaysian investors), log production more than doubled. Even with subsequent falls in timber output, environmental degradation remained endemic.

Much the same story emerges from the efforts of Pacific islanders to develop their marine resources, multiplied many times over by the establishment of 200-mile exclusive economic zones. Given the importance of fish and other sea foods in the local diet and as a source of export revenue, and the fact that the region's fisheries resources were exploited largely by distant-water fishing nations, the fisheries industry soon became a subject of considerable contention. During the 1980s the issue made headlines when first the Solomons and then Kiribati decided to oppose what they perceived to be predatory American tuna fishing practices. When the Solomon Islands seized the marauding *Jeanette Diana* in June 1984, the United States retaliated by banning all fisheries exports from that country. Only strategic considerations, prompted by Kiribati's acceptance of a Soviet offer – an example which the other Pacific island states might be tempted to emulate – led the United States to lift the trade ban and sign in April 1987 a multilateral fisheries treaty with 11 South Pacific states, including New Zealand. This belated recognition of the right of island states to license tuna fishing did much to allay island sensitivities, but it could not radically alter the asymmetric relationship between the small Pacific states and the dominant fishing nations.[251] According to one estimate, the tuna harvest of North American and East Asian boats operating in Micronesian waters was valued in 1994 at $1.7 billion, of which only 5 per cent was returned to the islands. Confronted with the power of external corporate interests, Forum Fisheries Agency (FFA) members attempted to speak with one voice. Regional co-ordination, it seemed, was the only strategy which could at least partially offset their small size, negligible influence and limited access to capital and technology.

Fiji's diversification policies point to the most serious attempt to date by a Pacific island state to reduce the vulnerabilities arising from excessive dependence on one or two export commodities. Rising exports of fish and timber products as well as manufactured goods, coupled with an expanding tourist industry which had by the early 1980s become Fiji's principal source of foreign exchange, reduced reliance on sugar as a proportion of total exports from close to 75 per cent in the early 1980s to 38 per cent in 1990.[252] Under Rabuka, Fiji sought to liberalize its economy and follow in the footsteps of Asia's NIEs. To attract foreign capital, tax-free zones were established, thereby enhancing other available incentives, including cheap labour, a reasonable infrastructure and favourable access to western markets. Though the mix of instruments was quite successful in increasing Fiji's manufactured production and exports (in clothing, footwear, furniture and food products), it was far from emulating the performance of the East Asian tigers. The difficulties encountered by Fiji's smaller, traditional industries combined with a steadily rising import bill, itself a byproduct of rising living standards and increasing energy and machinery requirements, meant that import costs easily outstripped export gains. As a consequence, Fiji's balance of trade deficit rose to 15 per cent of GDP at the end of the 1980s, while its external debt accounted for 39.3 per cent of GDP and debt service for 18.4 per cent of overseas earnings.

By the end of the 1990s Fiji's key industries remained precariously poised. The sugar industry had to face not only sharply declining production levels, attributable to cyclones, drought and industrial disputes, but uncertainty about the future of the Sugar Protocol to the Lomé Convention beyond 2000. Under this arrangement Fiji was able to rely on guaranteed sales at two to three times the world price. The marked increase in visitor arrivals during the mid-1990s – just under 340 000 in 1996 – was only marginally affected by the East Asian financial crisis, but future growth would increasingly depend on greater investment in infrastructure. In the case of the garment industry, Fiji had relied on access concessions such as those offered under the South Pacific Regional Trade and Economic Co-operation Agreement (SPARTECA), but continued access at comparable levels was far from guaranteed. Nor were the prospects of the gold industry, in particular those of the Emperor gold mine at Vatukaula, especially promising, given steadily falling gold prices on the world market.[253]

It remains to say a word about the economic reform agenda pursued by the World Bank, the IMF, the Asian Development Bank and the Australian and New Zealand governments. To this end the principle of conditionality was increasingly attached to both grants and loans. Recipients were expected not only to liberalize their trade and financial arrangements, but to introduce more effective systems of accountability and transparency and more generally to apply principles of 'good governance'.[254] Using the South Pacific Forum as the principal mechanism, Australia had attempted from 1994 to establish a new set of economic norms and practices to which Pacific island governments would conform. These included a regional timber code to encourage a more sustainable forestry industry in PNG,

Vanuatu and the Solomon Islands; a collective approach to negotiations with distant-water fishing nations; the rationalization of Pacific island airlines; and the establishment of procedures to monitor progress in the structural reforms within each economy. In line with the neo-liberal agenda espoused by core governments and multilateral institutions, increasingly powerful external pressures, both material and ideational, were now bearing upon Pacific island economic and social organization.

External Security

Economic vulnerabilities were inevitably reflected in other forms of externally induced insecurity. Though not altogether absent, insecurity in its classical sense was perhaps less in evidence than the twin dangers of nuclear and environmental despoliation. The aim here is to illustrate rather than fully describe or explicate the phenomenon. Military sources of insecurity or military instruments of security were most relevant to Papua New Guinea's experience, probably because of its size relative to other Pacific island states, its proximity to two larger and more powerful states, Australia and Indonesia, and the strategic dilemma posed by West New Guinea's troublesome incorporation into Indonesia. In the early 1980s, the anti-Indonesian activities of the Free Papua Movement (OPM) and the counterinsurgency operations of the Indonesian military sent some 11 000 West Papuans fleeing into PNG territory, placing considerable financial and diplomatic strains on Port Moresby. The 1979 border agreement between Indonesia and Papua New Guinea had failed to offer an effective remedy, let alone prevent border violations.[255] To moderate tensions, the two countries concluded in 1986 a Treaty of Mutual Respect, Friendship and Co-operation. A subsequent thaw in bilateral relations saw Indonesia sponsor Papua New Guinea's admission as an observer at ASEAN meetings and the latter's accession to the Treaty of Amity and Co-operation in 1987. Barely a year later tensions resurfaced following a series of Indonesian military incursions across the PNG border in pursuit of OPM guerillas.

The strategic uncertainties created by separatist tendencies in West New Guinea would continue to preoccupy PNG and Australian military planners right through the 1990s, and provide a continuing justification for the close military links between the two countries. Australian assistance to the PNG defence forces reached a peak of A$52 million in 1991 but steadily declined to A$11.7 million in 1996–7, before rising to A$19 million in 1997–8. The framework of co-operative activities announced in October 1997 as part of the New Defence Partnership envisaged 12 major programmes with the emphasis on defence management. Strategic planning and core military skills, including border security, were also targeted for special attention.[256]

The US policy of strategic denial provided the only other notable manifestation of military insecurity. In 1976, the ANZUS partners, having endorsed claims that the Soviet Union was intent on developing a regional military presence, committed themselves to thwarting Soviet objectives by cementing closer strategic and diplomatic ties with the South Pacific islands. A three-pronged strategy combining economic aid, regional institution-building and low-level defence co-operation was seen as the most effective instrument for dissuading local governments from establishing diplomatic or economic links which the United States deemed inimical to its interests. The ANZUS connection was meant to provide a protective umbrella, with much of the responsibility for implementing the strategy delegated to the two junior partners, Australia and New Zealand.[257] Yet the assumptions of strategic denial, even when read in the context of the second Cold War, were not altogether plausible. In no other part of the world was the Soviet Union so devoid of friends, access or influence. The Pacific islanders for their part, preoccupied as they were with more intractable domestic and external challenges to their security, had little inclination to become embroiled in the East–West conflict. The policy of strategic denial was, it seems, aimed as much at securing and legitimizing western interests in the region as at excluding a Soviet naval presence.

In pursuit of their wider strategic interests, Britain, the United States and subsequently France had made of the Pacific a nuclear playground, as each sought to expand and refine the capabilities of its nuclear arsenal. Under a special arrangement with Australia, Britain conducted 12 nuclear explosions and some 30 minor trials at Monte Bello, Emu, Maralinga and Christmas Island. At the Bikini and Eniwetok atolls in the Marshall Islands some 67 US atomic and hydrogen bombs were detonated between 1946 and 1958. The inhabitants of Eniwetok did not return to their atoll until 1980. Two decades later it was still not possible to determine the full extent of the clean-up costs at Bikini atoll or the date at which resettlement could safely proceed. Several other atolls had also received doses of radiation fall-out far exceeding the limits set by the International Commission on Radiological Protection.[258]

France's decision to establish a nuclear testing site at Mururoa atoll in 1963 would prove even more controversial. Testing in the atmosphere began in 1966 but was moved underground in 1975, in the hope of deflecting mounting local and international criticism. South Pacific opposition to the French programme would nevertheless continue to be voiced with varying degrees of intensity over the next two decades. President Chirac's decision to resume testing in 1995 after a three-year moratorium substantially raised the diplomatic stakes, with organized advocacy groups clamouring for tough retaliatory measures against France.[259] Responding to stronger than anticipated public sentiment at home, the Australian government felt obliged to assume leadership of the wide-ranging publicity campaign initiated by the South Pacific Forum. Though France eventually announced a permanent end to its nuclear testing programme in January 1996, there was little likelihood that the controversy on the human impact of the French nuclear-testing programme would subside until a comprehensive, independent and transparent study had been made of the health effects on workers at the test site and residents of neighbouring atolls.[260]

Atomic testing was in any case only part of a multifaceted programme that also included missile testing, transportation of plutonium and nuclear wastes, transit by nuclear-powered and nuclear-armed ships, and the establishment of nuclear-related command, control and communications facilities. There were, in other words, clear limits to how far Pacific Island states and territories could pursue their nuclear-free preferences. Even Australia, by far the region's most influential state, had to temper its anti-nuclear inclinations in deference to great power interests and priorities. The South Pacific Nuclear Weapons Free Zone established in 1985 at the initiative of the Labor government in Australia was a carefully crafted document designed to give voice to regional anti-nuclear sentiment but without offending the United States or curbing any of its current nuclear-related activities.[261] Despite Australia's persistent entreaties, the United States did not become a signatory to the treaty until March 1996, by which time nuclear-free zones had become a useful post-Cold War instrument of US non-proliferation policy.

What Australia and New Zealand could not achieve was unlikely to be within the reach of much weaker polities. To salvage this constitutional roadblock to the possible nuclearization of the island, Palau had waged a sustained legal and political struggle over a period of 14 years during which one Palauan president was assassinated, another took his own life and several other anti-nuclear activists were subjected to various forms of harassment and intimidation. The Compact of Free Association negotiated with the United States eventually came into force in November 1994, but with Washington retaining sole responsibility for the defence and security of the territory.[262] Palau's economic dependence had visibly restricted the range of available policy options.

When it came to environmental security, the external pressures with which Pacific islands had to contend were perhaps not as daunting, but no less pervasive or restrictive.[263] The possible ecological degradation of the seas could not but cause profound disquiet to the Pacific peoples, given the importance of the marine environment as a source of food and the tendency of external powers to regard the vast expanse of ocean as a convenient solution to problems of waste management. The decision of the United States to establish the Johnston Atoll Chemical Agent

Disposal system was to prove especially contentious. The incineration facility on Johnston Atoll, situated 717 nautical miles west-south-west of Hawaii, was issued in August 1985 a ten-year permit by the US Environmental Protection Agency to begin storing and treating toxic chemical weapons, including mustard gas and nerve agents. From June 1990 weapons shipped from Germany, Okinawa and the Solomon Islands were undergoing incineration.[264] For several years, Pacific island states, individually and collectively through the South Pacific Forum, would consistently call for the closure of the facility, but with relatively little success. The first sign of a breakthrough would not come until September 1997, when the US Senate banned further transport of chemical weapons to the atoll.

At its twenty-sixth annual meeting in September 1995, the Forum adopted the Waigani Convention to Ban the Importation into Forum Island Countries of Hazardous and Radioactive Wastes. Under the treaty, the area from which the import and storage of imported wastes would be excluded encompassed the national territories together with the seas enclosed by their exclusive economic zones. There were, however, several loopholes in the convention: transshipment of radioactive wastes had not been banned; no limits were placed on the generation of wastes within the region; and wastes produced by French nuclear testing did not come under the Convention's jurisdiction. Concerns over the transport by sea of plutonium and high-level nuclear wastes through the Pacific Ocean had gathered momentum, despite strenuous efforts by the consortium of Japanese, British and French interests to reassure regional governments that these shipments met the highest international safety standards. The fact remained that Pacific micro states could wield only limited leverage, and that these limits were as much a reflection of domestic weakness as of external pressure.

For Pacific islands, the prospect of rising sea levels associated with the so-called 'greenhouse effect' posed perhaps the greater long-term danger to environmental and economic security. Many of them, for example Kiribati, the Marshall Islands, Tuvalu, Nauru and the Northern Marianas, were made up largely of low-lying islands, and even populations located on higher ground were likely to prove vulnerable to storms and cyclones. The issue was widely perceived as one of physical survival, hence the frequent pleas for urgent action to reduce the risks of global warming. Not surprisingly, climate change became the most contentious issue at the 1997 meeting of the South Pacific Forum.[265] In line with the hardline negotiating stance it had adopted in the lead-up to the Kyoto Conference, the Howard government was determined to prevent any endorsement for binding greenhouse gas emission reductions. As a consequence the strong views of the island leaders were substantially watered down to accommodate Canberra's position. Despite the publication shortly before the meeting of a confidential Australian government report containing highly disparaging assessments of island governments and their leaders, Australia's economic and strategic muscle was sufficient to ensure that its views would prevail. The position of the Pacific micro states was partially vindicated by the Framework for Climate Change Convention agreed to in Kyoto in December 1997, which required the main developed economies to reach reduction targets of 6–8 per cent. The Pacific island countries had been pressing for much higher targets and a much shorter implementation time frame, hence their profound disappointment with the modest results at Kyoto. The outcome of the Conference was made even more unpalatable for the South Pacific by virtue of the conference's decision to allow Australia (and two other developed economies) to increase its emissions by 8 per cent between the base year 1990 and 2010. Island concerns on global warming, however legitimate, had to contend with the hierarchical structure of regional and global power relations.

Conscious of their marginality, the Pacific island states had sought to widen their range of options and curb the influence of core and semi-peripheral interests on their decision-making processes by engaging in various forms of regional co-operation. Beginning with the South Pacific Forum in 1971, the newly independent states had created an array of regional and sub-regional institutions, notably the Forum Fisheries Agency (1979), the South Pacific Regional Environmental Programme (1980) and the South Pacific Organization Co-ordinating Committee (1988). In addition, a great many subsidiary organizations, several of them operating under the Forum umbrella, gradually assumed important co-ordinating and administrative functions. Complementing these organizational arrangements were a number of agreements, notably the South Pacific Regional Trade and Economic Cooperation Agreement (SPARTECA), the South Pacific Nuclear Free Zone (SPNFZ) treaty and the convention for the Prohibition of Fishing with Long Driftnets, all of which, notwithstanding substantial differences in areas of competence and scope of operation, had one common objective, namely to expand the legal framework of South Pacific security.

Other initiatives were directed at sub-regional consultation, of which the most prominent was the Melanesian Spearhead Group. Founded by Papua New Guinea, the Solomon Islands and Vanuatu in 1985 – Fiji joined in 1996 – the Group's primary purpose was to enhance diplomatic influence by developing a more coherent sense of Melanesian identity and solidarity. Its effectiveness was most clearly evident when it sought to moderate regional (including Australian) responses to the Fiji coups. It was equally vocal, though perhaps less effective, when it came to pressing for self-determination in New Caledonia, where the initiative rested largely with the South Pacific Forum. On issues considered highly sensitive by any one member, neither regional nor sub-regional institutions seemed well placed to exercise much influence. The Bougainville conflict was particularly instructive in this regard. The most successful attempt at mediation originated not from any regional mechanism, where competing interests and perceptions rendered any sustained initiative virtually unthinkable, but from New Zealand, a neighbouring state with no direct stake in the conflict.

A CONCLUDING NOTE

In surveying a number of peripheral and semi-peripheral polities, the intention was not to offer a comprehensive account of their external relations. Much less was it to evaluate the way policies were formulated and applied. Rather it was to establish the degree to which periphery and semi-periphery could articulate and pursue interests or objectives independently of the core. What emerges from this analysis is the ability of regional players, even the smallest South Pacific island states, to exercise a degree of influence over the shape of their external environment.[266] How much influence, in what context and with respect to what issues varied greatly.from case to case. As a general proposition, however, it is arguable that the late 1980s and early to mid-1990s had produced a conjunction of domestic and external factors favourable to a greater self-assertion in the peripheral and semi-peripheral zones of Asia Pacific.

The waning discipline of Cold War ideologies, the rise of multipolarity, greater competition between major centres of power and rapid economic expansion in much of East Asia had helped to generate a mood of greater self-confidence but also a keener appreciation of the possibilities for change. Australia and Canada were now intent on pursuing an active policy of engagement with Asia. Though strikingly different in leadership style and diplomatic ethos, both Malaysia and Indonesia had fostered a greater sense of Southeast Asian identity and cohesion. Particularly in Malaysia's case, the distinctive and sustained advocacy of 'Asian values' tinged with vehement anti-American rhetoric found expression in a range of sub-regional, regional and even global diplomatic initiatives. South Korea took advantage of its relatively smooth transition to democratic politics and the impressive success of its export-oriented industrialization strategy to diversify its relations with regional and external powers and raise the profile of its diplomacy, even on the highly delicate and contentious issue of inter-Korean relations. As for the Pacific islands, though their preferences carried little weight outside of the South Pacific, they had identified the issues of immediate interest to them, namely decolonization, economic development and environmental security, and were beginning to harness the institutional resources needed to make their voices heard.

These manifestations of relative autonomy and the diplomatic and economic conjuncture which made them possible must not, however, be exaggerated. There were clear limits, internally as much as externally induced, to the capacity of the periphery and semi-periphery to define, let alone aggressively or successfully to prosecute, their perceived interests. The ramifications of economic vulnerability were particularly conspicuous in the experience of the South Pacific island states, but they also impinged on the foreign policies of Southeast Asian countries, and even of Australia and Canada. In the fiercely competitive environment of globalized markets, these states were acutely aware of the powerful pressures pulling them towards increased trade liberalization and financial deregulation, the limitations of their productive base, the fragility of their financial systems and their continued dependence on foreign capital or technology. In this sense, the various regional arrangements to which they subscribed were dictated as much by economic necessity as by political preference. Even the powerful *chaebol* of South Korea could not escape the painful readjustment provoked by the financial crisis. Economic weakness was in many cases compounded by political or cultural uncertainty. The instabilities generated by problems of leadership succession, ethnic divisions, economic downturn or environmental degradation constrained the effectiveness of diplomatic initiative and institutional innovation. The cultural distance separating Australia and Canada from Asia made the task of regional economic integration politically hazardous at home and diplomatically contentious abroad.

Externally, all peripheral and semi-peripheral states had to contend with the pressures exerted by core states and core economic players. Australian and Canadian attitudes to the China–Taiwan dispute, and even more starkly South Korea's relations with the North, had to operate within an alliance framework whose parameters were set largely by US strategic priorities. The non-aligned status of Indonesia and Malaysia offered a degree of insulation from external influence, but it could not altogether escape the pervasive influence of the United States, mediated by alliances with third parties (for example, ANZUS), international financial institutions (notably the IMF) and the policies of friends and allies (in particular, Australia and Canada).

For both periphery and semi-periphery, external relations generally and security policy in particular, which had both an internal and external dimension, could not in any case be separated from economic conditions. Here the degree of leverage was even more conspicuously constrained, with several South Pacific territories, some enjoying the trappings of sovereignty and others not, largely dependent on the transfer of funds from metropolitan or semi-peripheral centres as the case may be (for example, Papua New Guinea, Palau, New Caledonia, French Polynesia). Even the semi-periphery, notwithstanding sustained growth of manufacturing capacity as in Malaysia or relative technological sophistication as in Canada or Australia, was vulnerable to a range of external economic pressures, variously manifested in acute dependence on a few export commodities or export markets, sudden and uncontrolled financial flows, or large and often unpredictable swings in international interest rates and exchange rates. Two main options were available to peripheral and semi-peripheral societies as they sought to counterbalance or limit the impact of these external pressures: the cultivation of social cohesion, political stability and economic development at home, and multilateral co-operation, especially in a regional setting, abroad. The first option, while dependent on the complex interplay of politics and culture, could not itself be insulated from external influences. We turn our attention to the domestic environment in the next chapter and leave the discussion of multilateral mechanisms and processes to the companion volume, *Regionalism in the New Asia-Pacific Order*. It is already apparent, however, that these two strategic options are not independent variables in the equation but closely interlinked, and in part constrained by interest articulation and power configuration within the core.

NOTES

1. While 'dependency' is the most frequently used term, there is considerable variation in terminology. Andre Gunder Frank, for example, prefers the imagery conveyed by metropolis and satellite. For the purpose of this analysis, dominant/dependent, centre (or core)/periphery and metropolis/satellite will be used interchangeably. One of the most influential exponents of dependency theory has been Andre Gunder Frank, author of *Latin America: Underdevelopment or Revolution:Essays on the Development of Underdevelopment and the Immediate Enemy* and *Capitalism and Underdevelopment in Latin America* (both published in New York by Monthly Review Press in 1969). Much of his work, however, reflects the influence of Paul Baran, who may be considered the pioneer of this approach and possibly the most important contemporary innovator in the Marxist theory of imperialism. In addition to *The Political Economy of Growth*, New York: Monthly Review Press, 1957, see Paul Baran and P. Sweezy, *Monopoly Capital*, Harmondsworth, Middlesex: Penguin, 1963; and P. Baran, *The Longer View*, New York: Monthly Review Press, 1974; S. Bodenheimer, 'Dependency and Imperialism: The Roots of Latin American Underdevelopment', *Politics and Society*, 1(3), May 1971, 327–58; Fernando Henrique Cardoso, 'Dependency and Development in Latin America', *New Left Review*, no. 74, July–August 1972, p. 83–95; Johan Galtung, 'A Structural Theory of Imperialism', *Journal of Peace Research*, VIII(2), 1971, 81–117; P. Jalée, *The Third World in World Economy*, New York: Monthly Review Press, 1969; Theotonio dos Santos, 'The Structure of Dependence' *American Economic Review*, LX, May 1970, 231–6.
2. See D. Ray, 'The Dependency Model of Latin American Underdevelopment: Three Basic Fallacies', *Journal of Interamerican Studies and World Affairs*, XV, 1973, 4–20; Dudley Seers (ed.), *Dependency Theory: A Critical Reassessment*, London: Frances Pinter, 1981.
3. This aspect of dependency theory is common to several writers, including Frank, dos Santos, Galtung and Cardoso.

4. For example, Arghiri Emmanuel, *Unequal Exchange: A Study of the Imperialism of Trade*, New York: Monthly Review Press, 1972; S. Amin, *Accumulation on a World Scale*, 2 vols, New York: Monthly Review Press, 1974.
5. Johan Galtung provides the following classification of the main institutional mechanisms which sustain dependence: multinational corporations (BINGOs), international governmental organizations (IGOs), military alliances (MIGOs), international press agencies, shipping and air companies and other communications systems (CONGOs), international non-governmental organizations (INGOs).
6. See Joseph Camilleri, 'Dependence and the Politics of Disorder', *Arena*, nos. 44–5, 1976, 34–58.
7. Immanuel Wallerstein, 'Semi-Peripheral Countries and the Contemporary World Crisis', *Theory and Society*, 3(4), Winter 1976, 461–84.
8. Immanuel Wallerstein, *The Capital World-Economy*, Cambridge: Cambridge University Press, 1979, pp. 26–33.
9. The need to distinguish between autonomy, sovereignty and strength as attributes of statehood is elaborated in Camilleri and Falk, *The End of Sovereignty?*, pp. 31–9, 85–8.
10. See James N. Rosenau, *Along the Domestic–Foreign Frontier: Exploring Governance in a Turbulent World*, Cambridge: Cambridge University Press, 1997, pp. 99–117.
11. Stanley Hoffman, 'What Should We Do in the World?', *Atlantic Monthly*, 264(4), October 1989, 84–96.
12. Recently notions of 'middle power', and more specifically 'middle power initiative' or 'middle power leadership', have gained considerable currency. See, for example, Carsten Holbraad, *Middle Powers in International Politics*, London: Macmillan, 1984; Bernard Wood, *The Middle Powers and the General Interest*, first in the series *Middle Powers in the International System*, Ottawa: North–South Institute, 1990; Cranford Pratt (ed.), *Middle Power Internationalism: The North-South Dimension*, Montreal: McGill-Queen's University Press, 1990. Such notions have been applied to foreign policy-making either in individual case studies (see Michael K. Hawes, *Principal Power, Middle Power, or Satellite?*, North York, ON: York Research Programme in Strategic Studies) or in comparative studies, notably Andrew F. Cooper, Richard A. Higgott and Kim Richard Nossal, *Relocating Middle Powers: Australia and Canada in a Changing World Order*, Melbourne: Melbourne University Press, 1993. However, to avoid the state-centric quality of much 'middle power' theorizing, and to highlight the interconnections between security and economy on the one hand, and domestic politics and foreign policy on the other, the terms periphery/semi-periphery seem preferable to small power/middle power.
13. For a clear exposition of the case for the widening of the security agenda, see Barry Buzan, 'Rethinking Security after the Cold War,' *Cooperation and Conflict: Nordic Journal of International studies*, 32(1), March 1997, 5–28; also J.A. Camilleri, 'Security: Old Dilemmas and New Challenges in the Post-Cold War Environment', *Geo-Journal*, 34(2), 1994, 135–45.
14. See Sung-joo Han, 'South Korean Politics and Its Impact on Foreign Relations', in Robert A. Scalapino, Seizaburo Sato, Jusuf Wanandi and Sung-joo Han (eds), *Asia and the Major Powers: Domestic Politics, and Foreign Policy*, Berkeley, Cal.: Institute of East Asian Studies, University of California, 1988, pp. 163–4.
15. See James Cotton, 'From Authoritarianism to Democracy in South Korea', *Political Studies*, 37, 1989, 244–59; also Chalmers Johnson, 'South Korean Democratization: The Role of Economic Development', *Pacific Review*, 2(2), 1989, 1–10.
16. For a penetrating analysis of South Korea's security ideology, or its 'dominant security paradigm,' see Chung-in Moon, 'South Korea: Recasting Security Paradigms', in M. Alagappa, *Asian Security Practice: Material and Ideational Influences*, Stanford, CA: Stanford University Press, 1998, pp. 264–87.
17. See James Cotton, 'Bilateral Accomplishments and Multilateral Tasks in Northeast Asian Security', *Contemporary Southeast Asia*, 20(2), August 1998, 146.

18. Chung-in Moon, 'South Korea: Recasting Security Paradigms', pp. 274–5.
19. *Challenges of Building a Korean Peace Process: Political and Economic Transition on the Korean Peninsula*, Special Report by the United States Institute for Peace, June 1998, p. 5.
20. See speech by ROK Foreign Minister, Gong Ro-Myung, at Council of Foreign Relations, New York, 26 September 1996.
21. *FEER*, 18 April 1998, 25.
22. *Challenges of Building a Korean Peace Process*, pp. 5–6.
23. See Konstantin Sarkisov, 'New Developments on the Korean Peninsula and Regional Security', in *Korean Peninsula Security and the US–Japan Defence Guidelines*, IGCC Policy Paper no 45, October 1998, p. 19.
24. BBC, *SWB*, 16 February 1998, FE/3152, D/1.
25. Bill Meldrum and James Cotton, 'The US–DPRK Agreed Framework, KEDO, and "Four-Party Talks": The Vicissitudes of Engagement', *Issues and Studies*, 34(11/12), November/December 1998, 140.
26. *FEER*, 22 October 1998, 18.
27. *FEER*, 15 July 1999, 19.
28. *FEER*, 24 June 1999, 20–21.
29. *FEER*, 10 February 2000, p. 24.
30. *Age*, 16 June 2000, p. 9.
31. *Age* (News Extra), 17 June 2000, p. 7.
32. For a more detailed outline of North Korean–US/IAEA negotiations, see Sang Hoon Park, 'North Korea and the Challenge to the US–South Korean Alliance', *Survival*, 36(2), Summer 1994, 81–5.
33. The background to the crisis and North Korea's nuclear intentions are examined in Andrew Mack, 'The Nuclear Crisis on the Korean Peninsula', *Asian Survey*, XXX111(4), April 1993, 339–59.
34. James Cotton provides a careful examination of the twists and turns of American thinking in 'The North Korea–United States Nuclear Background and Consequences', *Korean Observer*, XXV1(3), Autumn 1995, 32–44.
35. See Lee Dong-bok, 'Dealing with North Korea: The Case of the Agreed Framework', *Journal of Northeast Asian Studies*, 24(2), Summer 1994, 91–101; also Kathleen C. Bailey, 'The Nuclear Deal with North Korea: Is the Glass Half Empty or Half Full?', *Comparative Strategy*, 14, June 1996, 137–48.
36. Cotton, 'Bilateral Accomplishments and Multilateral tasks', p. 147.
37. See US, Japan, ROK Joint Statement on North Korean Issues, 24 September 1998.
38. *New York Times*, 27 May 1999, 2 June 1999, 17 June 1999.
39. See Frank Ching, 'Promising Accord on Korea', *FEER*, 30 September 1999, 32.
40. See US, Japan, ROK Joint Statement on North Korean Issues, 24 September 1998.
41. 'Foreign Policy Agenda of the Republic of Korea in the New Century', address by the ROK Foreign Minister to the Graduate School of International Studies of Korea University, 11 December 1998.
42. A more detailed account of the reinforcement of US military capabilities is given in Jae-Jung Suh, 'Duality to Reciprocity: America's Two-war Doctrine and Peace on the Korean Peninsula', paper presented to the Conference on Alternative Security Systems in the Asia-Pacific, Bangkok 27–30 March 1997, pp. 5–7.
43. *The Military Balance 1995-96* (IISS), p. 226.
44. It was difficult to avoid the conclusion that the Republic of Korea now had the military capability to defeat a North Korean blitzkrieg without US ground or air support and without losing much ground. See J.J. Suh, 'Blitzkrieg or Sitzkrieg? Assessing a Second Korean War', *Pacifica Review*, 11(2), June 1999, 151–76.
45. *SIPRI Yearbook 1996*, p. 466.

46.   For a discussion of the entrapment–abandonment dilemma as it impacted on NATO during the 1980s, see Jane M.O. Sharp, 'NATO's Security Dilemma', *Bulletin of the Atomic Scientists*, 43(2), March 1987, 42–4. The implications of US deterrence policy for South Korea are examined in Patrick M. Morgan, 'US Extended Deterrence in East Asia', in Tong Whan Park (ed.), *The US and the Two Koreas: A New Triangle*, Boulder, Col.: Lynne Rienner, 1998, pp. 57–63.

47.   *FEER*, 1 July 1999, 26.

48.   See Byung-joon Ahn, 'The Impact of US–Japan Defense Cooperation Guidelines on East Asian Security', in *Korean Peninsula Security and the US–Japan Defense Guidelines*, pp. 8–10.

49.   See Kim Dae-jung's address before the Japanese Diet, 8 October 1998.

50.   Andrew Mack, 'The Nuclear Crisis on the Korean Peninsula', *Asian Survey*, XXXIII(4), April 1993, 341.

51.   Jae-Jung Suh, 'Duality to Reciprocity', p. 10.

52.   See 'North Korea's Decline and China's Strategic Dilemmas', US Institute of Peace Special Report, October 1997, p. 3.

53.   The full extent of the famine in North Korea could not be ascertained from official figures. The only estimate published by Pyongyang indicated 250 000 deaths during 1995–8, but other estimates put the number of deaths as high as 3 million (see *Le Monde Diplomatique*, November 1999, 15).

54.   See Young-dae Song, 'Assessing Collapse Possibilities of the North Korean Regime', paper presented at a conference organized by the National Institute of National Intelligence, Seoul, December 1996.

55.   In any case, the scenario of a rapid or imminent disintegration of the North Korean political system may have been overstated. See Norman D. Levin, 'What If North Korea Survives', *Survival*, 39(4), Winter 1997–98, 156–74.

56.   Bjung-Joon Ahn, 'Prospects for Korea under the IMF and Kim Dae-jung', *Korea Focus*, 6(3), 1998, 7.

57.   *Korea Times*, 10 July 1997.

58.   *Seoul Hangyore*, 10 July 1997.

59.   Dewi Fortuna Anwar, *Indonesia's Strategic Culture*, Brisbane: Griffith University, Centre for the Study of Australia–Asia Relations, Australia–Asia Papers no. 75, May 1996, pp. 4–7.

60.   See Harold Crouch, *The Army and Politics in Indonesia*, Ithaca, NY: Cornell University Press, 1978, pp. 221–44.

61.   See Dewi Fortuna Anwar, *Indonesia and the Security of Southeast Asia*, Jakarta: CSIS, 1992, p. 14.

62.   See Mochtar Pabottingi, 'Indonesia: Historicising the New Order's Legitimacy Dilemma', in Muthiah Alagappa (ed.), *Political Legitimacy in Southeast Asia*, Stanford, Cal.: Stanford University Press, 1995, pp. 224–56.

63.   Ibid., pp. 506–7.

64.   Bob Lowry, *Indonesian Defence Policy and the Indonesian Armed Forces*, Canberra: Australian National University, Strategic and Defence Studies Centre, 1993, p. 23.

65.   Mark Farrer, 'Regional Airpower: Combat Capable or Hollow Shell?', *Asia-Pacific Defence Reporter*, 1998 Annual Reference Edition, p. 22.

66.   For an examination of the historical origins of that principle, see J. Soedjati Dji Wandono, 'Indonesia's Post Cold War Foreign Policy', *Indonesian Quarterly*, 22(2), 1994, 90–102.

67.   Ali Alatas, 'Security in the Asia Pacific Region: An Indonesian and ASEAN Perspective', address to the Council on Foreign Relations, New York, 20 December 1996.

68.   See Jin Song, 'The Political Dynamics of the Peacemaking Process', in Michael W. Doyle, Ian Jonstone and Robert O. Orr (eds), *Keeping the Peace: Multidimensional UN Operations in Cambodia and El Salvador*, Cambridge: Cambridge University Press, 1997, pp. 63–4.

69.   See Lee Lai To, 'Defusing Rising Tensions in the Spratlys: An Analysis of the Workshops on Managing Potential Conflicts in the South China Sea', *American Asian Review*, 12(4), Winter 1994, 187–209.

70. See Ali Alatas, 'Managing the Potential of the South China Sea', *Indonesian Quarterly*, 17(2), 1990, 111.

71. See opening address by Ali Alatas to Sixth Workshop on Managing Potential Conflict in the South China Sea, Balikpapan, 10 October 1995.

72. See opening address by Ali Alatas to the Ninth Workshop on Managing Potential Conflicts in the South China Sea, Jakarta, 1 December 1998.

73. See for example, Iman Sudarwo (First Assistant to the Indonesian State Minister for Research and Technology), keynote speech to the Sixth KSP International Forum; also Ali Wardhana, 'Indonesia, Asia Pacific and the Global Economy at the Beginning of the 21st Century', *Indonesian Quarterly*, 23(4), 1995, 332– 41; President Suharto's Independence Day Speech, 3 September 1996.

74. Tugabus Feridhanusetyawan, 'Social Impact of the Indonesian Economic Crisis', *Indonesian Quarterly*, 26(4), 1998, 335.

75. The MPR consisted of 700 members, comprising the 500 members of the DPR (including the appointed TNI members), plus 135 regional representatives and 65 social group representatives (for example, labour, business, religious and women's groups). For a useful survey of the election results and of the complexities of the ensuing presidential race, see Stephen Sherlock, 'After the Elections, After East Timor: What's Next for Indonesia?', Australian Parliamentary Library, Information and Research Services, *Current Issues*, Brief no. 5, 1999–2000.

76. See *FEER*, 28 October 1999, 12–13; Michael van Langenberg, 'End of the Jakartan Empire', *Inside Indonesia*, no. 61, January–March 2000, 8.

77. See *Indonesia's Crisis: Chronic but now Acute*, Jakarta, ICG Indonesia Report No. 2, May 2000, p. 19.

78. *FEER*, 2 September 1999, 16–8.

79. *Weekend Australian*, 13–14 May 2000, 13.

80. *Australian*, 6 June 2000, 11.

81. The domestic politics/external environment nexus is examined in Bob Lowry, 'Indonesia: Political Futures and Regional Security', ANU Australian Defence Studies Centre, Working paper no. 53, Canberra, 1999.

82. See Bob Lowry, Stage Set for Final Showdown with Wiranto', *Australian*, 18 January 2000, 8.

83. *FEER*, 30 March 2000, 26–27.

84. *Australian*, 15–16 April 2000, 13; *Age*,19 April, 11.

85. See excerpts of interview between Minister of Foreign Affairs with journalists from Portugal on the question of East Timor, Jakarta, 2 February 1999.

86. See Brian Woodley's report from Dili, 'Red and White Terror', *Australian*, 1–2 May 1999, 19, 22.

87. For details of the UN-administered referendum, see Anthony Smith 'East Timor: Opting for Independence', *New Zealand International Review*, 24(6), November–December 1999, 6–9.

88. *FEER*, 28 October 1999, 20–21.

89. For an analysis of the UN's handling of the East Timor crisis, see William Maley, 'The UN and East Timor', *Pacifica Review*, 12(1), February 2000, 63–76.

90. *Australian*, 3 November 1999, 7.

91. Ian James Storey, 'Indonesia's China Policy in the New Order and Beyond: Problems and Prospects', *Contemporary Southeast Asia*, 22(1), April 2000, 166.

92. Musa Hitam, 'Malaysia's Doctrine of Comprehensive Security', *Foreign Affairs Malaysia* (hereafter referred to as *FAM*), 17(1), 1984, 94.

93. Ibid., p. 96.

94. See Abdullah Ahmad, *Issues in Malaysian Politics*, Singapore: Singapore Institute of International Affairs, 1988, p. 5.

95. For a valuable insight into Mahathir's notion of the Malaysian nation (*bangsa Malaysia*), see Chaudran Jeshurun, 'Malaysia: The Delayed Birth of a Strategic Culture', in Ken Booth and Russell Trood (eds), *Strategic Cultures in the Asia-Pacific Region*, Melbourne: Macmillan, 1999, pp. 241–3.
96. K.S. Nathan, 'Malaysia: Reinventing the Nation', in Alagappa (ed.), *Asian Security Practice*, p. 524.
97. Mahathir Mohamad, *Malaysia: The Way Forward*, Kuala Lumpur: Centre for Economic Research and Services, Malaysian Business Council, 1991, p. 2.
98. *SIPRI Yearbook 1998*, p. 224.
99. *Asia-Pacific Defence Reporter*, 1998 Annual Reference Edition, p. 53.
100. See Chaudran Jeshurun, 'Malaysian Defence Policy Revisited: Modernization and Rationalization in the Post-Cold War Era', *Southeast Asian Affairs 1994*, p. 199
101. *FEER*, 14 December 1989, 36–7.
102. See Mahathir's speech to the Fourth Meeting of the ASEAN Heads of Government, Singapore, 27 January 1992, *FAM*, 25(1), January 1992, p. 32
103. Mahathir speech to the International Trade and Investment Conference, 'Malaysia and China in the 21st Century: Prosperity through Cooperation', Kuala Lumpur, 23 January 1995 (http://smpke.jpm.my:...an.pm/1995/950123.txt, pp.1–2).
104. B.A. Hamzah, 'Sea Lanes of Communication Security: A Malaysian Perspective', Lau Teik Soon and Lee Lai To (eds), *The Security of the Sea Lanes in the Asia-Pacific Region*, Singapore: Heinemann Asia, 1988; Johanes Sarsito, 'Coastal Management in an Enclosed Sea Environment: A Case Study of the Malacca Strait', in Sam Bateman and Stephen Bates (eds), *Shipping and Regional Security*, Canberra: Australian National University, Strategic and Defence Studies Centre, 1998, pp. 55–66.
105. See Andrew Tan, 'Problems and Issues in Malaysia–Singapore Relations', Australian National University, Strategic and Defence Studies Centre Working Paper No. 322, Canberra, July 1998.
106. Musa Hitam, 'Malaysia's Doctrine of Comprehensive Security', p. 95.
107. Mahathir Mohamad, Speech to the Second Summit of the Group of 15, Caracas, 27 November 1991, *FAM*, 24(4), December 1991, p. 85.
108. Mahathir Mohamad, Speech to the Non-Aligned Movement Summit, Jakarta, 1 September 1992, *FAM*, 25(3), September 1991, pp. 59–60.
109. Statement by Datuk Abdullah Haji Ahmad Badawi, Minister of Foreign Affairs, Vienna, 18 June 1993, cited in J. Tang (ed.), *Human Rights and International Relations in the Asia-Pacific Region*, London: Pinter, 1995, p. 236.
110. The 'Look East' policy has been usefully described as 'a two-pronged strategy for Malaysia's economy on the road to rapid industrial growth, and at the same time to prod its predominantly Bumiputra population into becoming economic achievers' (Johan Saravanamuttu, 'Look East Policy: The Real Lessons', in K.S. Jomo (ed.), *Mahathir's Economic Policies*, 2nd edn, Kuala Lumpur: Insan, 1989, p. 24.
111. Mahathir Mohamad, address to 'The First East Asian Young Leaders Congress', Kuala Lumpur, 5 August 1994, (http://smpke.jpm.my.1...an.pm/1994/94805.txt, pp. 1–2).
112. Mahathir Mohamad, 'New Government Policies', memorandum, 28 June 1993, in Jomo, *Mahathir's Economic Policies*, pp. 9–11.
113. Noordin Sopiee, 'Malaysia's Visionary Plan Was "Born of Consensus" ', interview in *Asian Business Review*, September 1993, 48.
114. Samuel Huntington, 'The Clash of Civilizations', *Foreign Affairs*, 27(3), 1993, 22–49.
115. For two significant Malaysian contributions to this process, see *Towards a New Asia*, a report for the Commission for a New Asia convened by Noordin Sopiee, Kuala Lumpur, 1994; Anwar Ibrahim, *The Asian Renaissance*, Singapore: Times Books International, 1996.
116. Mahathir Mohamad, Address to the Europe/East Asia Economic Forum, Hong Kong, 14 October 1992 (http://smpke.jpm.my:l...n.pm/1992/921014b:txt, pp. 1–2).

117. Mahathir Mohamad, Address to the Institute of Mitsui and Company for Trade and Economic Studies Incorporation, Tokyo, 19 October 1992, *FAM*, 25(4), December 1992, pp. 18–9.
118. Mahathir Mohamad, Address to the Asia Society Conference on 'Asia and the Changing World Order', Tokyo, 13 May 1993, *FAM*, 26(2), June 1993, p. 45.
119. Mahathir, Mohamad, Address to the Kyushu-Asian Summit for Local Authorities, Kyushu, 21 October 1994, (http://smpke.jpm.my.l...an.pm/1994/941021.txt), pp. 4–5.
120. Mahathir Mohamad, *A New Deal for Asia*, Selangor Darul Eshan: Pelanduk Publications, 1999, p. 94.
121. See Johan Saravanamuttu, 'Malaysia's Foreign Policy in the Mahathir Period, 1981–1995: an Iconoclast Come to Rule', *Asian Journal of Political Science*, 4(1), June 1996, 6–7.
122. Speech by Prime Minister Mahathir Mohamad at the Non-Aligned Summit, Durban, 3 September 1998 (delivered by Foreign Affairs Minister Abdullah Badawi, *FAM*, 31(3), September 1998, 54–8.
123. Mahathir Mohamad, Address to the 51st session of the UN General Assembly, 27 September 1996, *FAM*, 29(3), September 1996, 59–65..
124. Abdullah Badawi, Statement to 53rd Session of the UN General Assembly, 28 September 1998.
125. Between 1985 and 1999 Malaysia contributed more than 10 000 military personnel to 12 UN peacekeeping operations, including UNTAG in Namibia, the UN Transitional Authority in Cambodia, the UN operation in Mozambique, and UNPROFOR in Bosnia-Herzegovina.
126. See David Camroux, *'Looking East'. . . and Inward: Internal Factors in Malaysian Foreign Relations during the Mahathir Era, 1981–1994*, Centre for the Study of Australia–Asia Relations, Griffith University, Australia-Asia Paper no. 72, October 1994, p. 12.
127. See Meredith L. Weiss, 'What Will Become of *Reformasi*? Ethnicity and Changing Political Norms in Malaysia', *Contemporary Southeast Asia*, 21(3), December 1999, 431; also *FEER*, 24 June 1999, 9–11.
128. Even in the 1990s many reference works dealing with Asia Pacific still did not include Canada, for example *Asia-Pacific Defence Reporter* (Annual Reference Edition) and *Asia Yearbook*.
129. See Brian L. Job, 'Canadian Interests and Perspectives Regarding the Emerging Pacific Security Order', North Pacific Cooperative Security Dialogue Research programme, York University, Working Paper no. 2, 1992, p. 10.
130. David Cox, 'Canadian Defence Policy in the Pacific', in M. Goldie and D. Ross (eds), *Pacific Security 2010: Canadian Perspectives on Pacific Security into the 21st Century*, Aurora Papers no. 10, Ottawa: Canadian Centre for Arms Control and Disarmament, August 1991, p. 65.
131. See *Independence and Internationalism: Report of the Special Joint Committee of the Senate and of the House of Commons on Canada's International Relations*, Ottawa: Supply and Services, Canada, 1987, pp. 77–80; *Canada's International Relations: Response of the Government of Canada to the Report of the Special Joint Committee of the Senate and the House of Commons*, Ottawa: Supply and Services, 1986, pp. 59–61; Brian Mulroney, Prime Minister of Canada, 'Singapore Lecture', Ottawa: Office of the Prime Minister, 16 October 1989.
132. See Martin Rudner, 'Canadian Development Assistance to Asia: Programs, Objectives, and Future Policy Directions', *Canadian Foreign Policy*, 1(3), Fall 1993, 67–93.
133. Paul M. Evans, 'The Emergence of Eastern Asia and Its Implications for Canada', *International Journal*, XLV11, Summer 1992, 516–17.
134. Statement by Raymond Chan, Secretary of State (Asia-Pacific), to Asia Pacific Foundation meeting with Heads of Mission, Vancouver, 13 January 1995.
135. Address by Lloyd Axworthy, Minister of Foreign Affairs, Tokyo, 4 April 1997.
136. 'Immigrant Population – 1996 Census', *Statistics Canada*, Ottawa, November 1997.

137. See Barbara McDougall, Secretary of State for External Affairs, 'Cooperative Security in the 1990s from Moscow to Sarajevo', Statement 93/36, 17 May 1993.
138. Lloyd Axworthy, 'Between Globalization and Multipolarity: The Case for a Global Humane Foreign Policy', Ottawa:, Department of Foreign Affairs and International Trade, 1998 (http://www.dfait-maeci.gc.ca/english/foreign/humane,htm, p. 6).
139. See Joe Clark, 'Canada and Asia Pacific in the 1990s', speech to the Victoria Chamber of Commerce, Victoria, British Columbia, 17 July 1990, Canada, External Affairs and International Trade, Statement 90/40; also speech to the 45th Session of the UN General Assembly, 26 September 1990, Statements and Speeches 90/13; also 'The Canadian Initiative for a North Pacific Co-operative Security Dialogue', a position paper of External Affairs and International Trade, Canada, 3 December 1990.
140. See Notes for a Speech by Joe Clark, Secretary of State for External Affairs, to the North Pacific Security Dialogue, Victoria, British Columbia, 6 April 1991.
141. See Stewart Henderson, 'Zone of Uncertainty: Canada and the Security Architecture in Asia Pacific', *Canadian Foreign Policy*, 1(1), Winter 1992–93, pp. 113–14.
142. *1994 Defense White Paper*, Ottawa:, Supply and Services, 1994, p. 12.
143. 'The Presence of the Canadian Navy in the Asia-Pacific Region', Canada, Navy, Office of Public Affairs, February 1997.
144. The market-driven character of Canada's aid programme is elaborated in Ronald C. Keith, 'China and Canada's "Pacific 2000 Strategy"', *Pacific Affairs*, 65(3), 1992, 319–33.
145. Paul Gecelovsky and T.A. Keenleyside, 'Canada's Human Rights Policy in Practice: Tiananmen Square', *International Journal*, L(3), Summer 1995, 570–71.
146. Ibid., 583–4.
147. 'Canada–China Bilateral Trade' DFAIT, 1999 (http://www.dfait-maeci.gc.ca/asia/ viewdoc... t-e.asp?continent=Asia&code=10&name=76514).
148. Tony Clarke, *Silent Coup: Confronting the Big Business Takeover of Canada*, Canadian Centre for Policy Alternatives, and James Lorimer, 1997, p. 100.
149. Address by Art Eggleton to Canada–China Business Council, Toronto, 29 May 1996 (http://www.dfait.maec.../96_state/96_026e.htm).
150. See Address by Art Eggleton, Minister for International Trade, to the Canadian Chamber of Commerce in Japan, Tokyo, 23 April 1996 (http://www.dfait_maec.../96_state /96_014e.htm).
151. Art Eggleton, Address to the Korea–Canada Business Council, Seoul, 13 January 1997 (http://www.dfait-maeci.gc.ca/engl...ews/statem~1/97_state/97_002e.htm).
152. Address by Sergio Marchi, Minister for International Trade, to the Canada–Korea Business Council, Mississauga, Ontario, 30 September 1997.
153. Address by Sergio Marchi, Minister for International Trade, to the Hong Kong Bank of Canada Forum on East Asia, Toronto, 24 October 1997 (http://www.dfait.maeci.gc. engl...ews/statem~1/97~state1/97_044e.htm).
154. Clarke, *Silent Coup*, p. 101.
155. Address by Raymond Chan, Secretary of State (Asia-Pacific), to Malaysia–Canada Business Council, Kuala Lumpur, 11 August 1994 (http://www.dfait-maeci.../94state/94-43eng.html).
156. Address by Raymond Chan to Malaysia–Canada Business Council, Vancouver, 16 February 1996 (http://www.dfait_maec.../96_state/96_005.htm).
157. J.A. Camilleri, *An Introduction to Australian Foreign Policy* (4th edn), Brisbane: Jacaranda Press, 1979, p. 24.
158. Address by Prime Minister E.G. Whitlam to the Singapore Press Club, 8 February 1974.
159. See *Australia and the Third World*, Report of the Committee on Australia's Relations with the Third World, Canberra: AGPS, 1979.
160. *Australian Foreign Affairs Record* (hereafter referred to as *AFAR*), 54(9), September 1983, 514. See also Michael C. Pugh, *The ANZUS Crisis, Nuclear Visiting and Deterrence*, Cambridge: Cambridge University Press, 1989, pp. 33–9.

161. See Kim Beazley's speech to the New South Wales Branch of the Australian Institute of International Affairs, 27 July 1985, in *Backgrounder*, no. 489, 31 July 1985, p. A12; also address to the Australian Institute of International Affairs, 9 February 1986, p. 12.
162. *Review of Australia's Defence Capabilities*, Report to the Minister for Defence by Paul Dibb, Canberra: AGPS, 1986.
163. *The Defence of Australia 1987*, presented to the Parliament by Defence Minister Kim Beazley, March 1987, Canberra, AGPS, 1987.
164. Address to ASEAN–Australia Forum, Canberra, 3 May 1994, p. 4.
165. 'Australia's Regional Security', Ministerial Statement by Gareth Evans, Minister for Foreign Affairs and Trade, December 1989, in Greg Fry (ed.), *Australia's Regional Security*, Sydney: Allen & Unwin, 1991, p. 172.
166. Ibid., p. 214.
167. Gareth Evans and Bruce Grant, *Australia's Foreign Relations in the World of the 1990s*, Melbourne: Melbourne University Press, 1991, p. 107.
168. See address by Gareth Evans, 24 February 1991, in *Monthly Record*, 62(2), February 1991, 42.
169. For a critical New Zealand perspective of Australia's subservience to US security policy, see David Lange, 'Of Defence, Dinosaurs and Dogma', *Australian*, 1 August 1990, 11.
170. *Backgrounder*, 19 October 1990, 3.
171. *Monthly Record*, 62(4), April 1991, 127.
172. *Strategic Review 1993*, Canberra: Defence Centre, 1993, p. 39.
173. Fry, *Australia's Regional Security*, pp. 188–90.
174. *Strategic Review 1993*, pp. 22, 28.
175. Gareth Evans, 'The World after the Cold War: Community and Co-operation. An Australian View', *Round Table*, no. 329, 1994, 33.
176. Address by Gareth Evans, Minister for Foreign Affairs, to the Canada–Australia Conference on Co-operation in the Asia-Pacific Region, Canberra, 28 July 1995.
177. Address by Gareth Evans, Minister for Foreign Affairs, Institute of Diplomacy and Foreign Relations, Kuala Lumpur, 20 February 1995.
178. Gareth Evans and Paul Dibb, *Australian Paper on Practical Proposals for Security Cooperation in the Asia Pacific Region*, Canberra: Department of Foreign Affairs and Trade and Strategic and Defence Studies Centre, ANU, 1994.
179. Address by Gareth Evans to the 1994 Pacific Rim Forum, Beijing, 27 October 1994, p. 2.
180. *Strategic Review 1993*, p. 29.
181. Striking evidence of Australia's dominant position was provided by the 25th South Pacific Forum meeting, which decided to act on Keating's firm advice and develop a more assertive multilateral response to the region's dwindling fishing and forestry resources (*Australian*, 2 August 1994, 2).
182. *Australian*, 25 May 1994, 10.
183. Address to the Institute for Contemporary Asian Studies, Monash University, 19 July 1990, in *Monthly Record*, 61(7), July 1990, 424–5.
184. For useful background to the Australian initiative, see *Weekend Australian*, 12–13 November 1994, 21.
185. Speech by Prime Minister Paul Keating to the Australia–Asia Institute, Brisbane, 28 October 1994, p. 8.
186. *Australian*, 18 November 1992, 3.
187. Australian Department of Foreign Affairs and Trade, *In the National Interest: Australia's Foreign and Trade Policy*, White Paper, Canberra, 1997, pp. 36–51, 55, 58, 60–1, 63, 65–7.
188. See Bob Hawke's public statements during his visit to Japan in September 1990, in *Monthly Record*, 61(9), September 1990, 622.
189. See 'Australia's Security in Asia: The Strategic Relationship', (Bob Hawke's Asia Lecture, 24 May 1991), *Monthly Record* 62(5), May 1991, 205.
190. *Reports from Japan* (published by Embassy of Japan, Canberra), Spring 1995, p. 1.

191.   Address by Alexander Downer, Minister for Foreign Affairs, to the IISS/SDSC Conference, 'The New Security Agenda in the Asia Pacific Region', Canberra, 2 May 1996, p. 9.

192.   Naoko Sajima, *Japan and Australia: A New Security Partnership*, Australian National University, Strategic and Defence Studies Centre, *Working Papers*, no. 292, January 1996, pp. 23–5.

193.   See Ken Berry, *Cambodia – From Red to Blue: Australia's Initiative for Peace*, Sydney: Allen & Unwin in association with the Department of International Relations, Australian National University, Canberra, 1997, p. 6.

194.   See statement by Gareth Evans, *Commonwealth Parliamentary Debates,* Senate, vol. S137, 24 November 1989, Canberra: Commonwealth Government Printer, 1990, p. 3300.

195.   *Age*, 30 August 1990, 1.

196.   *Monthly Record*, February 1991, 45.

197.   Richard Woolcott, 'Our Timor Troubles', *Weekend Australian*, 6–7 March 1999, p. 29 (Richard Woolcott was Australian Ambassador to Indonesia during 1975–8, and later headed the Australian Department of Foreign Affairs).

198.   See statement of Hugh White, Deputy Secretary of the Defence Department, to a preliminary inquiry (*Age*, 10 June 1999, 11); also numerous reports received by the UN Assistance Mission in East Timor (*Weekend Australian*, 19–20 June 1999, 13).

199.   See Robert Garran, 'Downer's Secret Plan for East Timor's Future', *Australian*, 22 February 1999, 1–2.

200.   See John Lyons, 'The Secret Timor Dossier', *Bulletin*, 12 October 1999, 25.

201.   *The Age*, 10 June 1999, 11.

202.   'Angry Indons Tear Up Security Treaty', *The Age*, 17 September 1999, 1; 'Habibie Attacks Australia's Role', *The Australian*, 22 September 1999, 6; Gun Attack on Embassy, *Age*, 22 September 1999, 1; 'Friends No More', *The Economist*, 25 September 1999, 36; Michael Maher, 'The Perils of Peace', *Bulletin*, 28 September 1999, 30–31; Michael Maher, 'The Blame Game', *Bulletin*, 12 October, 32–6.

203.   Fred Brenchley, 'The Howard Doctrine', *Bulletin*, 28 September 1999, 24.

204.   See J.A. Camilleri, 'Problems in Australian Foreign Policy, January – June 1991', *Australian Journal of Politics and History*, 37(3), 1991, 386–8.

205.   John Howard's remarks at the 1997 South Pacific Forum, altogether ruling out the possibility of Bougainvillean independence, were indicative of the dominant strand in Australian official thinking (*Australian*, 19 September 1997, 5).

206.   John Henderson, 'Bougainville: The Uncertain Road to Peace', *New Zealand International Review*, May–June 1999, 10–3.

207.   For detailed consideration of these episodes, see Rita Camilleri, *Attitudes and Perceptions in Australia–Malaysian Relations 1985–1996*, MA thesis, La Trobe University, 1998.

208.   For a careful examination of the cultural undertones of these incidents, see Harold Crouch and Peter Searle, 'Recalcitrant or *Realpolitik*? The Politics of Culture in Australia's Relations with Malaysia', in Richard Robinson (ed.), *Pathways to Asia: The Politics of Engagement*, Sydney: Allen & Unwin, 1996, pp. 56–84.

209.   The complex interaction between the cultural and the political is clearly articulated in Camilleri, *Attitudes and Perceptions,* pp. 167–8.

210.   See Andrew Tan, *Problems and Issues in Malaysia–Singapore Relations*, Canberra: ANU Strategic Defence Studies Centre, Working Paper no. 314, December 1997.

211.   *Australia's Strategic Policy*, Canberra: Department of Defence, 1997, p. 24.

212.   Gareth Evans, Minister for Foreign Affairs, Address to the Chinese Association of Victoria and the Chinese Chamber of Commerce of Victoria, 24 August 1995.

213.   Ibid., p. 5.

214.   See John Moore, Speech to Tamasek University, Singapore, 23 February 1999, p. 5.

215.   Gary Klintworth, 'Sino-Australian Defence Relations Reach New Heights', *Asia-Pacific Defence Reporter*, 25(5), August–September 1999, 4.

216.   *Age*, 15 July 1999, 9.

217. *Australian,* 14 July 1999, 4.
218. See Gareth Evans, Address to the Australian Business Asia Forum, Sydney, 3 November 1994, p. 1.
219. *Australia's Strategic Policy,* p. 32.
220. See Greg Sheridan, 'Forward Defence', *Weekend Australian,* 6–7 December 1997, 27.
221. See Joint Communiqué, Australia–United States Ministerial Consultations, Sydney, 30–31 July 1998.
222. The deficiencies of Australia's strategic intelligence capabilities are clearly highlighted in Gary Klintworth, 'Does Australia Need Strategic Intelligence?', *Asia-Pacific Defence Reporter,* February/March1999, 46–7.
223. While acknowledging the challenges posed by a rapidly changing geopolitical environment, a great many Australian commentators tended to take the durability of the alliance as given, and to overlook, or at least underestimate, the factors likely to weaken the assumed coincidence of US and Australian strategic and diplomatic objectives. See, for example, Russell Trood and William T. Tow, 'The Strategic Dimension', in William T. Tow, *Australian–American Relations: Looking toward the Next Century,* Melbourne: Macmillan Education Australia, 1998, pp. 113–15.
224. Evans, Address to Malaysian Institute of Diplomacy, p. 6.
225. *Australian,* 16 September 1996.
226. See T.I.J. Fairbairn, 'Pacific Island Economies: Structure, Current Developments and Prospects', in N. Douglas and N. Douglas (eds), *Pacific Islands Yearbook,* 17th edition, Suva: Fiji Times, 1994, pp. 11–24.
227. See Stewart Firth, 'Sovereignty and Independence in the Contemporary Pacific', *The Contemporary Pacific,* 1(1–2), Spring and Fall 1989, 78–9.
228. See Sinclair Dinnen, 'State, Societies and Order in Papua New Guinea,' in Dauvergne (ed.), *Weak and Strong States,* pp. 38–59.
229. Sinclair Dinnen, 'Restorative Justice in Papua New Guinea', *International Journal of the Sociology of Law,* 25(3), 1997, 245–62.
230. *Age,* 3 July 1999, 21; *Australian,* 7 July 1999, 13.
231. See Sean Dorney, *Papua New Guinea: People, Politics and History since 1975,* Sydney: Random House Australia, 1990; R.J. May and M. Spriggs (eds), *The Bougainville Crisis,* Bathurst: Crawford House Press, 1990; Ken Ross, *Regional Security in the South Pacific: The Quarter-Century 1970–95,* Canberra: Australian National University, Strategic and Defence Studies Centre, 1993, pp. 109–15.
232. The Bougainville crisis had a profound impact on the role of the PNGDF and PNG politics more generally. More specifically, it demonstrated the limitations on the use of force for purposes of internal conflict resolution. See R.J. May, *The Changing Role of the Military in Papua New Guinea,* Canberra: Australian National University, 1993, pp. 57–71.
233. Though not officially accepted, some estimates suggest that as may as 20 000 may have been killed.
234. See Stuart Macmillan, 'Bringing Peace to Bougainville', *New Zealand International Review,* March–April 1999, 3.
235. The complex relationship between social structure and political life in Fiji is examined by Nicholas Thomas, 'Regional Politics, Ethnicity and Custom in Fiji', *Contemporary Pacific,* 2(1), Spring 1990, 131–46; see also Brig. V. Lal, *Power and Prejudice: The Making of the Fiji Crisis,* Wellington: New Zealand Institute of International Affairs, 1988.
236. Several useful accounts of the coup are already on offer, notably Stephanie Lawson, *The Failure of Democratic Politics in Fiji,* Sydney: Oxford University Press, 1991; Michael C. Howard, *Fiji: Race and Politics in an Island State,* Vancouver: University of British Columbia Press, 1991; 'As the Dust Settles: Impacts of the Fiji Coup', special issue of *Contemporary Pacific,* 2(1), Spring 1990. Yet these early attempts at interpretation need to be refined and even modified in the light of subsequent events, and closer attention paid to the implications of economic restructuring during the 1980s and 1990s.

237. See John Henderson, 'The Fiji Election', *New Zealand International Review*, XXIV(4), July–August 1999, 13–7.

238. *Pacific News Bulletin*, 14(6), June 1999, 1–2, 7, 10.

239. See *FEER*, 18 February 1999, 26–7.

240. See David A. Chappell, 'New Caledonia', *Contemporary Pacific*, 10(2), Fall 1998, 445.

241. *Pacific News Bulletin*, 13(11), November 1988, 12.

242. For a detailed outline of the new constitutional arrangements, see Jean-Jacques Quesraynne, 'The South Pacific: a New Frontier?', *New Zealand International Review*, XXV(1), January/February 2000, 7–12.

243. *Pacific News Bulletin*, 14(6), June 1999, 6, 15.

244. Ramesh Thakur, 'Introduction to the South Pacific', in R. Thakur (ed.), *The South Pacific: Problems, Issues and Prospects,* London: Macmillan, 1991, p. 23.

245. See Stephen Bates, 'South Pacific Island Perceptions of Security', in Peter Polomka (ed.), *The Security of Oceania in the 1990s, Vol. 2: Managing Change*, Canberra: Australian National University, Strategic and Defence Studies Centre, 1990, p. 43.

246. Steve Hoadley, *The South Pacific Foreign Affairs Handbook,* Sydney: Allen & Unwin in association with the New Zealand Institute of International Affairs, 1992, pp. 174–5.

247. Cited in Peter Larmour, 'Migdal in Melanesia', in Dauvergne (ed.), *Weak and Strong States*, pp. 84–5.

248. Karin von Strokirch, 'The Region in Review: International Issues and Events, 1996', *Contemporary Pacific*, 9(2), Fall 1997, 449–50.

249. *Pacific Research*, 8(1), February 1995, 25.

250. Peter Dauvergne, 'Weak States and the Environment in Indonesia and the Solomon Islands', in Dauvergne (ed.), *Weak and Strong States*, p. 145.

251. See David J. Doolman, *Tuna Issues and Perspectives in the Pacific Islands Region*, Honolulu: East–West Centre, University of Hawaii, 1987; George Kent, *The Politics' of Pacific Island Fisheries*, Boulder, Col.: Westview Press, 1980; Ludwig Scharmann, 'The UN Convention on the Law of the Sea and Its Implications for Third World Countries: The Case of Tuna Fishery in South Pacific Countries', *Ocean and Shoreline Management*, 15, 1991, pp. 309–24; Geoffrey Waugh, 'The Politics and Economics of Fisheries in the South Pacific', in Stephen Henningham and R S. May (eds), *Resources, Development and Politics in the Pacific Islands*, Bathurst, NSW: Crawford House Press, 1992; Alfred Sasako, 'Fishy Deals – Is the Pacific Losing Out?', *Pacific Islands Monthly*, July 1996, p. 8; Ronnie Alexander, 'Regional Cooperation and Security in the Pacific: The Fisheries and Nuclear Free Regimes', paper presented to the Conference on Alternative Security Systems in the Asia Pacific, Bangkok, 27–30 March 1997.

252. This overview of the gradual restructuring of Fiji's economy in the 1980s is based largely on Steve Hoadley's excellent account in Hoadley, *South Pacific Foreign Affairs Handbook,* pp. 95–104.

253. See the economic overview provided by the Australian Department of Foreign Affairs and Trade, *Fiji Country Brief*, March 1999.

254. See World Bank, *Pacific Island Economies: Building a Resilient Economic Base for the Twenty-First Century*, Washington: World Bank, 1995.

255. See Robin Osborne, *Indonesia's Secret War: The Guerilla Struggle in Irian Jaya*, Sydney: Allen & Unwin, 1985, pp. 246–85; R.J. May (ed.), *Between Two Nations: The Indonesia–Papua New Guinea Border and West Papua Nationalism,* Bathurst: Robert Brown and Associates, 1986; Dorney, *Papua New Guinea*, pp. 246–85.

256. Australian Department of Foreign Affairs and Trade, *Papua New Guinea Country Brief*, February 1999.

257. See Richard A. Herr, 'The Changing Geo-politics of ANZUS: The Place of the South Pacific', *World Review*, 23(1), April 1984, 30–31.

258. 'Marshall Islands to Renegotiate Compact with US', *Pacific News Bulletin*, 14(6), June 1999, 1–2.

259. Karin von Strokirch, 'The Political Fallout from French Testing in the Pacific', *Pacific Research*, 8(3), August 1995, 5–8.

260. See Karin von Strokirch, 'French Polynesia', *Contemporary Pacific*, 11(1), Spring 1999, 217–9.

261. See Michael Hamel-Green, 'The Not-so-Nuclear Free Zone: Australia's Arms Control Policy in the South Pacific Region', *Interdisciplinary Peace Research*, 1(1), 1989, 37–59.

262. 'Independence for Palau', *Pacific Research*, 8(1), February 1995, 25.

263. See Stephen Henningham, *The Pacific Island States: Security and Sovereignty in the Post-Cold War World*, London: Macmillan, 1995, pp. 71–90.

264. 'Chemical Weapons on Johnston Atoll', *Pacific News Bulletin*, 12(10), October 1997, 3.

265. Karen von Strokirch, 'The Region in Review: International Issues and Events, 1997', *Contemporary Pacific*, 10(2), Fall 1998, 421–3.

266. For a useful exposition of the continuing role of agency in the post-Cold War context, see Greg Fry, *South Pacific Security and Global Change: The New Agenda*, Canberra: Australian National University, Department of International Relations, Working Paper no. 1999/1.

5.   State, economy and civil society

If much of our analysis has been devoted to the policies and relations of states, it is not because of any underlying premise that states are the pre-eminent, let alone exclusive, actors on the Asia-Pacific geopolitical or geoeconomic stage. The fact that they often occupy a central place in both theoretical and policy debates about the future direction of the region nevertheless merits attention. The more important consideration is that states still offer a useful vantage point from which to probe the role of other actors and the complex and evolving networks of international interaction. The point is not to construct or deconstruct the state, but to contextualize it, to situate it within its internal and external milieu, to explore the interface between domestic and international political space. In line with our earlier exposition, the state will be treated as both agent and victim of the competitive dynamic that characterizes both the state system and the world economy. More than that, the state is seen to provide the locus of activity for other actors, be they subnational, supranational, international or transnational in their structure or mode of operation.

CLARIFYING KEY CONCEPTS

The focus of this chapter is on Pacific Asia rather than Asia Pacific: that is, on those societies which are culturally distinct from the West and have at different stages and with different degrees of success pursued policies of export-oriented industrialization. Attention will be directed primarily to those Asian states that have been closely identified with one or other of the three recent waves of industrialization: the first comprising Korea, Taiwan, Hong Kong and Singapore; the second the more economically advanced ASEAN countries; and the third China. Periodic references will also be made to the Japanese experience, partly because it is instructive in its own right, but especially because of the profound influence it has exerted on the economic and political trajectory of virtually every country in the region. Using the state as our conceptual point of departure, we wish to examine three closely related questions: how we are to interpret the economic functions performed by the state; the extent to which changes to the legal and political apparatus of the state are explicable in terms of democratization; and, if a case can be made for such a trend, how it impinges on the triangular relationship between state, economy and civil society.

Any attempt to grapple with these conceptually elusive, not to say empirically tangled, questions must begin with at least a partial clarification of terms. It is customary to describe the modern state as a boundary-maintaining system exercising sovereign jurisdiction over a given territory and population. It is clearly the case that since the industrial revolution states have, notwithstanding periodic fluctuations between *laissez-faire* and interventionist policies, helped to organize and regulate economic activity within and across national boundaries. To this end states have been instrumental in establishing a system of legal rights for the maintenance of property relations, standardizing money as the medium of exchange, furnishing the material infrastructure necessary for industrial development, and introducing taxes and subsidies and imposing tariffs and a range of other trade and financial controls designed to protect domestic industries. To this must be added two other important state functions, namely security (protection from both internal and external threats), which rests largely on the state's coercive powers, and legitimation (widespread acceptance of existing political institutions) based on the establishment of a value consensus or unifying culture, often expressed in terms of national identity or national interest.[1]

The elaborate administrative, legal and military, not to mention ideological, apparatus that East Asian states have established in the performance of these functions has often been cited as evidence of the strength of these states (about which more shortly). Regrettably the notion of strength lends itself to diverse and even conflicting interpretations. It cannot, for example, be assumed that state strength is synonymous with state sovereignty or its 'softer' variant, state autonomy. The concepts are related but not identical. In Wallerstein's model core states are deemed to have strength in that they are able to tax more plentiful surpluses and offer dominant economic interests the infrastructure and the financial, organizational and military protection they need to gain control of international markets. By contrast peripheral states are weak because they have much less control over international transactions and because their dominant interests depend for their survival largely on the strength of core states.[2] Strength – and capability – as envisaged here is first and foremost a relational concept which is best situated in an international setting. If one accepts this line of reasoning, then strength and capability must be distinguished from sovereignty and autonomy, which explicitly refer to the freedom of the state to define and assert its will independently of both outside forces and domestic private interests.

To avoid unnecessary confusion there is also a case for distinguishing between strength and centralization, if by the latter is meant the degree of control the state is able to exercise at its centre over the entire machinery of government.[3] Understood in this sense, the centralization of authority, as evidenced in one-party systems and military rule (for example, the Philippines under Marcos or even Indonesia under Suharto), may be a sign of weakness rather than strength if its function is primarily to obscure and entrench the dependent status of that society and its dominant elite. Conversely, the state may be strong but not highly centralized (for example, the United States). Strength, and possibly centralization, may assist a state to overcome the domestic or external resistance to its sovereign will. They are at best necessary but not sufficient conditions of sovereignty. Two other observations are relevant here. Precisely because of its relational quality, strength cannot be within the reach of every state. Hypothetically at least, centralization may be a universal option, but it may deliver neither strength nor sovereignty.

At face value the internationalization of trade, production and finance, which has steadily gained momentum over the last half century, has greatly circumscribed the scope for national economic management. Paradoxically, however, states have acquired even greater capabilities in a bid to fashion effective instruments for the organization and regulation of economic activity. Such instrumental intervention, including the creation of a vast panoply of international organizations, must not, however, be confused with autonomy, let alone sovereignty. To come to terms with the state's changing profile and modalities of action, we must characterize more clearly the relationship between the state on the one hand and the economy and civil society on the other. Both dualities, state–economy and state–civil society, have of course a long and complex history, but each is undergoing profound transformation under the relentless impact of continuous product innovation, and in particular the information revolution. All states, regardless of their size or complexion, have been constrained to accept the competitive logic of the world market. While functioning within a quasi-anarchic system of states, they also have to negotiate with transnational firms and international organizations since these have acquired a decisive role in shaping the balance of costs and benefits, risks and opportunities which governs the structure of the globalizing economy.

While previous chapters have considered the state–economy nexus, the connection between state and civil society has thus far received less attention. Civil society is hardly a new concept. Indeed the term *societas civilis* goes back to the time of Cicero, although it then was virtually synonymous with the state. However, as Ehrenberg has incisively observed, 'the Roman notion of *res publica* implied the existence of *res privata* as a correlative sphere', in which family, property and a network of rights sustained the network of intimate associations and particular interests.[4] In its subsequent reincarnations in post-Renaissance European thought, the concept would acquire a range of meanings, each predicated on a different relationship to the state. For both Hobbes and Rousseau, though in sharply divergent paths, the development of civil society represented an important threshold in, and a catalyst for, the emergence of political society, that is, the state. For others, notably for Hegel, civil society referred to the system of economic needs and the formation of economic classes and organizations, a view which predisposed Marx to 'equate civil society with the economic relations of bourgeois society'.[5]

The point of this brief historical digression is to emphasize at the outset that civil society, if it is to offer us rich analytical insights, cannot be reduced, as popular discourse would have it, to an amalgam of social movements and non-governmental organizations of progressive or liberal disposition. As Garry Rodan makes clear, any number of forces in civil society may subscribe to values and internal organizational principles and practices that are 'blatantly elitist and anti-democratic'.[6] In other words, exponents of the liberal tradition who wish to celebrate civil society because they equate it with various notions of political pluralism, liberal democracy and the fulfilment of individual aspirations,[7] may be unnecessarily straitjacketing the concept and in the process depriving it of its explanatory potential. Rodan is right to draw attention to the limitations of this perspective, which he characterizes as

> the idealisation of civil society; the fostering of a zero-sum conception of the relationship between state and civil society; the obscuring of attempts to gain state power to shape relationships in civil society; and the conceptual concealment of ambiguous but significant relationships between state and society.[8]

The liberal tendency to view civil society through rose-coloured glasses is indeed doubly problematic. First, it is premised on a misleading, not to say highly negative, representation of the state; second, the pluralist conception of democracy on which it rests is itself narrowly conceived, privileging as it does highly individualistic and market-oriented notions of interest articulation.

If civil society is not to degenerate into an apologia for western liberalism, then it must allow for a wide range of values, ideological preferences and forms of association, a more nuanced, yet more encompassing understanding of democracy, and a multifaceted and highly variable relationship with the state. It is, for example, possible to envisage a state exercising the array of legal, administrative and other levers and controls at its disposal either to circumscribe or expand the freedom of action available to the constituents of civil society. Similarly, civil society may significantly influence the definition and achievement of state objectives, either by setting normative standards of state conduct or by facilitating or alternatively impeding the mobilization of human and material resources on which the state ultimately depends for the performance of its functions. State and civil society are thus engaged in an interdependent, dialectical relationship, in which neither party can eliminate the other without endangering its own existence. In this sense, state and civil society may be described as two distinct but mutually constitutive forms of political space. It is not a question therefore of either the authoritarian state destroying civil society, or of a flourishing civil society dispensing with the functions of the state, or of choosing between the state's addiction to authoritarianism and civil society's inherently democratic propensities.

As the East Asian experience indicates, a state may opt to restrict the political space available to civil society in the interests of consolidating the power of an unpopular regime or of obviating criticism and organized protest against particular policies and practices. No state, however, can altogether neutralize or eradicate civil society, unless the latter is so narrowly defined as to equate it with a sphere of activity over which the state may exercise absolute control. In postulating that civil society requires 'the existence of an independent public space from the exercise of state power, and then the ability of organizations within it to influence the exercise of state power',[9] Bernhard comes unnecessarily close to adopting such a definition, for, wittingly or otherwise, civil society is made to function only by the grace of the state. If, on the other hand, allowance is made for the fact that civil society can function both actively and passively, overtly and covertly, in direct or indirect relationship to the apparatus of the state, then civil society may be said to operate within a political space that overlaps with but is nevertheless separate from that of the state.

Two important conclusions emerge from the preceding analysis. The first points to the comprehensiveness yet amorphousness of civil society, comprising as it does every conceivable type of association. Formed to advance particular interests and objectives, these associations include nuclear and extended families, clans and villages, local neighbourhoods, craft guilds, unions and firms, groups for leisure and charity, and religious, cultural, sporting and professional organizations. What is distinctive about them is their voluntary or spontaneous character, their sense of identity and belonging, their contribution to a public space which functions side by side with, yet independently of, the state. These associations do not exercise legally enforceable jurisdiction over their members; they give rise to multiple overlapping and intersecting layers of organization; they penetrate each other's space and in the process establish or re-establish communities that cut across spatial boundaries.

The second conclusion reinforces an earlier observation. The associations that comprise civil society need not be any more or less democratic in ethos or practice than the state itself. If democracy – and the twin principles of representation and participation which it subsumes – is deemed valuable, whether as a means to an end or as an end in itself, then it must be integral to the workings of both state and civil society. Indeed, it is difficult to see how the state apparatus can function democratically in the context of a civil society whose practices and institutions are prone to domination and oppression. Similarly, it is unlikely that the democratic ethic will easily flourish in a civil society that is perennially subjected to a tyrannical state. There is nevertheless a striking difference between state and civil society. Though both are equally susceptible to the authoritarian virus, civil society, precisely because of its inherent plurality and diversity, is less likely to be as uniformly authoritarian in its decision-making processes as the highly centralized state. To this extent at least, the centralization of state power can never be fully replicated in civil society. The latter will always reflect, however imperfectly, something of the multiple cultural and normative influences that have punctuated its history. By examining, then, the evaluation of the state–civil society relationship in East Asian countries over the last few decades, it should be possible to shed additional light not only on their political cultures, but on their economic performance, external relations and changing perceptions of their place in the region.

Pacific Asia, we are perennially reminded, constitutes a rich mosaic of polities, economies and cultures. Yet one notable thread appears to unify its recent history. Virtually all states in the region, notwithstanding their different traditions, have sought legitimation in terms of one or more of the following objectives: preservation of security and territorial integrity (often focusing more on internal than external threats); cultural and political reassertion (especially significant for societies still recovering from the humiliating experience of colonial occupation and other forms of western domination); and economic growth (designed to satisfy steadily rising material expectations). To add icing on the cake the state, whether in Indonesia, Malaysia or Singapore, would often project itself as the standard bearer of national identity and national purpose. In return for these promised benefits, society was expected to acquiesce in the state's management of the economy and its handling of the instruments of coercion. Though it varied considerably in conception and execution from one country to another, a social contract had seemingly emerged, with the state entrusted with the task of producing a range of public goods and society assuming primarily the role of consumer.

The metaphor of a social contract is, no doubt, misleading if it is depicted as the outcome of pubic deliberation of available options, or of some measurable and credible test of public opinion. More often than not civil society was not consulted. Policies were announced and laws enacted in the expectation that, once successfully implemented, they would gain widespread public acceptance. This was at best a tacit social contract which left several questions unanswered. One question, in particular, has turned out to have far-reaching implications: what would be the consequence of either success or failure? If the state did, in fact, deliver its side of the bargain, which would presumably mean, among other things, higher levels of security and economic well-being, would that success strengthen or weaken the existing state–society nexus? Conversely, what would be the impact if, for whatever reason, a substantial gap arose between the promise and performance of the state? Would the state apparatus continue to enjoy a relatively free hand in handling the society's affairs, or would pressure emerge for a reassessment of the terms of the existing contract? What if, on the other hand, the state's performance were to prove uneven – no doubt a more realistic outcome? What if, in other words, its legislative programme and administrative practice tended to favour some constituencies at the expense of others, or at least more than others? What if the state's actions were seen to privilege a particular class or stratum of society, ethnic community, political party or family? How would, for example, the siphoning off of state resources affect the actual or potential fault-lines of the polity, be they ethnic, religious, economic or ideological? Would it be possible to contain any ensuing discontent within the existing framework of state–society relations, or would the latter come under increasing critical scrutiny? Needless to say, the forms and consequences of the social contract have varied markedly both between and within countries. Side by side, however, with the unique circumstances of different cultural settings and different stages of development has been a certain shared experience reflecting in part similar domestic and international pressures. To analyse these differences and commonalities we must focus more closely on the two dualities, state–economy and state–civil society, and on the complex triangular relationship which they necessarily imply.

THE STATE–ECONOMY NEXUS

Our analysis of the relationship between state and economy in East Asia unavoidably begins on well-trodden ground, but only as a stepping stone to a more fruitful line of inquiry. Intrigued by East Asia's economic dynamism, many observers have identified the role of the 'strong state' as the key to economic success.[10] This school of thought is in many ways an understandable reaction to the economic orthodoxy of market-led development, with its stress on the relative absence of price distortions and trade restrictions. As Linda Weiss incisively argues, the two successive waves of neo-liberal analysis have sought to discount the role of the state by arguing either that growth in fact followed the lifting of political controls ('free-market' theory),[11] or that such controls had a 'self-cancelling or "neutralising" effect' ('simulated free-market' theory). By contrast, Weiss, an exponent of the strong-state thesis, suggests that by protecting domestic industries (through a range of import restrictions, tax exemptions and credit subsidies) and assisting export industries, the state created 'a powerful built-in "bias towards" exports and against imports'.[12] She refers in this context to 'governed market' theory pioneered by Robert Wade,[13] which emphasizes the role of industry policy in encouraging heavy investment in internationally competitive high-growth industries, and subsequently in high-technology sectors.[14]

A somewhat distinct, though closely connected approach, which Weiss finds more compelling and to which she herself contributes, is that of 'governed interdependence' theory. Here East Asian development is explained by reference to a complex but state-mediated network of public–private institutions. The function of this network is said to be the socialization of risk associated with investment decisions, in particular the raising of capital, choice of technologies, targeting of markets and development of a skilled workforce.[15] In a useful overview of the state–business partnership in East Asia, Richard Appelbaum and Jeffrey Henderson highlight various elements of state intervention, including encouragement of higher value-added, higher-wage and more technology-intensive forms of production; legislation to discourage speculative investment; supply of credit and financial guarantees; investment in the creation of new technologies; protection of selected domestic industries; use of price controls; and establishment of rigorous performance standards for companies receiving state guaranteed credits. They conclude that in the partnership with industry, the state in Japan and the NIEs has been firmly in the driver's seat.[16]

For Weiss the distinguishing feature of East Asian competitiveness is more subtle. It expresses the institutional capacity of the state to collaborate with industry, but in ways which enable it to set goals, co-ordinate policies and mobilize resources. This capacity is manifested in the high calibre of the bureaucracy, the high level of expertise within core economic ministries, and the effectiveness of interdepartmental co-ordinating agencies (for example, ROK's Economic Planning Board). As a consequence, the state's apparatus is sufficiently robust and self-conscious to insulate it from individual interests and pressure groups. Insulated or 'autonomous' though it may be, the bureaucracy is nevertheless said to be closely linked to industry through a range of policy networks which provide useful mechanisms for the exchange of information and joint decision-making between the public and private sectors. Mirroring the capacity of state structures is the effectiveness of industrial organizations, in particular the centralization of business structures within and across specific industries, enabling the private sector to make a coherent and sustained input to the policy-making process. To restate the overall argument, both state and industry in East Asia are said to have developed the organizational underpinning needed to engage in a successful policy partnership.[17]

There can be no disputing the enormous influence which the new scholarship on state intervention has had on our understanding of East Asian industrialization. That the World Bank, long regarded as a bastion of neo-liberal orthodoxy, should have begun by the early 1990s to acknowledge the role of the state was perhaps a measure of that influence. Its 1993 report, entitled *The East Asian Miracle*, though still wedded to the neo-liberal development model, had at least conceded the linkage between government intervention and export promotion.[18] Another 1993 report went so far as to attribute 'the rapid productivity and economic growth of the region' to 'the combination of modest distortions, macroeconomic stability, and effective government spending', as well as to such factors as 'consensus building and efficient bureaucracies'.[19] Subsequent publications went even further in revising the notion of market-driven development. By 1997, the World Bank had become an active proponent of at least certain forms of state intervention, including regulatory frameworks for creating competition, managing the contracting process and overseeing monopolies. Acting in partnership with the private sector, the state was expected to ensure more efficient financing and delivery of infrastructure.[20]

The pattern of business–government relations across Pacific Asia is not, of course amenable to a simple or single generalization. Drawing on the substantial literature now available, a closer but selective look at the experience of a few individual countries may nevertheless yield a few important insights. There is, as we shall see, much evidence to support the 'strong state' thesis; but strength needs to be clearly defined, carefully distinguished from autonomy and substantially qualified to take account of the impact of international and transnational influences. It should already be apparent that political institutions as well as corporate structures, and industrial policy itself, are undergoing profound change as they move from one phase of economic development to another.

Japan's post-war economic resurgence is no doubt attributable in part to the role of strategically located government agencies, notably MITI, the Bank of Japan and the Ministry of Finance, and to the close interconnections between political leadership, bureaucracy and business. The long period of Liberal Democratic Party rule provided an effective umbrella whereby senior civil servants and business leaders could set the priorities and strategies of the developmental state relatively unfettered by judicial restriction or public scrutiny.[21] Paralleling and reinforcing this triangular relationship has been the organization of the business sector itself, which, as we saw in Chapter 2, developed close links between distributors and manufacturers and between small and large firms, as well as a complex network of overlapping shareholding arrangements.[22] None of this is to suggest that the 'iron triangle' was monolithic or that the bureaucratic apparatus itself was always able to pursue a single-minded industrial policy.

There is much to Kent Calder's argument that the disbursement of government credit and other benefits was not so much a case of 'picking winners' as of establishing a more encompassing and durable partnership dominated by neither state nor industry.[23] Though labour was largely excluded from this model of 'corporate-led strategic capitalism', changes in Japan's domestic and international environment, particularly after the 1973–4 oil crisis, made both industry and organized labour more favourably disposed to labour participation in decision-making across a wide range of policy issues. Indeed, there is much evidence to support the conclusion that 'by the early 1980s, all opposition parties except the JCP had . . . joined the neo-corporatist regime erected in the wake of the 1973 oil crisis as a consortium of the LDP, the government bureaucracy, and both big business and the main labour organizations'.[24]

The role of the state in Korea's economic development has been the subject of numerous detailed studies.[25] Here we confine ourselves to a few observations which draw on that literature and are central to the argument we wish to advance. That the political leadership, especially after the military coup of 16 May 1961, saw itself as overseeing South Korea's rapid industrialization is clear enough. Through the monitoring conducted by the Economic Planning Board (EPB) and a combination of cheap credit and tariff protection, the Park Chung Hee regime was able to discipline the private sector, rewarding firms for productive investment and success in export markets and penalizing others for poor performance.[26] The allocation of bank credit was a particularly powerful instrument, for industrial capitalists soon understood that unless they complied with government directions, they would be deprived of their major source of cash flow, namely the state-controlled financial institutions. By the late 1970s, South Korea's state-sponsored industrial strategy was well on the way to achieving the ambitious targets it had set for the motor vehicle, shipbuilding and electronics industries.[27]

Two important qualifications must, however, be made to this line of argument. First, the close association between government and business was not as immune to the influence of vested interests as notions of 'state autonomy' or 'bureaucratic insulation' would suggest. Indeed, much of the initial impetus for the shift to export-oriented production came from big business, especially from Lee Byung-chul, founder of the Samsung group.[28] It is arguable that the state's facilitating role was crucial but largely reactive, and that the perceptions of the leading *chaebol* were the critical factor in identifying export opportunities and determining investment decisions. The period of heavy-chemical industrialization beginning in 1973 certainly reflected the state's diversification objective, but the execution of the policy entailed a good deal of negotiation with the large business groups whose participation was essential to the success of the project. To secure their co-operation the state had to offer 'a combination of guarantees, equity participation, and increasingly distorted incentives in the form of tax concessions and preferential low-interest credit'.[29] Increasingly, the state was obliged to serve as the guarantor of corporate profitability.

Significantly, the *chaebol* were concentrated in the southeast of the country, which, as it happened, was also the home region of a disproportionately large number of government leaders and senior bureaucrats. The less favoured regions and the bulk of small and medium-sized firms had relatively little contact with government and were generally denied access to preferential loans.[30] Second, the state's drive for industrial restructuring in the 1980s was aimed at rationalizing business concentration and reducing overcapacity. It was accompanied by a number of measures to liberalize the financial sector and privatize state-owned commercial banks. These policies, spearheaded by the EPB but clearly bearing the imprint of international pressures, encountered strong resistance from the main association of large business interests, the Federation of Korean Industries, but also from within the bureaucracy, notably the Ministry of Finance and the Ministry of Commerce and Industry. These tensions gathered momentum during the Roh Tae Woo and Kim Young Sam periods, when greater attempts at transparency exposed the extent to which the government–business nexus had been oiled by vast financial contributions by business conglomerates in return for political favours. The prison sentences imposed in 1996 on the chairmen of Daewoo and Samsung simply confirmed how endemic corruption had become in Korea's political economy.[31]

Paradoxically, financial deregulation further weakened the state's capacity to control the market, in part by enhancing *chaebol* financial autonomy through greater access to private credit. By the late 1980s state activism in industrial policy had grown weaker and was largely confined to a few sectors. The government's function was now seen primarily as setting the macroeconomic parameters conducive to investment. Much less in evidence was the 'hands-on' strategy which had previously given shape and content to industrial policy. As Chung-in Moon has persuasively argued, state and business could no longer be described in terms of a patron–client relationship.[32] Under Kim Young Sam, notions of economic efficiency and the autonomy of capital were used to justify increasing industrial concentration in the *chaebol* and the corresponding weakening of the state's monitoring capacity.

With the rapid rise in the bankruptcy rate of small and medium enterprises and the steady decline of its middle-class support, the government became increasingly reliant on the support of big business.[33] To give effect to its financial deregulation programme, it liberalized interest rates for various savings accounts, abolished guidelines for bank loans to manufacturing industry, relaxed controls on city banks opening overseas branches, and converted investment banks into merchant banks. Significantly, the drastic reduction of the government's supervisory capacity coincided with a marked expansion of foreign borrowing by both banks and big business. Liberalizing policies would gain additional impetus in the wake of the 1997 financial crisis. Responding to the powerful international constraints bearing upon Korea, the Kim Dae-jung administration proceeded to establish a more robust and coherent financial regulatory regime under the direction of the Financial Supervisory Commission. It set stricter reporting standards for company accounts, and undertook with mixed success a substantial reorganization of the largest *chaebol*.

Despite notable similarities with South Korea, Taiwan's somewhat different political history and strikingly different geopolitical context were bound to produce distinctive outcomes in relation to both the form and content of state intervention. The Taiwanese government, acting through the Economic Stabilization Board, played a decisive role in steering the economy towards export-led growth. The Chiang Kai-shek regime's firm grip on power, coupled with strong US military and economic support, made it possible for a technocratic elite to function with relative antonomy, develop a highly skilled economic bureaucracy and pursue industrial policies which have been described as 'scientific, modern and pragmatic' in both style and content.[34] State-owned enterprises were able to produce many of the basic materials (such as cotton, iron, steel, refined petroleum) which private firms bought at relatively cheap prices as part of a drive to develop key industries, including textiles, machinery and plastics. The state sector was also directly involved in the development of capital-intensive industries, including petrochemicals, ship-building, petroleum refining and nuclear power, as well as the armaments industry with which they formed a vertically integrated production system.

In the wake of Taiwan's increasing diplomatic isolation following Beijing's admission to the UN and the shock waves produced by the 1973–4 oil crisis, the government embarked upon a more self-reliant development strategy. A major programme was launched to improve infrastructure and promote research and development in a range of technologies, including computers, robotics, machine tools, semiconductors, telecommunications, robotics and biotechnology.[35] Operating under the umbrella of the uninterrupted rule of the Kuomintang (KMT), the Taiwanese technocracy was intent on retaining the initiative in industrial policy, a task made easier by the fact that most indigenous businesses were of relatively modest size, at least when compared with the South Korean industrial conglomerates. On the other hand, Taiwan's very success, reflected in persistent trade surpluses, made it vulnerable to growing international pressure for market liberalization and financial deregulation. In response to these and other pressures, decisions were taken to shift Taiwan's labour-intensive manufacturing and textile industries offshore, and in particular to take advantage of the new investment opportunities offered by China's decision to open up its economy and establish a number of special economic zones.

At first glance, the state appears to have played a less conspicuous role in Hong Kong's development. The growth of the colony's manufacturing prowess is often attributed to the flexibility and adaptability of its small-scale businesses. Much of Hong Kong's infrastructure, including its public transport, electricity, telecommunications and port facilities, was operated by the private sector. Even its sophisticated financial sector evolved more in response to regional demand than state intervention. The function of government, other than providing a well-administered legal system, was confined to maintaining conditions for political and macroeconomic stability.[36] Indeed, what proved especially attractive to fund managers and foreign banks was the absence of exchange controls, Hong Kong's low taxation policies, its strategic location, both regionally and globally, and its geographical and psychological proximity to China, notably the close family and business ties that connected it to Guangdong's booming economy.[37] Another contributing factor may have been the government's ability to register budgetary surpluses through the 1980s and early 1990s. The quality of the state educational system, the maintenance of a basic social safety net and perhaps most importantly the provision of affordable public housing [38] also played a part in developing a highly skilled workforce while at the same time minimizing labour costs. It nevertheless remains the case that Hong Kong's economic fortunes prior to June 1997 were inextricably linked to its exceptional legal and political status as an intermediary between Asia and the West and a focal point in the liberalization and modernization of the Chinese economy.

Though Singapore shared much of Hong Kong's commitment to free market policies and export-led growth, the two city-states and former British colonies offered a study as much in contrasts as in similarities. The Singaporean experience from the early 1960s rested very much on the managerial skills of an activist state. Central to the bureaucratic management of the economy was the Economic Development Board, whose task it was to oversee the development of the manufacturing sector and create conditions favourable to both local and foreign investment. To this end, the Singapore government, resting on a close alliance between the People's Action Party (PAP) and the civil service[39] and on Lee Kuan Yew's pervasive influence, first as Prime Minister and subsequently as Senior Minister, sought to establish firm control over the labour force by suppressing communist activity, eliminating independent trade unions and developing instead a special relationship with the National Trade Union Congress.[40] The state's role, however, was not confined to creating a macroeconomic, industrial or fiscal environment conducive to private investment. Through the establishment of a number of statutory boards and state-owned enterprises, themselves subsidiaries of one of three government holding companies, the state was able to influence directly the trajectory of Singapore's industrial development, the choice of technologies and the achievement of employment goals.[41] To this must be added the government's sustained efforts to upgrade Singapore's technological capacity and develop more sophisticated industries, which explains the very substantial investment in education and training programmes. Finally, mention must be made of the institutional measures taken to enhance Singapore's comparative advantage in the provision of financial services and as a market for foreign exchange and other financial transactions.[42] Given the extent and intensity of the state's intrusiveness, some observers have gone so far as to describe the Singapore model of economic development as socialism by another name. Yet such a conclusion is misleading for it equates bureaucratic activism, which is after all but a means to an end, with the end itself. More importantly, it fails, as we shall see, to distinguish the internal and external dimensions of state autonomy. While the state apparatus may be omnipresent within Singapore itself, it remains an open question as to how effectively that apparatus can influence, let alone control, the major players and forces that directly impact on the Singaporean economy.

To complete this brief overview of institutional processes, it may be useful to say a word about the Malaysian experience. As we have already noted, the introduction of the New Economic Policy, which assumed concrete form with the Second Malaysia Plan (1971–5), was an attempt by the state to attenuate Malay resentment of interethnic economic inequalities through a strategy of affirmative action. In line with this policy, the proliferation of non-financial public enterprises (which rose from 109 in 1970 to 656 in 1980) was paralleled by greatly increased resource allocation to the public sector (from RM4.6 billion for the period 1966–70 to RM31.1 billion during 1976–80),[43] made possible in large measure by the dramatic expansion of the state's oil revenues. Through Petronas, the state had assumed control over Malaysia's oil and gas reserves and through the Malaysia Mining Corporation substantial control over the tin industry. One of the principal objectives of government policy had been achieved, namely greater Malay ownership of the agricultural, manufacturing, financial and banking sectors. By the early 1980s the state was ready to support a new development phase, namely a targeted industrialization programme which, as the 'Look East' policy clearly suggested, was patterned on the model pioneered by Japan and subsequently adopted by South Korea and Taiwan. The new industrial policy, which crystallized with the First

Industrial Master Plan (1986–95), was designed to achieve specific growth targets in selected industries, notably in steel, cement, motor vehicles, heavy engineering and electronics.[44] The new approach, while it envisaged the expansion and upgrading of Malaysia's industrial capabilities, was not however predicated upon continuing high levels of state intervention.

The development of Malay capitalism, manifested in the emergence of an expanding Malay managerial class, did give rise to various forms of cronyism, in particular bureaucrats-turned-businessmen who were little more than 'rent seekers'.[45] On the other hand, it also created a new stratum of Malay entrepreneurs possessed of considerable technical and professional skills, eager to take advantage of the new business opportunities that might accompany a shrinking public sector and a corresponding transfer of resources to the private sector. The recession of 1985–6, characterized by a collapse in commodity prices, rising public debt and a decline in private investment, served as the catalyst for a concerted programme of economic liberalization and financial deregulation. Instructively, Mahathir's drive for privatization was supported by various social classes and ethnic groups. An important segment of the Malay business elite was now more concerned with creating conditions for greater growth than for more equitable distribution.[46] Less dependent on continued state and party patronage, this group of Malay capitalists had become 'more closely integrated with Chinese and/or foreign capital'.[47] Chinese capitalism had itself markedly changed. With the exception of that diminishing segment of the Chinese business elite linked primarily to the Chinese chambers of commerce, Chinese capital had much in common with the emerging *bumiputra* capitalist class.

Enough has been said to suggest that in Malaysia's case the state was intimately connected with the emergence of an indigenous business elite. The policies of the state were clearly instrumental in sustaining the conditions for capital accumulation and ensuring that indigenous capitalists obtained a sizeable share of the spoils and opportunities associated with economic growth. The five-year plans under the New Economic Policy and the subsequent Industrial Master Plans, as well as the periodic responses to crises, for example the 1985–6 recession and more strikingly the 1997 financial crisis, can be interpreted as attempts by the state to maintain the momentum of growth and extend or at least protect the gains made by the indigenous capitalist class. Though the timing, political setting and policy instruments used differed in each case, the same general conclusion applies to Japan, South Korea, Taiwan, Hong Kong and Singapore, and to a greater or lesser extent to the capitalist upsurge in other parts of Southeast Asia.[48] Less clear, however, is the extent to which the Southeast Asian state, even in Malaysia's case, was able to develop the political structure necessary for the purpose. Equally unclear is the extent to which those policies – both the institutional strategies adopted and instruments used – and even the objectives they were meant to serve were shaped by the state or by external influences largely outside its control.

The preceding survey is not intended to provide a detailed account of the role of the state in the contemporary development of East Asia's economies. Rather the aim is to illustrate the main features of the 'strong state' thesis and to acknowledge that it sheds useful light on the important economic and political transformation taking place in the region and on the nexus between state and economy, that is, between business and politics, which has been central to that transformation. Yet the thesis explains both too little and too much. Distinct from, though not altogether unconnected with, the unresolved definitional problems raised by the notion of the 'strong state' are two crucial questions. First, if the strong performance of East Asia's economies is to be explained by reference to state strength, how are we to explain weak economic performance, or for that matter serious shortcomings in other areas of public policy? Second, if state strength is the key variable accounting for East Asia's economic dynamism, how are we to explain this commonality in state practices and institutions in what is generally portrayed as a highly heterogeneous region?

In a sense both questions allude to a common methodological problem: is the political economy of East Asia essentially uniform across time and space, and therefore explicable in terms of some relatively constant factor? Or is variability a distinguishing characteristic of economic and political outcomes, in which case a number of variables need to be integrated into the equation?

Turning first to the second question, exponents of the 'strong state' thesis have attempted to provide an answer by linking political norms and institutions with social and cultural influences, or to put it more simply, by proposing culture as the key to East Asian exceptionalism.[49] This proposition will be explored at some length when we come to discuss the state–civil society relationship. Suffice it here to say that, unless carefully formulated, cultural explanations run the risk of crude reductionism.[50] Even if it could be argued that the formation of a strong state in South Korea and Japan had its origins in feudal Confucianism, the same explanation could not be applied so easily to the political economies of Hong Kong, Taiwan, post-Maoist China, not to mention Malaysia, Indonesia or Thailand. Indeed, to attribute the rise of East Asia to Confucianism or some other generalised civilizational ethos or system of acculturation is, as Mark Berger and others have cautioned, to construct a 'new orientalism'.[51]

This latest conceptualization of the problem may be more instructive for what it tells us about dominant North American and West European discourses on modernization than about the dynamics of economic growth in East Asia. Not so long ago, an older 'orientalism' relied on the same essentialist cultural categories to explain, not the strength, capability or success of the East, but the weakness, inadequacy and failure of its traditions and institutions. Indeed, it is arguable that the recent pattern of East Asia's economic development owes as much to Anglo-American market liberalism as it does to indigenous political cultures. As Weiss herself concedes:

> Today, one of the biggest threats to state coordinating power (and thereby long-term growth) stems from the rise of American trained neo-classical economists to influential positions in the governments of Taiwan and Korea. Their growing significance in policy making circles has led to increasing efforts, especially within the Korean government, to let markets do the job of coordination.[52]

By the mid-1980s western concepts and institutional practices had a profound impact not only on the way East Asian economies – the Chinese economy very much included – did business with the rest of the world, but across the spectrum of macroeconomic and even microeconomic policies. The traumatic events of July 1997 merely served to deepen and accelerate this trend.

One may go further and suggest that the celebration of East Asia's economic dynamism, though clearly reflected in the triumphalist narratives favoured by domestic elites, ultimately rests on acceptance of prevailing western conceptions of economic success, and the corresponding emphasis on exponential rates of GNP growth, steadily rising levels of per capita energy usage, and rapidly expanding individual consumer affluence. We are thus brought back to our first question and the need to evaluate more objectively the assumed solidity and longevity of East Asia's economic success. It is in part the addiction to the western model and dependence on transnational capital which accounts for the relative neglect in public policy, at least until recently, of the environmental implications of unplanned and unregulated growth. The strong state, it seems, has not been strong enough or independently minded enough to integrate into its planning processes such costs as acute air pollution resulting from high levels of sulphur dioxide and other gaseous emissions, acid rain, overuse of pesticides, water contamination, unregulated waste dumping, deforestation and inadequate nuclear safety standards.[53] These environmental consequences, it should be noted, are integral not merely to considerations of health and aesthetics, but to the developmental calculus itself, that is, to future prospects for sustained economic growth. Any assessment of the performance of the East Asian state would also need to take account of other costs, including trade and technological dependence (manifested in the heavy reliance of several East Asian economies on the US market and Japanese technology), the vulnerability of the agricultural sector to liberalization of the domestic market, and the mass exodus from the countryside to the cities, all of which in varying degrees accompanied policies of export-oriented industrialization.

The 'strong state' hypothesis, persuasive though it may seem, is on closer reflection both too limiting and too encompassing to be read as an adequate account of the East Asian economic experience. In no way does this conclusion lend added credence to the neo-liberal argument. It merely reinforces the view that East Asian industrialization must be properly contextualized, in both spatial and temporal terms. The export-led growth of the manufacturing sector has occurred at different times and assumed different forms in different economies. To this extent at least the East Asian 'economic miracle' must be seen as one phase in a qualitatively evolving process. The evidence is of sequential and highly differentiated development. To describe that development in the present tense is therefore highly tendentious. It is to bestow on what is a complex and in all probability a relatively brief historical phase a permanence and uniformity it does not possess.

Let us then set East Asia's economic performance in its proper international and historical setting and in so doing connect it to the analysis outlined in Chapter 2. For Henderson and Appelbaum, five important phases have contributed to the region's transformative dynamics: Japanese industrialization between the Meiji Restoration of 1867–8 and the First World War; the impact of western colonialism in the region; the conjunction of decolonization and geopolitical and ideological bipolarity; overlapping with the third phase, a period of expanding world trade associated with the 'long boom' in the industrialised western world between the late 1940s and early 1970s; and in the most recent phase the onset in many core economies of turbulence and bouts of prolonged recession.[54] This periodization no doubt needs to be considerably elaborated and refined but it does convey something of the important external influences that have shaped the contemporary East Asian experience.

Japan's significance in any explanatory scheme cannot be overstated. It represents the first wave of East Asian industrialization but is also an important catalyst for every subsequent wave. Japan's internal social structures and cultural forms were undeniably central to its economic success in the twentieth century, but so was commercial and technological contact with the West.[55] Conversely, the Japanese state contributed not only to Japan's own economic modernization, but to that of other East Asian societies, not least those that succumbed to Japanese military expansion, notably Manchuria, Korea and Taiwan. Japanese colonial rule in the Korean peninsula was instrumental in building the necessary physical infrastructure, implanting 'a model of a highly articulated, disciplined bureaucracy, later to be adopted by South Koreans',[56] establishing, courtesy of the *zaibatsu*, the framework for the subsequent development of South Korea's *chaebol*, and creating the conditions for the emergence of an indigenous working class. Imperial control in both Taiwan and Korea, relying as it did on a hierarchical military administration, also bequeathed to both societies a deeply embedded institutional predisposition to bureaucratic discipline and authoritarian state forms.[57] The impact of colonialism assumed a different form but was no less striking in Hong Kong and Singapore. Relatively efficient legal and bureaucratic systems were an important feature of the British legacy as were the extensive networks of trading houses and specialized services.[58]

In the more recent period two factors, one of global dimensions and the other with a sharper regional focus, were to exert a profound and lasting impact on East Asian industrialization. The first refers to the dual movement that has characterized the trajectory of the core capitalist economies in the latter half of the twentieth century. The sustained growth they experienced during the 1950s and 1960s established the necessary conditions for newcomers to penetrate the rapidly expanding markets for manufactured products. Paradoxically, the subsequent downturn that afflicted many of the core economies reinforced the trend. The severe pressure on profit margins, which set in motion the global relocation of manufacturing industries, especially clothing, textiles, footwear and electronics, provided another window of opportunity for East Asian export-led industrialization. The second factor, which may be described as the distinguishing feature of East Asia's regional political economy, has been Japan's emergence as a major industrial and financial centre. For more than three decades Japan would supply much of the capital and technology and, to a lesser but not negligible extent, the psychological confidence and institutional model that would underpin East Asian industrialization.

Placed in this context, the strong, authoritarian East Asian state may be said to have served an indispensable function within the changing international division of labour. Given the relative abundance of unskilled and underemployed labour, particularly in industries that relied on a largely female workforce, and the existence of bureaucratized, often highly militarized, political systems capable of enforcing labour discipline, East Asia was ideally placed to host manufacturing enterprises in search of higher profit margins. To the extent that the state could offer additional incentives, whether in the form of tax concessions, subsidized infrastructure, or low levels of health, environmental, work safety and financial oversight, East Asian economies became immensely attractive to both domestic and foreign capital. Within this highly generalized pattern there was much scope for improvization and differentiation of market strategies. Empirical studies of the footwear industry, for example, have established that, whereas South Korean firms succeeded in capturing a sizeable share of the extraordinarily dynamic athletic footwear market in the United States, Taiwanese producers tended to concentrate on the already established market in plastic and vinyl shoes.[59]

Different market niches for particular consumer goods must themselves be differentiated from different types of export production. Gerefi identifies five such types, of which three are crucially important to East Asian industrialization: *the commercial subcontracting role* involving the production of finished consumer goods by locally owned firms, which are then distributed and marketed by large retail chains and their agents; the *export platform role*, where production is concentrated in export-processing zones that deliver a range of special advantages to foreign capital; and the *component supplier role* in which subsidiaries of foreign firms manufacture parts or sub-units of consumer goods, which are then either assembled and marketed by the parent company in the country of destination or sold to diverse buyers on the world market.[60] Different market niches and different economic roles reflect the disparities in technological, managerial and commercial capabilities between countries, and between the different stages of industrial development within the same country. More than that, they indicate the complex ways in which the East Asian semi-peripheral economies have attempted to gain an international competitive advantage by performing at any given moment specific functions with an increasingly globalized economy.

This last point is worth stressing because it highlights the dynamic character both of the international division of labour and of the functions performed by particular economies and particular states. The industrial strategies pursued by East Asian states and the institutions and mechanisms developed for the purpose are therefore attributable as much – if not more – to a rapidly evolving division of labour as to the norms of an enduring political culture. Even if the 'strong state' accurately describes the extensive regulatory and co-ordinating functions it performed in the early stages of industrialization, it does not follow that such functions would continue to be performed indefinitely into the future. Higher wages and higher levels of unionization, coupled with rising demands for social welfare, at a time of closer integration into the regional and global division of labour, were likely to yield higher costs of production, more intensive competition for access to capital and technology, accompanied by increasing pressures for trade liberalization and financial deregulation, and often unpredictable capital flows directed to real estate, stock market and currency speculation.

On the vastly altered geoeconomic stage of the 1990s East Asian states were placed under enormous pressure by a combination of core states and transnational economic and financial actors to depart from their well-rehearsed scripts, and this at a time of profound internal social and political upheaval when they were especially vulnerable to outside pressure.

East Asian states were not all equally affected by the new circumstances, and their responses were far from identical. As the 1997 'financial crisis' demonstrated, the obvious differences between first-tier and second-tier economies were compounded by significant disparities within both tiers. Whereas the Taiwanese and Singaporean economies continued to perform relatively well, aided by strong trading accounts and foreign exchange reserves, South Korea and Hong Kong experienced severe recession. Whereas some felt obliged to accept IMF conditionalities (Indonesia, Thailand, South Korea), others experimented with limited capital controls (Malaysia). Yet these were essentially variations on a theme. The dynamics of globalization now permeated the structure of all East Asian economies. In the process new subnational spaces were emerging, whether metropolitan centres or export processing zones, linked more to transnational economic spaces than to their national hinterlands. Paralleling this trend were new regional zones and networks, whether natural economic territories or free trade groupings, further accelerating the free flow of capital, labour and technology.[61] As a consequence the East Asian state of the 1990s had to operate within an environment far more conducive to deregulation, which did not, however, mean the withdrawal of the state from all forms of economic regulation. Indeed, by the end of the decade the main thrust of the IMF's message to East Asian governments was the need to accelerate the restructuring of their corporate and financial systems.

In a sense, international financial institutions were calling upon the East Asian state to continue playing a highly activist, indeed interventionist role, but in accordance with the logic of the global capital market. Once East Asia's economies had achieved industrial take-off and entered the era of mass consumption, the state was expected to oversee a transitional regime which would see the industrial and financial assets of those economies opened up to international competition.[62] Taking advantage of continuous technological innovation and the proliferation of financial instruments, actors in the market place were now able to respond to changing prices with remarkable speed and flexibility. The task of the state was no longer to identify strategic industries, let alone to protect them, but to sustain the conditions most conducive to these market activities. It was not so much a case of managing the national economy as of keeping 'the fundamentals' right and of developing robust financial institutions and transparent legal, administrative and accounting systems and procedures.[63] The tenor of the World Bank's advice in this regard was unmistakable: 'East Asia needs to move faster in developing regulatory frameworks for creating competition, managing the contracting process, and regulating monopolies'.[64] This is not to say that the response to globalization was uniform across Pacific Asia, or that East Asian developmental states, whether broadly or narrowly defined, were about to 'converge on Anglo-American norms and institutions'.[65] On the other hand, it is equally clear that the erosion of developmentalism or the onset of 'normalization' was more advanced than exponents of the strong state were prepared to acknowledge. The state in Japan and Taiwan might continue to support the development and commercialization of new technologies, but the global context in which interventionist policies now took shape was likely to exert decisive influence over the content, structure and success of such policies. In any case, how each state approached the task of financial regulation or economic co-ordination would vary considerably from state to state, as would economic outcomes and the levels of consent and resistance. Economic policy could not be indefinitely insulated from societal demands and aspirations.

STATE AND CIVIL SOCIETY

We have been at pains to show that the 'strength' of the East Asian state, while it offers useful insights into the political economy of these countries, captures only one slice of a complex reality. We are, however, on much safer ground when pointing to highly centralized political systems. In common with much of the post-colonial world, East Asian states have justified centralization as the only available antidote to the dangers of fragmentation and polarization. Needless to say, institutional forms have assumed a different complexion depending on time and place, with power and authority variously concentrated in the leader, the dominant political party, the bureaucracy, the military, or some combination of these.

Individual leaders have undoubtedly played a key role in maintaining elite cohesion, while at the same time making elite rule acceptable to a wider constituency or even the population as a whole. Mao Zedong and Deng Xiaoping in China, Chiang Kai-shek in Taiwan, Ho Chi Minh in Vietnam, Norodom Sihanouk in Cambodia, Suharto in Indonesia, Mahathir in Malaysia and Lee Kuan Yew in Singapore are among the more obvious examples. The functions performed by different leaders have, of course, varied considerably, as have the sources of their power, their claims to legitimacy, ideologies and decision-making styles. Of particular interest in this context is the typology proposed by David Brown, who postulates five principal types of elite cohesion, each requiring different leadership roles: neo-patrimonialism; charisma; corporatism; class; and dominant consociationalism.[66] Although conceptually distinct, these five types in practice often intersect and overlap.

This is especially the case in contemporary East Asian politics, where all five types are represented, but where three appear to have deeper roots and to have decisively shaped the evolution of political institutions and the growth of civil society.

The neo-patrimonial model, most strikingly evident in Suharto's style of leadership, saw different elements of the military, business and ethnic elites offer their support to the leader in return for a share of the resources which he controlled. To a greater or lesser extent, Park Chung Hee, Deng Xiaoping and Ferdinand Marcos may be said to conform to this model. Equally important has been the charismatic leader (for example, Sukarno, Mao, Ho Chi Minh, Sihanouk) whose principal claim to legitimacy is his role as 'the father figure of the nation' rather than his ability to disburse resources or influence. More significant in the recent experience of industrializing states has been the corporatist model where the leader – Chun Doo Hwan, Lee Kuan Yew, Mahathir are obvious instances – considers himself to be overseeing a bureaucratic or technocratic apparatus equipped to deliver 'efficient management' of the economy and offering private enterprises and associations access to state resources and decision-making structures, but with the state retaining primacy in defining and facilitating legitimate interest articulation. A brief reference should perhaps be made to Brown's fifth type, 'dominant consociationalism', which seeks to maintain the stability of an ethnically plural state by devising some acceptable power-sharing formula. In East Asia, post-1969 Malaysia is perhaps the only striking example of consociationalist politics, because in almost every other instance the overwhelming dominance of one ethnic bloc effectively precluded any incentive or opportunity for institutional power-sharing. Even in the case of Malaysia, constitutional arrangements consciously sought to protect the interests of the Malay majority.

Critically important though it has been to the functioning of the state, the role of the strong leader cannot be viewed in isolation from other political institutions. Indeed, one of the main functions of leadership has been to maintain the cohesion and effectiveness of the dominant institution, or less frequently some equilibrium between competing institutions. More often than not it is the political party which has provided the institutional framework for the exercise of leadership. For all the vicissitudes of their respective histories, the Chinese Communist Party (CCP) in China and the Kuomintang (KMT) in Taiwan would perform that function without break for 50 years. In each case, the1990s would see a gradual erosion of the monolithic control once exercised by the party, but despite the restructuring of polity and economy, both the CCP and the KMT were intent on retaining their pervasive influence on the political process. In China's case, the CCP's agonizing experiment with the socialist market economy and the draconian ban on the Buddhist sect, Falun Gong, and the resulting 'three stresses' campaign formally launched in June 1999, could be read as different expressions of the same strategic intent, namely self-preservation. In the former case the aim was to satisfy material aspirations, thereby consolidating the regime's legitimacy, and in the latter to eliminate a potential channel for independent political mobilization[67] and at the same time arrest the corrosive effect of corruption on the Communist Party's badly tarnished image.

In Southeast Asia, the dominant party was integral to the political economy of Singapore and Malaysia, and to a lesser extent Indonesia. Under Lee Kuan Yew's leadership, the People's Action Party (PAP), which had established its dominance as far back as 1954, used the collapse of the merger with Malaysia in 1965 as added justification for a highly disciplined, not to say authoritarian, model of leadership. The PAP projected itself as the party of strong and meritocratic government, offering representation within its ranks to non-Chinese minorities and depicting political opposition as a regressive irresponsible force.[68] The strengthening of party power, including recourse to extra-parliamentary methods of coercion, not least the Internal Security Act, was presented as the unavoidable instrument for defeating the communist movement and promoting economic growth. Having tamed all political opposition, the PAP had effectively achieved a monopoly of power, exercising its hegemony over every arm of the state, including the bureaucracy, judiciary and military.[69]

In Malaysia, the multiethnic ruling coalition, the Barisan Nasional, was the vehicle chosen to establish an arrangement based on elite accommodation between the Malay majority and the non-Malay minority communities. In return for receiving patronage benefits, the non-Malay elites were prepared to accept Malay political leadership expressed through the United Malays National Organization (UMNO). Formed in 1946 to give voice to Malay national consciousness, UMNO came to dominate government in the post-independence period, with constitutional provisions progressively eroded, particularly in the wake of the intercommunal riots of May 1969. Despite the determined efforts of opposition parties, in particular the largely Chinese Democratic Action Party (DAP) and the Malay Islamic Party (PAS), UMNO was able to assert its dominance in part through manipulation of electoral boundaries and periodic recourse to the Internal Security Act, but also through extensive control over the media and enactment of emergency legislation.[70] Notwithstanding the trappings of constitutional parliamentary democracy, autocracy or 'soft authoritarianism' seemed more appropriate labels for the Malaysian and Singaporean political systems, at least during the heyday of Mahthir's and Lee Kuan Yew's rule. To argue that in both countries power had become increasingly centralized in the leader and the party through which he operated is not, however, to obscure the significant differences between the two systems. Politics in Malaysia was generally more open, with greater opportunities for public debate and more visible signs of division within the overall power structure and UMNO itself. The fact nevertheless remains that in each case the centralization of power and authority had been achieved, though by different means and to different degrees, at the expense of the autonomy of other institutions, whether it be the parliament, the judiciary or the media, and additionally in the case of Malaysia the royalty or regional government.

Centralization of power and authority was also a distinguishing feature of Indonesia's New Order, although in this case the four streams, or *aliran*, that had emerged as integral aspects of Indonesia's national consciousness in the post-independence period, namely Islam, nationalism, communism and the role of the military, could not so easily be assimilated into a monolithic power structure. Sukarno's strategy of using his personal authority to balance one stream against another achieved at best partial and temporary success. Following the bloody transition from Sukarno to Suharto and the effective destruction of the PKI, the military sought to reinforce their primacy *vis-à vis* all other political forces by assuming a dual responsibility (*dwifungsi*) for national defence and national development.[71] The latter objective was essential to the New Order's strategy of widening its support base and strengthening its political legitimacy.[72] To this end new institutions would gradually emerge designed to create a politically stable framework which, in addition to entrenching the power of the military, would establish the social and economic structures conducive to a programme of sustained economic modernization. The particular emphasis attached to agribusiness, manufacturing and financial services was not, however, explicable purely in terms of poverty alleviation or the more abstract commitment to wealth creation. The additional resources which the developmental process was likely to place at the state's disposal were seen as critical to the task of funding the politics of patronage and in the process buttressing the 'New Order pyramid' based on a politically active military, a centralized bureaucracy and, above all, a dominant presidency.[73] The formation of Golkar, a party consisting of linked functional groups and funded largely by ABRI and the bureaucracy, served primarily as an extension of military and bureaucratic interests. Unlike the PAP in Singapore or UMNO in Malaysia, its primary function was to legitimate rather than co-ordinate the state apparatus.

Enough has been said to indicate that the political systems of both Northeast and Southeast Asia, even when they shared the common goal of export-led industrialization, differed considerably in their formal as well as informal institutions and conventions. The respective roles performed by leaders, political parties, the armed forces and the bureaucracy, the leverage they each wielded and the power relationships between them were far from uniform across the region, or even within each sub-region. It may nevertheless be possible to generalize to this extent: state power and authority tended to be highly centralized, usually in the hands of a dominant leader or political party. Where, for one reason or another, no single party had achieved a hegemonic position, the tendency was for the leader to be closely aligned with, or rely for his power base on, the military (for example, South Korea, Indonesia). In almost every instance the relative status and power enjoyed by the bureaucracy had increased over time, although the trend was more conspicuous in countries at a more advanced stage of industrialization (as with South Korea and Singapore). With the partial exception of Singapore, bureaucratic standards of rationality were somehow able to co-exist with, and at times strengthen, pre-existing or even newly emerging patron–client relationships.

The centralist tendencies of the polities we have just described were largely antithetical to notions of 'openness' or political pluralism. During the 1970s and 1980s traditions of vigorous public debate and loyal opposition were generally unfamiliar or uncongenial to the body politic, or forcibly marginalized by regimes which regarded them as threatening their very survival. Several influences, however, some of domestic, others of international provenance, would in due course combine to produce a markedly different political environment, and to encourage among both established and emerging political players a different calculus of political risks and opportunities. The particular mix of influences, their interaction, timing and trajectory, would vary from country to country. Increasing integration into the world economy inevitably created tensions between the winners and losers from trade liberalization and financial deregulation, between the proponents of rapid modernization and its twin concomitants, urbanization and secularization on the one hand, and traditionalists whose support was rooted in rural or religious settings[74] on the other. The vastly increased purchasing power of a sizeable middle class, the acute vulnerability of important strata of society to either sudden or prolonged economic downturn – graphically demonstrated in the aftermath of the 1997 financial crisis – coupled with the revival of suppressed religious and cultural identities or the emergence of new ones, were bound to generate powerful pressures for change. In much of the literature it is often readily assumed that such pressures would sooner or later manifest themselves in a concerted drive for greater democracy. Such a conclusion is, as we shall see, at least premature and possibly misleading.

The experience of democratization as it slowly and at times painfully unfolded in South Korea in the late 1980s and 1990s, or somewhat more consistently in Taiwan, is not necessarily the model that was followed elsewhere. In the Philippines, the departure of the Marcos regime pointed to a more dramatic break with the authoritarian past, in sharp contrast to the resistance to change which variously characterized the Chinese, Malaysian and Singaporean political systems. In each case, the democratic impulse, nowhere fully developed but equally nowhere entirely absent, functioned within a unique national environment, giving rise to distinctive processes and outcomes. We shall return to these in the ensuing examination of the role of culture and the evolution of civil society. A few observations about the demise of the New Order in Indonesia may nevertheless be pertinent here, not simply because of the intrinsic importance of these events or of their diplomatic and strategic implications for the region, but because they serve to highlight in unusually dramatic fashion the structures and agencies that are simultaneously facilitating and impeding the transition to new political forms and practices.

In a bid to legitimize the New Order and strengthen the authority of his own position, Suharto, drawing upon symbols deeply rooted in Javanese culture, had consciously fostered a culture of paternalistic dependency.[75] Projecting himself as *bapak pembangunan* ('father of development'), he cultivated a patrimonial system, with ABRI, the bureaucracy and Golkar functioning as the coercive, technical and political-ideological pillars sustaining New Order rule. The distribution of benefits associated with rapid economic growth, particularly after the early 1980s, was sufficiently widespread to limit the incidence and intensity of dissent, which is not to say that corruption itself was not widespread or that those in positions of power did not take advantage of their office to amass immense fortunes. According to one estimate, five of the top ten indigenous taxpayers in 1993 were either children or close relatives of the president. Collectively, they had acquired large interests in petrochemicals, satellite communications, road construction, the clove and citrus fruit industries and the national car project. Many of the largest Chinese business empires were closely connected to the president or had financial ties to members of his family.[76]

Two distinguishing features of the New Order need emphasizing here: first, the fragility of the elite consensus on which it rested; and second, the pressures periodically emanating from below, whether in the form of peasant unrest, student protest, Islamic discontent or ethno-regional separatism. The preservation of the New Order and Suharto's leadership depended on preventing either tendency from reaching critical proportions, and perhaps more crucially on ensuring that the two tendencies did not interact to set off an uncontrollable chain reaction. Both tasks remained relatively manageable so long as the economic climate allowed the dispensation of sufficient largesse among the elites and offered the less privileged strata of society a reasonable prospect of material progress. It is not surprising therefore that the mismanagement of several military-run enterprises in the early 1970s and the collapse of the oil boom in the mid-1980s should have been seen as endangering the stability of the New Order. In both instances, the government reacted by effecting significant policy shifts which were themselves potentially destabilizing since they entailed a realignment in the relative status and power of different elites and intellectual currents. Despite the apparent success of export-oriented industrialization in the early 1980s and 1990s, the government's freedom of action was severely circumscribed by the intense competition for policy ascendancy between neo-liberal technocrats and economic nationalists, and for political influence between ambitious generals and well-connected business groups.[77]

The delicate juggling act on which Suharto's leadership rested and the precarious balance between elite and popular expectations on the one hand and the economy's capacity to deliver on the other meant that domestic and international demands for the loosening of political controls had to be treated with great caution. A few tentative steps towards political liberalization in the early 1990s were soon halted with the banning in June 1994 of three widely read popular magazines, *Tempo*, *Detik* and *Editor*, the jailing of journalists and the fierce crackdown on more radical forms of political activism. A watershed was reached in June 1996 when Megawati Sukarnoputri, daughter of former President Sukarno, was removed from the leadership of the Indonesian Democratic Party (PDI). Her removal was dictated by fear – a sense that, unless her political fortunes were nipped in the bud, she might become an irresistible symbol of popular discontent that would help to energize and mobilize a nationwide opposition movement.[78] The exclusion of Megawati and her supporters from the officially sanctioned list of PDI candidates for elections scheduled in 1997, the eruption of violent demonstrations in Jakarta and the subsequent storming of PDI headquarters constituted a defining moment in Indonesian politics.

With the Suharto regime already strained to the limit, it simply remained for the suddenness and ferocity of the 1997 financial crisis to administer the *coup de grâce*. Not only did the economic downturn drastically curtail the government's capacity to maintain existing employment levels, especially in the cities, but the conditionalities of the IMF package meant sharp increases in the price of food and other essential commodities and withdrawal of government support for banks and large business ventures whose survival depended on the injection of public funds. At its most vulnerable moment in more than 30 years, the New Order was effectively deprived of the economic levers which may have enabled it to survive in the short to medium term. With Suharto's dethronement in mid-1998 and B.J. Habibie's accession to the presidency, Indonesian politics entered a tumultuous period of prolonged and intense student protests in the cities, violent clashes across the ethnic and religious divide in several provinces, the progressive breakdown of law and order in East Timor, with varying degrees of TNI complicity before and after the UN-administered self-determination ballot of 30 August 1999, and new revelations of corruption, of which the Bank Bali scandal would prove the most damaging to Habibie's political fortunes.

This was nevertheless a period of significant transition, marked by the progressive fracturing of the New Order coalition of interests and extensive political reforms, including provisions for a democratically elected legislature and a much freer press. The June 1999 elections, which saw Megawati's PDI secure a substantially larger share of the national vote than Golkar, endowed Indonesian politics with a degree of pluralism scarcely imaginable even six months earlier. The election in October 1999 of Abdurrahman Abdurrahman as President and Megawati Sukarnoputri as Vice-President and the subsequent appointment of a 32-member, overwhelmingly civilian and reformist cabinet[79] was the culmination of a transitional period which promised a more proactive parliament, a more independent judiciary and a civil society more likely to command the attention of the political and bureaucratic elites. What emerges from this sequence of events is not that Indonesia had entered a new era of stable democratic politics – the immediate future was likely to prove no less unpredictable than the recent past – but that the New Order, despite its façade of stability and strength, had in several important respects failed to establish a strong institutional base. While Suharto had for the best part of 30 years managed through skilful manipulation of money politics and the military's supremacy to centralize power in his own hands, the state nevertheless remained a fragile edifice poorly equipped to withstand the political and economic tremors of the late 1990s.

THE POLITICS OF LEGITIMATION

By virtue of the centralization of power and authority and the corresponding marginalization of civil society, legitimation had for many East Asian states become the *sine qua non* of political stability. Several distinct but closely related principles became central to the legitimation project. Of these the most obvious, though not necessarily the most important, was the promise of economic prosperity and physical security, a familiar theme in much of European history. To achieve these ends, the state was precluded from making respect for individual rights and liberties a high priority, for it operated in a hostile environment by reason not only of the essential anarchy of the international system – a notion hardly unfamiliar to the western mind – but of its own economic, technological and military backwardness. Individual rights and democratic processes were a luxury which the Asian state, preoccupied with the requirements of sheer survival, could ill afford. Particularly for the less developed economies, modernization discourse became inextricably linked with the politics of legitimation. Rather than the claims of the individual, the state had to focus on the collective good, which might well dictate the growth of more effective forms of bureaucratic control.[80] Japan's economic success both before and after the Second World War, and later the strong performance of the tiger economies, was presented as vindication of this principle. There was, however, more to the state's legitimation strategy than a professed commitment to raising living standards. The particular formulation might vary from state to state, but almost invariably an appeal would be made to a sense of collective pride, variously expressed as a return to an idealized past, an affirmation of religious faith or a critique of western domination.

To return to a theme we have previously canvassed, though in a slightly different context, the search for political legitimacy had to be culturally grounded. It had to be embedded in a set of ideas and symbols, a collective state of mind which bestowed on the nation its sense of identity, purpose and social solidarity.[81] For many states these ideas and symbols were derived from the colonial experience itself; that is, the state's legitimacy rested in part on the struggle for independence and on post-colonial attempts to create a national identity distinct from western interests, policies and institutions. China under Mao, Indonesia under Sukarno and Malaysia under Mahathir all endeavoured to project their respective political programmes as forms of state-building designed to counter the hegemonic intentions of the West. Influential as this perspective may have been, it was clearly not enough. It had somehow to be complemented by a more positive message, one unambiguously rooted in their own civilizational experience.

To establish the legitimacy of a highly centralized system, it was necessary to reconstruct from the classical tradition a particular conception of the relationship of individual and collectivity, one which would reinforce the authority of the state as the embodiment of the collective good, but at the same time permit the individual to exercise consumer choice and the firm to make investment decisions. The claim has frequently been made that South Korean, Japanese, and in particular Chinese societies found in their common Confucian heritage the necessary foundations for an authoritarian political system capable of stimulating capitalist economic development.[82] In contrast to the western model of state-building, with its emphasis on rationality, efficiency and individualism, this oriental model was said to rest on 'human emotional bonds, group orientation and harmony'.[83] The idea that neo-Confucianism may have served as the ethical foundation of East Asian economic dynamism – some have referred to it as the functional equivalent of the Protestant ethic in the early rise of European capitalism[84] – is not, however, the immediate focus of our analysis. What concerns us here is not so much the economic as the political function of Confucianism, not its contribution to economic development *per se* but its concept of the state.

Confucian political thought, it has been argued, privileges hierarchy and expertise. It is the aim of both virtuous man (*junzi*) and virtuous government to conform to *Dao* – the way to recreate in the present 'the perfectly ordered arrangement of virtuous rule and universal harmony' that once existed in the distant past.[85] The Confucian world view is centred on five fundamental relationships (*wulun*), namely affection between parent and child; righteousness between ruler and subject; distinction between husband and wife; order between old and young; and sincerity between friends. The aim of these relationships is to cultivate the perfect virtue of love or benevolence (*ren*) and uphold the principle of reciprocity (*shu*). Societies within the East Asian 'Sinitic sphere' have over the centuries espoused with varying degrees of authenticity and intensity these Confucian core values as a way of underpinning the legitimacy of the state and mobilizing wider support for the existing regime.

The Meiji Restoration in Japan in the latter half of the nineteenth century offers a striking manifestation of this tendency, the influence of which would extend well into the twentieth century and far beyond Japan's borders. The overthrow of the Tokugawa Shogunate in 1867 and the restoration of the imperial authority of the Meiji dynasty ushered in the establishment of a politically unified and modernized state. Integral to this political project was the propagation of new loyalties and the transformation of a predominantly peasant population into citizens of a centralized state. Education policy, by emphasizing traditional Confucian and Shinto values, would play a major part in inculcating this new ideological orientation. The Imperial University Order of 1886 rendered the university a servant of the state for the training of high officials and elites in various fields, and was followed by sweeping changes to the school system and the introduction of a rigid, regimented curriculum designed to foster 'a good and obedient, faithful and respectful character'. These reforms culminated in 1890 in the Imperial Rescript on Education (Kyoiku Chokugo) which, while giving support to modernization, made complete loyalty to the Emperor the defining characteristic of Japanese national identity.[86]

Several contemporary East Asian states, it is argued, have sought legitimacy and support for their modernization programmes by pursuing a similar strategy, by having recourse, implicitly or explicitly, to the same Confucian values. In line with a Confucian world view, they have adopted harmony as the fundamental principle for the right ordering of the social and political realm, from which is said to derive the subsidiary principle that each individual must fulfil an ordained relationship and accept the authority of the state. Applied to a modern setting, these principles require that citizens give effect to the judgements of professional experts who effectively perform the role of the *junzi* of an earlier age. To give effect to this strategy, the People's Action Party in Singapore openly promoted during the 1980s the inculcation of a Confucian ethos, through changes to the school curriculum and greater emphasis on Mandarin language training and usage. Prime Minister Lee had clearly articulated this strategy as early as 1979:

> The litmus test of a good education is whether it nurtures citizens who can live, work, contend and co-operate in a civilized way. Is he loyal and patriotic? Is he, when the need arises, a good soldier, ready to defend his country and so protect his wife and children and his fellow citizens? . . . Is he clean, neat, punctual and well-mannered?[87]

In the teaching and learning of Mandarin he saw the possibility of transmitting 'the norms of social and moral behaviour', which he equated with 'Confucianist beliefs and ideas of man, society and the state'. The introduction of *Confucian Ethics* in schools as one of the six options for the moral education programme was explicitly defended as 'an attempt to check the powerful influence of materialistic and individualistic values on young Singaporeans'. The Confucian cultural tradition was portrayed as contributing much to Singapore's economic, social and political development. It required the leader to rule with virtue, 'to lead by moral example' and to have 'the welfare of the people at heart at all times'.[88] These and other cultural techniques have been described by Chua Beng Huat as 'deep ideological penetration in the social body' intended to produce 'collective welfare' and 'social harmony' on the one hand and 'passive acceptance of hierarchical authority and paternalism' on the other.[89] In the words of Stephanie Lawson, a sharp critic of the Singaporean model, the preoccupation with Confucian ethics was designed to exclude the western option of 'oppositional politics' and, by placing harmony and consensus at the core of Singapore's political ideology, to make of 'state and society . . . an undifferentiated organic whole', with the PAP as its dominant organ.[90]

While the state's instrumental use of political Confucianism was most explicitly acknowledged in Singapore, it was far from absent in the constitutional, legislative and communicative practices of other East Asian states. The rediscovery or reinvention of the Confucian tradition was helpful in widening the freedom of action available to the 'virtuous rulers and in justifying the precise regulation of duties through a centrally administered state apparatus. The Confucian tradition was, it seemed, well suited to the economic imperatives of technocratic planning. Indeed, the Singaporean model held considerable attraction even for socialist states, notably China and Vietnam, intent on developing market economies while retaining authoritarian political structures. Deng Xiao Ping, who made no secret of his admiration of the Singapore model, was not averse to the rehabilitation of Confucian ideas. Indeed, Jiang Zemin as Party Secretary described Confucius as 'one of China's great thinkers', and went on to recommend thorough study and future implementation of 'his five ideals',[91] an attitude subsequently echoed in the pronouncements of leading scholars and public figures, who saw in Confucian thought and practice a signpost for national unification, the establishment of 'harmonious relations between the Han and minority nationalities', and even for the struggle against corruption.[92]

The appeal to Confucian values as a source of legitimacy was nevertheless fraught with difficulty. To begin with, it was not readily apparent how a set of norms and ritual practices steeped in tradition and focused on recreating the harmony of a distant utopian past could be transposed to the dramatic push to modernize and the associated disruption of everyday life. Nor was it entirely clear that in most so-called Confucian societies the Confucian ethic had the moral or emotional resonance often attributed to it. How Confucian, after all, was the Singaporean society of the 1980s? As Chua points out, the Chinese, who had in the main arrived in Singapore as displaced peasants from southern China, shared an understanding of Confucianism that 'was at best a distilled folk version of familialism'.[93] To mount its educational programme in Confucian ethics, the Singapore government had found it necessary to rely on the expertise of overseas scholars. The Institute of East Asian Philosophies established in 1983 made remarkably little headway in the dissemination of Confucian teachings, and the elective on Confucian ethics, which attracted considerably fewer school students than comparable subjects on Buddhism or Bible study, was abandoned a few years later, ostensibly for fear of provoking religious tensions.

One other consideration severely constrained the promotion of Confucianism as official or quasi-official ideology. To invoke the Confucian tradition as a legitimizing strategy was to open up a Pandora's box of competing textual interpretations and ethical preferences. The writings of Confucius, not to mention the many contributors to the neo-Confucian tradition, could be used to support widely diverging views of human nature, of the relationship of individual to society and of the nature of political obligation. Though often presented as an essentially conservative social and political philosophy, a virtual prescription for autocratic rule, Confucianism could also be read – as did a number of distinguished scholars in the field – as a reform-oriented programme geared to maximizing the possibilities for self-transformation and humane governance.[94] To set virtuous rule as the norm and to posit such virtue as a necessary condition for transforming the moral and economic condition of society is in effect to set extraordinarily high standards not only for the ruler, who is to cultivate virtue in exemplary fashion, but for the scholar bureaucracy that is mandated to translate virtue into administrative competence. Were the ruler and his administrators to fall short of these expectations, Confucianism as a legitimizing instrument might well become a double-edged sword.

The appeal to Confucian values was in any case applicable only to those societies which comprised the 'Sinitic sphere'. It was not a feasible option for a great many Southeast Asian polities where Confucian influence was relatively weak or where Islam, Buddhism or Christianity had become firmly established as the dominant religion. To seek legitimacy by reference to any one of these religious traditions was likely to prove just as risky an undertaking. Buddhism in Thailand, perhaps Islam in Indonesia and to a lesser extent in Malaysia, might provide a useful bridge between the sacred or spiritual dimensions of culture and the requirements of social cohesion and state-building. A great many movements of resurgent Islam did, in fact, engage with national politics in both Malaysia and Indonesia. The Malay Islamic Party (PAS), which identified Islam as the ideology of Malay nationalism, though forming the government in one or more states, was unable to replicate this electoral success at the national level. National government in Malaysia, as in Indonesia, did from time to time endeavour to establish its Islamic credentials, but generally remained wedded to notions of cultural and religious plurality.[95] Under pressure from more radical Islamic currents, UMNO felt obliged during the 1990s to elevate Islam to a higher status in its ideology, but the Mahathir government remained resistant to the comprehensive Islamization of the government apparatus. As a broad generalization, Malaysian and Indonesian political elites had eschewed the religious path to legitimacy, for they were not persuaded that religious symbolism held the key to social or political cohesion. Apart from the dangers posed by religious fundamentalism,[96] not least the deep divisions it might provoke within the same community of believers, was the likelihood of escalating tensions between different religious traditions, particularly in places where religious affiliation closely coincided with ethnic identification. Such considerations were decisive in Malaysia given the delicate intercommunal balance,[97] and not altogether absent in Indonesia or the Philippines, where sizeable religious minorities had periodically sought to articulate or redress their grievances or where, conversely, religious majorities had sought to entrench their dominant position.[98]

Even if the divisive impact of religious differentiation could somehow be contained or obviated, there was no guarantee that the state could effectively capture the religious impulse or the various institutional forms through which it expressed itself. Rather than the state successfully using religion as a vehicle for its own legitimation, it was just as likely that religious organizations and their leadership would use the state to advance their own cause or, failing that, would subject the conduct of the state to uncompromising and debilitating criticism. Whether such a critique reflected a fundamentalist or a liberal understanding of religious faith was in a sense tangential to the political outcome. Either way, the state stood to get its fingers burnt, which in part explains the tendency of most East Asian states, where religious practice was deeply embedded, to oscillate between firm commitment to secularist policies and institutions and at best arm's-length embrace of any politico-religious project.

It should, then, come as no surprise that East Asian attempts to legitimate the centralization of authority should have generally avoided any ideological formulation that was culturally particularist, historically specific or context-bound. Intent on fending off pressures for greater democratization emanating from both within and without, the state turned to the construction of a value system, namely a system of 'Asian values', sufficiently encompassing to avoid exacerbating intercommunal friction yet suitably crafted to appeal to popular sensitivities and aspirations. This is not to say that national symbols, national histories and a sense of national purpose were not commonly invoked to assist in the process of state-building.[99] Some states, where the society (as in China, Japan, Korea and Vietnam) had undergone a period of prolonged yet unifying cultural evolution, were better placed to pursue this path than others (most obviously Malaysia, Singapore, Indonesia) which were relatively recent creations, reflecting the interacting influences of migration and colonization. Yet, to a greater or lesser extent, all states had to do more than just play the national card. National consciousness, important as it was for purposes of social cohesion, could not of itself guarantee the durability of centralist practices and institutions. Nationalism as ideology was not necessarily antithetical to democratic principles or to the devolution of power.

Perhaps the most prominent exponent of a distinctively Asian model of development was Singapore's Lee Kuan Yew, who insisted on the need for Asian societies to cultivate traditional core values which were common to all of them and set them apart from other civilizations, notably the 'West'.[100] Several other articulate Singaporeans, including Ambassador Tommy Koh and Kishore Mahbubani (permanent head of the Ministry of Foreign Affairs)[101] also contributed to what came to be known as the 'Singapore School'.[102] Proponents of the 'Asian Way' were not, however, confined to Singapore but included Malaysian Prime Minister Mahathir, a sharp critic of the universalist claims of the western value system, and the Indonesian and Chinese political elites who rejected western social and political norms as alien to their respective political cultures. 'Asianization' has been aptly described as a government-initiated process designed to differentiate between 'Self and Other', namely Asia and the West, and on the basis of that differentiation mount a critique of western political liberalism.[103]

With few exceptions East Asian governments tended to emphasize the need for centralized authority and political control, given ethnic tensions and the priorities of economic development, and to describe international scrutiny of political and legal arrangements as unacceptable interference in their internal affairs. Appealing to Asian cultural traditions, they argued for the primacy of community and family values and the importance of status and authority relations, as distinct from western notions of individual freedom and democratic or adversarial politics. Mahathir expressed this view more succinctly than most:

> I believe there is a stratum of common values and beliefs that most Asians follow as a guide through the world. Those shared values can be called 'Asian', just as there is a body of common values that can be called 'Western'.
>
> First of all, Asian values are community- and family-oriented. We place greater value on the family and on the needs and interests of the community than on the individual and his or her rights to absolute personal freedom.
>
> Asian values also include respect for authority. Authority is seen to guarantee stability for the entire society; without authority and stability there can be no civility.[104]

A preference for morality over law as the basis of government, a profound commitment to education and acceptance of the unique authority residing in the state[105] were said to offer a viable alternative to western individualism.[106]

The 'Asian Way' thesis, it is fair to say, derived its significance at least as much from its political potency as from its intellectual coherence. It is nevertheless useful to specify the key elements which were explicitly or implicitly contained in the notion of a distinctive Asian ethic. For purposes of analytical convenience we reduce the disparate arguments and classifications to seven elements:[107]

1. *Cultural difference* The divergence of cultural and to a lesser extent economic and political circumstances was most clearly enunciated in the Bangkok Declaration, issued in May 1993 at the conclusion of the Asian regional preparatory meeting for the Vienna World Conference on Human Rights. The Declaration argued that human rights, though universal in nature, 'must be considered in the context of a dynamic and evolving process of international norm-setting, bearing in mind the significance of national and regional peculiarities and various historical, cultural, and religious backgrounds'.[108] This view echoed the Chinese government's sentiments, which it elaborated in its 1991 White Paper, *Human Rights in China*:

> Owing to tremendous differences in historical background, social system, cultural tradition and economic development, countries differ in their understanding and practice of human rights.[109]

In much the same vein the official statement *Shared Values* issued by the Singapore government also in 1991 highlighted the relationship between individual and community as distinguishing Asian from western values. The emphasis on the community, the paper argued, 'has strengthened social cohesion, and enabled Singaporeans to pull together to surmount difficult challenges collectively, more successfully than other societies'.[110]

2. *Centrality of family values* A second and closely related element of the 'Asian Values' approach was the importance attached to the family. Although most obviously associated with Confucian morality, the politically decisive role of familial solidarity and kinship ties is equally evident in the non-Confucian societies of Southeast Asia.[111] Situated at the heart of a complex network of clan associations, the family, which often shaped political allegiance, was seen as vital to both economic success and cultural cohesion. To the extent that it weakened the ties that bind families and communities, individualist conceptions of society were disruptive of social stability and economic progress.

3. *Duties and obligations* It was not just individualism that was under challenge, but the very notion of rights, since the emphasis was on upholding the family as the building block of society and resolving differences by consensual rather than adversarial politics. Not surprisingly, this interpretation of the relationship between individual and society often acquired Confucian overtones in its stress on the role of leadership and the respect that was due to authority figures generally, and political leaders in particular. The Singapore paper puts it this way:

> The concept of government by honorable men (*junzi*), who have a duty to do right for the people, and who have the trust and respect of the population, fits us better than the Western idea that a government should be given as limited powers as possible, and should always be treated with suspicion unless proven otherwise.[112]

4. *Social and economic development* What, then, was the primary responsibility of government? Given the economic backwardness of Asia, the first priority of state policy was to develop the economy, hence the primacy of social and economic over civil and political rights. Without economic development, that is, without steady progress in nutrition, education, health and employment, the conditions did not exist for the meaningful exercise of political rights. In the words of a senior adviser to the Malaysian government:

> T]he primary responsibility of any Government is to ensure the well being of its people. The security of the majority in the country cannot be sacrificed for the sake of maintaining the rights of the minority of individuals who choose to go against the rule of law.[113]

Expressed a little differently, the argument was that the centralization of power and authority was the price that had to be paid to achieve the political conditions conducive to economic development.

5. *Internal security* The interests of the community, as distinct from the interests of individuals, also required that particular interests be subordinated to larger political goals, and especially to the need for political stability and cohesion. Singaporean, Malaysian, Indonesian and other Asian leaders often pointed to the threat posed by internal subversion or racial agitation, which they saw as justifying the curtailment of a number of civil rights, including the right to associate and assemble and the right to exercise free speech and expression. Such practices as detention without trial and other deviations from the normal standards of criminal law were defended on similar grounds.

6. *State sovereignty* Asian governments consistently reaffirmed the principle of non-interference in the internal affairs of states. Even when they conceded the universality of human rights, they insisted that the way these rights were interpreted and applied came under each state's domestic jurisdiction and was not the concern of other states or of the international community. Chinese public statements consistently reiterated the point that state sovereignty was the only basis for the implementation of human rights.

7. *Rejection of western dominance* A number of Asian governments, most strikingly China and Malaysia, took the argument further, claiming that attempts to develop mechanisms for global governance, and in particular for monitoring and enforcing human rights standards, reflected a desire on the part of the West, notably the United States, to maintain global hegemony. Mahathir's decision to impose capital controls in response to the 1997 financial crisis and his subsequent denunciation of the role of foreign speculators and of western economic interests generally were presented as an understandable and justifiable response to western pretensions of continued dominance, and as further evidence of the need for firm prime ministerial control over the decision-making process.[114]

The 'Asian Values' concept, which gained wide currency in the early to mid-1990s, no doubt served a useful purpose from the Asian state's perspective. However, it was not always possible to disentangle the domestic and international contexts in which it was used. The assertion of Asian Values was in part intended to disarm the international, predominantly American, offensive on democracy and human rights, but the domestic audience was its primary target. The rhetorical emphasis on Asian as distinct from western interests and on East Asia's sense of achievement and confidence in the future undoubtedly struck a responsive chord with many who resented the continued determination of the North to set the international political and economic agenda and its presumption that the South had little option but to comply. In that sense, Mahathir's Look East policy, his critique of the US and Australian roles in APEC, his denunciation of the international community's failure to protect human rights in Rwanda, Chechnya and especially Bosnia, and his frequent diatribes against the IMF, currency speculators and the proponents of global deregulation were all carefully crafted to appeal to Malaysian and wider Asian interests and sensitivities.[115] In this he was probably more successful than many of his detractors were prepared to concede. The issue for many in Southeast Asia as in other parts of the Third World was not so much western or US domination as globalization, though from the perspective of the South the two were closely entwined. Mirroring and reinforcing the rapid acceleration of trade, and with it investment and technology flows across national boundaries, was the globalization of information flows and the global homogenization of culture, which threatened existing values and lifestyles and accepted patterns of cultural identity.[116]

The pressures of globalization were nevertheless complex, diffuse and contradictory. Globalization produced both winners and losers, affirmative as well as dissenting voices. Raising the spectre of foreign interference and calls to Asianization were likely to elicit different responses from different constituencies. Within Malaysia itself, distinctions would need to be drawn between the attitudes and aspirations of moderate and radical Muslims, small landholders and the professional classes, intellectuals and industrialists. Agents of political change, be it the *Reformasi* movement in Malaysia, the student movement in Indonesia or Falun Gong in China, were clearly not persuaded by the 'Asian Values' thesis. Many saw this as a case of special pleading, in which their own governments were trying to deflect the domestic and international spotlight away from their own policies and practices. Rather than simply challenging questionable Western assumptions and practices, they were perhaps attempting to obscure their own reluctance to act in ways which would disturb entrenched privilege. The stance of governing elites, though more widely publicized both at home and internationally, was often sharply at odds with that of indigenous peoples, ethnic minorities, intellectual networks and religious organizations. Generalized descriptions of Asian Values did not sit comfortably with the intellectual and political heterogeneity of many Asian societies. In Indonesia and Malaysia, for example, Islam contained a plurality of religious and political tendencies and had to contend with a great many other influences, not least Hindu, Christian and Confucian. Notwithstanding deferential attitudes to authority, the pronouncements of Asia's political elites were not universally accepted as the authentic representation of the norms and traditions underpinning their respective societies and cultures.

Nor could Asian governments entirely obscure the essential ambiguity of the communitarian argument which they frequently used to distinguish the Asian experience. What exactly was envisaged by the term community? Did it refer to ethnic, indigenous, religious or any number of smaller communities that made up the larger society? Or was community a codeword for the state itself? Underlying many of the pronouncements celebrating the Asian way was the assertion that culture, community and state were somehow inextricably linked or simply different manifestations of the same phenomenon. This was the argument used by the state to claim the authority to interpret culture and define community. Yet a good deal of evidence suggests that state, community and culture, far from being synonymous, were often in uneasy tension with each other. The democracy movements in the Philippines, China and Burma and the nationwide student protests in Indonesia attested to this disjuncture. At issue here was the complex structure and evolution of civil society and its relationship to the state, a subject to which we shall presently turn our attention.

The 'Asian Values' thesis encountered another, though closely related, difficulty: East Asia's religious and cultural diversity. Even Confucian Asia represents, as we have noted, multiple tendencies and countertendencies. When it comes to the normative impulses of civilizational entities, the dividing line between uniqueness and commonality is a slender and elusive one. Notions of an 'Asian way' entail therefore a vulgar homogenization and gross oversimplification of what is a multifaceted and complex social reality.[117] Lacking clearly delineated geographical or demographic boundaries, glib references to Asian culture or Asian values were not easily manipulable to serve what were essentially statist interests and objectives. In any case, Asian governments themselves did not reflect a politically homogeneous orientation. Chinese and Japanese legal institutions and practices, for example, operated in accordance with quite different principles and conventions. Even within ASEAN there were marked differences between member states with regard to the constitutional entrenchment of human rights, the independence of the judiciary, the plurality of political parties, the vigour of public debate and freedom of the press. Nor were political conditions within one country likely to be static, as events after 1985 would graphically demonstrate, first in the Philippines, Taiwan and South Korea, and later in Thailand and Indonesia. By the end of the 1990s all the indications were that the trend would continue to spread and intensify, but with considerable national variations. The ability of Asian governments to act or speak in unison as a way of buttressing their domestic legitimacy appeared severely constrained.

DEMOCRATIZATION AND THE GROWTH OF CIVIL SOCIETY

In the introduction to this chapter, stress was placed on the multidimensional quality of civil society, its separateness from, yet interdependence with, the state, and its capacity to manifest either democratic or authoritarian tendencies, or some combination of the two. Here the notion of democracy itself requires clarification, for the democratic tradition, rooted as much in the affective as in the rational character of human existence, is itself diverse and subject to continual refinement and renegotiation. To put it simply, there is more to the democratic tradition than the tenets of political and economic liberalism. Despite the claims of universalism that have been made for it by the agents or functionaries of US hegemony, the liberal world view, with its emphasis on anonymous individuals engaging in a multiplicity of contracts based on rational choice, is but one strand in the democratic tradition. To confine the state's role to securing the conditions for the making and honouring of such contracts is to offer a rather limiting view of both the state and civil society. Distinct from American notions of representative democracy, where the accent is on the separation of powers, open debate and conflicting interest groups, is the European model of social democracy and its variants, where representation and open debate function within the context of an active and involved citizenry.[118] Nor do these two types exhaust the range of possibilities. For if participation is deemed central to the concept of democracy, then, as Held suggests, what is envisaged is a political project of 'double democratization',[119] that is, the simultaneous democratization of state and civil society. It is not only the institutions of state but those of civil society, including family, school, university, office, factory, theatre, sporting club, religious community, trade union, professional association and advocacy group, that are amenable to participatory forms of organization.

Once this perspective is adopted, it is but a small step to apply it to the economy itself. Economic democracy, after all, refers simply to the participation of all those engaged in the production and distribution of goods and services in the decisions relevant to the organization of these productive and distributive processes. In other words, the economy cannot, by virtue of being labelled the 'private sector', be insulated from the participatory ethic.[120] It need hardly be said that state, economy and civil society are not self-contained, hermetically sealed entities. The boundaries between them are themselves blurred and open to periodic redefinition. Members of families are simultaneously factory or office workers and citizens of the state. These different facets of social life cannot be neatly compartmentalized. It is highly improbable that authority and participation as experienced in one arena can be insulated from the other two. There is much to be said for Mittelman's view that the state, as it interacts with civil society, 'becomes a terrain of struggle', and that civil society is 'both outside and inside the state'.[121] But the argument can be taken one step further. How civil society interacts with the state will in part depend on how civil society is organized, how it helps to shape the perceptions of individuals not just in their roles as members of society, but as citizens, producers and consumers.

Bearing in mind our comprehensive conception of civil society, but also the distinctions and interconnections we have established, what does the evidence tell us about the evolution of civil society in contemporary East Asia? To begin with, a few general observations. One obvious trend has been the quantitative growth of civil society, in particular the proliferation of technical and professional groups and associations that form an integral part of an industrializing economy. Complementing this trend has been the growing number of public interest, research and philanthropic organizations. According to one study, the Indonesian NGO development sector had expanded dramatically in the space of two decades, with the number of independent organizations in the early 1990s ranging from 4000 to 6000. In Thailand, following a decade of dramatic growth, there were 8408 general non-profit associations and 2966 foundations registered with the National Cultural Commission. By the early 1990s, more than 14 000 NGOs and 'people's organizations' had registered with the Philippines Department of Interior and Local Government. According to a nationwide investigation conducted in China in 1991, 89 969 organizations had been accorded *shetuan* status out of 118 691 applications, a *shetuan* being a social organization formed voluntarily but registered with the state and collectively engaged in economic activities or public affairs.[122]

More revealing perhaps is the qualitative dimension of civil society activism. Especially striking in this context was the mushrooming of umbrella networks and associations. Indicative of this aggregative trend was the formation in the Philippines of the Caucus of Development NGO Network (CODE-NGO) representing some 3000 individual organizations.[123] Other significant networks included the Philippine Partnership for the Development of Human Resources in Rural Areas (Phil DHRRA), consisting of some 60 development organizations, and the Philippine Support Service Agencies (PHILSSA), a network of support services in such areas as education and training, research and documentation, and legal and technical assistance. In Thailand, the NGO-Co-ordinating Committee for Rural Development (NGO-CORD), the National Council for Social Welfare and the Thai Volunteer Service Foundation (TVS) had approximately 220, 640 and 400 member organizations respectively. A more *ad hoc* but surprisingly effective initiative was the formation in 1995 of the Assembly of the Poor, a network of rural villagers and urban dwellers adversely affected by state and private sector development projects. As of 1997 some 133 organizations had associated themselves with the initiative.[124] The Malaysian Environmental and Conservation Network, SAVE (Society Against Family Violence) in Singapore and Wahana Lingkungan Hidup (WALHI), an Indonesian coalition of environmental organizations, were all part of the same aggregative process.

A more important qualitative difference in the functioning of civil society was the emergence of more independently minded organizations prepared to address politically sensitive environmental and human rights issues, draw attention to the negative consequences of rapid economic growth, advance notions of popular participation and democracy and promote grassroots development projects more attuned to local knowledge and traditions.[125] NGO visibility differed markedly from one country to another, from a pervasive presence in the Philippines to a moderate profile in South Korea and Thailand and virtual non-existence in Laos and Burma.[126] NGO activism was not, in any case, an entirely reliable indicator of the way *public space* was constructed, its autonomy defined *vis-à-vis* the state, or the degree to which it enhanced the democratization of state and civil society.

For a more sharply focused and variegated picture of the evolution of civil society in the region, we must turn to the unique experience of a number of countries. As might be expected, rapid industrialization in South Korea and Taiwan saw a marked increase in the number of white-collar workers – as a proportion of the total South Korean workforce the number rose from 4.8 per cent in 1965 to 17.1 per cent in 1985.[127] The growth of the student population and of the intelligentsia more generally is widely credited with having had a democratizing influence in South Korean politics. Even more striking was the expansion of organized labour, as reflected in the number of trade unions and the level of union membership, which rose from 1.1 million in the summer of 1987 to 1.5 million in September 1988.[128] The emergence of autonomous unions soon led to more widespread industrial collective action,[129] but also to greater contacts and co-operation between students and workers, which in turn influenced the attitudes and policies of both groups and eventually set the stage for a more diverse oppositional movement.[130] In Taiwan the labour movement was politically less militant. Though it boasted a higher rate of unionization than South Korea – 22.3 per cent in 1986 compared to 7 per cent in South Korea in the same year[131] – Taiwanese unions were generally under corporate management or KMT control. It was only after the process of democratization got under way and martial law was rescinded in 1987 that independent unions were formed. Even then organized labour operated largely in the industrial rather than the political arena, with the initiative for promoting a liberal democratic agenda resting primarily with politicians, intellectuals and other segments of the middle class.

Hong Kong again presents a somewhat different configuration, with influential interests prior to the 1980s confined principally to business organizations such as the Hong Kong Chamber of Commerce or the Chinese Manufacturers' Association. The colonial government would seek the views of business leaders or appoint them to various consultative and statutory bodies,[132] but Hong Kong's social movements had few organizational resources and relatively little public visibility. They tended to press for moderate reforms in such areas as education, housing and public services and, given Hong Kong's economic prosperity and political stability, generally found it difficult to challenge the territory's 'quasi-bureaucratic authoritarian structure' or translate *ad hoc*, single-issue campaigns into a larger programme of democratic mobilization.[133] However, Sino-British negotiations on Hong Kong's future, which got under way in 1982, proved something of a watershed. With the top-down reforms being introduced by the British government came an explosion of new interest groups: the Hong Kong Policy Viewers, Green Power, Progressive Society, Meeting Point, and Hong Kong Affairs Society to name only a few.[134] The Sino-British Joint Declaration published on 26 September 1984 was widely seen as offering a unique window of opportunity. Subsequent indications that China might obstruct the proposed course of Hong Kong's democratization endowed the process with added impetus. The Joint Committee on the Promotion of Democratic Government (JCPDG) was formed in October 1986 with a membership of 95 organizations. An alliance of student and educational bodies, trade unions, social services, political groups, religious bodies and community organizations, the JCPDG became the flagship of Hong Kong's democracy movement.[135] The decade that followed would see the increasing politicization of civil society, notably greater levels of participation in public debate, more assertive forms of advocacy and the emergence of new political parties. Yet the labour movement remained relatively weak, certainly weaker than its counterparts in Taiwan and South Korea. Between 1976 and 1987 a marked decline in union membership coincided with a rapidly expanding workforce,[136] an outcome to which the structure of Hong Kong's economy, labour market conditions and trade union factionalization had contributed and which in the longer run would colour the objectives and strategies of the democracy movement.

Civil society in its various Southeast Asian settings presented a picture of even greater contrasts, reflecting perhaps greater economic and cultural disparities, but also different degrees of political repression. At one end of the spectrum was Singapore where, in the name of functional efficiency, the government had meticulously identified the interest groups with which it would do business, and established the consultative and administrative mechanisms through which these professional, business and ethnic organizations could connect with the public policy process.[137] Only a few environmental and women's organizations, notably the Nature Society, the Association of Women Lawyers and the Association of Women for Action and Research, appeared able to operate outside the realm of officially sanctioned interest-based politics. Even for such groups, opportunities for political activism were narrowly circumscribed by the state, whether through restrictive legislation, court action or the possibility of deregistration. The Societies Act, for example, effectively precluded any voluntary association from publicly voicing its views on matters outside the direct interests of its declared constituencies.[138]

At the other end of the spectrum was the highly politicized civil society of the Philippines, where anti-colonial struggle against Spain, opposition to US economic and military domination and more recently the popular protests that eventually toppled the Marcos regime had fostered a participatory culture unknown in any other part of Southeast Asia. Many of the citizens' movements and coalitions which spearheaded the democracy movement, though they lost momentum during the Aquino years, nevertheless played a key role in the development of national campaigns around such issues as agrarian reform, the removal of US bases, the handling of foreign debt, and wages and working conditions for factory workers. Perhaps a more revealing indicator of the pervasiveness of civil society was the focus on community development, with an estimated 20 000 NGOs and people's organizations operating in villages, towns and, in a few instances, across entire provinces and regions (for example, Philippine Rural Reconstruction Movement, Philippine Business for Social Progress), and some 36 000 mostly NGO-initiated co-operatives, many of which were also connected to government programmes. Reference must also be made to the increasingly important role of national advocacy involving churches, academia, media and other professional groups. This trend gained added impetus after the Ramos government publicly committed itself to a 'social reform agenda' that offered civil society access to a number of consultative and participatory mechanisms. Government–NGO consultative processes assumed particular importance on issues of environment, social development, population, women's rights and labour conditions, and were reflected in government positions taken at a number of UN-sponsored world conferences, at Rio de Janeiro, Cairo, Copenhagen and Beijing, to name a few.[139] The rapidly developing multidimensional relationship between state and civil society in the post-Marcos period remained nevertheless ambivalent, with the state having to contend with multiple pressures emanating from domestic and foreign commercial and financial interests as well as internally from the bureaucracy and the armed forces, and civil society caught between the risks of political isolation and the loss of autonomy implicit in the politics of co-option.

Situated somewhere between these two ends of the spectrum were the civil societies of Indonesia and Malaysia, although in the former case the dramatic events that culminated in Suharto's resignation in 1997 and the subsequent turbulence of the Habibie interregnum enormously widened the public space available to civil activism. In the highly restrictive political conditions of the New Order, civil society organizations had lost much of their former autonomy, with journalists obliged to practise the 'culture of silence', university students precluded from engaging in overtly political protest, and trade unions, farmers' and fishermen's associations, youth and women's organizations required to operate within officially recognised national umbrella organizations.[140] A substantial gap eventually emerged, especially in the area of development, between NGOs prepared to participate in official programmes and those which were highly critical of the New Order and engaged instead in various forms of consciousness-raising. Others still preferred to focus on self-reliant local development.[141] The general trend, however, was towards greater emphasis on participatory values and, over time, more vigorous advocacy around such issues as 'the environment, child labour, street traders, rights of women, landless peasants and workers'.[142] Given the state's restrictions on public space, attention from the 1970s on increasingly turned to political and structural change and to the defence and expansion of legal rights.

By the late 1980s a number of organizations were beginning to emerge specifically aimed at democratic reform, with some calling for the liberalization of existing institutions (as in the case of the Forum for Democracy, founded in 1991 with Abdurrahman Abdurrahman as its first chairman) and others pressing for more comprehensive structural change (for example, the Centre for People's Democracy, a coalition of labour groups, students, farmers, landless peasants and pro-East Timor independence groups).[143] Important elements of the labour movement, in particular such unions as PPBI (the Centre for Working Class Struggles) and SBSI (Indonesia Prosperous Workers' Union), were now intent on consolidating their independence. More extensive links between students and workers on the one hand, and between students and peasant organizations on the other gradually gave rise to more effective forms of coalition-building, both locally and nationally.[144] One important coalition was the International Forum on International Development (INFID) which, encompassing a wide cross-section of Indonesian and international NGOs, provided a useful negotiating forum for competing ideological currents and connected 'the micro developmental and macro political levels' of civil society activism.[145]

Indicative of the rising political temperature, INFID's Twelfth Conference held in September 1999 identified the following issues as deserving close attention: human rights violations; the role of the military; state violence; corruption; implementation of development and emergency aid; debt; and privatization.[146] In addition to pressing for the abolition of the military's 'dual function', INFID called on the military to decrease its 'territorial' role, particularly in Aceh and Ambon, and cease its 'improper involvement in the Indonesian economy'. INFID's conception of nation-building was one based on 'respect for diversity and difference within a strong framework of human rights and pluralism'. Whether civil society had the breadth or depth to pressure the state into accepting this vision for Indonesia remained to be seen.

In Malaysia state controls, particularly during the Mahathir period, had left civil society even less room for manoeuvre. The Internal Security, Official Secrets, Police, Printing Presses and Publications, Trade Unions and Societies Acts were expressly designed to limit the space for communication within and between civil society organizations. The government's approach was to limit consultative processes to NGOs (for example, the National Council of Women's Organizations, the Federation of Malaysia Consumers' Association) which espoused acceptable attitudes and policies. Though a good number of think-tanks and research institutions had been established, these were generally either funded by government or intended to provide government with policy advice. The Institute for Strategic and International Studies (ISIS), which often reflected the thinking of Prime Minister Mahathir, eventually became independent of government financing, but one of its primary functions continued to be the development of ideas and proposals on economic and security policy for consideration by government. The Malaysian Strategic Research Centre established in 1993 had close links to Defence Minister (subsequently Education Minister) Najib Tun Razak, while the Islamic Institute for Policy Research was similarly connected to Deputy Prime Minister Anwar Ibrahim, and was in any case intended to establish a bridge between Islamic teachings and the government's vision of modern economic development. The need to operate within the accepted limits of official tolerance was equally evident in the actions and strategies of consumer associations and environmental organizations (for example, the Environmental Protection Society, the Malaysian Nature Society, Sahabat Alam Malaysia and the Centre for Environment, Technology and Development Malaysia).[147]

Two other clusters of civil society activism were particularly significant because they addressed the highly sensitive area of civil and political rights and issues of domestic and global justice. The first cluster included such human rights organizations as Voice of Malaysia (Suara Malaysia) and Aliran, a number of student, trade union and women's groups and the Malaysian Bar Council, all of which were often critical of the government's failure to respect democratic rights. The second cluster, linked in part through the Malaysian Action Front (MAF) and comprising such organizations as the Movement in Defence of Malaysian Islam and Just World Trust (subsequently renamed the International Movement for a Just World), had greater public visibility and was generally less susceptible to the state's critical eye. These various groups were to a greater or lesser extent protected either by their focus on Islam or their ability to use the government's rhetoric on North–South issues to articulate a sharp critique of the international economic and political system. This second cluster, though it echoed some of the positions favoured by the Prime Minister, was also congenial to Anwar Ibrahim's thinking. Not surprisingly, many of these groups acquired a higher public profile, but also a more complex relationship to the political process.

The *Reformasi* movement unleashed by Anwar's loss of political office and subsequent jailing provided a broad umbrella for a multiplicity of groups advocating social, political and economic change of one kind or another. What gave *Reformasi* much of its appeal was precisely the opportunity for new forms of intellectual and political interaction, with opposition to Mahathir's authoritarian style constituting the primary unifying factor. While the majority of its activists were young, middle-class Malay men, the two overlapping human rights-based coalitions that initially gave voice to the *Reformasi* platform (Gagasan and Gerak) were eventually superseded by the Barisan Alternatif. Common to all these networking arrangements was the attempt to integrate both Islamic and secular tendencies, a perspective that became the defining concern of the Movement for Social Justice launched by Wan Azizah, and its successor body, Parti Keadilan Nasional. The *Reformasi* movement's declared goal was to overcome the gender, class, religious and ethnic divides of Malaysian society.

Two other initiatives, though they had little immediate impact, were nevertheless symbolically instructive. An array of women's groups launched the Women's Agenda for Change which, in addition to highlighting a range of gender inequalities, drew attention to issues of work, religion, culture, sexuality and domestic violence.[148] In August 1999, 11 influential ethnic-Chinese groups issued a manifesto calling, *inter alia*, for the repeal of the Internal Security Act, the amendment of other security laws to bring them into line with international human-rights covenants, legislation to make the Anti-Corruption Agency accountable to parliament, and the introduction of a Race Relations Act to combat racism and racial discrimination. Sponsored by Chinese organizations that had rarely entered the political arena, the manifesto was also notable for its advocacy of wide-ranging political reforms rather than ethnically inspired demands. Within the space of a few weeks, it had received the endorsement of some 2000 local and national Chinese community organizations.[149] The other notable aspect of the *Reformasi* project was its likely impact on Islamic dissent and the future relationship of Islam to the political process. The use of mosques as a platform for criticism of government policy became more common, and various Islamic non-governmental organizations became more openly allied with opposition parties.[150] Responding to the threat, the government removed a number of imams from state mosques and attempted to co-opt others. These two not entirely unconnected developments, Anwar's fall from grace and the growth of Islamic sentiment may not have decisively altered the balance between state and society, but they had yet to run their full course.

To conclude this brief survey, a word about China: here was a state whose institutional and ideological underpinnings were antithetical to the very notion of an autonomous civil society. Indeed, by order of the State Council Order No. 43 promulgated in October 1989, all non-governmental associations had to be registered by the Ministry of Civil Affairs after approval by the 'relevant professional leading organs'.[151] The registration process required each association to submit a detailed account of its objectives, structure and proposed activities. Obliged to operate within this rigid framework, all professional associations were inextricably linked to the state. On the other hand, the rapid growth of these organizations, some of which had budgets, offices and staff independent of their supervising unit, indicated a limited loosening of state controls.

Nowhere was this trend more apparent than in the related spheres of education and research. Surveys conducted in Beijing and Guangzhou Universities in 1986 and 1989 respectively found a steady growth in the number of autonomous groups and the number of students participating in their activities.[152] A similar trend was discernible with professional societies, promotional groups and the diverse collection of think-thanks, foundations and research institutes. There was also evidence of intellectuals and professionals attempting to establish their own academic and professional bodies as a way of maximizing their relative independence. Side by side with the well-established and government-funded institutes, in particular the Chinese Academy of Social Sciences and its various institutes, China Centre for International Studies, China Institute of Contemporary International Relations, China Institute of International Studies and Shanghai Institute of International Studies,[153] were a number of other institutes (for example, the Academy of Chinese Culture, Young Economists' Association, Capital Steel Research Institute) that were less dependent on state funding, more in control of their research agenda and more inclined to use less conventional tools of analysis.[154] Mirroring this trend was the establishment of private schools with their corresponding educational bodies,[155] and the attempts of journalists to attach increasing importance to notions of professionalism and expertise.

Quite apart from the proliferation of newspapers which accompanied the introduction of economic reforms was the changing organization of the media. Rather than confining themselves to official sources, the financially independent newspapers were more inclined to expose official corruption, including police misconduct, and to broach such sensitive issues as AIDS and the government's telecommunications monopoly.[156] None of this is to suggest that the media could as yet delve into taboo political subjects or give a voice to dissenting views, let alone encourage political reform. Nevertheless, a new and as yet unpredictable pattern of social expression was beginning to unfold. Complementing and reinforcing the limited relaxation of institutional controls in the related but strategic realms of media and education was the proliferation of autonomous civil organizations. According to one estimate, there were as of 1999 at least 200 000 unregistered community organizations spanning the entire range of human activity, 'from a sewing circle to a triad society'.[157] The reluctant but steady withdrawal of the Communist Party from the multiple crises of everyday life – accentuated by the modernization drive it had itself unleashed – had resulted in a multitude of new associations attempting to fill the gap in such diverse areas as health, AIDS, sexual relationships, the environment, domestic violence and the rights of migrant workers. China's economic transformation could not but usher in a comparable, if less immediately visible, social transformation.

Reflecting in part major gaps in the existing literature on the changing pattern of associational life, the preceding snapshots of civil society across Pacific Asia offer at best a partial and impressionistic survey of what was a fluid and multifaceted phenomenon. There was nevertheless reason to think that these sociological trends had, and would continue to have, far-reaching ramifications for the evolution of civil society and its relationship to the state. With few exceptions, civil society had acquired a richer and more variegated organizational texture, especially in the context of family, religion and work, and partly as a consequence, its political space has intruded with increasing frequency and intensity into the political space traditionally occupied by the state. Such a conclusion in no way underestimates the powerful political and economic constraints which still stifled in much of East Asia the full expression of civil society's energies and affinities. Even in Japan, where the formal structures of representative democracy were most firmly established, the state remained extremely jealous of its prerogatives, and the bureaucracy generally antipathetic to interaction, let alone effective dialogue, with civil society.[158] Nor were the constraints purely external to civil society. They were in a sense integral to the wider culture, and to a greater or lesser extent to the normative orientation of ethno-religious and other societal forces which, though intent on expanding their own freedom of action, were not always comfortable with extending that same freedom to other social actors. The democratization of civil society still had a long way to go.

Notwithstanding the need for caveats and qualifications, it is none the less possible to generalize to this extent: the deepening and widening of civil society activism had paralleled and encouraged the democratization of the state. This was as true of the events that led to the demise of martial rule in the Philippines as it was of the end of military rule in Thailand and of the Suharto regime in Indonesia. Conversely, the liberalization of state structures had made possible a more convivial environment for the continued flowering of social movements and networks. The argument cannot, however, rest on just these two relatively simple propositions. To begin with, the democratization of civil society was not a sufficient condition for the democratization of the state. The failure of the democracy movements in China and Burma provides at least circumstantial evidence for this third proposition. Where the authoritarian state was strong as well as centralized, that is, where the state apparatus was sufficiently unified and the official ideology continued to provide the only viable framework for civil order and civic conduct (Lee Kuan Yew's Singapore and to a lesser extent Mahathir's Malaysia come to mind), civil society seemed unable to exert decisive influence over constitutional and political arrangements.

It emerges, then, that the state–civil society nexus, important as it is, cannot of itself fully explain the pace or quality of political change. For this purpose, it is necessary to reintroduce the economy into the equation. Indeed, for some, the key variable which accounts for democratization in East Asia is the shift to export-oriented industrialization. Here the argument usually takes one of two forms. The first version emphasizes the twin processes of liberalization and marketization; that is, the unavoidable tendency of industrializing economies to reduce government controls and subject themselves to more competition in the world market. The authoritarian developmental state, which performed a crucial function in the early stages of industrialization, must now reshape itself to permit the necessary restructuring of industry, financial system and labour market. In keeping with the requirements of a more mature and complex economy, the very nature of state intervention must change to 'a transparent, market-government, democratic policy-making process'.[159] This formulation neatly dovetails with the second version of the argument: with the formation of a domestic capitalist class, new demands arise, compounded by pressure from international capitalists, for a smaller public sector and for new strategic alliances.[160]

There is, as we have seen in earlier chapters, much to support the view that export-oriented industrialization gives added impetus to the logic of internationalization. That an industrializing economy gives rise to a growing middle class is equally evident. What is much less clear is whether these two developments have actually had a democratizing impact on the state and political culture more generally. Is it the case, as so many have argued, that what brought to an end the cycle of authoritarian rule in South Korea[161] and Taiwan[162] and possibly in Thailand and the Philippines, and what promises to do it in Singapore and China, is the emergence of a middle class increasingly attracted to western values and life-styles and to notions of accountability, transparency and multiparty politics?[163] Or are Girling and others closer to the mark when they argue that the emergence of a new business class, rather than strengthening democratic institutions, may simply entrench money politics and the corrupt practices associated with the buying of votes and politicians?[164]

The nexus between economic modernization and democratization cannot, obviously, be reduced to a simple cause-and-effect relationship. Greater social mobility and changes to class structure may well exert pressure for political liberalization, but they do not predetermine political outcomes. Chung-Si Ahn characterizes the relationship in the following terms:

> Economic development certainly sets the stage for democratization and shapes the structural contour of the transition process ... But the very process of democratization cannot be automatically deduced from the structural parameters of economic development and its concomitant societal change.[165]

Crouch and Morley offer us a more subtly calibrated formulation of the same argument:

> [I]n the Asia-Pacific region, as elsewhere, the correlation between economic growth and political change is generally curvilinear; characteristically economic growth does not drive the state to give up its arbitrary power gradually as social forces gain in strength ... Rather, in these circumstances, it is more apt to hold out as long as it can, giving in to democratization only at a higher level of growth when the balance of power between it and society has finally tipped – not partially, but as a whole.[166]

This notion of a critical threshold – the tipping of the balance in favour of political change – is indeed helpful, but it does leave unanswered a number of crucial questions. Crouch and Morley are right to ascribe a role to geographical, social, political and international factors, but what is it about these factors, singly or collectively, which is likely to tilt the economic balance in favour of political change? Can these factors indefinitely retard political liberalization even in conditions of sustained, high-level economic growth: the Singapore case readily suggests itself? Conversely, can these non-economic factors make way for democratization even at much lower levels of economic development – an outcome well illustrated by the Philippine experience?

None of these questions lends itself to a simple answer. Positing the emergence of the middle class as the missing link between economic and political liberalization is itself unsatisfactory. The middle class is after all a highly ambiguous concept, and its emergence and even consolidation may have quite contradictory cultural and political consequences. The middle class is rarely a homogeneous entity. The professionals, civil servants, white-collar workers, small-business people, students and intellectuals who make it up do not necessarily share the same interests, worldviews or aspirations. The question is not primarily whether or not a middle class has emerged, or even how large or how wealthy it is, but the balance in political outlook and motivation between its constituent units, and between them and other important segments of society, be they peasants, landlords, industrial workers or leading industrialists and financiers. Even within the professional class, substantial attitudinal differences may exist between the so-called 'caring professionals' (for example, journalists, teachers, nurses, counsellors, social workers) and the more technically minded or business-oriented variety (surveyors, engineers, accountants, computer technicians, market research and public relations consultants).[167] The middle class, in other words, might just as easily fuel the politics of dissent as the politics of contentment. To grasp the dynamic of political change, and more specifically democratization, it is therefore necessary to go beyond the state–economy and state–civil society dualities and place them in a triangular relationship. The glaring deficiency of many explanatory models is precisely their tendency to interpret the political role of the middle class in terms of the state–economy duality and to overlook the complex relationship between the middle class and civil society, and the implications of that relationship for the strength, centralization and even sovereignty of the state. At this point, a few empirical observations may help to illuminate the conceptual puzzle posed by the East Asian experience.

The democracy movement in South Korea, which emerged in the 1970s and gathered momentum during the 1980s, was the product of several societal changes and ideological currents. One of the most important consequences of the export-oriented industrialization programme was the decline of the farming sector and the appearance of a large working class, although for the best part of 20 years the state would maintain strict control over trade unions and firmly suppress labour protest. However, by the mid-1980s the labour movement, though not directly involved in the democracy struggle, had substantially enhanced its organizational muscle and, potentially at least, posed a major challenge for the authoritarian regime.[168] Rapid industrialization also gave rise to a large middle class, and with it came a rapidly expanding student population. The democracy movement itself was nurtured by three guiding principles: nationalism (*minjok*-ism), democracy (*minju*-ism) and populism (*minjung*-ism).[169] The populism of the 1980s may have had its roots in the peasant rebellions of an earlier era, but it was specifically directed against the prevailing politico-economic order and the more obnoxious features of state-led capitalism. Its conception of democracy involved not just the establishment of political freedoms and the rule of law but the 'liberation of underprivileged people from the system that oppressed them'.[170] Led by students and intellectuals, and to a lesser extent by religious groups and opposition politicians, the movement had by 1985 acquired a single national umbrella organization, the Democracy–Reunification–People Alliance, which then opted to support the rejuvenated New Democratic Party. This was a delicately poised alliance between a radical social movement pressing for the removal of the existing regime and the introduction of a new 'people's constitution', and a relatively moderate group of politicians whose primary objective was the institution of a fair system of direct presidential elections.

Uneasy though it was, the alliance nevertheless had the necessary ingredients for success. The moderating influence exerted by the parties in opposition persuaded large segments of the relatively conservative middle class to support the democracy movement. On the other hand, the more militant stance of students and intellectuals prompted the regime to initiate top-down democratic reform for fear that failure to act might generate mass support for their radical agenda. This worst-case scenario had to be avoided at all costs, for it was distinctly possible that organized labour, encouraged by its growing industrial muscle, would choose to play a more direct role in the democracy campaign than had hitherto been the case. Mindful that the idea of the working class as the central agent of social change featured prominently in the thinking of the intelligentsia, the state felt impelled to make sufficient concessions to forestall such a possibility. The mass protests which culminated in the democracy declaration of June 1987 and the ensuing wave of strikes would soon pave the way for an open presidential election.

The gradual and moderate reforms introduced during the first three presidential administrations were, each in its own way, designed to reduce the appeal of populist radicalism and at the same time reassure the new middle class of white-collar, service and professional workers. Even Kim Dae-jung, who came to office with a reputation as the champion of democracy and human rights, made caution a distinguishing feature of his reform agenda. In a series of presidential amnesties between March 1998 and August 1999 some 250 political prisoners had been released, but more than 200 prisoners of conscience were still in Korean jails. During the same period, more than 300 arrests had been made under the National Security Law and several hundred unionists and striking workers had been arrested for 'illegally' engaging in industrial action.[171] Proposed amendments to the National Security Law before the parliament would define more narrowly what constituted an 'anti-state' organization and distinguish more precisely between legitimate dissent and Pyongyang-inspired subversion,[172] but there was no question of abolishing the law or dismantling the elaborate security framework on which it rested. The democratization of South Korea at the end of the 1990s may therefore be interpreted as a precarious compromise between competing economic interests and ideological currents, temporarily reinforced by US influence[173] and the continuing division of Korea.

The Taiwan experience was, if anything, more directly attributable to external factors. As in the case of South Korea, the United States had made democratization an important part of its diplomacy, for its special relationship with Taipei would gain considerably in legitimacy to the extent that Taiwanese democracy could be contrasted with one-party rule in China. The approaching end of the Cold War and the diminishing threat of communism made such a scenario both more feasible and less threatening. For the KMT leadership, however, there was a more pressing concern, namely Taiwan's political identity, which above all hinged on its present and future relationship with China. Elite uncertainty about Taiwan's status had been accentuated by the success of Beijing's diplomacy not only in unseating Taipei at the UN but in drastically reducing its official ties with other states and in excluding it from virtually all intergovernmental fora and organizations.

Largely in response to this dilemma the KMT sought, tentatively under Chiang Ching-kuo but more assertively under Lee Teng-hui, to strengthen its hold on power by abandoning the pretence that it constituted the *de jure* government of the whole of China and substituting the claim that it was the legitimate government of an independent island state. To strengthen that claim, and therefore its own prospects for political survival, the KMT regime opted, as in the case of South Korea but in the absence of a comparable oppositional force, for a programme of technocratically guided democratic reform. As David Jones has observed, the process of democratization was not unleashed by an increasingly confident and autonomous middle class, but by a government which had concluded that its organizational access to resources and effective control of the means of communication would guarantee it victory in any carefully stage-managed electoral contest.[174] Nor was the likelihood of a deteriorating relationship with Beijing, which might accompany such a strategy, viewed with alarm. On the contrary, as Lee Teng-hui's comfortable victory in the 1996 presidential elections would show, increased tensions across the

Taiwan Strait might work to the KMT's advantage by enhancing its credentials as the guarantor of Taiwanese independence and prosperity. No doubt, increased electoral activity and the politicization which it encouraged were likely to resonate with a substantial cross-section of the Taiwanese middle class, but in the absence of a vibrant civil society intent on creating its own political space, it was unlikely that the process of democratization would stray far beyond the confines set by the governing elite.

In Hong Kong no less than in South Korea and Taiwan, the external factor would prove decisive in the territory's political evolution. Here again, a sizeable middle class had emerged by the end of the 1980s. As a proportion, those whose monthly household income was in excess of HK$15 000 had increased from 0.5 per cent in 1976 to 24.9 per cent in 1991. During the same period, the proportion of the population owning their own homes would rise from 23.2 per cent to 42.6 per cent.[175] Economic prosperity coupled with political stability had generally discouraged any serious challenge to British rule. The anxieties provoked by China's much less favourable economic and political circumstances had, if anything, enhanced the legitimacy of the colonial government. Indeed, it was only the prospect of imminent decolonization which concentrated the mind of the British government, prompting it in its tortuous negotiations with China to press for the introduction of a number of democratic provisions. It was only in the wake of those negotiations that it proactively but cautiously set about the task of reforming the legislature.

As already indicated, a range of civil society organizations responded positively to the initiative, but the enthusiasm for reform was neither intense nor universal. Indeed, the most influential elements of the business and professional communities formed an alliance in August 1986 with the express purpose of slowing down the pace of reform. The more privileged sections of society could see little to be gained from antagonizing Beijing, the territory's future master, or from subjecting the business of government to electoral volatility and democratic pressure for increased social welfare and higher business taxes.[176] In the tumultuous and somewhat confused period of Chris Patten's governorship, the initiative in the democratization campaign would steadily shift from social movements to political parties. The Tiananmen events of June 1989 certainly reinforced the democratic sensitivities of the middle class and the wider population, but after a wave of rallies organized in support of the democracy movement in China, tensions emerged within the pro-democracy political opposition, both between the two social movement umbrella organizations, and between them and the three pro-democracy parties.[177] Hong Kong's expanding middle class had not been matched by a growing democracy movement, in part because the relatively meagre political resources of civil society had been diverted, perhaps prematurely, to the formation of fledgling political parties. In the last two years of Patten's governorship, relative satisfaction with the economic *status quo* and fear of provoking Beijing's displeasure placed additional constraints on active popular participation. This tendency became even more striking after June 1997 with significant elements of the Hong Kong business community applying strong pressure on the government to resist demands for any expansion of democratic institutions. As one business leader put it, a 'centralized government ensures the tax-exempt minority does not swamp the taxed majority'.[178]

The trajectory of Southeast Asian polities has varied sharply with time and place and does not therefore easily lend itself to a generalized overview. With the exception of Singapore, their more recent drive for export-oriented industrialization and generally lower levels of economic development have meant a smaller and weaker middle class. Yet there is no clear correlation between the size or strength of the middle class and progress in democratization. If, for the purpose of analytical convenience, we confine our attention to three countries, Indonesia, Malaysia and Singapore, it is arguable that by the end of the 1990s the strength of democratic institutions was inversely proportional to the strength of the middle class. Plausible though it may be, however, this proposition is no more solidly based than its antithesis. What the evidence in each of these three instances suggests is not that rapid economic growth will give rise to, or for that matter impede, a more democratic or pluralist set of political institutions, but that an authoritarian-developmental regime can initiate and withstand a prolonged period of such growth. Regime change may occur – as with post-Suharto Indonesia – but the size or strength of the middle class is unlikely to be the determining factor, although economic transformation (past and present) will almost certainly influence the quality and solidity of the new institutional order.

In the Indonesian case, the very weakness of the middle class and the extraordinary concentration of the private business sector in the hands of the small and vulnerable ethnic Chinese minority may well have contributed to Suharto's downfall. The patrimonial regime which Suharto had painstakingly built over a long period rested on precarious economic and military foundations which could not withstand the seismic shocks unleashed by the financial crisis and the heightened tensions associated with ethnic and religious discontent. In other words, Suharto could no longer rely on the 'performance legitimacy' which political stability and economic growth had previously conferred on his regime. The withdrawal of legitimacy, most dramatically symbolized by sustained student protests, had not however resulted from any organized middle-class mobilization or, indeed, from any discernible set of common middle-class interests.[179] The transitional period ushered in by the Habibie and Abdurrahman presidencies was not the product of an inherently liberal or reformist middle class, but more a response to inchoate but widespread social resentment that cut across the class, ethnic and religious divisions of Indonesian civil society.

The ambivalent implications of socio-economic change were equally apparent in Malaysia, giving rise simultaneously to authoritarian controls and increased democratic resistance.[180] Despite periodic crises, the Malaysian state, through a process which Harold Crouch has aptly described as 'incremental authoritarianism',[181] had ensured the continued concentration of power in the Malay political elite – a process which Mahathir had skilfully reinforced and on which he stamped his dominant personality and developmentalist vision of the future. In the course of two decades, Malaysia's occupational class structure had undergone a radical change, with the middle class expanding from 20.0 per cent in 1970 to 32.6 per cent in 1990, and agricultural employment registering a corresponding decline from 44.9 percent to 28.3 per cent. These trends were reflected in each of the three main communities, but in 1990 agricultural employment was still highest among Malays (37.4 per cent) whereas the Chinese community had by far the highest proportion employed in middle-class occupations (43.2 per cent).[182] The state had significantly restricted the political space in which the middle class could negotiate and articulate its interests, but it is equally the case that many of the elements comprising the middle class were, as the principal beneficiaries of Malaysia's economic success, reluctant to disturb the political *status quo* or the interethnic compromise on which it rested.

Here, it is worth noting in parenthesis that, while the incidence of poverty at the national level had declined during the 1980s and early 1990s, the income gap had widened. Comparing the income of the top 20 per cent of households with the bottom 20 per cent, the UNDP's 1996 Development Report concluded that Malaysia had the highest income inequality of any country in Asia.[183] Aside from intra-elite dissent, which periodically afflicted the UMNO structure, oppositional forces were confined primarily to political groupings stressing ethnic and religious affinities, with PAS deriving much of its electoral support from poor Malay peasants, and the Democratic Action Party (DAP), although formally a multiracial party, securing most of its votes from the non-Malay, especially Chinese, communities. It is arguable that the parting of the ways between Mahathir and his deputy Anwar Ibrahim in 1998, the latter's subsequent jailing and the attempts of his supporters to launch a multiracial reform movement, signalled more than just another split within UMNO. Anwar's prolonged trial had certainly dramatized in the minds of many the less acceptable features of the authoritarian state, and perhaps strengthened the view among students and intellectuals that transparency and accountability were ideas whose time had come.[184] The long-term success, however, of such a reformist agenda was likely to depend on the formation of a viable coalition spanning the ethnic divide, and appealing at least as much to the losers as to the winners of rapid economic growth.

Even in the absence of the potentially divisive ethnic affiliations that characterize Malaysian society, the Singaporean middle class, much wealthier and better educated than its Malaysian counterpart, was no more successful in shaking off the authoritarian mantle of the state. Singapore's ruling elite was not under any discernible pressure to liberalize the political system and, as a consequence, the political space available for 'autonomous organizations in civil society' remained sharply circumscribed. A large new middle class, made up of graduates employed by an expanding public sector, had internalized a professional ethic based on respect for expertise, deference and group conformism. Though to a degree these characteristics were shared with South Korea and Taiwan, they were in Singapore's case exacerbated by what Jones has apply described as 'the claustrophobic nature of Singaporean life'.[185]

Conscious of Singapore's smallness, lack of resources and external vulnerability – messages which the state propagated at every opportunity – the middle class had over time acquired an identity remarkably attuned to the official ideology. In that sense, *kiasu* behaviour, understood as the widely shared commitment to achieving success in a competitive but highly regulated environment, represented a critical point of equilibrium between 'individual life and national destiny', between the society's underlying anxiety or fear of failure and the state's role as guardian of physical security and economic well-being. If Yao Souchou is at all right in concluding, on the strength of a qualitative survey of public attitudes, that 'the state discourse has become the conventional wisdom with which people see the world',[186] it is difficult to see how middle-class affluence can be construed as the driving force for regime change. By the late 1990s, there were hints in both official and private discourse that a more open and flexible style of government might be a desirable long-term objective, but there was no evidence of a schism between state and civil society. There was certainly no suggestion that the middle class was about to engage in political imagining of a kind that significantly deviated from that prescribed by the state.

It remains to say a word about China's vastly different circumstances. Had two decades of furious economic growth generated a climate for comprehensive political change? To be more precise, did the emergence of a sizeable middle class and the continuing restructuring of the economy on which its future depended foreshadow a loosening of political controls, and the imminent or even gradual decline of the Chinese Communist Party as the principal repository of state power and authority? It is clear that China's economic modernization had resulted in substantially higher per capita incomes, particularly for the urban middle class, and that the ensuing accumulation of capital and wealth had led to much greater social mobility. Struck by the sheer scope and speed of this transformation, many observers argued that changing networks of power would sooner or later accompany the new class structure emerging in both urban and rural China. The growth of a market economy was said to have given rise to the 'new rich' and a new entrepreneurial class, which the existing political hierarchy would somehow have to accommodate. Changes in social stratification had already contributed to 'a new cluster of values, notably the acceptance of individual striving and market competition', and greatly enhanced the currency of such notions as 'personal interests, material incentives, differential rewards, economic efficiency and market distribution'.[187] Assuming this to be a highly generalized but essentially accurate portrayal of modernizing China, the question remains: what are the political implications of socio-economic change? Was there reason to think that China could not emulate the Singapore model, that democratization was the necessary byproduct of economic liberalization, that the gamble of the Chinese Communist leadership to use economic reform as the key to political survival was fundamentally flawed? To this large and multifaceted question only the future could provide a conclusive answer.

There were nevertheless good grounds for suggesting that material affluence could not of itself establish the conditions for political ferment. Contemporary China now afforded greater opportunities for the expression of social freedoms, whether in fashion, music or food,[188] but it was not at all clear that the freedom to consume would necessarily be translated into a widespread movement for political reform. Indeed, the individualism characteristic of a consumerist culture was as likely to prejudice as to enhance the democratic prospect. Far from nurturing the growth of a civil society conducive to pluralistic or participatory politics, rampant materialism might simply be the reward offered by the state in return for the co-option of dissent.[189]

The preceding line of argument is not meant to suggest that the Chinese state was not vulnerable to pressure or that it was not already experiencing slow but steady normative and institutional change. There was, especially at the local level, evidence of a greater diffusion of financial and organizational resources, widespread development of leadership and conflict resolution skills and, increasingly, demands for greater transparency and accountability in government. It did not follow, however, that local trends would necessarily be transposed to the national arena, or that the introduction of mechanisms designed to increase the transparency and efficiency of economic decision-making would spill over onto the political arena and such sensitive issues as human rights and multiparty politics. The Chinese state at the end of the 1990s had to contend with numerous threats to its integrity, not least those arising from regionally based economic disparities, periodic tensions between the urban and rural sectors of the economy, and separatists tendencies based on ethno-religious identity. In response to one or more of these mutually reinforcing challenges to its authority, the state, particularly in moments of acute internal dissension, might be prepared to devolve functions and powers to regions, cities and localities. Whether or not, and the extent to which, such a trend materialized, and whether decentralization would be accompanied by democratization – an outcome which, as the disintegration of the highly centralized Soviet state had shown, was in no way assured – would in part depend on the emergence of a robust and 'cosmopolitan' civil society.

THE DYNAMICS OF CHANGE

Rapid industrialization may have characterized much of Pacific Asia, but political change was   neither uniform nor unilinear. The proposition that an expanding middle class will necessarily bring in its wake the democratization of the state is, in the light of recent historical experience, clearly unsustainable. On the other hand, it is the case that authoritarianism was under increasing challenge and that in several, though by no means all, cases the centralization of power and authority had been eroded and varying degrees of political pluralism tolerated and even encouraged. To make sense of this intriguing phenomenon two distinct but not entirely contradictory interpretations have been advanced. The first, most succinctly expressed by David Martin Jones, argues that change was technocratically managed, driven by a ruling elite 'often ideologically and economically and sometimes ethnically homogeneous with the middle class', and intent on anticipating the aspirations of the middle class or the problem of political succession.[190] Far from responding to a societal demand for 'a communicatory democracy', political reform or constitutional innovation sought to satisfy the psychological needs of an expanding middle class but in conformity with the Confucian-collectivist ethic.[191] By contrast the second interpretation, favoured by, among others, Hewison, Robison and Rodan, emphasizes the inability of the authoritarian state to withstand the powerful pressures exerted by the internationally oriented segment of the middle class. The democratic option became particularly attractive when none of the available mechanisms could effectively mediate or resolve conflicts internal to the middle class, or when the advantage accruing to the middle class from more transparent market-driven decision-making processes outweighed the benefits conferred by the authoritarian state, whether through protection, subsidy or patronage.

Both interpretations are analytically useful because each in its own way illuminates the complex interplay between middle class and governing elite, yet neither is entirely satisfactory. The first interpretation places too much weight on the collectivist ethic of Pacific Asian political cultures and on the capacity of the state to manage crises and manipulate competing interests and influences, and too little weight on the powerful international pressures that inevitably accompany export-oriented industrialization. The second interpretation, on the other hand, fails to distinguish between the political reforms that are essential to the efficient functioning of a market-driven economy and the wider institutional and constitutional changes that are integral to the democratic ethic. It is not therefore able to identify with any clarity those factors or agents likely to encourage one reform agenda as against the other. Our own analysis suggests instead that democratization, which by definition is a fluid and multidimensional process, gains momentum at those unique moments when the authoritarian state's performance is on the decline and civil society's assertiveness is on the rise. Any number of endogenous and exogenous factors may contribute to either or both trends.

Of the factors that account for the diminishing efficacy of authoritarian controls, five are worth highlighting. First is the demise of ideological bipolarity. Quite apart from its obvious geopolitical repercussions, the end of the Cold War deprived communist and anti-communist states alike (China, Vietnam, South Korea, Malaysia) of one of the most powerful instruments of legitimation at their disposal. The ideological argument was especially potent because it helped to synthesize in the public imagination both internal and external threats to security and to project the centralized state as the only agent capable of responding to those threats. Second is the state's increasing vulnerability to external economic shocks, whether it be the oil crisis of the early 1970s, the debt crisis of the 1980s or the financial crisis of the late 1990s. In each case, the states most directly affected were obliged to make often highly unpopular economic policy adjustments, which on the one hand weakened their capacity for patronage and on the other substantially strengthened civil society activism, often in ways that cut across ethnic and even class divisions. Third is the increasing force of centripetal tendencies, reflected in separatism of various kinds, religious and ethnic polarization or tensions in centre–periphery relations. The combined effect of these tendencies was to expose the inherent weaknesses of supposedly strong states and to compound the problem of succession – Suharto's Indonesia is the obvious example, but Mahathir's Malaysia might also prove to be a case in point.

The fourth and closely related factor is elite dissension, which is likely to gain added impetus from the increasingly powerful challenges to which the state is subjected. The search for adaptive responses inevitably provides opportunities for aspiring leaders and competing factions to question the *status quo* and to propose political reforms of one kind or another as a way of undermining the incumbent's hold on power (that in essence was Anwar's strategic response to the 1997 financial crisis). Such challenges may not deliver democratization but they do provide more fertile soil for social and political movements to articulate their respective demands and create new arenas for dialogue and negotiation. Unresolved succession problems were instrumental in both South Korea and Indonesia in generating a new kind of civic politics. Fifth is the corrosive effect of corruption. It is not only that corrupt practices impede the efficient allocation of resources, but that they undermine the legitimacy of the state. Once corruption has permeated those institutions that are at the core of the state's legitimacy, notably the judiciary and police forces and, in the case of the one-party state, the party itself, then the conflict is no longer one between aggrieved citizen and corrupt official, but between state and citizenry. That was presumably the disease to which the Suharto regime eventually succumbed and which the Chinese state was desperately trying to combat.

Yet this analysis would be incomplete if the variables in question were not themselves set in the context of a globalizing economy. Paralleling the internationalization of East Asia's economies was the internationalization of its societies, and most strikingly of its middle classes. The discipline imposed by transnational corporations, financial markets, the Bretton Woods institutions, GATT/WTO and APEC had drastically curtailed the state's freedom of action, but at the same time created or accentuated a great many social grievances which, in time, would affect almost every sector of the economy and every stratum of society. It is as if the policies and mechanisms of trade liberalization and financial deregulation had become the conduit for new forms of interest articulation and aggregation. As a consequence the authoritarian or 'strong' state had to find new ways of organizing political space, a task for which it was not always intellectually or institutionally well equipped. Already weakened by the internationalization of capital and the rapidly diminishing costs of communication and transportation, the bureaucratic apparatus of the state had to contend with an ever-widening assortment of social actors who were developing their own channels of interest mediation and representation. Bureaucratic and political attempts at co-option, including plans for decentralization and participation, even when successful, often unleashed a dynamic which the state could not fully comprehend, let alone control. Nowhere was this trend more strikingly evident than in the environmental implications of globalization. Export-oriented industrialization and the ensuing transboundary flows of population, knowledge, technology and capital had, by virtue of their widespread and enduring environmental effects, produced in much of East Asia the beginning of an attitudinal shift. Civil society was emerging as a major site of contestation, with diverse social actors seeking to restructure politics and reorganize the allocation of resources. The decay of nationalist, communist and other revolutionary movements had brought to an end an important chapter in the history of East Asia's political economy, but the transition to neo-liberal capitalism had opened a new chapter of social and political ferment at least as turbulent and absorbing as the one that preceded it.

NOTES

1. For a fuller historical and conceptual treatment of the functions of the state, see Camilleri and Falk, *The End of Sovereignty*, pp. 24–31, 83–4; also Barry Supple, 'The State and the Industrial Revolution 1700–1914', in Carlo M. Cipolla (ed.), *The Industrial Revolution 1700–1914*, London: Fontana, 1973.
2. Immanuel Wallerstein, *The Modern World System II: Mercantilism and the Consolidation of the European World Economy 1600–1750*, New York: Academic Press, 1980, p. 113.
3. This distinction is often overlooked even in otherwise perceptive accounts of the state; for example, Peter B. Evans, Dietrich Rueschmeyer and Theda Skocpol, 'On the Road toward a More Adequate Understanding of the State', in P.B. Evans, D. Rueschmeyer and T. Skocpol (eds), *Bringing the State Back In*, Cambridge: Cambridge University Press, 1985, pp. 350–1.
4. See John Ehrenberg, *Civil Society: The Critical History of an Idea*, New York: New York University Press, 1999, pp. 19–27.
5. For a brief but illuminating exposition of these intellectual currents, see Yoshikazu Sakamoto, 'Civil Society and Democratic World Order', in Stephen Gill and James Mittelman (eds), *Innovation and Transformation in International Studies*, Cambridge: Cambridge University Press, 1997, pp. 207–19.
6. Garry Rodan, 'Civil Society and Other Political Possibilities in Southeast Asia', *Journal of Contemporary Asia*, 27(2), 1997, 157.
7. See Chandran Kukathas and David W. Lovell, 'The Significance of Civil Society', in Chandran Kukathas, David W. Lovell and William Maley (eds), *The Transition from Socialism: State and Civil Society in the USSR*, London: Longman Cheshire, 1991; Yehudah Mirsky, 'Democratic Politics, Democratic Culture', *Orbis*, 37(4), 1993, 567–80; Larry Diamond, 'Rethinking Civil Society: Toward Democratic Consolidation', *Journal of Democracy*, 5(3), 1994, 4–17.
8. Rodan, 'Civil Society and other Political Possibilities in Southeast Asia', p. 160.
9. Michael Bernhard, 'Civil Society and Democratic Transition in East Central Europe', *Political Science Quarterly*, 108(2), 1993, 308.
10. Among the many studies that have contributed to the critique of neo–classical orthodoxy, of particular note are the interpretations offered by Chalmers Johnson, *MITI and the Japanese Miracle*; T. Gold, *State and Society in the Taiwan Miracle*, Armonk, NY: M.E. Sharpe, 1986; various contributors in F.C. Deyo (ed.), *The Political Economy of the New Asian Industrialism*, Ithaca, NY: Cornell University Press, 1987; A.H. Amsden, 'Third World Industrialization: "Global Fordism" or a New Model?', *New Left Review*, no. 182, 1990, 5–31.
11. Linda Weiss, 'Sources of the East Asian Advantage: An Institutional Analysis', in Robinson (ed.), *Pathways to Asia*, pp. 174–5.
12. Ibid., p. 176.
13. See Robert Wade, *Governing the Market: Economic Theory and the Role of Government in East Asian Industrialization*, Princeton, NJ: Princeton University Press, 1990; also 'The Visible Hand: The State and East Asia's Economic Growth', *Current History*, 92(578),

1993. 431–40.

14.   Weiss, 'Sources of the East Asian Advantage' p. 177.
15.   Ibid., p. 178.
16.   J. Henderson and R.P. Appelbaum, 'Situating the State in the East Asian Development Process', in R.P. Appelbaum and J. Henderson (eds), *States and Development in the Asian Pacific Rim*, London: Sage, 1992, pp. 20–22.
17.   Weiss, 'Sources of the East Asian Advantage', pp. 182–7; See also Linda Weiss, 'Governed Interdependence: Rethinking the Government–Business Relationship in East Asia', *Pacific Review*, 8(4), 1995, 589–616.
18.   World Bank, *The East Asian Miracle: Economic Growth and Public Policy*, Oxford: Oxford University Press for the World Bank, 1993, pp. 366–8.
19.   World Bank, *Government Policy and Productivity Growth: Is East Asia an Exception?*, Lessons of East Asia Series, Washington, DC: World Bank, 1993, p.18.
20.   World Bank, *World Development Report 1997: The State in a Changing World*, Oxford: Oxford University Press for the World Bank, 1997, p. 163.
21.   Johnson, *MITI and the Japanese Miracle*, p. 322; also Daniel I. Okimoto, *Between MITI and the Market: Japanese Industrial Policy for High Technology*, Stanford, Cal.: Stanford University Press, 1989.
22.   See David Martin Jones, *Political Development in Pacific Asia*, Cambridge: Polity Press, 1997, pp. 65–6.
23.   Kent Calder, *Strategic Capitalism: Private Business and Public Purpose in Japanese Industrial Finance*, Princeton, N.J.: Princeton University Press, 1993, pp. 72–102.
24.   Haruhiro Fukui and Shigeko N. Fukai, 'The End of the Miracle: Japanese Politics in the Post-Cold War Era', in Mark T. Berger and Douglas A. Borer (eds), *The Rise of East Asia: Critical Visions of the Pacific Century*, London: Routledge, 1997, p. 49.
25.   See, for example, Leroy Jones and Il Sakong, *Government, Business and Entrepreneurship in Economic Development: The Korean Case*, Cambridge, Mass.: Harvard University Press, 1980; Yun-han Chu, 'State Structure and Economic Adjustment of the East Asian Newly Industrializing Countries', *International Organization*, 43, Autumn 1989, 647–72; Stephen Haggard and Chung-in Moon, 'Institutions and Economic Policy: Theory and a Korean Case Study', *World Politics*, 42, January 1990, pp. 210–37; Byung Sun Choi, 'The Structure of the Economic Policy-making Institutions in Korea and the Strategic Role of the Economic Planning Board (EPB)', *Korean Journal of Policy Studies*, 2(1), 1991, 1–25; Jung-En Woo, *Race to the Swift: State and Finance in Korean Industrialization*, New York: Columbia University Press, 1991; H.-J. Chang, 'Political Economy of Industrial Policy in Korea', *Cambridge Journal of Economics*, 17(2), 1994, 131–57.
26.   Frank B. Tipton, *The Rise of Asia: Economics, Society and Politics in Contemporary Asia*, Melbourne: Macmillan Education, 1998, p. 426.
27.   See Jones, *Political Development in Pacific Asia*, pp. 72–4.
28.   This proposition is developed at some length by Timothy C. Lim, 'Power, Capitalism, and the Authoritarian State in South Korea', *Journal of Contemporary Asia*, 28(4), 1998, 457–83.
29.   David C. Cole and Yung Chul Park, *Financial Development in Korea, 1945–1978*, Harvard East Asian Monograph, 106, Cambridge, Mass.: Harvard University Press, 1983, p. 277.
30.   Tipton, *The Rise of Asia*, p. 427.
31.   Jones, *Political Development in Pacific Asia*, pp. 76–7.
32.   Chung-in Moon, 'Changing Patterns of Business–Government Relations and Regime Transition in South Korea', in A. MacIntyre (ed.), *Business and Government in Industrialising Asia*, Sydney: Allen & Unwin, 1994, p. 161.
33.   See Yeon-ho Lee and Hyuk Rae Kim, 'The Dilemma of Liberalisation: Financial Crisis and the Transformation of Capitalism in South Korea', paper presented at the Conference, 'From Miracle to Meltdown: The End of Asian Capitalism', Fremantle, 20–22 August 1998, p. 12.
34.   Jones, *Political Development in Pacific Asia*, p. 81.

35. Wade, *Governing the Market*, pp. 97–8.
36. See A.J. Youngston, *Hong Kong Economic Growth and Policy*, Hong Kong: Oxford University Press, 1982, pp. 86–91, 115–23, 132–6.
37. L.C. Chew, *Lessons of East Asia. Hong Kong: A Unique Case of Development*, Washington, DC: World Bank, 1993.
38. See M. Castells, L. Goh and R.Y. Kwok, *The Shek Kip Mei Syndrome: Economic Development and Public Housing in Hong Kong and Singapore*, London: Pion, 1990; G. Schiffer, 'State Policy and Economic Growth: A Note on the Hong Kong Model', *International Journal of Urban and Regional Research*, 15(2), 1991, 180–96.
39. See Chan Heng Chee, 'The PAP and the Structuring of the Political System', in K. Singh and P. Wheatley (eds), *The Management of Success: The Moulding of Modern Singapore*, Singapore: Institute of Southeast Asian Studies, 1989; J. S. T. Quah, 'Political Consequences of Rapid Economic Development: The Singapore Case', in S. Nagel (ed.), *Asian Development and Public Policy*, London: Macmillan, 1994.
40. For a fuller account of the Singapore government's approach to industrial relations, see S. Haggard, *Pathways from the Periphery: The Politics of Growth of the Newly Industrializing Countries*, Ithaca, NY: Cornell University Press, 1990; T. W. Soon and C. J. Tan, *Lessons of East Asia. Singapore: Public Policy and Economic Development*, Washington, DC: World Bank, 1993.
41. A succinct but useful overview of the Singapore model of economic management is offered in Jones, *Political Development in Pacific Asia*, pp. 94–8 .
42. See W.G. Huff, *The Economic Growth of Singapore: Trade and Development in the Twentieth Century*, Cambridge: Cambridge University Press, 1994, pp. 299–360.
43. Khoo Boo Teik, 'Democracy and Authoritarianism in Malaysia since 1957: Class, Ethnicity and Changing Capitalism', in Arek Laothamatas (ed.), *Democratization in Southeast and East Asia*, Singapore: Institute of Southeast Asian Studies, 1997, p. 55.
44. See Kim Ong-Giger, 'Malaysia's Drive into High-technology Industries: Cruising into the Multimedia Super Corridor', in *Southeast Asian Affairs 1997*, Singapore: Institute of Southeast Asian Studies, 1997, p. 188.
45. Peter Searle *The Riddle of Malaysian Capitalism: Rent-seekers or Real Capitalists?* Sydney: Asian Studies Association of Australia in association with Allen & Unwin and University of Hawaii Press, 1999, p. 244.
46. Khoo Boo Teik, 'Democracy and Authoritarianism in Malaysia since 1957', pp. 66–8.
47. Searle, *The Riddle of Malaysian Capitalism*, p. 245.
48. See L. Jones, 'Big Business Groups in South Korea: Causation, Growth and Politics', in Lee-Jay Cho and Yoon Hyung Kim (eds), *Korea's Political Economy: An Institutional Perspective*, Boulder Col.: Westview Press, 1994; G. White (ed.), *Developmental States in East Asia*, London: Macmillan, 1988; Ruth McVey (ed.), *Southeast Asian Capitalists*, Ithaca, NY: Southeast Asia Program, Cornell University, 1992.
49. For a striking illustration of this approach, sometimes referred to as the 'oriental' model of economic development, see Hung-chao Tai, 'The Oriental Alternative: A Hypothesis on East Asian Culture and Economy", *Issues and Studies*, 25, March 1989, 10–36.
50. For a fuller outline of the pitfalls of cultural reductionism, see P.W. Preston, *Pacific Asia in the Global System*, Oxford: Basil Blackwell, 1998, pp. 218–20.
51. Mark T. Berger, 'The Triumph of the East? The East Asian Miracle and Post-Cold War Capitalism', in Berger and Borer (eds), *The Rise of East Asia: Critical Visions of the Pacific Century*, pp. 262–7; see also Meredith Woo-Cummings (Jung-en Woo), 'East Asia's America Problem', in Meredith Woo-Cummings and Michael Loriaux (eds), *Past as Prelude: History in the Making of a New World Order*, Boulder, Col.: Westview Press, 1993, p. 138.
52. Weiss, 'Sources of the East Asian Advantage', p. 189.

53.   See Walden Bello, and Stephanie Rosenfeld, *Dragons in Crisis: Asia's Miracle Economies in Distress*, San Francisco, Cal.: Institute for Food and Development Policy, 1990, pp. 12–13. For more recent assessments, see Dupont, *Environment and Security in Pacific Asia*, pp. 10–16; R T. Maddock, 'Environmental Security in Southeast Asia', *Contemporary Southeast Asia*, 17(1), June 1995.

54.   Henderson and Appelbaum, 'Situating the State in the East Asian Development Process', pp. 5–6.

55.   Though they view differently the relative importance of internal and external influences on Japanese industrialization, most informed observers recognize the dual conjuncture. See F. Moulder, *Japan, China and the Modern World Economy*, Cambridge: Cambridge University Press, 1977; Michio Morishima, *Why Has Japan 'Succeeded'?* Cambridge: Cambridge University Press, 1982.

56.   Kim, 'From Neo-mercantilism to Globalism', p. 85.

57.   See A.H. Amsden, 'Taiwan's Economic History: A Case of "Étatisme" and a Challenge to Dependency Theory', *Modern China*, 5(3), 1979, 341–79; B. Cummings, 'The Origins and Development of the Northeast Asian Political Economy: Industrial Sectors, Product Cycles and Political Consequences', in Deyo (ed.), *The Political Economy of the New Asian Industrialism*, pp. 48–83.

58.   Henderson and Appelbaum, 'Situating the State in the East Asian Development Process', p. 8.

59.   See Gary Gereffi, 'New Realities of Industrial Development in East Asia and Latin America: Global, Regional and National Trends', in Appelbaum and Henderson (eds), *States and Development in the Asian Pacific Rim*, pp. 102–5.

60.   Ibid., pp. 106–10.

61.   See Bob Jessop, 'Reflections on Globalisation and its (il)logic(s)', in Kris Olds *et al.* (eds), *Globalisation and the Asia-Pacific Contested Territories*, London: Routledge, 1999, pp. 32–6.

62.   A possible consequence of this transition was 'a massive transfer to foreign ownership'. See Saskia Sassen, 'Servicing the Global Economy: Reconfigured States and Private Agents', in Olds *et al.* (eds), *Globalisation and the Asia-Pacific*, p. 154.

63.   See Cayetano Paderanga, Jr., 'Globalisation and the Limits to National Economic Management', in Olds *et al.* (eds), *Globalisation and the Asia-Pacific*, pp. 163–80.

64.   World Bank, *World Development Report 1997*, p. 163.

65.   Weiss, 'Developmental States in Transition', *Pacific Review,* 13(1), 2000, p. 22.

66.   David Brown, 'The Search for Elite Cohesion', *Contemporary Southeast Asia,* 15(1), June 1993, 111–30.

67.   The official rationale for the decision to ban Falun Gong is outlined in *Peace*, no. 52, September 1999, pp. 11–12. For outside assessments, see Liz Sly, 'A State of Paranoia', *Bulletin of the Atomic Scientists*, 55(5), September–October 1999, 38–43; Susan V. Lawrence, 'Successful Summer', *FEER* , 19 August 1999, 16–18; L. Holland, 'Breathtaking', *FEER*, 11 November 1999, 20–21; 'Sect Defies Beijing Crackdown', *Age*, 26 April 2000, 8.

68.   Stephanie Lawson, 'Confucius in Singapore: Culture, Politics, and the PAP State', in Dauvergne (ed.), *Weak and Strong States*, p. 125.

69.   See John Girling, 'Democracy and Civil Society: Growth Model and Area Diversity', *Contemporary Southeast Asia*, 15(2), September 1993, pp. 240–41.

70.   See Harold Crouch, *Government and Society in Malaysia*, Sydney: Allen & Unwin, 1996, pp. 77–95.

71.   Jones, *Political Development in Pacific Asia*, pp. 30–33.

72.   M. Din Syamsuddin, 'Political Stability and Leadership Succession in Indonesia', *Contemporary Southeast Asia*, 15(1), June 1993, 13–14.

73. See R. William Liddle, 'Suharto's Indonesia: Personal Rule and Political Institutions', *Pacific Affairs*, no. 58, 1985, pp. 68–90; Michael R.J. Vatikiotis, *Indonesian Politics under Suharto*, London: Routledge, 1993, pp. 32–59.

74. See L. Pye with M. Pye, *Asian Power and Politics: The Cultural Dimensions of Authority*, Cambridge, Mass.: Harvard University Press, 1985, p. 115; also Vatikiotis, *Indonesian Politics under Suharto*, p. 2.

75. Harold Crouch, 'Indonesia's Strong State', in Dauvergne (ed.), *Weak and Strong States*, pp. 106–7.

76. See A. MacIntyre, 'Power, Prosperity and Patrimonialism: Business and Government in Indonesia', in A. MacIntyre (ed.), *Business and Government in Industralising Asia*, Sydney: Allen & Unwin, 1994; also Adam Schwartz, *A Nation in Waiting: Indonesia in the 1990s*, Boulder, Col.: Westview Press, 1994, pp. 133–61.

77. See Ariel Heryanto, 'Indonesia: Towards the Final Countdown?', in *Southeast Asian Affairs 1997*, Singapore: ISEAS, 1997, pp. 107–26.

78. *FEER*, 9 September 1999, pp. 8–21.

79. *Age*, 27 October 1999, 13.

80. See Cotton, *The Pacific Century*, p. 147.

81. For a fuller treatment of the cultural foundations of state practice see, C. Jenks, *Culture*, London: Routledge, 1993, pp. 25–44; also P.W. Preston, *Political Cultural Identity: Citizens and Nations in a Global Era*, London: Sage, 1997.

82. Tu Wei Ming has seen in the East Asian political economy 'an amalgam of the family or collectively oriented values of the East and the pragmatic, economic-goal oriented values of the West' (*Confucian Ethics Today: The Singapore Challenge*, Singapore: Federal Publications, 1984, p. 110).

83. See Hung-chao Tai, 'The Oriental Alternative: An Hypothesis on Culture and Economy', in Hung-chao Tai (ed.), *Confucianism and Economic Development: An Oriental Alternative?*, Washington, D.C.: Washington Institute Press, 1989, pp. 6–7; also Michio Morishima, *Why Has Japan Succeeded?*; Roy Hofheinz, Jr and Kent E. Calder, *The East Asia Edge*, New York: Harper & Row, 1982, pp. 41–5, 109–13.

84. Henderson and Appelbaum, 'Situating the State in the East Asian Development Process', p. 16.

85. See Arifin Bey, 'Confucianism's Contribution to the Modernization of Japan', in Osman Bakar and Cheng Gek Nai (eds), *Islam and Confucianism: A Civilizational Dialogue*, Kuala Lumpur: University of Malaya Press, 1997, pp. 173–90.

86. See Mark R. Mullins, Shimazono Susumu and Paul L. Swanson (eds), *Religion and Society in Modern Japan: Selected Readings*, Berkeley, Cal.: Asian Humanities Press, 1993, p. 81.

87. Lee Kuan Yew's *Letter to Moral Education Team*, cited in Khun Eng-Kuah, 'Confucian Ideology and Social Engineering in Singapore', *Journal of Contemporary Asia*, 20(3), 1990, 375.

88. Curriculum Development Institute of Singapore, *Confucian Ethics*, Textbook for Secondary Three, Singapore: Educational Publishers, 1985, pp. 120–1.

89. Chua Beng Huat, 'Culturalisation of Economy and Politics in Singapore', in Robison (ed.), *Pathways to Asia*, p. 93.

90. Stephanie Lawson, 'Confucius in Singapore: Culture, Politics, and the PAP State', in Dauvergne (ed.), *Weak and Strong States*, pp. 127–8.

91. 'Confucius: Still a Subject of Interest', *Beijing Review*, 25–31 December 1989, 17–21.

92. 'Confucius on State, "Confucius the Commoner"', *Beijing Review*, 33(18), 1990, 2–33.

93. Chua Beng Huat, *Communitarian Ideology and Democracy in Singapore*, London: Routledge, 1995, p. 28.

94. See T. de Bary, *Neo-Confucian Orthodoxy and the Learning of Mind-and-Heart*, New York: Columbia University Press, 1981; Tu Wei-ming, *Humanity and Self-Cultivation: Essays in Confucion Thought*, Berkeley, Cal.: Asia Humanities Press, 1978.

95. See Amyn B. Sajoo, *Pluralism, in 'Old Societies and New States'*, Singapore: Institute of Southeast Asian Studies, 1994, pp. 31–65.

96.	Hussin Mutalib, 'Islamisation in Malaysia: Between Ideals and Realities', in Hussin Mutalib and Taj ul-Islam Hashmi (eds), *Islam, Muslims and the Modern State: Case Studies of Muslims in Thirteen Countries*, London: Macmillan, 1994, pp. 152–73.

97.	See A. B. Shamsul, 'Religion and Ethnic Politics in Malaysia' in Charles F. Keyes, Laurel Kendall and Helen Hardacre, *Asian Visions of Authority: Religion and the Modern States of East and Southeast Asia*, Honolulu: University of Hawaii Press, 1994, pp. 99–116; see also Shanti Nair, *Islam in Malaysian Foreign Policy*, London, Routledge, 1997, pp 91–100.

98.	See Douglas Ramage, *Politics in Indonesia: Democracy, Islam and the Ideology of Tolerance*, London: Routledge, 1995; also C. W. Watson, 'Muslims and the State in Indonesia', in *Islam, Muslims and the Modern State*, pp. 174–96.

99.	See R. William Liddle, 'Coercion, Co-operation, and the Management of Ethnic Relations in Indonesia', in Michael E. Brown and Šumit Ganguly (eds), *Government Policies and Ethnic Relations in Asia and the Pacific*, Cambridge, Mass.: MIT Press, 1997, pp. 273–320.

100.	Fareed Zakaria, 'A Conversation with Lee Kuan Yew', *Foreign Affairs*, 73(3), March–April 1994, 109–26.

101.	Kishore Mahbubani, 'The Pacific Impulse', *Survival*, 37(1), Spring 1995, pp. 105–20. For an earlier version of his argument and its implicit criticism of 'western values', see 'The Dangers of Decadence: What the West Can Teach the East', *Foreign Affairs*, 72(4) 1993, 10–14.

102.	See Bilahari Kausikan, 'Asia's Different Standard', *Foreign Policy*, 92(3), Fall 1993, pp. 24–41; for a more analytically incisive exposition of the construction of 'Asianness', see John Ingelson, 'The "Asian Ethic" ', in R. Bell (ed.), *Negotiating the Pacific Century: The New Asia, the United States and Australia,* Sydney: Allen & Unwin, Australian Centre for American Studies, 1996, pp. 254–64.

103.	See Chua Beng Huat, 'Culturalisation of Economy and Politics in Singapore', pp. 98–9; also Michael Freeman 'Human Rights, Democracy and "Asian Values" ', *Pacific Review*, 9(3), 1996, pp. 352–66; Karo Bessho, *Identities and Security in East Asia*, Adelphi Paper 325, Oxford: Oxford University Press for International Institute for Strategic Studies, 1999, pp. 53–60.

104.	Mahathir Mohamad, *A New Deal for Asia,* Selangor: Pelanduk Publications, 1999, p. 69.

105.	For a further characterization of the neo–Confucian ethic, see Reg Little and Warren Reed, *The Confucian Renaissance,* Sydney: Federation Press, 1989, pp. 4–6.

106.	See Li Xianghu, 'The Post-Cold War Challenge from Asia', *New Perspectives Quarterly,* 9(1), Winter 1992, p. 15.

107.	For this exposition I am indebted to Yash Ghai's illuminating analysis (see Yash Ghai, 'Human Rights and Governance: the Asia Debate', Asia Foundation Center for Asia Pacific Affairs, Occasional papers, no. 4, November 1994).

108.	Final Declaration of the Regional Meeting for Asia of the World Conference on Human Rights of 2 April 1993 (Bangkok Declaration), UN Doc A/CONF: 157/AS RM/8; A/CONF:157/PC/59, 7 April 1993, pp. 3–7. Both the Bangkok Declaration and the NGO counter-declaration are reproduced in James T. Tang (ed.), *Human Rights and International Relations in the Asia-Pacific Region*, London: Pinter, 1995.

109.	See State Council, *Human Rights in China*, Beijing: Foreign Language Press, 1991; a second paper on human rights was issued by the Chinese government in 1995 under the title *Progress of Human Rights in China.*

110.	Singapore Government, *Shared Values,* Singapore: Singapore National Printers, 1991.

111.	See Alan Dupont, 'Is There an Asian Way?', *Survival*, 38(2), Summer 1996, p. 24.

112.	See Singapore Government, *Shared Values,* 1991.

113.	Tun Daim Zainuddin, 'Rhetoric and Reality of Human Rights Linked to Basic Needs', *New Straits Times*, 28 July 1996, 16.

114.	For Mahathir's most comprehensive assessment of the 1997 crisis and its implications for Malaysia, see his speech to the Annual Seminar of the World Bank in Hong Kong, 20 September 1997, in *Human Rights: Views of Dr Mahathir Mohammed*, Kuala Lumpur: compiled by World Youth Foundation, 1999, pp. 142–55.

115. See Long Wong and Beverley Blaskett, 'Manipulating Space in a Post-Colonial State: The Case of Malaysia', in Camilleri, Jarvis and Paolini (eds), *The State in Transition,* pp. 173–88.
116. See Taufik Abdullah, 'Islamic Society and the Challenge of Globalization', in J.A. Camilleri and Chandra Muzaffar (eds), *Globalization: The Perspectives and Experiences of the Religious Traditions of Asia Pacific,* Petaling Jaya: International Movement for a Just World, 1998, pp. 51–62.
117. Much the same argument is made by Michael Freeman, 'Human Rights, Democracy and "Asian Values" ', *Pacific Review,* 1996, 365.
118. Here I am indebted to the succinct exposition of the diverse democratic traditions offered by Preston, *Pacific Asia,* pp. 244–6.
119. See the connection established between 'autonomy and democracy' in David Held, *Democracy and the Global Order: From the Modern State to Cosmopolitan Governance,* Cambridge: Polity Press, 1995, pp. 192–201.
120. The formulation advanced here has some affinity with that proposed by Sakamoto, 'Civil Society and Democratic World Order', pp. 217–19.
121. James H. Mittelman, 'Resisting Globalization: Environmental Politics in Eastern Asia', in Gill and Mittelman (eds), *Innovation and Transformation,* p. 77.
122. Tadashi Yamamoto (ed.), *Emerging Civil Society in the Asia Pacific Community,* Singapore: Institute of Southeast Asian Studies and Tokyo: Japan Center for International Exchange, 1995, pp. 5–6.
123.   Much of the information that follows is drawn from Yamamoto (ed.), *Emerging Civil Society,* pp. 8–9.
124.   Bamrung Kayotha, 'Forum of the Poor in Thailand', paper presented to 'Focus on Alternative Security Systems in the Asia-Pacific' Conference, Chulalongkorn University, Bangkok, 27–30 March 1997.
125. See John Clark, *Democratising Development: The Role of Voluntary Organizations,* London: Earthscan Publications, 1991; Kevin Hewison, 'Nongovernmental Organizations and the Cultural Development Perspective: A Comment on Rigg (1991)', *World Development,* 21(10), 1993, pp. 1699–708; Philip Eldridge, 'Human Rights and Democracy in Indonesia and Malaysia: Emerging Contexts and Discourse', *Contemporary Southeast Asia,* 18(3), December 1996, 298–319; *Report of NGO Symposium on a Social Development Agenda for the ESCAP Region into the Twenty-First Century, Bangkok, 12–15 July 1994,* Bangkok: UN Economic and Social Commission for Asia and the Pacific (SD/NGOSYM/Rep).
126. See Rajni Kothari, 'The NGOs, the State and World Capitalism', *New Asian Visions,* 6(1), 1989, 40–58; Adi Sasono, 'NGOs and Social Movements in Developing Democracy: The Southeast Asian Experiences', *New Asian Visions,* 6(1), 1989, 14–26.
127. See Hagen Koo, 'Middle Classes, Democratization and Class Formulation', *Theory and Society,* 20(4), August 1991, 485–509.
128. Mark Clifford, 'Young Turks Strike Back', *FEER,* 22 September 1988, 30.
129. See Jiang-jip Choi, *Labor and the Authoritarian State,* Seoul: Korea University Press, 1989; George E. Ogle, *South Korea: Dissent within the Economic Miracle,* London: Zed Books, 1990.
130. Yin-wah Chu, 'Labor and Democratization in South Korea and Taiwan', *Journal of Contemporary Asia,* 28(2), 1998, 198–9.
131. Ibid., p. 191.
132. Lo Shiu Hing, 'Political Participation in Hong Kong, South Korea and Taiwan', *Journal of Contemporary Asia,* 20(2), 1990, 239.
133. Ming Sing, 'Economic Development, Civil Society and Democratization in Hong Kong', *Journal of Contemporary Asia,* 26(4), 1996, 488.
134. Lo Shiu Hing, 'Political Participation in Hong Kong, South Korea and Taiwan', p. 243.
135. Ming Sing, 'Economic Development, Civil Society and Democratization in Hong Kong', p.490.

136. See Ng Sek Hong, 'Labor', in Joseph Cheng (ed.), *Hong Kong in Transition*, Hong Kong: Oxford University Press, 1986, p. 273.
137. Garry Rodan, 'Civil Society and Others Political Possibilities in Southeast Asia', p. 172.
138. See Cesar P. Cala, 'Civil Society in the Philippines', in Proceedings of First Asia-Pacific Civil Society Forum, Seoul, 11–14 August 1995, pp. 183–95; also Cesar Cala and Jose Grageda (eds), *Studies on Coalition Experiences in the Philippines*, Manila: PCJC-HRD, 1994.
139. See David G. Timberman, *A Changeless Land: Continuity and Change in Philippine Politics*, New York: M.E. Sharpe, 1991, pp. 374–400; David Rosenberg, 'Sociocultural Development in the Philippines', in Thomas W. Robinson (ed.), *Democracy and Development in Southeast Asia*, Washington, D.C.: AEI Press, 1991, pp. 213–34.
140. Andra L. Corothers and Estie W. Suryatna, 'Review of the NGO Sector in Indonesia and Evolution of the Asia Pacific Regional Community Concept Among Indonesian NGOs', in Yamamoto (ed.), *Emerging Civil Society*, p. 124.
141. For a fuller account of these three models, see Philip Eldridge, *NGOs in Indonesia: Popular Movement or Arm of Government?*, Working Paper no. 55, Monash University, Centre of Southeast Asian Studies, 1989.
142. P. Eldridge, 'Human Rights and Democracy in Indonesia and Malaysia', p. 306.
143. Ibid., pp. 306–7.
144. Garry Rodan, 'Civil Society and other Political Possibilities in Southeast Asia', pp. 173–4.
145. P. Eldridge, 'Human Rights and Democracy in Indonesia and Malaysia', p. 308.
146. *Challenges Facing Civil Society in a Changing Indonesia*, Statement by the 12th INFID Conference, Bali, 14–17 September 1999.
147. James H. Mittelman, 'Resisting Globalization: Environmental Politics in "Eastern Asia" ', p. 79.
148. Weiss, 'What Will Become of *Reformasi*?', p. 430.
149. *FEER*, 7 October 1999, 20.
150. S. Jayasankaran, 'Politics of the Pulpit', *FEER*, 16 September 1999, 22.
151. Zhang Ye, 'Chinese NGOs: A Survey Report', in Yamamoto (ed.), *Emerging Civil Society*, pp. 93–107.
152. Jermain Lam and Ka-ho Mok, 'Economic Prosperity or Democracy: Dilemma of Development in Hong Kong and China', *Journal of Contemporary China*, 61(6), 1997, 475.
153. See Shohei Muta and Makito Noda, 'Status of Research Institutions in China: A Trend Report', in Yamamoto (ed.), *Emerging Civil Society*, pp. 358–66.
154. Lam and Mok, 'Economic Prosperity or Democracy', p. 476.
155. See K.H. Mok, 'Private Challenges to Public Dominance: The Resurgence of Private Education in Pearl River Delta', *Contemporary Education*, 33(1), 1997, 43–60.
156. Bay Fang, 'Colourful Crusaders', *FEER*, 7 May 1998, 13.
157. *FEER*, 7 May 1998, 11.
158. Indicative of the bureaucracy's attitude to civil society was its deeply ingrained assumption that, whereas NGOs reflected particular interests, only the government was authorized to express the public interest. The extremely onerous procedures and requirements for the registration of non-profit organizations was itself symbolic of this attitude. See Toshihiro Menju (with Takako Aoki), 'The Evolution of Japanese NGOs in the Asia Pacific Context', in Yamamoto (ed.), *Emerging Civil Society*, pp. 149–51.
159. Kevin Hewison, Richard Robison and Garry Rodan, 'Political Power in Industrializing Capitalist Societies: Theoretical Approaches', in K. Hewison, R. Robison and G. Rodan (eds), *Southeast Asia in the 1990s: Authoritarianism, Democracy and Capitalism*, Sydney: Allen &Unwin, 1993, p. 29.
160. See Surin Maisrikrod, 'The Making of Thai Democracy: A Study of Political Alliances among the States, the Capitalists and the Middle Class', in Laothamatas (ed.), *Democratization in Southeast and East Asia*, p. 159.

161. See Sung-Joo Han, 'South Korean Politics in Transition', in L. Diamond, J.J. Linz and S.M. Lipset (eds), *Democracy in Developing Countries*, Boulder, Col.: Lynne Reinner, 1989, pp. 267–304. For a more nuanced analysis, see Sung-Joo Han and Oknim Chung, 'South Korea: Economic Management and Democratization', in James W. Morley (ed.), *Driven by Growth: Political Change in the Asia-Pacific Region*, rev. edn, Armonk, NY: M.E. Sharpe, 1999, pp. 197–223. See also Tun-jen Cheng and Chia-lung Lin, 'Taiwan: A Long Decade of Democratic Transition', in Morley (ed.), *Driven by Growth*, pp. 227–34.

162. Lo Shiu Hing, 'Liberalization and Democratization in Taiwan: A Class and Functional Perspective, in Laothamatas (ed.), *Democratization in Southeast and East Asia*, pp. 215–36; Graham Field, *Economic Growth and Political Change in Asia*, London: Macmillan, 1995, pp. 153–82.

163. See Chung-Si Ahn, 'The State, Society and Democratization in South Korea: The Impact of Deepening Industrialization', in Stuart Nagel (ed.), *Asian Development and Public Policy*, London: Macmillan, 1994, pp. 32–43.

164. John Girling, *Interpreting Democracy, Capitalism, Democracy, and the Middle Class in Thailand*, Ithaca, NY: Cornell Southeast Asia Program Publications, 1996.

165. Chung-Si Ahn, 'Economic Dimensions of Democratization in South Korea', in Laothamatas (ed.), *Democratization in Southeast and East Asia*, pp. 248–49.

166. Harold Crouch and James W. Morley, 'The Dynamics of Political Change', in Morley (ed.), *Driven by Growth*, p. 327.

167. Such evidence is specifically cited in Sing, 'Economic Development, Civil Society and Democratization in Hong Kong', p. 492.

168. See Hagen Koo, 'The State, *Minjung*, and the Working Class and South Korea', in Hagen Koo (ed.), *State and Society in Contemporary Korea*, Ithaca, NY: Cornell University Press, 1993.

169. This argument is developed at some length by Sejin Pak, 'Two Forces of Democratization in Korea', *Journal of Contemporary Asia*, 28(1), 1998, 45–73.

170. Ibid., p. 62.

171. *Le Monde Diplomatique*, November 1999, 14.

172. *FEER*, 30 September 1999, 21.

173. It is worth noting that through its military presence in Korea and the political pressure it brought to bear on South Korean governments, the United States had, at least indirectly, strengthened the democracy movement. By appealing to nationalist sentiment, opposition to US troops in Korea endowed the movement with a degree of legitimacy it may not otherwise have had. Similarly, US advocacy of political liberalization afforded the movement a degree of protection that may otherwise have been denied to it.

174. Jones, *Political Development in Pacific Asia*, pp. 158–9.

175. These figures are drawn from the *Hong Kong Annual Digest of Statistics* and cited by Lam and Mok, 'Economic Prosperity or Democracy', p. 468.

176. This sentiment was if anything strengthened in the aftermath of Hong Kong's return to China. See 'Rearguard Action', *FEER*, 6 April 2000, 28–9.

177. This argument is developed at greater length in Sing, 'Economic Development, Civil Society and Democratization in Hong Kong', pp. 494–5.

178. *FEER*, 6 April 2000, 28.

179. See Jamie Mackie, 'Indonesia: Economic Growth and Depoliticization', in Morley (ed.), *Driven by Growth*, pp. 136–8.

180. See Zakaria Haji Ahmad and Sharifah Munirah Alatas, 'Malaysia: In an Uncertain Mode', in Morley (ed.), *Driven by Growth*, pp. 176–96.

181. Harold Crouch, *Government and Society in Malaysia*, Sydney: Allen & Unwin, 1996, pp. 96–113.

182. Ibid., pp. 183–5.

183. *Malaysian Human Rights Report*, Petaling Jaya: Suaram Komunikasi, 1998, p. 11.

184. Simon Elegant, 'Ferment on Campus', *FEER*, 4 November 1999, 21–2.

185. Jones, *Political Development in Pacific Asia*, p. 144.

186.   Yao Souchou, 'Consumption and Social Aspirations of the Middle Class in Singapore', in *Southeast Asian Affairs 1996*, Singapore, Institute of Southeast Asian Studies, 1996, p. 350.
187.   Lam and Mok, 'Economic Prosperity on Democracy', p. 473.
188.   Suzanne Ogden, 'The Changing Context of China's Democratic Socialist Institutions', *In Depth*, Winter 1993, pp. 237–56.
189.   See Martin F. Farrell, 'Global Power or East Asian Tinderbox? China in the Post-Deng Post-Cold War Era', in Berger and Borer (eds), *The Rise of East Asia*, pp. 69–72.
190.   Jones, *Political Development in Pacific Asia*, p. 149.
191.   Ibid., p. 160.

6. Concluding reflections

The transformative dynamic that brought the Cold War to an end had yet to run its full course. More than a decade after the collapse of the Berlin Wall, it was still not possible to characterize the post-Cold War system or the principal axes of conflict and co-operation with any degree of confidence. There was certainly no identifiable concept or principle which even approximated the unifying logic of the Cold War. The normative, sociological and geopolitical attributes of ideological bipolarity that had dominated international diplomacy and political discourse more generally for over 40 years had largely disappeared from public view. However, change was so pervasive and relentless and its consequences so contradictory yet interconnected that no single script could do justice to the intriguing drama that was unfolding on the geopolitical and geoeconomic stage.

Though the dénouement and the time it would take for it to emerge could still only be dimly perceived, three trends were nevertheless readily discernible First, power in the emerging international order had become more concentrated but at the same time more diffuse. Strategic unipolarity, grounded in America's overwhelming military might, coexisted with geopolitical multipolarity associated with the rise of new centres of economic power and the declining political utility of military power. Second, the increasing interpenetration of national economies and the rapidly expanding network of commercial, financial and technological interdependencies coincided with the sharpening of tensions both within the core, and between the core and the periphery. Third, states, while they still occupied centre stage in formal international decision-making processes and institutions, in practice exercised steadily diminishing control over key aspects of economic and security policy. All three trends had to a greater or lesser extent assumed global, regional and sub-regional dimensions.

Nowhere was the diffusion of power and wealth more striking than in East Asia. Japan first, then the newly industrializing economies and later the ASEAN-4 and China had experienced remarkable rates of GDP growth and almost exponential rates in the growth of their manufactured exports. A distinguishing feature of East Asia's political economy was the relative success of the state in setting economic objectives and devising appropriate strategies. Contributing to and taking advantage of the diffusion of power, East Asian states, though presiding over economies that spanned

427

vastly different stages of development, seemed by the late 1980s well placed to pursue more autonomous, even more assertive, economic and security policies. Exuding a new mood of self-confidence, grounded in part on economic performance, many of these polities were beginning to diversify their policies and relationships. What endowed the East Asian renaissance with its obvious potency was the prospect of Japanese or Chinese leadership. Japan, by flexing its economic muscle, and China, by relying on its geopolitical weight, would no doubt offer different forms and styles of leadership and be more comfortable leading on different issues and in different settings. The role that Beijing might play in recasting the regional security environment was more an issue for the future, which is not to say that it did not already concentrate the minds of scholars and policy-makers alike. Japan's economic clout on the other hand was a *fait accompli*. By the end of the 1980s Japan had already established a commanding position in several East Asian economies. It was largely thanks to Japanese capital that South Korea, Thailand and Indonesia had been able to bypass in the early 1980s the formal requirements of IMF and World Bank structural adjustment programmes. In the 1997 financial crisis, it was once again only Japanese capital that could have allowed these same economies to ignore the IMF's policy prescriptions.

Mindful of the actual and potential challenges to its economic interests and strategic priorities, the United States embarked in the 1980s on a major counteroffensive, although its full implications did not become apparent until the advent of the Clinton Administration. While US policy, concerned to extract full advantage from its triumph in the Cold War, was global in both conception and execution, the attention and energy devoted to Asia cannot be underestimated. Relying on an extensive array of unilateral and multilateral instruments, the American state set out to consolidate its strategic presence in Asia, regain the high moral ground through its advocacy of democracy and human rights, and rein in East Asia's economic dynamism and autonomy. A concerted campaign, directed first at Japan but eventually encompassing most of East Asia, sought to enhance US access to Asian markets. Though containment of Soviet, or for that matter Chinese, power no longer served as the official rationale, the United States remained firmly committed to the forward projection of military power. In the East Asian context this meant the retention and upgrading of military alliances, notably with Japan, South Korea and Australia; a continuing commitment to Taiwan; a reinvigorated defence relationship with the Philippines; and, more generally, enhanced access to air, naval, intelligence and missile testing facilities along the rimlands of Asia and across the Pacific. Strengthening and at the same time legitimizing America's pervasive presence in the region was the high profile of its human rights diplomacy, which had two key objectives: first, to wield domestic and international leverage over China's political elites; and second, to enlist the support of East Asia's expanding intellectual, professional and business classes, who were increasingly critical of the authoritarian developmental model and more at ease with the ethos and practice of economic and professional globalization.

Gently at first, but with increasing vigour during the Clinton years, economic priorities assumed centre stage in US diplomacy. The accent was on removing barriers which East Asian states had erected by 'trade-distorting' exercises in industrial policy. Trade liberalization was to be complemented by financial deregulation, an agenda which would be facilitated greatly by the 1997 financial crisis. The sudden outflows of foreign capital had left several of East Asia's worst-hit economies highly vulnerable to IMF leverage. South Korea, Thailand and Indonesia were expected to remove limitations on foreign ownership, accelerate the privatization of state enterprises and restructure the banking system in accordance with norms defined by their foreign creditors. The wide-ranging trade, investment and financial reforms favoured by the IMF closely coincided with the openly stated preferences of the US Treasury. These specific initiatives formed part of the larger neo-liberal project which had seen a systematic attack on key UN institutions and programmes, notably UNCTAD, intent on bridging the North–South divide. A corresponding drive to institutionalize an international trading system around free market principles had informed the US role in the Uruguay round of the GATT negotiations, the creation of the World Trade Organization in 1994 and the new negotiating round inaugurated by the Seattle meeting in November 1999.

The neo-liberal agenda aggressively pursued by successive US administrations may be read as an attempt to promote the interests of powerful US industrial and financial corporations which, by virtue of their competitive advantage and their greater capacity to forge global strategic alliances, stood to gain from increasingly deregulated markets. US policy, however, was both more complex and more ambitious. Though not fully articulated, the intention was to shape the ideas and norms that would govern the restructuring of the world economy, thereby ensuring that economic globalization continued to serve western and in particular US interests. To this extent at least, US policy was still wedded to a hegemonic project, the most obvious consequence of which was to make globalization indistinguishable from westernisation.

However successful the authoritarian developmental state may have been in delivering economic growth, it remained highly vulnerable to external pressure, especially in the context of an increasingly pervasive neo-liberal economic and political agenda. Japan aside, East Asia's economic growth was highly dependent on continuing access to foreign capital and technology. Moreover, virtually all East Asian economies, Japan included, were crucially dependent on the US market. They were all to varying degrees subjected through the 1980s and 1990s to increasing unilateral US pressure, accentuated in several instances by high levels of strategic dependence or sustained international criticism of their human rights record. Vulnerability to external shocks associated with sudden changes in capital flows or international interest rates was compounded by domestic weakness, variously induced by fragile financial and political institutions, elite dissension or ethnic separatism. The net effect of these, at times mutually reinforcing, pressures was to limit the capacity of East Asian states to pursue the politics of patronage, on which depended the viability of the existing power structure and, on occasion, the very cohesion of the body politic. The fall of the Suharto regime was but the most dramatic manifestation of this trend. Unifying symbols developed in an earlier phase, whether nurtured by nationalist sentiment, appeals to Asian solidarity or resentment of western domination, seemed much less efficacious in the vastly altered circumstances of a rapidly globalizing economy. As an added complication, East Asian states had to grapple with the spillover effects of financial and political contagion, not to mention the transboundary ramifications of environmental degradation, piracy, large population movements, pollution and transnational crime.

The widening gap between promise and performance, to the extent that it weakened the legitimacy of the authoritarian state, helped, notably after the mid-1980s, to create new forms of political space and accelerate the pace of political reform. The trend, however, was far from uniform or universal. Some states, for example Deng Xiaoping's China and Suharto's Indonesia, actively resisted the expansion and diversification of civil society. Others, notably the Philippines under Aquino and Korea under Kim Dae-jung, were more sympathetically disposed to the opening up of political space. Even here, however, the tendency was for free space to be occupied by the more privileged elements of society. Conversely, no state could be immune to the changing patterns of social and economic power resulting from rapid industrialization. Most obvious was the emergence of an increasingly large and differentiated middle class, at least sections of which were intent on giving voice to new interests and identities and to exercising greater pressure on the policy-making process. The reawakening of civil society had become commonplace, but the responses of governing elites varied widely, with some willing, at least in principle, to experiment with participatory politics and others still wedded to coercive or co-optional strategies.

Socio-economic transformation had created a climate more conducive to political reform, but its implications for democracy were far from clear. In Korea, as in Taiwan or Thailand, wider political participation did not necessarily mean the displacement of powerful political elites. Substantive democracy did not automatically follow the consolidation of procedural democracy. The interests of the new middle classes did not always accord with the requirements of democratization. How much and what kind of democracy remained highly contested questions. Answers would emerge only gradually, and reflect the complex and still evolving relationship between state, economy and civil society. The interests of business and even professional and bureaucratic elites could not in any case be divorced from regional and global production strategies and capital flows and the international division of labour on which they rested. A globalizing economy was likely to foster a globalizing middle class whose members shared common aspirations and subscribed to common norms, the cumulative effect of which would be to erode the state's capacity to manage the national economy and reduce the scope and efficiency of democratic institutions.

Care, however, must be taken not to overstate the commonality of interests between the emerging middle classes of South Korea, Taiwan and Thailand, let alone Malaysia, Indonesia and China, or between them and their counterparts in the western world. In responding to the 1997 crisis, East Asian governments and private enterprises in both the industrial and banking sectors diverged as much as they converged when it came to perceptions of risks and opportunities and preferred strategies for economic recovery. In other words, greater civic activism was not of itself a sufficient condition for continued democratization. Such an outcome would depend on something more than the development of electoral politics, namely the extent and quality of social mobilization. More specifically, it would depend on the establishment of new channels of interest articulation and aggregation. Institutions giving expression to a range of social and political grievances and providing effective and independent channels through which they could be expressed were only just beginning to emerge. The upsurge of Falung Gong activities in China, student protests in Indonesia and the *Reformasi* movement in Malaysia were an accurate barometer of growing social and political ferment in Asia. At the same time they pointed to a state generally discomfited by the phenomenon and inclined to question the motivation or political literacy of those involved. Ill-equipped to practise the politics of dialogue, it tended to find refuge in the politics of division and, where the challenge persisted, to resort to the politics of veiled or even naked coercion.

In no instance did the authoritarian developmental state give way to a fully fledged democratic polity. Arguably, Taiwan had made greater progress than China in developing laws and institutions consistent with notions of representative and participatory democracy. Perhaps the same could be said of Abdurrahman's Indonesia if compared to Mahathir's Malaysia. But virtually every East Asian state, Japan included, could best be described as a hybrid political system given to recurring oscillations between authoritarian and democratic impulses. Reflecting the fluidity of economic and social arrangements and heightened domestic political polarization, these swings of the pendulum had a temporal dimension (that is, concessions to democratic politics might be made at a given moment but not necessarily followed through), a spatial dimension (they might apply in some parts of the country but not in others) or a functional dimension (they might apply to particular issues or areas of policy but not to others).

Needless to say, the foregoing generalizations would be seriously misleading if they obscured the marked differences between states or if they gave the impression that East Asian politics had somehow failed to measure up to the high standards of western democratic theory and practice. To refer to East Asian states as hybrid political systems is not to imply that western states were the models of democracy that oriental states had to emulate. Nor is it to overlook the conspicuous shortcomings of the western liberal tradition. It is simply to stress the heterogeneous influences that were moulding East Asia's recent political history and were likely to shape its future trajectory. These influences could in large measure be traced back to the dynamics of social and economic change on the one hand, and deeply ingrained cultural traditions on the other, which perhaps helps to explain why the drive to modernize generated recurring tensions within the body politic. While the polarization of values and interests assumed a different profile in different national settings, it generally revolved around two distinct yet closely related contradictions: the first between centralized authority and democratization, and the second between westernization and respect for tradition. Connecting but not necessarily resolving these two contradictions was the elusive search for national identity and the consequent attempts of the state to define its place in the region. Ironically, this political objective preoccupied not only Asian states grappling with the demands of post-colonial or post-occupation reconstruction, but also Australia and Canada, two states firmly anchored in the western tradition but desperately keen to establish their credentials as members of the emerging Asia-Pacific community.

Nowhere did the legacy of the Second World War impose a heavier psychological burden than in Japan. For McCormack, central to any understanding of contemporary Japanese political discourse and practice was the country's failure to address the question of war responsibility.[1] Three decisions could be said to symbolize the politics of denial: the granting of immunity to Japan's wartime supreme commander, the emperor; the refusal to give due consideration to the issue of war crimes; and the persistent failure to acknowledge responsibility for the suffering inflicted on neighbouring countries. Among Japan's conservative leaders the widely held though seldom publicly expressed view was that the adoption of a peace constitution, framed by the occupying state, was penance enough for any sins that Japan may have committed. In this sense, the constitution posed two agonizing dilemmas for which no Japanese government was able to offer a lasting resolution: how to reconcile the constitutional commitment to democratic principles with continuing adherence to the imperial tradition still pivotal to Japan's self-understanding; and how to balance the constitution's pacifist intentions with the desire for a return to 'normalcy', understood as Japan's right to exercise power and influence commensurate with its wealth.

For the political elites who had not entirely accepted what they perceived to be the second-class status imposed on Japan by virtue of its defeat in the war and subsequent US occupation, the constitutional limitations on Japan's freedom of action had to be overcome, whether by gradual reinterpretation, supplementary legislation or outright revision. In a sense, the review of the constitution initiated in the latter part of 1999 was an attempt to explore how much change would be acceptable to the electorate, and what might be the promising avenues for achieving it. The approach most closely associated with Ozawa Ichiro – and exemplified by the *Yomiuri* proposals – was designed to challenge the constitutional *status quo* by mobilizing increasing popular disenchantment with political corruption at home and diplomatic impotence abroad.[2] 'Pacifism in one country' was criticized as unprincipled and unsustainable. Rather than continuing to buy its security on the cheap by excessive reliance on the US protective umbrella, Japan, it was argued, had to make a more substantial contribution to international security by direct participation in UN peace operations, even if that would entail an eventual contribution to a UN standing army. Apart from appealing to Japan's sense of international civic responsibility, these proposals took care to soften the apparent radicalism of constitutional revision by placing the stress on national emergencies. References, for example, to the Kobe earthquake and the Sarin attack in the Tokyo underground were intended to focus on scenarios where a more assertive security strategy was likely to be viewed as entirely reasonable and unproblematic, and to deflect attention from international conflict, where the use of force would tend to be both controversial and unpredictable in its consequences.

Fearful of losing the battle for hearts and minds, especially in the wake of the Socialist Party's *volte face* on the constitutionality of the Self-Defense Forces and the Security Treaty with the United States, Japanese intellectuals and others with a strong disposition to a more pacifist conception of internationalism conceded the need to legitimize the existence of the armed forces but sought to limit their functions.[3] Through supplementary legislation military capabilities could be restricted to purely defensive missions (in direct defence of Japanese territory), abandoning claims to the defence of 1000-mile sea lanes and precluding their involvement in domestic political life. Japan's internationalist credentials could be enhanced by supporting UN operations by other than military means, initiating or supporting a range of regional and global disarmament proposals, promoting co-operation and reconciliation with neighbours and enacting an International Co-operation Law which would drastically expand Japan's development aid programme and ground it more firmly on principles of equity and sustainability. Though views differed on the highly contested issue of the

US military presence in Japan, the general drift of opinion within this constituency was for a gradual reduction of US military personnel and facilities, eventually leading to their complete withdrawal.

These conflicting perspectives on Japan's constitutional and security options did not exhaust the range of possibilities under discussion, nor did they predict the likely outcome. They did, however, offer valuable insights into the profound soul-searching that would engage Japan's political, bureaucratic, economic and intellectual elites over the coming decade and beyond. At stake in this contest was Japan's identity as state, nation and economy, and the part that power and force would play in determining its place in the region and the world. In shaping its future external relations, Japan had yet to determine how Asianization or engagement with Asia would relate to persisting 'imperial and *Kokutai* myths of Japanese uniqueness, exclusiveness and superiority'.[4] Deeply embedded in the society's collective psyche, these myths were ideally suited to the articulation of a political agenda intent on liquidating the humiliation of the past, while reasserting the unique virtues and interests of the Japanese nation. Prime Minister Yoshiro Mori's contentious reference to Japan as 'a divine nation centred on the emperor[5] vividly demonstrated the continuing pull of traditionalist sentiments and attachments. It remained to be seen whether the previous 50 years, apart from inculcating more idealistic visions of the future, had established the economic and political foundations – both nationally and internationally – capable of sustaining that idealism.

The same fundamental challenges confronted modern China, although its economic and political superstructure had a markedly different profile. As previous chapters have been at pains to emphasize, what preoccupied China's political leadership above all else was the need to consolidate the country's territorial and political unity. It was as if the regime's claim to legitimacy depended on restoring to China its dignity and sense of importance, expunging the humiliation suffered at western hands, and satisfactorily managing the unfinished business of China's civil war, not to mention the Cold War. With the return of Hong Kong and Macao, the spotlight turned to Taiwan precisely because its separation from the mainland powerfully symbolized the continuing intrusion of western power and influence into what China considered to be its legitimate domain. More fundamentally still, Taipei's estrangement from Beijing raised the question of identity. For China, at least as much as for Taiwan, it was a living reminder that the Chinese state as the guardian of Chinese civilization had yet to regain its status as the 'middle kingdom', that it had yet to be granted the respect and recognition to which it was accustomed and to which it still aspired. In that sense, the Taiwan dispute, rightly or wrongly, was perceived, as much outside as inside China, as a litmus test of the efficacy of China's domestic and international policies.

Notions of Chinese integrity and sovereignty, endlessly reiterated but seldom defined, meant however more than just recovering control over colonized territories. They were predicated on the need to contain internal divisions and separatist tendencies. In practice, it was necessary to keep within the fold a number of provinces, more specifically the ethnic minorities concentrated in the northern, northwestern and western regions of China. Tibet, Xinjiang and Inner Mongolia, though neither demographically nor economically vital to China's future development, were nevertheless regarded as strategically valuable, not simply because of the vast territory they comprised, but because they performed a critical function in establishing China's credentials as one of the world's centres of geopolitical gravity. As Martin Farrel has incisively observed:

> Tibet gives China a presence on the South Asian land mass . . . Xinjiang . . . links China to the strategically vital Middle East. Inner Mongolia connects China to the steppes of central Asia . . . Manchuria provides a bridge to China's status as a player in Northeast Asia . . .[6]

China's outlying regions bring it into direct contact with, or at least close proximity to, the other three major centres of power in Asia – India, Russia and Japan – thereby making it central to their strategic calculations. At the same time, they furnish an invaluable shield against external threats, and to the extent that the financial, military and diplomatic costs of their continued incorporation into a unitary Chinese state can be kept to an acceptable level, they maximize the prospect of preserving China's political and juridical unity. To put it crudely, effective control over China's periphery was seen as an indispensable buffer against the dreaded domino effect that resulted in the Soviet Union's and the former Yugoslavia's remarkably swift disintegration.

Conceptually elegant and politically appealing as it may seem, the quest for a unified China posed a number of excruciatingly difficult dilemmas. While realization of the objective held enormous promise for the survival and legitimacy of the Chinese Communist Party as for the identity and security of the Chinese state, it also carried a substantial and perhaps ultimately intolerable price. Aside from the financial and military costs associated with maintaining or acquiring control over territory over long distances and in cultural and political settings where Beijing's rule might be less than welcome, whether it be in Tibet or Taiwan, China's governing elites had to entertain a number of political costs. The use of threat of force to achieve unification was in itself likely to prove debilitating both for the state and the party. If nothing else it would expose and accentuate a legitimation deficit for the existing system of authority, particularly at a time when widespread political corruption and the gradual reawakening of civil society were already placing both state and party under mounting strain. Moreover, coercive strategies were likely to tarnish China's international reputation and provide external actors with additional ammunition with which to wage an anti-China campaign which, whatever its motives, could severely damage Chinese diplomatic, economic and strategic interests.

The unification objective was also likely to compound the problem of national economic management. By placing under its authority regions of such disparate economic expectations and stages of development, the centre was more or less committed to remedying rising inequalities of wealth and income. The alternative would be to devolve power and authority to cities and regions, the net effect of which might be exacerbate economic asymmetries and weaken the centre's capacity to control and integrate the peripheries. Coercive centralization at home would greatly complicate Beijing's attempts to develop a *modus vivendi* with the United States and consolidate its economic opening to the world. By the same token a fragmenting China would be less likely to command the attention of powerful external actors, be they states or international organizations, and less capable of resisting the penetration of external influences.

The complex and largely unresolved nexus between the imperatives of security and identity on the one hand and those of democratization and political stability on the other was equally evident in the political trajectory of the semi-periphery. With the demise of the New Order, Indonesia had in a sense to reinvent itself. The solutions which the Suharto regime had brought to the twin problems of internal security and identity had lost whatever credibility they once enjoyed. In the bleak political and economic climate of the late 1990s, the transitional leadership of Habibie and Abdurrahman would no longer rely on military force or the politics of patronage to preserve the country's social cohesion or territorial integrity. The chaos and destruction amidst which East Timor was severed from Indonesia's sovereign jurisdiction were indicative of the state's paralysis, with competing interests and constituencies opting for sharply diverging strategies. Whereas significant elements of the military were intent on protecting their turf by turning to the politics of division and coercion, a number of political groupings and social movements were strenuously trying to consolidate and expand the role of democratic institutions. Though no clear sense of direction had yet emerged, the Abdurrahman presidency was engaged in a precarious balancing act. It was endeavouring to hold the line on further fragmentation of the Indonesian state while refusing to adopt the military's strong-arm tactics; to give freer rein to Islamic sentiment while standing firm on the need for religious tolerance and interethnic dialogue; to take advantage of US, and more generally western, economic and psychological support (especially useful in dissuading key generals from staging a coup) while making Asia the focus of a more independent diplomacy. It would be several years before the contours of this strategic blueprint acquired more definite shape, and perhaps even longer before any assessment could be made of the prospect of reconciling these antithetical tendencies and of constructing the social and political coalitions needed to sustain the strategy.

Much the same pattern had emerged in Malaysia, although in this case the political formula on which the country's future cohesion would depend was if anything even less certain. Mahathir's 20-year reign was fast approaching its end, but his survival in the face of adversity and partial success in the 1999 general election had in a sense postponed the renegotiation of Malaysia's multiethnic compact, and of the constitutional and legal arrangements that would more closely correspond to the country's vastly altered circumstances. The enormous energy expended on developing a distinctive post-colonial diplomacy, often highly critical of the West, would probably emerge as an enduring legacy of the Mahathir period, as would the attempt to construct a cohesive East Asian community and a more sharply delineated institutional framework. The birth of the *Reformasi* movement was perhaps indicative of future trends, but a new public sphere had yet to crystallize. The issues of national identity and culture had yet to be subjected to informed public debate, yet only in that context could a consensus eventually emerge on a more appropriate relationship between state and civil society. Without a resilient public sphere it would be difficult to sustain a more nuanced conception of the new Asia and of the material and intellectual resources that Malaysia might contribute to such a project.

At first glance, political institutions in Australia and Canada appeared to enjoy much higher levels of stability and legitimacy than their Asian counterparts, and internal conflicts to intrude less conspicuously in the making of foreign policy. Be that as it may, in both societies the same complex dynamic connected issues of identity with political economy and geopolitical orientation. As relatively advanced economies with strong historical affiliations with Europe and extensive strategic and economic ties with the United States, both Australia and Canada were now intent on cultivating closer economic and political ties with Asia. Largely for economic reasons, they had both invested in the 1980s and 1990s considerable diplomatic energy and at least modest financial resources, in a bid to gain acceptance as significant players in the Asia-Pacific region. Yet cultural distance remained a significant obstacle. Australian governments argued with increasing insistence that, at least by virtue of geography, Australia had no option but to become more closely enmeshed with Asia. However, given that geography was a relative constant in the equation, it was not self-evident why the case for engagement should be so much stronger now than before. Not surprisingly, Asian governments tended to be sceptical of both Australian and Canadian motivations. If in the past racial and cultural barriers had prevented these two European outposts from identifying with Asian interests and aspirations, was there reason to think that these barriers had lost their former potency or relevance? Might a more accurate interpretation be that the cultural divide, far from dissipating, had simply been sidestepped in the interests of doing profitable business with Asia, and that otherwise traditional alliances, geopolitical perspectives and cultural/ideological affinities would persist more or less intact? Though a crude overstatement of Australia's and Canada's Eurocentric worldview, this reading did nevertheless point to a number of unresolved tensions in both Canadian and Australian political culture. Indicative of the state of play were the ambiguities of the constitutional debate in each country and the inability of policy-making elites to fashion a new cultural and political vocabulary that resonated with their own electorates, and a national identity capable of synthesizing the demands of history and geography and balancing security threats with economic opportunities.

In various ways and to varying degrees all the countries of the region were ensnared by three major contradictions. First, they needed to reconcile the powerful pressures of national identification with the requirements of economic regionalization and globalization. Second, their policies, while driven by the competitive dynamic of global markets, had nevertheless to integrate notions of inter-regional as well as intra-regional interdependence. Third, they had to acknowledge the residual hegemony of the United States, in particular its overwhelming military supremacy, but at the same operate within an environment that was increasingly multipolar in ethos and structure.

In using the term 'hybrid' to describe many of the political systems and political cultures of Asia Pacific, we have done no more than point to the profound tensions which beset the formulation of policy and the construction of identity, and the consequent ambiguities which characterized the responses of states and civil societies. These contradictory pressures did not, however, operate solely within the confines of national politics. They were equally in evidence, albeit in different forms, in the very processes of globalization. We may therefore speak of a hybrid international system, not only in the sense that unipolarity co-existed with multipolarity or that states and non-state actors increasingly occupied the same political space, but in that globalization had acquired a logic and a momentum distinct from the economic and political agents that had spearheaded the trend.

In the twentieth century the United States may have been the prime mover in the internationalization of economic activity, but the phenomenon, once it got under way, could not be conceived of as the property of the United States, as entirely malleable to the wishes and interests either of the American state or of American capital. While commanding enormous influence in the world's markets, US corporate interests were themselves hardly immune to the vagaries of globalization. There is no disputing that in the knowledge-intensive sector – in electronic software and hardware, biotechnology, lasers, optoelectronics and liquid crystal technology, to name a few of the more obvious industries – US firms, especially when supported by government, exercised enormous leverage over the pace and quality of technological and industrial development in other advanced economies, the NIEs and the Third World. Yet that leverage fell far short of determining outcomes. US capital, which was anything but monolithic, and the fragmented American state could not, either separately or in tandem, control the world's financial and industrial markets. Nor could they dictate terms to the growing number of international institutions created to monitor, adjust and stabilize the rapidly evolving international trading and financial regimes. These limitations on US power were clearly visible at the WTO Seattle negotiations in November 1999, where the United States failed to secure broad agreement for its agenda. Its priorities, which included transparency in government procurement, reform of the WTO's dispute settlement system, a broader information-technology agreement and the phasing out of tariffs in a range of industrial sectors (chemicals, energy products, environmental products, fish, forest products, jewellery, medical and scientific equipment and toys), met with a decidedly frosty response. Japan had no intention of liberalizing fish and forestry products; the European Union and South Korea as well as Japan were steadfastly opposed to lower tariffs or reduced domestic support for agriculture; and Third World governments, better informed and organized than in previous negotiations, had little appetite for further liberalization.

This latest tussle in the increasingly fierce struggle to reshape the ground rules that would govern the future international division of labour had obvious and far-reaching implications for Asia Pacific. First, it demonstrated the sharp conflicts of interest among core states and core economies, which both the periphery and semi-periphery, not least in the Asia-Pacific region, could turn to their advantage. They might, for example, attempt to extract greater concessions from competing core actors in return for varying degrees of support for their respective positions. Alternatively, they could pursue a range of collective regional strategies in which Japan or China could play a leadership role. Such strategies, it is worth noting, were just as likely to have a negative as a positive thrust, intent as much on thwarting unwelcome change as on advancing preferred outcomes.

By the late 1990s globalization, or at least the radical neo-liberal creed that had served as its driving engine for more than two decades, was under mounting challenge. Though the sharpest critique had originated in the largely marginalized constituencies of both North and South, more powerful voices of dissent were beginning to make themselves heard. With 11 out of 15 EU governments pursuing a centre-left agenda, the political mood in Europe had noticeably changed. The Declaration of Paris agreed at the Socialist International Conference in November 1999 called for a 'critical relationship with capitalism', and a 'fairer distribution of benefits'. The declaration was more than just rhetoric: it reflected the initiatives already undertaken by a number of European governments to enhance social cohesion through a mixture of wage moderation, job creation and increased funding for education, health and culture. French Prime Minister Lionel Jospin explicitly referred to a new social contract which would require an 'active state' to regulate capitalism and promote equality of opportunity. Nor could the task of managing and humanizing globalization be left entirely to the state. New forms of regional and global regulation would have to be devised to impose on the market socially acceptable standards and priorities.

Europe's cultural and political traditions could not, of course, be readily transposed to Asia's vastly different circumstances. Environment, human rights and labour standards did not have the same political resonance as in Europe, but considerations of cultural and religious identity, social safety nets and security of employment were highly valued public goods which could not be delivered without taming the market. In Asia Pacific, globalization posed major challenges not only to the national state, but to a range of regional institutions. The uneasy relationship between state and civil society was itself indicative of the internalization of globalizing influences, but also of the slow but steady growth of regional and global organizations, which often seemed, at least by virtue of their scope and membership, better suited to handle the pressures associated with transboundary flows. At the beginning of the twenty-first century, the peoples and states of Pacific Asia were confronted with exceedingly difficult choices: whether or not to enhance regional collaboration; by what mechanisms and for what specific objectives; and with what implications for the relationship between state and society, and between state and market. Hybridity was as much a distinguishing characteristic of the region as of the nation-state or the international system. Regionalization posed several as yet unresolved questions: how to define the region, how to reconcile identity and difference, what forms of leadership to accept and encourage, and how to relate to other regions, other cultures and other centres of power. In short, how to negotiate the challenge of globalization in the context of social fragmentation and geopolitical multipolarity.

NOTES

1. Gavan McCormack, *The Emptiness of Japanese Affluence*, Sydney: Allen & Unwin, 1996, p. 187.
2. The background to these proposals and their content are examined in McCormack, *The Emptiness of Japanese Affluence*, pp. 204–10.
3. Many of these ideas were encapsulated in a set of proposals published by the Iwanami Publishing House, and in modified form by *Asahi Shimbun* on 3 May 1995 (see McCormack, *The Emptiness of Japanese Affluence*, pp. 213–16).
4. Ibid., p. 173.
5. *Australian*, 17 May 2000, 10.
6. Martin Farrell, 'Global Power or East Asian Tinderbox? China in the Post-Deng, Post-Cold War Era', in Berger and Borer (eds), *The Rise of East Asia*, p. 75.

Select bibliography

This bibliography refers mainly to some of the more useful secondary source material available in books, monographs and articles. For primary sources consult the notes for each chapter.

Agnew, John and Stuart Corbridge, *Mastering Space: Hegemony, Territory and International Political Economy*, London and New York: Routledge, 1995.

Agnew, John, *Geopolitics: Re-visioning World Politics*, London and New York: Routledge, 1998.

Akaha, Tsuneo, 'Japan's Response to Threats of Shipping Disruptions in Southeast Asia and the Middle East', *Pacific Affairs*, 59 (2), Summer 1986, 255–77.

Akaha, Tsuneo, 'Japan's Security Policy After US Hegemony', *Millennium*, 18 (3), Winter 1989, 435–54.

Akaha, Tsuneo, 'Russia in Asia in 1994: An Emerging East Asian Power', *Asian Survey*, XXXV (1), January 1995, 100–10.

Akaha, Tsuneo, 'Beyond Self-defense: Japan's Elusive Security Role under the New Guidelines for US–Japan Defense Cooperation', *Pacific Review*, 11 (4), 1998, 461–83.

Alagappa, Muthiah, 'The Major Powers and Southeast Asia', *International Journal*, XLIV (3), Summer 1989, 541–97.

Alagappa, Muthiah, 'Soviet Policy in Southeast Asia: Towards Constructive Engagement', *Pacific Affairs*, 63 (3), Fall 1990, 320–50.

Alagappa, Muthiah (ed.), *Asian Security Practice: Material and Ideational Influences*, Stanford, Cal.: Stanford University Press, 1998.

Aldrich, R., *France and the South Pacific since 1940*, London: Macmillan, 1993.

Alonzo, Ruperto P., 'Japan's Economic Impact on ASEAN Countries', *Indonesian Quarterly*, 15 (3), July 1987, 472–87.

Anderson, C., 'Survey Taiwan' *The Economist*, 7 November 1998, 3–22.

Anderson, Jennifer, *The Limits of Sino-Russian Strategic Partnership*, Adelphi Paper 315, Oxford: Oxford University Press for the International Institute for Strategic Studies, 1997.

Andrew, A., *The Rise and Fall of a Middle Power: Canadian Diplomacy from King to Mulroney*, Toronto: Lorimer, 1993.

Arase, D., 'Japan's Evolving Security Policy after the Cold War', *Journal of East Asian Affairs*, 8 (2), Summer–Fall 1994, 396–410.

Arase, D., 'A Militarized Japan?', *Journal of Strategic Studies*, 18 (3), September 1995, 84–103.

Armstrong, D., 'Chinese Perspectives on the New World Order', *Journal of East Asian Affairs*, 8 (2), Summer–Fall 1994, 454–81.

Arnold, W., 'Political and Economic Influences in Japan's Relations with China since 1978', *Millennium*, 18 (3), Winter 1989, 415–34.

ASEAN Secretariat, *ASEAN Statistical Indicators*, Singapore: Institute of Southeast Asian Studies, 1997.

Asher, D., 'A US–Japan Alliance for the Next Century', *Orbis*, 41 (3), Summer 1997, 343–74.

Asian Development Bank, *Asian Development Outlook 1997 and 1998*, Oxford: Oxford University Press, 1997.

Asian Development Bank, *Asian Development Outlook 1999: Update, Asian Development Bank*, London: Oxford University Press, 1999.

Aspen Strategy Group, *Harness the Rising Sun: An American Strategy for Managing Japan's Rise as a Global Power*, Aspen Strategy Group Report, Washington, DC: Aspen Institute, 1993.

Australian National Korean Studies Centre, *Korea to the Year 2000: Implications for Australia*, Canberra: East Asia Analytical Unit, Department of Foreign Affairs and Trade, 1992.

Badawi, Abdullah Ahmad, 'On Malaysia–Russia Relations', *International Affairs* (Moscow), 4 (4), 1977, 174–78.

Baker, R. (ed.), *The ANZUS States and Their Region: Regional Policies of Australia, New Zealand and the United States*, Westport, Conn.: Praeger, 1994.

Baker, R. and G. Hawke (eds), *ANZUS Economics: Economic Trends and Relations among Australia, New Zealand, and the United States*, Westport, Conn.: Praeger, 1992.

Ball, Desmond (ed.), *The Transformation of Security in the Asia/Pacific Region*, London: Frank Cass, 1996.

Bauer, Joanne R. and Daniel A. Bell (eds), *The East Asian Challenge for Human Rights*, Cambridge: Cambridge University Press, 1999.

Beeson, M., Jayasuriya, K. and Robison, R. (eds), *Politics and Markets in the Wake of the Asian Crisis*, London: Routledge, 1999.

Bell, R., T. McDonald and A. Tidwell (eds), *Negotiating the Pacific Century: The 'New' Asia, the United States and Australia*, St Leonards, NSW: Allen & Unwin, 1996.

Bello, Walden, 'East Asia on the Brink of Depression?', *Pacifica Review*, 10 (2), June 1998, 95–109.

Bello, Walden, and Stephanie Rosenfeld, *Dragons in Distress: Asia's Miracle Economies in Crisis*, San Francisco, Cal.: Food First, 1990.

Benwang, S., 'The Impact of the Kosovo War on International Situations', *International Strategic Studies*, 54 (4), October 1999, 1–9.

Berger, Mark T. and Douglas A. Borer (eds), *The Rise of East Asia: Critical Visions of the Pacific Century*, London and New York: Routledge, 1997.

Bergsten, C. Fred and Marcus Noland (eds), *Pacific Dynamism and the International Economic System*, Washington, DC: Institute for International Economics, 1993.

Bernstein, Richard and Ross H. Munro, *The Coming Conflict with China*, New York: Alfred A. Knopf, 1997.

Bernstein, Richard and Ross H. Munro, 'China: The Coming Conflict with America', *Foreign Affairs*, 76 (2), March–April 1997, 18–32.

Berry, Ken, *Cambodia – From Red to Blue: Australia's Initiative for Peace*, St Leonards, NSW: Allen & Unwin, and Canberra: Department of International Relations, Research School of Pacific and Asian Studies, Australian National Uni:·ersity, 1997.

Bertrand, J., 'False Starts, Succession Crises, and Regime Transition: Flirting with Openness in Indonesia', *Pacific Affairs*, 3 (3), Fall 1996, 319–40.

Betts, R., 'Wealth, Power and Instability: East Asia and the US after the Cold War', *International Security*, 18 (3), Winter 1993–4, 34–77.

Bilveer, S., 'East Asia in Russia's Foreign Policy: A New Russo-Chinese Axis?' , *Pacific Review*, 11 (4), 1998, 485–503.

Blakeslee, G., 'The Establishment of the Far Eastern Commission', *International Organization*, 5 (3), August 1951, 499–514.

Blanchette, A. (ed.), *Canadian Foreign Policy, 1977–1992: Selected Speeches and Documents*, Ottawa: Carleton University Press, 1992.

Blank, S., 'The New Russia in the New Asia', *International Journal*, XLIX (4), Autumn 1994, 874–907.

Blank, Stephen, 'Russian Policy and the Changing Korean Question', *Asian Survey*, XXXV (8), August 1995, 711–25.

Blank, Stephen, 'Which Way for Sino-Russian Relations?', *Orbis*, 42 (3), Summer 1998, 345–60.

Bobrow, D., 'Hegemony Management: The US in the Asia-Pacific', *Pacific Review*, 12 (2), 1999, 173–97.

Booth, K. and R. Trood (eds), *Strategic Cultures in the Asia-Pacific Region*, London: Macmillan, 1999.

Bosworth, Stephen W., 'The US and Asia', *Foreign Affairs*, 71 (1), Winter 1991–2, 113–29.

Brown, E., 'Japanese Security Policy in the Post-Cold War World: Threat Perceptions and Strategic Options', *Journal of East Asian Affairs*, 8 (2), 1994, 327–64.

Brown, Michael E., Sean M. Lynn-Jones and Steve E. Miller (eds), *East Asian Security*, Cambridge, Mass.: MIT Press, 1996.

Bullock, M. and R. Litwak, *The US and the Pacific Basin: Changing Economic and Security Relationships*, Woodrow Wilson Center Special Studies no. 2, Washington, DC: Woodrow Wilson Center Press,1991.

Buzan, B, 'New Patterns of Global Security in the 21st Century', *International Affairs*, 67 (3), 1991, 431–51.

Cable, V., 'What Is International Economic Security?', *International Affairs*, 71 (2), 1995, 305– 24.

Calder, K., *Pacific Defense: Arms, Energy, and America's Future in Asia*, New York: William Morrow, 1996.

Callahan, William A., 'Rescripting East/West Relations, Rethinking Asian Democracy', *Pacifica Review*, 8 (1), May–June 1996, 1–25.

Camilleri, Joseph A., *Chinese Foreign Policy: The Maoist Era and Its Aftermath*, Seattle, Wa.: University of Washington Press, 1980.

Camilleri, Joseph A., *The Australia–New Zealand–US Alliance: Regional Security in the Nuclear Age*, Boulder, Col.: Westview Press, 1987.

Camilleri, Joseph A., 'Problems in Australian Foreign Policy, July–December 1990', *Australian Journal of Politics and History*, 37 (2), 1991, 184–99.

Camilleri, Joseph A., 'Problems in Australian Foreign Policy: January–June 1991', *Australian Journal of Politics History* 37 (3), 1991, 375–95.

Camilleri, Joseph A., 'Security: Old Dilemmas and New Challenges in the Post-Cold War Environment', *GeoJournal*, 34 (2), October 1994, 135–45.

Camilleri, Joseph A. and Jim Falk, *The End of Sovereignty? The Politics in a Shrinking and Fragmenting World*, Aldershot, Hants.: Edward Elgar, 1992.

Camilleri, Joseph A. and Chandra Muzaffar (eds), *Globalisation: The Perspectives and Experiences of the Religious Traditions of Asia Pacific*, Selangor Darul Ehsan: International Movement for a Just World, 1998.

Camilleri, Joseph A., Anthony P. Jarvis and Albert Paolini (eds), *The State in Transition: Reimagining Political Space*, Boulder, Col.: Lynne Reinner, 1995.

Camroux, D., *Looking East . . . and Inwards: Internal Factors in Malaysian Foreign Relations during the Mahathir Era, 1981–1994*, Australia-Asia Paper no. 72, Brisbane, Queensland: Faculty of Asian and International Studies, Griffith University, October 1994.

Carpenter, Ted Galen, 'Washington's Smothering Strategy: American Interests in East Asia', *World Policy Journal*, XIV (4), Winter 1997–8, 20–31.

Case, William, 'Semi-democracy in Malaysia: Withstanding the Pressures for Regime Change', *Pacific Affairs,* 66 (2), 1993, 183–205.

Central Commitee of the Communist Party of China, *Selected Works of Deng Xiaoping, Vol. III: 1982-1992*, Beijing: Foreign Language Press, 1994.

Chan, Adrian, 'Confucianism and Development in East Asia', *Journal of Contemporary Asia*, 26 (1), 1996, 28–45.

Chan, Adrian, 'In Search of Civil Society in China', *Journal of Contemporary Asia*, 27 (2), 1997, 242–51.

Chan, S., 'National Security in the Asia Pacific: Linkages among Growth, Democracy and Peace', *Contemporary Southeast Asia*, 14 (1), June 1992, 13–32.

Chan, Steve (ed.), *Foreign Direct Investment in a Changing Global Political Economy*, London: Macmillan Press, 1995.

Chang, H.-J., H.-J. Park and C.G. Yoo, 'Interpreting the Korean Crisis: Financial Liberalisation, Industrial Policy and Corporate Governance', *Cambridge Journal of Economics*, 22, 1998, 735–46.

Chang, M., 'Greater China and the Chinese "Global Tribe"', *Asian Survey*, 35 (10), October 1995, 955–67.

Chang, Parris H., 'Don't Dance to Beijing's Tune', *China Journal*, 36, July 1996, 103–11.

Chang, Ya-chun, 'Peking–Moscow Relations in the Post-Soviet Era', *Issues and Studies*, 3(1), January 1994, 83–99.

Chee, C. (ed.), *Leadership and Security in Southeast Asia*, Singapore: Institute of Southeast Asian Studies, 1993.

Chee, C. (ed.), *The New Asia-Pacific Order*, Singapore: Institute of Southeast Asian Studies, 1997.

Cheeseman, Graeme and Robert Bruce (eds), *Discourses of Danger and Dread Frontiers: Australian Defence and Security Thinking after the Cold War*, St Leonards, NSW, and Canberra: Allen & Unwin in association with the Department of International Relations and the Peace Research Centre, Australian National University, 1996.

Cheng, J., 'China's Japan Policy in the Mid-1990s: Adjusting to the Evolving Multipolar World', *Pacifica Review*, 8 (2), November–December 1996, 1–30.

Chowdhury, A. and I. Islam, *The Newly Industrialising Economies of East Asia*, London: Routledge, 1993.

Christensen, Thomas J., 'China, the US–Japan Alliance, and the Security Dilemma in East Asia', *International Security*, 23 (4), Spring 1999, 49–80.

Chu, Shulong, 'The Russian–US Military Balance in the Post-Cold War Asia-Pacific Region and the "China Threat"', *Journal of Northeast Asian Studies*, 13 (1), Spring 1994, 77–95.

Clark, C. and S. Chan (eds), *The Evolving Pacific Basin in the Global Political Economy: Domestic and International Linkages*, Boulder, Col.: Lynne Reinner, 1992.

Clark, S., 'Japan's Role in Gorbachev's Agenda', *Pacific Review*, 1 (3), 1988, 276–89.

Commission for a New Asia, *Towards a New Asia*, Kuala Lumpur, 1994.

Cooper, Andrew F., Richard A. Higgott and Kim Richard Nossal, *Relocating Middle Powers: Australia and Canada in a Changing World Order*, Melbourne: Melbourne University Press, 1993.

Copper, J., 'A US Negotiating Role in Resolving Beijing–Taipei Differences?', *Journal of East Asian Affairs*, 12 (2), Summer–Fall 1998, 384–417.

Corbet, H., 'Issues in the Accession of China into the WTO System', *Journal of Northeast Asian Studies*, 25 (3), Fall 1996, 14–33.

Corning, Gregory P., 'US–Japan Security Cooperation in The 1990s: The Promise of High-tech Defence', *Asian Survey*, 29 (3), March 1989, 268–86.

Cotton, James, 'Bilateral Accomplishments and Multilateral Tasks in Northeast Asian Security', *Contemporary Southeast Asia*, 20 (2), August 1998, 137–53.

Cox, R., 'Middlepowermanship, Japan and the Future World Order', *International Journal*, XLIV (4), Autumn 1989, 823–62.

Crone, Donald, 'Does Hegemony Matter? The Reorganisation of the Pacific Political Economy', *World Politics*, 45 (4), July 1993, 501–25.

Crowe, W. and A. Romberg 'Rethinking Security in the Pacific', *Foreign Affairs*, 70 (2), Spring 1991, 123–40.

Curtis, Gerald L. and Michael Baker (eds), *Japan's Foreign Policy after the Cold War: Coping with Change*, Studies of the East Asian Institute, Columbia University, Armonk, NY: M.E. Sharpe, 1993.

da Cunha, D. and J. Funston (eds), *Southeast Asian Affairs 1998*, Singapore: Institute of Southeast Asian Studies, 1998.

Dauvergne, Peter (ed.), *Weak and Strong States in Asia-Pacific Societies*, St Leonards, NSW: Allen & Unwin, and Canberra: Department of International Relations, Research School of Pacific and Asian Studies, Australian National University, 1998.

De Castro, R., 'Changes in US Post-Cold War Hegemony: The Case of the East Asian-Pacific Region', *AUSSENPOLITIK*, 46 (2), 1995, 168–75.

Deguang, Zhang, 'A Strategic Partnership into the 21st Century', *International Affairs* (Moscow), 4 (4), 1977, 164–8.

Deny, Yong, 'Chinese Relations with Japan: Implications for Asia-Pacific Regionalism', *Pacific Affairs*, 70 (3), Fall 1997, 373–91.

Dibb, P., *Towards a New Balance of Power in Asia*, Adelphi Paper 295, London: Oxford University Press for International Institute for Strategic Studies, 1995.

DiFilippo, A., *Cracks in the Alliance: Science, Technology, and the Evolution of US–Japan Relations*, Aldershot, Hants: Ashgate, 1997.

Djiwandono, J. Soedjati, 'Indonesia's Post Cold War Foreign Policy', *Indonesian Quarterly*, 22 (2), 1994, 90–102.

Dobson, W., *Japan in East Asia: Trading and Investment Strategies*, Singapore: Institute of Southeast Asian Studies, 1993.

Dobson, Wendy and Chia Siow Yue (eds), *Multinationals and East Asian Integration*, Ottawa: International Development Research Centre and Singapore: Institute of Southeast Asian Studies, 1997.

Dorrance, C., 'US Security Interests in the Pacific Islands', *World Review*, 23 (1), April 1984, 4–20.

Dorrance, C., *The United States and the Pacific Islands*, Washington Papers no. 158, Westport, Conn.: Praeger and Washington, DC: Center for Strategic and International Studies, 1992.

Drifte, R., *Japan's Foreign Policy*, Chatham House Papers, London: Royal Institute of International Affairs/Routledge, 1990.

Drifte, R., 'Japan's Security Policy and Southeast Asia', *Contemporary Southeast Asia*, 12 (3), December 1990, 186–97.

Drysdale, Peter, and Dong Dong Zhang (eds), *Japan and China: Rivalry or Cooperation in East Asia?*, Canberra: Australia–Japan Research Centre, 2000.

Dua, A. and D. Esty, *Sustaining the Asia Pacific Miracle: Environmental Protection and Economic Integration*, Washington, DC: Institute for International Economics, October 1997.

Dupont, A., *The Environment and Security in Pacific Asia*, Adelphi Paper 319, Oxford: Oxford University press for International Institute of Strategic Studies, 1998.

Du Rocher, Sophie Boisseau, 'Le Japon et l'Asie du Sud-Est: Un Nouveau Partenariat', *Politique Étrangère*, 57 (3), 1992, 541–9.

Economics Department, (Japan Research Institute), 'The Japanese Economy in 1996: The Creation of New Markets and the Need for Fiscal Re-engineering', *Japan Research Quarterly*, 5 (1), Winter 1995–6, 3–47.

Edwin, M., *The Allied Occupation of Japan*, New York: American Institute of Pacific Relations, 1948.

Eldridge, Philip, 'Human Rights and Democracy in Indonesia and Malaysia: Emerging Contexts and Discourse', *Contemporary Southeast Asia*, 18 (3), December 1996, 298–319.

Emmott, B., 'The Economic Sources of Japan's Foreign Policy', *Survival*, 34 (2), Summer 1992, 50–70.

Evans, G. and B. Grant, *Australia's Foreign Relations in the World of the 1990s*, Melbourne: Melbourne University Press, 1991.

Evans, P., 'The Emergence of Eastern Asia and Its Implications for Canada', *International Journal*, XLVII (3), Summer 1992, 505–28.

Falkenheim, P., 'The Soviet Union, Japan, and East Asia: The Security Dimension', *Journal of Northeast Asian Studies*, 8 (4), Winter 1989, 43–59.

Frankel, J. and M. Kahler (eds), *Regionalism and Rivalry: Japan and the United States in Pacific Asia*, Chicago, Ill.: University of Chicago Press, 1993.

Friedberg, A., 'Ripe for Rivalry: Prospects for Peace in a Multipolar Asia', *International Security*, 18 (3), Winter 1993–4, 5–33.

Fry, G. (ed.), *Australia's Regional Security*, Sydney: Allen & Unwin, 1991.

Fukui, Haruhiro and Shigeko N. Fukai, 'The Role of the United States in Post-Cold War East Asian Security Affairs', *Journal of Asian and African Studies*, 33 (1), February 1998, 114–33.

Gallagher, M., 'China's Illusory Threat to the South China Sea', *International Security*, 19 (1), Summer 1994, 169–94.

Gang, X., 'A Comment on Russia's Great Power Diplomacy', *International Strategic Studies*, 54 (4), October 1999, 42–50.

Garby, C. and M. Bullock (eds), *Japan: A New Kind of Superpower?*, Washington DC: Woodrow Wilson Center Press, 1994.

Garnaut, Ross, *Open Regionalism and Trade Liberalization: An Asia-Pacific Contribution to the World Trade System*, Singapore: Institute of Southeast Asian Studies, and Sydney: Allen & Unwin, 1996.

Garrett, B. and B. Glaser, 'Chinese Perspectives on Nuclear Arms Control', *International Security*, 20 (3), Winter 1995–6, 43–78.

Gecelovsky, P. and T. Keenleyside, 'Canada's International Human Rights Policy in Practice: Tiananmen Square', *International Journal*, L (3), Summer 1995, 564–93.

Gertov, M., 'South Korea's Foreign Policy and Future Security: Implications of the Nuclear Standoff', *Pacific Affairs*, 69 (1), Spring 1996, 8–31.

Ghai, Yash, 'Autonomy with Chinese Characteristics: The Case of Hong Kong', *Pacifica Review*, 10 (1), February 1998, 7–22.

Gilpin, R., 'Where Does Japan Fit In?', *Millennium*, 18 (3), Winter 1989, 329–42.

Goldie, M. and D. Ross (eds), *Pacific Security 2010: Canadian Perspectives on Pacific Security into the 21st Century*, Aurora Papers no. 10, Ottawa: Canadian Centre for Arms Control and Disarmament, August 1991.

Goldstein, Avery, 'Great Expectations: Interpreting China's Arrival', *International Security*, 22 (3), Winter 1997–8, 36–73.

Gordon, Bernard K., 'Japan, the United States, and Southeast Asia', *Foreign Affairs*, 56 (3), April 1978, 579–600.

Gordon, Bernard K., 'Asian Angst and American Policy', *Foreign Policy*, 47, Summer 1982, 46–65.

Haber, D., 'The Death of Hegemony: Why "Pax Nipponica" is Impossible', *Asian Survey*, 30 (9), September 1990, 892–907.

Haggard, Stephen and Robert R. Kaufman, 'The Political Economy of Democratic Transitions', *Comparative Politics*, 27 (3), 1997, 263–83.

Hao, J. and Z. Qubing, 'China's Policy toward the Korean Peninsula', *Asian Survey*, 32 (12), December 1992, 1137–56.

Harding, Harry, 'A Chinese Colossus?', *Journal of Strategic Studies*, 18 (3), September 1995, 104–22.

Harland, B., *Collision Course: America and East Asia in the Past and the Future*, Singapore: Institute of Southeast Asian Studies, 1996.

Harris, Stuart, and James Cotton (eds), *The End of the Cold War in Northeast Asia*, Melbourne: Longman Cheshire, and Boulder, Col.: Lynne Reinner 1991.

Harris, Stuart, 'The Economic Aspects of Security in the Asia/Pacific Region', *Journal of Strategic Studies*, 18 (3), September 1995, 32–51.

Harris, Stuart, 'The Taiwan Crisis: Some Basic Realities', *China Journal*, 36, July 1996, 129–34.

Harris, Stuart, *The China–Japan Relationship and Asia-Pacific Regional Security*, Working Paper no. 1996/7, Canberra: Research School of Pacific and Asian Studies, Australian National University, October 1996.

Harris, S. and A. Mack, *Asia-Pacific Security: The Economics–Politics Nexus*, St Leonards, NSW: Allen & Unwin in association with the Department of International Relations, Research School of Pacific and Asian Studies, Australian National University, 1997.

Harrison, Selig S. (ed.), *Japan's Nuclear Future: The Plutonium Debate and East Asian Security*, Washington, DC: Carnegie Endowment for International Peace, 1996.

Hart-Landsberg, Martin and Paul Burkett, 'Contradictions of Capitalist Industrialization in East Asia: A Critique of "Flying Geese" Theories of Development', *Economic Geography*, 74 (2), April 1998, 87–110.

Hassall, G., 'Democracy in Asia Revisited', *Asian Studies Review*, 21 (2–3), November 1997, 2–18.

Hatch, W. and Kozo Yamamura, *Asia in Japan's Embrace: Building a Regional Production Alliance*, Cambridge: Cambridge University Press, 1996.

Hayashida, M., M. Inouchi, H. Kanayama and E. Ueda, *East Asia and Japan: Japan's Diplomatic Strategy for Seeking Common Interests*, IIPS Policy Paper 134E, September 1994 (ftp://ftp.glocom.ac.jp/pub/IIPS/Policy Paper/ IIPS134E.txt).

Head, Brian W. and Allan Patience (eds), *From Fraser to Hawke*, Melbourne: Longman Cheshire, 1989.

Hefner, Robert W. (ed.), *Market Cultures: Society and Morality in the New Asian Capitalisms*, St Leonards, NSW: Allen & Unwin, 1998.

Helleiner, E., 'Money and Influence: Japanese Power and the International Monetary and Financial System', *Millennium*, 18 (3), Winter 1989, 343–58.

Henderson, S., *Canada and Asia Pacific Security. The North Pacific Cooperative Security Dialogue: Recent Trends*, North Pacific Cooperative Security Dialogue Working Paper no. 1, Ontario: York University, 1991.

Henningham, S. and D. Ball, *South Pacific Security: Issues and Perspectives*, Canberra: Strategic and Defence Studies Centre, Research School of Pacific Studies, Australian National University, 1991.

Herspring, Dale R., 'Russia's Crumbling Military', *Current History*, 97 (621), October 1998, 325–8.

Higgott, R., 'Pacific Economic Cooperation and Australia: Some Questions about the Role of Knowledge and Learning', *Australian Journal of International Affairs*, 46 (2), November 1992, 182–97.

Higgott, Richard, Richard Leaver and John Ravenhill (eds), *Pacific Economic Relations in the 1990s: Cooperation or Conflict*, St Leonards, NSW: Allen & Unwin 1993.

Hoadley, S., *The South Pacific Foreign Affairs Handbook*, Sydney: Allen & Unwin, 1992.

Holbraad, C., *Middle Powers in International Politics*, London: Macmillan, 1984.

Holgerson, K., *The Japan–US Trade Friction Dilemma: The Role of Perception*, Aldershot, Hants.: Ashgate, 1998.

Holsti, O. and James Rosenau, *American Leadership in World Affairs: Vietnam and the Breakdown of Consensus*, Boston, Mass.: Allen & Unwin, 1984.

Hook, G. and M. Weiner, *The Internationalisation of Japan*, London: Routledge, 1992.

Hook, Steven W. and Guang Zhang, 'Japan's Aid Policy since the Cold War: Rhetoric and Reality', *Asian Survey*, 38 (11), November 1998,1051–66.

Horner, Charles, 'The Third Side of the Triangle: The China–Japan Dimension', *National Interest*, 46, Winter 1996–7, 23–31.

Horsnell, Paul, *Oil in Asia: Markets, Trading, Refining and Deregulation*, Oxford: Oxford University Press for the Oxford Institute for Energy Studies, 1997.

Howe, C. (ed.), *China and Japan: History, Trends, and Prospects*, Oxford: Clarendon Press, 1996.

Hsin-hai, C., 'The Treaty with Japan: A Chinese View', *Foreign Affairs*, 26 (3), April 1948, 505–14.

Hu, Weixing, 'China's Taiwan Policy and East Asian Security', *Journal of Contemporary Asia*, 27 (3), 1997, 374–91.

Hu, Xiaobo, 'A Milestone as Well as a Millstone: The Jiang–Clinton Summit', *Issues and Studies*, 33 (12), December 1997, 1–18.

Huang, Y., *FDI in China: An Asian Perspective*, Singapore: Chinese University Press/Institute of Southeast Asian Studies, 1998.

Hughes, C., 'China and Liberalism Globalised', *Millennium*, 24 (3), Winter 1995, 425–45.

Hughes, Christopher, 'Globalisation and Nationalism: Squaring the Circle in Chinese International Relations Theory', *Millennium*, 26 (1), 1997, 103–24.

Hughes, Helen, 'Why Have East Asian Countries Led Economic Development?', *Economic Record* 71 (212) March 1995, 88–104.

Huntington, S., 'The Lonely Superpower', *Foreign Affairs*, 78 (2), March–April 1999, 35–49.

Ikenberry, G. John, 'The Future of International Leadership', *Political Science Quarterly*, 111 (3), Fall 1996, 385–402.

Inoguchi, T., 'Japan's Role in International Affairs', *Survival*, 34 (2), Summer, 1992, 71–87.

Inoguchi, T., *Japan's Foreign Policy in an Era of Global Change*, London: Pinter, 1993.

Institute of Southeast Asian Studies, *Southeast Asian Affairs 1993*, Singapore: ISEAS, 1993.

Institute of Southeast Asian Studies, *Southeast Asian Affairs 1996*, Singapore: ISEAS, 1996.

Institute of Southeast Asian Studies, *Southeast Asian Affairs 1997*, Singapore: ISEAS, 1997.

Isami, T., 'A New Dialogue for Japan, ASEAN, and Oceania', *Japan Echo*, 20, Special Issue, 1993, 72–6.

Islam, I. and A. Chowdhury, *Asia-Pacific Economies: A Survey*, London: Routledge, 1997.

Ivanov, O., 'Russia–APEC: A New Stage of Cooperation', *International Affairs* (Moscow) ,4 (4), 1977, 165–73.

Japan Review of International Affairs, 'Conference Report: The Future Role of the United States in the Asia-Pacific Region', *Japan Review of International Affairs*, 5 (1), Spring–Summer 1991.

Ji, You, 'Taiwan in the Political Calculations of the Chinese Leadership', *China Journal*, 36, July 1996, 119–25.

Ji, You, *The Armed Forces of China*, St Leonards, NSW: Allen & Unwin, 1999.

Jian, Chen, *The China Challenge in the Twenty-first Century: Implications for US Policy*, Washington, DC: United States Institute of Peace, June 1998.

Job, B., *Canadian Interests and Perspectives Regarding the Emerging Pacific Security Order*, North Pacific Cooperative Security Dialogue Working Paper no. 2, Ontario: York University, 1991.

Jockel, J. and J. Sokolsky, *Canada and Collective Security: Odd Man Out*, New York: Georgetown University Press and Praeger, 1986.

Johnson, C., *MITI and the Japanese Miracle: The Growth of Industrial Policy, 1925–1975*, Stanford, Cal.: Stanford University Press, 1982.

Johnson, C. 'Economic Crisis in East Asia: The Clash of Capitalisms', *Cambridge Journal of Economics*, 22, 1998, 653–61.

Johnson, C., 'Japan in Search of a "Normal" Role', *Daedalus*, 121 (4), Fall 1992, 1–33.

Johnson, C. and E. Keehn, 'East Asian Security: The Pentagon's Ossified Strategy', *Foreign Affairs*, 74 (3), July–August 1995, 103–12.

Johnston, Alastair Iain and Robert S. Ross (eds), *Engaging China: The Management of an Emerging Power*, London and New York: Routledge, 1999.

Johnstone, Christopher B., 'Strained Alliance: US–Japan Diplomacy in the Asian Financial Crisis', *Survival*, 41 (2), Summer 1999, 121–38.

Jones, David Martin, *Political Development in Pacific Asia*, Cambridge: Polity Press, 1997.

Jones, Randall, Robert King and Michael Kien, 'Economic Integration between Hong Kong, Taiwan and the Coastal Provinces of China', *OECD Economic Studies*, 20, Spring 1993, 115–44.

Jongsuk, C., *Culture and International Relations*, New York: Praeger, 1990.

Kanet, Roger E. and Susanne M. Birgerson, 'The Domestic–Foreign Policy Linkage in Russian Politics: Nationalist Influences on Russian Foreign Policy', *Communist and Post-Communist Studies*, 30 (4), 1997, 335–44.

Kataoka, T. and R. Myers, *Defending an Economic Superpower: Reassessing the US–Japan Security Alliance*, Boulder, Col.: Westview Press, 1989.

Katz, Richard, *Japan: The System that Soured: The Rise and Fall of the Japanese Economic Miracle*, Armonk, NY: M.E. Sharpe, 1998.

Katzenstein, Peter J. and Nobuo Okawara, *Japan's National Security: Structures, Norms and Policy Responses in a Changing World*, Ithaca, NY: East Asia Program, Cornell University, 1993.

Katzenstein, Peter J. and Nobuo Okawara, 'Japan's National Security: Structures, Norms and Policies', *International Security*, 17 (4), Spring 1993, 84–118.

Katzenstein, P. and T. Shiraishi (eds), *Network Power: Japan and Asia*, Ithaca, NY: Cornell University Press, 1997.

Keddell, J., *The Politics of Defence in Japan: Managing Internal and External Pressures*, New York: M.E. Sharpe, 1993.

Keith, R., 'China and Canada's "Pacific 2000 Strategy"', *Pacific Affairs*, 65 (3), Fall 1992, 319–33.

Kelly, David and Anthony Reid (eds), *Asian Freedoms: The Idea of Freedom in East and Southeast Asia*, Cambridge: Cambridge University Press, 1998.

Kelly, James, 'US Security Policies in East Asia: Fighting Erosion and Finding a New Balance', *Washington Quarterly*, 18 (3), Summer 1995, 21–35.

Kennedy, B., 'Curbing Chinese Missile Sales: From Imposing to Negotiating China's Adherence to the MTCR', *Journal of Northeast Asian Studies*, 25 (1), Spring 1996, 57–68.

Kennedy, Paul, *The Rise and Fall of the Great Powers: Economic Change and Military Conflict from 1500 to 2000*, New York: Random House, 1987.

Kent, A., 'China, International Organizations and Regimes: The ILO as a Case Study in Organizational Learning', *Pacific Affairs*, 70 (4), Winter 1997–8, 517–32.

Kim, H., 'The United States and Korea: Dynamics of Political and Security Relations in the 1990s', *Korea and World Affairs*, 19 (1), Spring 1995, 5–28.

Kim, S., 'China's Pacific Policy: Reconciling the Irreconcilable', *International Journal*, L (3), Summer 1995, 461–87.

Kimura, Hiroshi, 'Primakov's Offensive: A Catalyst in Stalemated Russo-Japanese Relations?', *Communist and Post-Communist Studies*, 30 (4), 1997, 365–77.

Kimura, Masato and David A.Welch, 'Specifying "Interests"': Japan's Claim to the Northern Territories and Its Implications for International Relations Theory', *International Studies Quarterly*, 42 (2), June 1998, 213–44.

Klintworth, G., 'China: Status Quo Power or Regional Threat?', *Journal of East Asian Affairs*,12 (2), Summer–Fall 1998, 364–83.

Krugman, Paul, 'The Myth of Asia's Miracle', *Foreign Affairs*, 73 (6), November–December 1994, 62–78.

Lam, J., 'Chinese Policy towards Hong Kong: Prevention of Peaceful Evolution', *Journal of East Asian Affairs*, 12 (1), Winter–Spring 1998, 267–90.

Lam, Willy Wo-Lap, 'The Factional Dynamics of China's Taiwan Policy', *China Journal*, 36, July 1996, 116–18.

Laothamatas, A. (ed.), *Democratization in Southeast and East Asia*, Singapore: Institute of Southeast Asian Studies, 1997.

Lawson, Stephanie, 'Culture, Democracy, and Political Conflict Management in Asia and the Pacific: An Agenda for Research', *Pacifica Review*, 6 (2), 1994, 85–98.

Layne, C., 'A House of Cards: American Strategy toward China', *World Policy Journal*, XIV (3), Fall 1997, 77–95.

Layne, C., 'Rethinking American Grand Strategy: Hegemony or Balance of Power in the Twenty-First Century?', *World Policy Journal*, 15 (2), Summer 1998, 8–28.

Leaver, R. and D. Cox (eds), *Middling, Meddling, Muddling: Issues in Australian Foreign Policy*, St Leonards, NSW: Allen & Unwin, 1997.

Lee, C. and H. Sato (eds), *US–Japan Partnership in Conflict Management: The Case of Korea*, Monograph Series no. 5, Claremont, Cal.: Keck Center for International and Strategic Studies,1993.

Lee, Chyungly, 'US Leadership in the Asia-Pacific Region: Some Help From Economic Strategies?', *Issues and Studies*, 34 (4), April 1998, 42-71.

Lee, Jaymin, 'East Asian NIEs' Model of Development: Miracle, Crisis, and Beyond', *Pacific Review*, 12 (2), 1999, 141–62.

Lehner, U., *The Asia Factor in US–Japan Relations*, Pacific Economic Paper no. 246, Canberra: Australia Japan Research Centre, Australian National University, 1995.

Lentner, H., 'Implications of the East Asian Economic Crisis for East Asian Economic Policies', *Journal of East Asian Affairs*, 13 (1), Spring–Summer 1999, 1–32.

Lewis, J. and X. Litai, *China's Strategic Seapower: The Politics of Force Modernization in the Nuclear Age*, Stanford, Cal.: Stanford University Press, 1994.

Li, Rex, 'Unipolar Aspirations in a Multipolar Reality: China's Perceptions of US Ambitions and Capabilities in the Post-Cold War World', *Pacifica Review*, 11 (2), June 1999, 115–49.

Lim, Timothy C., 'Power, Capitalism, and the Authoritarian State in South Korea', *Journal of Contemporary Asia*, 28 (4), 1998, 457–83.

MacIntyre, A., 'Ideas and Experts: Indonesian Approaches to Economic and Security Cooperation in the Asia-Pacific Region', *Pacific Review*, 8 (1), 1995, 159–72.

Mack, Andrew, 'The Nuclear Crisis on the Korean Peninsula', *Asian Survey*, 33 (4), April 1993, 339–59.

Mack, Andrew and John Ravenhill (eds), *Pacific Cooperation: Building Economic and Security Regimes in the Asia-Pacific Region*, Boulder, Col.: Westview Press, 1995.

Mack, Andrew, *Island Disputes in Northeast Asia*, Working Paper no. 1997/2, Canberra: Research School of Pacific and Asian Studies, Australian National University, September 1997.

Mackinder, Halford, 'The Round World and the Winning of the Peace', *Foreign Affairs*, 21 (4), July 1943, 595–605.

Mackinder, Halford, *Britain and the British Seas*, Westport, Conn.: Greenwood Press, 1969.

Maddison, A., *Chinese Economic Performance in the Long Run*, Paris: OECD Development Centre, 1998.

Maddock, R., 'Environmental Security in East Asia', *Contemporary Southeast Asia*, 17 (1), June 1995, 20–37.

Mahan, A., *The Interest of America in Sea Power, Present and Future*, Boston, Mass.: Little Brown, 1911.

Mahan, A., *The Influence of Sea Power upon History, 1660–1783*, London: Methuen, 1965.

Mahan, A., *Retrospect and Prospect: Studies in International Relations Naval and Political*, New York: Kennikat Press, 1968.

Mahathir Mohamad, *Human Rights: Views of Dr Mahathir Mohamad*, Melaka: World Youth Foundation, July 1999.

Mahbubani, Kishore, 'Japan Adrift', *Foreign Policy*, 88, Fall 1992, 126–45.

Mahbubani, Kishore, 'The Pacific Way', *Foreign Affairs*, 74 (1), January–February 1995, 100–11.

Mahbubani, Kishore, 'An Asia-Pacific Consensus', *Foreign Affairs*, 76 (5), September–October 1997, 149–58.

Malhotra, Kamal, *East and Southeast Asia Revisited: Miracles, Myths and Mirages*, Focus Papers, Bangkok: Focus on the Global South, November 1997.

Manning, R., 'Future Shock or Renewed Partnership? The US–Japan Alliance Facing the Millennium', *Washington Quarterly*, 18 (4), Autumn 1995, 78–98.

Maswood, S., 'Does Revisionism Work? US Trade Strategy and the 1995 US–Japan Auto Dispute', *Pacific Affairs*, 70 (4), Winter 1997–8, 533–54.

Maynes, C., '"Principled" Hegemony', *World Policy Journal*, XIV (3), Fall 1997, 31–6.

McCormack, Gavan, *The Emptiness of Japanese Affluence*, St Leonards, NSW: Allen & Unwin, 1996.

McGillivray, M. and G. Smith (eds), *Australia and Asia*, Melbourne: Oxford University Press, 1997.

McLennan, A., 'Balance, Not Containment: A Geopolitical Take from Canberra', *National Interest*, Fall 1997, 52–63.

Mediansky, F.A. (ed.), *Australian Foreign Policy: Into the New Millennium*, Melbourne: Macmillan, 1997.

Melanson, R., *American Foreign Policy since the Vietnam War: The Search for Consensus from Nixon to Clinton*, Armonk, NY: M.E. Sharpe, 1996.

Mendl, W., *Japan's Asia Policy: Regional Security and Global Interests*, London: Routledge,1995.

Menon, Rajan and Daniel Abele, 'Security Dimensions of Soviet Territorial Disputes with China and Japan', *Journal of Northeast Asian Studies*, 8 (1), Spring 1989, 3–19.

Meyer, P., 'Russia's Post-Cold War Security Policy in Northeast Asia', *Pacific Affairs*, 67 (4), Winter 1994–5, 495–512.

Milner, Anthony and Mary Quilty (eds), *Australia in Asia: Communities of Thought*, Melbourne: Oxford University Press, 1996.

Mochizuki, M., J. Auer *et al.*, *Japan and the United States: Troubled Partners in a Changing World*, Special Report of the Institute for Foreign Policy Analysis, Washington, DC: Brassey's, 1991.

Mochizuki, Mike, 'Toward a New Japan–US Alliance', *Japan Quarterly*, 3, July–September 1996, 4–12.

Moon, C.I., 'Complex Interdependence and Transnational Lobbying: South Korea and the United States', *International Studies Quarterly*, 32 (1), March 1988, 67–89.

Moore, T., 'China as a Latecomer: Toward a Global Logic of the Open Policy', *Journal of Contemporary China*, 5 (12), July 1996, 187–208.

Mori, Kazuko, 'The Impact of Sino-Soviet Détente', *Pacific Review*, 1 (3), 1988, 290–95.

Morley, J. (ed.), *Driven by Growth: Political Change in the Asia-Pacific Region*, New York: M.E. Sharpe, 1993.

Morley, J. (ed.), *Driven by Growth: Political Change in the Asia-Pacific Region*, rev. ed, Studies of the South East Asia Institute, Columbia University, Armonk, NY: M.E. Sharpe, 1999.

Murphy, W., 'Power Transition in Northeast Asia: US–China Security Perceptions and the Challenge of Systemic Adjustment and Stability', *Journal of Northeast Asian Studies*, 23 (4), Winter 1994, 61–84.

Muscat, R., *Thailand and the United States: Development, Security and Foreign Aid*, New York: Columbia University Press, 1990.

Naisbitt, John, *Megatrends Asia: Eight Asian Megatrends that Are Reshaping Our World*, New York: Simon & Schuster, 1996.

Nathan, Andrew J., 'China's Goals in the Taiwan Strait', *China Journal*, 36, July 1996, 87–93.

Naya, Seiji and Akira Takayama (eds), *Essays in Honor of Professor Shinicho Ichimura*, Honolulu : East-West Center, and Singapore: Institute of Southeast Asian Studies, 1990.

Nelsen, Harvey W., 'Japan Eyes China', *Journal of Northeast Asian Studies*, 14 (4), Winter 1995, 81–90.

Nesadurai, Helen E.S., 'In Defence of National Economic Autonomy? Malaysia's Response to the Financial Crisis', *Pacific Review*, 13 (1), 2000, 73–113.

Nester, W., 'Rules of Engagement: Psychological and Diplomatic Dynamics of American–Japanese Relations', *Asian Survey*, 35 (4), April 1995, 323–35.

Nye, Joseph S., 'East Asian Security: The Case for Deep Engagement', *Foreign Affairs*, 74 (4), July–August 1995, 90–102.

Oba, T., 'Japan's Role in East Asian Investment and Finance', *Japan Review of International Affairs*, 9 (3), Summer 1995, 246–51.

O'Hanlon, Michael, 'A New Japan–US Security Bargain', *Japan Quarterly*, 44 (4), October–December 1997, 12–19.

Okazaki, Hisahiko, 'Southeast Asia in Japan's National Strategy', *Japan Echo*, 20, Special Issue, 1993, 52–63.

Okazaki, Hisahiko, and Sato Seizaburo, 'Reflecting the Role of Japanese Military Power', *Japan Echo*, 18 (1), Spring 1991, 20–5.

Olds, Kris, Peter Dicken, Philip F. Kelly, Lily Kong and Henry Wai-chung Yeung (eds), *Globalisation and the Asia Pacific: Contested Territories*, London: Routledge, 1999.

Olsen, E., *The Evolution of US Maritime Power in the Pacific*, Working Paper no. 246, Canberra: Strategic Defence Studies Centre, Australian National University, April 1992.

Pak, Seijin, 'Two Forces of Democratisation in Korea,' *Journal of Contemporary Asia*, 28 (1), 1998, 45–73.

Papayoanou, P. and S. Kastner, *Assessing the Policy of Engagement with China*, Institute on Global Conflict and Cooperation, Policy Paper no. 40, San Diego: University of California, 1998.

Park, Tong Whan (ed.), *The US and the Two Koreas: A New Triangle*, Boulder, Col. and London: Lynne Reinner, 1998.

Parker, G., *Geopolitics: Past, Present and Future*, London: Pinter, 1998.

Pempel, T. J., 'Regime Shift: Japanese Political Economy in a Changing World Economy', *Journal of Japanese Studies,* 23 (2), 1997, 333–62.

Petras, James, 'The Americanization of Asia: The Rise and Fall of a Civilization', *Journal of Contemporary Asia,* 28 (2), 1998, 149–58.

Pincus, J. and R. Ramli, 'Indonesia: From Showcase to Basket Case', *Cambridge Journal of Economics,* 22 (2), 1998, 723–34.

Pollack, Jonathan D., 'China's Taiwan Strategy: A Point of No Return?', *China Journal,* 36, July 1996, 111–16.

Preston, P.W., *Pacific Asia in the Global System: An Introduction,* Malden, Mass.: Blackwell, 1998.

Puckett, R. (ed.), *The United States and Northeast Asia,* Chicago, Ill.: Nelson-Hall, 1993.

Qingguo, Jia, 'Reflections on the Recent Tension in the Taiwan Strait', *China Journal,* 36, July 1996, 93–7.

Ravenal, E., 'The Nixon Doctrine and Our Asian Commitments', *Foreign Affairs,* 49 (2), January 1971, 201–17.

Reich, Simon, 'Miraculous or Mired? Contrasting Japanese and American Perspectives on Japan's Economic Problems', *Pacific Review,* 13 (1), 2000, 163–93.

Renwick, N., 'Ending the US–Japan Alliance: The Search for Stable Peace in North East Asia after the Cold War', *Interdisciplinary Peace Research,* 4 (2), October–November 1992, 3–30.

Risse-Kappen, Thomas (ed.), *Bringing Transnational Relations Back In: Non-state Actors, Domestic Structures and International Institutions,* New York: Cambridge University Press, 1995.

Robinson, Wayne, 'Japan's Security Debate: Uncovering the Political', *Pacifica Review,* 6 (1), May–June 1994, 31–59.

Robison, R. (ed.), *Pathways to Asia: The Politics of Engagement,* St Leonards, NSW: Allen & Unwin, 1996.

Rodan, Garry, 'Civil Society and Other Political Possibilities in Southeast Asia', *Journal of Contemporary Asia,* 27 (2), 1997, 156–78.

Rosenberger, Leif Roderick, 'Southeast Asia's Currency Crisis: A Diagnosis and Prescription', *Contemporary Southeast Asia,* 19 (3), December 1997, 223–51.

Ross, Robert S., 'The Geography of the Peace', *International Security,* 23 (4), Spring 1999, 81–118.

Roy, Denny, 'Hegemon on the Horizon? China's Threat to East Asian Security', *International Security,* 19 (1), Summer 1994, 149–68.

Roy, Denny, 'Current Sino-US Relations in Strategic Perspective', *Contemporary Southeast Asia,* 3, December 1998, 225–40.

Roy, Denny, 'Tensions in the Taiwan Strait', *Survival,* 42 (1), Spring 2000, 76–96.

Said, S., 'Suharto's Armed Forces: Building a Power Base in New Order Indonesia, 1966–98', *Asian Survey,* 38 (6), June 1988, 535–52.

Sales, Peter M., 'Cambodia after UNTAC: The Ambivalent Legacy of a United Nations Peace-Keeping Operation', *Pacifica Review*, 8 (1), May–June 1996, 81–92.

Saravanamuttu, J., 'Malaysia's Foreign Policy in the Mahathir Period, 1981–95: An Iconoclast Come to Rule', *Asian Journal of Political Science*, 4 (1), June 1996,1–16.

Saravanamuttu, Johan, 'The Southeast Asian Development Phenomenon Revisited: From Flying Geese to Lame Ducks?, *Pacifica Review*, 10 (2), 1998, 111–25.

Sarkisov, Konstantin, 'The Northern Territories Issue after Yeltsin's Re-election: Obstacles to a Resolution from a Russian Perspective', *Communist and Post-Communist Studies*, 30 (4), 1997, 353–63.

Sasae, Kenichiro, *Rethinking Japan–US Relations*, Adelphi Paper 292, Oxford: Oxford University press for International Institute for Strategic Studies, December 1994.

Sato, K., 'International Use of the Japanese Yen', *World Economy*, 22 (4), June 1999, 547–84.

Satoh, Y., 'Emerging Trends in Asia-Pacific Security: The Role of Japan', *Pacific Review*, 8 (3), 1995, 531–43.

Scalapino, R., 'The US Commitment to Asia', *Journal of Strategic Studies*, 18 (3), September 1995, 68–83.

Scalapino, R., S. Sato, J. Wanandi and S-J. Han (eds), *Asia and the Major Powers: Domestic Politics and Foreign Policy*, Berkeley, Cal.: Institute of East Asian Studies, 1988.

Searle, Peter, *The Riddle of Malaysian Capitalism: Rent-seekers or Real Capitalists?*, ASAA Southeast Asia Publications Series, St Leonards, NSW: Asian Studies Association of Australia (ASAA)/Allen & Unwin/University of Hawaii Press, 1999.

Shambaugh, D. (ed.), *Greater China: The Next Superpower*, Oxford: Oxford University Press, 1995.

Shambaugh, D., 'Containment or Engagement of China? Calculating Beijing's Responses', *International Security*, 21 (2), Fall 1996, 180–209.

Shambaugh, D., 'Chinese Hegemony over East Asia by 2015?', *Korean Journal of Defense Analysis*, Summer 1997, 7–28.

Shambaugh, D., 'Sino–American Strategic Relations: From Partners to Competitors', *Survival*, 42 (1), Spring 2000, 97–115.

Shambaugh, D., 'The Insecurity of Security: The PLA's Evolving Doctrine and Threat Perceptions towards 2000', *Journal of Northeast Asian Studies*, 13 (1), Spring 1994, 3–25.

Sheridan, K. (ed.), *Emerging Economic Systems in Asia: A Political and Economic Survey*, St Leonards, NSW: Allen & Unwin, 1998.

Shih, C.-Y., 'Defining Japan: The Nationalist Assumption in China's Foreign Policy', *International Journal*, L (3), Summer 1995, 539–63.

Shinn, J. (ed.), *Weaving the Net: Conditional Engagement with China*, New York: Council on Foreign Relations, 1996.

Shirk, S., 'Chinese Views on Asia-Pacific Regional Security Cooperation', *Analysis* (National Bureau of Asian Research), 5 (5), December 1994, 1–13.

Shlapentokh, Vladimir, 'Russia, China, and the Far East: Old Geopolitics or a New Peaceful Cooperation?', *Communist and Post-Communist Studies*, 28 (3), 1995, 307–18.

Shuja, S., 'China after Deng Xiaoping: Implications for Japan', *East Asian Studies*, Spring 1999, 69–94.

Shulong, Chu, 'National Unity, Sovereignty and Territorial Integration', *China Journal*, 36, July 1996, 98–102.

Simon, Sheldon W., 'The Clinton Presidency and Asian Security: Toward Multi-lateralism', *Australian Journal of International Affairs*, 47 (2), October 1993, 250–62.

Simon, Sheldon W., 'Is There a US Strategy for East Asia?', *Contemporary Southeast Asia*, 21 (3), December 1999, 325–43.

Smith, Sheila, 'Wider Implications of the Bilateral Alliance', *Japan Quarterly*, 44 (4), October–December 1997, 4–11.

Soeya, Y., 'The Evolution of Japanese Thinking and Policies on Cooperative Security in the 1980s and 1990s', *Australian Journal of International Affairs*, 48 (1), May 1994, 87–95.

Soeya, Y., 'The Japan–US. Alliance in a Changing Asia', *Japan Review of International Affairs*, 10 (4), Fall 1996, 265–75.

Solarz, S., *Clinton's Asia Policy*, Singapore: Institute of Southeast Asian Studies, 1994.

Song, Young-sun, 'Prospect for US–Japan Security Cooperation', *Asian Survey*, 35 (12), December 1995, 1087–1101.

Spar, D., 'Co-developing the FSX Fighter: The Domestic Calculus of International Co-operation', *International Journal*, XLVII (2), Spring 1992, 265–92.

Stankiewicz, Michael (ed.), *Korean Peninsula Security and the US–Japan Defense Guidelines*, an IGCC Study Commissioned for the Northeast Asia Cooperation Dialogue VII, Policy Paper 45, San Diego: Institute on Global Conflict and Cooperation, University of California, October 1998.

Steinbruner, John, 'Problems of Predominance: Implications of the US Military Advantage', *The Brookings Review*, 14 (4), Fall 1996, 14–17.

Steven, Rob, *Japan and the New World Order: Global Investments, Trade and Finance*, London: Macmillan Press, 1996.

Stubbs, R., 'Malaysian Defence Policy: Strategy versus Structure', *Contemporary Southeast Asia*, 13 (1), June 1991, 44–56.

Stubbs, R., 'States, Sovereignty and the Response of Southeast Asia's "Miracle" Economies to Globalization', in D.A. Smith, D. J. Solinger and S. C. Topik (eds) *States and Sovereignty in the Global Economy*, London and New York: Routledge, 1999.

Sudo, S., 'Japan and the Security of Southeast Asia', *Pacific Review*, 4 (4), 1991, 333–44.

Syamsuddin, M., 'Political Stability and Leadership Succession in Indonesia', *Contemporary Southeast Asia*, 15 (1), June 1993, 12–23.

Taylor, T. and S. Sato, *Future Sources of Global Conflict*, London: Royal Institute of International Affairs, 1995.

Thakur, Ramesh (ed.), *The South Pacific: Problems, Issues and Prospects*, London: Macmillan, 1991.

Thakur, Ramesh, 'Australia's Regional Engagement', *Contemporary Southeast Asia*, 20 (1), April 1998, 1-21.

Thakur, R. and C. Thayer (eds), *Reshaping Regional Relations: Asia-Pacific and Former Soviet Union*, Boulder, Col.: Westview Press, 1993.

Thurston, Anne F., *Muddling toward Democracy: Political Change in Grassroots China*, Peaceworks no. 23, Washington, DC: United States Institute of Peace, August 1998.

Tipton, F., *The Rise of Asia: Economics, Society and Politics in Contemporary Asia*, Melbourne: Macmillan, 1998.

Tomoda, S., 'Japan's Search for a Political Role in Asia: The Cambodian Peace Settlement', *Japan Review of International Affairs*, 6 (1), Spring 1992, 43–60.

Tong, K., 'Revolutionising America's Japan Policy', *Foreign Policy*, 105, Winter 1996–7, 107–24.

Tow, William, *Encountering the Dominant Player: US Extended Deterrence Strategy in the Asia-Pacific*, New York: Columbia University Press, 1991.

Tow, William (ed.), *Australian–American Relations: Looking toward the Next Century*, Melbourne: Macmillan, 1998.

Tso, Allen Y., 'Foreign Direct Investment and China's Economic Development', *Issues and Studies*, 34 (2), February 1998, 1–34.

Tuathail, Gearóid Ó., *Critical Geopolitics: The Politics of Writing Global Space*, London: Routledge, 1996.

Unger, Danny, and Paul Blackburn (eds), *Japan's Emerging Global Role*, Georgetown, Boulder, Col. and London: Institute for the Study of Diplomacy and Lynne Reinner, 1993.

United Nations Conference on Trade and Development (UNCTAD), Division on Transnational Corporations and Investment, *World Investment Report 1995: Transnational Corporations and Competitiveness*, New York and Geneva: United Nations, 1995.

United States Institute of Peace, *'Trialogue': US–Japan–China Relations and Asian-Pacific Stability*, Special Report, Washington, DC: US Institute of Peace, September 1998.

Ursacki, T. and I. Vertinsky, 'Canada–Japan Trade in an Asia-Pacific Context', *Pacific Affairs*, 69 (2), Summer 1996, 157–84.

Valencia, M., *China and the South China Sea Disputes*, Adelphi Paper 298, Oxford: Oxford Univesity Press for International Institute of Strategic Studies, 1995.

van Ness, Peter, 'Competing Hegemons',*China Journal*, 36, July 1996, 125–8.

van Vranken Hickey, Dennis, 'The Taiwan Straits Crisis of 1996: Implications for US Security Policy' *Journal of Contemporary China*, 7 (19), November 1998, 405–19.

Wah, C., 'The Five Power Defence Arrangements: Twenty Years After', *Pacific Review*, 4 (3), 1991, 193–203.

Wampler, R., *Power and Prosperity: Linkages between Security and Economics in US–Japanese Relations since 1960*, Policy paper no. 39, San Diego, Cal.: Institute on Global Conflict and Co-operation, April 1998.

Wan, Ming, 'Spending Strategies in World Politics: How Japan Has Used Its Economic Power in the Past Decade', *International Studies Quarterly*, 39 (1), March 1995, 85–108.

Wang, S., 'Estimating China's Defence Expenditure: Some Evidence from Chinese Sources', *China Quarterly*, 147, September 1996, 889–911.

Wardhana, Ali, 'Indonesia, Asia Pacific, and the Global Economy at the Beginning of the 21st Century', *Indonesian Quarterly*, 23 (4), 1995, 331–41.

Weeks, Stanley B. and Charles A. Meconis, *The Armed Forces of the USA in the Asia-Pacific Region*, St Leonards, NSW: Allen & Unwin, 1999.

Weiss, Linda, 'Developmental States in Transition: Adapting, Dismantling, Innovating, not "Normalizing"', *Pacific Review,* 13 (1), 2000, 21–55.

Weiss, M., 'What Will Become of the *Reformasi*? Ethnicity and Changing Political Norms in Malaysia', *Contemporary Southeast Asia*, 21 (3), December 1999, 424–50.

Welfield, J., *An Empire in Eclipse: Japan in the Postwar American Alliance System*, London: Athlone Press, 1988.

Whiting, Allen S., 'China and Japan: Politics versus Economics', *Annals, American Academy of Political and Social Sciences*, 519, January 1992, 39–51.

Wishnick, E., 'Prospects for the Sino-Russian Partnership: Views from Moscow and the Russian Far East', *Journal of East Asian Affairs*, 12 (2), Summer–Fall 1998, 418–51.

Woodiwiss, Anthony, *Globalisation, Human Rights and Labour Law in Pacific Asia*, Cambridge: Cambridge University Press, 1998.

World Bank, *Global Economic Prospects and the Developing Countries*, Washington, DC: World Bank, 1993.

World Bank, *China 2020: Development Challenges in the New Century*, Washington, DC.: World Bank, 1997.

World Bank, *East Asia: The Road to Recovery*, Washington, DC: World Bank, 1998.

Wortzel, L., 'China and Strategy: China Pursues Traditional Great-Power Status', *Orbis*, 38 (2), Spring 1994, 157–75.

Wu, Renhong, 'China's Macroeconomy: Review and Perspective', *Journal of Contemporary China*, 7 (19), 1998, 443–58.

Xinbo, Wu, 'Changing Roles: China and the United States in East Asian Security', *Journal of Northeast Asian Studies*, 25 (1), Winter 1996, 35–56.

Yahuda, M., 'The Foreign Relations of Greater China', *China Quarterly*, 1993, 687–710.

Yamamoto, T., *Emerging Civil Society in the Asia Pacific Community*, Singapore: International Institute of Strategic Studies, 1995.

Yeon-ho, Lee, 'The Failure of the Weak State in Economic Liberalization: Liberalization, Democratization and the Financial Crisis in South Korea', *Pacific Review*, 13 (1), 2000, 115–31.

Young, Alwyn, 'Lessons from the East Asian NICS: A Contrarian View', *European Economic Review*, 38, 1994, 964–73.

Yuan, J.-D., 'United States Technology Transfer Policy toward China: Post-Cold War Objectives and Strategies', *International Journal*, LI (2), Spring 1996, 314–38.

Yuan, J.-D., 'Studying Chinese Security Policy: Toward an Analytic Framework', *Journal of East Asian Affairs*, 13 (1), Spring–Summer 1999, 131–97.

Yue, Chia Siow, 'Trade, Foreign Direct Investment and Economic Development of Southeast Asia', *Pacific Review*, 12 (2), 1999, 249–70.

Zakaria, Fareed, 'The Myth of America's "Free Security"', *World Policy Journal*, XIV (2) Summer 1997, 35–43.

Zhang, D., 'Negotiating for a Liberal Economic Regime: The Case of Japanese FDI in China', *Pacific Review*, 11 (1), 1998, 51–78.

Zhang, Jialin, 'US–China Relations in the Post-Cold War Period: A Chinese Perspective', *Journal of Northeast Asian Studies*, 24 (2), Summer 1995, 47–61.

Zhang, Ming, 'The Emerging Asia-Pacific Triangle', *Australian Journal of International Affairs*, 52 (1), 1998, 47–61.

Zhao, Suisheng, *Power Competition in West Asia: From the Old Chinese World Order to Post-Cold War Regional Multipolarity*, London: Macmillan, 1998.

Index

DATE DUE

HIGHSMITH #45230

Printed
in USA